D0236288

THE
LORD'S
COMPANION

THE
LORD'S
COMPANION

edited by

BENNY GREEN

PAVILION
MICHAEL JOSEPH

DEDICATION

In gratitude,
for the pleasure he has always given me,
this book is respectfully dedicated to
Denis Charles Scott Compton
(Middlesex, Arsenal, and England).

Published in Great Britain in 1987 by
Pavilion Books Limited
196 Shaftesbury Avenue, London WC2H 8JL
in association with Michael Joseph Limited
27 Wrights Lane, London W8 5TZ

Introduction, notes and selection © Benny Green 1987
Wisden extracts © John Wisden & Co. Ltd.
Other copyright holders are acknowledged on page 460.

Designed by Kevin Shenton

All rights reserved. No part of this publication
may be reproduced, stored in a retrieval system, or
transmitted, in any form or by any means, electronic,
mechanical, photocopying, recording or otherwise,
without the prior permission of the copyright owner

British Library Cataloguing in Publication Data
The Lord's Companion.
1. Cricket
I. Green, Benny
796.35'8   GV917
ISBN 1-85145-132-3

Typeset and printed in Great Britain by
Butler & Tanner Ltd, Frome and London

INTRODUCTION

THE casual stroller through the northern purlieus of central London, having
arrived on the threshold of that land of stucco villas and quiet walled
gardens where once the well-appointed town gentleman set up his mistress in
discreet splendour, is brought up short by an astonishing apparition on the
corner of St John's Wood Road and Wellington Road. It is a frieze cut into a
large white stone tablet set in a brick wall, in which a group of able-bodied,
noble-minded sportsmen and sportswomen gaze expressionlessly at unseen
opponents and off-stage scoreboards. One glance at the lady tennis player's sun
vizor, the ballooning amplitude of the golfer's plus fours, the prep school caps
of the cricketers, the functional severity of the lady swimmer's costume, tells
us that the frieze is a priceless period piece, whose unspoken invocation, obvious
though it is in the postures of the sculpted, is cut into the stone above the heads
of the figures: 'Play Up, Play Up, and Play the Game'. In the bottom right-hand
corner there is the date 1934 and the name of the artist, Gilbert Bayes;
underneath is a plaque announcing that the bas-relief was the gift of one
Alderman Isaacs. The traffic belches past on its furious way to Swiss Cottage and
points north; from time to time the occupant of a car, waiting at the adjacent
traffic lights, can be seen gazing incuriously at this strange device, which looks
less like a feature of the real, modern London than something out of a forgotten
novel by Talbot Baines Reed or Ernest Raymond. Certainly it looks to have little
business in the fag-end of the twentieth century. And yet there it is, not only
naked and unashamed, but also undefaced by the spray-guns of barbarism,
protected from the times by its own chasteness.

The sculpture is a brave if modest flourish, but it is the only one the investigator
will find on his tramp round the perimeter of Lord's Cricket Ground. Wellington
Road, which begins, so to speak, at the northern rim of the sculpture, proceeds
for nearly two hundred yards without any adornment apart from a Green Line
bus timetable. The first breach in the ten-foot high brick wall comes when the
road makes a ninety-degree turn into a side street where stands the first

indication that somewhere inside lies an arena of considerable dimensions. Large green-painted double doors display the plea 'Do Not Obstruct'; just inside the entrance, to the right, is a doorman's hut. A few paces further down the street is an opening for cars, and then, fifty yards due west, some turnstiles. So far all the signals have been plain enough; the green fields glimpsed through the various openings and apertures in the wall comprise some sort of sporting island set in the very heart of the town.

But then the impressions become slightly confused, almost as though to venture down the road would be to drift into a time-warp where dundrearied men in frock-coats sit in beeswaxed drawing-rooms reading of Mr Gladstone's latest fulminations against the iniquity of the Universe, God Almighty and the Conservative Party, although not necessarily in that order. Two small houses mark the end of the brick wall, at which the side street modulates abruptly into a private road called Cavendish Close, whose houses are so hushed that even to set foot in the roadway seems like an unpardonable breach of some long-discarded code of etiquette instituted by the Forsytes. The trespasser, hoping to unravel the emerging mystery of the missing cricket ground, presses on, only to realise, after about ninety yards, that his path is barred by a white-painted brick wall. He can advance no further, and can only gaze at the great house frowning down upon him from behind the black wrought-iron gates. The wall is blind except for a small wooden door let into the brickwork, and painted white also, so that it all but disappears in the context of the wall about it. There is no visible lock, no keyhole, no bolts. The interloper feels like Alice confronted by the tiny door to the garden of flowers, except that at least she could peep through the keyhole. Possessing neither the glass key of ownership nor the wondercake of privilege which will gain him entry, he has no choice but to beat a retreat, back through the hushed close, past the gates and back along Wellington Road, baffled by the apparent inaccessibility of this so famous stadium and yet rather proud on its behalf, as though the mystery of the cul-de-sac only enhances its charm still further. Perhaps an approach from the opposite direction, along the southern perimeter, will resolve the enigma?

At first all goes well. St John's Wood Road, presenting the public face of the ground to the outside world, proceeds for about three hundred and sixty yards, incorporating gates, doors and turnstiles before arriving at the arched facade of the new Mound Stand. For all cricket lovers the promenade represents so many enthralling days, days of lazy quietude, days of sunlit sensation and drizzling disappointment. Then the Grace Gates, a trysting-place as celebrated in its own way to the sporting fraternity as the pillars of the Lyceum Theatre to students of Sherlockiana, or the portico of St Paul's Church to Shavians. After the Gates a short continuation of the boundary wall before the façade of the Lord's Tavern, whose frontage measures, either through whimsical caprice or even more whimsical contrivance, exactly twenty-two yards. Then the end of the territory and a large new block of flats on the corner site.

Heartened by having traced out the full southern limits, the investigator turns right into Grove End Road and the line of quaint old houses looking as though they might have direct access to the ground. Like all modestly aristocratic homes, their numbering is perverse enough to derange the apprentice postman, going from 2a to 2, proceeding in even numbers until the last one in the line, which, not content with being No. 14, also calls itself The Vines. But at least Grove End Road is navigable, a fact which raises the spirits of the investigator as he turns at an angle of ninety degrees once more down Elm Tree Road. According to the geometry of his experience, this road should lead directly to the other side of that white brick wall, yet here are ordinary houses marching eastwards. For two hundred yards or so Elm Tree Road behaves in a perfectly conventional manner. And yet, and yet. The roof of the north stand is occasionally glimpsed *behind* the houses, which suggests that somehow, between its own extremities and the workaday world the MCC has cunningly contrived to create an impenetrable buffer state comprised of privately-owned bricks and mortar, gardens and conservatories. The roof of the north stand disappears, reappears reminding the explorer of a thousand afternoons when in strolling round the ground his curiosity was tickled momentarily by the upper windows of the houses visible from the back alley behind the bars and printing shop. These must be the fronts of those same houses. Where does the road finally arrive at the walls of Lord's, and what of that white painted barrier? The questions are never answered, because Elm Tree Road, after flirting with the hopes of its investigator for a while, waving before his eyes those tantalising intermittent glimpses of the north stand roof, suddenly veers off sharply to the north, directly away from the cricket ground, wandering off into a road of villas and finally losing itself in the labyrinth of Swiss Cottage. Once again the investigator retreats, having confirmed once and for all the suspicion he has been harbouring for years, that Lord's Cricket Ground, corporeal though it outdoubtedly is, retains certain affinities with the mansions of fable, among which is that it is impossible to circumnavigate it. Another aspect of the uniqueness of Lord's, the only sporting arena in the world which defies anyone foolish enough to wish to surround it.

When, on the morning of 17 June 1939, I first entered Lord's, it was with the same frisson of joyous anticipation I recalled from some years earlier on my introduction to Highbury Stadium. Lord's proved to be very different. Whereas the visit to Highbury had been under the supervision of my father, this time he left me at the gates with two of my sporting associates whose identity had, for purposes of historical accuracy, better be clarified. They were Dave Morris, the dairyman's son, and Ronnie Hamid, whose grandfather's head had been seen on an old Malayan postage stamp. They had been to Lord's before, I had not, and they took some pleasure in the proprietory guided tour of the facilities which they gave me. There were few other spectators to impede our laughing, hooting progress. No doubt there were fanatics expressing their passion by dozing in the long-legged chairs in the Long Room, but for us there was only the promise of the wide open spaces of the Mound Stand.

I can remember quite clearly my sensations as, clasping the brown paper bag containing my lunch of two buttered rolls and an apple, I gazed about me. For one thing this was nothing like any football stadium I had seen. It was much wider, much flatter, somehow more serene, quaint even. I can recall gazing at the north grandstand, with its little balconies, in deep wonder which instantly

bloomed into an affection which has never faded. Even after I had broken into
the exchequer of sixpence by purchasing a match-card, I was more interested
in the place than the players, although all three of us were well enough versed
in the history of the game to know that in a fixture like MCC v. Cambridge
University, there were bound to be both coming heroes and some rapidly
disappearing over the horizon. And when we examined the small print, we saw
that MCC included an England captain, no less, in A. P. F. Chapman, who
disappointed us bitterly by being out for five runs. Memory also tells me that Jim
Smith hit one or two towering hits. When I came to look up the details half a
lifetime later, I was almost afraid to look, just in case Jim Smith had done nothing
of the sort. But there it is in Wisden:

J. Smith.... c. Shirreff.... b. Webster....15.

It comes back to me also that long before the end of the day's play we were all
thoroughly fed up with ourselves and each other, and longed for stumps to be
drawn and my father to return to the Grace Gates at six o'clock in the evening
to escort us home. I think we whiled away the last hour or so antagonising two
members of the ground staff by assing about with a large roller parked by the
Nursery End sight-screen. But the adventure glowed in recollection, and I knew
I would come back, again and again, one day.

I suppose all three of us should have been acutely aware of the shadow of
war already racing across the green turf. We had been through the Munich
crisis, had seen them digging trenches in the parks, been fitted for gas masks,
been told to register in case of evacuation. But none of this grown-up rubbish
had anything to do with the likes of us. What did we care for the front pages of
the newspaper? Like all civilised young gents, we read the papers from the back
forwards. There was only cricket in the sun, and pennies in the pockets of our
short pants to buy chocolate bars from Dark's little sweet-shop at the back of
the Mound Stand. And so we galloped around the estate, pausing to watch a
few overs of the cricket every now and then, making erudite hieroglyphics on
our match-cards, picking up empty cigarette cartons to see if any careless addict
had left the cigarette cards inside. What we were doing, all unwittingly, was
taking a golden fragment of boyhood and placing it in the time-capsule of Lord's.
Two summers later, when I returned, we were all living in another world. Dave
and Ronnie had moved on to other schools in other parts of the country, great
silver elephantine bags floated in the sky, chocolate was rationed, all the cricketers
now had military or naval prefixes, and the spectators were sporting much
khaki. But Lord's had not visibly changed, and that was its benison. The
changelessness must have been an illusion, but as the inevitability of gradualness
has always been part of the Lord's philosophy, the wanderer returning to St
John's Wood has for nearly two hundred years, ever since Thomas Lord was
ejected by the canal-builders, been able to avail himself of the emollient of
permanence in a shifting world. Exactly how much it has shifted becomes
apparent in the following pages. Dave drives a London cab now, and once, when
by a perfect fluke I hailed his vehicle en route to Lord's, he delivered me there
and refused to take any fare. For old time's sake, he said. As for Ronnie, he

went to work in Malaya many years ago, but at least he is still alive. One or two of my constant Lord's companions have not been so fortunate, but their spirit seems to linger on, high in the Mound Stand on quiet Saturday afternoons, or in the pavilion tea-bar when the rain drums down, or along that curious walkway behind the north stand which looks up at the back windows of those houses perched midway between a cricket ground and humdrum London proper. But they have rebuilt the Mound Stand now, and they have removed the old bookstall to that little house separating the ground from the Nursery. Behind that house there is a betting tent and an Indoor School, and the Press Box is new and modernistic. The old Tavern has vanished in the name of some footling expediency. Even so, I can claim, if my recollections insist on it, that nothing ever changes at Lord's.

BENNY GREEN

THERE have been three Lord's, but the disparity between their respective lifespans has all but obliterated any consciousness of the existence of the first two. The embryonic Lord's, on the site of the present Dorset Square, lasted twenty-four years; the second, at North Bank, St John's Wood, disappeared after only three; the third is still with us and is, at the time of writing, 173 not out. The first closure was brought about by the expiry of the lease and the energy of those speculative builders whose monuments were so spectacular a feature of London life towards the end of the eighteenth century. The second closure was forced upon the owners by the cutting of the Regent's Park Canal. At one or two points in the nineteenth century there were similar threats to the present ground, but the gallant intercession of moneyed gentlemen always staved off disaster. Innumerable accounts of these early viccisitudes have been published, none more succinct than the one to be found in Prince Ranjitsinhji's *Jubilee Book of Cricket* (1897), dedicated 'By Her Gracious Permission to Her Majesty the Queen Empress'.

How much of the book Ranjitsinhji actually wrote is problematic. The list of contents formally acknowledges the contributions of 'various writers', and a prefatory note confesses with princely politeness that the author 'has received special assistance from W. J. Ford; Professor Case; Mr C. B. Fry; The Master of Trinity College, Cambridge; and Mr Gaston of Brighton.' Whoever these worthies were, their reputations have long since vanished, with the exception of Fry, whose many-layered life is as well known today as that of any late Victorian luminary. It seems likely that much of the lucidity and some of the pretensions to literary style in Ranjitsinhji's book are really due to Fry, who may well be responsible for this brisk summary of the background to the founding of Lord's. Fry, however, as becomes a true gentleman, makes no reference in his own autobiography either to Ranjitsinhji's book or his own part in it.

The MCC is acknowledged to be the great cricket authority throughout the world. Like many famous institutions, its success has been at times checkered. In the latter part of the last century Thomas Lord, a cricketer of some weight in his day, was in the habit of frequenting the Artillery Field at Finsbury. This was the oldest ground of which we have the scores reserved of the early matches. On one occasion Lord there met the Earl of Winchilsea and the Hon. Colonel Lennon, both of whom were great supporters of the game. These promised Lord their patronage if he would find a suitable ground. In 1787 he selected the spot where Dorset Square now stands, and from that year 'Lord's' and the MCC became accomplished facts. The first match of note was June 20, 21, 22, 1787, between England and the White Conduit Club, with six given men, when England won by 239 runs. On June 27, 1788, MCC played the White Conduit Club, and amongst the players who participated for the MCC were Lord Winchilsea, Lord Strathavon, Sir Peter Burrell (of Sussex), and the Hon. A. Fitzroy, the MCC winning by 83 runs. Subsequently Lord, owing to a dispute with his landlord, Mr Portman, about an addition to the rent, gave up this site and took another ground at North Bank, Regent's Park, in the year 1810. This ground was only in existence for a period of three years, for when the Regent's Canal was planned the course was taken through the cricket-ground. Lord was, however, by no means discouraged, for in 1814 the present site in St John's Wood Road was secured, and it is a singular fact, though often overlooked by chroniclers, that the cricketers of the present day actually play on the same sward as did old

Small, the crack batsman of the famous old Hambledon Club – in fact the turf, after it was taken from the old ground in Dorset Square and relaid on the North Bank pitch, was transferred to the St John's Wood enclosure. The old pavilion unfortunately was destroyed by fire just after the conclusion of the first Winchester v. Harrow match on the 28th of July 1823. Nearly all the records and many important documents in connection with the game were destroyed – such documents, for instance, as scores and notes of matches; while it is stated that Lord had over £2,000 due to him for subscriptions. But the books were burned and Lord was anxious to retire. The situation was critical, speculating builders were on the alert, and but for the prompt action of Mr William Ward, MP for the City of London, the ground would speedily have been studded with villas. Mr Ward purchased the lease at a high price, drawing a cheque for £5,000, and giving it to Lord. In the year 1836 Mr Ward, from altered circumstances, retired from his mansion in Bloomsbury Square and sold the lease of Lord's to Mr John Henry Dark, who became the proprietor. Nine years earlier, however, in 1827, the first university match was played at Lord's, and that year the remuneration of professional cricketers was fixed at a standard of £6 per head for the winning side and £4 for the losers. In 1843 his late Royal Highness the Prince Consort became a patron, while the following year I find there were 465 members on the roll of the club.

In 1863 Mr Dark proposed to part with his interest in Lord's ground for £15,000, the remainder of the lease being twenty-nine and a half years. A committee was appointed to report on the matter, and in 1864 the sum of £11,000 was agreed upon by Mr Dark for the purchase of his premises, which comprised the tavern, racquet and tennis court, billiard-room, and cricket-ground. The ground landlord, Mr Moses, offered to renew the ground-rent for ninety-nine years at £550 per annum: it had previously been £150. In 1865 Mr Marsden (late Moses) offered to sell outright for £21,000. This was eventually reduced to £18,150, and the following year Mr William Nicholson, a member of the MCC committee, and captain of the Harrow Eleven in 1843, in the most handsome manner advanced the money on a mortgage of the premises at £5 per cent, which he afterwards reduced to £4 per cent. At a special general meeting on May 2, 1866, Mr Nicholson's proposal was unanimously adopted, and from that period, when the famous old club could call the ground its own, the progress year by year has been remarkable. Two or three years ago this same gentleman, Mr W Nicholson, purchased a large piece of ground at Harrow and presented it to his old school. He was formerly MP for Petersfield, High Sheriff for Hants, and president of the MCC.

By the year 1878 the whole of the loan advanced by Mr W Nicholson for the purchase of the ground had been paid. When Mr Nicholson purchased the freehold in 1866 the club had a muster-roll of 980 members and an income of £6,000 odd. Today I find from the MCC report the club has a membership of 4,197. The hundredth anniversary of the MCC was celebrated by a dinner held in the tennis court on the 15th of July 1887. The invited guests, numbering about two hundred, included past presidents, those who had played in the Gentlemen v. Players matches at Lord's twice, and other distinguished supporters of the game. In September 1889 the Hon. Sir Spencer Ponsonby Fane, KCB, laid the first stone of the present handsome pavilion, which cost the club, according to the MCC statement of accounts for 1890, over £15,000.

K. S. RANJITSINHJI, *The Jubilee Book of Cricket*, 1897

THE Fry–Ranjitsinhji account of things is the conventional one, but it is hardly much more than the skimming of the surface of somewhat deep waters. Who was Thomas Lord? What were his origins, and how did he come to control the destiny of an exclusive club for gentlemen? He appears to be a much vaguer figure than most histories of the game seem willing to admit. Neither his dates nor his antecedents, nor the dates of his several children, are anything like as precise as historians would have us believe, and even the famous portrait by Morland, with its alert eyes and complacent mouth, is recognised as a likeness only because his patrons said it was. Lord's function was to provide a closed-in space not far from central London where his aristocratic customers could play their game and socialise in private. Although Lord in his young days was a cricketer himself, it seems likely that had his patrons required a football ground, or a hockey pitch, or a running track, then he would have obliged with just as much enthusiasm as he brought to the creation of the ground bearing his name. Attempts at precise biographical summary have appeared in recent years, but the apparent exactitude of the facts may be a shade misleading. His year of birth has never been confirmed beyond dispute, and even the corroboration of his existence implied by the documentation of his playing career is fogged by contradiction, so that we can never quite be sure what type of bowler he was. But because founding fathers are always required to be securely based personalities, it is perhaps just as well for the peace of mind of a grateful posterity that the founder of the finest games-playing acreage in the world is now, although perhaps not quite a substantial figure, at least reasonably well-lit by the flickering torches of the eighteenth century.

He was a man of handsome presence and possessed a bonhomie which was almost irresistible. On one occasion, after attending a great gathering of notables of which two Russian Grand Dukes were the central figures, his great friend, Sir John Hall, Master of the Dock, observed to him: 'Lord, you were the handsomest man present', a verdict which, without flattering him, was considered just. Lord was a well-proportioned man of medium size, being 5 feet 9 inches in height and weighing 12 stone. He was often in the King's presence, and for many years, whilst renting a wine merchant's office in Upper Gloucester Street, supplied the wine for the Royal table. He was the first Protestant member of his family, and in 1793 married Amelia Smith (née Angell), who belonged to a well-known North London family and was the widow of a proctor.

As a cricketer, Lord, without ever being in the first flight, was a capable performer. Had he been able to devote all his time and energies to the practical side of the game he would, no doubt, have made a name for himself as an all-round player, but there were matters of more moment to demand his attention. Still, he played frequently, and with success, for Middlesex. *Scores and Biographies* says that 'In the field Lord generally stood point, and his underhand bowling, for which he was noted, was slow'. In Sutton's *Nottingham Cricket Matches*, however, we are told, on first-hand authority, that in 1791 his bowling was 'extremely rapid', being so fast that the play of the Nottingham men was 'utterly inadequate to contend with it'. Perhaps his pace was originally fast and, as in the case of many other players, became slower with the passing of the years. His batting was at times distinctly serviceable, his best feat being perhaps to score 56 for Middlesex at Lord's in 1790 against the MCC, who had Beldham and Clifford to bowl for them.

LORD HARRIS AND F. S. ASHLEY-COOPER, *Lord's and the MCC, 1914*

He was in many respects a typical example of the late eighteenth-century entrepreneur. Born in Yorkshire in 1755, the son of a gentry farmer who was stripped of his possessions after supporting the Young Pretender in 1745, Lord first came into contact with the London aristocracy while employed as a bowler and general factotum by the White Conduit Club. From his earliest dealings, there is little doubt that Lord was motivated more by the chance to make a profit than by any love of the game. Before the purchase of the first Lord's, the rate books of St Marylebone indicate that he was the lessee of the Allsop Arms. As well as trying to find a permanent home for the MCC, he was involved in a series of transactions involving property in Gloucester Street, Orchard Street and Wardour Street. The success of these transactions enabled Lord to become a respected citizen in the neighbourhood of St John's Wood, for in 1807 he was elected to the Marylebone Vestry. To these property dealings he later added a flourishing business in wines and spirits. On the sale of Lord's in 1825, he retired to West Meon where he died in 1829.

CHRISTOPHER BROOKES, *English Cricket*, 1978

THIS account of Lord's business acumen, with its implication that there is something reprehensible about it, does no more than hint at the truth about Lord, which was that his career as a cricketing entrepreneur was largely an accident, of which he was able to take spectacular advantage through his ability to mix with his betters without angering them either by uncouth habits or social pretensions. This account of him, by one of the liveliest of the Victorian writers on cricket, confirms the impression of a shrewd operator who knew how to manipulate money and property and who, like most entrepreneurs of his time, enjoyed the whole business thoroughly. Like a great many self-made men, however, he was to learn that a gift cannot be bequeathed as easily as the assets it creates.

Whether Dorset Square was Lord's first experience of the pains and pleasures of dealing with land is not known; but if so it was to be the first of many. The fit of shyness, or sense of absurdity, which comes over a man when he is first requested to place his finger on the seal and say, 'I declare this as my act and deed', must soon have been forgotten and the thing have become mere matter of routine. The records at the Middlesex Registry shew him to have had many dealings, buying and selling, taking leases and granting them, borrowing money on mortgage and lending it. A peppercorn became as familiar to him as a glass of wine, a building agreement no stranger than an invoice. In 1791 he took a lease of land in New Road, now Gloucester Street, and mortgaged it. He had other property in Gloucester Street and in New Street and Orchard Street, in Wardour Street and in Dorset Place. One deed shows him in 1829 raising £2,000 by a mortgage to Thomas Trusty Trickey, a gentleman whose parents had already done their best to remedy an initial misfortune; at least, as some other deeds show, when he agreed to take a lease of other building land from the Portman family, and the houses were erected and the leases granted, it was the builder, not he, who failed. His son, Thomas Lord the younger, the sole devisee of his father's property, for a time was 'Thomas Lord of Gray's Inn, gentleman'. Perhaps Lord senior, in placing his son in the Law, exaggerated, as others have done who have paid for the preparation of deeds, the profits made by those who prepare them.

Perhaps Mr Lord junior (1794–1875) despised the slight pecuniary rewards of his profession; in any case he followed the hounds with more enjoyment than he followed the law. He was rather erratic, according to family recollection, ran through a fortune fox-hunting, and let his business take care of itself to a certain extent. Apparently it had to do this for years together. Between 1822 and 1843 his name appears as a practising London attorney in only nine years; but in those nine years he had offices at eight different addresses. At each he was ready to welcome business; he was solicitor for an association to protect small vessels in the Thames, and coasting vessels, against damage by steamers; he was a Parliamentary agent, British and foreign; Irish and Scotch agent; a 'foreign law agent for recovering foreign debts' and prepared to act in 'transmitting deeds to all places on the Continent'. He is buried at Sidmouth, Devon.

E. B. V. CHRISTIAN, *At the Sign of the Wicket*, 1894

IT seems from these accounts and others that Lord was one of that group of self-made entrepreneurs which was responsible for the absorption of the St John's Wood area into the main body of London. At the end of the eighteenth century it was still very much the style to regard the present site of the ground as a suburban and even a sylvan retreat, notwithstanding the plans for Regent's Park so soon to be approved by the Prince Regent and instigated by John Nash. It comes back to me that on the walls of my old adolescent prison, Saint Marylebone Grammar School, founded in 1792, there used to hang a painting showing the lone figure of a man retreating into a vista of sun-soaked meadows scattered with trees, horses, and a few quiescent sheep. The painting was called 'Across the Fields to Marylebone', and was hanging there as a symbol of the year of the school's foundation. So Lord's speculations in Wardour Street, followed by the domestic quietude he enjoyed in St John's Wood, may be seen as an ancient version of the tactic by which a stockbroker announces his triumphant City career by retreating to Sunningdale or Esher. The imprecision of the facts pertaining to Lord's and, more particularly, to the Marylebone Cricket Club, has been best described by that perverse but intermittently brilliantly original historian of the game, Rowland Bowen:

The clubs are called the White Conduit Cricket Club and the Marylebone Cricket Club, because that is what they were often called at the time, and of course the second is still properly so-called. But both 'White Conduit' and 'Marylebone' were topographical terms and they may well have been merely descriptive and not formal names. There is no evidence in fact of a formal White Conduit Cricket Club: what is known is of gentlemen from the Star and Garter Club who frequented, with others, the White Conduit Fields to play cricket and who, without others, moved to Marylebone. Any formal organisation called the Marylebone Cricket Club may well not have come into existence at that time or indeed for another three or four years. It may, however, have had a formal organisation of a much smaller scope rather before, just as those dining clubs which still exist, and which have regular dinners usually at one favourite restaurant and which usually need some kind of rules to ensure cohesion. The rules of the Marylebone Cricket Club suggest strongly that it began in that sort of way, for how otherwise could its first rule be to state when the Anniversary Dinner should be held? That is exactly what one would expect from a group of gentlemen who associated for their convivial purposes at the Star and Garter tavern, and played cricket together in north London. All early records of the club were lost in the fire in 1825 – had they not been it is reasonably certain that they would have disclosed a date for the club either much before 1787 (which is no more than a date for Lord's first ground) when members first went out to Islington, or a few years later – but not 1787 which has no significance in terms of the history of the club.

ROWLAND BOWEN, *Cricket, A History of its Growth and Development*, 1970

BOWEN is being perverse as usual. In arguing against the existence of any written proof that the MCC dates from 1787, he is assaulting the holy writ of the club rather than of the ground which is its home. In placing the Marylebone Cricket Club on the same unwritten foundation which has managed to sustain the constitution of England for rather a longer period, Bowen has evidently made up his mind not to admit the vital importance to any club of any kind of secure and recognised premises. To say that the opening by Thomas Lord of the first Lord's ground has 'no significance in terms of the history of the club' is as absurd as suggesting that Pugin's emblematic excesses at Westminster have 'no significance' in terms of public attitudes to parliamentary democracy, or that the Tower of London is disconnected from perceptions of the temperament of William the Conqueror. It might seem a shade absurd to discuss a mere cricket ground in the context of the Houses of Parliament or the Tower, but then Lord's is not a mere cricket ground. It is also a familiar monument and a public facility whose importance is known even to those who abhor the game for which it stands. But Bowen, for all his curmudgeonly diatribes, serves a useful function when he reminds the modern world that it knows far less of the origins of most things generally, and Lord's in particular, than it usually likes to pretend.

The roots of Bowen's distaste are revealing. Although in social terms his roots were what are sometimes laughingly referred to, even today, as 'gentlemanly', he was all his life implacably opposed to that concept of an idyllic English society divided between rich, land-owning toffs and poor hired lackeys. The early history of the Marylebone Cricket Club is scattered with well-appointed, well-educated, well-moneyed English gentlemen who looked on the club and its ground as their own private property, which in a sense it was, and who reacted accordingly to any attempted innovations, affecting either the rules or the premises. Being gentlemen, these grandees were usually gamblers and always drinkers. It was therefore perfectly reasonable that Lord, in administering his club, should encourage the institutions of prize money in important games and betting facilities for the spectators, and also an inn where players and spectators alike might toast each other:

A grand match will be played on Thursday, 31st of May, 1787, in the new Cricket-ground, the New Road, Mary-le-bone, between nine gentlemen of the county of Essex, with two given men, against eight gentlemen of Middlesex, with two gentlemen of Berkshire, and one of Kent, for One Hundred Guineas a side.

The wickets will be pitched at ten o'clock, and the match will be played out. No dogs will be admitted

The Times, 29 May 1787

On Monday, August 30th, began playing a grand match of Cricket, in Lord's Ground, Mary le Bonne, and finished on Thursday, September 2nd: four gentle men of the Mary le Bonne Club, with seven of Hants, against All England for 1,000 Guineas.

The Times, 4 September 1790

For many years the majority of the great matches were played for stakes, and bookmakers could be seen regularly at Lord's calling out the odds in front of the Pavilion. Foremost among the betting-men were the notorious Jim and Joe Bland, Simpson, a gaming-house keeper, Dick Whitlom, of Covent Garden, and Toll, of Esher, each of whom, to make his betting safe, was not above keeping a player out of the way by a false report that his wife was dead. In the circumstances can one be surprised that the Bishop of London forbade his clergy to take part in the chief matches? The frequency with which the word 'gentlemen' turns up in these early reports of cricket at Lord's goes some way to explaining how its proprietor, a nobody from the north, so rapidly ingratiated himself at the very apex of London society. The game in which he was involved happened by a sheer fluke of circumstance to be the preserve of the landowning oligarchy of the time, and it was literally impossible for Lord to administer the premises without coming into almost daily contact with some of the most powerful men in England. As one example among several, there was the Duke whose life and career were so tightly interwoven into the tapestry of English history that to read even the briefest of biographical notes evokes irresistible thoughts of the monarchy, the Empire, and not least of the twenty-ninth chapter of *Vanity Fair*:

Numbered amongst the earliest members of the Club were the Hon. Charles Lennox, afterwards 4th Duke of Richmond, and HRH the Duke of York, brother of George IV and William IV. The first-named was one of the finest gentlemen players of his time, and one of the first great cricketers to show the game in Scotland. In 1789 he fought a memorable duel on Wimbledon Common with the Royal Duke in consequence of a quarrel concerning the appointment of Lennox to the command of a battalion in the Coldstream Guards, of which York was colonel, without reference to him, an undoubted breach of military etiquette. Lennox, whose second was Lord Winchilsea, was in grim earnest and shot away a curl from the Duke's forehead, but HRH did not return the fire and did not intend doing so. The latter said that if Colonel Lennox was not satisfied, he might fire again. The pair were reconciled the following year on Lord's ground, during a match between England and Hampshire. Lennox subsequently became Viceroy of Canada, in which country he died of hydrophobia resulting from the bite of a pet fox. It was his Duchess, it may be recalled, who gave the historic ball on June 15th, 1815, the night before Quatre Bras.

LORD HARRIS AND F.S. ASHLEY-COOPER, *Lord's and the MCC*, 1914

A LIFE, as the saying goes, packed with incident. And yet the Duke of Richmond was by no means the most fascinating, or the least predictable, of Lord's clients. As the business – for that was what it was – flourished, the proprietor adopted the classic tactic of living over the shop, able to observe the swift rush of developments brought about by his introduction of a little urbanity into the leafy glades of the district. For with the Dukes came the riff-raff, and with the sporting ethics the drinking habits, and it is unfortunate that the views have not survived of those residents of St John's Wood who, until the coming of Lord and his sporting circus, had been able to enjoy the quiet pleasures of the bucolic life.

Thomas Lord settled down on the spot. His house at the north-east corner of the ground overlooked the pitch. There he stayed until a couple of years before his death in 1832. His last two years had been spent in retirement in the Hampshire village of West Meon. Meanwhile, another institution had grown up nearby, Lord's Tavern, the famous pub used by patrons of the game. Squire Osbaldeston must have been a familiar frequenter of this place.

GORDON MACKENZIE, *Marylebone*, 1972

OSBALDESTON certainly was a frequenter of Lord's, but only for so long as he was able to control his own temper. A member of that élite which regarded Lord's ground as a private club, Osbaldeston went his way without regard for the finer points of the law, and eventually received the ultimate accolade, of elevation into English fiction:

Lord received much help and encouragement from one of the great sporting characters of the time, George Osbaldeston, known as 'Squire' Osbaldeston. Steeplechase rider, renowned master of foxhounds, dedicated cricketer and cricketing enthusiast, he fought a celebrated duel with Lord George Bentinck, son of the 4th Duke of Portland and friend of Disraeli. The venue, rather appropriately perhaps in view of their lawless intentions, was Wormwood Scrubs, and the two performers in the splendid drama seem to have gone through the life-saving antics sometimes resorted to. Bentinck, it is said, fired first, missed, and bawled out, 'Now, Squire, it's two to one in your favour!' 'Why then, the bet's off,' yelled Osbaldeston, and fired into the air. Reconciliation, however, seems to have been delayed for several years, perhaps because neither of the honourable gentlemen was able to display any justificatory wound. That was in 1831, when the Squire had reached the ripe age of forty-four. The same year he matriculated in that peculiar sport of the Corinthian age, the equestrian 'spectacular'. He won a thousand-guinea bet that he would not ride two hundred miles in ten consecutive hours by completing the course in 8 hours 42 minutes. Since he changed his horse at the end of every four miles, he must have used fifty horses in this mad marathon, and come away with a pretty sore seat – surely Sir Walter Scott's hard-riding Sir Hildebrand Osbaldistone in *Rob Roy* must have been taken from him, perhaps unconsciously, since the name is hardly changed. Osbaldeston was a thick-set man of great muscular strength. Cricket absorbed him so wholly in his later years that he settled down at 2 Grove Road, St John's Wood, within walking distance of Lord's. There he died, at seventy-nine, in 1866.

GORDON MACKENZIE, *Marylebone*, 1972

THIS portrait is no more than partial. As one of the archetypes of the early Lord's membership, and one of those heroes of the prehistory of cricket, Osbaldeston loomed large in the life of his own times, and was the beneficiary of a lightning sketch by Thomas Creevey (1768–1838), who, being such an amiable gossip, could hardly have been a contemporary of Osbaldeston without observing him closely: 'Though only five feet high, and in features like a cub fox, he is a very funny little chap; clever in his way, very good-humoured and gay, and with very good manners.' A publication called *The Sporting Magazine* added the detail that he was 'remarkably large about the chest ... his face is good-looking, but he has lost some of his front teeth from a fall, and when he speaks you perceive it'. Much closer detail, and some anecdotage, is placed, most appropriately, in the first history of Lord's:

He was a famous rider, hunter, and shot, and one of the hardest and straightest men across country ever seen. Among his many remarkable feats were to kill ninety-eight pheasants in a hundred shots, and, in 1831, aged forty-four and weighing over eleven stones, to ride two hundred miles in 8 hours 42 minutes, using twenty-eight horses, after backing himself to do the distance in ten hours. His duel with Lord George Bentinck the same year is historic, and as is well known, he refereed the Caunt–Bendigo match for the Championship of England in 1845. He has been described as 'the Greatest sportsman the world ever knew since the days of the Assyrian Nimrod', high praise indeed, but who would be bold enough to question its accuracy? An active open-air existence was almost life and breath to him, and one can understand him giving up Parliament, 'as it was not exactly in accordance with his tastes'. Once, whilst hunting, he plunged into the Witham and rescued a boy from drowning, and on another occasion, during a ball, rode fifty miles (twenty-five out and home) in order to procure a choice bloom for a lady whom he thereby protected from the banter of a somewhat unfriendly rival. The 'Squire' was always as fearless as honest, and, as the *Dictionary of National Biography* truly remarks, no one who knew him would imagine for a moment that he was capable of doing anything approaching an ungentlemanly action. He died at 2 Grove Road, St John's Wood, on August 1st, 1866, in his eightieth year.

LORD HARRIS AND F.S. ASHLEY-COOPER, *Lord's and the MCC*, 1914

THIS item of hagiology would have astonished Osbaldeston's teachers and tutors at Eton and Brasenose, who were never able to impart to Osbaldeston the rudiments of a formal education. Instead this hero of the times expended most of his energy in the slaughter of as many wild animals as could be found for him to execute. Among those who were suitably impressed by the gentlemanly lineaments of a man who could kill ninety-eight pheasants out of a hundred was another, later historian of Lord's, Sir Pelham Warner who, ever the unconscious humorist, says of Osbaldeston that he had 'charming manners' and was 'pretty handy with his fists'. Whether or not his manners were all that charming, the Squire certainly liked to play cricket for money, and it was a celebrated wager with a much less likeable man which caused Osbaldeston's sad breach with the Marylebone club.

As a cricketer Osbaldeston, though a splendid hard-hitting batsman, was best known as a bowler, said to be the fastest who had yet appeared, and in conjunction with William Lambert he was ready to challenge any other pair in England. He challenged for a match of fifty guineas Lord Frederick Beauclerk and T.C. Howard, to decide who were the stronger pair. Just before the match Osbaldeston was taken ill, and suggested a postponement. 'No. Play or forfeit,' said Lord Frederick. 'I won't forfeit. Lambert shall play you both, and if he wins have the money', was Osbaldeston's reply. Lord Frederick argued that such a match was nonsense, but Osbaldeston held his ground, and said, 'If you don't play we shall claim the stakes.' In the result Lambert made 56 in the first innings and 24 in the second – total 80. He dismissed Lord Frederick and Howard for 24 and 44 – total 66 – and so won by 14 runs. Lambert, however, showed great guile. Lord Frederick had an irascible temper, and, wides not counting, Lambert bowled them to him till he lost his temper, and then bowled him with a straight one. Lord Frederick was not too magnanimous, and took a revenge that does not redound to his credit. In a moment of pique Osbaldeston removed his name from the list of members at Lord's. Later in life he came to live at 2 Grove Road, St John's Wood, and sought re-election. Lord Frederick prevented his readmission as a member by determined opposition, though both Budd and Ward pleaded for his reinstatement.

SIR PELHAM WARNER, Lord's, 1946

Τ HIS incident is no more than typical of Lord Frederick Beauclerk, who has the dubious honour of being English cricket's first authenticated oaf. A gifted cricketer who said he expected to make £600 a season out of profits made in matches played for stakes, Beauclerk was sometimes suspected of having been involved in the fixing of matches. Warner in his eulogy insists that nothing was ever proved, and will unbend no further than to admit that Beauclerk, who 'had his enemies', was considered so beyond the pale that *The Times* spurned him at his death by pointedly omitting to publish an obituary notice, even though he was recognised as one of the most famous sportsmen in England. But then Warner always was committed to the legend that cricket in England has been played exclusively by companies of angels and virgins, and that nothing untoward was ever done or said or even thought of by a gentleman. But even Messrs Harris and Ashley-Cooper are honest enough to admit that Lord Frederick, for all his antecedents and his prowess, seems to have been the sort of man who prompted his hosts to count the dinner spoons after he had paid a visit. They say: 'One fears that many a scheme which nowadays would cause one to be shunned by right-thinking folk was hatched under his periwig. There was, to express the matter charitably, a side to his character which recalls Horace's description of Achilles:

Irascible, inexorable, keen.

When engaged in a match he would not hesitate to employ any means which might assure him of victory, and when, as occasionally happened, he lost an event which he had set his heart upon winning, he would attempt to bribe Bentley to suppress the score. His Lordship was undoubtedly a very fine cricketer, but his scheming was deplorable.'

The man to take Beauclerk's measure is the sardonic, embittered Bowen, who perceives the nature of Beauclerk's temperament so well that it is almost as though he sees in his lordship certain echoes of himself:

There was one man who made his mark on all the earlier part of the period both through his cricket and through his gambling. This was Lord Frederick Beauclerk. He was a clergyman, and from 1828 till his death vicar of St Albans. He was a very fine batsman and a very fine bowler, and he also possessed a sharp tongue and a bad temper. He often seems a kind of equivalent to the former Bishop of Autun, the eventual Duc de Talleyrand-Perigold; a cleric without, it would seem, the faintest interest in being a clergyman, or any kind of Christian, and one can well imagine a man like Beauclerk, once he had survived the initial terror of a revolution, becoming in the end one of its most distinguished servants.

Even amongst all the hagiography that exists about cricketers, an unqualified eulogy of Beauclerk has never been seen, and that is significant. But he was a fine cricketer. He scored more centuries than anyone except William Ward (who hit nine), and Fuller Pilch with ten; and he hit more fifties than anyone. If it had not been that he played before anyone thought to take a note of the bowling or even to give the bowler's name for batsmen caught or stumped, it is likely that Beauclerk would have shown similar eminence as a bowler. It is by no means improbable that Beauclerk was the first man to take 100 wickets in a season, but we shall never know.

ROWLAND BOWEN, *Cricket, a History of its Growth and Development*, 1970

Beauclerk, Osbaldeston, Ward, Budd and company, being the leaders of the gentlemanly element in English cricket, had no illusions about the racy and sometimes gamey nature of the environment in which the big matches were played. Dorset Square was, after all, within easy walking distance of places like Somers Town and Seven Dials, many of whose inhabitants were no more particular than Lord Frederick when it came to honouring their moral commitments:

Colonel Greville had his pockets picked on Monday last at Lord's ground of cash to the amount of £30. The pickpockets were so daring on Monday evening in the vicinity of Lord's Cricket Ground that they actually took the umbrellas of men and women by force, and even their watches and purses, threatening to stab those who made resistance. They were in gangs of between twenty and thirty, and behaved in a manner the most audacious.

The Press, 1802

Because he was such an outrageous character, a cricketing virtuoso with the ethics of a streetfighter and a temper difficult to control, Beauclerk features in several anecdotes of early days at Lord's. In one of these, we see him outcheated by an even greater cricketer, the immortal 'Silver Billy' Beldham. It took place not so long before the building speculators chased Thomas Lord and his members out of their Dorset Square home forever. The following account seems to suggest that Lord Frederick remained unaware of the advantage taken of him, which somehow seems difficult to believe:

Beldham, Robinson and Lambert played Bennet, Fennex and Lord Frederick Beauclerk, a notable single-wicket match at Lord's, 27th June, 1806. Lord Frederick's last innings was winning the game, and no chance of getting him out. His Lordship had then lately introduced sawdust when the ground was wet. Beldham, unseen, took up a lump of wet dirt and sawdust and stuck it to the ball, which pitching favourably, made an extraordinary twist, and took the wicket. This I heard separately from Beldham, Bennett and also Fennex, who used to mention it as among the wonders of his long life.

JAMES PYCROFT, *The Cricket Field*, 1851

HAD Beauclerk realised what had been done to him, he would have put on his celebrated cabaret act designed for the discomfiture of those who dared to get the better of him on the field of play. It should be explained that in a career lasting thirty-five seasons Beauclerk always wore the same uniform, white stockings, nankeen breeches, a scarlet sash, and a white beaver hat, which, according to H. S. Altham, 'when frustrated, he was apt to dash to the ground'. Here is one instance among many:

I have very frequently known Tom Walker to go in first and remain to the very last man. He was the coolest, the most imperturbable fellow in existence; it used to be said of him that he had no nerves at all. Whether he was only practising, or whether he knew that the game was in a critical state, and that much depended upon his play, he was the same phlegmatic, unmoved man – he was the Washington of cricketers. Neither he nor his brother was active, yet both were effective fieldsmen. Upon one occasion, on the Mary-le-bone grounds, I remember Tom going in first, and Lord Frederick Beauclerk giving him the first four balls all of an excellent length. First four or last four made no difference to Tom – he was always the same cool, collected fellow. Every ball he dropped down just before his bat. Off went his lordship's white hat – dash upon the ground (his constant action when disappointed) – calling him at the same time 'a confounded old beast'. – 'I doan't care what ee zays,' said Tom when one close by asked if he had heard Lord Frederick call him 'an old beast'. No, no, Tom was not the man to be flustered.

JOHN NYREN, *The Cricketers of My Time*, 1833

NOT all Beauclerk's opponents were as unconcerned by his histrionics as Tom Walker. Not long after Thomas Lord had moved to his third and final ground, the MCC, captained by Beauclerk, sent a team up to Nottingham to play against Twenty-Two of the locals. Nottingham at this time, June 1817, was a town rendered potentially dangerous by the activities of the Luddites, and the magistrates warned Beauclerk and his men that if they continued playing after seven o'clock they, the magistrates, would not be responsible for the consequences. At seven o'clock promptly stumps were pulled up, but before the players could reach the safety of the pavilion, the crowd had swarmed on to the pitch. Beauclerk was reported as being highly alarmed, but his fears proved groundless; the crowd desired only a close look at men who dared to play against Twenty-Two. But it was in this match that his years of presumption and self-indulgence finally caught up with his lordship. One of his professional fielders, a player called Stearman, was reproved by Beauclerk, in front of the rest of the side, for slackness in the field. Stearman then lost his temper and, when the chance came, fielded a ball and returned it so violently at Lord Frederick as to dislocate a finger. His lordship foolishly neglected the injury, which almost ended in lockjaw, and is said to have curtailed his active career by at least ten years. Our final glimpse of this extraordinary man is of a pathetic, senile old roué defiantly keeping his temper on the boil to the very last:

Lord Frederick might be seen at the entrance-gate of the old pavilion, generally smoking a cigar, and attended by a little snapping white cur, which never bit anyone, but examined the calves of every one who went in and out, and growled. (His lordship was the only man allowed to take a dog on the ground.) Sir Spencer Ponsonby-Fane recalls Lord Frederick sitting by the scorers, on the field of play, and peremptorily ordering off the ground any spectator who was unfortunate enough to incur his displeasure. As to the gradual change time wrought in him, Mr Pycroft has said: 'At first I used to see his lordship taking a bat to show some tyro "how fields were won"; then, after a few seasons in which he sat in the pavilion as the Nestor of the MCC, he was fond of leaning on some friend's arm, or seeking a sheltered corner and shrinking from every breeze; and last of all he used to appear in his brougham, his health and strength fast failing, with a lady nurse at his side.'

LORD HARRIS AND F.S. ASHLEY-COOPER, *Lord's and the MCC*, 1914

W HAT amuses the modern reader about Lord Frederick is not so much his scoundrelism but the fact that it should have been harboured beneath so aristocratic and so ostensibly pious an exterior. As Bowen reminds us, Beauclerk's success in concealing his religious pretensions was by no means unusual in the Church of England at the time, nor was it a rare spectacle to see someone of noble birth go about his daily business unimpeded by anything so inhibiting as a morality. Once again in taking his lordship's measure, we have to dismiss from our minds any thought of Lord's as the lofty defender of the faith into which it eventually evolved, but to realise that the ground was a countrified hotbed of drinking, gambling and cheating filled with the sort of dissolute young men who later passed through the pages of Thackeray's novels. A visitor to Lord's in Lord Frederick's heyday would no more have expected to find good conversation, ethical concern, respect for the proprieties, than anyone would today visiting a greyhound track or a professional boxing match.

Just in front of the pavilion at Lord's at every great match sat men ready, with money down, to give and take the current odds upon the play. Many well-known bookmakers were to be found regularly amongst them, and even the famous Crockford and Gully occasionally appeared there. William Beldham has related how Gully would often take him aside and discuss the theory of the game with him, but that, being nothing of a player himself, he never became anything of a judge. These Marylebone 'legs' unfortunately were not content with straight-forward business, but resorted to every sort of trick to make their money safe. The same old player told Pycroft how they would go down into Hampshire quite early in the season to 'buy us up'; but it was at the great cricketer's hostel of the 'Green Man and Still' in Oxford Street that their chief business was done. Here all the leading professionals would come to lodge for the big London matches. The best of wine and beef was their normal fare, living such as five guineas for a win and three guineas for a loss could never pay for, and many a young countryman fresh to, and dazzled by, the glamour of London life, must have fallen an easy victim to the free drinks and wiles of the 'legs'. Ultimately of course, the rogues overreached themselves. In one of the Surrey v. All England games of the period, Surrey were represented by a very fine side, and thought to have the match in their pocket. Much to Beldham's surprise, however, he found that the 'legs' were laying seven-to-four against them; but 'this time they were done, for they backed in the belief that some Surrey men had sold the match; but Surrey then played to win'.

The climax came when two of the worst offenders fell into a quarrel at Lord's. Their unguarded recriminations were wafted through the open pavilion windows, and Lord Frederick immediately hauled them before the Committee; they were both in a towering rage, and, being powerful men, were ordered to stand on opposite sides of the table, from which they proceeded to hurl accusations at each other as to the bribes each had received. With the taunts falling in so accurately with the painful recollections of many present as to matches lost and won against all reasonable expectation, the Committee had no choice left open to them. The guilty pair were warned off Lord's for ever, and one of the greatest cricketers of all time then passed ingloriously out of the game.

H. S. ALTHAM, *A History of Cricket*, 1926

A PLAYER almost as renowned as Beauclerk in his time was E. H. Budd, a big-hitting batsman who enjoyed seeing the crowd at Lord's begin to back away when they saw that he was warming to his work of hitting the bowlers as hard and as high as possible. Budd, a magnificent athlete and an impressive figure of a man, is one of the most engaging reminiscers of this early period of cricket history, and had a happy knack of making his anecdotage leap off the page, being one of the very first proficient players to realise, probably instinctively, that much of the truth about a cricketer is revealed, not on the field of play, but in the world at large. Beauclerk said of his colleague, 'Budd always wants to win the game off a single ball'. Budd returned the compliment by observing, of one of Beauclerk's devious betting stratagems, 'It was in my estimation anything but creditable in a clergyman, the brother of a duke.' In chatting to one C. A. Wheeler, compiler of a volume of pleasing gossip entitled *Sportascrapiana*, Budd paints a vivid picture of young men-about-town in the years before Victorian sobriety inhibited so many bumptious spirits:

We remember well an amusing tale of Budd being at Lord's ground playing a match, which we give in his own words: 'A great fellow was there, a City merchant, and he bet me five guineas I did not get him out in twenty balls, and he subsequently denied having made the bet, saying "It's a lie, and you are no gentleman." "Say that again and I'll knock you down." He did what I asked, and I did what I had promised. Lord Frederick Beauclerk said it served him right; but Barton, a lawyer, came up, saying "For —s sake, Budd, stop; he's a tremendously rich man, and will take the law of you." "I don't care," I said, "no man shall say that with impunity." Several friends then began excuses for his infirmity of temper, and at last it was hushed up on my undertaking to provide a fish dinner and wine for the party, at King's Hotel, adjoining Lord's.

'I sent to Billingsgate for a peck of periwinkles. I got splendid silver covers from Bott, one of the King's pages, who lived near, and a gallon of British wine, from Dales in the Haymarket; and thus, on the appointed day, after a game of cricket, a dinner of periwinkles only was served. Before the covers were removed, the guests wondered why a large pin was laid for each man at table. The offended individual was the more irate by my thus (as he said) adding insult to injury; and pleaded that as I had not performed my contract, he would bring his action after all, if it cost him £1,000. Two of the party (Bartons) were lawyers, and I gave them a shilling each to take the risk, and there the affair ended. Long after this I was playing in a match and my periwinkle friend was on the ground; thinking, perhaps, I did not know him, he asked me to give him a ball. I did so, and with a jerk sent one in like lightning, that took his hand with a force quite equal to the former blow I had given him. I saw the blood running, but did not see that he wanted any more of it.'

E. H. BUDD, quoted in C. A. WHEELER, *Sportascrapiana*, 1867

THE Victorians would never have tolerated Beauclerk for a moment, but even as his lordship was perpetrating his outrages, the temper of the times was slowly beginning to change, at least in cricket. With the new century arrived a group of grandees whose attitudes were occasionally to anticipate the later obsession with playing up and playing the game, men who did much to elevate the casual enterprise of Thomas Lord into something perilously close to a secular religion. Among these was Benjamin Aislabie, who, in the portrait by Henry Dawe, retains into old age the open demeanour of a happy schoolboy as he sits at a table contentedly clasping the MCC Committee Minute Book.

One hundred years ago no figure was more familiar at Lord's than that of Benjamin Aislabie, who was born in London in January 1774 and educated at Eton. He was connected with the MCC for forty years, being elected a member in 1802 and acting as Honorary Secretary, to the satisfaction of all, from 1822 until his death twenty years later. He was extremely fond of the game, which he understood thoroughly, and for many years arranged the great matches and often played in them. As a cricketer he was of no account, and during the last ten years or so that he appeared weighed nineteen or twenty stone, always having someone to run and field for him, and whilst at the wicket creating considerable amusement. Nothing pleased him more than to take teams to play against the Public Schools, and in *Tom Brown's Schooldays* we are told how 'old Mr Aislabie stood by looking on in his white hat, leaning on a bat, in benevolent enjoyment', and after dinner 'made the best speeches that ever were heard'. He was the author of several cricket verses, songs and alphabets, some of which he occasionally sang at the club's Anniversary Dinners, and was a most agreeable companion. Mr Herbert Jenner said it was due entirely to his personal charm that he continued his membership, and Mitford described him as 'the father of cricket and the great *fautor* of the Marylabonne Club'. It is a proof of his popularity that in 1823 he was elected President of the Club. At Lord's his bust and an oil painting commemorate him.

Aislabie by profession was a wine merchant and for some years lived at Lee Place, which, in allusion to his size, used to be called by some of his friends the Elephant and Castle. Concerning Aislabie's size and weight, Mr Philip Norman wrote: 'In 1826, as Herbert Jenner and he were on their way to Kingscote to play in a match, they put up at the Plough Inn, Cheltenham, where there was a weighing machine. After much persuasion, Aislabie was induced to mount thereon; he said it was of no use, as he knew his weight to an ounce – exactly seventeen stone. He carefully took out his pocket-book, purse, and bunch of keys. To the surprise of everyone, including a tall chambermaid, the machine registered nineteen stone.' Aislabie, it may be added, was custodian of the club snuff-box. One day, shortly before his last illness, he left it in charge of Dark, who put it away carefully and forgot all about it until 1867, when he at once restored it to the MCC.

HENRY DAWE, quoted in LORD HARRIS AND F. S. ASHLEY-COOPER,
Lord's and the MCC, 1914

MEN like Aislabie have become renowned only within the limits of cricket history, but in 1805 there suddenly descends on Lord's the figure of a boy destined to become one of Europe's most notorious men, and one of the very few for whom the modern world retains a breathless fascination. In the summer of 1805 Lord Byron was seventeen years old, and impatiently performing the rituals of his final term at Harrow School. Congenital lameness had cruelly handicapped him, but not enough, evidently, to prevent his attempts to assert himself on the cricket field. The most readable of his many biographers, André Maurois, conveys the impression of a turbulent, obstinate youth, half-rake, half-scholar, a problem child whose classical learning was acknowledged by his teachers, and so dominated his attitudes that even the school playing fields seemed analogous to the legends of Olympus: 'There is always a small band of demi-gods who rule in an English public school,' writes Maurois, 'and of this sanctified band Byron was now part. The slopes of Harrow Hill, overlooking the plains where the ploughman toiled and the rival teams waged their cricketing battles, made him think of Homer's Mount Ida, from whose summit the Gods looked down upon the works and wars of mortals.' But it apparently made him think also of gilding the lily in an attempt to conceal the modest nature of his cricketing gifts. Byron, who was to sentimentalise in print about the days when he and his schoolmates were 'together joined in Cricket's manly toil', was fortunate to have reached Lord's ground at all.

The score-sheet of the Eton v. Harrow match played at Lord's on August 2, 1805, records that one of the Harrow batsmen, George Gordon, Lord Byron, played innings of seven and two. Byron refers to this match in a letter to Charles Gordon in which he wrote: 'We have played Eton, and were most confoundedly beat; however, it was some comfort to me that I got eleven notches in the first innings and seven in the second, which was more than any of our side, except Brookman and Ipswich, could contrive to hit.' It will be seen that Byron presumes to exaggerate his scores, but this is not so remarkable as the fact that he played at all. Owing to his lameness he had to have someone to run for him, and quite apart from this he does not seem to have been a very good player. Charles Lloyd, the Harrow captain of 1808, remarks that 'Byron played in the Eleven, and very badly too. He should never have been in the Eleven had my counsel been taken.'

No doubt Byron wished to play at Lord's, and, being Byron, managed to be chosen. In spite of his handicap he appears to have enjoyed his cricket. In his first publication, *Hours of Idleness*, which appeared in 1807, he recollects how he and his fellows

> ... beneath the noontide sun,
> In rival bands, between the wickets run,
> Drive o'er the sward the ball with active force,
> Or chase with nimble feet its rapid course.

He also reminds 'Alonzo, best and dearest of my friends', how

> Together we impell'd the flying ball:
> Together waited in our tutor's hall:
> Together joined in Cricket's manly toil.

One of Byron's contemporaries at Harrow said: 'Though Byron was lame he was a great lover of sports, and preferred hockey to Horace, relinquished even Helicon for duck-puddle, and gave up the best poet that ever wrote hard Latin, for a game of cricket on the common.' Many years later Byron wrote that in his schooldays he was 'always cricketing–rebelling–fighting ... and in all manner of mischiefs', which suggests that he regarded cricket as simply an activity in which he could exercise his tempestuous personality. He continues the letter quoted earlier on by saying that 'after the match we dined together and were exceedingly friendly; not a single discordant word was uttered by either party. To be sure, we were most of us rather drunk, and went together to the Haymarket, where we kicked up a row ... how I got home after the play, God knows!' The victorious Etonians after the match addressed the following epigram to their opponents:

> Adventurous boys of Harrow School,
> Of cricket you've no knowledge;
> You play not cricket, but the fool
> With Men of Eton College.

Byron, it is said, took up the challenge on behalf of Harrow and sent the following reply:

> Ye Eton wags, to play the fool
> Is not the boast of Harrow School;
> What wonder then at our defeat?
> Folly like yours could ne'er be beat.

A neat reply, displaying Byron to better advantage as a poet than a cricketer, even though he himself claimed (with considerable 'poetic licence') to have been the third most successful batsman on the side.

GERALD BRODRIBB, *All Round the Wicket*, 1951

Mr R. J. P. Broughton of Harrow, said that they went to Lord's by coach or post-chaise. The coach was the cheaper, but they preferred to go by chaise, and so saved up for it. A chaise held three, and the cost was thirty shillings, or ten shillings each boy. As a rule ten or twelve of these vehicles would start from the school. At a given word they would go off at a gallop, and all the way to London it was one mad, wild race. They used to pass and repass, and if the postboys were not particularly skilful in managing the horses accidents were inevitable. Generally there were one or two smashes. One year the race was more than usually exciting. It was literally neck and neck until one of the chaises skidded in a rut, and then there was a collision. Those behind, unable to stop, crashed on to the broken vehicles, adding to the confusion and producing some accidents. After this racing was strictly forbidden. Broughton had a curious experience in the match with Eton in 1834. Whilst fielding in the first innings, he and W. S. Buckingham, both going for a catch at short-leg, collided and both became insensible. They were carried into the pavilion and laid side by side on the table until they came round again. The umpire said that, between them, they had held the ball long enough to make a catch: but nobody had appealed.

LORD HARRIS AND F. S. ASHLEY-COOPER, *Lord's and the MCC*, 1914

ALTHOUGH Eton v. Harrow 1805 has been known ever since as Byron's Match, historians have regretfully pointed out that in strict terms the match does not belong in the pantheon at all. Eighty-four years later this tiny issue was apparently still smouldering in the minds of some Old Harrovians, including Lord Bessborough, who wrote to *The Harrovian* in November 1889 to the effect that the respective captains of Eton and Harrow in 1805 had not arranged the match, that the Harrow captain, Byron's friend J. A. Lloyd, was not a member of the school at the time, and went on, with some relevance to the dispute over Byron's runmaking in the match: 'There is no authentic record of the game of 1805. The score, which is inserted in *Scores and Biographies*, is taken from a half-sheet of paper sent anonymously through Frederick Lillywhite to the Hon. Robert Grimston, who forwarded it to the editor of *Bell's Life in London*, for what it was worth, and from that paper it has been copied in *Scores and Biographies*.' Here is a corner of Byronian scholarship strangely neglected by the prodigious Byron industry. Was the poet telling lies about his scores? Or was the mysterious unidentified sender of Bessborough's half-sheet an enemy of Byron, an embryonic critic, perhaps? Nobody knows, but it is revealing that Lord Harris and Mr Ashley-Cooper prefer anonymous notes to dissolute poets, for they state as a matter of fact that Byron against Eton scored 'only seven and two'. Both Bessborough and Grimston were to play their part in the evolution of Lord's in the years after Byron's death, but in an attempt to clarify the picture of the ground at the time of Byron's one appearance as a player there, it is necessary to examine Thomas Lord's policy, not as a cricket manager but as an impresario open to any likely offer:

Although Lord's was primarily a cricket ground, various sports were practised there. There were frequent hopping matches, and John Bentley alone won twenty-nine there. The ground, too, was occasionally used as an exercise ground by the St Mary-le-bone Volunteers, and more than once there was a consecration of colours presented by Lady Jane Dundas to various regiments of the Royal East India Volunteers. Furthermore, M. Garnerin made his second balloon ascent in the country from Lord's ground on July 5th, 1802, accompanied by Mr E. H. Locker, in the presence of the Prince of Wales, who was attended by several ladies of distinction and an immense number of nobility. As the aeronaut and his companion were about to ascend they were handed the following letter:

> Lord's Cricket Ground
> July 5th, 1802

> We, the undersigned, having been present at the ascension of M. Garnerin, with his balloon, this afternoon, and witnessed the entire satisfaction of the public, beg leave to recommend him to the notice of any gentleman in whose neighbourhood he may happen to descend.
> Signed: GEORGE P. W.
> BESSBOROUGH
> G. DEVONSHIRE
> CATHCART

The wind was too high to allow Garnerin to descend by parachute, as he intended, and the two adventurers alighted at Chingford, having travelled seventeen miles in just over fifteen minutes.

LORD HARRIS AND F. S. ASHLEY-COOPER, *Lord's and the MCC*, 1914

IN encouraging anybody who cared to show himself off in any activity vaguely sporting, Thomas Lord was creating a precedent which was followed for most of the nineteenth century. Today the thought of the MCC hiring the ground out to 'other games' seems too outlandish to countenance, and as for the action of the administrators of The Oval some years ago in allowing a programme of popular music to be performed inside the ground, such a thing would probably cause death by apoplexy among the club members. But it was not always so. Harris and Ashley-Cooper state that Lord Frederick Beauclerk took part in many running contests at Lord's, and also displayed his ability to blow live creatures to pieces whether he intended eating them or not. This claim is substantiated in more than one periodical of the time:

Lord Frederick Beauclerk was the first at the winning-post, for the Gold Medal, on Saturday, the 12th inst., at Lord's Ground, Mary-le-Bone. His Lordship retired, for the second time, with the annual honours of the Club, from having killed forty of sixty pigeons; though the shooting this year was very inferior to that of the former season.

Sporting Magazine, June 1813

VIOLENCE of a very different kind attended the birth of Lord's second ground. The premises at North Bank were officially taken over on 8 May 1811, after great care had been taken to remove the Dorset Square turf and replant it on the new ground, so that 'the noblemen and Gentlemen of the MCC can play on the same footing as before'. Unfortunately for Lord, very few of the said noblemen and Gentlemen had any desire to play on the new ground on whatever footing, and in the three seasons, from 1811 to 1813, the club played only three matches there. In 1813 Lord Liverpool's government decreed that the Regent's Canal should be cut through the centre of the ground, but the Eyre family, who owned the acreage, agreed to allow Thomas Lord to rent another plot. At a rent of £100 per annum, Lord was ready to reopen on the present premises when beset by a singular disaster.

A shocking accident occurred on Thursday at the New Lord's Cricket-ground public house, Mary-le-bone fields. The landlady of the house had occasion to use a small quantity of gunpowder, and whilst in the act of taking the same from a paper, containing a pound weight, a spark from the fire caught it and it went off with a great explosion. The landlady, her sister, and two little girls who were in the room were seriously burnt. The two former are in a dangerous way. The explosion broke every pane of glass in the room and also set it on fire.

St James's Chronicle, 5–7 May 1814

THERE is something oddly disingenuous about this report, which leaves unspoken the thought that very few public-house landladies of the period could have had either access to or the need for gunpowder in the administration of their professional duties. Further light is shed on this obscure scene by J. L. Carr, who, in his delightful *Dictionary of Extraordinary English Cricketers*, includes the following entry: 'Mrs Emma Locksley, landlady of the New Lord's Tavern, in a fit of despair, blew up her house, her sister-in-law, and herself.' The roots of Mrs Locksley's despair have never been located, but have never been attributed to the proximity of boring batsmanship. Well aware that his members had shown some distaste for the white elephant of North Bank, Lord did everything in his power to make ground number three too attractive and well-appointed to ignore. He began investing capital in a string of improved amenities:

The ground had to be carefully prepared, a tavern, pavilion and various smaller buildings erected, and the whole site enclosed by a high fence. So occupied was he in attending to the welfare of the MCC members that he had not time to provide new accommodation for himself: until 1816, in fact, he continued to reside in Upper Gloucester Street, but in that year built two small houses at the south-east corner of the ground, in one of which he lived until he left London fourteen years later. Where he laboured with such energy was then quite a rural spot, there being no houses between it and the Eyre Arms on the one side, or between it and the Swiss Cottage on the other. In 1814, however, St John's Wood Church was built, and almost simultaneously many houses were erected in the immediate vicinity. Clearly Lord was only just in time to save the site from the builders.

His efforts notwithstanding, however, it was very long indeed before the new ground could compare at all favourably with the first. For many years there were two ponds on it, and W. H. Slatter, the Clerk of Works at Lord's, informs us that his father, the well-known Steevie, who was born in 1818 and was engaged at Lord's for about forty years, taught himself to swim in one of them; he tied one end of a rope to a tree and passed the other round his body, so that when tired or in difficulties he could haul himself out.

LORD HARRIS AND F. S ASHLEY-COOPER, *Lord's and the MCC*, 1914

L ORD'S official opening of his new ground, overshadowed by the disintegration of Mrs Locksley and her dependents, eventually went ahead, and its proprietor was pleased to note far more enthusiasm for it than for the North Bank compromise. Gentlemen riding out from town to participate found adequate stabling facilities and some excellent sport. They also found the opportunity to practise their repertoire of strokes, for in 1818 was hired the first practice bowler at Lord's. A well-scrubbed young man in formal dress with shining topper held deferentially in white-gloved hands, William Caldecourt looks altogether too bookish and mild-mannered to be very effective as a cricketer. However, the facts contradict outward appearances. Caldecourt turns out to have been an unsung anticipator of Sir Garfield Sobers:

It was in 1818 that 'Honest Will' Caldecourt, then only fifteen years of age, but receiving a man's pay, was engaged at Lord's as a practice bowler, a position he retained for forty seasons. He had commenced his connexion with the club six years before as a ground-boy upon Lord's second enclosure, and for over thirty years few figures were more familiar at headquarters. Besides being a well-known coach at Harrow and Cambridge, and famous as an umpire, he was long remembered for scoring six sixes off a six-ball over in a match between Watford and Hertfordshire, a feat which was counted so remarkable by Mr Ward that he paid two guineas for the ball as a memento of the performance.

LORD HARRIS AND F. S. ASHLEY-COOPER, *Lord's and the MCC*, 1914

M EANWHILE Lord continued to improve amenities at the ground, doing what he could to achieve that elaboration of the premises which not only was deemed appropriate to the expectations of gentlemen, but which would continue to command the allegiance of those gentlemen. Although business seemed brisk enough, evidently it was not brisk enough to the point where it satisfied Lord's entrepreneurial ambitions. In 1825 he received a lease on the property from the Eyres, and proceeded to lay plans for building seven pairs of houses, leaving a truncated playing area in the south-west corner. Contemporary opinion suggests that Lord was increasingly doubtful that the ground could be made to pay its way through cricket alone, and there seems little question that the unsentimental Lord, had he been convinced of the financial advantages, was prepared to build houses to cover the entire site. At this point there stepped in one of the legendary saviours of the ground.

Mr William Ward, who was destined to play so important a part in the history of the MCC, was born at Highbury Place, Islington, almost within hail of the old White Conduit ground in 1787, and was a large and powerfully built man, 6 foot 1 inch in height and weighing 14 stone. His schooldays were passed at Winchester, and he became one of the best-known financiers of his generation. As a youth he spent some time at Antwerp at a banking-house, but was taken into partnership by his father in 1810 and elected a Director of the Bank of England seven years later. If to this we add that he was returned to Parliament in the Tory interest for the City of London in 1826, that he retired from public life in 1835, when beaten by the Whigs, and that in 1847 he published *Remarks on the Monetary Legislation of Great Britain*, we shall have mentioned the chief events of his career apart from his cricket.

Pycroft says that he made a serious business of his practice. 'He once,' remarked Caldecourt, 'gave me a guinea because, discovering a weak point in his play, I bowled him out twice one morning. Ward would also practise at eighteen or nineteen yards, instead of twenty-two, to increase his difficulty. After that he found play at twenty-two yards comparatively easy.' He was fond of making curious matches with his friends, and more than once handicapped himself by using a walking-stick instead of a bat. Like most men who have practised intelligently and been coached well, he was able to play with credit to himself until well advanced in years. Even Mynn at his best found him a difficult batsman to contain, and it has been said that his average in the last year he played was seventy. His style was perfectly upright, and therein perhaps lay the secret of his success. When he had begun to increase in weight, and to lose some of his effect, Lord Frederick Beauclerk, in his amiable way, suggested that he was 'too big to play cricket', a remark which, being repeated to Ward, had not a little to do with his rejuvenescence.

LORD HARRIS AND F. S ASHLEY COOPER, *Lord's and the MCC*, 1914

ACCOUNTS vary in small details regarding Ward's lightning speed of action once he realised that Lord was prepared to bury the cherished ground under a pile of bricks and mortar, but the essentials of the story of his intervention have never been contradicted. There seems no doubt that it is to Ward, more than any other man of his age, more even than to Thomas Lord, that we owe the existence of the friendliest, most attractive, most nearly perfect cricket ground in England.

Last of the great gentlemen players of the period comes William Ward. Parliamentary representative for the City of London, Director of the Bank of England, and an unrivalled hand at picquet, his abiding fame rests mainly on two accounts. In 1825 Lord seems to have become anxious as to his financial position, and began at last to play with the idea of turning the ground into a building estate. Ward recognised the danger in a flash, went to Lord and asked him his price for the lease. 'Five thousand,' was the reply. Ward drew his cheque-book from his pocket, Lord passed into honourable retirement, and Lord's was saved from an unimaginable fate. To this same Ward's credit stood, until Holmes beat it in 1925, the record for the highest score ever made at headquarters, 278, on July 24th, 1820, for MCC v. Norfolk.

LORD HARRIS AND F. S. ASHLEY-COOPER, *Lord's and the MCC*, 1914

It was reported that the ground was for sale, and Mr Ward remarked to Lord, 'It's said you are going to sell us.' Lord said he would dispose of the ground if he could get his price. 'What is your price?' said Ward; and having the reply, £5000, Mr Ward said, 'Give me your pen and ink.' A cheque was at once drawn for the amount, and the purchase was thought a good investment. 'I have heard,' said Mr Budd, 'that he settled it on his sisters.' Mr Ward, who was a Bank of England director, was highly esteemed by City men, as indeed he was by a wide circle of acquaintances, and was also a great man in the cricket world. He often used to back Mr Budd thus: according to who was bowling against Mr Budd, Mr Ward would give £20 to £25 to anyone who would give him £1 for every run scored by Mr Budd at the one innings, knowing that he was making a pretty safe thing, Mr Budd's average being twenty-nine in all the great matches.

C. A. WHEELER, *Sportascrapiana*, 1867

IMMEDIATELY on acquiring control, Ward began investing considerable sums of money in the improvement of facilities, especially the wooden pavilion erected by Lord in 1814. Intent on achieving that elaboration of the premises which he deemed appropriate to the needs of gentlemen like himself, Ward set to work. But those gods towards whom so many classically educated men of Ward's generation deferred were waiting to mock his pretensions.

About half-past one yesterday morning a fire broke out in a large building called The Pavilion, erected in the cricket-ground near the school of the orphans of the clergy, on the St John's Wood Road. From the nature of the materials, which were chiefly of wood, although lately enhanced and beautified at a great expense, the fire in a very short time defied the power of the fire-engines and water, if there had been a sufficient supply of the latter, which happened not to be the case. In about half an hour after the commencement of the fire, the whole Pavilion was reduced to a heap of ruins, saving only the foundation, which is about three feet high of brick-work. So strong was the fire that the wooden rails round the building were partly destroyed. There was a very valuable wine-cellar well-stored in the Pavilion, belonging to the gentlemen of the various clubs who frequently play in the ground, which shared the same fate with the building. Happily no houses were near enough to the spot to be in the least danger, but some of the trees in the adjoining grounds were scorched. Yesterday a grand match of cricket was to have been played between the young gentlemen of Eton and Harrow Schools.

The Times, 30 June 1825

DESTRUCTION OF THE ASSEMBLY, BETTING AND DRESSING ROOMS
AT LORD'S CRICKET GROUNDS

About one o'clock yesterday morning a fire was discovered in the above orna-mental buildings, attached to the far-famed grounds belonging formerly to Mr Lord, but now in the possession of a Mr Ward, in which, perhaps, some of the greatest cricketers have played and alternately won and lost thousands.

The building was situated at the northern extremity of the play-ground and so remote from any resource of water, that the efforts of those who surrounded the burning fabric were rendered completely ineffectual. By a quarter to two o'clock several of the town engines were on the road leading to the gates of the ground, but the freshness of the wind had by this time so wound up the burning element that the most appalling fears were evinced; in fact, so emblazoned was the horizon that to those who witnessed the reflection of the light in the Strand and on the adjacent Bridges, the conflagration seemed very near, and hundreds of persons stood for some time looking with wonder at the rapid strides it made. By half past two o'clock no less than twenty to thirty engines were at the gates and on the grounds but, as we before stated, were rendered wholly useless from the situation of the building. It is but justice to state that we never witnessed a more ready attendance of firemen belonging to the different Fire Offices, but such was the appearance in the element that many were led astray; in fact, several of the engines went round by Maida Hill, and came to the spot from the North road. So late as half past four, engines from the more distant London stations continued to arrive; but by this time the fire had nearly burnt itself out, and all that was left to those who were admitted to witness it was the mass of burning timber that lay on the ground. Our Reporter, who was on the spot, endeavoured by every means to find out by what accident the fire had taken place, but all he could learn was, that a party had been in the ground in the afternoon, and after their departure the rooms had been left in supposed security. That the fire was caused by accident there can be no doubt, but how the accident occurred must remain a mystery. By five o'clock there only remained the burnt-out embers of the fabric, and the engines were ordered to return to their respective stations.

The stronger proof of the extent of the flames on the horizon was such that the fire-engines from Poplar and the adjacent parts were on the spot. It is a curious fact that a grand match was to have been played yesterday in the grounds, between the Scholars of Harrow School and Eton College and that some of the parties enjoyed themselves there in the early part of Thursday.

Morning Post, 30 July 1825

By many incendiarism was suspected, 'for there never was any fire in the Pavilion during the season, beyond a lighted candle to enable gentlemen to smoke their cigars'. W. H. Slatter suggests that a thunderstone caused the destruction, and in support of his theory states that, when the foundation of the present Pavilion was being laid, one was found embedded in the earth on the site occupied by the original building.

LORD HARRIS AND F. S. ASHLEY-COOPER, *Lord's and the MCC*, 1914

THIS great calamity was followed by the beating of many a committed breast, none more violently than the one belonging to the Reverend James Pycroft, who, carefully losing all sense of proportion in his opening statement, and in the process dropping a cunning hint that he had been the beneficiary of an impressively expensive education, nonetheless kept his head to the extent of letting posterity know of the relentlessly mercantile style of Thomas Lord. Evidently unmoved by the disaster, Lord, who, contrary to general belief in the aftermath of the fire, had managed to retrieve some of the club's records, later *sold* them to the club, as Pycroft, with apparent innocence, records:

What the destruction of Rome and its records by the Gauls was to Niebuhr, what the Fire of London was to the antiquary in his walk from Pudding Lane to Pie Corner, such was the burning of the pavilion at Lord's, and all the old score-books – it is a mercy that the old painting of the MCC was saved – to the annalist of cricket. 'When we were built out by Dorset Square,' says Mr E. H. Budd, 'we played for three years where the Regent's Canal has since been cut, and still we call our ground Lord's, and our dressing-room the Pavilion. How many a time have I looked over the old papers of Delany and Sir H. Mann, but the room was burnt, and the old scores perished in the flames.'

(The disastrous fire occurred in the early morning of Friday, 29th June, 1825, and the scene must have been curious when ten hours after the outbreak, the Eton v. Harrow match was commenced. By some incendiarism was suspected, but there is evidence to suggest that the fire was caused by a thunderstone. It may be well to record that not all the score-books were destroyed, for Lord afterwards sold several to the MCC. Possibly they had been stored in the premises occupied by Lord in the corner of the ground as a dwelling-house and so have escaped destruction.)

JAMES PYCROFT, *The Cricket Field*, 1851

WARD promptly rebuilt the pavilion, and the institution of Lord's began slowly to advance out of the miasma of its own pre-history. There were two bones of contention in these years, one closely allied to the other: the dangerous condition of the pitches, and the dubious legality of any bowling which was not purely under-arm. Many of the gentlemen-batsmen of the day were bitterly opposed to the new, round-arm approach for the obvious reason that it exposed pitilessly the flaws in their technique. Lord's ground stood out for a while against the innovations of the round-arm fast bowlers, and was scandalised by the events of 1822 when the Kentish bowler John Willes brought the county side to Lord's to play against the MCC. Willes was a known round-armer, a man whose persistent use of the blasphemous delivery had often caused crowds to invade the pitch and bring the game to a premature close. Willes remained dedicated to the cause, and was determined that he and it should be accepted at Lord's. His persistence resulted in the most eccentric retirement from the game ever recorded.

On July 15th, 1822, the end of Willes' missionary attempt came. He opened the bowling for Kent against the MCC at Lord's, but was promptly no-balled by Noah Mann, son of the old Hambledon Noah, and godson of Sir Horace: Willes threw down the ball in disgust, jumped on his horse, and rode away out of Lord's, and out of cricket history.

H. S. ALTHAM, *A History of Cricket*, 1926

ALTHOUGH history was on the side of Willes and his horse, the reluctance of the batsmen to accept the round-arm style of delivery can best be understood in the context of the primitive pitches of the period, in which regard Lord's was no better and perhaps a great deal worse than all the others.

I remember that, at Lord's, the creases were cut out in the turf about an inch deep. It was a bad plan. The lines were not always cut straight, and they were always being filled up, so that the umpires used to take a stump now and then to scratch them out afresh with the point, as they were very liable to become choked up with dirt or trodden over. They were often not clearly discernible. I don't remember to have seen them at any other ground than Lord's, but without doubt the system was in use in days of yore. I remember very well when Lord's was sheep-fed. Shortly before a match the sheep were penned in the north-east corner of the ground. A light roller only was used, and the bents of grass were just skimmed off on the morning of the match, or sometimes on the day before. I don't think that much water was ever used to get the pitch in order, and at times the ground was not only very fiery, but positively dangerous if the bowling was fast. The cracks in the ground were often enormous, but I do not think that a ball was ever lost in one of them.

NB: At Lord's and The Oval the only boundary in Mr Walker's time was the pavilion, and for some years even a hit to the pavilion had to be run out.

V. E. WALKER, quoted in W. BETTESWORTH, *The Walkers of Southgate*, 1900

Eighty years ago, and for long afterwards, the wickets at headquarters partook very much of the Grampian Hills. 'Lord's in those days,' wrote Mr Pycroft, 'in a hot summer was clay baked to the hardness of brick, as different from any other ground as a metal billiard table is quicker than a wooden one; only those used to Lord's ever did justice to their play.' Caldecourt, never deficient in pluck, when ordered to assist as an emergency said he would as soon stand up for a fight, for the blows he expected. Frequently the deliveries of very fast bowlers bounded over the batsman and wicket-keeper into long-stop's hands. For a few seasons Alfred Mynn and Redgate terrorised batsmen by their pace, and Lord Verulam, asked who was the faster, said, 'I was hit by both, and I really cannot say which hurt the most.' Early members were wont to declare that Redgate was the best bowler ever seen at Lord's, but he ran violently up to the wicket, threw his whole body into his work, and delivered the ball with great effort to himself. Unfortunately, he did not live carefully, and in consequence his career was short, but he loved the game to the last and, when unable to walk, used to attend the matches at Trent Bridge in a bath-chair. 'His weakness was known,' says Felix, 'and there was a general conspiracy to pass the tankard.'

LORD HARRIS AND F. S. ASHLEY-COOPER, *Lord's and the MCC*, 1914

THE decline of poor Redgate was typical of a problem besetting the professional cricketers of the day, who lived well enough while still active in the higher reaches of the game, but were often hard put to stay fed and clothed once their playing days were over. We read frequently of teenagers emerging from the coal mines on to the cricket field, enjoying their day and then returning in middle age to the same coal mines. Even the briefest biographies of the working-class cricketer draw a sedate veil over the later years of once-famous players, the euphemism usually being a reference in the style of 'as to the hardships of his later years there is no need to dwell on those unhappy times...'. The pathos of famous men reduced to penury was one which troubled plebeian and patrician alike, and in time all sorts of benefit funds and testimonials were engineered to cushion retirement. One victim among many in the early years was the great star of the early Hampshire sides:

Hampshire for a few years were seen annually at Lord's, where Tom Beagley, their best batsman, invariably did well. In the Gentlemen v. Players match of 1821, arranged in celebration of the Coronation of George IV, he carried out his bat for 113, hitting freely and well against the bowling of Lord Frederick Beauclerk and Budd. He was considered the best long-stop of his time, and in an old poem was referred to as:

> ... Worthy Beagley, who is quite at the top –
> With the bat he's first-rate, a brick wall at long-stop.

He married the beautiful Catherine Forjonnel, but, despite her devotion and exertions, it was only a timely subscription organised by the MCC in 1851 which saved him from want.

LORD HARRIS AND F. S. ASHLEY-COOPER, *Lord's and the MCC*, 1914

I recall him sitting neglected and alone under the lime-trees at Lord's while the ground was resounding with just such cheers for others, in his day unborn, which once had been raised for him. At length a benefit was attempted, in acknowledgement of his former services; but the weather rendered it of little worth to him, and time after time we saw him looking more threadbare and more pitiful, till at last a notice in 'Bell' told us what Thomas Beagley had been and what, alas! he was.

'Do you see that old man sitting there?' we said to one of the first of the amateurs; 'that man is Thomas Beagley.'

'Thomas who?' was the reply.

JAMES PYCROFT, *The Cricket Field*, 1851

L ORD'S in the 1830s was sufficiently well recognised as the centre of the game, and had been established as such for long enough, for there to exist a body of sentimentalists experienced enough in spectating to bemoan the loss of the old innocence. As bowlers countered the techniques of all-conquering batsmen by developing round-arm bowling, and as batsmen countered by developing defensive play, resorting to protective pads and gloves, and as the occasional serious accident strengthened the case for better pitches, so the cricket itself became more sophisticated, its techniques more firmly established. There is no question that all-round skills were increasing, and no question either that this improvement caused considerable heartburn among the old school:

Cricket is quite national, and, from early habit, I never come to London without visiting the ground at Mary-le-bone, where, indeed, though admiration is greatly excited by the perfection with which the game is executed, yet there is a feeling present, which, I think, rather checks the exhilarating remembrance of our earlier pleasure. The play there seems to partake too much of the cold character of science, and to have something of the insensibility and hardness of mechanism about it; and there is a cautious slowness in its progress which shows how much the wary understanding and how little the promptness of the heart is engaged.

THE REV. CHARLES TOWNSHEND (attrib.), 1835

O NE of the key dates in the history of Lord's is 30 June 1835, when the Eyres, acting on the direction of Thomas Lord junior, granted to Ward a lease on the ground for the next fifty-nine years at a yearly rental of £150. In July Ward transferred the lease to a man whose influence on the ground was to be even greater than that of Thomas Lord himself. James Henry Dark, born in the Edgware Road, the son of a poor saddler, in 1795. He was engaged as a fielder at the old Dorset Square ground when only ten years old, and, following Lord from ground to ground, saw all the grandees from Beauclerk to W. G. Grace. His memoirs, had he bothered to write them, may well have been one of the great cricket books, but Dark, who grew into a forbidding figure, bewhiskered and draped in a cape, was reticent to the end. He had been a good enough cricketer to represent the Players, and later won some respect as an umpire. One contemporary study describes him as 'a mischievous performer, hitting all over the ground. He is of a somewhat pugnacious aspect, and apparently of a rather irascible temper, but a good fellow nevertheless. In make he is rather short, but broad-shouldered and sturdy.' By the time he bought the Lord's lease from Ward for £2,000 and an annuity of £425, he was already a power at the ground, and it was not long before people began referring to Lord's as Dark's. His effect on arrangements was wholly benign, and it could be said that he as much as any man ensured the future of the ground.

The noblemen and gentlemen who dined at the Pavilion expressed their entire approbation of the splendid condition of the ground and the improvements that have already taken place. A beautiful garden has been added to it, and nearly four hundred trees planted round the ground. The Pavilion has been tastefully decorated, and all the premises have undergone a thorough repair at a great expense.

Bell's Life, 15 May 1837

The Marylebone Club, having been established in year 1787, it is resolved that a Jubilee Match shall take place at Lord's Ground on the second Monday in July, 1837, for the benefit of the Players; twenty-two of whom shall be chosen to perform on that day. The Earl of Thanet and the Lord Frederick Beauclerk are requested to make the selection; and every Member of the Club is solicited for a subscription of One Pound towards the promotion of the sport on this interesting occasion.

BENJAMIN AISLABIE (SECRETARY OF THE MCC), 25 July 1836

The Pavilion has undergone a complete renovation, especially in the interior, and is lighted with gas. A new assembly-room has been built over the parlour of the Tavern, and the long-room at the east end of the Tavern is now converted into a billiard-room. At the west end a piece of ground, which had long been in a neglected state, is now turned into an excellent bowling green, the whole of which is railed in. Mr Dark has also taken a large portion of the nursery ground on the north side, which is intended for an archery ground.

Bell's Life, 13 May 1838

The chief event of 1838 was the laying of the foundation-stone of the Tennis Court by Mr Aislabie on October 15th. The building involved Dark in an outlay of over £4,000, but it tended very considerably to increase the membership of the Club. In the apartments attached to the Tennis Court, Mr Dark has made every provision for the comfort of his patrons. They can be furnished with as many as 100 warm baths and 100 cold baths per diem, with dressing-rooms; couches have also been provided for their temporary use after a heavy practice, and there are two of the best billiard-tables that can be manufactured.

WILLIAM DENISON, *Sketches of the Players*, 1846

MORE even than Lord before him, Dark was clearly aware of the extra-cricketing potential of a well-appointed ground within comfortable distance of the West End and the City. And unlike Lord, Dark did not have to worry about breaching any traditions; by the time he came into his property Lord's was well known as a place where anything might happen, and occasionally did.

On May 1, 1828, a large crowd assembled to see John Joseph Grandserre attempt to cover twenty miles on a velocipede in two hours twenty minutes, for a wager of 2,000 guineas between several noblemen. The ground being too soft for the purpose, the Frenchman consented to perform on the public pathway outside. He travelled for two hours fifteen minutes under the greatest disadvantages, 'it being out of the power of the constables to prevent the crowd occasionally pressing round him, and an unusual number of dogs kept crossing his path'. There being doubt as to the distance covered, all bets were declared off.

The Times, 1838

In *The Times* of September 13, 1837, is an account of an abortive attempt by an aeronaut named Hampton to demonstrate the utility of a newly-invented parachute. An endeavour was made to ascend in a half-inflated balloon, the result being that the chimney stack of a neighbouring cottage was wrecked and the car became entangled in a tree. 'A promise was made to attempt the parachute ascent tomorrow, with a free admission for those who had paid, which restored something like order.'

Two billiard-rooms were provided in the old tennis court in 1838–39, and thirty-six years later were converted into one and a balcony thrown out from it. Afterwards, for a few seasons, well-known billiard professionals were engaged to play matches there on Mondays during the season. The room was renovated during 1894–5 and was, of course, demolished when the court made way for the Mound. A billiard-room, however, was provided in the new courts, behind the pavilion, but during 1905–6 was converted into dressing-rooms and the table purchased by Mr Lacey.

In 1838 a bowling-green was laid out by Dark and an archery ground provided, and doubtless both were well patronised. On May 10, 1869, the Committee were 'unanimously of opinion that the University Sports could not be held at Lord's', and on May 29, 1871, they refused permission to a Mr Aldridge, who appeared in person, to liberate 1,000 pigeons on the ground. At the Annual General Meeting of 1875 Dr Gaye lamented that the club had refused the use of the ground for a Clown XI to perform for charitable purposes; on May 27, 1895, the use of the Nursery Ground for drilling the Middlesex Volunteers was declined; on April 24, 1911, it was decided that leave could not be granted for the practice ground to be utilised for tent-pegging; and on another occasion the MCC declined to sanction Lord's being used as a recruiting ground.

In the spring of 1842 Dark, at his own expense, had prepared an admirable running-ground, 640 feet long and 7 feet 6 inches wide, in a straight line, so that those 'who wish to run 200 yards on good level ground can do so to advantage, and have the distance roped down the middle. Upwards of sixty loads of gravel and other hard substances have been used in forming the line, and to make it as level as possible the ground in many places has been raised upwards of a foot. It is now considered the best 200 yards sprint near London.'

By no means all the members approved of these wide-ranging extra-curricular activities. Some of them insisted that the MCC, being a cricket club, should confine activities on the ground to cricket. But Dark, being the holder of the lease, was able to call the tune – most of the time. Among the most apoplectic opponents of any innovation was the Hon. Robert Grimston, who, at a later stage in his life, violently contradicted his own abhorrence to change by evolving into the Earl of Verulam. Regarding Lord's, the Hon. Robert nurtured one pastoral passion and one sporting aversion. Among the amenities he cherished were the sheep; among the facilities he loathed were Dark's cursed tennis courts.

The Lawn Tennis grounds were his special aversion. 'I wish they would take away those beastly "skittle grounds",' he remarked one day, and when a bill came for making the asphalt courts he said, 'I shall move that the bill be not paid, and that we give instructions to have it all taken up, and have the ground ploughed and sowed with grass seeds...'

Lord's forty years ago was practically a country ground, as it was almost open country northwards and westwards. An old-fashioned tavern, with trees in front, was the hostelry, and the pavilion was somewhat of a rustic kind, with shrubbery in front. The tennis court was the only building except the Tavern, and the members only numbered from 300 to 400, and the professional bowlers were few in number compared with those of today. There were no nets, but ground boys did the scouting; and strangers for a small payment on non-match days might have a wicket and some wonderful bats and balls, of unknown age and date, facetiously supposed to have been made by Steevie, a great character and ground man, in his leisure hours. The money payment of course was no object to the Club, and the privilege was great to those who wanted a little amusement, and the stumps were pitched in out-of-the-way places for strangers, often on very rough ground.

FREDERICK GALE, *Life of the Hon. Robert Grimston*, 1885

There were few outward trappings of the game that the Victorians could refrain from improving. It is related that the Honourable Robert Grimston, coming to Lord's one day when he had not been expected, found one of the new-fangled lawn mowers being used to cut the grass on the wicket. Plunging his hand into his fob of sovereigns, Grimston went to a group of navvies at work on a nearby trench, and led them back with their pickaxes to smash up the devilish contrivance. Dark might be in nominal control of Lord's ground, but while the Honourable Robert knew it, the pitch would be mown by grazing sheep, as it always had been.

JOHN ARLOTT, *Cricket*, 1953

A MORE formidable and certainly more enduring grandee was the Right Hon. Sir Spencer Cecil Brabazon Ponsonby-Fane, sixth son of the 4th Earl of Bessborough, nephew by marriage of Lord Frederick Beauclerk, and brother of the 6th Earl. Like so many of his time and class Sir Spencer acquired additional names without apparent effort; they accrued to him like barnacles to the hulk of a privateer. He was over fifty before collecting 'Fane', this attachment being a pre-requisite of his inheriting the estate of Lady Georgina Fane. Although his life's career was cricket, Sir Spencer indulged in considerable secondary activities as a diplomat which confirmed his reputation inside the cricket world as an administrator of sorts. In 1840 he entered the Foreign Office, and later became Private Secretary to my lords Palmerston, Clarendon and Granville. He served as Attaché at Washington, 1846–7; was Comptroller of the Lord Chamberlain's Office until 1901, was Gentleman Usher to the Sword, and earned some notoriety as the man who brought to London from Paris the treaty ending the Crimean War. Much of the fascination regarding Sir Spencer is due to his longevity and the length of his association with Lord's. He first played for MCC as a teenager in 1839, and became treasurer in 1879, a position he held till his death thirty-seven years later. In the photographic portrait taken late in life by Elliott and Fry, his dewlaps and keen nose give him the air of a weary but patient turtle. The quiet disenchantment of his expression speaks of generations of power and self-indulgence, while the venerable cut of his lapels and the slightly rakish angle of his straw boater evoke comparisons with, of all Edwardian cricket-haters, Sir Max Beerbohm. Sir Spencer never wrote his cricketing memoirs, which is a pity. Judging from his essay introducing the history of Lord's published by Lord Harris and F. S. Ashley-Cooper, the old boy had much of interest to tell us:

It was about eighty years ago that I was first taken to Lord's, where my brother Frederick, afterwards Lord Bessborough, was playing for Harrow against Eton. Some time after, whilst I was still a lad, Mr Dark, then proprietor of the ground and who paid all expenses connected with it, presented me with a bat and the 'Freedom of the Ground' as he called it. From that time I was there continually, and I may almost say have lived there up to the present day.

Oh! what changes I have seen and taken part in, not only in the scene itself but the nature and exponents of the game. It is only natural that in such a length of time such changes should have taken place, but it is almost impossible to compare the rough and simple habits of those times with the luxury of the present day.

In the then pavilion, a small one-roomed building, surrounded with a few laurels and shrubs, and capable of holding forty or fifty members, I can see Mr Benjamin Aislabie, the Secretary of the Club, a big fat man over twenty stone in weight, fussing about with a red book in which he was entering subscriptions for some desired match, of which the funds of the Club could not afford the expense. And here sat Lord Frederick Beauclerk, then the Autocrat of the Club and of cricket in general, laying down the law and organising the games. On these he always had a bet of a sovereign, and he himself managed them whilst sitting alongside the scorers at the top of the ground, whence he issued his orders to the players. He himself had then given up playing.

Then there was the public-house, a long, low building on the south side, separated from the ground by a row of clipped lime-trees, and a few green benches on which the thirsty spectators smoked long pipes and enjoyed drinks. Round the ground there were more of these small benches without backs, and a pot-boy walked round with a supply of beer and porter for the public, who had no other means of refreshing themselves. Excepting these benches there were no seats for spectators. At the south-east corner of the ground there were large stacks of willow-blocks to be seasoned and made into bats in the workshop adjoining. On the upper north-east corner was a large sheep-pen. In the centre of the ground, opposite the pavilion, was a square patch of grass which was kept constantly rolled and taken care of. No scythe was allowed to touch it, and mowing machines were not then invented. The rest of the ground was ridge and furrow – not very easy for fielding on, nor made any easier by the number of old pitches which abounded, for on non-match days the public could have a pitch for a shilling, a sum which included the use of stumps, bat and ball, the last-named selected from half a dozen or so from the capacious breech pockets of 'Steevie' Slatter, Mr Dark's factotum, which never seemed to be empty.

The grass, as I have said, was never mowed. It was usually kept down by a flock of sheep which was penned up on match-days, and on Saturdays four or five hundred sheep were driven on to the ground on their way to the Monday Smithfield Market. It was marvellous to see how they cleared the herbage. From the pitch itself, selected by Mr Dark, half a dozen boys picked out the rough stalks of the grass. The wickets were sometimes difficult – in a dry north-east wind, for instance; but when they were in good order it was a joy to play on them, they were so full of life and spirit. The creases were cut with a knife and, though more destructive to the ground, were more accurate than those marked subsequently with white paint.

Sir S. Ponsonby-Fane, in his introduction to
Lord Harris and F. S. Ashley-Cooper, *Lord's and the MCC*, 1914

Another semi-legendary figure in the cricket history of the period, and a man closely associated with Lord's, was Nicholas Wanostrocht, who played under the name of N. Felix, and who excelled in many arts unconnected with cricket. He had adopted the pseudonym through fear that his career as a schoolmaster might be compromised by his cricketing reputation; some of the parents of his pupils at his school in Camberwell expected their pedagogues to be of a more sober cut than Wanostrocht felt inclined to achieve. But in time cricket so preoccupied him and so absorbed his energies, that his school declined. He started up again at Blackheath but again failed. John Arlott has defined him as 'one of the first truly scientific cricketers. A gifted man – he was an accomplished painter, he could play any musical instrument, was a sound classical scholar and a fair writer – it seems strange that Felix eventually threw in his lot entirely with cricket. His playing career continued until he had a stroke after playing the match Horsham v. Ifield at Horsham on 14 July 1854. He made 1 and 0 in his two innings, but he took several wickets, including the last which fell in the game. Years later he pencilled in the margin of his copy of *Scores and Biographies* opposite the score of this match: "After this match I was most kindly admonished by Almighty God, being struck down by paralysis when in the enjoyment of good health." After his illness he continued to travel with Clarke's All-England Eleven, made all the side's after-dinner speeches, reported their matches for *Baily's Magazine*, kept a diary of their tours, illustrated with his delightful water-colours ... His book, *Felix on the Bat*, was the first elaborate cricket publication, carrying some remarkable illustrations by G. F. Watts, who had been an evening pupil at Felix's school.'

This versatile man, of Flemish descent, played out many of the comedy-dramas of his career at Lord's.

N. Felix, whose real name was Nicholas Wanostrocht, was of Flemish descent and was born in October 1804 at Camberwell, in a spot very convenient on account of the coaches going to and from London every hour. He was very popular at Lord's, where, on June 1–3, 1846, a match, attended by the Prince Consort, was played in his honour, Felix's Eleven against Fuller Pilch's Eleven. In 'Lillywhite' we read: 'The Prince came on horseback, attended by some of the elite of the land; he was enthusiastically received, and was invited to see the Pavilion, and to inspect the implements of war, etc, etc, peculiar to the noble game. He turned and left the spot, saw a little more of the passing game, thanked the noblemen and gentlemen of the MCC for their attention, and remounted his horse, and every head was uncovered as he left the ground.' Felix was a very versatile man, inventor, writer, musician, classical scholar, and accomplished artist. He invented the catapulta and also tubular index batting gloves, the patent of which he sold to Robert Dark at Lord's.

JOHN ARLOTT, *Cricket*, 1953

A. Mynn, who was bowling, delivered a ball off which a catch was given to N. Felix, who was fielding point. Now Felix was a jocose, amusing fellow, who even during the process of the match would play antics. On missing that catch he immediately fell to the ground, held his head down, tucked up his knees and folded his arms round his knees, in fact made himself as much into a ball as possible. Mynn – I recollect the occasion as well as if it had been yesterday – walked up to him, took hold of him by the collar of the flannel jacket, and in a jocose manner also held him up, with one arm extended at full length for a second or so. Now Felix, though rather short, weighed, I should guess, about 11 stone. This anecdote will prove Mynn's great strength, I think. I saw it myself, when looking on from the pavilion at Lord's.

ARTHUR HAYGARTH, in conversation, recalling the 1846 season

IT should not be imagined, from the scientific basis of Felix's theories of batsmanship, or from the constant refining by Dark of the facilities available to members, that Lord's was much improved as a field for playing cricket. There remained for some years an element of the old Georgian raffishness and a certain offhand approach to the condition of the playing area. It should be kept in mind, however, that in these years when a lot more besides cricket took place at the ground, not all the executants carried the same expectations regarding the tending of the turf. The point is brought out by the events of 1844, followed by the description of yet another patrician member whose changes of name may well have baffled family annalists:

In August 1844, the Ioway Indians encamped at Lord's, where they exhibited their skill in archery, ball play and dancing, the last-named on an elevated platform. The troupe consisted of fourteen persons, including the Great Mystery Man.

LORD HARRIS AND F. S. ASHLEY-COOPER, *Lord's and the MCC*, 1914

In 1845 Lord's was still very primitive. Lord Cottesloe (T. F. Fremantle of the Eton XI of 1848) recalls 'a small assembly of amateurs and members of the Club in the Pavilion, low benches put in a circle round the ground at a good distance, and on which sat a few spectators, and pot-boys coming round and calling out, "Give your orders, gents". There would be a few carriages with boys' relations and friends. You could hit and run out a sixer then, or if this was to leg or to the off, to the extreme corner, the ball went into an immense pile of half-made bats, piled there to get seasoned.'

GAMBIER PARRY, *Annals of an Eton House*, 1907

L IKE Thomas Lord before him, Dark enjoyed living on the premises, in one of the very few Lord's buildings apart from the pavilion itself. This contemporary account of the ground is the only one which discloses the identity of Dark's neighbour just to the west of the ground. Edwin Landseer (1802–1873), immortalised through his avuncular lions in Trafalgar Square, and celebrated in the front parlours of a million seaside boarding-houses by 'The Stag at Bay' and 'Monarch of the Glen', was himself something of a stag at bay as Dark's tenancy drew to a close, his morbid taste for cruelty for its own sake eventually undermining his sanity. Perhaps he would have been advised to follow Dark's hint and take Sunday tea on a plain where wounded animals were conspicuous only by their absence.

Dark's house was in the left-hand corner of the ground going in, and the only other buildings were the pavilion – a green-painted wooden building, with a kind of dressing-room at the back – the Tennis Court, and a rustic tavern with bow windows with a row of very leafy trees in front. On one side of the pavilion stood a row of pollard trees, and behind them were the beautiful gardens, four acres in extent, belonging to Landseer, the great animal painter. Improvements, however, were made gradually. The telegraph board, chronicling the total number of wickets down and score made by the last man, was introduced in 1846; two years later a small room was built on the north side of the pavilion for the professionals, who had previously been obliged to come through the entrance gate to the ground to have their innings; in 1848, also, score-cards were first issued at Lord's, from a portable press, in the Sussex v. MCC match; and during 1849–50 the ground was drained. The scorers' 'perch', an elevated platform about eight feet from the ground, affording no protection from the sun or rain but placing its occupants out of reach of the curious, had been introduced a few seasons earlier. For some years at four o'clock on Sundays Lord's was opened free to the public, who called there after visiting Bagnigge; small tables were dotted round the ground, and waiters were in attendance to supply refreshments; but the arrangement, not proving a success, was soon discontinued.

LORD HARRIS AND F. S. ASHLEY-COOPER, *Lord's and the MCC*, 1914

OCCASIONALLY one of these early worthies would invent a new tactic, or introduce a new device, which has since been discarded by the modern world. One of these forgotten innovators was a man whose bowling action sounds as though it were somewhat original, whose resolution as an umpire was liable to cause him trouble, but whose real significance may well be the thoughtfulness with which he countered the problem of his own obesity. Since the Victorians, umpires' girths have tended to be less generous than they once were, but even so, sports goods manufacturers of the new age, so busy marketing protective equipment for batsmen, might spare a thought for the umpire, and revive a very useful and serviceable gadget:

One of the most popular cricketers was James Dean, known as The Ploughboy and Joyous Jemmy, who was a nephew of the Broadbridges and was engaged at Lord's from 1837 to 1861. At one time he was known as Dean Swift, as his bowling was fast, and concerning his delivery Mr Gale has said that he 'rolled himself like a hedgehog quickly towards the crease and "exploded" and out shot a ball which came deadly straight with good pitch and strong curl.' Mr Haygarth summed him up admirably as 'good at all points of the game, able, willing and obliging, a hard-working cricketer, and an honest man.' On one occasion he was pursued by the friends of an eleven in the country after he had decided in his office as umpire against them: the decision lost them the match, and after undergoing their abuse and ill-usage he succeeded in reaching the Tavern at Lord's. Having identified himself by a plaintive assurance that he was poor little Jemmy Dean, he was admitted by the window and escaped his followers. After retiring from match-play he was in frequent demand as an umpire, and, having become very portly, occasionally carried a stick with a clip at the end which enabled him to pick up fallen bails without being obliged to stoop for them himself.

LORD HARRIS AND F. S. ASHLEY-COOPER, *Lord's and the MCC*, 1914

BY NOW Lord's ground was old enough to have acquired an aura, if not of antiquity, then at least of permanence. As early as 1846, in a work called *Sketches of the Players*, William Denison could write that 'The severance of Lord's from its almost immemorial rights and uses, would cause many a pang and deep regret', it being understood that the use of the phrase 'almost immemorial' to define a period of less than seventy years was just the writer's way of bluffing any hypothetical land developers into retreat. One morning, in the stunned days following the belated ending of the Great War, a pseudonymous correspondent confided to readers of *The Times* his recollections of Lord's in the year of the Great Exhibition. The details he recalls, especially regarding headgear and catering arrangements, serve as a reminder to the modern reader that for all the elaboration of amenities provided by Dark, and the growing sophistication of the players, cricket at Lord's at that time would have presented a bizarre sight to the spectators of the next century. The mysterious 'Senior' is offering proof that after three-quarters of a century, Lord's had still to emerge fully-fledged from its own pre-history:

Sir, I was at Lord's in 1851 and 1852, and saw the following matches – Eton and Harrow; Eton and Winchester: and Harrow and Winchester. In one of these the captain of the Eton eleven was the brother of one of my school-fellows, which gave many of us a desire to see the match. This captain wore a tall black hat, being, I believe, the last non-professional player to do so. The 'professionals' continued to wear the hat much longer. It was in fact a sort of badge of the profession.

In the days referred to the arrangements for refreshments at Lord's old ground were such as would now be considered simple and anything but luxurious. Visitors had luncheon standing up at a long counter in an open shed to the left of the entrance gate. There one could get little, if anything, to eat, except sandwiches and pork pies. Once when I was there a member of the Eton eleven came into the refreshment shed and asked for 'shandy gaff' – the first time that I had ever heard the word.

In the middle of the last century it was a common belief – at any rate in South-Eastern England – that the inhabitants of the 'shires' could not play cricket. The only people credited then with ability to play it were those who belonged to Kent, Sussex, Surrey, Middlesex, Essex, &c.

Your obedient servant,

SENIOR

Letter to *The Times*, 16 August 1919

IT WAS through the 1860s that Lord's faced its most dangerous challenge yet from the land speculators. In 1860 the Eyre Estate decided to put up the freehold of Lord's to public auction. In retrospect it seems insane that the club should have disdained to bid, but despite the entreaties of Dark, they stood aside and allowed the ground to become the property of Mr I. Moses for £7,000. Three years later Dark offered to sell his interest in the ground and the Tavern for £15,000. The matter was discussed by Messrs Fitzgerald, Nicholson and Broughton, who welcomed the chance. Later Broughton wrote that by now the club saw the advantage of owning the ground, if only to be free of Dark, who, 'although an honest and straightforward man, was a bit of a despot, and things did not always work smoothly. I remember that when our honorary secretary at one of our Committees pointed out to him that the boots and shoes of members were not properly cleaned, he replied, "Go and clean 'em yourselves".'

At another meeting attended by Messrs Kynaston, Broughton, Nicholson and Fitzgerald, on December 22nd at 2 Portland Place, Dark's suggestion to sell his interest in the ground without the Tavern for £8,000 was considered and it was resolved that valuers report to the Committee thereon. At this time Dark was seriously ill – he made his will on January 17th, 1864 – and matters were delayed, but on February 23rd the valuers wrote saying that Dark's proposition was that £11,000 should include the Tavern, racket court, tennis court, etc., but exclude three houses, and that some arrangement be made about his brother's widow, who had the bat and ball trade. Moses asked £550 per annum rent, giving the club the option of buying off any portion of the rent beyond £200 per annum at 25 years' purchase, term 99 years.

LORD HARRIS AND F. S. ASHLEY-COOPER, *Lord's and the MCC*, 1914

NEGOTIATIONS drifted on, and were finally resolved to the satisfaction of the MCC thanks to the generosity of William Nicholson, who now did for the Lord's of the 1860s what his predecessor William Ward had once done for the founding fathers. Nicholson (1824–1909), was a Harrow wicketkeeper–batsman of some reputation who joined the MCC in 1845, served on the Committee, became President in 1879, and served as a Trustee for the last forty-three years of his life. In 1843 he had captained Harrow. Exactly fifty years later he bought a large piece of ground there and presented it to the school. A Liberal MP in the House from 1866 to 1874 and a Conservative from 1880 to 1885, the great achievement of his life was to ensure the future of Lord's ground.

> Great as Mr Nicholson's skill as a player undoubtedly was, it is probable that he will always be remembered for the unstinted support he was ever ready to accord the game. In *Cricket* of January 1886 it was told how, when the fate of Lord's was almost in the balance, before the sudden increase of wealth from Eton and Harrow and University matches, Mr Nicholson stood in the gap, and after all England had been drawn for subscriptions to save the ground – for few escaped Mr Roger Kynaston and his red book – he advanced the money as mortgage on a security which the outside public would not take. Little was said about it, as men who do such things do not talk about them, but there is no doubt he saved Lord's from the builders. The celebrated Mr William Ward did a similar thing many years before. He drew a cheque for £5,000 and gave it to Lord for the lease, and as it happened this turned out a good investment, as indeed did Mr Nicholson's mortgage also, though he ran the risk for the love of cricket, and the sum advanced was a large one – a very long way into five figures. This action on his part should cause his name always to be gratefully remembered, not only by members of the Marylebone club, but by all English cricketers in whatever part of the world they may be domiciled. His generosity enabled the old club to purchase the freehold of Lord's; but for him the ground might have been built over and the MCC, the recognised head of the game, have been rendered homeless.

Wisden, 1909

WHILE the financiers played their games in the background, the cricket world was animated by what seemed to be a more immediate danger, more important than landlords or items of millinery or the state of the food counters. This was the condition of the playing area. It seems odd that Dark, so efficient and thoughtful an administrator, and a man so keen to improve the quality of life for the members at Lord's, should have considered a running track and the Tennis Court to have priority over the hiring of a groundsman capable of creating a pitch which rendered life less dangerous for batsmen. Indeed, Dark lived long enough to witness the inevitable, the death of a batsman through bad pitch preparation. Whether Dark simply ignored the problem, or did not know how to cope with it, he certainly had frequent warnings, in the form of constant complaints from members. What makes it all doubly hard to understand is the fact that many other first-class grounds had long since mastered the problem of providing safe wickets. One well-known writer-player even hinted at the possibility of removing the important matches from Lord's altogether, to grounds better fitted.

Gentlemen v. Players at Lord's, June 29 and 30, 1868.
Had I been a wicket-keeper or a batsman at Lord's during the match I should have liked (plus my gloves and pads) to have worn a singlestick mask, a Life Guardsman's cuirass and a tin stomach-warmer. The wicket reminded me of a middle-aged gentleman's head of hair, when the middle-aged gentleman, to conceal the baldness of his crown, applies a pair of wet brushes to some favourite long locks and brushes them across the top of his head. So with the wicket. The place where the ball pitched was covered with wet grass wetted and rolled down. It never had been, and never could be, good turf. I send a specimen or two for your inspection.

I have no hesitation in saying that in nine cricket-grounds out of ten within twenty miles of London, whether village or county club grounds, a local club could find a better wicket, in spite of drought and in spite of their poverty, than the Marylebone club supplied to the Players of England.

FREDERICK GALE, *circa* 1890

Lord's was terribly bad, and it was said that the only respect in which its pitch resembled a billiard table was the pockets. Imagine then what it must have been like to face such men as Jackson and Tarrant, Harvey Fellows, Marcon, and Kirwan. Boundaries were, as a rule, unknown; their gradual introduction, dating from the sixties, had an adverse effect on deep fielding, and especially on throwing, to which the progressive urbanisation of the country also contributed. Nets were unknown for practice at Lord's until 1866, and for considerably longer in the north. The hours of play at Lord's were noon to 7 p.m. on the first day, 11 to 7.30 on the other two. Lunch was at 3 p.m., and lasted only thirty-five minutes; there was no tea interval. The telegraph was first instituted at Lord's in 1846, at The Oval two years later.

H. S. ALTHAM, *A History of Cricket*, 1926

Speaking of wickets in general in the early 1860s, W. G. wrote this: 'Up to this time many of the principal grounds were so rough as to be positively dangerous to play upon, and batsmen were constantly damaged by the fast bowling. When the wickets were in this condition the batsmen had to look out for shooters and leave the bumping balls to look after themselves. In the 'sixties it was no unusual thing to have two or three shooters in an over; nowadays you scarcely get one shooter in a season. At this time the Marylebone ground was in a very unsatisfactory condition – so unsatisfactory that in 1864 Sussex refused to play at Lord's owing to the roughness of the ground. When I first played there the creases were not chalked out, but were actually cut out of the turf one inch deep, and about one inch wide. As matches were frequently being played, and no pains were taken to fill up the holes, it is quite easy to imagine what a terrible condition the turf presented.' He added that he could remember the time when he could go on to the pitch and pick up a handful of small pieces of gravel. In 1865 a large piece of the ground was levelled and returfed. Lord's gradually improved, but in 1870 it was still capable of an almost murderous condition. It was in that year that he made an historic 66 against Freeman and Emmett. 'Tom Emmett and I,' said Freeman, many years afterwards, 'have often said that it was a marvel that the Doctor was not either maimed or unnerved for the rest of his days or killed outright. I often think of his pluck when I watch a modern batsman scared if a medium-paced ball hits him on the hand; he should have seen our expresses flying about his ribs, shoulders and head in 1870.'

BERNARD DARWIN, *W. G. Grace*, 1934

DARK appears to have remained indifferent, although there were funds available for extensive improvements. Even as batsmen were being felled and bruised by balls flying up from the uneven pitch, Dark was investing surplus funds in amenities which must have seemed like frivolous luxuries to the victimised batsmen. More land was acquired, and more sophisticated buildings erected. It seemed indeed as though Dark was now thinking more of property values and profits from subsidiary income than of the true business of Lord's, which was to provide cricket of the highest standard played in the best possible conditions. One wonders what consolation it was for batsmen with bruised ribs and bloody noses to go into a more sophisticated Tavern to nurse their wounds, or to think of how pleasant life must be for spectators at the Eton v. Harrow game:

Soon after the pavilion had been enlarged it was decided to pull down the Tavern which had been built for Lord in 1813–14 and erect a new one. Tenders for the work were invited, and that of £3,983.3s. by Messrs Ager was accepted. Mr Nicholson offered to advance a sum not exceeding £4,000 for the purpose at five per cent, and the work, commenced in December 1867, was completed by the end of the following May. Mr Day continued as tenant, the arrangement being that he should pay £300 rent the first year, £350 the second and £400 yearly afterwards. Not until 1897 did the club become its own caterer, the supply of refreshments being let out to a contractor until that year. A further improvement was effected during 1869–70, for at the Anniversary Dinner in 1870 it was announced that Guy's Gardens, situate at the east end of the ground, had been purchased for £1,750. Hitherto £20 had been paid annually for the exit of carriages through the Gardens during the Eton v. Harrow match, but the acquirement of the property of course added to the area of the ground in addition to saving that expense.

LORD HARRIS AND F. S. ASHLEY-COOPER, *Lord's and the MCC*, 1914

THE dangers presented by the Lord's pitch must have been considerable at any time, but doubly so in spells of hot weather when, in the absence of rain, the irregular turf was baked to the consistency of concrete. Such a season was 1868, when at least two batsmen seemed unperturbed by the threat of injury. The season also saw the death at the age of forty of one of the best loved and most gifted of the professionals, Billy Buttress of Cambridgeshire, described in Altham's history as the 'father of leg-break bowling'. Buttress was a medium-pace bowler who, says Altham, 'on a wicket that gave him any assistance was most deadly'. The brevity of Buttress's career and life was due largely to the thirst he was forever attempting to quench, a weakness which sometimes threatened the salvation of his side. His fellow-professionals on one occasion took drastic measures to ensure his sobriety. Yet it may well be that this brilliant cricketer was best-respected of all for the facetiousness with which he indulged an odd gift better suited to the stages of the emergent Music Halls of his prime.

The summer of 1868 was one of the finest England has ever known, with very little rain, except for a period in August. There were some notable matches at Lord's–MCC v. England and of course, Gentlemen v. Players, in which W. G. scored a wonderful 134 out of a total of 201 on a very fiery wicket. He also obtained ten wickets for 81 runs, and he was not yet twenty years of age. In the Eton v. Harrow match C. I. Thornton (Eton) hit a ball over the pavilion, the ball flying high and out of the ground for six. Lord Harris in *A Few Short Runs* writes: 'I was in with him at the time. He had just previously hit one against the old Armoury, which occupied the site of the members' luncheon-room, and one over D Block, and when he followed these big hits – very big for a boy – by that astounding drive over the pavilion, I thought it was all right for Eton, but he was bowled by a shooter almost the next ball.' This exploit was all but repeated in 1877 by H. E. Meek (Harrow), who hit a ball on to the top of the pavilion, whence it bounced over. Thornton's went clean over.

SIR PELHAM WARNER, *Lord's*, 1946

BUTTRESS had a failing for pints. His weakness was well known, and occasionally he would be entrusted to the care of Caffyn or another steady professional after stumps were drawn. Once, at the end of the second day's play in an important match at Lord's, it was recognised that the result would depend almost entirely on the fitness of Buttress on the following morning. Therefore some of the players entered into a conspiracy whereby his sobriety could be assured. After he had changed, he was enveigled into the basement of the old Pavilion or Tavern to inspect a cellar, which was supposed to possess, for that occasion only, some remarkable feature. Quite unsuspecting the plot, Buttress walked in, whereupon the door was slammed to and hastily bolted. He remained prisoner until shortly before play was resumed, and then worked off his anger at the expense of the opposing side, who could make no stand against him and were easily beaten. On another occasion, when it was his turn to bat, he was discovered perched in one of the lime trees. Asked for an explanation, he replied, 'What's the good of me going in? If I miss 'em I'm out. If I hit 'em I'm out. Let's start the next innings!' Poor Buttress was a skilful ventriloquist, and nothing pleased him more than to delude old ladies in a crowded railway carriage into the belief that a savage dog was under the seat.

Had Buttress lived a little longer, he might have witnessed an event which many felt was inevitable. The match between MCC and Nottinghamshire at Lord's in June 1870 is one of the saddest in all the history of cricket. Despite some attempt by the groundsman, Jordan, to improve the Lord's playing area, the cricketers continued to complain. After the end of the MCC–Notts match, at least one of them complained no more:

Despite Jordan's efforts, the wickets provided at Lord's continued for several years to be far from protection or even safe. There had been much dissatisfaction expressed with the pitch provided for Gentlemen v. Players in 1868, and the criticism was renewed in 1870 when, batting for Nottinghamshire v. MCC, George Summers was struck so severely on the head by a ball from Platts that the injury proved fatal. It was thought that the ball pitched on a stone: however that may be, Daft, who was next on the list, went in with a towel round his head. It is possible that if good medical advice had been followed, Summers would have recovered, but he was removed to Nottingham against the judgement of a London doctor, and upon arrival was submitted to a herbal treatment. He had played a grand game for 41 in his first innings, and his last scoring stroke was a five. The MCC spent £30 in the erection of a tombstone to his memory.

LORD HARRIS AND F. S. ASHLEY-COOPER, *Lord's and the MCC*, 1914

During the MCC v. Nottinghamshire match there was a sad accident, a ball bowled by Platts getting up straight and hitting Summers, of Nottinghamshire, on the cheek. He retired, but the story goes that he was given brandy, the last thing to do in the circumstances, and, further, sat in a hot sun at Lord's the next day before returning to Nottingham that evening. As a result he died a few days later, and was buried at Nottingham, where the MCC put up this stone to his memory:

> This tablet is erected to the memory of George Summers by the
> Marylebone Cricket Club to mark their sense of his qualities as
> a cricketer and to testify their regret at the untimely accident
> on Lord's Ground which cut short a career so full of promise,
> June 19, 1870, in the 26th year of his age.

Alfred Shaw, in *Alfred Shaw, Cricketer*, says that every care was taken of Summers, and that he did not leave his hotel until just before starting on his journey to Nottingham. The exact care that was taken of this unfortunate player after he had been hit seems, therefore, to have been in dispute, but I prefer to rely on Alfred Shaw's version. Shaw was a most reliable man, and is unlikely to have been incorrect in such a matter. *Wisden* records that the wicket was 'excellent', but that the ball pitched on a pebble which had worked up. The next batsman, Richard Daft, went in with a towel round his head and scored 53, following a beautiful innings of 117.

SIR PELHAM WARNER, *Lord's*, 1946

DARK himself soon followed poor Summers, although not through any injury sustained at cricket. He had lived a long and successful life, and could justly claim to have established the Lord's ground as a permanent feature of London life and a recognised centre for several games, but mainly cricket, as well as providing a headquarters for what was evolving into the recognised administrative body of the game. No man spent his life so close to the ground, in spirit as well as geographically. It was after his death that there were disclosed family links with one of the more famous of Dickens's later characters. One of Dark's descendents also makes reference to the same Landseer whose gardens abutted on to the ground. Perhaps the presence of the painter drew engravers to the area.

On October 17, 1871, J. H. Dark passed away, at the age of seventy-six. He had been connected with Lord's for fifty-nine years (1805–1864), 'having, perhaps, done more for MCC than any other individual', says Alfred D. Taylor, in his *Annals of Lord's and History of the MCC*. He was a somewhat taciturn, silent man, out of whom information was not easily extracted, but he was so much a part of the club that at one period Lord's was often referred to as Dark's. Dark was a good hitter and fieldsman, and a most capable umpire. He played once, in 1835, for the Gentlemen v. Players, in the match in which the Gentlemen were allowed to choose any two of the Players, except Lillywhite, to assist them. They chose J. Cobbett and S. Redgate, and the former bowled Dark for a duck. The Players won by six wickets, Lillywhite taking in all twelve wickets.

Dark was known as 'the Boss', and for many years selected the Players' team. He was born in the Edgware Road, on 24 May 1795, and died in a house in St John's Wood Road, which he built overlooking the ground. He had lived all his life within its hail, and his name is inseparably connected with Lord's. His grave is in Kensal Green, and a red granite slab is inscribed: 'Sacred to the Memory of Mr James Henry Dark, who died Oct. 17, 1871, aged 76. For many years "Proprietor of Lord's Cricket Ground".'

Sir, In your interesting MCC Number, and in the subsequent correspondence which you have published, there have been references to my great-

great-uncle, James Henry Dark, who bought Lord's from Lord and afterwards sold it to the MCC.

There may, perhaps, be some small historic interest in the detail of the connexion of my family with Lord's and with cricket. James Henry Dark was one of several brothers who were the sons of a Liskeard sadler. One of his brothers, John Dark, was dust contractor to the old St Marylebone and Paddington vestries. He appears to have known Dickens, and there is a family rumour that he was the original of Boffin, the golden dustman.

Another brother, Ben Dark, founded the cricket bat and ball manufactory which was inherited by my father. The bats were made in a workshop at Lord's and the balls at a factory at Hildenborough in Kent.

James Henry Dark had no children, but his brothers were extremely prolific. When he was a young man, my father had 66 first cousins. The consequence was that though James Henry and his brothers left considerable sums of money, it was divided among so many heirs that the legacies were of small account.

I was born in a house in St John's Wood Road, owned by my grandfather, which had a private entrance into Lord's. My father had another house next door but one, which also had a private entrance into Lord's; and my grandfather's widowed sister-in-law had a third house, farther east and also looking over the ground. When I was a small child the bat and ball business was known as Matilda Dark and Sons, and I quite remember my great-grandmother, a very old lady, who lived in some rooms over the workshops. St John's Wood Road was, indeed, in those days a veritable colony of my family.

One of my grandfather's sisters married James Bromley, the engraver, who reproduced several of the more famous Landseers. They, too, lived in St John's Wood Road, and the landlord of Lord's Hotel was the husband of one of my grandmother's sisters.

To the west of the hotel there was a building known as the Armoury, which belonged to my grandfather and was the headquarters of the Fifth Middlesex Volunteers, which, when there was no match on that day, always paraded in Lord's before

their route march. In those long ago days the
'Licensed Victuallers' Fête and Gala' took place
regularly in Lord's in September, and on summer
Sunday evenings the hotel did a roaring open-air
trade, tables being set out within the grounds.

What is now the practice ground was then a
nursery, and I remember the beautiful row of
chestnut trees that used to ornament the eastern
side of the ground.

The falling in of leases was primarily responsible
for the ending of the Darks' connexion with Lord's.
Workshops had to be moved elsewhere, and my
father, who was a gifted craftsman, had no sort of
idea of business, and the once flourishing and
almost famous manufactory declined to almost
nothingness. Thanks however to the gracious
kindness of the MCC, the family connexion with
Lord's went on until the death of my father at the
age of 85, seven years ago. Darks had been making
cricket bats for a hundred years. Since then they
have been making them no longer.

SIDNEY DARK, Letter to *The Times*, 30 June 1937

Dark in fact bought Lord's from William Ward, who had bought it from Lord.

O NE of the more priceless ironies of the Summers tragedy is that it was witnessed in
comparative comfort by the gentlemen of the Press. Ever since Lord's opened, the
reporters had been obliged to find for themselves what facilities they could, and it was
not until the end of Dark's regime that some acknowledgement was made that perhaps
after all those who reported events at the ground were entitled to a little extra
consideration, if only to enable them to perform their professional duties. Their burden
had been eased a little in 1846 with the introduction of Lord's first scoreboard, showing
runs, wickets down and the score of the last man out. Another key date was 26 June
1848, when a printing tent was put into working order, and the public, to say nothing
of the reporters, were able for the first time, to buy a 'card of the match'. Sir Pelham
Warner, in his attempt to paint the blackest picture possible, overlooks the introduction
of scoreboard and match-cards, but even with these amenities life must at times have
been difficult for the gentlemen of the Press, who were finally accounted for around the
time poor Buttress was supping his last ale.

Until a grandstand was built during the winter of 1867–68 there was no
accommodation for the Press. Previous to this the reporters had to stand their
chance of getting a seat anywhere. There were shrubberies at each end of the
pavilion, and Mr Knight, the only recognised newspaper representative, who
wrote for *Bell's Life*, which later changed its name to *The Sporting Life*, stood all

day in the bushes inside the rails, this being the only place from which to view the cricket on a crowded day, with no scoreboard or cards to tell him the state of the game, and having to record the score of the whole of the match in his own score-book.

SIR PELHAM WARNER, Lord's, 1946

By the time the 1870s opened, English cricket was beginning to take on the shape into which it was to settle for generations to come. The death of Dark marks one point at which the fortunes of Lord's took a new turn. The debut on the ground of the teenaged W. G. Grace in 1865 marks another. A sort of rudimentary, unofficial County Championship was beginning to interest spectators, but most significant of all, the great set pieces of the season, Gentlemen v. Players, Eton v. Harrow, Oxford v. Cambridge, were now not only great cricketing events but dates in the social calendar. The Public Schools fixtures were usually better attended than the county games, and the time was swiftly approaching when a doting parent would no more think of not putting in an appearance at the Eton–Harrow match than of cutting Ascot or Henley. The cricket match had the added advantage of taking place virtually on Belgravia's doorstep. As the more readable cricket writers were almost exclusively products of the Public Schools and University system, much of the cricket reporting of the day tended to show an imbalance in favour of the amateurs which readers of a more egalitarian age have sometimes found Pooteresque. But there can be little doubt of the sensational and unprecedented Varsity match of 1870. Oxford had been set 179 to win, and had reached 175 for seven wickets. F. C. Cobden now came on to bowl one of the most famous overs in the history of the Varsity match, in the history of Lord's, in the history of Victorian cricket:

> We say with confidence that never can one over bowled by any bowler at any future time surpass the over that Cobden was about to deliver then, and it deserves a minute description. Cobden took a long run and bowled very fast, and was for his pace a straight bowler. But he bowled with little or no break, had not got a puzzling delivery, and, though effective against inferior bats, would never have succeeded in bowling out a man like Mr Ottaway if he had sent a thousand balls to him. However, on the present occasion Ottaway was out, those he had to bowl to were not first-rate batsmen, and Cobden could bowl a good yorker.
>
> You might almost have heard a pin drop as Cobden began his run and the ball whizzed from his hand. Mr Hill played the ball slowly to cover-point, and rather a sharp run was made. As the match stood, Oxford wanted 2 to tie and 3 to win, and three wickets to go down: Mr Butler to receive the ball. The second ball that Cobden bowled was very similar to the first, straight and well up on the off stump. Mr Butler did what anybody else except Louis Hall or Shrewsbury would have done, namely, let drive vigorously. Unfortunately he did not keep the ball down, and it went straight and hard a catch to Mr Bourne, to whom everlasting credit is due, for he held it, and away went Mr Butler—amidst Cambridge shouts this time. The position was getting serious, for neither Mr Stewart nor Mr Belcher was

renowned as a batsman. Rather pale, but with a jaunty air that cricketers are well aware frequently conceals a sickly feeling of nervousness, Mr Belcher walked to the wicket and took his guard. He felt that if only he could stop one ball and be bowled out the next, still Mr Hill would get another chance of a knock and the match would probably be won. Cobden had bowled two balls, and two more wickets had to be got; if, therefore, a wicket was got each ball the match would be won by Cambridge, and Mr Hill would have no further opportunity of distinguishing himself. In a dead silence Cobden again took the ball and bowled a fast ball well up on the batsman's legs. A vision of the winning hit flashed across Mr Belcher's brain, and he raised his bat preparatory to performing great things, hit at the ball and missed it, and he was bowled off his legs. There was still one more ball wanted to complete the over, and Mr Belcher, a sad man, walked away amid an uproarious storm of cheers.

Matters were becoming distinctly grave, and very irritating must it have been to Mr Hill, who was like a billiard-player watching his rival in the middle of a big break; he could say a good deal and think a lot, but he could do nothing. Mr Stewart, *spes ultima* of Oxford, with feelings that are utterly impossible to describe, padded and gloved, nervously took off his coat in the pavilion. If ever a man deserved pity, Mr Stewart deserved it on that occasion. He did not profess to be a good bat, and his friends did not claim so much for him; he was an excellent wicket-keeper, but he had to go in at a crisis that the best bat in England would not like to face. Mr Pauncefote, the Oxford captain, was seen addressing a few words of earnest exhortation to him, and with a rather sick feeling Mr Stewart went to the wicket. Mr Hill looked at him cheerfully, but very earnestly did Mr Stewart wish the next ball well over. He took his guard and held his hands low on the bat handle, which was fixed fast as a tree on the block-hole; for Mr Pauncefote had earnestly entreated Mr Stewart to put the bat straight in the block-hole and keep it there without moving it. This was not by any means bad advice, for the bat covers a great deal of the wicket, and though it is a piece of counsel not likely to be offered to W. G. Grace or Stoddart, it might not have been inexpedient to offer it to Mr Stewart. Here, then, was the situation—Mr Stewart standing manfully up to the wicket, Mr Cobden beginning his run, and a perfectly dead silence in the crowd. Whiz went the ball; but alas!—as many other people, cricketers and politicians alike, have done—the good advice is neglected, and Stewart, instead of following his captain's exhortation to keep his bat still and upright in the block-hole, just lifted it: fly went the bails, and Cambridge had won the match by two runs! The situation was bewildering. Nobody could quite realise what had happened for a second or so, but then—Up went Mr Absolom's hat, down the pavilion steps with miraculous rapidity flew the Rev. A. R. Ward, and smash went Mr Charles Marsham's umbrella against the pavilion brickwork.

Wisden, 1871

THIS game, known ever since as 'Cobden's Match', soon became part of the beloved mythology of cricket. For fifty, sixty, seventy years afterwards, *Wisden* was meticulous in recording the death of anyone who had happened to participate in that match, even in the most modest and ineffectual capacity. It was as if association with Cobden was in itself an acceptable qualification for entry into the pantheon. As for Cobden himself, when he died 62 years later in New South Wales, he had accomplished nothing more. He had, however, accomplished enough. And he had accomplished it before the most fashionable crowd of the season at the most fashionable ground in the world. Nor was the hysteria in the Lord's pavilion that day by any means a matter of ageing reverends and retired colonels reliving the enthusiasms of their boyhood. Many of the most vociferous idolaters of Cobden were themselves considerable cricketers, destined to achieve much more than he. At least one of them had the distinction of putting an end to another tense finish in another Lord's set piece of 1870. Here is a description of the last moments of Cobden's match:

The sudden storm of cheers which broke out after the most intense stillness during which the bowler advanced to deliver the last ball was altogether remarkable: elderly gentlemen, noted for their serious deportment, leaped on seats (unmindful of gout) and cheered themselves hoarse, and it was only with difficulty that Bos Absolom, in his joy, was restrained from throwing the chairs and forms on the pavilion roof over the parapet.

LORD HARRIS AND F. S. ASHLEY-COOPER, *Lord's and the MCC*, 1914

AND here a description of the last moments of the Gentlemen v. Players match. The Players, needing 154 to win, had reached 144 for nine wickets when W. Price, who looked well set, was joined by the last man, Southerton:

No hands clapped, no voice cheered him as he walked to the wickets, so quiet, so strangely quiet, at that moment were the spectators, who, however, cheered wildly when Price by a cut for 2 made it 8 to win, and louder still when a leg bye, and a single by each batsman, brought it 5 to win; but there the match finished, as directly after a catch at cover-point settled Price (c. Absolom b. G. F. Grace), and in this way at 7.30 the 1870 match ended in a victory for the Gentlemen by 4 runs.

Wisden, 1871

THE unfortunate Southerton, left not out and yet defeated, might have found consolation in the fact, had he only known it, that his son, S. J. Southerton, was to become at least as famous as he in the annals of the game, although not as a player. S. J. became editor of *Wisden* in 1934, and within two years had achieved the ultimate apotheosis of all cricket journalists. As the Almanack puts it: 'Southerton, having proposed the toast of 'Cricket' at the dinner of The Ferrets Club at The Oval, sank down, and in a few minutes his life had ebbed away.' His father, being less distinguished, merely died, but, being a professional cricketer, took no part in the elaborate social ceremonies connected with the great Public Schools matches, which were by now as much a part of the Lord's calendar as they were of the national education system. Indeed, the time was fast coming when the size and unruliness of crowds at the Eton–Harrow matches was to throw the administrators of the ground into a quandary and at last to draw severe censure from *Wisden* itself. Hints of the chaos to come were first evident in the 1869 match in which Eton, starved of victory for seven seasons, won by an innings. Grown men went berserk, and none berserker than the schoolmasters themselves. Among distinguished Old Etonians who witnessed the triumph was Henry S. Salt, iconoclastic close friend of Bernard Shaw, who loved cricket. At the end of the 1869 match, says Salt,

... there was an orgy of wild excitement such as I had never dreamed of and have never witnessed since; and in the thick of it, as I afterwards remembered, I saw the Provost of Eton, Dr Goodford, transformed into a Bachanal, dancing bare-headed, and waving his hat like the maddest of us all.

H. S. SALT, *Memories of Bygone Eton*, 1928

BUT the overtones of bacchanalia were carefully expunged from the match report in *Wisden*, whose editors preferred to concentrate on the social éclat of the occasion. Although there are unintentionally comic overtones in the gushing account of frocks, honourable institutions, the fine old game and the social season, the report does convey something of the surface brilliance of the occasion, leaving no doubt in the minds of readers that to have attended such an event was to have touched the hem of royalty itself:

ETON v. HARROW
Lord's, July 9, 10, 1869

That this, the most attractive match of the season, annually increases in popularity with the fair and fashionable portion of English society Lord's ground bore brilliant testimony on Friday the 9th of last July, on which day £100 more was taken at the gates for admission than was ever before taken in one day at Lord's. The weather was fortunately fine; the attendance marvellous, both in numbers and quality; and the old ground, as it that day appeared, a fitting subject for a companion picture to Frith's 'Derby Day'. One writer described the Grand Stand as being 'as gay as a bank of Summer Flowers', and so it was, for two-thirds of the occupants were 'The Ladies of England', whose gay, varied and brilliant hued attires pleasantly contrasted with the dark, sombre clad, dense mass of 'he' humanity that thronged the seats and roof of the Pavilion, a majority of whom 'had been' Public School Boys, many of whom 'are' distinguished members of the highest and most honourable Institutions of the Country. As many of the Drags of 'The Four in Hand Club' as could gain admission to the ground were grouped together at the NW end of the Pavilion. Around the ground flanking the ropes, closely clustered (at most parts six deep) were 600 carriages of the nobility and gentry, each vehicle fully, most of them 'fairly' freighted. The tops of the wood-stacks had occupants, so had the window-sills of the Racket Court, and the top of Mr Dark's garden wall; and how vast was the number of visitors each day may be estimated from the facts that on Friday 'about' £770 and on Saturday 'nearly' £500 was taken at the gates for admission money. In fact, the Eton and Harrow match at Lord's has now become one of the most prominent events of the London Season; for years to come may it so continue to be, and thus materially aid in keeping alive the interest of the fine old game, at present so manifest and general, among its very best supporters, 'The Gentlemen of England'.

Wisden, 1870

THE crowds at this match were so dense that the MCC was obliged to introduce a new rule which, in retrospect, marks the end of the old ground created by Thomas Lord. From 1869 on no spectator at the Eton–Harrow match was allowed to enter the ground on horseback. But the fixture, elevated in tone though it may have been, was in that same year the scene of sharp practice not altogether reconcilable with the actions of a gentleman. The Eton captain, the Hon. G. Harris, soon to transmute himself into Lord Harris, went on to bowl, and was so incensed by the tactics of the Harrow batsman C. A. Wallroth, who had been stealing runs by backing up before the ball left the bowler's hand, that he broke the wicket before releasing the ball, thus running out Wallroth. Harris later said, 'There was quite a fuss about it', and Warner, dashing as usual with pathetic eagerness to paper over the gaps in his idealised picture of the game, insists that Harris was acting 'quite correctly'. In spite of Warner, Harris had in fact acted like a lout, it being, then and since, an unwritten law that before resorting to such a device, the bowler should give the batsman a warning. And indeed, there remained for the rest of his life certain social backwaters where Harris was not accepted. One of Wallroth's sisters, who witnessed the outrage, later married the famous cricketer Alfred Lubbock, and to the end of her long life, which ended in 1943 in her 96th year, never forgave Harris. Warner says that when he attempted to argue the case with her, she protested, 'That George Harris! I shall never forgive him!' In the following year the Eton–Harrow match became ever more glorious, with the arrival of Royalty, and the inception of the pretty convention by which the spectators, including the ladies, transformed the playing area into a swirl of colour and high fashion.

ETON v. HARROW
Lord's, July 8, 9, 1870

Their Royal Highnesses the Duchess of Cambridge and the Prince and Princess of Teck, with a host of the nobility, honoured this match with their presence at Lord's. The Grand Stand was thronged, a large majority of its occupants being ladies. The Pavilion seats and roof were crowded with members and their friends. 'The Ring' was deeper and more densely packed and the outer ring of carriages more extensive than at any preceding match. Such an assemblage of rank, fashion and numbers had never before been seen even at Lord's. It was computed that quite 30,000 visitors attended the ground on those memorable two days; at all events so much as £790 was taken for admission on the Friday and £660 on the Saturday—this £1,450 being nearly £200 in excess of any previous receipts for admission to the match. The weather was fortunately favourable and attendance of ladies commensurately large. Down by Mr Dark's house, up by the NE corner, and fronting the whole row of well-known dwarf chestnut trees, the accidental but graceful grouping of ladies elegantly attired, added a picturesque brilliancy to the old ground not seen at other matches. Two sights unusual on cricket grounds and curious by contrast, were witnessed at this match; the first occurred on the Friday, when on the 'boys' retiring to luncheon the whole playing area of the ground was covered by a gay company promenading; the other on the Saturday, when on rain commencing falling at noon the youthful cricketers were suddenly surrounded by a dense ring of some thousands of opened umbrellas. Weather, attendances and exciting finish considered, there surely never was played a more successful Eton v. Harrow match than this of 1870.

Wisden, 1871

THE day would come when a later age would look back incredulous at the casual style of life taken for granted at Lord's in the 1860s. When contemporary events drift back to the point where they become history, the effect is always the same, of wonder that the crude and the unsophisticated could ever have been endured. The Eton and Harrow boys of the 1860s, swigging their ale on the grass while the vast crowd of fully 3,000 people followed the play, were regarded by everyone, including themselves, as among the most soigné creatures in England. When their grandchildren peered back at them through the pages of *The Cricketer*, the effect was very different.

It was a different Lord's from the trim and highly organised arena that we know. A scythe and a flock of sheep did duty for the roller and close-set mowing machine. Most of the ground was ridge and furrow, and in dry weather the wicket must have been lively indeed. Even in the 1860s it was good advice to 'expect every ball to shoot and you will be in time if she rises; if watching too eagerly for the rise you will be too late if she shoots'. Pads were rare, and gloves never seen. Attendances, compared with modern times, were small – 3,000 being a very big gate, but there were a great many more carriages and coaches on the ground than is or could be the case today. Many gentlemen used to watch the game from horseback. Every boy playing in the matches at Lord's had to pay 7s. 6d. for the privilege to Mr Dark, and, instead of the elaborate lunches of today, you might have seen Etonians and Harrovians lying about on the grass with a pint of half-and-half and bread and cheese. The Harrow supporters used for preference to drive to the match in post chaises, ten or twelve of which would start simultaneously from the school, and race precariously the five or six miles to St John's Wood. The hours of play were from 10 a.m. to 7.30 p.m., with little more than half an hour for lunch, and no tea interval. For many years the Wykehamists played in tall white beaver hats, but Eton and Harrow in straws.

It all sounds strange and primitive to modern ears, but we may be very sure that there were as fine players then as there are now, and many a modern batsman might have found it difficult to get into double figures under the arduous conditions of the time. As match followed match, public interest and attendances increased, until, in 1866, the crowd was so large as to interfere with the play, and necessitate the introduction of the boundary system. Of enthusiasm, we may be sure there was no lack. At times, indeed, barracking is not too strong a word to apply to the habits of the rival partisans. A yearly feature of the match was the at first wordy and eventually active warfare of two 'town cads' hailing respectively from Eton and Harrow. They would be plied with bitter beer ad lib to bring them to the necessary pitch of fluency and quarrelsomeness, and at last from the one that hailed from Eton would come the taunt that never failed to herald a fight: 'All the good I sees in 'Arrow is that you can see Eton from it if you go into the churchyard.'

The Cricketer, 9 July 1921

AₙD we in our turn look back and regard the sophisticates of 1921 with a condescending smile, just as one day the cricket lover of the future will glance at us and wonder at our quaint gaucheries. Meanwhile, matches in the early days continued to be full of incident to be coveted later by historians of the game. In June 1871, in a match between the club and the Royal Engineers, the final scores included 111 extras. A few days later, in a match against Gloucestershire, the visitors fielded no fewer than four members of the Grace family. And in May 1872 a one-day experimental match was staged in which the stumps were one inch higher than usual, and the wickets one inch wider. Later that same week Surrey dismissed the club for 16, eight of the MCC batsmen, including W. G. Grace, failing to score. In July came the Eton–Harrow match, and it is clear enough from the report in *Wisden* that the size of the crowd and the unruly behaviour of some of the Gentlemen of England was beginning to cause concern.

ETON v. HARROW
Played at Lord's July 12 and 13, 1872
Never before was congregated on Lord's Ground so numerous and brilliant a company as that which on the 12th of last July crushed and crowded on to that famous cricket arena to witness the first day's play in this, 'the fashionable match of the season'. Every seat in the spacious grand stand had been secured several days prior to the match, and up to the close of the day preceding, applications for 'seats in the stand' were continuously arriving. On 'the day before the battle commenced', so extensive a use had been made of members' privileges in regard to standing room for their carriages, and so numerous had been the applications from non-members for space for their vehicles, that every available foot of the old ground set apart for carriage standing was secured; so, in order to lessen public disappointment as much as possible, the Committee caused to be inserted in the morning journals of Friday the following:

Notice.
'In consequence of the great number of applications for carriages on the part of the members, the Committee regret that they will be unable to accommodate any more visitors' carriages today at Lord's Ground.
By order of the Committee,
Lord's Ground, July 12   R. A. Fitzgerald, Secretary, MCC'

The crush at the gates on the first day was great and lasting beyond all precedent, the crowd waiting their turn to pay and pass on to the ground extending in a line some distance up St John's Wood Road, and for hours the 'clack' 'clack' of the turnstiles resounded as rapidly and as regularly as the men in the two boxes could take the admission shillings. On the Saturday, the storms that fell at mid-day doubtless deterred hundreds from visiting Lord's; but when all was over, the tell-tales notified that

On the Friday,	and	On the Saturday,
16,450 visitors had paid and passed through the turnstiles		11,005 visitors had paid and passed through the turnstiles

The number that paid on the Friday exceeded by nearly 3,000 those that paid on the first day of the match in 1871, and although the number paying on the second day was about 130 fewer than on the second day in '71, the aggregate numbers that paid on the two days was considerably greater, and by those best qualified to ascertain, it was computed that—Club members and carriage company included—there were 38,000 visitors on Lord's Ground during the two days of the Eton and Harrow match of 1872.

Friday was a superb day for cricket and other out-door pleasures, and when about 5.30 that afternoon The Prince and Princess of Wales and Prince Arthur came on the ground, the scene at old Lord's was indeed 'splendid'. Grand stand, pavilion, carriages, and the space between the carriages and ropes set apart for visitors on foot were all as crowded as they possibly could be. The four-in-hand enclosure at the top end of the pavilion was packed with drags, not one of which had room for another outside passenger; and stand, drags, and carriages were all made bright and glorious by a crowd and wealth of brilliantly attired beauteous women, such as can be seen nowhere out of grumbling but glorious Old England.

Wisden, 1873

THE Lord's authorities were gradually becoming aware that popularity for the game was beginning to outstrip the way the ground was being administered. Season after season new refinements were added to the facilities, but still there were popular occasions when it became difficult almost to the point of impossibility to control the crowd. Through the 1870s the club struggled with considerable resource to contain the problem:

Among the minor improvements and conveniences effected during the 1870s may be mentioned the introduction of turnstiles in 1871, in which season it was estimated that during Eton v. Harrow over 38,000 persons attended and more than 600 vehicles were admitted. 1872 saw the introduction of a travelling post-office on the ground and the installation in the old Tennis Court of the clock, the gift of Lord Ebury and for long the target of ambitious leg-hitters; whilst during 1873–74, to promote the comfort and convenience of members and their friends introduced on special occasions, an embankment was constructed which supported four rows of seats capable of accommodating 400 persons. During 1875–76 a practical architect and surveyor was appointed at a fixed salary, and the Annual Report of 1878 recorded that 'since last season a new lodge has been substituted for the old one, and a new workshop, store-room, stable, etc. have also been erected at a cost of about £1,000.'

LORD HARRIS AND F. S. ASHLEY-COOPER, *Lord's and the MCC*, 1914

The Marylebone Club had offered a Champion County Cup for competition at Lord's. Several counties, after deciding to compete, declined to enter the contest and MCC withdrew the offer, but Kent and Sussex agreed to play their round at Lord's. Kent won by 52 runs, as described in *Wisden*, 'on dangerous and bad wickets. A new and very fast bowler, Mr Coles, battering and bruising several of the Sussex men and finally disabling George Humphreys. Mr Coles had ten Sussex wickets—eight bowled.' This was the only match played for the Cup. Subsequent to this match the preparation of wickets at Lord's was left to the superintendence of the umpires who were elected a week previous to the match being played; the result was good wickets for the remainder of the 1873 season.

Wisden, 1940

IN retrospect it seems very much as though the threat of mob violence presented itself only on very rare occasions, most of which appear to have been the Eton–Harrow matches. The 1873 game provided the worst exhibitions of misbehaviour so far in the series, and the MCC Secretary, the benign R. A. Fitzgerald, was obliged to issue a manifesto which confessed to the club's inability to keep control, and a threat to discontinue the match unless improvements were made in future. Fitzgerald's reference to 'unseemly behaviour', and vague talk of disorder left readers of *Wisden*, in whose pages the manifesto was published, wondering exactly what had happened. At least one publication was more explicit:

The disturbance that occurred after the finish of the Eton and Harrow match has caused the Committee of the Marylebone Cricket Club to issue the following manifesto: – 'The Committee regret that, notwithstanding all their efforts to prevent a scene of confusion at the termination of the Schools' Match, their efforts were frustrated by the unseemly conduct of some persons on the ground. Such scenes as those witnessed on Saturday would not occur if the partisans of both schools were to assist the authorities in checking the immoderate expression of feeling at the conclusion of the match. The Committee appeal to the old and young members of the two schools to assist them in future in preventing a repetition of such disorder, which must inevitably end in a discontinuance of the match. – By order of the Committee, R. A. FITZGERALD, Sec. MCC.' We could venture to wish that the Committee had been a little more explicit, and had said where the 'scene of confusion' was, as it is just possible that they may refer to a crowd at the gate, which is said to have behaved itself ill. But we have little or no doubt that the crowd in front of the pavilion is what is referred to, and we must admit that it is very properly found fault with. The noise and confusion were extreme, and lasted for a most unreasonably long time. If the police and those of the ground men who helped them had not been very peaceful and good-tempered the result of the scrimmage might have been really serious, and as it was certain hats were broken and many toes trodden on, and it is said that one policeman was a good deal injured. But, though we do object much to such horse-play, we cannot help thinking that too much has been said about it in some quarters. People who were not at Lord's, but who read the accounts of the match in Monday's papers, must have thought that there was something very like a free fight between Eton and Harrow going on, as soon as the match ended in favour of Harrow. Now, we who write were on the top of the pavilion, just beyond the centre, during the whole of the row, and we can fairly say that we did not see one single blow struck in anger throughout. As far as we could understand the situation, the Eton boys, after Mr Hadow and Mr Shand on the Harrow side had been borne victoriously through the crowd, wanted to treat Mr Buckland to the same sort of glorious but uncomfortable manifestation of sympathy. Probably Mr Buckland either did not know this, or did not care for the honour, or was dressing and not presentable – anyhow, he did not respond, and the crowd surged up against the police in the vain hope of getting at him. This is the belief of those who could see best, being up above the crowd, *sua sine parte pericli*, not a dozen yards from the centre and kernel of the row, the middle entrance of the pavilion. That there was really no violence worth mentioning may be proved sufficiently by the fact that more than one ex-Etonian near us had a brother or friend in the thick of the crowd, without feeling the faintest anxiety for his fate or even for the symmetry of his costume. 'Just like a bully at the wall,' said one of them at our elbow, using the technical name for their most crowded game at football, and he could not have hit the thing off better in one sentence. It was just like a rough game, such as football, and was, as far as the boys went, just as harmless. One rough fellow, not a boy, but a middle-aged man, tipped a policeman's hat off, but he did it from behind, and looked most innocently in the opposite direction when the policeman, who did not exactly like the liberty taken with his uniform, turned upon him. A few more of his stamp would have put the whole place in an uproar; but he was, most luckily, not seconded. And now that we have entered our protest against the somewhat exaggerated way in which this not very terrible disturbance has been treated, we must say that the Committee are perfectly right in resolving to put down anything of the kind in future years. We must not expect too much of boys; but they really ought to learn to moderate their transports and confine themselves to the use of their voices. Even these might be advantageously toned down in some cases. 'Well hit!' and 'Well bowled!' are fair cries enough; but 'Well fielded!' when an adversary misses a catch, and 'Well asked!' when the umpire gives his decision in favour of the batsman, are, to put it mildly, errors in taste and judgement. We do not want boys to 'take their pleasures sadly, after the manner of their country', for they will surely, like the rest of us, find plenty of sadness later on in life. But we venture to hope that they will henceforward have sufficient self-command to refuse to follow the bad example set to them by the 'persons of unseemly conduct' referred to by the Committee. Some of these worthy folks, hangers-on at the schools and other parasites and partisans of the most contemptible kind, are known to do what they can, year after year, to make and keep up a row, and they must have succeeded beyond their hopes on Saturday last. If one or two of them were taken in the act, and had a short but appropriate allowance of treadmill administered to them for their pains, society would be able to get on pretty well without them for a while, and they would learn a lesson that would be useful to them in future years. We commend this point to the attention of the MCC Committee for 1874.

The Times, 21 July 1873

COMPLAINTS of a different kind were raining down on the heads of the MCC management. Although the Dark philosophy of continually improving facilities was carried on into the 1870s, little improvement was to be seen in the most important area of all. It is as though the Committee, having made an inventory of all that required to be done, then placed the condition of the pitch at the very bottom. One of the last beneficiaries of the improvements had been the scorers. Under the old, primitive arrangements, they had been perched on high seats unprotected from the sun and rain. In 1865 they were at last provided with a covered box. But the pitch itself remained a danger to life and limb. Three years after the death of Summers, correspondents were still railing against the very real danger of serious physical injury being sustained by the batsmen at Lord's.

Oxford v. Cambridge, 1873
We must add in conclusion that very little can be said in favour of the wickets provided for this match. There has been not a single good wicket at Lord's yet this season. It is almost an insult to common sense to suppose that a club with an income of £10,000 a year cannot find the means of covering half a dozen acres with turf adapted to the game of cricket. There are other clubs in London whose committees can provide wickets for any number of great matches, in which cricketers may play without any fear of their teeth being knocked down their throats, or their arms being disabled.

The Saturday Review,

IN the meantime, Fitzgerald's appeal evidently had its effect, for the 1874 match, although attended by as large a throng as ever, was noted for the improved conduct of all present. The popular Press, however, may have been so disappointed by this lack of newsworthiness at a match swiftly becoming notorious for its rowdiness, that it invented unruliness where none was apparent. At any rate, Fitzgerald was obliged to publish a disclaimer in *Bell's Life*. This disclaimer was later reproduced in *Wisden*:

ETON v. HARROW
Played at Lord's, July 10, 11, 1874

Shortly after the termination of the Eton and Harrow match of 1873 it was rumoured that the admission charges to the ground would, in all probability, be increased at the 1874 match. A proposition to that effect was advanced at the club's annual May meeting; it was subsequently discussed by the Committee, and the result was the publication in the usual cricket chronicles of the following announcement:

ETON v. HARROW
To The Editor

'Sir,—I am instructed to ask you to publish the following resolution, passed at a meeting of Committee on June 8 last:

Resolved—"That it is desirable to make arrangements for diminishing the number of persons at the Eton and Harrow match, on July 10 and 11. and that, with that view, the price of admission on that occasion for each person on foot be raised from 1s. to 2s. 6d."

It was also resolved—"That the masters and boys of each school be admitted free, by tickets."

I am, your obedient servant,

R. A. Fitzgerald, Secretary, MCC'

So numerous were the applications for carriage standings, that a week prior to the match the Secretary found it necessary to issue a public notice, of which the following formed parts:

CARRIAGE ARRANGEMENTS

'No further application for carriage tickets can be entertained. The Secretary has issued as many tickets as the space at his disposal admits of.

Members' carriages will be admitted by ticket on Thursday, July 9, from 10 a.m. to 7 p.m., to take up position on the ground.

The Committee particularly request that at the conclusion of the Eton and Harrow match everybody present on the ground will abstain from undue exhibition of party feeling. The co-operation of the members of the club is earnestly solicited to carry out this resolution. Hoisting is strictly prohibited.

By order of the Committee,

R. A. Fitzgerald, Secretary, MCC'

The seats in the Grand Stand had all been secured a week prior to the match, and as the demand for more seats continued numerous and pressing, a temporary stand was erected at the east end of the grand, and all the seats in the temporary were quickly secured. Over 400 carriages of the members of the club entered and were admirably positioned on the ground during the day prior to the match, and the official records of the numbers of visitors who paid the 2s. 6d. and passed through the turnstiles on to the ground during the two match days were:

9,039 on the Friday, and 6,325 on the Saturday.

On the Friday the weather was bright and hot, very hot, and the closely packed human ring that encircled the cricketers, the fair-ly, fashionably, and fully occupied seats on the new embankment, and the wealth of beauty and rank that filled and graced the two Grand Stands and the 430 carriages, eloquently told that Eton v. Harrow at Lord's was still the great event of the London fashionable season, and that for aught it would have affected the wonderful attraction of the match, the admission charge might as well have been raised to half-a-guinea as to half-a-crown.

THE LATE ETON AND HARROW MATCH
To the Editor of *Bell's Life in London*

'Sir,—I shall feel obliged by your publishing the following facts in connection with the late Eton and Harrow match. Numerous unauthenticated statements have appeared in the papers, and in justice to MCC I trust you will permit me to correct them:

1. No money was taken for any carriage taking up position on the ground.

2. 430 carriages belonging to members only were admitted.

3. 9,039 persons paid admission on the first day, 6,325 persons on the second day; in 1873 15,808 persons paid admission on the first day, and 11,214 persons on the second day.

4. 1,000 free passes were sent to each school, and upwards of 1,000 tickets, each admitting four persons, were allotted to the members; 6,000 persons may fairly be computed to have had free admission to the ground on each day of the match.

The admirable order preserved by this assembly, and the kind attention shown by all persons to the published regulations of the Committee, eminently deserve a public recognition. The increased tariff of admission fulfilled the expectations of the Committee; it not only tended to check the attendance by several thousands, but it was especially conducive to the good order that prevailed.

In grateful acknowledgment of the help I personally derived from the visitors themselves,

I remain, your obedient servant,

R. A. Fitzgerald. Secretary, MCC'

Wisden, 1875

Not all Mr Fitzgerald's responsibilities in 1874 were as stern. Later that summer the club acted as hosts to the most exotic guests since the arrival of the Aborigine side of 1868. The American visitors, hopeful of exhibiting the arts and general style of their game, would have been mortified to have read in the *Wisden* of the following year mention of the dread word: Rounders.

THE AMERICAN BASE BALL PLAYERS IN ENGLAND, 1874

Twenty-two base ball players from America visited England at the back end of the cricket season, 1874, 'their mission'—it was semi-officially stated—'being to give the English a practical insight into the workings of base ball.' The twenty-two comprised eleven members of the Boston (red stockings) and eleven of the Philadelphia Athletes (blue stockings), the two leading base ball clubs in the United States, where the game holds the same high and popular national position cricket does in England. The visitors' stay in this country was limited to one month. They quickly got to work, making their first appearance in flannel on an English ground the 30th of July, at Edgehill, the ground of the Liverpool Cricket Club. They were a finely-framed, powerful set of men and, although 'Base Ball' did not take the popular fancy here, the splendid long-distance throwing and truly magnificent out-fielding of the Americans at once won the full and heartily-expressed admiration of Englishmen, who frankly and freely acknowledged the Americans' superiority to the generality of English fielders.

Nine Bostons v. Nine Athletics played, with varying success, base ball matches on the Liverpool Club's cricket ground at Edgehill; on the Manchester Club's ground at Old Trafford; on the Marylebone Club's ground, 'Lord's'; on Prince's ground, at Belgravia; on the Richmond Club's ground in the Old Deer Park, Richmond; at the Crystal Palace, Sydenham, on the Surrey County Club's ground, 'The Oval'; on the Yorkshire County ground, Sheffield, and at Dublin.

THE AMERICANS AT LORD'S

Considerable interest was excited in cricketing circles last summer by public announcements that representative teams of the two leading Base Ball Clubs of America would, at the back end of our cricket season visit England and by playing their national game on our principal cricket grounds, endeavour to acclimatise that game in this country. The interest created by this announcement was increased by the statement that the Americans had also (but somewhat reluctantly) agreed to play a cricket match against an English Club team on each ground they played their base ball match on. Of course Lord's was one of the grounds selected for these displays and respecting this visit of the Americans to head quarters, the following announcement was published:

ELEVEN GENTLEMEN OF MCC v. EIGHTEEN GENTLEMEN OF AMERICA

'August 3, 4, 5, 1874.— The Committee of the Marylebone Club have granted the use of Lord's Ground during the above days to the American gentlemen, who intend to give an exhibition of their prowess at cricket as well as their national game of base ball.

The proceeds of the match will be handed over to the American gentlemen, to meet the large expenditure incurred by their visit to England. The programme will be as follows:

On Monday, August 3, a match will commence between Eleven Gentlemen of MCC and Eighteeen of America.

Play will be suspended at 3 p.m. on Monday, August 3, when two selected nines (Americans) will commence a game of base ball.

The cricket match will be resumed on Tuesday morning, August 4, and at its conclusion a second match of base ball will be commenced, the sides to be selected, as may be arranged, between a mixed English and American nine.

A dinner will be given at the Tavern, Lord's Ground, at 8 p.m. on August 3, to which the visitors and other distinguished Americans will be invited by the MCC.

Members of the MCC who may wish to be present at the dinner are requested to give early notice of their intention to the Secretary of the MCC. Dinner tickets £1 1s. each. The chair will be taken by the President of the club, the Marquis of Hamilton.

The admission to the ground on each day of the match will be 1s. for persons on foot; 2s. 6d. will be charged for each carriage. Admission to the Grand Stand 1s. The members' enclosure will be reserved for visitors introduced by the members of the club.

By order of the Committee,

R. A. Fitzgerald, Sec. MCC'

Monday, August 3rd, was one of our Bank Holidays and, fortunately, a day of splendid weather, but unfortunately, it was also the opening day of the annual Canterbury Cricket Week: nevertheless, there was a large company present to welcome the strangers to Lord's, so many as 3,580 having paid the 1s. and passed on to the old ground that day.

Prior to the commencement of the cricket match, the Americans surprised and delighted the company with a display of their ball-throwing and catching abilities: the great height and distance they threw was marvellous and their correct judging, cool, clever waiting for, and easy catch of the ball from those big throws, was really wonderful: each throw and catch eliciting a hearty cheer. Having evidently greatly gratified the company with this display, they turned out at 12.25 to commence the cricket match:

12 GENTLEMEN OF MCC v 18 OF AMERICA

The MCC batting was commenced by Mr Alfred Lubbock and Mr Courtenay, to the bowling of H. Wright (medium round) and McBride (fast underhand) who took three strides to the wicket and then let fly a tremendously fast grubber that rarely rose from the ground an inch after it pitched; this kind of bowling quickly settled Mr Courtenay and Mr Round and at first somewhat stuck up Mr Alfred Lubbock, who, however, soon got into something like his old fine form of play, scored 24 runs, and was then clean bowled by H. Wright. Mr Lubbock left with the score at 34 and at 41 a clever catch at point settled Mr Lucas for 12. One more run was scored and then—at five minutes past two—they retired to luncheon and preparations were forthwith made for commencing:

THE BASE BALL MATCH
ATHLETIC CLUB 9 v. BOSTON CLUB 9

The Boston men were the Base Ball champions of America and The Athletics (of Philadelphia) the ex-champions. The marking out the diamond-shaped base ground, and the subsequent play of the sides was watched with marked interest by the audience, but they had not proceeded far with the match before many of the spectators were impressed with the idea that they were witnessing a modernised, manly—and unquestionably an improved—edition of that most enjoyable old game of their boyhood—Rounders, the most patent differences being:—a cricket-sized ball is used at base ball, instead of a ball of tennis size, as at rounders; throwing the ball at the striker when running from base to base is allowed at rounders, but is properly barred at base ball; and instead of the ball being struck with a stick of broom-handle thickness held in one hand, as at rounders, it is at base ball struck by a formidably-sized club, clutched and wielded by both hands, a form of play that, to become efficient in, evidently requires lengthened practice and much skill.

The play proceeded to the evident advantage of the Bostonians all through; and after a contest of two hours and ten minutes' duration, the Boston Champions won by 27 to 7, the following being the score, as published in *Bell's Life*:

Athletics

	Runs	First Base hits	Put out	Assisted to put out
McMullen (centre field)....	1	3	4	0
McGeary (short stop)......	1	1	1	5
Anson (first base).........	1	3	10	0
McBride (pitcher).........	1	2	0	0
Murnan (right field).......	1	2	2	0
Batten (second base)......	1	2	3	2
Sutton (third base)........	1	1	0	3
Clapp (catcher)...........	0	1	6	1
Gedney (left field)........	0	2	1	0
Totals	7	17	27	11

Bostons

	Runs	First Base hits	Put out	Assisted to put out
C. Wright (short stop).....	4	4	4	0
Barnes (second base)......	4	2	3	5
Spalding (pitcher)	4	4	0	0
McKey (catcher)..........	3	4	4	0
Leonard (left field)	2	3	1	0
O'Rouke (first base).......	2	2	7	0
H. Wright (centre field)....	1	2	5	0
Hall (right field)..........	1	3	0	0
Schafer (third base).......	3	1	3	2
Totals	24	25	27	7

Runs Scored in Each Innings

	1	2	3	4	5	6	7	8	9	Totals
Athletics	3	0	0	0	1	1	1	0	1	7
Boston	3	7	4	0	5	0	5	0	0	24

Bases by errors: Boston 9 times, Athletics 1. Runs earned: Athletics 6, Bostons 11. Umpire, Mr Thomas Beales, of the Boston Club. Duration of game, two hours ten minutes.

Play in the cricket match was resumed at 6 o'clock, Mr V. E. Walker and Mr Bird continuing the MCC batting. Mr V. E. Walker hit freely and got well hold of the bowling, but was at last settled by a good ball from H. Wright and was out for 27 – the highest score hit in the match. Then play ceased for the day, the MCC score standing at 88 for five wickets, Mr Bird not out, 15. The Americans fielded very smartly and effectively before luncheon, but subsequent to their base ball struggle their fielding was loose and ineffective.

In the evening the Americans were entertained at dinner by the Marylebone Club, the President of the Club, the Marquis of Hamilton, presiding, supported by the Treasurer, Mr R. Burgoyne and the Secretary, Mr R. A. Fitzgerald. It was understood that 50 gentlemen sat down to dinner.

Tuesday, August 4th, was a woeful wet day, so wet that play in the cricket match could not be resumed until 2.30 and then under such difficulties to the batsmen that twelve overs sufficed, to finish off the MCC innings, which had become part of cricket history, by 3 o'clock, the wickets having fallen as under:

1/2 2/8 3/34 4/41 5/88 6/90 7/92 8/92 9/102 10/105 11/105

The Americans then batted to the bowling of Mr Appleby and Mr Rose. Most of the strangers went in for hard hitting, Mr Spalding heading the lot with 23, an innings that included a splendid on-drive down to Dark's house and two or three other hard cracks. They had made 73 runs for ten wickets when a fierce rainstorm of twenty minutes' duration literally swamped the ground; however, being desirous of finishing off that innings and then closing the mach, they went at it again later on and the finish was so close and exciting, that when the Americans had only two wickets to fall, they wanted 6 runs to defeat MCC's total; when they had only one wicket left they wanted 3 runs; and when their last man was caught out they were two runs ahead of MCC, a result they were evidently proud of and justly so, for this MCC 12 was undoubtedly the best English team the Americans met at cricket throughout their brief tour. The American wickets fell as follows:

1/2 2/9 3/23 4/34 5/38 6/41 7/56 8/68 9/71
10/73 11/87 12/87 13/87 14/91 15/100 16/103 17/107

The match was not played out.

MCC		America	
C. Courtenay b McBride ...	0	H. Wright b Rose.........	2
*A. Lubbock b H. Wright ..	24	J. D. McBride b Rose	5
J. Round b McBride.......	0	A. G. Spalding b Appleby ..	23
A. C. Lucas c Schafer		W. Anson c FitzGerald b	
b McBride	12	Rose	2

G. E. Bird c McVey b H.
Wright 15
V. E. Walker b H. Wright .. 27
A. Anstruther c Batten b G.
Wright 0
*F. P. U. Pickering b H.
Wright 9
*E. Lubbock b G. Wright. .. 0
*R. A. Fitzgerald c Hall
b G. Wright 4
*W. M. Rose b G. Wright .. 0
*A. Appleby not out 0

B 9, l-b 3, w 2... 14
───
105

R. C. Barnes b Pickering ... 5
G. Wright b Rose......... 12
E. B. Sutton b Pickering ... 3
W. Fisher run out 3
A. J. Leonard b Rose 13
S. Wright c A. Lubbock b
E. Lubbock 0
C. A McVey b Pickering ... 10
J. O'Rourke b E. Lubbock .. 4
J. Sensenderfer b Pickering. 0
T. Batten c Appleby b Pick-
ering 4
J. McMullen b Pickering... 5
G. Hall c Round b Pickering 5
H. C Schafer c A. Lubbock
b Pickering 5
G. Beales not out........ 1

B 2, l-b 2, w 1... 5
───
107

*Played in America in 1872.

American Bowling

	Overs	Mdns	Runs	Wkts
H. Wright	52	32	43	4
McBride...............	37	19	34	3
G. Wright	16	9	14	4

MCC Bowling

	Overs	Mdns	Runs	Wkts
Pickering...............	15.3	4	23	8
Appleby...............	15	4	26	1
Rose..................	12	3	35	5
F. Lubbock	8	4	13	2

Wisden, 1875

THE man responsible both for order at the Eton–Harrow matches and for visits from colonial baseball professionals was R. A. Fitzgerald, one of the outstanding secretaries of the Club in its Victorian years. Born in Berkshire in 1834, and elected an MCC member in 1858, Fitzgerald accepted the honorary secretaryship in 1863, and was tireless in the club's interest until ill-health at last forced his retirement. W. G. Grace was one of his firmest advocates, writing later that 'the period of reform and improvement at Lord's began, I think, when my old friend Fitzgerald was elected honorary secretary of the MCC. He became paid secretary in 1868 and held the post thirteen years, resigning on grounds of ill-health in 1877. An assiduous and energetic official, he initiated numerous improvements, both as regards the ground and the management of the club. His popularity may be judged from the fact that when he became secretary the MCC membership was 651, when he resigned it was 2080.'

When Fitzgerald first accepted the post he lived in a house overlooking the ground, but once he married he moved to Chorleywood, Herts. Fitzgerald was particularly noted for his speech-making, at Anniversary Dinners and other semi-official functions. At one dinner he observed that he had 'at times been compelled to use language that was unpleasant for him to utter and for others to hear, but he believed that without it he could not have got the workmen out of the pavilion'. Later he was offered an annual salary of £400 for his work, and on accepting this arrangement, he reminded his colleagues that during his reign the club had become for the first time independent owners of the ground, a new pavilion had been erected, two-thirds of the ground had been re-levelled, a grandstand had been built, the tennis court restored and a new Tavern built. Perhaps the best way of conveying the spirit of the man is to read the opening paragraphs of his *Wickets in the West*, his account of the English tour of America and Canada in 1872. The prose, although slightly laboured in its attempt to entertain and amuse, is not altogether a failure, and evokes overtones of the style soon to be popularised by Jerome K. Jerome.

Fitzgerald's declining health was probably at least partly due to overwork, and at one stage his doctor ordered him abroad in an attempt to separate him from his duties. But he returned, and left again. On this second departure, Fitzgerald published an appeal addressed to 'Secretaries and to all Cricketers Whom It May Concern':

Gentlemen: I am on the point of leaving England, by medical advice, for a couple of months. The Committee have kindly made arrangements for conducting the business of the Club during my absence, and all letters, till further notice, may be addressed to H. Perkins, Esq., Acting-Secretary, MCC, Lord's Ground, NW, who will give prompt attention to the same. I have only to request that the same courtesy may be extended to Mr Perkins as has been shown to myself for several years past. I trust to return with fresh vigour to my usual place in June; and I leave England with confidence that the general routine of business is left in excellent hands, and that the rules and regulations in force will be respected as hitherto by the frequenters of Lord's Ground.

I am, Gentlemen,

your obedient servant,

R. A. Fitzgerald, Secretary, MCC

BUT Fitzgerald never did regain his health, never did resume his duties. At last he tendered his resignation and retired to the peace of Hertfordshire, where, after years of suffering, he died, on 28 October 1881. Meanwhile the affairs of the club passed into the capable hands of Perkins, a formidable character, a bearded patriarch whose career as a lawyer and regular member of the staff of *The Times* qualified him eminently both for the composing of manifestos and the handling of the ever-more convoluted business of the club.

Even in his last days as secretary, Fitzgerald was obliged to defend his policies from diehard members who took exception to every change on principle. He was well able to take care of himself, and used with skill the ploy which a great many indispensable men are inclined to fall back on, the threat of resignation:

At the Annual General Meeting of the club on May 5, 1875, a fierce attack was made, not for the first time, by Mr Willoughby, who criticised the expenditure on the Tavern, derided the match-list as rubbishing, and asserted that professionals were reluctant to play at Lord's, being better treated elsewhere. He objected strongly to the introduction of a lawn-tennis court, and criticised the attitude of the Secretary to members. Another member objected to the admission of carriages to Lord's. The Secretary, Robert Fitzgerald, declined to reply *seriatim* to Willoughby's strictures, and defended lawn tennis as 'an athletic and popular game'. It would appear to have been a lively meeting, in which the cut and thrust of debate went too far, and at the subsequent dinner, which lasted until midnight, Fitzgerald said that he regretted the alleged lack of courtesy on his part, and added that if it were true it was excess of zeal for the interests of the club. He offered to resign, but this brought general support for his retention of office, and the members separated in mellow mood, after the splendid dinner provided by Mr Crick, the caterer.

LORD HARRIS AND F. S. ASHLEY-COOPER, *Lord's and the MCC*, 1914

AMONG those whose approval of and support for Lord's was by no means unqualified were the editors of *Wisden*, who clearly felt that democratisation could be taken too far. Remembering the exclusivity of the club when it was a small organisation serving primarily as a retreat for well-bred gentlemen, it rather surprisingly tended to bemoan the introduction of new facilities and the patronage of spectators unable to claim even a single change of name in the course of their lives:

GENTLEMEN OF MCC v. THE ROYAL ARTILLERY, Lord's
June 3 and 4, 1875

Two quiet days at Lord's were enjoyed by the few visitors who witnessed the cricket in this match—the oldest now played by MCC. Barring a few welcome summer showers, the weather was bright and hot and the happy absence of crowd, cads, card-criers and other unpleasantries necessarily suffered at a great match, increased the enjoyment which would have been thorough had better out-cricket been played by both teams, especially by the gunners.

Wisden, 1876

A FEW days after this, *Wisden* was celebrating one of the great games of the season. Stimulated to poetic heights by the decline in the weather, the reporter then went on to describe the pleasures of a well-attended match, at least comparatively speaking, and finally to document a memorable piece of bowling. Modern readers will be enchanted to see that Shaw's scorebook figures incorporate eating arrangements:

ALFRED SHAW's MAGNIFICENT BIT OF BOWLING
41 overs (36 maidens) for 7 runs and seven wickets—6 bowled

MCC AND GROUND v. NOTTINGHAMSHIRE
Played at Lord's, June 14, 15, 1875

Wind and weather alone considered, this was the most un-enjoyable match ever played out at Lord's, for throughout those two days the wind blew big and bitter blasts from the WSW, so cold that the air was more fitting for Ulsters and mid-winter than summer suits and midsummer and so strong that—in addition to other casualties—the wind broke clean in half the trunk of a full-sized sturdy elm tree that stood at that end of the Regent's Park nearest to Lord's Ground.

The attendances included most of the familar faces seen on London grounds when a great match is being played by first-class cricketers, a strong contingent of 'cricket critics' (grey beards and smooth chins) and a fairly large number of members; and if the gatherings were not, numerically, up to the form such a match deserved, that must be debited to the exceedingly ungenial cricketing weather; as it was 1,214 paid for admission the first day, and 1,439 on the second, and there can be no doubt but that had the match days been favoured with those sunny skies and seasonable warmth, cricketers—and all other men—naturally expect in 'leafy June', the ground would have been largely attended, especially as it was Richard Daft's first match in London that season.

The batting was unequal and most certainly did not master the bowling, not withstanding so many of the batting cracks of the period played. Only 440 runs were scored for the forty wickets down. Mr W. Grace was one hour at wickets scoring his 10 runs and one hour and ten minutes making his 35; he was thoroughly put on his defence by Alfred Shaw and one of the few batting treats of the match was the defence of Mr W. Grace against the rare bowling of Alfred Shaw; over after over was played in truly great form, shooters being got down upon with marvellous sharpness, but those enjoyable struggles between ball and bat ended in victories to Shaw, who clean bowled the crack in each innings. In his innings of 10 Mr Grace made only 3 runs (all singles) from Alfred Shaw's bowling and in his second innings of 35 runs only three of them (all singles) were obtained from Shaw's bowling. Mr I. D. Walker was one hour scoring his 13 runs, including a splendid cut down the ground for 5 from McIntyre and Mr I. D. was nearly an hour making his 12 runs all of which were from McIntyre's bowling. Mr Hadow was precisely thirty-eight minutes at wickets for his first innings of one run and in his second he went in fourth wicket down and took his bat out for 8, so it can be readily imagined how very carefully Mr Hadow played. Mr Webbe (the colt from Oxford) was undeservedly out in his second innings, being called by Mr Grace to a desperately sharp run and being splendidly thrown out from cover-point by Wyld. Mr Duncan (the colt from Cambridge) played with much steadiness a not out innings of 18 runs, made by five 2s and eight singles and equally steady was the batting of Mr Ridley during his one hour's play for 15 runs. Clayton hit as Clayton usually does when they let him stay—i.e., freely and hard, though for all that his 22 took him forty minutes to knock together. But the best batting for MCC—and in the match— was Mr Buller's 45; that was a brilliant display of truly fine all round hitting, comprising a superb on-drive up to the NE corner of the ground for 5 from Oscroft's bowling, four 4s—off-drive and cut from J. C. Shaw, on-drive from Oscroft and a magnificent leg hit from Morley, the ball pitching about a dozen yards from the racket court; in addition to those hits Mr Buller made seven 3s, three of them from Alfred Shaw's bowling; but although Mr Buller made three 4s, a 3 and two singles in his 17, he did not score one of those runs from Alfred Shaw. Mr Renny-Tailyour's 6 was a one hit innings—a grand on-drive from Morley, who shortly retaliated by clean bowling his man and with the following ball he as brilliantly bowled Mr Duncan. The Nottinghamshire innings was productive of further proof of good batting promise in Arthur Shrewsbury, who stayed forty minutes at wickets for 8 runs against the bowling of Mr Grace and Mr Ridley. None played the Oxford lobs in better form than this lad, who is not 21 years old, but who possesses the confidence of a veteran and shaped in a form that foretells a prominent batting career in the cricket of the future. Martin McIntyre was exactly one hour and ten minutes making his 41, the highest Notts. score; he played with unusual steadiness; he was missed at short-leg by Mr Duncan when he made 22 and finished his innings with a very fine drive up the ground for 4—the only 4 he made, his other hits being one 3, eleven 2s and 12 singles. Daft appeared somewhat nervous on commencing his first innings and was some time ere he settled down; he was ninety-five minutes at wickets for his 25 runs, which were not made in 'his old form' as reported; but in his second innings he quickly got into something like that 'old form', played all the MCC bowling with his usual ease, grace and skill, saw seven wickets fall, the score increased from 4 to 75 and took his bat out for 35, an innings that included three good drives for 4 each and—his last hit—a superb off-drive from Mr W. Grace's bowling for 5.

The fielding of Mr Herbert at leg and long-off, of Mr Renny-Tailyour at square-leg and of Selby at cover-slip and long-off was A1; the very fine form in which they flew over ground after the ball and saved runs elicited frequent, loud and deserved cheering. But the cream of the fielding was the effective way in which Mr Ridley, Alfred Shaw, Morley and Mr W. Grace fielded their own bowling; that was indeed fine and enjoyable cricket, and atoned for several shortcomings in the field by others.

The bowling was very remarkable. McIntyre ended the play before dinner on the first day by bowling Lord Harris with a brilliant bailer— a better ball was never bowled; but on the second day Mc. commenced with an over that included two wides, a hit for 4 and a 2. Morley, on the first day, started with six successive maiden overs; on the second day, one of his overs was finished off with a hit for 6, but in his following over he clean bowled two wickets. Mr Ridley, on the first day, bowled three wickets in five successive balls; on the second day he started with seven overs for one run and two wickets and finished with ten overs and three balls for five runs and two wickets. Mr W. Grace, in the match, bowled 83 overs for 86 runs and nine wickets; and although Mr Hadow failed to floor a wicket, only four of his 14 overs were hit. But successful as some of those bowlers undoubtedly were, all of them were entirely put to shade by the brilliant ball work done in the match by Alfred Shaw who, all told, bowled 95 overs (71 maidens) for 46 runs and nine wickets—

averaging in the match less than half a run per over for 95 overs, and a shade over 5 runs per wicket for nine wickets.

Alfred commenced the bowling on the first day with a maiden over; two singles were scored from his second over and one from his third; then he bowled seven overs for one run and a wicket and when dinner was called at 2.30, he had bowled 44 overs (31 maidens) for 27 runs and two wickets; after dinner, he was hit a bit and they scored a 2 from each of his last overs; nevertheless, his bowling in that innings totalled up

Overs	Mdns	Runs	Wkts
54	35	39	2

If the reader runs his eye down the names of the eleven MCC batsmen, he will see they include several Gentlemen of England status and some of the most accomplished batsmen and finest hitters of the period, making the above a most successful bit of bowling; but it was as nothing to what followed from the clever right hand of the same great master of the ball, who, in the old Club's second innings, actually bowled

Overs	Mdns	Runs	Wkts	
41.2	36	7	7	(six bowled)

Such marvellous bowling as this to such high-class batsmen has no equal in the history of the game. It brought out the full defensive powers of Mr W. Grace, Mr I. D. Walker, Mr Hadow, Mr Ridley and Mr Buller; none of these great hitters being able to get the ball away for runs and during their stay at wickets the attack from Alfred Shaw and their defence was indeed 'splendid cricket', that will long be remembered with admiration by those who sat out that bitterly cold, boisterous, but memorable Tuesday at Lord's. To worthily portray on paper the many rare excellencies of Alfred Shaw's bowling in that second innings of MCC's is wholly beyond the power of the compiler of this little book, but he will give those who missed witnessing it an opportunity of estimating its excellence and success by the following full and careful chronicle of every ball bowled by Alfred Shaw in MCC's second innings:

```
....   ....   ....        ....   ....   ....   ....   .I..   ....
....   ....   ....        ....   I...   ....   W...   ..I.   ....
....   II.W   ....        ..W.   ....   ....   ....   ....   ....
....   ..W   (Dinner)   .  .    ....   ..W.   ....   ....   ....
....   ....   ....        ....   ....   ...W   2...   .W
```

The 2 hit (scored by Clayton) was a pure fluke, and so was one of the singles; bearing this in mind, considering that this bowling was delivered to some of the most skilled batsmen of the day, remembering also that six of their wickets were clean bowled, it will be conceded that those 41 overs and two balls for 7 runs and seven wickets by Alfred Shaw is the most wonderful display of the mastery of the ball over the bat ever delivered by bowler. Nevertheless, MCC won the match by 62 runs.

MCC and Ground

W. G. Grace Esq. b Alfred Shaw	10	– b Alfred Shaw 35
I. D. Walker Esq. b Alfred Shaw	13	– st Biddulph b Alfred Shaw . 12
W. H. Hadow Esq. b Martin McIntyre	1	– not out 8
A. W. Ridley Esq. b William Oscroft	15	– b Alfred Shaw 8
C. F. Buller Esq. c Alfred Shaw b Morley	54	– b Alfred Shaw 17
A. J. Webbe Esq. b William Oscroft	0	– run out 0
Lord Harris b Martin McIntyre	3	– b Alfred Shaw 0
H. W. Renny-Tailyour Esq. c Alfred Shaw b Martin McIntyre	4	– b Morley 6
A. S. Duncan Esq. not out .	18	– b Morley 0
A. W. Herbert Esq. b Martin McIntyre	0	– b Alfred Shaw 0
R. Clayton c and b William Oscroft	22	– b Alfred Shaw 2
B 7, l-b 4, w 2 ...	13	B 1, l-b 6, w 3 ... 10
	153	93

Nottinghamshire

William Oscroft lbw b W. G. Grace	4	– b W. G. Grace 3
F. Wyld b Clayton	6	– b Ridley 0
Arthur Shrewsbury b W. G. Grace	3	– c and b W. G. Grace 8
Richard Daft c and b W. G. Grace	25	– not out 35
Martin McIntyre c Harris b W. G. Grace	41	– c I. D. Walker b Ridley 4
J. Selby not out	15	– c W. G. Grace b Ridley 1
Alfred Shaw c Hadow b Ridley	5	– st Webbe b W. G. Grace ... 7
William Shrewsbury b Ridley	0	– b W. G. Grace 5
Biddulph b Ridley	0	– b W. G. Grace 0
F. Morley c and b Ridley...	9	– c and b Ridley 6
J. C. Shaw b Ridley	3	– c and b Ridley 5
B 2, l-b 1	3	B 1 1
	114	75

Nottinghamshire Bowling

	Overs	Mdns	Runs	Wkts	Overs	Mdns	Runs	Wkts
Alfred Shaw ...	45	35	39	2	41.2	36	7	7
M McIntyre	39	18	48	4	10	2	35	–
Morley	21	13	20	1	25	13	30	2
W. Oscroft	13.3	6	19	3	6	1	16	–
J. C. Shaw	6	2	14	–				

MCC and Ground Bowling

	Overs	Mdns	Runs	Wkts	Overs	Mdns	Runs	Wkts
Mr W. Grace...	45	20	43	4	38	18	43	5
Clayton	18	6	28	1				
Mr Ridley......	14.1	8	15	5	38.3	24	31	5
Mr W. Hadow..	14	10	13	–				
Mr R. Tailyour .	8	3	12	–				

Umpires: John West and Nixon.

Wisden, 1876

WHILE Alfred Shaw was trundling away, there was taking place one of the most significant changes in the history of the administration of Lord's. In November 1874 the club at last took effective steps to end the long period in its history when its pitches were a cause of reproach and complaint. The appointment as Ground Superintendent of Peter Pearce, known as Percy, heralded a new era. Having had extensive instruction in the maintenance of lawns, and furthered his experience at the Hove county ground, Pearce arrived at Lord's well equipped to deal with the problem. Indeed, there were those, including some bowlers, who felt he was dealing with it far too well. What had for so long a rock-strewn path for batsmen suddenly became a featherbed under the tender ministrations of Percy Pearce. Correspondents who had only a season or two before been grumbling about the appallingly bad condition of the Lord's wicket, now began grumbling about its appallingly good condition:

Gentlemen v. Players, 1876
There is a certain amount of novelty attached to the idea of a cricket ground being 'too good' for the purpose of a great match, yet such an idea is entertained by the Marylebone Club, and Pearce, the new groundsman, has orders not to improve it further. Better wickets than those of Monday were not needed, and to their condition the heavy scoring can to a large degree be attributed.

The Field, 1876

Time was when a good wicket at Lord's was the exception but now, happily, thanks to Pearce, the groundsman, the playing portion of the arena is in faultless condition, and a batsman can concentrate his energies on the defence of his 'timber' without, as formerly, having any misgiving as to his personal safety.

The Standard, 27 June 1876

AT least as prestigious in its way as Eton v. Harrow was the University match, the only fixture in the cricket calendar which could match it in standards of *haute couture* and blueness of blood. So important was this aspect of the match thought to be, perhaps excusably so, that *Wisden* invariably began its report with a review of the fashions on parade. This partial view of the first-class cricket of the day was already being challenged by those who sensed that the time had come for a more co-ordinated approach to the administration of the game, the selection of representative teams and the arranging of fixtures. No breath of any of this ruffled the sedate pages of *Wisden*:

OXFORD v. CAMBRIDGE
Lord's, June 25 and 26, 1877

The innings over, the visitors crowded on to the playing portion of the ground in great numbers; in fact, Lord's ground was then literally covered by the fashionable throng. The gaily dressed ladies slowly promenading; the thickly packed crowd swaying to and fro in front of the pavilion; the mass of people outside the ropes down at the bottom of the ground, perforce moving onwards at a snail's pace, and at times coming to a dead block, unable to move either way; and the chock at the top of the ground when the police mandate rang out, 'Clear the ground, Clear the ground there; Ladies, do pray clear the ground', formed a sight that those in a position to look down on can never forget, for truly said a twenty years regular attendant at Lord's, 'It is a sight that never had an equal on a cricket ground.'

But at last the entreaties of the police cleared the ground sufficiently to finish off the match; at five o'clock the brothers Webbe were lustily cheered as they walked to the wickets to hit off the required 47 runs, and thereby square up the ill-fortune attending their first innings.

Wisden, 1878

B UT behind the scenes the MCC was under heavy fire, just as in England at large the power of the old land-owning aristocracy was being eroded by the new industrial rich. The MCC had always been primly indifferent to the idea of a well-organised annual county championship, apparently fearful that the developing strength of the county clubs might soon constitute a threat to its taste for absolutism. But the days when the counties were the poor relations socially speaking were already past. Several shires now boasted ennobled connections on their committees. There was also the much more important factor, of public demand. The MCC would ignore this appetite for first-class cricket at its peril. In 1874 the club, seeking to forestall plans for a championship between the counties, proposed its own counter-stratagem, a series of regional representative matches, at Lord's, naturally, between sides chosen from the north, south-east and west. But the public failed to respond. Attendances at Lord's fell to the point where, as we have seen, *Wisden* could rejoice in the tranquillity to be found during matches there.

But Fitzgerald, ailing though he was, continued to fight resolutely to the last ditch on behalf of the old order, claiming that falling attendances were due to the partial absence from the ground of W. G. Grace and the way in which too much cricket had blurred the demarcation lines between Gentlemen and Players. Among the opponents of this specious defence was one of the most renowned of the Gentlemen, R. A. H. Mitchell, the deity who presided over cricket at Eton:

I cannot think that Mr Grace's advent to the field of cricket can have in any way contributed to the decline of cricket. It is professionals whose names we miss.

Why is this? Those who say there is too much cricket appear to me to be stating only half the truth. There is too much cricket under the imperfect management of the MCC. The MCC, occupying as it does the first position of any club in England, holds in its hands the remedy for the present state of affairs. What is wanted is a policy of reconciliation with due regard to the interests of other clubs. Hitherto, the MCC has arranged their matches independently, and the argument advanced has been, 'We arrange our matches and others must make their own arrangements accordingly.' I hope the hard logic of facts may break down so infatuated a theory. Let the MCC invite representations from the county clubs and the all-England Elevens to meet together in the autumn and arrange their matches for the next year in such a way as may be most convenient to all. In such matches as the Gentlemen v. Players, I should like to see permission given to the Players to select their own side.

R. A. H. MITCHELL in *Bell's Life*, 1875

Let the Marylebone Secretary, if he has the time, pay a visit to the Kennington Oval, or to Prince's, whilst a good county match is proceeding without Mr Grace, and he will at either place receive a direct denial to his preposterous statement. The real fact of the case is that the public are more fond of cricket than ever, but they will not visit any ground that does not lay an attractive programme before them.

Bell's Life, 1875

Two accidents were now to come to the aid of the beleaguered MCC. One was the illness and retirement of diehard Fitzgerald, followed by the appointment of the harder-headed Perkins. Among the important amendments to the club rules was one ensuring that the proportion of playing members be maintained: 'Cricketers possess the first claim on the Club, and it is not thought conducive to their best interests to suffer the welfare of the Club to depend upon so uncertain a basis as the popularity of certain great matches.'

The second stroke of fortune enabling Lord's to thrive was one which ironically wiped out one of its two London rivals. Prince's Ground, in Hans Place, Sloane Street, was, socially speaking, a formidable challenger to Lord's, having an earl as its president, and a committee incorporating five earls, a marquis, six peers and two colonels. The ground was considerably larger than Lord's, covering thirteen acres. But those acres were coveted by land developers, who, almost before Prince's had got under way in 1871, began chipping away at its perimeter. In 1876 *Wisden* reported the 'cutting off of the NE corner', and speculated on the possibility of the land being 'magnificently mansioned over'. Those fears proved all too well grounded, but by then one of the more attractive tenants at Prince's had had a dispute with the management and decided to move on to pastures new. Those pastures were to be at Lord's.

In 1877 cricket at Lord's benefited greatly by the appearance there of the Middlesex Club, which had migrated from its former headquarters at Prince's, and the addition of a few county matches to the Marylebone programme will certainly strengthen it in a point where it has been undeniably weak of late years. For some time there has been a complaint that there was not so much first-class cricket at Lord's as the revenue and position of the club warranted, and beyond all doubt, with the exception of the two fashionable meetings of the season, there had been for some time to the outside world an air of monotony and apathy about the cricket at Lord's. The addition of the Middlesex fixtures filled a decided blank in the Marylebone programme, and there was certainly more life in the appearance of matters at headquarters than in the previous year.

Lillywhite's Almanack, 1878

There was no charge at that time for the use of the ground, but the county generally made a donation to the MCC, larger or smaller according to the state of its finances. These arrangements have varied from time to time, and today Middlesex pay a rent of £1,100 a year and take the gate money, but no stand money, Middlesex paying all the expenses of the matches – professionals, umpires, scorers, gatekeepers, entertainment tax, luncheons and teas for the teams. Middlesex are limited to a membership of 1,200 who have the *entrée* to the pavilion for Middlesex matches, and for all other matches at which a member of the MCC is entitled to introduce a friend into the pavilion. This modus operandi has proved of advantage both to the club and to the County. It has proved what may be called 'a happy marriage', and those who criticise it can learn from the remarks of Lillywhite how Lord's before Middlesex played there had a meagre list of first-class fixtures.

SIR PELHAM WARNER, *Lord's*, 1946

THE troubles experienced by the MCC were those of a private, exclusive club with pretensions to autocratic rule over the game at large. By the end of the 1870s the MCC had to decide whether to be one or the other, for it patently could no longer be both. The steadily increasing crowds at first-class matches, the patronage of rival clubs by members of the aristocracy, the rise of strong county sides, the steady increase in the number of column-inches devoted to the game in the national Press, all these were factors in the forcing of MCC's hand. The club had either to broaden its approach or fail once and for all to broaden its influence. In the end the fortuitous incident of Perkins' appointment and the arrival from Prince's of the Middlesex eleven pushed the club in the right direction. But for at least the next three generations, the growing status of the MCC as the final arbiter of cricketing affairs and the custodian of its morality was balanced – some would say impeded – by its strict adherence to the traditions of a past in which the contests of schoolboys and students were considered the most important fixtures of all. This excess of sentiment was neither wholly foolish nor wholly undesirable. Some of the University cricketers were also international virtuosi, and some of the memories engendered by the participants at Lord's contributed to the common stockpot of legend surrounding that extinct breed, the Victorian Gentleman:

Oxford won the University match of 1877 by ten wickets, F. M. Buckland scoring 117 not out and taking seven wickets for 52 runs. In Cambridge's second innings the Hon. Alfred Lyttelton was superbly caught low down at short leg by F. G. Jellicoe, a brother of the Admiral of the Fleet, a good left-arm bowler, but a notoriously bad fieldsman. Years afterwards at a Foreign Office reception Lyttelton and the Admiral met, and the first words Lyttelton said were, 'How's that wretched brother of yours, who caught me out in such an outrageous way in the Varsity Match of '77?'

Wisden, 1913

As the MCC somewhat reluctantly attempted to put its house in order, the game over which it presumed to preside was exploding into something unsuspected and perhaps unintended by the old grandees. The casual historian of the game, leafing back through the annals, cannot help sensing that 1878 was a watershed for English cricket. Not only were Middlesex installed at last in what was to be their permanent home, but the general public was about to see in cricket an imperial significance which had hitherto played no appreciable part in cricketing affairs. There had been some rudimentary tours in which English sides had nonchalently challenged Fifteen, or Eighteen, or even Twenty Two of the opposition, but it was not until 1878 that the truth sank in that one colonial country at any rate could put into the field an eleven able to reduce the might of England to acute embarrassment. There was also a literary footnote about to be added to cricket history. The poet and cricket-lover Francis Thompson went to Old Trafford one day in 1878 to witness the first match ever played there between the home county and Grace's Gloucestershire. The experience was to symbolise for Thompson the poignancy of lost innocence, which permeates his poem 'At Lord's'. Thompson's choice of title is in its way the finest tribute ever paid to the ground, for the actual inspiration for the poem came from his experiences at Old Trafford. In this context of emergent county and international cricket, the continuing concern over what to do about the Eton–Harrow match seems like a fading echo of the MCC's own lost innocence.

THE ANNUAL MEETING

The 91st Anniversary Meeting of the Marylebone Club was held at Lord's on Wednesday, the 1st of May, 1878. T. Burgoyne, Esq. (The Treasurer), in the chair. The Secretary, H. Perkins, Esq., read the report, the most publicly-interesting items of which were as follows, as extracted from *Bell's Life* of May the 4th. 'A sum of £4,428 was received from matches last season and £2,385 expended.' ... 'Last year the total number of members, including those on the abroad list, amounted to 2,304 and there are now no less than 443 candidates for membership.' ... 'Since last season a new lodge, a new workshop, a new storeroom, stable, etc., have been erected at a cost of about £1,000; and all buildings and other property of the Club are in good repair.' ... 'The question of the admission of carriages at the Eton and Harrow match is becoming a difficult one. Last year many members were refused carriage tickets owing to want of space; and if the number of applications for carriage tickets goes on increasing, the admission of carriages may have to be stopped altogether. It having come to the knowledge of the committee last season that carriage tickets were in several cases disposed of to persons who were not members of the Club, the committee desire to remind members that carriage tickets are not transferrable and that it is most unjust that strangers should have carriage tickets when many members cannot obtain them.' . . . 'Since last year three more volumes of Scores and Biographies have been published, bringing the records of Cricket up to the end of 1870.'

Wisden, 1879

EVERYTHING else, however, which happened in 1878 was dwarfed by the presence in England of the first representative Australian touring side, managed and captained by two men, John Conway and David Gregory, prepared to go to almost any lengths to do down their hosts. On 27 May they were due at Lord's, and it was the events of this day which mark the beginning of that fervent international rivalry which was to degenerate in less than fifty years to cynical intimidation, the exchange of insults by players and of diplomatic notes by politicians, culminating in the contemporary lunacy by which a nation's prestige is presumed to be at stake every time one of its representative teams of athletes takes the field. For good or ill, that process took root on 27 May 1878 at Lord's, when Gregory's Australians came to Lord's, hardly noticed by the general public.

The season of 1878 is a landmark in cricket history, for the Australians paid their first visit to this country, under the captaincy of D. W. Gregory, one of a family of seven brothers, five of whom played for New South Wales, and an uncle of S. E. and J. M. Gregory. James Southerton, in his description of the tour of James Lillywhite's Eleven in Australia in 1876–77, had written in high praise of several of the Australian cricketers, but little notice of his warnings had been taken, and our visitors arrived almost unheralded and certainly unsung. They started badly in bitterly cold weather at Nottingham, where they lost by an innings and 14 runs, but in their next match, against the MCC at Lord's on May 27, they administered a severe shock to our complacency. In one day, in the short space of four and a half hours of actual play, on a very sticky wicket, they defeated a powerful side by nine wickets, and the fame of Australian cricket was established for all time. Nine of the MCC Eleven were clean bowled in the second innings. The result created a great sensation, and *Punch* celebrated it in the following lines:

> The Australians came down like a wolf on the fold:
> The Marylebone cracks for a trifle were bowled;
> Our Grace before dinner was very soon done,
> And Grace after dinner did not get a run.

Wisden, in a long description of the game, said:

This, one of the most remarkable matches ever played at Lord's, was commenced at three minutes past twelve, and concluded at twenty minutes past six the same day. Only 128 overs and 2 balls were bowled, and but 101 runs, from the bat, scored in the match.... Allan began; the first ball he delivered Grace hit to leg for 4, the second got Grace caught out at short square-leg, and thereupon out rang lusty cheers, and shouts of 'Bravo, Allan! Well done, Australia!' ... At three minutes to four the second innings was commenced; at ten minutes to five that innings was over for 19 runs!

A stream of at least 1,000 men rushed frantically up to the pavilion, in front of which they clustered and lustily shouted, 'Well done, Australia!' 'Bravo, Spofforth!' 'Boyle, Boyle!' the members of the MCC keenly joining in the applause of that 'maddened crowd', who shouted themselves hoarse before they left to scatter far and wide that evening the news how in one day the Australians had so easily defeated one of the strongest MCC elevens that had ever played for the famous old club.

Here is the score of the match:

MCC v. THE AUSTRALIANS
Played at Lord's, May 27, 1878
Result: The Australians won by nine wickets

MCC

First innings		Second Innings	
W. G. Grace, c. Midwinter, b. Allan	4	b. Spofforth	0
A. N. Hornby, b. Spofforth	19	b. Boyle	1
C. Booth, b. Boyle	0	b. Boyle	0
A. W. Ridley, c. A. Bannerman, b. Boyle	7	b. Boyle	0
A. J. Webbe, b. Spofforth	1	b. Spofforth	0
F. Wyld, b. Boyle	0	b. Boyle[1]	5
W. Flowers, c. and b. Spofforth	0	b. Boyle	11
G. G. Hearne, b. Spofforth	0	b. Spofforth	0
A. Shaw, st. Murdoch, b. Spofforth	0	not out	2
G. F. Vernon, st. Murdoch, b. Spofforth	0	b. Spofforth	0
F. Morley, not out	1	c. Horan, b. Boyle	0
Leg bye	1		
Total	33	Total	19

THE AUSTRALIANS

C. Bannerman, c. Hearne, b. Morley	0	b. Shaw	1
W. Midwinter, c. Wyld, b. Shaw	10	not out	4
T. Horan, c. Grace, b. Morley	4	not out	7

A. C. Bannerman, c.
    Booth, b. Morley   0
T. W. Garrett, c. Ridley, b.
    Morley   6
F. R. Spofforth, b. Shaw. . . .   1
D. W. Gregory, b. Shaw. . . .   0
H. F. Boyle, c. Wyld, b.
    Morley   2
W. L. Murdoch, b. Shaw . . .   9
F. E. Allan, c. and b. Shaw.   6
G. H. Bailey, not out . . . . . .   <u>3</u>

      Total   41   Total (1 wkt.)   12

BOWLING ANALYSIS
The Australians

First Innings	O.	M.	R.	W.	Second Innings	O.	M.	R.	W.
Boyle	14	7	14	3	Boyle	8.1	6	3	6
Spofforth	5.3	3	4	6	Spofforth	9	2	16	4
Allan	9	4	14	1					

MCC

	O.	M.	R.	W.		O.	M.	R.	W.
Shaw	33.2	25	10	5	Shaw	8	6	4	1
Morley	33	19	31	5	Morley	8	4	8	0

Umpires: A. Rylott and M. Sherwin

[1] In W. H. Bettesworth's *Chats on the Cricket Field* (Merritt and Hatcher, 1910), p. 116, a note (written by F. S. Ashley-Cooper) confirms that in the MCC second innings Wyld was bowled by Boyle, and not by Spofforth. He says, 'This error is to be found in *Scores and Biographies*, *Wisden's Almanack*, Ayers' book on the tour, and even on the official score-card. The score was given correctly, however, in Lillywhite's *Companion and Annual* and in Conway. Boyle took six for 3.'

Wisden, 1879, quoted in Sir Pelham Warner, *Lord's*, 1946

A MORE colourful account, but one no less near the truth, was provided by H. S. Altham in his *A History of Cricket*. Here is one of those all too rare moments when a specialist cricket writer, sensing that, divorced from its social context, the greatest sporting sensation in the world may be rendered innocuous, ventures, as it were, out into the streets to discover exactly how great was the sensation caused by Gregory's men. The boys of the previous generation were now, many of them, something in the City; newsprint and word of mouth were both powerful disseminators of instant gossip around the town. For the first time, London going about its daily business, was sensitive to shifts in the balance of sporting power. Through that world of clopping horses and toppered gents, of modest clerks and publicans, there circulated the invisible waves of sporting awareness, culminating in Altham's telling detail about the ultimate focusing of curiosity on a hotel.

It was on May 27th that English cricket suffered the shock of its life. When, on a showery morning after a heavy night's rain, and with 'casual water' standing in puddles on the ground, the Australians drove in their brake on to Lord's ground, they passed practically unrecognised by the 500 or so spectators that had by then mustered; twelve hours later England was ringing with the news that the flower of its cricket had been beaten in a single day, and crowds came flocking to the Tavistock Hotel in Covent Garden to look on the men who had thus flung open a new era in the history of the game.... The news of the sensational cricket had brought London swarming up to Lord's, and when at 4 p.m. Grace and Hornby opened the club's second innings to Spofforth and Boyle, more than 5,000 people, in a state of intense expectancy, filled the ring.... The scene at the finish beggared description, and the winners could not have been more heartily cheered had Sydney or Melbourne been the scene of their victory.

H. S. ALTHAM, *A History of Cricket*, 1926

IN this climate of thriving interest in the game, crowds at Lord's grew larger for the more attractive fixtures, especially if W. G. Grace was involved. Already he had attained the status of deity, not only for the mastery of his batting and the guile of his bowling but for the irresistible verve of his personality. His young protégé Gilbert Jessop was one day to claim for him the distinction of sharing with Gladstone and General Booth the honour of being one of the three best-known men in England, and if by 1878 his fame had still not quite achieved that apex, he was still indisputably the world's best-loved cricketer. In this season of 1878 he very nearly announced his retirement, but the presence of the Australian tourists deterred him, and he continued to do what he had been in the habit of doing for several seasons past, reconciling his cricketing genius with his studies in the medical schools. It was not till the following year that he finally became a doctor, but in cricketing terms he was the most eminent professor of them all, not only capable of winning matches on his own, but apparently also quite able to humour a crowd into good behaviour, as he did at Lord's one afternoon:

NORTH v. SOUTH

Played at Lord's, June 10, 11 and 12, 1878, for the benefit of the MCC Professional Cricketers' Fund. Whit Monday 1878 broke bright, breezy and hopeful for the enjoyment of the holiday folks, and up to the early afternoon of that day the people streamed up St John's Wood Road to Lord's so continuously that—notwithstanding a showery stormy afternoon that undoubtedly lessened the attendance—the official return stated that 10,858 paid their 6d. for admission. Lord's Ground on that day was indeed a sight, the equal of which had never been seen on a Whit Monday. The people thronged the Grand Stand— they crowded to inconvenience the players' seats at the north end of the pavilion—they filled to an inch the embankment seats at the NE and SW corners—they completely blocked up the Tavern steps— they sat as closely together as they could sit on the garden wall tops—every window looking on the ground was filled with lookers- on, and not only did the visitors stand five or six deep behind the ring, but at top and bottom of the ground, they swarmed in hundreds before the ring, thereby materially contracting the fielding space and rendering 'hits to the people' not worth more than half the runs they were booked for. But for all that, the 10,000 present were, as a rule, a jolly and good-tempered crowd, and when Mr W. G. Grace went to and entreated them, in his well known bland and courteous manner, to get back a bit and give a little more fielding space, they laughed at, chaffed and shook hands with the crack in the most enjoyable, merry and free-and-easy form; and by this and other ways practically proved that 'the enlightened foreigner' who wrote 'the English took their pleasures churlishly' knew nothing about the matter, and wrote a famous fib.

Wisden, 1879

HAVING established their strength, the Australian tourists continued to enjoy a successful summer. Losing only three matches, they coped with the poor weather by drawing on their brilliant bowling skills rather than their batting, which was adequate but not on a level with that of Grace and company. In Spofforth, the 'Demon', they had one of the greatest fast bowlers in history, and there is no doubt that the high professionalism of the tourists contributed much to make 1878 the summer when modern cricket could be said to have evolved. Once more, Warner is at pains to present a picture of splendid fellows manfully accepting victory and defeat with the same smiling good nature:

The Australians played two other matches at Lord's v. Middlesex, whom they beat by 98 runs, a game memorable for a magnificent innings of 113 by the Hon. E. Lyttelton, in honour of which Spofforth presented him with a walking-stick, which he used to point to with pride, and v. Cambridge University, under Edward Lyttelton's captaincy, who beat them by an innings and 72 runs. It was in this game that Charles Bannerman made an historic hit off the bowling of P. H. Morton, who was on at the pavilion end. The ball pitched short of the ring, bounded over the low stand on the left of the pavilion, and cleared Lord Londesborough's drag, striking the wall behind with a lovely thud. Twenty-five years later I met Charles Bannerman in New Zealand, and in conversation with him I asked him if he remembered this hit, and he replied, 'Lord bless you, sir! I can feel her on the bat now!'

SIR PELHAM WARNER, *Lord's*, 1946

WE are not told how Bannerman knew so many years in advance of the rest of the world of Warner's coming knighthood, but then, 1878 was a year of a great many portents. For much of it the rain fell, trying the skills of Peter Pearce to the limit as he struggled to prepare pitches worthy of the cricketers. His efforts did not go unnoticed:

THE GROUND

Due consideration being given to the extremely wet spring that cricket-ground keepers had to contend against in 1878, high praise is due to Peter Pearce for the excellent form into which he had worked the old ground. Five-and-twenty years attendance at Lord's fails to bring to mind the old battle-field looking so smooth, so firm, so well covered with herbage, so free from spots and blotches, so green, or so apparently fit for the fights of a season, as it appeared on the 2nd of May, when it was indeed 'in high class condition', but the frequent and heavy rainstorms that subsequently fell materially discounted the care, skill and labour that had been lavished and—for a time—the mucky, messy, muddy wickets played old scratch with true cricket, and upset all calculations and anticipations, excepting those of slow bowlers, whose efforts were almost irresistible on the slippery pasty turf that cricket was, unavoidably, played on during that most miserable month of May, nineteen of whose thirty-one days were thorough wet ones. Moreover two-thirds of June was—for enjoyable cricket—as miserable as the May days, for, up to the 20th, scarce a day of 'the leafy month' passed away without copious rain-storms pelting down, drenching the old ground and making the cricketing community as miserable as maniacs; but all things come to those who can wait, and on the 20th, 21st and 22nd June the sun shone out with true summer brilliancy and heat, and all were then hopeful that thenceforth fair weather, good wickets, good cricket and good attendances, would be the rule at Lord's Ground in 1878.

Wisden, 1879

A T the end of the season the MCC issued one of the most wonderfully ambivalent manifestos in its history, pertaining to the vexed question of professionalism and when was a Gentleman not a Gentleman. It was an open secret that some amateurs, especially the Graces, took money for playing cricket, even though they were categorised as Gentlemen. W.G. had charged the selectors a fee of £3,000 for captaining England in Australia five years before, and his brother E.M., the Gloucestershire secretary, would think nothing of doubling admission prices at the last minute and declaring the match a Grace 'Benefit'. There was nothing reprehensible in any of this. As one of the greatest public entertainers in the world, a man like Grace was surely entitled to profit from his genius. The difficulty lay not in the acceptance of money, but in the bland denials that any cash had changed hands at all. Grace and several of his fellow-amateurs wanted the money without surrendering their status as Gentlemen. The MCC Committee's statement at the end of the 1878 season certainly made it permissible for them to do this. This statement says, with spectacular absence of the slightest equivocation, that an amateur could collect his expenses, or his 'pecuniary assistance', without relinquishing his Gentlemanly standing.

In strict terms, an amateur was nothing of the sort. It was understood that the essence of a Gentleman-cricketer was his willingness to play the game and meet his own expenses by drawing on those personal resources which made him a Gentleman in the first place. What, then, was the real difference between the Amateur and the Professional, if it was not a question of drawing money for playing? The Committee's statement makes clear that the distinction was not a financial one, but a social one. A Gentleman was one who had had an expensive education. A Professional was one who had not. In which regard it was perfectly logical for Grace to have earned enormous sums out of cricket and remained an amateur, for he had been trained as a professional man and was about to enter one of the gentlemanly professions. What was wrong with the MCC attitude was not its acknowledgement that a cricketer ought to be able to collect expenses, but that the difference between Gentlemen and Players was purely financial, when in fact it was social, and, in a sense political. But the statement published in *Bell's Life* at the end of the 1878 season seems to have gone unremarked.

Qualification to Play in the Match Gentlemen v. Players at Lord's
The Committee of the MCC have passed the following resolution: 'That no gentleman ought to make a profit by his services in the Cricket Field, and that for the future, no Cricketer who takes more than his expenses in any match shall be qualified to play for the Gentlemen against the Players at Lord's; but that if any gentleman feels difficulty in joining the match without pecuniary assistance, he shall not be debarred from playing as a Gentleman by having his actual expenses defrayed.' This rule has been strictly observed by the MCC since the management of the Finances of the Club has been in its own hands.

Bell's Life, 2 November 1878

IF 1878 had been soggy, the following season was positively saturated. Nothing Pearce could do made much difference to the Lord's turf. Most of the country suffered too, and the execrable playing conditions were reflected in the batting figures. Not even Grace managed to score a thousand runs, but, as an all-rounder, he could at least console himself with the 113 wickets he took at a cost of just over thirteen runs each. From May to August the rain came spattering down, bringing despair to county treasurers and disenchantment to the doughtiest of spectators:

Rain, pitiless and persistent, made the four months of the cricket year cheerless for players, altogether uninviting and dismal for spectators, and no one of either class could possibly have been truly sorry when the last day of August brought the game to a standstill.

Lillywhite's Annual, 1880

The season 1879 was the wettest ever known at Lord's. Rain fell more continuously and for a greater length of time than the oldest frequenter of the ground could remember. All the care, labour and attention of Pearce, the Ground Superintendent, and his men, was frustrated by the almost ever-recurring heavy rainstorms that from early May to the back-end of July fell over and drenched the old ground out of all form for playing true cricket.

Wisden, 1880

AND yet for Grace it was one of the most memorable summers of his life. Obliged to miss the first few weeks of the season in order to complete his final studies for his medical examination, he finally entered the arena in June, knowing that before the summer's end he was to be the recipient of official recognition of his towering influence over the English game. Two years earlier the Duke of Beaufort, President of the MCC, had suggested support for a national testimonial involving as many county and other cricket clubs as could be persuaded to co-operate. The occasion came at Lord's on 23 July 1879, the second day of the match between Over Thirty and Under Thirty. The outstanding speech was made by Lord Charles Russell, one of the great panjandrums of the club. He had first played for MCC in 1837, and was well known in political circles as the half-brother of Earl Russell.

PRESENTATION TO MR W. G. GRACE

The presentation to which allusion has been made above took place at the most appropriate spot which could have been selected—viz., in front of the pavilion at Lord's. It consisted of a sum of money and a marble clock, bearing this inscription:—'Presented to W. G. Grace, on July 22nd, 1879, on the occasion of the match Over Thirty v Under Thirty, played in his honour at Lord's', and two bronze ornaments representing Egyptian obelisks.

Lord Fitzhardinge, who had kindly undertaken to make the presentation, regretted his inability to control the weather, as he thought there were few such interesting occasions as that which had brought them together. Referring to the testimonial, his Lordship said that the original idea had been to purchase a practice for Mr Grace: but he had talked the matter over with the Duke of Beaufort, and they thought that Mr Grace was old enough and strong enough to take care of himself—(laughter and cheers)—and they would leave him to choose a practice for himself. The total amount, deducting expenses, which would be placed to Mr Grace's credit, including the value of the clock and the ornaments, was about £1,400 (cheers). He had, accordingly, great pleasure in presenting this testimonial to Mr Grace, and he could only say, on behalf of the people of Gloucestershire, that they wished him as much success in his profession as he had reaped in the cricket field (loud cheers).

Mr W. G. Grace, after stating that he was not a speech-maker, made a short and appropriate reply, in which he thanked them all for the manner in which they had got up the testimonial. It had far exceeded his expectations, and whenever he looked at the clock he should remember the occasion on which it was presented to him.

Lord Charles Russell, who had been asked as one of the oldest members of the Marylebone Club to say a few words on the occasion, said 'he was not satisfied with the amount. He thought £1,400 was an odd sum to present to any one, and he pledged his word it would be £1,500 before they were done with it. He was an old cricketer, and the enjoyment he had had in the cricket-field for many years past was in seeing Mr Grace play cricket. He looked upon cricket as the sport of the people, from the prince to the peasant, he was delighted to see that it was increasing in popularity year by year, and that in some respects also it was being better played. He had seen better bowling than was seen now. He had certainly seen greater men in that department of the game than Mr Grace, but he would say, with a clear conscience, that he had never seen a better field—(cheers)—and he had never seen anyone approach him as a batsman.

(Cheers.) More than agility was wanted in playing cricket. The game must be played with head and heart, and in that respect Mr Grace was eminently prominent. He had often seen an England Eleven playing an up-hill game steadily and well; a sudden change had placed the game in their favour, and a change came over the field, such as there would be were the sun now to break out over their heads. Looking at Mr Grace's playing, he was never able to tell whether that gentleman was playing a winning or a losing game. he had never seen the slightest luke-warmness or inertness in him in the field. (Cheers.) If they wanted to see Mr Grace play cricket, he would ask them to look at him playing one ball. They all knew the miserably tame effect of the ball hitting the bat instead of the bat hitting the ball, whether acting on the defensive or offensive. In playing a ball, Mr Grace put every muscle into it, from the sole of his foot to the crown of his head (laughter); and just as he played one ball so he played cricket. He was heart and soul in it. He had never heard a bell ring for cricketers to go into the field, but Mr Grace was in first. And that was a great matter in cricket playing. The game was a game of laws and regulations. If they relaxed these, then it became merely a pastime fit for young men who had nothing else to do, or some middle-aged men who wanted to get an appetite. (Laughter and cheers). The Marylebone Cricket Club held its ground for the practice and promotion of good sound cricket, and it was for that reason they had such great delight in taking part in this testimonial to Mr Grace, who was in every respect of the word a thorough cricketer. (Loud cheers.) Allusion had been made to HRH the Prince of Wales having joined the subscribers; it might be presumption in him to speculate on his Royal Highness's motives for doing so, but he must hazard an opinion that HRH was grateful to Mr Grace for affording him an opportunity of showing his respect for the one great game of the people, requiring in those who play it the national essentials of patience, fortitude, and pluck, and fostering the respect for law and love of fair play which are characteristic of us English people. (Loud cheers.)

Wisden, 1880

AMONG those Lord's characters whose careers encompassed the 1870s was a man whose family name is scattered through cricket history of the period with dynastic persistence. Thomas Hearne (1826–1900), a batting star of the 1860s, retired from the Middlesex side in 1872, by which time he had already been established for years as head of the ground-staff. He continued playing, but a severe stroke ended his career in 1876, after which he made an astonishing recovery, working at Lord's for the next twenty-one years. His eldest son, Tom junior, later became Ground Superintendent at Lord's, and his second son, George F., was appointed Pavilion Clerk. Three of his nephews, G.G., Frank and Alec, enjoyed success with the Kent side. Among the distinctions earned by the family was George F.'s captaincy of the St John's Wood Ramblers, later Cross Arrows, for thirty-six consecutive seasons. It would appear from the following recollection by Harris and Ashley-Cooper that when old Tom retired from active cricket, the first-class game was still plagued by those who attempted to smuggle on to the field of play bats whose width was greater than their owners' sense of decorum.

One of the best-known figures at Lord's for many years was Tom Hearne, who was engaged there from 1861 until 1897 and succeeded Grundy as head of the ground-staff in 1872. Mr Gale has said, 'Old Tom Hearne, the Field-Marshal of the professionals, was, I fancy, as an infant hung on the knocker at Lord's, as I cannot imagine the club ever having existed without him within its gates.' When quite young he visited Lord's one day, and, after watching the game for some time, asked his neighbour who was batting. 'That? Why, it's Jemmy Dean!' was the reply, in tones which did not conceal astonishment that the identity of so famous a cricketer should be unknown. The first question was quickly followed by another, 'And is he considered first-class?' The person addressed, beginning to fear that his leg was being pulled, replied indignantly, 'Of course he is!' 'Then,' said Tom to the stranger's astonishment, 'so am I!' And soon afterwards he proved the truth of the remark, for he developed into a first-rate bat and a useful bowler. His jerking at the nets, whereby he produced a good off-break, was very popular with the members for it provided excellent practice. *Wisden* truly remarked that 'in personal character no professional cricketer stood higher, and all through his life he enjoyed the respect of every one who knew him'. About forty-five years ago he could occasionally be seen seated at the exit from the pavilion, with a gauge for measuring the width of bats as the players went in, for, not only were bats more liable to spread then than now, but doubtless some unscrupulous cricketers got unfair ones made for them by small manufacturers.

LORD HARRIS AND F. S. ASHLEY-COOPER, *Lord's and the MCC*, 1914

AT least once in the 1880s the legal expertise of Mr Perkins seems to have failed him, according to the account given by Warner. The occasion was one of the famous cause célèbres of the 1880s, a schools match in which the rules were bent to the point where they snapped altogether. The preamble to Warner's account adds to the gallery of Lord's workers a man hardly ever mentioned except by the faithful:

A new telegraph board, which altered the batsmen's totals as the runs were made, was first used in the match between the Australians and an England Eleven on September 13, and appropriately the first run on it was credited to W.G. Part of the proceeds of the game, together with a diamond ring, was given as a testimonial to J. A. Murdoch, the Assistant Secretary of the MCC. He was a tall, well-built man with good features, who with his pointed grey beard, eyeglass, and good manners looked like a diplomat of the old school. Years later he was destined to be the manager of the first team the MCC ever sent abroad, when his tact, courtesy, and resourcefulness were great assets.

A peculiar incident occurred in the fourth innings of the Rugby and Marlborough match, which Rugby won by 37 runs.

Law XIV ('The Over') then ran: 'The bowler may not change ends more than twice in the same innings, nor bowl more than two overs in succession.'

The law was altered in 1889 as follows: 'The bowler may change ends as often as he pleases, provided that he shall not bowl two overs in succession in the same innings.' *Wisden* gave this version of the matter:

RUGBY v. MARLBOROUGH
Played at Lord's, July 28, 29.

This proved to be one of the most interesting and well-contested of the public school matches played during the season of 1886, and it was made specially remarkable by a very singular incident which occurred late on the second afternoon. When Kitcat, the Marlborough captain, was disposed of it was discovered that Bengough, the Rugby captain, had by some oversight been allowed to go on twice at each end, and in his first over from the pavilion wicket (the second time he had been on that end) he got Kitcat caught at cover-point. A long discussion ensued; but it was decided by the umpires that Kitcat, having been fairly caught, could not go in again. As a result, however, of the objection of the Marlborough captain, Bengough was not allowed to bowl another ball in the innings after he had completed his over. The affair gave rise to a great deal of correspondence, and, indeed, it was not thoroughly settled at the time whether or not the umpires had acted rightly. Of course, it was a clear oversight on the part of the umpires that Bengough went on at this wrong end, but the universal opinion afterwards was that, Kitcat having been fairly caught, the umpires had no option but to give him out.

The decision given does not seem sound. The trouble arose through the umpires, T. Mycroft and Wheeler, failing to observe that Bengough, admittedly unwittingly, had broken the existing law. I agree entirely with the decision of the umpires that Kitcat was out, for the breach of the laws by Bengough in bowling again was the responsibility of the umpires, and of them alone, as 'the sole judges of fair and unfair play', and no penalty should have been inflicted on the bowler. As it was, appeal was made to Mr Perkins, the Secretary of the MCC, who ruled that Kitcat was out, *but that Bengough should not bowl again.*

Thus at the Headquarters of the game a special penalty, unknown to the laws, was inflicted by a court, one of which was the Secretary of the club, to whom no appeal lay; for the laws are quite clear that the umpires are the sole arbiters.

Appeal should not have been made to Mr Perkins, nor should he have entertained the same; but, having done so, it is remarkable that one who had been a successful barrister should have given an *ad hoc* decision both unknown to the laws and without precedent to sustain it.

SIR PELHAM WARNER, *Lord's*, 1946

BOTH Bengough and Kitcat later enjoyed county cricket, with the same club, Grace's Gloucestershire, although Kitcat was by far the more successful of the two, making several good scores and forcing himself into the Gentlemen's side in 1897. He was one of those amateurs obliged to become a professional once his schooldays were over, and it was generally agreed that business commitments impeded what might have been a more spectacular career. Kitcat lived on until 1942, but poor Bengough was unfortunate enough to be one of that group of cricketers who die far away from the camaraderie of the pavilion. He was given out in 1934 in, of all cricketless places,

Laramie, USA, where at any rate his misdemeanour at Lord's half a century earlier would not have much harmed his reputation with the locals.

In the 1880s several big hitters staked their claims to immortality at Lord's, whose steadily increasing reputation as an august, almost ecclesiastical institution seems to have inspired the irreverence of batsmen who took pleasure in smashing things, especially glass. The great connoisseur of this branch of calculated vandalism is Gerald Brodribb, meticulous annotator of the bizarre, the freakish and the spectacular:

In 1885 S. W. Scott of Middlesex hit a ball from W. G. Grace right into the Tavern at Lord's, 'scaring the barmaid nearly out of her wits'; the ball bounced back off the wall of the bar on to the grass. Soon after, in the very same innings, W.G. was again hit through the same door into the bar, this time by Sir Timothy O'Brien, whose hit smashed some claret glasses. It is not known what the barmaid said about the second hit. S. W. Scott, who told this story, says he never saw a ball hit into the Tavern before or since. In 1865 E. M. Grace, with one of his famous pulls, had hit a ball most gleefully through the window of an upper room of the Tavern, and it was humorously suggested that the landlord should frame the broken pane and keep it as an heirloom. There is something infinitely satisfying about a glass-smashing hit, and the boy who hits a ball through the neighbour's cucumber frame may well feel that, whatever the cost and penalty, it was worth it. A broken window at Lord's would seem especially awe-ful. W. G. Grace once drove a ball through the Committee Room window, and I believe windows in the Long Room have in comparatively recent times been smashed by both Jim Smith and Trueman, who no doubt enjoyed it immensely. Hammond, with a more precise straight drive, once put a ball through the open door of the Long Room, but the ball bounced right against one of the show-cases without damaging it.

GERALD BRODRIBB, *Hit for Six*, 1960

ONE big hitter justifiably jealous of his reputation was William Herbert Fowler (1857–1941), a giant of a man who registered some of the longest recorded hits of the nineteenth century, including one famous one at Lord's. Fowler was something of an all-rounder, and does not bother to mention in his letter that before he made his big hit on that day in 1882 he had already done the hat-trick when bowling. In addition to making runs for Somerset, Fowler was a famous golfer who represented England against Scotland for three successive years from 1903, and later designed several well-known courses in England and America.

Sir, Several of my friends have asked me to write to you on the subject of 'Over the pavilion at Lord's'. There seems to be considerable difference of opinion as to what has happened in the past. It is strange that I have never heard of W. G. Grace having done it. I was playing regularly from 1879 to 1890, and all this time I lived under the impression that C. I. Thornton (Eton v. Harrow 1868) and myself were the only two who had carried the pavilion and also the wall behind. My hit was in 1882, and was off the Derbyshire fast bowler George Hay. The ball went over the top of the flagstaff on the northern end of the pavilion. Bill Ford told my brother Howard that the ball was travelling faster than any he had ever seen; he was sitting in front of the pavilion. After the day's play was over, Hearne, the groundsman, and I chained the distance from the Nursery wicket to the base of the wall, and we made it 134 yards (recorded 157 yards elsewhere). This may be of interest now in reference to where the wickets are now placed. The ball before the one I hit off George Hay for six was bowled by T. Mycroft, and I hit it past mid-off and ran five for it. The match was MCC v. Somerset.

W. HERBERT FOWLER, Letter to *The Times*, 30 May 1935

NB: The old pavilion, to which the writer refers, was much lower than the new building which was opened in 1900.

WISDEN reported these and other events, although not quite either with Brodribb's sense of style or Fowler's hurt feelings at being forgotten. Among the happenings which the Almanack so dutifully recorded were the occasional extra-cricketing crises which are bound to arise from time to time at even the best-regulated grounds. The grieving descendents of Captain Hyde may console themselves with the thought that for such a gentleman there could have been few more pleasurable ways of taking his leave.

AUSTRALIANS v. MIDDLESEX
Lord's, June 24, 25, 26 1886

The play on the opening day was thoroughly good and enjoyable. Middlesex scored a very respectable first innings, Spillman and J. G. Walker being by far the most prominent of the batsmen; and then the Australians, in an hour and a quarter, put on 96 runs without losing a wicket, Jones being not out 52, and Scott not out 42, at the close of play. The ground was in splendid condition, and the company was very large. It must be mentioned here as a matter of record that Captain Hyde, a retired captain of the Peninsular and Oriental Company's service, died suddenly on the ground during the game. The deceased gentleman was a well-known frequenter of Lord's Ground, and his face and figure were doubtless familiar to hundreds of people.

Wisden, 1887

THE Thackerayan captain, alas, died just too soon to enjoy the junketings of 1887, a year distinguished for two anniversaries, the fiftieth of the Queen's reign, and the hundredth of the MCC's. Victoria's Golden Jubilee celebrations involved the Kings of Belgium, Denmark, Saxony, Portugal and assorted Crown Princes, none of whom had even a rudimentary grasp of cricket. The MCC birthday celebrations were much better arranged, and included a three-day match at Lord's between the club and an England eleven. A month before this game, Warner, having arrived in England from his native Trinidad in order to attend Rugby School, came to Lord's for the first time, and was lucky enough to see the future Professor Higgins, Duke of Wellington and mentor of Rudolph Rassendyll take an early wicket. A few weeks later Warner was back, to watch the game marking the club's hundredth birthday:

The first time I saw Lord's was on Friday, May 20, 1887. Only recently arrived in England from the West Indies, I had as a boy devoured the pages of *The Field*, which in those days gave a great deal of space to cricket, *Wisden*, and *The Times*. I had seen in the *Illustrated London News* a group of the Australian team, in which G. E. Palmer was wearing a stiff-fronted shirt, and nothing would satisfy me until I was given one exactly like his! The dramatic moments in the famous Test Match at The Oval in 1882, A. G. Steel's 148 at Lord's two years later, Ulyett's wonderful catch-and-bowl of G. J. Bonnor in the same match, and Shrewsbury's 164 on a sticky wicket for England against Australia at Lord's in 1886 were vivid in my imagination. I used to dream of cricket! It was, therefore, with a thrill of anticipation and delight that I passed through the turnstile at the main gate[1] and watched the play from a seat in front of the ivy-covered tennis court, with the great clock in the middle, where the Mound now stands. I can recall vividly even now the first wicket I ever saw taken at Lord's – C. A. Smith, from the Nursery end, clean bowling F. E. Lacey with what looked from the ring a very good one.

W. G. Grace was one of the club side, and during the luncheon interval he passed near by, and I gazed with undisguised admiration, not to say awe, on the greatest personality the cricket world has ever known, or ever will know. With his black beard and giant figure, with an MCC cap crowning his massive head, he bestrode the cricket world like some Colossus, and little did I dream then that one day I should play with and against him.

A month later my preparatory school was taken in a body to Lord's to see the MCC play England during the Centenary week, in which nearly all the great cricketers of the day were taking part. Of the players in that match none survives today, but I can see Lord Hawke, with his cap worn back to front, and A. J. Webbe catching Louis Hall at short leg, right under the bat, as if it were but yesterday. I can recall, too, A. E. Stoddart's and Shrewsbury's great first-wicket partnership of 266; Ulyett's powerful hits over deep extra cover's head off Barnes, of Nottinghamshire, scattering the spectators in Block A; George Lohmann's artistic and cleverly flighted bowling; and Johnny Briggs at cover. It all comes back 'quick like a shot through the brain'.

Here is the score of this great match:

[1] The main entrance is still in the same place as it was when the present Lord's was opened.

MCC CENTENARY MATCH
MCC v. ENGLAND
Played at Lord's, June 13, 14, and 15, 1887
Result: England won by an innings and 117 runs

MCC

First Innings		Second Innings	
Dr W. G. Grace, b. Lohmann	5	c. and b. Briggs	45
A. N. Hornby (capt.), c. and b. Briggs	16	b. Bates	6
W. Barnes, b. Briggs	8	c. and b. Bates	53
A. J. Webbe, c. Briggs, b. Lohmann	0	c. Pilling, b. Bates	14
W. Gunn, b. Lohmann	61	c. Shrewsbury, b. Briggs	10
G. G. Hearne, b. Briggs	8	c. Barlow. b. Lohmann	6
J. G. Walker, c. Hall, b. Lohmann	3	b. Briggs	25
Hon. M. B. Hawke, b. Lohmann	16	b. Briggs	10
W. Flowers, b. Lohmann	19	c. Lohmann, b. Bates	43
J. T. Rawlin, not out	18	c. W. Read, b. Bates	4
M. Sherwin, b. Bates	17	not out	1
Byes 3, wide 1	4	Byes 4, leg bye 1	5
Total	175	Total	222

ENGLAND

A. Shrewsbury, c. Barnes, b. Rawlin	152	G. Ulyett, c. Sherwin, b. Barnes	46
A. E. Stoddart, c. and b. Rawlin	151	L. Hall, c. Webbe, b. Barnes	0
R. G. Barlow, l.b.w., b. Rawlin	0	J. Briggs, b. Barnes	9
M. Read, c. Sherwin, b. Flowers	25	G. A. Lohmann, not out	9
W. W. Read (Capt.) c. Webbe, b. Barnes	74	R. Pilling, c. Gunn, b. Barnes	0
W. Bates, c. Hornby, b. Barnes	28	Byes 8, leg byes 12	20
		Total	514

BOWLING ANALYSIS
ENGLAND

First Innings	O.	M.	R.	W.	Second Innings	O.	M.	R.	W.
Lohmann	57	29	62	6	Lohmann	32	13	60	1
Briggs	55	22	84	3	Briggs	39	8	77	4
Bates	5	2	5	1	Ulyett	21	8	34	0
Barlow	2	2	0	0	Bates	28.3	15	46	5
Ulyett	8	3	20	0					

M.C.C.

	O.	M.	R.	W.		O.	M.	R.	W.
Barnes	74.2	30	126	6	Flowers	74	29	122	1
Rawlin	90	39	140	3	Hearne	9	3	19	0
Grace	36	16	65	0	Webbe	13	5	22	0

Umpires: John West and T. Mycroft

SIR PELHAM WARNER, *Lord's*, 1946

WARNER, writing in 1946, looks back to that day so long ago and tells the reader that the changes in the ground since then have rendered it almost unrecognisable from the Lord's into which he stepped off the boat from Port of Spain. 'Only three buildings remain – Block A, on the left of the pavilion as one looks at the wickets, the Hotel, and the members' luncheon room. There was no big scoring-board or 'Father Time'; the stands were few and small, and there was nothing like the seating capacity we are accustomed to in these days. The northern end of the Nursery had only just been purchased by the MCC. But the atmosphere then was the same as now.' That atmosphere was acknowledged, if not described, by *The Times*, which used the occasion as a chance to review the history of the club since its foundation.

The Centenary at Lord's

Rarely has a club attained such longevity and then found itself in the zenith of its fame as that which the Marylebone Club are celebrating this week at Lord's. Its formation in 1787 arose, it would seem, through an almost chance meeting of the Earl of Winchilsea and the Hon. Colonel Lennox. These gentlemen induced Thomas Lord – a cricketer himself of no small repute – to open a ground at St Mary-le-bone on the site where Dorset-square now stands. Subsequently Lord's removed to the North Bank, and thence to the ground in the St John's-wood-road, where its headquarters now exist. The first recorded match on Lord's original ground was on May 31, 1787, in which T. Lord himself played. It was followed within just a week of a century ago by a match between England and the White Conduit Club (with six men given) at Lord's. This practice of a side having players allowed them was far more general then and for many years subsequently than at present. Indeed, during the latter end of the last century matches usually depended on the individual prowess of a player, and sometimes the contests were made for heavy sums. These were either risked by the players themselves or else provided by some wealthy patron – much in the same manner as we now have professional oarsmen, runners, walkers, and others, supported by some admirer. We find in 1794 on Lord's Ground a match being played between Eight Gentlemen of the Marylebone Club (and four men given) against Eleven Gentlemen of London for 500 guineas a side. In this Thomas Lord took part, and in the double innings obtained 12 wickets. Even 50 years before this it is stated that in 1735 a great match was played at Moulsey Hurst, in Surrey, between his Royal Highness the Prince of Wales and the Earl of Middlesex, eldest son of the Duke of Dorset, for £1,000 a side; eight of the London Club and three out of Middlesex played for the Prince and the Kentish men for the Earl. One glimpse of the altered state of the metropolis is caught from the fact of Marylebone playing London, thus implying that Mary-le-bone, as it was then spelt, was distinctly an outlying district. The playing for heavy stakes naturally led to much betting and certain quarrels. This was particularly the case in single-wicket matches, which were then and until quite recent years very popular. Thus we find 'the lion of Kent, the bold and manly Alfred Mynn', so noted for his personal achievements. Gradually, however, the ability of the individual merged into the reputation of the club, which, when once firmly established, caused single-wicket matches to be of rarer occurrence. Even then for a time betting existed; but it gradually ceased. Though, at its outset, the records of the Marylebone Club are so bare as to leave its earliest doings almost in a cloud, it is certain that, once well established, it has always held the indisputable position it now so deservedly occupies. It must be remembered that the laws which governed the game a hundred years ago were in a very crude state. If for nothing else, the early attention to and careful revision of these laws by the Marylebone Club would alone entitle them to the respect of all lovers of the game. It could have been by no means so easy a task as cricketers may be prone to imagine that the laws were gradually formulated into their present shape. Not only has cricket such a charm for the players themselves, but throughout the summer it affords healthy recreation to hundreds of thousands, and is watched with a keenness, a subdued feeling of enjoyment, and withal an enthusiasm quite free from the artificial excitement and feverishness engendered by betting. Thus the inherent vitality of cricket is proved beyond question. To enumerate the long roll of exploits with which the name of the Marylebone Club is associated would be to give the history of cricket since it has become indisputably the national game. It is gratifying also to reflect that the freehold of the ground on which they play is now their absolute property – obtained after many vicissitudes. It is now without doubt the ambition of all cricketers, whether amateur or professional, to appear in a match at Lord's, and in the chronicles of the scores the appearance of a player at Lord's seems to be made almost the starting-point of his career. We are, perhaps, apt to think that players of the past were much superior to those of the present. Yet it is probable that two teams never entered the field so skilful at all points as those celebrating the centenary at Lord's. In glancing at the names of the players engaged in the match, it is curious to note that neither in the Marylebone nor in the England team is there a representative of a county which in bygone days has produced so many good cricketers. Sussex at one time could put a team into the field able to vie with any in England. In fact, it is not too much to say that the name of Lillywhite was a household word in connexion with the game. On more than one occasion Sussex has met England single-handed and defeated them. Yet at the present time it does not, in the opinion of those intrusted with the selection of the teams, possess a single player, able to take part in this centenary match. Nor can the elevens chosen, with any show of reason, be found fault with. In the two teams, Gloucestershire furnishes Dr W. G. Grace (the greatest cricketer of his and, in the opinion of most people, any other day); Lancashire sends Mr A. N. Hornby, Pilling, Barlow, and Briggs; Nottinghamshire,

Barnes, Gunn, Flowers, Shrewsbury, and Sherwin; Yorkshire, the Hon. M. B. Hawke, Bates, Hall, Rawlin, and Ulyett; Surrey, Mr W. W. Read, Lohmann, and Maurice Read; Middlesex, Messrs A. J. Webbe, J. G. Walker, and A. E. Stoddart; and Kent, G. G. Hearne.

The weather yesterday was charming, and if it is true that it can never be too hot for cricket the votaries of the game had nothing left to wish for. Long before the hour set for a beginning many took up their positions. The whole of the covered seats were crowded, as were also those along the tennis side of the ground. Members also fully availed themselves of their opportunities. The seats in front of the pavilion and members' enclosure were well filled and the roof itself was crammed.

Within a few minutes of 12 o'clock the appearance of England in the field showed that Marylebone had won the toss. Mr Hornby and Dr Grace opened the innings, and Lohmann delivered the first over from the pavilion end. After a single by Mr Hornby Briggs bowled from the Nursery end. In the fourth over Lohmann, fielding at slip, injured his hand and retired for a few minutes. Meanwhile Bates bowled in his place. The fielding and bowling were very close. Mr Hornby at last drove Briggs finely to the off for four, and soon afterwards he repeated the stroke. At 19, however, Mr Hornby returned the ball. Barnes joined Dr Grace, but with only four added the latter was beaten by a ball from Lohmann. Two for 23. Mr Webbe's stay was brief and unproductive, as without alteration in the figures he was out to a brilliant catch by Briggs, who secured the ball high up with his left hand, running from cover-point. Three for 23. Gunn joined Barnes. Runs were still obtained with great difficulty, until at 36 Barnes was clean bowled. George Hearne and Gunn improved matters. An off-drive for two by the Kent man brought 50 on the telegraph board after an hour and a quarter's play. Two runs later, however, Hearne was bowled, and half the wickets were down. Mr Walker started promisingly, making a fine cut for two, but was then dismissed by a clever catch at slip. Six for 55. The Hon. M. B. Hawke was next on the order. He made a hard off-drive for four from Lohmann, and in the following over from that bowler his companion secured four by a similar hit. Although the bowling was twice changed, the total was 85 for six wickets at luncheon. Lohmann and Briggs conducted the bowling after the interval. Mr Hawke was at length clean bowled. Forty runs had been added since the fall of the sixth wicket. With seven batsmen out for 95 Flowers aided Gunn. The 100 was reached at 3 o'clock. Gunn completed his 50 at 3.20. Flowers was bowled at 125, and Gunn had Rawlin for a partner. The former soon had the misfortune to play on. He had been in two hours and 10 minutes, and his 61 were obtained in splendid style; his chief contributions were three fours, three threes, and 12 twos. Sherwin, the last man, and Rawlin hit freely, and put on 39. Bates now clean bowled Sherwin, and the innings was over at a quarter past four. Pilling had kept wicket to quite his old style, and the total reached 140 before the first extra was recorded.

Shrewsbury and Mr Stoddart began the England batting at 4.35. Barnes and Rawlin were the bowlers. Now came one of the best displays of batting that has been seen at headquarters for some time. The bowling underwent almost every conceivable change, while the field was frequently varied. With the exception of a hard return chance by Mr Stoddart (the ball also glancing to mid-off), the batting was perfect, and they played out time, runs having been obtained at the rate of 80 an hour. The company on the ground numbered about 8,000, among whom were Prince Christian, Lord Charles Russell, Lord and Lady Londesborough, Lord Winterton, Lord Sondes, Lord Erskine, Lord Bessborough, Lord Bingham, Lord Anson, &c.

MCC AND GROUND 175 (Gunn 61; Lohmann 6 for 62) and 222 (Barnes 53, Dr W. G. Grace 45, Flowers 43; Bates 5 for 46, Briggs 4 for 77)
ENGLAND 514 (Shrewsbury 152, Mr A. E. Stoddart 151, Mr W. W. Read 74, Ulyett 46; Barnes 6 for 126)
Score after first day: MCC 175; England 196 for 0
England won by an innings and 117 runs

The Times, 14 June 1887

In his recollections of the Centenary Dinner, Warner invokes the name of the once-renowned George Goschen, who had, only a few weeks before, become part of the mythology of Victorian politics, through the misjudgement of one of his professional rivals. In 1887 Salisbury's Chancellor of the Exchequer, Lord Randolph Churchill, resigned, less on a matter of principle than as a show of strength. Lord Randolph walked out in the belief that nobody could do his job. Salisbury promptly appointed Goschen and proved that anyone could. Historians later achieved the impossible, of making Goschen seem romantic by dubbing him 'the man Lord Randolph forgot', since when he has become the man everyone has forgotten about. What he was doing at the MCC dinner nobody has ever been able to explain, as, on his own confession, he knew virtually nothing about the game.

The Right Hon. G. J. Goschen (afterwards first Viscount Goschen), at that time Chancellor of the Exchequer in Lord Salisbury's Government, was present at the dinner in the tennis court on June 15, 1887, to celebrate the Centenary, and in his speech remarked that so keen was his interest in cricket that, whatever the political situation, the first thing he looked at in *The Times* every morning was the cricket news. At the dinner was Monsieur Waddington,[1] Prime Minister of France in 1879, and French Ambassador to the Court of St James from 1883 to 1893. Curiously enough, he, like Goschen, was a Rugbeian, and, I believe, they were contemporaries at school.

During my Rugby days I used to play in Lord Goschen's cricket week at Seacox

[1] He rowed in the Cambridge Eight of 1849, the year of two races. The first was rowed on March 29, when all the Cambridge crew were Trinity men and beat Oxford by about eight lengths. Oxford, according to *The Story of the Inter-University Boat Race*, by Wadham Peacock (Grant Richards, 1901), were so disgusted with their defeat that they at once challenged Cambridge to row against them again in the same year. The second race took place on December 15, and was the only occasion when a foul occurred. Cambridge won by a length, but Oxford appealed, and the decision went against Cambridge. On that occasion Waddington was not in the crew.

Heath, in Kent, with a fair amount of success, and he came hurrying from Downing Street to see me play my first match at Lord's for Middlesex in 1895. Unfortunately I got a 'duck', and as I walked disconsolately up the pavilion steps he rose from his seat with 'Oh, Pelham, how did it happen? You never did this sort of thing at Seacox!'

SIR PELHAM WARNER, *Lord's*, 1946

WISDEN reported the festivities in much closer detail, including the bewildering information that Lord Harris had paid tribute to the Press in the most fulsome terms. For some years the arrangements at Lord's for newspaper reporters had been little more than farcical; six years after the Centenary Dinner the editor of *Wisden* was still fulminating against the club: 'At Lord's the arrangements for Press men are far from adequate, and, I imagine, it is only the uniform courtesy which one experiences from everyone connected with the Headquarters of cricket that has prevented strong representations being made to the MCC. The accommodation is far too tough and limited, and, indeed, quite unworthy of Lord's Cricket Ground.' But the Press had to wait some years before improvements were made.

THE CENTENARY OF THE MARYLEBONE CLUB
Banquet at Lord's

On Wednesday, June 15th, 1887, the centenary banquet of the Marylebone Club was held in the tennis court at Lord's Cricket Ground. The Hon. E. Chandos Leigh (president) occupied the chair and the company present included the French Ambassador (M. Waddington), the Right Hon. G. J. Goschen, MP, the Duke of Abercorn, Lord Latham, Lord G. Hamilton, MP, Lord Bessborough, Lord Clarendon, Lord Willoughby de Broke, Lord Londesborough, Lord Oxenbridge, Lord Darnley, Lord Winterton, Lord Downe, Lord Wenlock, Lord Lyttleton, Lord Belper, Lord Harris, Sir W. Hart-Dyke, MP, Sir A. L. Smith, Sir G. Berry, Sir Saul Samuel, Sir J. F. Garrick, Sir J. Chitty, Hon. W. Monk Jervis, Hon. Sir S. Ponsonby-Fane, Hon. E. Stanhope, MP, Hon. Alfred Lyttelton, Rev. T. A. Anson, Rev. G. J. Boudier, Rev. J. Hornby, Mr R. Broughton, Mr J. L. Baldwin, Mr W. Nicholson, Mr R. A. H. Mitchell, Mr C. E. Green, Mr A. Rutter, Rev. V. Royle, Mr W. N. Roe, Mr T. C. O'Brien, Mr J. G. Walker, Mr E. F. S. Tylecote, Mr J. Shuter, Mr W. W. Read, Mr W. G. Grace, Mr H. Perkins, Mr A. N. Hornby, Mr A. J. Webbe, Mr I. D. Walker, Mr W. H. Patterson, Mr A. W. Ridley, Mr A. Appleby, Mr D. Buchanan, Mr V. E. Walker, Mr W. H. Hadow, Mr Courtney Boyle, etc. After the loyal toasts had been duly honoured, Mr Justice Chitty proposed 'The Houses of Lords and Commons', coupled with the names of the Duke of Abercorn and the Right Hon. G. J. Goschen, the Chancellor of the Exchequer.

Mr Goschen, who was received with loud applause, remarked that it was extremely kind to give so cordial a reception to one whose only feat in the cricket field was recorded by Mr Justice Chitty. It was in a single-wicket match and as it was a true anecdote of his early years he did not feel called upon to deny it. He had been asked to return thanks for the House of Commons, and it had been most properly observed that this was not a political toast. Any introduction of politics at a gathering of this kind would remind one of the bore who came up to a cricket match at Lord's and made some remarks upon what was going on in the House of Commons. They knew what a reception he would have if he were to say 'The Ministry are out'. (Laughter.) In the course of an excellent speech the right Hon. gentleman went on to say that, however important the matters might be which engaged his attention as a politician, there was one part of the daily paper to which he invariably directed his attention the first thing in the morning, and that was the part containing the scores of the cricket matches in course of progress.

The Earl of Bessborough then proposed 'Success to Cricket and the MCC', tracing in the course of his speech the career of the club from its earliest beginnings.

The Chairman responded and Lord Latham proposed 'The Distinguished Visitors', to which toast M. Waddington and Sir Saul Samuel replied.

Viscount Lewisham, MP, then proposed 'The Great Army of Cricketers', to which there were six responses: 'The Church' (the Rev. Dr Hornby, Provost of Eton), 'The Army' (the Right Hon. E. Stanhope, MP), 'The Navy' (the Right Hon. Lord George Hamilton, MP), 'The Bench and the Bar' (the Hon. Mr Justice A. L. Smith), 'Medicine' (Mr W. G. Grace), and 'the Cricket Counties' (Lord Harris).

After his response to this toast, Lord Harris proposed the last toast of the evening, 'The Press', and in so doing bore full and generous testimony to the careful accuracy with which cricket matches were recorded in the papers, and to the large share which the Press had in promoting the popularity of the national game. Then, with the toast, 'Our Next Merry Meeting', a memorable evening came to an end.

Wisden, 1888

It will be noted that the club president in Jubilee year was the renowned Sir Edward Chandos Leigh, brother-in-law of Fitzgerald, uncle of H. D. G. Leveson-Gower, sometime Recorder of Nottingham and Counsel to the Speaker, and Oxford Blue. Sir Edward's dilemma on an unspecified date demonstrates the difficulties often experienced by the old guard at Lord's. Veterans like Leigh had lived through decades of history at the ground, and had presided over a growth which had taken it from the coterie recreation place of Beauclerk's day to one of the most prestigious sporting arenas in the world, with a membership of thousands, and potential audiences of tens of thousands. In these circumstances, Sir Edward's ordeal at the hands of an impenitent ticket collector was bound at last to happen.

During his long life – he died in May 1915, at the age of eighty-two – there can have been few better-known men at Headquarters than Sir Edward Chandos Leigh. He often wore a grey bowler hat, with an IZ ribbon round it, tilted over his nose, and he had a superb swagger, which, I hasten to add, was such a pleasant swagger that no one could possibly be offended by it. He was altogether a most charming personality; but, such is fame, he had failed to impress himself on one of the attendants at Lord's, who demanded to see his ticket.

'Ticket!' said Sir Edward in a horror-struck voice. 'Ticket! Don't you know me, fellow?'

'Ticket please, sir. That's the rule, sir.'

'Who is this fellow who does not know me?' he asked of quite a number of members who had by this time crowded round him. 'My good fellow, I was President of the MCC, and President, moreover, in the Jubilee year.'

Despite all protests, however, the attendant was obdurate, and in the end Chandos was forced to sign his name in the book.

SIR PELHAM WARNER, Lord's, 1946

IT is deeply revealing that Leigh retained to the very end of his long life a certain bitterness regarding the apparent indifference of his parents and family to his cricketing exploits as a schoolboy. Having attained the high peaks of school and university cricket, Leigh could never understand why none of his nearest and dearest showed any interest; like Winston Churchill, Leigh was obliged to find solace in the surrogate solicitude of his nurse. He also expresses the unspoken thought that he had perhaps been born too early to enjoy the more exotic fruits of an Eton–Harrow match.

In the old days the MCC was under the management of Mr Dark, but when the club took the ground into their own hands, vast improvements took place. In Mr Dark's day, the boys who played in the Eton and Harrow and Winchester matches had each to pay 7s 6d. for each match, and as most boys in those days were kept pretty short of money, and no luncheon was given them, you would see Eton and Harrow boys lying on the grass with a pot of half-and-half and bread and cheese as their luncheon. Nor was it the fashion for relations to come up and see the boys or even the University men play. All the time I was in the Harrow and University Elevens, I remember none of my relations coming up to see me play – only my old nurse. How different all this is now. Nothing but luncheons, drags, private boxes, and all the boys from Eton and Harrow (there is no Winchester match now) coming up to be feted, whereas in old days, the matches took place at the commencement of the holidays, and very few boys who were not in the Eleven came from either school.

SIR EDWARD CHANDOS LEIGH, Bar, Bat and Bit, 1913

IN the following year the Eton–Harrow match caused the divine afflatus to burst out of a recklessly partisan gentleman called E. E. Bowen, a Harrow master renowned for the composition of many of the famous 'Harrow Songs'. The match was won by Harrow by 156, due largely to the all-round cricket of F. S. Jackson, who made 21 and 59, and took eleven wickets for 68 runs. Jackson's father, the Right Hon. W. L. Jackson, Financial Secretary to the Treasury at the time, showed something less than financial astuteness by offering his son £5 for every wicket and £1 for every run made in the match. Immediately on returning to school after the match, Jackson found a cheque awaiting him for £135. The donor eventually attempted to make a fresh start in life by metamorphosing into Baron Allerton, but his son remained doggedly Jacksonian, his only indulgence in change for its own sake being his habit of switching caps in mid-match. In one day's play in a Test match, he was seen sporting in quick succession a Cambridge cap, an I Zingari cap and finally a Yorkshire cap. A bright political future was predicted for him, but instead he became Chairman of the Unionist Party. This is the only poem written about him:

'A GENTLEMAN'S A-BOWLING'
(Dedicated to F. S. Jackson, *Lord's*, 1888)

O Cabby, trot him faster;
O hurry, engine, on,
Come glory or disaster
Before the day be done!
Ten thousand folks are strolling,
And streaming into view,
A gentleman's a-bowling
(More accurately two).

With changes and with chances
The innings come and go,
Alternating advances
Of ecstasy and woe.
For now 'tis all condoling,
And now – for who can tell –
A gentleman's a-bowling.
It yet may all be well.

Light Blues are nimbly fielding,
And scarce a hit can pass;
But those the willows wielding
Have played on Harrow grass!
And there's the ball a-rolling,
And all the people see
A gentleman's a-bowling,
And we're a-hitting he.

Ten score to make, or yield her!
Shall Eton save the match?
Bowl, bowler! Go it, fielder!
Catch, wicketkeeper, catch!
Our vain attempts controlling,
They drive the leather – no!
A gentleman's a-bowling
And down the wickets go.

And now that all is ended,
Were I the Queen today,
I'd make a marquis splendid
Of every one of they!

> And still for their consoling,
> I'll cheer and cheer again
> The gentleman a-bowling,
> And all the other ten!

By E. E. BOWEN, a master at Harrow School

As Lord's moved sedately on towards its second century, there were occasional attempts by players to obey the letter of the laws while circumventing their spirit. A case in point was the University match, in which the captains, no doubt stimulated to daring improvisation by their intense studies, resorted to devices so dubious that MCC was obliged to look long and hard at the rules of the game. In 1893 the Oxford captain deciding that his best chance of saving the game was to follow on, instructed his batsmen to throw their wickets away – at which the Cambridge captain instructed his bowlers to throw runs away. The spectacle of two sides of more or less grown men, one trying not to stay in, the other trying not to get anyone out, was among the more risible on view in that season.

Cambridge took full revenge for their unexpected defeat in the previous year, winning by 266 runs in two days, during which the crowd was estimated at 39,000. The long spell of fine weather during May and June had caused the pitch to be on the worn side, and the scoring was only moderate—Cambridge 182 and 254 (of which 47 came from extras), Oxford 106 and 64, Jackson, with 38 and 57 and four wickets for 57 runs, finished his Cambridge career in brilliant fashion. Latham played a very good second innings of 54, and Bromley-Davenport (five wickets for 11 runs), Streatfield (four for 19), and Wells (seven for 66) bowled extremely well, as did Berkeley (nine for 94) for Oxford. *Wisden* reported the match as follows:

> Nine wickets were down for 95 [in Oxford's first innings], and then, on T. S. B. Wilson, the last man, joining W. H. Brain, an incident occurred which is likely to be talked about for a good many years to come. Three runs were added, making the score 98, or 84 short of Cambridge's total, and Oxford thus required only 5 runs to save the follow-on. The two batsmen were then seen to consult together between the wickets, and it was at once evident to those who had grasped the situation that the Dark Blues were going to throw away a wicket in order that their side might go in again. Had one of them acted on his own account, it is probable that the object would have been gained, but Wells, who was bowling from the pavilion end, saw at once what was intended and promptly set to work to frustrate it. Going over the crease, he bowled a ball wide to the boundary, and then, after an unsuccessful effort to bowl a wide all along the ground, sent another round-arm ball to the ropes, thus giving away eight runs, but preventing Oxford from going in a second time. The incident gave rise to a great deal of talk and discussion, to say nothing of special articles in various newspapers. We are inclined to think, however, that in some quarters the matter was treated far too seri-

ously, the point being overlooked that all the players immediately concerned were actuated entirely by the desire to do the best thing possible for their side. Particularly would we wish to exonerate Wells from all blame. He saw clearly that Oxford, with the idea of securing an advantage, meant to throw away a wicket, and we hold that he was perfectly justified in taking any means to prevent them that the law permitted. Whatever may be thought of the incident, it had the immediate effect of bringing the question of the follow-on under the consideration of the MCC Committee.

Cambridge had good cause to be apprehensive of a law which made it *compulsory* for the side which was 80 runs, or more, behind on the first innings to follow on, for in their match with the Australians that season at Fenner's they had led by 94 runs on the first innings. The wicket was almost certain to crumble on the third day, and had they been able to choose they would certainly have gone in again to bat. As it was, the Australians made 319 in their second innings, and on the last day, on a broken wicket, Cambridge were all out for 108. Thus the law penalised the side which had, up to half-time, played the better cricket.

During the winter of 1893–94 this law was the subject of much discussion, and at the Annual General Meeting of the MCC on May 2, 1894, the following alteration was proposed: 'The side which goes in second *may be required* to follow their innings if they shall have scored 80 runs less than the opposite side'; but, though the Hon. Alfred Lyttelton, in an able and vigorous speech, protested against postponement, on the proposition of the Chairman, the Earl of Dartmouth, it was resolved to refer the matter to the Committee to inquire into and collect the various opinions and report to a special meeting to be held in July. At this meeting, on July 10, the Committee proposed an increase to 100 runs in a three-day match, or 80 runs in a two days' match. This was carried, and came into operation in 1895. The law, be it noted, still made the follow-on compulsory. There was to be a dramatic sequel in the following year.

SIR PELHAM WARNER, *Lord's*, 1946

IF the sequel was indeed as dramatic as Warner says it was, it was also highly predictable, with the captains in the match bending the rules whenever they could, and the legislators following breathlessly behind, trying to close up the gaps in what was in essence an unwritten law of sportsmanship and common sense. While the arcana of cricketing tactics were being pondered at the two universities, Lord's was enjoying its lighter moments. In 1893 the country was being governed by Mr Gladstone's fourth and last ministry, an administration famous for including three future Prime Ministers in Messrs Asquith, Campbell-Bannerman and the Earl of Rosebery. None of them, however, was considered good enough to be given a place in the official Government cricket team which played a one-day match against the Opposition at Lord's on 29 July 1893. In the event the Opposition proved far too strong for the Gladstonians, a feature of their ascendency being the deadly bowling of Mr H. W. Forster. *Wisden* does not comment on one interesting aspect of this game, which was the unusual feat of Mr R. T. Reid, who became the first wicket-keeper in history to take two wickets without being present on the ground.

GOVERNMENT v. OPPOSITION
Played at Lord's, July 29, 1893

A match between members of Parliament representing respectively the Government and Opposition was played, but did not prove the attraction expected. However, the weather was most unfavourable. The Opposition, which included several well-known cricketers, won very easily, declaring their innings at an end when three wickets had fallen for 243 runs.

Government

Mr J. A. Pease, b. Forster	4	c. Whitelaw, b. Forster	7
Mr J. F. Leese, b. Beckett	22	c. Chelsea, b. Forster	6
Hon. Mark F. Napier, c. Walrond, b. Forster	40	not out	14
Mr H. J. Gladstone, b. Chelsea	12		
Mr George Newnes, st. Davenport, b. Forster	4		
Mr A. E. Hutton, c. Walrond, b. Forster	4		
Mr Wm Allen, c. Chelsea, b. Forster	3		
Mr R. K. Causton, b. Forster	2		
Mr C. E. H. Hobhouse, st. Davenport, b. Forster	4		
Mr J. M. Paulton, not out	1		
Mr R. T Reid, absent	0	b. Chelsea	11
B 5, l-b 2, w 1	8	L-b 1, w 1, n-b 1	3
	104		41

Opposition

Mr H. W. Forster, c. Allen, b. Napier	81
Viscount Curzon, st. Reid, b. Allen	97
Viscount Chelsea, c. Reid, b. Napier	44
Mr Walter long, not out	9
B 5, l-b 1, w 6	12
(3 wkts dec.)	243

Mr W. Bromley-Davenport, Mr Ernest W. Beckett, Hon. Sidney Herbert, Mr A. F. Jeffreys, Captain Grice-Hutchinson, Mr G. Whitelaw and Sir William Walrond did not bat.

Opposition Bowling

	Overs	Mdns	Runs	Wkts	Overs	Mdns	Runs	Wkts
Forster	17.3	3	49	7	13	5	17	2
Beckett	11	2	32	1	6	2	12	0
Chelsea	6	1	15	1	6	4	9	1

Government Bowling

	Overs	Mdns	Runs	Wkts
Gladstone	12	1	44	0
Napier	15	2	78	2
Pease	16	1	85	0
Allen	2.3	0	10	1
Hobhouse	4	0	14	0

Umpires: W. Price and T. Mycroft.

Wisden, 1894

By 1896 Mr Gladstone had gone and the Earl of Rosebery had followed him, leaving Lord Salisbury in command of the field. His administration was distinguished for its Lord President of the Council, the 8th Duke of Devonshire, honoured today as the probable prototype of P. G. Wodehouse's Clarence, 9th Earl of Emsworth. Mr Goschen, whose knowledge of sea-going matters was as profound as his grasp of the principles of cricket, was First Lord of the Admiralty, but the most interesting appointment of all was that of Mr Long, rewarded for the style in which he had made his valiant 9 not out against the Gladstonians by being appointed President of the Board of Agriculture. The new follow-on laws had become official, and it now remained for the Oxford and Cambridge captains to see what they could do to thwart them. While their plans were receiving the final polish, the Australians came to Lord's and were the victims of a bowling analysis so unprecedented that more than sixty years later the match-card was exhibited under glass at the St Marylebone Town Hall, where it was peered at by a succession of students of the game, much in the spirit of theologians examining the Dead Sea Scrolls. Dick Pougher (1865–1926) was a resourceful medium-pace bowler who scored many runs and took hundreds of wickets for his native Leicestershire. Evidently Lord's was one of his favourite grounds, for he did the hat-trick there twice, in 1887 and again in 1892. He once took fourteen wickets in a match there, but nothing he ever achieved, there or anywhere else, gained him the renown he won at Lord's in June 1896.

AUSTRALIANS v. MCC AND GROUND
Played at Lord's, June 11, 12, 1896

So far the Australians had had a career of uninterrupted success, but in this match—perhaps the most sensational of the whole tour—they met with a rude check, the MCC beating them by an innings and 18 runs. The game is already a historical one, the Australians being got rid of in their first innings by J. T. Hearne and Pougher for 18, the smallest score for which an Australian team has ever been dismissed in this country. George Giffen's illness compelled them to bat one short, but though his absence of course made a difference, it is hardly likely he would have been able to save his side from disaster. By winning in such sensational style the MCC at last took their revenge for the never-to-be-forgotten defeat in 1878. J. T. Hearne and Pougher bowled with extraordinary averages. Pougher, who went on with the total at 18 for three wickets, took five wickets, and not another run was scored. Nearly twenty-four hours' rain had considerably affected the ground, and the MCC gained a decided advantage in winning the toss, but even allowing for this, and two or three missed catches, they did uncommonly well to score 219. On the second day Darling played a fine innings, and J. T. Hearne again bowled splendidly.

MCC and Ground

Mr W. G. Grace, b. Trumble . 15
Mr A. E. Stoddart, st. Kelly,
    b. Trott 54
K. S. Ranjitsinhji, b. Trumble 7
Mr F. S. Jackson, c. and b.
    Trumble 51
W. Gunn, b. McKibbin 39

Mr G. MacGregor, b. Trumble   0
G. Davidson, b. Trumble....   0
Mr F. Marchant, b. McKibbin   20
A. D. Pougher, not out   9
W. Attewell, b. Trumble....   7
J. T. Hearne, b. McKibbin ...   1
     B 13, l-b 2, n-b 1....   16

            219

Australians

J. J. Kelly, c. and b. Pougher	8	b. Hearne	0
H. Graham, b. Hearne	4	b. Hearne	5
G. H. S. Trott, b. Hearne........	6	c. MacGregor, b. Hearne	14
S. F. Gregory, b. Hearne........	0	c. MacGregor, b. Hearne	28
F. A. Iredale, b. Hearne.........	0	b. Hearne	0
C. Hill, b. Pougher	0	b. Hearne	4
H. Trumble, b. Pougher........	0	b. Hearne	0
J. Darling, not out.............	0	c. Stoddart, b. Hearne	76
C. J. Eady, b. Pougher..........	0	c. Grace, b. Hearne ..	42
T. R. McKibbin, c. Davidson, b. Pougher	0	not out	3
G. Giffen absent ill.............	0	absent	0
		B 11..........	11
	18		183

Australian Bowling

	Overs	Mdns	Runs	Wkts
Trumble ..	34	8	84	6
Giffen	9	0	22	0
McKibbin .	19.2	2	51	3
Trott	13	1	35	1
Eady	8	2	11	0

MCC Bowling

	Overs	Mdns	Runs	Wkts	Overs	Mdns	Runs	Wkts
Hearne ...	11	9	4	4	50.3	22	73	9
Attewell ..	8	5	14	0	10	4	14	0
Pougher ..	3	3	0	5	28	15	33	0
Jackson ..					10	3	16	0
Davidson .					7	3	15	0
Grace					8	1	21	0

Umpires: W. A. J. West and J. Phillips.

Wisden, 1897

Almost before the dust had settled on the Australians, the University match was under way, amid scenes of unprecedented bitterness and even violence. Both sides included some of the most distinguished cricketers of their generation, and at least one undisputed genius in Gilbert Jessop. Oxford's victory was a brilliant affair, but not even the match-winning innings of G. O. Smith proved in the end to be as memorable as the juridical in-fighting which followed the events which took place on the field:

OXFORD v. CAMBRIDGE
Played at Lord's, July 2, 3, 4, 1896

In one respect at least, the University engagement of 1896, was the most remarkable of the series, the Oxford eleven being left to get 330 in the last innings, and hitting off the runs for the loss of six wickets. No such feat had ever been performed before in the University match, and the Oxford eleven deserve all possible credit for establishing a new and startling record. It is not so much, however, for this exceptional performance, as for the much discussed incident in regard to the follow-on rule, that the Oxford and Cambridge match of 1896 will be remembered. When the MCC, yielding to the fears of some famous players, rejected a drastic alteration of law 53, and contented themselves with increasing from 80 to 120 the number of runs, involving a follow-on, it was easy to foresee that, given the same circumstances, the incident which caused so much angry discussion in the University match of 1893 would inevitably be repeated. After an interval of three years, Mr Frank Mitchell, as captain of the Cambridge XI, followed the example set him in 1893 by Mr F. S. Jackson, and by palpably giving away runs to prevent his opponents from following on, forced the MCC to reconsider the whole question. Cambridge occupied nearly the whole of the first day in scoring 319, some admirable cricket of a very steady kind being shown by Burnup and Wilson, and at about a quarter to four on the Friday, they were leading on the first innings by 131 runs, with only one Oxford wicket to go down. Rightly or wrongly, Mitchell judged that it would be better for his own side to go in again than to field for the rest of the afternoon, and E. B. Shine, who was then bowling at the pavilion wicket, settled the matter by sending three balls—two of them no-balls—to the boundary for four each. These twelve runs deprived Oxford of the chance of following on, and immediately afterwards the Dark Blues' innings closed for 202 or 117 behind. As they left the field, the Cambridge eleven came in for a very hostile demonstration at the hands of the public, and inside the pavilion matters were still worse, scores of members of the MCC protesting in the most vigorous fashion against the policy that Frank Mitchell had adopted. In our opinion this display of passion was altogether illogical and uncalled for. We defended F. S. Jackson and C. M. Wells for what they did in the match of 1893, and believing that even in its amended form, law 53 is ill-adapted to modern cricket, we think Mitchell was quite entitled, in the interests of his side, to take the course he did. The incident gave rise to a long correspondence in the columns of *The Times*, and to show the difference of opinion that existed amongst the best authorities, diametrically opposite views were expressed by Lord Cobham and his younger brother, Edward Lyttelton. Lord Cobham strongly supported Mitchell's action, and Edward Lyttelton as strenuously opposed it.

Whether or not the angry demonstration they provoked unnerved the Cambridge batsmen, we cannot say, but on going in for the second time they started very badly. Cunliffe and Hartley bowled in splendid form, the former continually making the ball go down the hill with his arm, and when the sixth Cambridge wicket fell the score had only reached 61. N. F. Druce, however, came to the rescue of his side with a splendid innings, and received such valuable help from Bray that when rain came on and stopped play at twenty minutes to seven, the total had reached 154 with eight men out. Cambridge thus had considerably the best of the game, being 271 runs ahead with two wickets to fall. It was feared that the rain, which fell for some little time after the drawing of stumps, would spoil the ground, but as a matter of fact, it had just the contrary effect, the wicket, which had shown some slight signs of crumbling, rolling out better than ever on the Saturday morning. Cambridge carried their score to 212 and so set Oxford the tremendous task of getting 330 in the last innings. How brilliantly this task was accomplished is now a matter of cricket history. Up to a certain point they seemed to have no chance of victory, Mordaunt, Warner and Foster being out for 60 runs. The turning point came with the partnership of G. O. Smith and Pilkington, and once on the road to victory, the Oxford men never looked back. Cambridge made two or three mistakes in the field, but as to the fine quality of the batting there could not be two opinions. Pilkington, in about an hour and a quarter, helped to put on 84 for the fourth wicket, and then, during an hour and three-quarters of gradually increasing excitement, Smith and Leveson-Gower added 97 runs together, the latter being caught at the wicket with the total at 241. Eighty-nine runs were then wanted with five wickets to go down, and any little accident might have turned the scale in Cambridge's favour. Smith, however, found an invaluable partner in Bardswell, and between them the two batsmen made Oxford's success certain. Smith, who up to a certain point had played with scrupulous care, hit out most brilliantly, and in less than an hour 87 runs were put on. Then, with only two runs wanted to win, Smith, overcome by the excitement of the moment, jumped out to drive one of Cobbold's slows and was easily caught at slip. On his departure, Waddy joined Bardswell and a couple of singles gave Oxford the victory by four wickets, Bardswell, in making the winning hit, being missed in the long field by Burnup. G. O. Smith was congratulated on all hands upon his magnificent innings of 132.

Cambridge

Mr C. J. Burnup (*Malvern and Clare*)
  c. Mordaunt, b. Hartley......... 80   c and b Hartley... 11

Mr W. G. Grace jun. (*Clifton and*
  Pembroke) b. Hartley 0   b. Cunliffe 1

Mr H. H. Marriott (*Malvern and*
  Clare) c. Warner, b. Hartley..... 16   b. Cunliffe 1

Mr N. F. Druce (*Marlborough and*   c. Pilkington,
  Trinity) c. Smith, b. Cunliffe..... 14   b. Waddy 72

Mr C. E. M. Wilson (*Uppingham and*   c. Lewis, b.
  Trinity) c. Cunliffe, b. Hartley.... 80   Hartley 2

Mr W. M. G. Hemingway
  (*Uppingham and Kings'*) c. and b.
  Hartley 26   b. Cunliffe 12

Mr F. Mitchell (*St Peter's, York and*
  Caius) c. Leveson-Gower, b.
  Hartley 26   b. Cunliffe 4

Mr G. L. Jessop (*Private and Christ's*)   st. Lewis, b.
  c. Mordaunt, b. Hartley......... 0   Hartley 19

Mr E. H. Bray (*Charterhouse and*   c. Lewis, b.
  Trinity) c. Pilkington, b. Cunliffe . 49   Waddy 41

Mr P. W. Cobbold (*Eton and Trinity*)
b. Hartley 10   not out 23
Mr E. B. Shine (*Private and Selwyn*)   c. Hartley, b.
not out 10   Waddy 16
    B 4, l-b 1, w 2, n-b 1 8   B 5, w 1, n-b 5   11
                          319   212

Oxford

Mr P. F. Warner (*Rugby and Oriel*) run
out 10   run out 17
Mr G. J. Mordaunt (*Wellington and*
University) b. Jessop............ 26   b. Jessop 9
Mr H. K. Foster (*Malvern and Trinity*)
b Wilson 11   c. and b. Cobbold . 34
Mr G. O. Smith (*Charterhouse and*   c. Mitchell, b.
Keble) c. Bray, b. Wilson........ 37   Cobbold 132
Mr C. C. Pilkington (*Eton and*
Magdalen) b. Jessop 4   c. and b. Jessop ... 44
Mr H. D. G. Leveson-Gower (*Win-*
chester and Magdalen) b. Jessop... 26 c. Bray, b. Shine .. 41
Mr G. R. Bardswell (*Uppingham and*
Oriel) c. and b. Cobbold......... 0   not out 33
Mr P. S. Waddy (*Paramatta and*
Balliol) st. Bray, b. Cobbold...... 0   not out 1
Mr J. C. Hartley (*Tonbridge and Brase-*
nose) c. Marriott, b. Wilson...... 43
Mr F. H. E. Cunliffe (*Eton and New*) b.
Shine 12
Mr R. P. Lewis (*Winchester and*
University) not out............. 0
    B 12, l-b 4, n-b 8.......... 24   B 6, l-b 6, w 6, n-b 1 19
                          202   330

Oxford Bowling

	Overs	Mdns	Runs	Wkts	Overs	Mdns	Runs	Wkts
Cunliffe	55	25	87	2	33	11	93	4
Hartley	59.3	13	161	8	30	3	78	3
Waddy	24	10	35	0	11	3	28	3
Pilkington	29	19	24	0	3	1	2	0
Leveson-Gower	2	0	4	0				

Cambridge Bowling

	Overs	Mdns	Runs	Wkts	Overs	Mdns	Runs	Wkts
Jessop	37	15	75	3	30	8	98	2
Wilson	37	19	48	3	42	20	50	0
Shine	12.3	4	29	1	20	9	41	1
Cobbold	11	2	26	2	44.4	7	96	2
Burnup					2	0	3	0
Druce					7	2	11	0
Mitchell					2	1	12	0

Umpires: W. Hearn and W. A. J. West.

Wisden, 1897

It had been feared by many that when the follow-on law was kept on a compulsory basis trouble would follow. Those who opposed making the follow-on voluntary stressed overmuch the advantage of winning the toss, and did not realise sufficiently that the side which had gained a lead on the first innings was being penalised for having played the better cricket. The climax came in the University match. When F. Mitchell, the Cambridge captain, in order to avoid Oxford's following on, instructed E. B. Shine, as Jackson had instructed Wells three years before, to send down three balls – two of them no-balls – to the boundary there was a very hostile demonstration. On returning to the pavilion the Cambridge eleven were hooted at by the members of the MCC, and in the pavilion itself there were angry scenes, many members losing all control over themselves. Winged words were given and returned, Cantab was divided against Cantab, and brother against brother. The reader will remember that Alfred Lyttelton had pleaded for a voluntary follow-on, but now Lord Cobham supported Mitchell, and his brother, Edward Lyttelton, condemned him. When Oxford took the field they were greeted with loud and prolonged cheering, and when F. H. E. Cunliffe, from the pavilion end, in his first over, clean bowled W. G. Grace, junior, for o his dismissal was greeted with a yell of delight. Young W.G., however, made a 'pair', and both Dark and Light Blue partisans were genuinely sorry, and the Oxford team, even at a moment of extreme tension, did not forget to say so. We thought of the Grand Old Man and how deeply he would feel it. Six Cambridge wickets fell for 61 before the splendid bowling of Cunliffe and J. C. Hartley, but N. F. Druce played a beautiful innings, though I should have caught him at backward point, off Hartley, when he had scored some 20 or 30 runs. Had I been a six-footer I might have done so, but a hard cut touched only the tips of my fingers, though I jumped for the ball like a rough-haired fox-terrier I once owned, who put all other high-jumping dogs into the shade! E. H. Bray, P. W. Cobbold, and E. B. Shine gave Druce strong support, and Oxford were set 330 runs to make to win, a tremendous task in a fourth innings. But the wicket, which had shown definite signs of crumbling on the second afternoon – the reason for Mitchell's action – benefited, from an Oxford point of view, by rain during the night, and played easily enough. We had lost three wickets – Mordaunt, Foster, and myself – for 60 at lunch-time, but Leveson-Gower (41) and C. C. Pilkington (44) added 84 runs for the fourth partnership, and Leveson-Gower and G. O. Smith 97, when Leveson-Gower was caught at the wicket. 89 runs were wanted with five wickets to fall, and Cambridge still had a chance; but Bardswell never looked like getting out, and we were within 2 runs of victory when Smith jumped out to drive Cobbold and was caught at slip. As he came up the pavilion steps the members rose to him and took off their hats. He had played a magnificent innings of 132, and as long as their is a history of Oxford and Cambridge cricket the name of G. O. Smith will be emblazoned on its rolls.

Soon after Leveson-Gower had gone in to bat his mother, unable to stand the tension, left the ground, got into a hansom, and drove about Regent's Park. After an hour she returned, and as she walked through the entrance the gate attendant remarked, 'It's all right, ma'am. He's still there.' Leveson-Gower was a splendid captain. Always cheerful and encouraging, he managed his somewhat limited bowling most skilfully. He was a quick and smart fieldsman at cover-point, and a great man at a crisis as a batsman. Over and over again he came to the rescue and made runs when they were wanted.

It was not until the Annual General Meeting on May 2, 1900, that the law was changed to read as follows: 'The side which leads by 150 runs in a three-day match, by 100 runs in a two-day match, and by 75 runs in a one-day match shall have the *option* of calling on the other side to follow its innings.' To some it might appear that the MCC Committee moved slowly, but it should always be remembered that the MCC, very wisely, are generally reluctant to propose any new legislation until the opinions of cricketers all over the world have been ascertained, and this naturally takes time. At the same meeting the over was increased from five balls to six, and a declaration of the innings was made permissible at or after the luncheon interval on the second day.

SIR PELHAM WARNER, *Lord's*, 1946

Bʏ the time Mrs Leveson-Gower decamped in a hansom in search of balm for the spirit, the MCC Committee must have been in so battered a condition that the temptation to follow her and not come back must have been strong in their hearts. Only a fortnight before, when the Test against Australia began, nearly 30,000 people crammed into the ground and proved to be uncontrollable. *The Times* was horrified, telling its readers that 'Lord's has scarcely ever before been the scene of so much noisiness and rowdyism as was displayed yesterday when the crowds encroached on the ground.' Even more terrifying was the wrath of Lord Harris, who, in his autobiography, *A Few Short Runs*, said, 'It was a dreadful sight for those who love the strictness of first-class cricket as played at Lord's; and the Committee felt that every effort must be made to prevent the repetition of a scene so deplorable.' But the 1890s were not all blood and thunder. The most talented of the author-cricketers one day found himself in a particular set of difficulties rarely encountered by anybody:

I was playing for MCC against Kent, and faced for the first time Bradley, who was that year one of the fastest bowlers in England. His first delivery I hardly saw, and it landed with a terrific thud upon my thigh. A little occasional pain is one of the chances of cricket, and one takes it as cheerfully as one can, but on this occasion it suddenly became sharp to an unbearable degree. I clapped my hand to the spot, and found to my amazement that I was on fire. The ball had landed straight on a small tin vesta box in my trousers pocket, had splintered the box, and set the matches ablaze. It did not take me long to turn out my pocket and scatter the burning vestas over the grass. I should have thought this incident unique, but Alec Hearne, to whom I told it, assured me that he had seen more than one accident of the kind. W.G. was greatly amused. 'Couldn't get you out – had to set you on fire!' he cried, in the high voice which seemed so queer from so big a body.

SIR ARTHUR CONAN DOYLE, *Memories and Adventures*, 1924

EVEN odder were the effusions of an eccentric cricket writer of the period, E. B. V. Christian, who published straightfaced essays about 'A Socialist Cricket Match', 'The Cricketer's Innings Insurance Company Limited', and 'The Cricketer as Accountant', and worried himself over such abstruse issues as whether or not a batsman can be given out for holding the bails and stumps together to prevent the bowler knocking them over. In the 1890s Mr Christian, thinking he saw the way the winds of change were blowing, projected himself forward just a little into the future, where he found events at Lord's to be only slightly more bizarre than they had been:

It will long be remembered that Australia, winning the toss, sent in Giffen and Lyons; and the latter driving Attewell's first ball hard, it fell on to the 11.35 express for Sheffield. The batsmen, of course, ran; and the fieldsmen saw that it was hopeless to attempt to recapture the ball, which fell through the window of the guard's brake. The Englishmen cried 'Lost ball'; the umpire, however, ruled that a ball is not lost when you know where it is. After consultation it was decided to telegraph to the station-master to return the ball, and subsequently Mr Stoddart was sent by the 1.10 train to recapture what our sporting contemporaries still call the 'pilule'. The 1.10 is a slow train, and on arriving in the evening at Sheffield Stoddart found to his mortification that the station-master had sent the ball back by parcel-post. The parcel did not reach Lord's till 1.30 next day. Persons on the ground will not easily forget that the Englishmen sat watching in front of the pavilion, while the batsmen continued to run. When the weapon of attack was again secured Australia had scored 1,849, and the innings was declared closed. The score read thus:

Lyons   not out   1,849
Giffen   not out   0
Total, declared,   1,849

The Englishmen naturally failed to equal this gigantic total; but it was felt that the luck had been, to some extent, against them.

E. B. V. CHRISTIAN, *At the Sign of the Wicket*, 1894

MR Christian's penchant for fantasising was matched by Norman Gale's taste for sentimental versifying about the game. One of his heroes was that flawed idol Andrew Stoddart (1836–1915), an English international cricketer and Rugby Union player, captain of Middlesex and England, scorer of 484 in one innings in a game for Hampstead in 1886, a man whose life reached a limited excellence on the sports field but began to decline when he was too old to play. At last, beset by failing health and a collapsing marriage, Stoddart shot himself in his home only a stone's throw from Lord's. But in his prime, the black-moustached Stoddart, piped and blazered against adversity, was every schoolboy's hero, the very embodiment of manly vigour and good sportsmanship. The thought struck Norman Gale so forcibly that he was inspired to publish the following:

UP AT LORD'S

When Stoddart makes her hum
Up at Lord's,

Till the bowler bites his tnumb,
Up at Lord's,
How the Middlesex supporters
Turn vociferous exhorters
As he jumps on Lockwood's snorters,
Up at Lord's.

When Stoddart makes her hum
Up at Lord's,
And my country cousins come
Up at Lord's,
With their looks as sweet as honey
And their exclamations funny
I am prodigal of money
Up at Lord's.

When Stoddart makes her hum
Up at Lord's,
And the Surrey skipper's glum
Up at Lord's,
Oh! All my odds are even,
And (I hope to be forgiven)
'Tis a truly Cricket Heaven
Up at Lord's.

NORMAN GALE, *Cricket Songs*, 1896

GALE's effusions about his country cousins with their looks as sweet as honey represented a little less than the truth. That there was a genteel element among the Lord's regulars there is no question, but there was also the mass of spectators, among whom, then as now, were a few rowdies who were attracted as much by the opportunity to drink as by the cricket. Nor did the connoisseurs of the game always feel inclined to accept with much docility what was being served up to them. Two accounts of the 1899 season reflect this less cosy other side of the life to be found at Lord's. In the first, a game obviously heading for stalemate met with an original stroke of derision expressed in musical form, while in the second, one of the champions of village and country-house cricket, a member of that group of successful authors and dramatists who dedicated themselves to the game, gives an alarmingly uncharacteristic picture of the way a schoolboy might see the minatory aspect of a cricket crowd:

On the first day of the Middlesex match (1899) there was an unseemly demonstration on the part of the spectators, 'happily without precedent at Lord's Ground', says *Wisden*. Darling, the Australian captain, who eventually scored 114, took three hours to make his first 38 runs, and the spectators in the Mound Stand whistled the 'Dead March' in *Saul*, and kept time by stamping with their feet. Darling was suffering from a badly bruised heel, and the Middlesex bowling – J. T. Hearne, Wells, Rawlin, and Roche – was good, as was the fielding and the wicket-keeping of MacGregor.

SIR PELHAM WARNER, *Lord's*, 1946

In 1899, when, though we could not forsee it, the Boer War was about to come, there was another Test match at Lord's. By that time Francis Colmer, who still bears his erudition so apologetically, had taken charge of my education, and it was with him and with Arnold that I set out for headquarters on the 15th of June. I had then, being only thirteen, little sense of the social conditions in England; and I now recall with surprise the roughness of a cricket crowd, even at Lord's, in those distant days. Men, obviously, drank more than their sons drink now. One man, quite near to us, differing with another about the principles of Liberalism, threw a gingerbeer-bottle at the head of his antagonist. This was like the casting-down of a knight's glaive. In a twinkling the two men were at fisticuffs. In those days, too, silk hats were still commonly worn, but if any unwary fellow, adorned by one, approached our 'free seats', he became at once an Aunt Sally for all available oranges and newspaper-cannonballs.

CLIFFORD BAX, *People and Ideas*, 1936

THESE were the years when the memories of a lifetime were being preserved in the minds of schoolboys unaware that decades later they would look back and, for reasons neither they nor anyone else could explain, recall with photographic exactitude the cut of some player's flannels, the bend of his elbow, the sweep of his bat. A single session of play, an over, a single delivery even, would become etched in the memory for all time. One such schoolboy was Hugh de Selincourt (1879–1951), destined to be the author of the best novel ever written about any game, *The Cricket Match* (1924). De Selincourt was one of a group of writer-cricketers who kept alive the tradition of idyllic village games. Like Siegfried Sassoon, Edmund Blunden, Clifford Bax and Jack Squire, De Selincourt saw cricket essentially as part of the English landscape, and composed his rhapsodies accordingly. But he had an eye also for the whimsical and the absurd; one of his short stories told of a dream in which his modest village side defeated Warwick Armstrong's Australians. Just as far-fetched in its way, but apparently true, is this recollection of a game seen in boyhood.

A. G. Pelham made a lovely shot at Lord's on August 5th, 1892, when Monmouthshire were playing the MCC, though I should not recommend it to young players. He hurled his bat thirty yards over the umpire's head to leg and hit the ball through the slips for three, all at one fell swoop. It must be remembered that with the bat to help he would almost certainly have been able to run four, and one run may make all the difference to the winning of a match; so the last glad gesture of hurling his bat over the umpire's head was spirited but unwise.

HUGH DE SELINCOURT, *Over*, 1932

SOMEONE else whose mind harped back constantly to a day at Lord's was a well-known cricketer who inadvertently won a footnote to imperial history, although it is doubtful if he would have been pleased had he known the precise circumstances. Cyril Pelham Foley (1868–1936) was an opening batsman who did well for Eton, Cambridge,

Worcestershire and Middlesex, for whom his career from 1893 to 1906 was twice interrupted in unusual circumstances. In the Boer War he served with distinction and came home in temporary command of the 3rd Royal Scots. But it was his earlier military folly, as a member of the group which participated in the notorious Raid into Transvaal by Dr Leander Starr Jameson, which earned him the nickname of 'The Raider'. Jameson himself would have chosen a different epithet. In the days before the raid, when the conspirators were waiting impatiently to proceed, knowing that the element of surprise was their one effective weapon, Jameson communicated with one Robert White, in command at Mafeking: 'I am wiring you that Foley leaves tomorrow to join you at camp – use him and keep him there. Not intentionally but idiotically he has been talking too much.' In other words, desperately short of men though he was, Jameson preferred to go into battle without the liability of Foley's support. In spite of his idiocy, or possibly because of it, Foley rose to the rank of Lieutenant-Colonel and commanded the 9th East Lancashires in the Great War. In his retirement he published an intermittently diverting autobiography, in which the following Lord's memory appears:

On July 6th, 1893 something totally unprecedented in first-class cricket happened to me. We were playing Sussex at Lord's and a tremendous crowd was present directly due to the fact that it was the day upon which King George V was married, many of the countless thousands who lined the streets having come up to see the cricket. A Sussex bowler named Gutteridge bowled me a ball which narrowly missed my wicket, struck Butt, the wicket-keeper, on the pads and rebounded into the wicket. Butt replaced one bail and I the other. As I was preparing to receive the next ball, Henty, the umpire, said, 'You're out.' Although I had no right to query his decision, I was so flabbergasted that I said, 'What for?' To my astonishment he said, 'For handling the bail.' I walked out like a man in a dream.

On reaching the pavilion Buns Thornton said to me, 'What did they give you out for, Cyril?' I said, 'For handling the bail.' 'Go back,' said Buns, 'the umpire can't make rules.' However, I went upstairs and took my pads off.

The dressing-rooms in those days were at the back of the pavilion, and I never saw what occurred, but I believe the crowd invaded the ground, and there was a devil of a row. In about a quarter of an hour W. L. Murdoch, the Sussex captain, came up to the dressing-room and said to me, 'I'm awfully sorry this has happened, Cyril; I want you to go in again.' Of course I was quite ready to do this and managed to add some 30 odd runs to the fifteen I had already scored, much to the delight of the crowd. I believe I am the only person who has ever been accorded two innings without the sanction of the umpire. On getting to the wickets I asked Gutteridge why he had appealed and he said, 'Because you handled the bail.' That of course was not true. He really had appealed on the chance of Henty, the umpire, thinking that the ball had grazed the wicket in passing, but when he heard the latter give his decision, he thought he would back him up. It is amazing to think that there should have been two such complete idiots standing so close to one another at a given moment. Henty was, I am sorry to say, suspended for two years. Why he gave such a decision no one has been able to discover.

C. P. FOLEY, *Autumn Foliage*, 1935

By the end of the century the MCC was commonly referred to, grudgingly by its enemies, fulsomely by its supporters, as The Parliament of Cricket. *Wisden* helps to underline the parliamentary parallels by reporting a debate on the lbw laws precisely as though the theme were foreign policy and the place Westminster. In fact, this wonderful late Victorian set piece suggests that, at least in debate, the MCC members conducted their affairs with more dialectical thoroughness and efficiency than their counterparts to the south. Especially true does this seem regarding Alfred Lyttelton, whose spell a few years later as Colonial Secretary in Mr Balfour's farcical government of 1902–5 was distinctly less distinguished than his opening flourishes in the lbw debate. Lyttelton began his cabinet career as the Aunt Sally of the popular Press regarding the cynical use of Chinese cheap labour in South Africa, and ended it by drafting a scheme for the constitution of Transvaal so contentious that it proved to be one of the very few political flourishes of its day which drew the fire of British and Boers simultaneously. It seems that he was far too civilised and decent a man to be effective in politics, and history generally agrees with J. A. Spender, who defined him as 'one of the gentlest of men'. He was also one of the most dedicated when it came to the welfare of cricket, and spared none of his cerebral energies when it came to the vexed question of the lbw law.

THE LEG-BEFORE-WICKET QUESTION

The ordinary business having been concluded, the meeting was made special to consider the proposed alteration in the Law of leg-before-wicket. The proposal was that, in place of the present rule, Law 24 should read: 'If with any part of his person (except the hand) which is between wicket and wicket he intercept a ball which would hit his wicket, "Leg Before Wicket".' On the ballot being taken, there were 259 votes in support of the change and 188 against. There was thus a majority of 71 in favour of the change, but as no alteration in the laws of cricket can be carried by less than a two-thirds majority, the proposal fell to the ground. As the discussion was of exceptional interest, some of the best experts in England expressing in detail their views on a very vexed question, it has been thought advisable to print in *Wisden* the full official report.

The Chairman, the Right Hon. Spencer Ponsonby-Fane, GCB, said: 'The meeting will now be made special to take into consideration the alteration of the law of leg-before-wicket, and the Hon. Mr Lyttelton will move a resolution:'

The Hon. Alfred Lyttelton: 'Sir Spencer, my lords, and gentlemen. I have to move that Law 24 as it at present stands, which is that, "If with any part of his person he stops the ball, which in the opinion of the umpire at the bowler's wicket shall have been pitched in a straight line from it to the striker's wicket and would have hit it, 'Leg-before-wicket,'" be altered. I propose to substitute for those words in italics: "If with any part of his person (except the hand) which is between wicket and wicket, he intercept a ball which would hit his wicket, 'Leg before wicket.'" I do not suppose anybody who heard me read those words for the first time would quite understand what they mean. I expect you almost all have heard them: but very briefly I will explain that the proposal is to draw—if I may put it as a sketch—to draw a line from one wicket to another. That, of course, would mean a long thin parallelogram twenty-two yards long, and my proposal is, gentlemen, that that should be the bowler's territory, and that if a leg or any part of a batsman's person occupy that territory, and a ball hit the leg so occupying the territory which would have hit the wicket, then the batsman will be out. ("Hear, hear.") And the point of the alteration, as you will readily see, will be to prevent that bowler—the hard-working and admirable functionary—who can produce a break-back upon the ball or a twist upon the ball, and of course does not pitch the ball between wicket and wicket, that when he pitches the ball so, either on the off-side or leg side off the wicket, and can succeed in baffling that which was intended by Nature and cricketers—the bat—that the grosser article, the leg, or other parts of the person shall intercept the just reward of the bowler who has beaten the bat, and who would hit the wicket. Now, gentlemen, I do not intend to labour the question of the present circumstances of cricket—they are amply familiar to you all. I maintain, subject, of course, to the opinion of others quite as experienced, and quite as sagacious, that the present cricket is somewhat dull. ("Hear, hear.") Nothing can make it really dull: it still remains the best game in the world. But, on the other hand, to eliminate leg-hitting, to eliminate on-driving, to eliminate all these strokes on the leg side with which we were familiar twenty years ago is a very serious thing in the game, and it is hoped that if you carry this rule that at any rate the bowler will be encouraged to both twist the ball and break it from the off. But the really important thing is that the game is at present inconclusive. What in any game in the world—what if you went out to play tennis, or went out to play racquets, or went out to play football—what would you think if 50 per cent of the occasions on which you went out it was left undecided whether you were the better man or your opponent? I have not gone into details of statistics this year; but I remember going into them some little time ago—I think two years ago, a fairly typical year—and I remember taking out certain statistics at the time—I won't trouble you with them—which showed that about 50 per cent of the most important matches of the year were drawn. I remember the champion county drew 50 per cent of its matches—half the matches that it played were not concluded. The Australians drew, I think, sixteen out of thirty-five matches, and that though they are the finest bowlers and fieldsmen in the world. And last year, looking as I came up here, I find that out of thirty-three matches Surrey drew sixteen: out of twenty-two Essex drew twelve: out of twenty-one matches Derbyshire drew ten: out of eighteen matches Warwickshire drew thirteen: out of twenty-four Sussex drew nineteen—(laughter)—and I won't trouble you with the rest. But, my lords and gentlemen, may I ask you: Do you wish this state of things to continue unaltered? (Cries of "No" and "Yes.") Do you wish that we should fold our hands in this club and say that such a state of things as that should continue? I do not think I have ever heard anybody dispute that the game is made more tame and monotonous than ever it was. And here are the figures to show that it is inconclusive; that you cannot finish your matches, and cannot prove who is the better side. Then is it your wish that this state of things should continue? I must frankly admit that some persons entitled to great respect do wish no alterations to be made. The Committee itself, with a majority in favour of the proposal of eight to five, sent circulars to the Colonies and to the secretaries of the clubs in South Africa, and they seemed against the change. And although I think my friend Mr Warner wrote an article, I have not read it. (Laughter.) I will read it: but I was told that he inserted in the article the statement that the Australians, undoubtedly the persons most competent to judge in this matter after ourselves, were against the proposal. My friend Mr Warner, if he did make that statement, I am sorry, considering the education he had in my chambers; if he did, it is inaccurate, because we have a reply from the Australians, received within the last two days, which is in favour of the proposal which we now make. ("Hear, hear.") And, my lords and gentlemen. I am not surprised that they are in favour of it, because the evil in Australia is even greater than the evil here. But, being rich, and men of leisure, and being prepared to play five, six, or seven days if necessary, it does not press upon them quite so much as it does upon a more business-like community. There is the state of things; there is the grievance; there is that which I cannot say all, but which most people wish us to see altered, and can alteration be made in favour of the bowler, can it be made—I ought to say—in a more conservative way? But I ought, before I come to that aspect, just to add one word about second-class matches. I consider the evil to be even greater in second-class matches than it is in first-class. Now it is common for a man to go out and play second-class matches, every bit as good as we have here, single day matches, and he is a working man, and he gives, say, his Saturday up to cricket. Now, it may well happen to that man that he plays five matches running, and supposing he goes in fifth or sixth, the first four batsmen get 250 or 300 runs, the innings is declared closed, and he gets no innings. Perhaps he is on the other side on another occasion, and has the pleasure of fielding first for this 250 runs, and gets no innings himself, and the result is you may very easily play several Saturday matches and never get an innings at all. What wonder is it, then, that other and inferior games like golf—(laughter)—entice away the disappointed cricketer, and satisfy him with the sedater joys that belong to that game. Well, if that be so—and let me now come to what I was saying before—can you put forward a more conservative proposal than that which the Committee now submit to you? It is the least change you can make in the game; it is, I am told by those older than myself, it is a reverting, a return to the old days, that nobody in old days—before I can remember—that nobody ever put his leg in front of the wicket in order to intercept the ball. And for two admirable reasons; one, that he was too good a sportsman, and the other that he had too tender shins. But be that as it may, I have no doubt the question did not press in those days: now it does. I was very much amused with a letter I saw in *The Times* of this morning, and which I read on my way here. I was very much amused to see that certain friends for whom I have a great respect, Lord Hawke, Mr Warner, and others, think that if this rule is carried they would have to abandon the way in which they have been taught to play forward. ("Hear, hear.") They say that they have been taught to play forward—and evidently by very sound teachers—to play forward with their left leg close against the bat. Of course they have. I have seen 'W.G.' do that many thousands of times when I was keeping wicket, and the ball has hit his leg. They consider they will have to abandon that practice. Why should they?

Why should they not continue to play with their legs alongside their bats? They will have, at any rate, the chance that the umpire won't give them out; but if the bowler has succeeded in beating the bat, why should not he have his reward? ("Hear, hear.") And if any of these gentlemen who have learnt forward play in so admirable a way—if they succeed in playing forward in the proper way, and if they fail to hit the ball with the bat, which was intended to hit the ball, and if they intercept the ball with their legs, why should they not be out? And why should they alter their forward style of play because this rule is passed? That is the first point in this letter. Another point in the letter asserts that these gentlemen admitted that this alteration in the rule will do no good on hard wickets. May I say that I don't admit that at all, I utterly deny it, and I quote my friend Mr Steel, whom I remember very well coming back from Australia, where, you know, he played on very hard wickets. Palmer was a great Australian bowler in those days. I remember my friend Mr Steel and Mr Charlie Studd told me that Palmer could break the ball on a hard wicket; and they told me that in order to baffle him they used to put their legs out—("Shame")—in front alongside the bat, and it was absolutely legitimate, and therefore when he broke a ball which did not pitch straight he beat the bat, and they said, "We were safe because the ball hit our legs." Now that is what we want to prevent. That is why no bowlers now will try any enterprise. What is the good of twisting the ball, what is the good of breaking the ball, if the batsmen is able—notwithstanding the fact that you play on these faultless wickets—if the batsman is able to baffle the bowler, whatever device he tries? The plain result is that bowlers are compelled, instead of doing what is amusing, and what is a fine craft, trying to get a break and curl on the ball—and no wonder they are reduced to it, poor fellows!—they are reduced to bowling on the off side in the hope that by dint of mere monotony the batsman will be tempted to do something he ought not do, and be caught in the slips. I ask the meeting whether it is a caricature of the present cricket if I describe it as two bowlers bowling good length balls outside the off stumps, and hoping the batsmen will be tempted to play the ball into the hands of the slips. There is a lot of beautiful play and beautiful hitting; but it is the way on a good wicket which most bowlers are condemned to aim for. Now I think I have said enough, because one ought to be brief. May I just summarise what I have said on the evil existing both in first-class, and still more in second-class matches, of cricket becoming dull and cricket becoming inconclusive, quantities of drawn matches, quantities of occasions in single day matches when batsmen never get an innings at all, and as a result of this, gradual abandonment of second-class matches—("Oh!")—and frequent abandonment of first-class cricket by all gentlemen who are unable to give their whole time to it. That is frequently the result. Do you wish cricket to be monotonous? Do you wish it to be inconclusive? I am sure you do not. Now, if you do not wish the present state of things to continue, can any of you suggest a change more conservative? I am quite prepared to go further, but I think it right first to take the most conservative line, because obviously it would be said, if you do not take so moderate a reform as this you will take nothing. Therefore, I say you have an admitted evil, and you have a conservative remedy for it, and I hope you will vote for it.' (Cheers.)

Mr John Shuter: 'Sir Spencer, my lords, and gentlemen.—As a

comparatively recent convert to the proposed alteration in this law, I venture to second this proposition which Mr Lyttelton has so ably put before you. I feel that I can add very little indeed to help our cause beyond what he has said, for I so entirely agree with everything he has said, not only as regards first-class cricket, but especially as regards second and third-class cricket. I am quite certain of this, gentlemen, that we all here probably as cricketers have very great respect for the opinions of those gentlemen whose names appear at the bottom of that letter in *The Times* of this morning, to which Mr Lyttelton has referred. But, personally, I cannot help saying that I am beyond measure disappointed in that they have made absolutely no reference to the heavy scoring of the present day, which, to my mind, is the basis of the proposed alteration which is now before us. Personally, speaking with regard to the leg play and the leg glide, which is, of course, a very beautiful and very artistic stroke, I can only say that I was not taught to put the ball where it is put at the present day, and so the batsmen who now play that stroke, and play it so admirably and secure so many runs by it, if they are unable to play that stroke without putting their legs in front of the middle stump or middle and leg, all I can say is that they ought to suffer if anything should occur by way of an appeal to the umpire for lbw. I really add very little beyond that, except to say this, that I am very strongly of opinion that in fine weather the alteration in the rule will have a decided effect. There is one point upon which Mr Lyttelton did not touch, and that is with respect to the umpiring. I feel strongly on that point, because I think that the umpire's position, far from being made more difficult, will, I really think, be made easier—("Hear, hear")—for the simple reason that at the present moment he has to judge in an infinitesimal space of a second as to whether a ball pitches in a space of about that much, whereas under the new law he certainly may have at times, on a slow wicket, rather difficult decisions to give: if so he can give them in favour of the batsman. But in the ordinary case his judgement will be helped, and I think, although I am open to correction—and Mr Lacey, I believe, can correct me if I am wrong in saying so—that the first-class umpires have expressed the opinion that their position would be made easier instead of more difficult. Gentlemen, I do hope that, though I am sure we all have a very high opinion of all those present-day cricketers who are against this change, I hope that if you are conscientiously in favour of the change, you will not fail to record your vote in favour of it.'

Mr A. G. Steel: 'May I ask that the communication from Australia referred to by Mr Lyttelton be read to this meeting?'

Mr ——: 'May I ask if you received any answer from America?'

Mr W. E. Denison: 'From Philadelphia, yes.'

The Secretary: 'I have a letter from Major Wardill, who writes as secretary of the Melbourne Cricket Club.' (Reads letter).

Mr P. F. Warner: 'I believe there has been no meeting of the Australians, and that is merely a private communication from Major Wardill, and is not official. Just because there are certain cricketers in England who are in favour, therefore you say the whole body are in favour of it.'

Mr W. E. Denison: 'My lords, and gentlemen.—Perhaps, as regards the Australian matter, which I do not think is of particular importance, I may merely comment upon the fact that a most extraordinary number of influential names are conspicuous by their absence. There are only, out of those names that were read out, three of four who would carry any weight in this country, and we do not hear anything from the Hills and Darlings, and all those men who have made themselves conspicuous in the past. That is a matter of comparatively little importance at present, and I will just mention it directly in connection with some of the other countries who have been asked their opinion. Now, Mr Alfred Lyttelton has told you that this particular alteration which he has mentioned will conduce a very great deal to making the game more lively and more agreeable to the spectators. I myself am of the exact opposite opinion, and I think I may mention one or two points which will, I hope, induce the meeting to take the same view. Now, it would appear that this proposed alteration of the law is faulty in principle. Under the existing law, if a man gets lbw to a ball which is going straight from wicket to wicket, he has placed himself in a false position, from which it is impossible that he can make a correct stroke; and under the proposed law he will be given out, he will be penalised for placing himself in the only position in which he can make a correct stroke, and he will be cramped in consequence. A man's leg must come across on the off-side, and he will be penalised for having assumed the correct position to play the ball. Now, a man's legs must be somewhere, and I cannot think it can conduce to the liveliness of the game to penalise him for placing them in the proper position. Now, something has been said about the umpires, and the comparative ease with which umpires will now perform their duties to what they did before. Well, I really cannot see that the umpire is placed in a more favourable position; he appears to me to be placed in a position of extraordinary difficulty. As it is now, what he has to decide is, did the ball pitch straight and would it go on straight: but now you are going to ask him to decide whether a ball, perhaps with a curl from leg, or a break back, was going to hit the wicket, and whether the exact spot struck on the batsman's leg was in the line of impact between wicket and wicket. I venture to think that is a thing very few umpires will correctly decide, and there are plenty of mistakes made at present, and I think they will be very much multiplied if this law is brought into force. When you make a new law you make it, of course, with a certain object. Now a very distinguished cricketer, Mr MacLaren, said the other day to me, when speaking about this, that you would never have thought of this if it had not been for the long scores. That is to say, it is not an improvement in the game. Mr Lyttelton appears to think the game will be made more lively. My own impression is that given a cautious batsman, you bring before his mind another danger which he is not exposed to now, and that it will make him more cautious, and he will simply stop a good many balls which under the present regime he would have hit. But I do not think myself that on a fast, good, and easy wicket this law will have any effect except that of making the game a little duller than it is now. And although Mr Lyttelton has referred to Palmer, there are not many Palmers about now.'

A Voice: 'There will be, though.'

Mr Denison: 'But where the ball does not beat the bat, these people do not get out lbw; there is no occasion for them to do so—they can find the ball with the bat when they come forward. But if you come to a good ground in a difficult state, or the ordinary ground upon which half-day matches and league matches are played, I think you will find that cricket, which is already too difficult, will become absolutely impossible. I should like to see anybody try to play on one of those grounds on which now 60 or 70 is a good score. I think two curly bowlers upon wickets such as we sometimes see would make the game look rather absurd; but I do not wish to take up all these points on the particular merits and demerits of this proposed law, because I think everybody has been able to make up his mind upon it, one way or the other. But I have to say this as regards the opinions that have been given out—that we have very valuable evidence from Philadelphia. The Philadelphians are, of course, the leading cricket team of the States, and they wrote to us to say that they could not recommend us to adopt this law, for the reason that they had tried it—not for one match or two matches, or for a season, but for several years—and it proved unsuccessful. And they added to that statement that they were very sorry they could not adopt it, because the idea had commended itself to them. Therefore, you have had this scheme thoroughly and sympathetically tried and found to be a failure. But, gentlemen, instead of dwelling upon the particular merits or demerits of this proposal, I should rather ask you to consider the wider question, that is to say, the way in which the laws of cricket are to be brought forward by the Marylebone Club and enforced upon the cricket community. It is a very necessary thing, or a very desirable thing, at all events, that there should be some central law-abiding body, and up to this time the Marylebone Club has filled this position with very great success. And Why? Because every alteration made has had the assent and approval of the great body of cricketers; everyone of them has been a success, and they have never been asked to rescind any one. But there is no instance on record of the Marylebone Club endeavouring to pass into law any proposal to which there was a very strong and widespread objection. It has never been done, and I really do not see how you could keep your position as central law givers of cricket if you were to force on new laws which were perhaps strongly and deservedly objected to. Now the process by which this proposed law has come before you is this: It was proposed at a cricket sub-committee, and was looked upon with doubt; as a matter of fact, they were divided, and made no recommendation on the point. It was then taken to a small meeting of the general committee, at which it was adopted and passed into its next stage—that is, the stage when the opinions of certain cricketing bodies were asked upon it. Those bodies were the Counties, the Universities, the Australians (whose opinion you have just heard), the Philadelphians, the West Indians, and the South Africans; the captains I have mentioned. Well, of course, the opinion of the captains came first, and the way in which opinion was asked was by sending letters to the individual captains asking them to state their opinions and that of their eleven. Some the captains did not answer, but the whole of those who did answer were against the proposal; the remainder of them answered at a meeting of the captains, which was a somewhat memorable meeting, which was held at the beginning of this year, and that meeting was reported by Lord Hawke, its chairman—who I am sorry is not here from indisposition—was reported to the Marylebone Club as absolutely unanimous against this proposal.' A Voice: 'That has since been found out not to be so.'

Mr Denison: 'The meeting was absolutely unanimous against it: but it appears that out of, I think there were twelve of the fifteen captains present, I think it appears that it is possible—("Certain")—that four of those who were not present are now in favour of this proposal, but that does not make the meeting of the captains that was held any less unanimous, nor does it in the least weaken what I was going to say, which was this, that on receiving this report from Lord Hawke, we naturally on the cricket sub-committee rec-ommended to the general committee in the mildest terms that in view of the great weight of opinion against this proposal, it was not advisable to proceed with it any further at the present time. We could not have put it more gently than that; we could not have been more soothing to Mr Lyttelton's feelings than we were. One would have thought, perhaps, that an opinion of this sort coming from the committee that you appoint for the purpose might have had some weight; but at another small meeting of the general committee they decided by a small majority, which has been mentioned, of eight to five, to set aside the opinion of their own cricket sub-committee, to treat what was apparently at that time the unanimous opinion of the captains with contempt, and to persevere with their own plans and schemes. Well, since that time they have had also the opinion of the Philadelphians, who have tried this scheme and found it a failure. I do think that it is perfectly impossible that a meeting such as this should enforce upon the cricket world, or endeavour to enforce upon the cricket world, a new law to which such very strong exception has been taken. ("Hear, hear.") I do not know really what you keep the cricket sub-committee for if you are not going to take its advice. I have often heard of a proposal made by a sub-committee which has not been accepted by the general committee, but I do not think I ever heard of a general committee insisting upon making an alteration which the sub-committee appointed for the purpose, strongly warned them against. I do not know that I need add any more, except just to summarise and say that I object to this law, first on its merits. I object to it because it is wrong in principle, difficult to carry out, and also on the ground that it will not effect its object, but that it will effect an object which is not desired. But I object to it still more, because I consider that to force on by a general meeting of the Marylebone Club, to force upon a reluctant cricket world a measure to which so many eminent judges are entirely opposed, cannot be anything but injurious to cricket, and, I think, disastrous to the reputation of the Marylebone Club as a cricket law giver. For those reasons, gentlemen, I beg to move the rejection of this proposal.' (Cheers.)

Mr A. G. Steel: 'My lords, and gentlemen.—In the ordinary course of events my friend Lord Hawke would have seconded Mr Denison's proposal this afternoon, but, as you have heard, he is somewhat indisposed, and a few moments ago I was asked if I would second the proposal instead of Lord Hawke, and I at once said that I would be delighted to do so, because I am dead against this proposal. Many years ago I was a bowler, and in spite of that fact I am dead against the proposal, because I do not think it is in the interests of the game. Now, we have heard two—if I may say so—excellent speeches, one from Mr Lyttelton, and the other from Mr Denison, and I am not going to make a speech to-day. My object is to get up and tell you that, personally, I think it would be against the best interests of the game if this proposed alteration is carried to-day. Now, I do not so much object in principle to the off-side of the wicket—that is to the batsman if he puts his leg across the off-stump, and the ball whips back to hit the wicket, he should be out. I do not so much object to that, but I do object to it on the leg-side. I think it is an impossibility as we play the game at present to have this rule altered. It seems to me that you have only to have two medium-paced leg bowlers, under-arm, and no side will get any runs—you will have them all out lbw. As I said before, I am not going to make a speech, but I will ask you, remembering that the captains were against the proposal, and that there is an enormous amount of feeling amongst cricketers against it, I ask you heartily to say that this proposed alteration shall not take effect this afternoon.' (Applause.)

Mr R. A. H. Mitchell: 'Sir Spencer, my lords, and gentlemen.—I hope you will bear with me while I say a few words about the proposed alteration of the lbw rule, because it is one that I have personally supported now for about, at all events, seventeen years; because I was a supporter of it when the great alterations were made in the rules in, I think, the year 1884. I am not perfectly certain about the date. I should like to say a few words first on what appear to me to be the merits of the case. I must go back, I am afraid, to a time when most of those who are now playing first-class cricket had either not appeared on the scene, or were still in their nurse's arms; therefore I may be looked upon almost as an antedeluvian, but at that time the rule was the same; but we were taught, and I have had a good deal of teaching at cricket, and I have always taught players not to put their leg in front more than is absolutely necessary, and in my day there was no one who deliberately stopped the ball with his leg. That may have been stupidity: I cannot say. Someone spoke of "better sportsmen": but I cannot believe that—I do not believe we were better sportsmen than the cricketers of the present day. But we did not learn to do that, and I totally disagree with Mr Steel, sorry as I am to do so, about balls on the leg side. It would introduce certainly a different style from the present but if I may I will describe the stroke we were taught to play to a good-length ball. Of course, there was a good deal of bowling round the wicket then, and instead of putting your leg in front to a ball that was pitched off the wicket which would take the wicket, we were taught to put the leg a little to the left, and play straight at the ball. That I believe to be the true game. Now people are taught to put their leg in front and tuck it round. Which is the better style I must leave to your own decision. I know which commends itself to me. As to its being impossible, I know it is not impossible, because people in my days had to contend with as much bowling round the wicket as over the wicket. I quite agree it is impossible in the present style. If people will put their legs in front of the wicket, under the proposed alteration they will, of course, very rapidly go back to the pavilion; but you must remember those who support the rule wish to see them go back much quicker than they do now. I think a great deal of the arguments I have seen—I do not pretend to have read all the literature that has appeared upon the subject—but a great deal of what I have seen seems to me to condemn the proposed alteration on the ground that it will get the batsman out. That is what we wish to do. If you are content with the present state of the game which Mr Alfred Lyttelton has described, then, of course, I quite understand your objecting to any change in the law. I have read some of the letters which have appeared, and I think a great many of the people who have written them seem to forget that when the batsman goes to the wicket there is placed in his hands a piece of wood over four inches broad, which is supposed to meet the ball. It is idle to contend that the leg is for the defence of the wicket. I was always taught that the bat was. It seems to me that you can keep your leg clear of that line as long as you like. It is perfectly true that to play a fine ball correctly, pitched outside the off stump, it is necessary step across the wicket, but then surely the bat is to meet the ball, and if the ball beats the bat, you ought to pay for it. Now I should like to say a few words about umpiring, because, although, of course, I have had nothing like the experience that Mr Steel, for instance, has had in first-class cricket, still I am afraid I must claim to have had more than thirty years' umpiring: I stood umpire at Eton two or three times a week, therefore I cannot say I have no experience. When you are appealed to under the present rule, three things you have to decide. The easiest of all is the question of whether the man's leg is between wicket and wicket: that, I conceive, he has very little difficulty in deciding. The most difficult point is as to whether the ball pitched straight or not: you have to be intent on the game every moment, and even then you cannot tell. That is the real thing we shall get rid of under the proposed alteration. Of course, the umpire may make a mistake as to whether the ball would have hit the wicket or not; so he does under the present rule. He must make some mistakes; that is one of the unfortunate blots in the game. Umpires will make mistakes, and I do not think they will make more mistakes under the proposed alteration than they do now, because the great difficulty, to my mind, is removed. I should very much prefer, as an umpire, to have to umpire under the proposed alteration than under the rule as it exists now. Well, now, I should like to say a few words—I am afraid I am rather lengthy—but I should like to say a few words about our position as old cricketers in relation to those who are playing cricket now. I cannot follow Mr Denison through the questions about the committee or what they have done: I do not know them, and do not understand them, and there is no necessity to follow them, I remember a gentleman once saying something to me, it was about rather a difficult question, and I said, "Well, I should like to consult a friend upon it," and he said, "If I had not an opinion of my own, I should be sweeping a crossing now." And I think much about the same with regard to the Marylebone Club. We are a representative cricket body, let us do what we think best for the interests of the game. ("Hear, hear.") That is my view: but at the same time I have always held this, that those who are playing cricket at the time ought to have the principal say in the question, and that is the great difficulty that I feel. As you know, when a question arises like this, those who are against the game represent—I do not use the words in an invidious sense—represent the noisy party. Those who do not want this change, leave it alone so far as writing goes. I think so far as I can learn there may be, and perhaps is, a large body of the present players against it. But, gentlemen, I should like to say to present players this: That if we grant you that, that we do not want to force a change upon you that is unpalatable even though we think it a good one ourselves, remember, it places on you a strong responsibility, and the responsibility seems to be this: You must either say, "We are content with the game as it is; we don't care twopence whether we finish our matches or not, or whether the game is dull, but we like it as it is; we like long scores, and three days' gate money"; or, if you are not content with that position, then I think it is for you to bring forward some change to shorten the game. It is not enough to say that; you must be prepared to come forward and say what will improve the game, because it is perfectly certain there is a wide discontent amongst a large number with the present state of things, and we are discontented with it because we are afraid it is degenerating from a sport into a profession, and that we do not like. We believe it to be the national game; and we do not want to see it cut out or even impaired by any other games such as are attracting and may attract notice, but we want to see the game a real good sporting game. And with reference to that, I should like to say one word more. I think of a remark which Mr Denison made, that it would make the game slower. Now in my day I consider that, owing to the fact that we had not found out how to defend our wicket with our legs, we were very much on the alert to hit every bad ball, because we knew our time was not likely to be so long as it is now, and we wanted to make use of every opportunity. Under the present system no one wants to make use of any opportunity. They only want to stick there, knowing that the bowler will get tired. Your Palmer cannot go on trying to twist the ball on a good wicket when he finds it is only intercepted by the leg if it beats the batsman. That is what makes it dull, and the batsman plays a slow game, except a few who are most attractive. All I can say is I must apologise for having kept you so long, but my interest in the game must be my excuse.'

Mr Denison: 'I only wish to make an explanatory statement on what Mr Mitchell has said. He has asked why we did not propose any scheme. We did not propose one because there is only one scheme in possession of the house.'

Mr Mitchell: 'Not to-night; I do not mean that.' (Cries of 'Vote, vote!')

Mr Warner: 'Mr Lyttelton talked as if one should only play on the off-side, and never by any chance make a stroke on the leg-side. Has he never seen Ranjitsinhji, Fry, or MacLaren? Mr Lyttelton talked about the poor bowler. Such men as Albert Trott and Rhodes are absolutely opposed to any alteration. I do not say this from any selfish motives, because I know I am no bowler. I assure you I have the true interests of the game at heart, and as I have played all over the world I think I am entitled to express an opinion. This has been the finest game in the world for generations, and so I ask you to beware how you tamper with its present laws.'

The Chairman: 'You have all heard the admirable speeches that have been made, and I do not think anybody would be likely to alter his opinion if they spoke on for ever.'

Mr Harvey Fellows: 'My Lords, and Gentlemen.—I should like to say a few words. I should imagine that every fair-minded cricketer would be of opinion that the bowler should always have a free wicket. The batsman has a bat wherewith to defend it, and I think, in common fairness to the bowler, if he bowls a ball which beats the batsman, and would have hit the wicket if the batsman's legs were not in the way, the batsman ought to pay the penalty and be out. But, with reference to the batsman stopping the ball with his legs, if his legs were not before the wicket, of course it would not be out. What can be more unfair towards the bowler than that he should have the ball stopped by the body after having beaten the bat? Now, let me mention one subject about which we ought to be unanimous. Did we not all condemn the mode in which Shrewsbury used to play the ball with his leg? Where is the true cricket if the batsman is not to be confined to using his bat for the protection of his wicket? Now, with reference to the bowler, it is awfully hard upon him. And what is the present state of the law? I am sure you will all agree with me in one illustration. Take a fast bowler who bowls round the wicket. How can he get a leg-before-wicket, except he tosses what you call a yorker? And the idea of a fast bowler's ball pitching in a line between wickets ... (Cries of "Time" and "Vote.") The eyes of all cricketers are upon this meeting, and they will see whether votes will be given to support the true principle of cricket, namely, that the ball should not be stopped by a man's legs, but by the bat which he has for that purpose. All I can say is, gentlemen, that if you consider what is fair with reference to the bowler, you will alter this law so that a batsman should know that he has to stop the ball with his bat, and not with his leg.' (Cries of 'Vote, vote.')

Mr C. C. Clarke: 'I think the writers to the papers based their calculations, if you follow it carefully, on wet wickets. In every paragraph you see "wet wickets," and at the end they recommend you to try a change.' (Cries of 'Vote, vote.')

The Chairman: 'I will now take a show of hands upon the question.'

After the show of hands the Chairman said: 'Well, gentlemen, it is quite impossible for us to decide, and I therefore ask you to vote as you leave the room. The result will be announced in the Press tomorrow.

'I will take this opportunity of informing you that Lord Howe has consented to be President for the ensuing year.'

The figures were declared as follows:—For the proposition, 259; against, 188. Majority for, 71. This, however, being less than a two-thirds majority, the proposal was not passed.

Wisden, circa 1900

P ERHAPS now, as the last long summer evenings of the nineteenth century fade into history, it is the appropriate moment to mark the passing of an assortment of men who, each in his very different way, bequeathed much to Lord's. One contributed luncheon arbours, one the ground itself. One did not even know where the ground was, and the fourth found himself mowing a pitch one minute, playing on quite a different one the next. All four of these worthies lived well on into the new century, but they were essentially men and types who belonged to the Victorian age.

Harrison, George Pickering. A typical Yorkshireman of the old school, died aged 78 at Scarborough, his home, in September 1939.... Known familiarly as

'Shoey', an abbreviation of his trade as shoemaker, Harrison often umpired in first-class cricket, and at every Scarborough Festival in recent years his favourite corner in the pavilion was alive with humour and reminiscences. Of many tales told of him, one mentioned in *The Cricketer* goes back to his first match at Lord's. When accepting the invitation to play for the Colts, he asked Mr Henry Perkins, the MCC Secretary, to meet him at King's Cross as he had never been to London.

Wisden, 1940

Hearne, John Thomas. In June 1890 he received a telegram asking him to play for Middlesex that very day: 'I turned over my pitch-mowing job to someone else, dashed to the station and from a newspaper found that Middlesex were playing Notts. When I arrived at Lord's just before lunchtime I saw 99 for no wicket on the scoreboard. Not until reaching the dressing-room did I learn that my side were batting. If Notts had been at the wickets I should not have played in that match. I remember Mr Webbe leaning out of the pavilion window as I passed down the little alley to the players' room and saying, 'It is quite all right, but I nearly left you out.'

Wisden, 1944

Nicholson, William, DL, JP Great as Mr Nicholson's skill as a player undoubtedly was, it is probable that he will always be best remembered for the unstinted support he was ever ready to accord the game. In *Cricket* of January 1886 it was told how, when the fate of Lord's was almost in the balance, before the sudden increase of wealth from Eton and Harrow and University matches, Mr Nicholson stood in the gap, and after all England had been drawn for subscriptions to save the ground – for few escaped Mr Roger Kynaston and his red book – he advanced the money as mortgage on a security which the outside public would not take. Little was said about it, as men who do such things do not talk about them, but there is no doubt he saved Lord's from the builders.

The celebrated Mr William Ward did a similar thing many years before. He drew a cheque for £5,000, and gave it to Lord's for the lease, and as it happened this turned out to be a good investment, as indeed did Mr Nicholson's mortgage also, though he ran the risk for the love of cricket, and the sum advanced was a large one – a very long way into five figures. This action on his part should cause his name always to be gratefully remembered, not only by members of the Marylebone Club, but by all English cricketers in whatever part of the world they may be domiciled. His generosity enabled the old club to purchase the freehold of Lord's; but for him the ground might have been built over and the MCC, the recognised head of the game, have been rendered homeless. In 1879 Mr Nicholson was elected the president of the club.

Wisden, 1909

Slatter, William R. Born September 12, 1851, died in Harrow Hospital on August 16, 1929, aged 77. Son of the better-known 'Steevie' Slatter, he was engaged at Lord's for 57 years, originally as a pavilion dressing-room attendant in 1863, working his way up to become clerk of works. His reminiscences were published in a private circulation pamphlet in 1914, entitled *Recollections of Lord's and the Marylebone Cricket Club.* Some idea of the changes which time wrought during his long association with the ground can be gauged from the fact that he could recall seeing wild rabbits there. He designed and built the luncheon arbours surrounding the practice-ground.

Wisden, 1930

NICHOLSON's gallantry and generosity on behalf of the club was one of several examples of devotion to the cause without which the MCC, in its Victorian years, could not have survived. As land values rose, as St John's Wood became drawn into the central area of the capital, and as public transport became at once a vital public amenity and a source of great profit to shareholders, it was inevitable that so large a tract of land, standing as it did directly across the route from the north into the West End, should become the focus of speculative operators. And the fact that Lord's was a place dedicated to so innocent and pastoral a pursuit as cricket would have counted for less than nothing in City boardrooms. When on the completion of the railway line into St Pancras it was found necessary to bridge that Regent's Park Canal whose genesis had been the cause of Thomas Lord's second move, a grave-yard was unceremoniously dug up, leaving behind so horrifying a selection of bones and tresses of hair that the architects sent down an apprentice to supervise the respectful removal of these human remains. The apprentice was Thomas Hardy, who wrote of the occasion;

> O, Passenger, pray list and catch
> Our sighs and piteous groans.
> Half stifled in this jumbled patch
> Of wrenched memorial stones.
>
> We late-lamented, resting here,
> Are mixed to human jam,
> And each to each exclaims in fear,
> 'I know not which I am.'

Fortunately for the welfare of Lord's, its administrators were in no doubt which or who or what they were, and acted accordingly.

The enlargement of the property in the 'nineties was due to the attempt by railway promoters to get a Bill through Parliament which not only threatened the old market gardens, now the practice ground, but, if not successfully resisted, might have led to an attack on the sacred match-ground, for land for sidings for what is now the Great Central Railway was not to be had easily, and an open space like Lord's was naturally tempting to the covetous railway promoters. The

MCC, most fortunately, had two most competent guardians, the late Lord James of Hereford and Mr S. Bircham, whose intimate acquaintance with Parliamentary and Private Bill procedure was invaluable and so successful that they secured for the MCC immense advantages from an attack which, at first, seemed fraught with danger to the headquarters of cricket. It is highly unlikely that Lord's can ever be successfully attacked with a view to its playing grounds being reduced, for, though the property of a private club, it is really a public cricket-ground; and, provided the MCC adheres to its time-honoured policy of doing all in its power to enable the public to view the best cricket comfortably and economically, the public will take care that its privileges shall not be curtailed.

LORD HARRIS AND F. S. ASHLEY-COOPER, *Lord's and the MCC*, 1914

THE twentieth century opened amid a blaze of controversy as to whether it had yet opened at all. In terms of mathematical logic, clearly on 1 January 1900, the nineteenth century still had one year to run, much as a batsman on 99 not out still requires a single to become a centurion. But in terms of popular hysteria, neither mathematics nor logic came into it, and the world insisted on an orgy of celebration and optimistic speculation. In Noël Coward's *Cavalcade*, which opens at a few minutes to midnight on 31 December 1899, the noise of chimes and sirens wakens the Marriot children, whose father, poised with a glass of champagne, remarks, 'How very impolite of the twentieth century.' Northcliffe's *Daily Mail*, standard-bearer of the New Journalism, described those same few moments:

The hand of the clock has reached the quarter, and is pressing on imperceptibly to midnight, the hour that marks the doom of the nineteenth age of the Christian era. The crowd has grown strangely quiet. The triangular space that separates the minute hand from the hour diminishes slowly. The angle becomes acute, the hand steals on, is blended with its fellow. The nineteenth century is gasping out its breath – Boom! The first stroke of midnight crashes through the frosty air and is hailed by an annihilating roar of jubilation. The succeeding strokes are almost unheard; they are all lost in the tumult of cheering. Hurrah! The twentieth century has dawned.

IT WAS the same at Mafeking, where the beleaguered British garrison was encouraged by its games-mad commander, Baden-Powell, to celebrate with parties and sporting contests; at midnight the rain spattered down on the veld as the strains of 'Auld Lang Syne' drifted out across the Boer lines. But the cricket season of 1900 arrived with the long-awaited relief still not in sight. What the British had been waiting for finally happened on 17 May. There might have been some great set piece being staged on that day at Lord's. Instead, the ironies of history dictated that while the whole of London was going berserk, within the walls of Thomas Lord's old ground, MCC were pottering away to a victory over Northamptonshire, then still very much a minor county.

There were no Test matches that summer. The visitors were the West Indies, little more than an embryonic cricketing force. On their debut at Lord's in June, they were beaten by the Gentlemen of the MCC, despite a century by L. S. Constantine, father of Learie. In the Varsity match, Oxford were strongly fancied, but, although R. E. Foster made a brilliant century, had to settle for a draw. At Lord's the Committee was beset, as always, by the strictures of dissatisfied customers, including Mr Harry Furniss, the celebrated *Punch* caricaturist. Furniss was one of those splenetic characters who are never lacking in a cause to defend or an institution to assault. Hot-headed and unreasonable, a watched pot forever on the boil, he was forever embroiled in some quarrel so complicated as to defy resolution. In *A History of Punch*, the equable R. G. G. Price describes him as 'cantankerous, overbearing and pushing', a description with which the administrators at Lord's would certainly have agreed. Furniss seems to have loved his cricket, and certainly spent a great deal of time at Lord's, much of it, evidently, in search of pretexts for complaint. It is therefore surprising that he was not on the attack in the very first days of the season, when the MCC decided to conduct one of its more arcane experiments.

During the first weeks of the 1900 season the MCC enclosed Lord's with a net about two feet six inches in height, with the idea of making the batsmen run out their hits, but the experiment met with no success and was given up. It was first arranged that when the ball went over the netting three runs should be scored, and that when it was stopped by the net two runs should be added to those already run. This method was modified after a few trials, with no better result. The plan penalised big hits over the ropes, and was generally voted clumsy.

SIR PELHAM WARNER, *Lord's*, 1946

Bᴜᴛ by July Furniss had located his target. He decided that the aspects of bald commercialism creeping into Lord's were an affront to the dignity of the members, and succeeding in working himself up into such a climax of irascibility that he even hoped for a second pavilion fire which might destroy the eyesore which Lord's in his artist's opinion had now become. Furniss's splendidly comic outburst, rising to heights of derision in its suggested innovations which the Committee might consider introducing, ends with the most delicate question in cricket history, then and since. To what extent can cricket be saved from financial expediency? The panjandrums of Furniss's day had no answer. Neither have their descendents. Neither has anyone.

Sir, I am not surprised to read your cricket correspondent's complaint in today's issue regarding the unsportsmanlike treatment the Press has received at the hands of the officials at Lord's.

Your readers will recollect how the Empire was nearly shaken to its foundation when the members of Lord's had to decide who was to be the new secretary of the play-ground in St John's Wood! The Queen's-hall was filled with swelled heads, and, judging from your correspondent's note, the swelled heads elected one of their own body. After all, Lord's is to cricket what St Andrews is to golf;

but at St Andrews golf is the one thing considered, at Lord's cricket is a mere detail. At St Andrews golfers, lovers of the game, and even mere sightseers, and, may I add, members of the Press, are given every facility to enjoy the game. But, alas! Lord's is fast degenerating from a club of gentlemen cricketers into a show run for the sake of profit.

Under the old management, for many years, Lord's was an ideal retreat for the tired worker and the cricket lover. Then the stranger felt that by paying at the gate he was free to sit in peace, and with the aid of a good cigar it was the ideal place in which to spend a happy day. Not so now, to those seated on the paying stands. Boys, heavily laden with open baskets containing merchandise one sees on Hampstead-heath on Bank holiday or on a third-rate race course, but surely of little attraction to the frequenters of Lord's, trample continually on your toes and screech everlastingly into your ears 'Cigarettes, cigars, chocolates – Cigarettes, cigars, chocolates.' 'Correct card – Correct card.' 'Cigarettes, cigars, chocolates.' 'Correct card.' 'Speshul 'dition – latest cricket scores.' 'Cigarettes, cigars, chocolates.' 'Speshul 'dition – latest cricket scores.' 'Correct card.' 'Cigarettes, cigars, chocolates.' And to offend the ear still further these calls of screeching boys are sandwiched by 'Any seat, Sir, but the first four rows.' 'Any seat, Sir, but the first four rows.'

Why, in the name of reason and peace, cannot the fact that, after paying extra, you can occupy certain seats be written on a placard, or, better still, on the tickets?

In fact, we may soon expect swings erected in the practice-ground, shooting booths under the atrocious erection of the big stand, and knock-me-downs in and out of the many drinking booths now disfiguring the club – a club, once a quiet gentlemanly retreat, now a huge conglomeration of various monstrosities of masonry. In fact, I frankly confess, were I to see the buildings at Lord's, some winter's night, on fire, although I would not be guilty to incendiarism I would certainly not hurry to give the alarm, for, as an artist, I consider even the outside of Lord's Cricket Ground an outrage upon taste and an offence to the eye.

It is not enough that the committee of Lord's

should offend the eye by having turned the pretty
pitch of old into an ugly mass of sheds and patches
of erratic architecture, but they must also offend
the ear by turning it into a pandemonium as well.

Many use Lord's Club as a fashionable picnic
ground for five days in the year – genuine cricket
lovers are absent then and look to the Press to read
in detail the doing of the colts – but now it appears
that, during the paying-picnic days, the Press is
turned out of the stand and relegated to the tool
shed, or, perhaps, to the roller horse's stable.

Nearly every sport in this country is being ruined
by 'the gate' question – can we not save cricket,
and particularly Lord's, before it is too late?

HARRY FURNISS, Letter to *The Times*, 7 July 1900

FURNISS's broadside drew the fire of friends and enemies alike. On the following day
support arrived in the form of a letter from a member who took violent exception
to the development of the ground in its more democratic aspects. The smuggling in of
the Mound Stand under cover of winter must have been a stroke of strategic genius,
but its arrival did not amuse the old school, who looked back fondly to the days when
the MCC had been a small club of gentlemen and the premises it occupied a bolt-hole
for its members to escape the madding crowd. The letter also raises the sore point of the
comically inadequate provisions offered to the Press. There is a contradiction here. If
the correspondent deplored the invitation to the masses to attend the ground, then he
should surely have been campaigning against the admission of the Press at all, for it
was through widespread popular journalism that Lord's was being pushed inexorably
to the point where it would become secondary to the game it professed to administer.
The old shire horse, on which the grandee had once sat, was turning into a tiger.

Sir, As an old member of Lord's I am rejoiced to see
the letter of Mr Harry Furniss in *The Times* of to-day.
I have long been looking out for some expression of
the kind, and I am thankful that it has at last come.
You must not think that the members of the MCC
approve of the treatment awarded to the members
of the Press. The fact is there is much dissatisfaction
amongst the members of the MCC at the manner
in which matters have been conducted for the last
few years, and the waste of money that has been
prodigious. Two hundred new members at £200
each have partly paid for this waste, but otherwise
the money might as well been thrown into the sea.
Hideous buildings have been erected all over the
place, and, as Mr Harry Furniss says, the place

which was once 'a quiet gentlemanly retreat is now
a huge conglomeration of various monstrosities of
masonry'. In fact, I can excuse his not giving the
alarm of fire before all the hideous buildings were
burnt down, should such a fortunate accident
occur. It must not be supposed that the members of
the MCC had anything to do with the erection of
these monstrosities. We went away in August and
when we returned in May the hideous building
called the Mound stand stood before us. No one who
is not obliged will sit in it, scorched in the sun or
drenched in the rain according to our variable
climate. The members were never consulted about
all this deformation of the ground. No plans were
placed before them. The clock was placed where no
one in the pavilion could see it. Since then another
clock has been placed on one of the hideous
buildings, luckily far off, so that it is not constantly
shadowing the game; and now the members of the
Press have been placed on the top of that building,
so that if they cannot see the game they will be
enabled, by looking round the corner, to time it. I
do not wish to say these things anonymously, so,
at the risk of some censure.

GEORGE ROSE NORTON,
Letter to *The Times*, 9 July 1900

BUT Furniss and Norton had exposed their flank with a recklessness that was almost
indecent, and within a few days they were made to pay for it. The correspondent
whose gallantry did not, sadly, extend to the disclosure of his own name, was merciless
in making the point that what might be called the Fundamentalists at Lord's, those
older members who desired nothing to change forever more, anywhere, in any way,
were in fact complaining about success. The comic sarcasm of 'Old Cricketer's' opening
complaint, his reduction of the Furniss argument to a plea for a sanatorium, his reminder
that Lord's was supposed to be a cricket ground, not an art gallery, reduced even
Furniss to silence.

Sir, Mr Harry Furniss in his diatribe against the
management of the MCC charges the Committee
with running the club for profit. Supposing it were
run at a loss, would he consider that as a mark of
superior management? Mr Furniss also complains
that Lord's is no longer 'a retreat for the tired
worker'. But it would hardly satisfy the members or

the public to turn the place into a sanatorium. Mr Furniss forgets, as do many others, that in the place of the few hundreds who used to attend the matches there are now as many or more thousands, for whom it is the duty of the Committee, as far as possible, to provide sitting and seeing accommodation, besides giving them facilities for obtaining refreshments. That the new Mound seats when empty are a thing of beauty no one will contend. Neither will any one, I venture to say, be able to suggest how a fine architectural effect could have been combined with the utilitarian necessities of the case. With regard to the letter of 'B.S.', I would point out that he is entirely in error in thinking that the chances of candidates put down for election were prejudiced by the recent introduction of 200 life members. As a matter of fact, no one's election was put back by a single day, whilst some had their prospect of election actually accelerated by that proceeding.

This was fully explained by Mr Alfred Lyttelton when he presided at the general meeting, at which the resolution was passed by a very large majority.

AN OLD CRICKETER

P.S. Since writing the above I have seen the letter signed 'Sigma' in your impression of today, and as regards 'the waste of club funds' in buildings to which he refers, I would observe that, seeing that the Mound stand, which seats many thousands for whom there was no accommodation before, also pays a fair interest on its cost, I fail to see where the wastefulness comes in.

Letter to *The Times*, 12 July 1900

MCC did not reply; but for the Gentlemen v. Players match on 16–18 July the Press returned to the Grand stand. Next season a new Press box was opened opposite the pavilion; in January 1906 it was demolished by a severe storm. Thenceforth the Press were accommodated in an extension to the pavilion until 1958, when they were moved to the top of the new Warner Stand – a comfortable but poorly sited location overlooking mid-off or long leg.

THE controversy surrounding Press facilities was kept alive for the next seventy years, largely through the efforts of the Press itself, which could not understand why so benign an institution should receive such scurvy treatment. Neither *The Times* nor *Wisden*, perhaps the two most influential organs of the Press, was very pleased with developments, and both, in their attempts to remain aloof and yet show their anger, came comically close to Furniss's lampoon. The parenthetical stroke by the *Times* reporter was effective, but quite outclassed for comic effect by the apparently serious complaints by the magisterial Sydney H. Pardon, whose descriptions of the location of the Press Box during the Varsity match sound very like Furniss's sarcastic talk of tool sheds and the roller horse's stable:

> Although the matter does not greatly concern the public I cannot pass over without comment the treatment of the Press representatives at Lord's on the occasion of the Oxford and Cambridge, and Eton and Harrow matches. It was an ungracious and uncalled-for act to shift them from the grand-stand to the roof of the ground bowlers' house in the corner of the ground. Happily the protest in the newspapers was so loud and unanimous that the MCC bowed before the storm, and at the Gentlemen and Players match—immediately following Eton v. Harrow—the unhappy experiment was given up. I cannot see why the MCC should be so reluctant to build a proper Press-box—commanding an end-on view of the game—as a continuation of the new Mound stand. The plans for such a box were, I understand, passed by a sub-committee nearly a twelvemonth ago, but afterwards rejected by the general committee on the ground of expense. The MCC have spent thousands of pounds during the last few years to increase the accommodation for their members and the public and they might surely do for the newspapers what has been done at Manchester, Leeds and Nottingham. At all these three grounds within a comparatively short space of time a commodious Press-box with an end-on view of the cricket has been put up. It is hardly the thing for the first cricket club in the world to thus lag behind the counties in so simple a matter.
>
> S. H. PARDON, *Wisden*, 1901

With regard to the cricket, we are able to give only a few general observations. The Marylebone Club executive have recently shown much hostility to the Press at Lord's; and yesterday the cricket reporters were exiled from the grand-stand to a position in the north-east corner of the ground, from which it was impossible to secure an accurate idea of the play. Our representative's application to the secretary of the club for a place where the game could be followed was met with a curt refusal. The Oxford eleven were seen (by the more fortunate) to splendid advantage.

The Times, on the Varsity match, 1900

By the dawn of the new age, cricket was indisputably the national game. Its technical expressions had permeated even the conversations of those with no interest in or experience of the game. There was hardly a genteel middle-class family whose members had not sat dutifully by the boundary ropes watching some young sprig doing his stuff. The great public schools and University matches at Lord's were occasions so glittering as to transcend the merely sporting and evolve into the elegantly social. There is a famous photograph showing the playing area dotted with the parents and friends of the boys taking part in the Eton v. Harrow match of 1895. The ladies stroll under white parasols, their dresses sweeping the grass. Their top-hatted escorts, white-collared and sober-suited, take their partners on their arms, or stride purposefully towards some larger cluster of the élite. The sky is clear; the air seems to glow with a friendly warmth not entirely due to the sepia tint of the photograph. Here is fashionable society showing itself off at one of the great set pieces of the Season. Lord's in the lunch-hour, and perhaps the theatre in the evening, where the ladies, who had during the day been bombarded with the arcana of the game, might find something a little more suited to their interests.

One writer who was alive to the possibilites was a well-known musical comedy lyricist with the comically pseudonymous name of W. Risqué. In 1901 Risqué, who had dabbled before with cricket songs, collaborated with the renowned Leslie Stuart to write a show for the Lyric Theatre to be called *The Silver Slipper*. Stuart, one of the most gifted popular melodists of the turn-of-the-century period, had already made his reputation with songs like 'Lily of Laguna' and 'Soldiers of the Queen', but for *The Silver Slipper* he was required to describe in music some very different settings. The plot of the show carried its characters to the planet Venus and the Art Club in Paris. The leading character, a flighty young lady who had been guilty of scratching a fellow's patent boots by playing 'footy-footy', had once or twice been part of the throng on the Lord's grass, which drew from Risqué and Stuart a song whose words indicate more clearly than a thousand sociologists how completely cricket had entered the national consciousness, and how confident its authors were that their little musical squib would be duly understood and granted the accolade of laughing applause:

'She Didn't Know Enough About the Game'

Don't you know the little lady who is nearly seventeen,
Who pretends she's very clever though she ain't.
And in trying to convince you that she's anything but green,
The result is often very quaint.

Say they took her down to Lord's to see the Varsities at play.
Though she'd never seen a cricket match before,
She would soon be talking cricket and remarking on the wicket,
And the batting and the bowling and the score.

She didn't know enough about the game.
The little lady was not to blame.
But her saying to a friend, 'Oxford's batting at this end, you know,
And Cambridge at the other', made me clearly comprehend, you know,
She didn't know enough about the game.

W. H. RISQUÉ, to music by LESLIE STUART,
from *The Silver Slipper*, at the Empire, 1 June 1901

HOWEVER, those who make jokes about cricket are on shifting ground, for they can never know when even the most slapstick device might not suddenly become sober fact. Mr Risqué's pleasantry was to have priceless if accidental repercussions a few weeks later, when the 1901 Varsity match took place. It appeared that the young lady in *The Silver Slipper* was by no means the only person guilty of not being familiar enough with the rules of the game to be capable of following the play. Evidently the umpires were in the identical predicament.

After heavy scoring the University match was drawn. When Oxford's seventh wicket fell in their second innings forty minutes were left for play. At this point F. H. Hollins was apparently caught low down in the slips by E. R. Wilson, who, being clearly under the impression that he had made the catch, threw the ball up. Hollins walked away to the pavilion. C. H. B. Marsham, the batsman at the other end, appealed, as he had a perfect right to do, but neither umpire, W. Hearn or J. Phillips, would give a decision, Hearn saying that the bowler, P. R. Johnson, had obstructed his view, and Phillips, the umpire at square leg, that W. P. Robertson, the wicket-keeper, who was standing back, had covered Wilson when he held the ball. It was a most unsatisfactory business that *both* umpires should have been unable to follow the ball. I do not like umpires who refrain from giving a decision on such grounds. It is their business to see. An umpire should not be a motionless figure standing rigidly at attention, with his eyes fixed to his front, as if on parade. A slight inclination of the head is all that is required.

SIR PELHAM WARNER, *Lord's*, 1946

THE season of 1902 saw one of the most exciting Test series in history, although most of the thrills took place away from Lord's: at Birmingham, where Rhodes and Hirst bowled out Australia for 36; at Old Trafford, where Australia scraped home by three runs; and above all at The Oval, where Gilbert Jessop hit one of the greatest centuries in the history of representative cricket. The Lord's match in contrast was ruined by rain, but before the contest was abandoned, a small curiosity was added to the history of the ground:

Lord's Test v. Australia, 1902
A curious incident occurred whilst Jones was bowling. A sparrow near the pitch had been struck and knocked over by the ball. 'Jonah' was about to resume bowling when there were cries from some of the spectators of 'Kill it! Kill it!', one of whom dashed on to the outfield presumably to carry out the deed. He was accompanied by shouts of approval from a section of the crowd; this, of course, held up play. As he neared the stricken sparrow it recovered and, to the surprise of all, flew off, much to the amusement of spectators and players alike, and a few minutes elapsed before play could be resumed.

LIONEL H. BROWN, *Victor Trumper and the 1902 Australians*, 1981

THE accidental killing of birds in cricket matches, although rare, was by no means unique; the weekly magazine *Cricket* reported two instances of this type of accident in first-class cricket during the 1885 season alone. It also reported a much rarer instance of animal fatality the same year. During a cricket practice at Loretto School, a batsman in the nets drove a ball hard along the ground. At the point where the net ended and the turf began was a hole, from which emerged a large rat at precisely the moment when the ball arrived.

The rat was killed instantly. In reporting this incident, the editor of the magazine recalled that in 1866, when Middlesex was playing its home matches at Islington, they acted as hosts to the Nottinghamshire club. In the second innings Tom Hearne, 'just as he was about to bowl in the second innings, had a shot at a pigeon flying overhead and brought it down'.

Here was a skill which might have been utilised by those entrepreneurs forever attempting to make cricket 'more interesting'. In Punch, issue dated 14 August 1901, there appeared a Lord's fantasy dreamed up by a world-famous writer intimately familiar with the ground in all its aspects:

Cricket Prospects for 1902

'First-class cricket, properly organised and run as an attractive variety show, would be a fine paying concern.'

AN AMERICAN FINANCIER TO AN INTERVIEWER

The Anglo-American 'Willow-and-Leather' Syndicate (President: Mr Pierpont Morgan; capital, ten million dollars) beg to intimate that their season will open at Lord's on the first of April. They have obtained an exclusive lease of this well-known ground, and their list of star artists fairly licks creation.

Turnstiles open at 7 a.m. No free passes. One continuous round of amusement from 9 a.m. to 6 p.m. Program for each day of the opening week:

9 a.m.—Prince Ranji and Lord Hawke will take center. These aristocratic willow-wielders will then demonstrate on slow half-volleys, putting on 200 runs in the hour. Positively no disappointment. However often they are bowled or caught, they will continue to whack the sphere untill the hour be expired. The Prince and the Peer every morning from nine to ten!

10–11—Grand exhibition of bowling and fielding by the United Yorkshire troupe. (Specially and exclusively engaged.) Rhodes, Haigh and Hirst will perform the celebrated Hat Trick. There are no spots on the Yorkshire bowlers!

11–11.30—Comic interlude, entitled 'No-Ball; or, The Doubtful Deliverer and the Umbraged Umpire'. Messrs Mold and James Philips have been booked at fabulous cost to give this screamingly-funny performance each day of the opening week.

11.30–12.30—Charles B. Fry will lecture on 'The Use and Abuse of the Leg-Glance'. The glory of C.B. as the champion cricketing word-spinner needs no polish to increase its glitter. Wise words from a brave batsman daily at 11.30! (Schools admitted to this turn at reduced fees.)

12.30–2.0—The Champion Midgets! Splendid show by Messrs Abel and Quaiffe. Skill versus size. The little wonders will smack the pilule to the boundary every time. Followed by Abel's celebrated turn: 'How I walk back to the Pavilion.' Howls of delighted applause!

From 2 to 3—The entire troupe will be fed in the pavilion, and the public will be admitted to view the fascinating scene. But the practice of offering the performers buns and lumps of sugar is very dangerous and cannot be permitted.

At 3 precisely—Dr W. G. Grace will lead the way into the field, and will give his world-renowned performance, including the Deep-Square-Leg Trick, the Scratching-the-ground-with-a-Bail Trick, etc., etc. At the conclusion of his turn he will be umpired out 'lbw' to a leg-break, and will then speak a stirring monologue. (Copyright strictly reserved.)

4–5—The Oxford and Cambridge elevens will play tip-and-run. The scene on the ground will be a careful reproduction of the famous 'Varsity match. Beauty and brightness will be seated on real drags: Peers (warranted hall-marked). Cabinet Ministers and Judges will watch the proceedings from the pavilion. Real triple-distilled essence of British Aristocracy will pervade this turn. Huge attraction for visitors from the States.

5–6—America *versus* England. Magnificent International Match. America will be represented by (among others) Fry, Hayward, Jessop, Palairet, Hearne, etc. (all of whom conclusively can show American descent; Their pedigrees have been made specially for the Syndicate, and are unquestionably genuine). England will number among its foremost champions Messrs Timson, Snooks, Stubbs, etc., of the Lower Pottlebury Cricket Club. America will win! The Supremacy of the Eagle over the Decrepit Lion will be established daily! Unique scene!

The whole of the troupe will join in singing 'The Star-Spangled Banner' (solo verses by S. M. J. Woods, G. J. V. Weigall and S. M. Crosfield), at the conclusion of which stumps will be drawn for the day.

Punch, 14 August 1901

SIR Arthur Conan Doyle was here playing the fool, but there were occasions when his attempts to be serious were much funnier. It was Doyle who suggested to the MCC that left-handedness should be outlawed in cricket, it hardly being required to add that Sir Arthur himself batted and bowled right-handed. It says much for the sanity of the Committee that it rejected his idiotic proposal and that nothing more was ever heard of it. But Doyle, as the creator of Holmes and Watson, remained one of the nation's most popular tourist attractions; there was at least one colonial visitor whose introduction to Lord's was rendered memorable by the proximity of the sworn enemy of left-handedness.

To young colonial cricketers it was not only distances which lent Lord's an enchantment unmatched. So much history had taken place on the ground, so many reputations made, so many decisions taken, so many legends born, that, to the aspirant out on the rim of empire, it seemed that no career was quite consummated without an appearance at St John's Wood. Among those who were imbued with this ambition to get to Lord's was Daniel Reese (1879–1953), one of the pioneers of New Zealand cricket. Reese made his first-class debut for Canterbury in 1895, after which his progress was rapid. Three years later he was part of the first-ever New Zealand touring side, which visited Australia, and from 1907 to 1921 he captained Canterbury and New Zealand. The best left-handed batsmen of emergent New Zealand cricket, he later enjoyed a distinguished career as businessman and administrator. In 1903 he made his first trip to London, where he played four matches for W. G. Grace's London County eleven. In one of them, against the MCC, he finally achieved his ambition, not only stepping on to the Lord's turf but, in the process, reaching within one pace of the world's first consulting detective. Not surprisingly, the experience stayed with him for the rest of his life, and is described in his autobiography, *Was It All Cricket?*

My first big match for London County was against MCC at Lord's. It was to prove, perhaps, the most remarkable match I have ever played in. Bad weather from the previous week continued, and on the first day of the match there was a drizzling rain, and no one thought of going to the ground. Tuesday was again wet, but on Wednesday there was brilliant sunshine. When my cab pulled up at the entrance gate at Lord's, who should arrive at the same time, from the opposite direction, but W. G. Grace. When he alighted from his hansom and saw me, he gave a hearty greeting and said, 'Come along with me, Reese.' Perhaps he appreciated the feelings that a youngster from so far afield would experience on entering the famous ground for the first time. At any rate, we were soon through the gates, and there met Sir F. E. Lacey wearing his I Zingari blazer and flannels, for he had been having a knock at the nets. 'Here Lacey, meet young Reese from New Zealand.' After a pleasant welcome from the MCC secretary we moved on, but had not gone many yards before W. G. called out, 'Here Doyle, meet a young New Zealander.' It was none other than the famous Conan Doyle. In this way I was fairly carried into the precincts of the home of the MCC...

Lord's is the only cricket ground where I had the experience of being able to have a hot plunge-bath after a hard day in the field. With a steward in attendance, the service was typical of that of an ocean liner, where bathroom attendants are always on hand.

DANIEL REESE, *Was It All Cricket?*, 1948

A LORD'S debut of a very different kind was experienced by Elias 'Patsy' Hendren (1889–1962), one of the outstanding international batsmen of his day. Maker of 57,610 runs and 170 centuries, including seven for England, Hendren was as much loved for his impish humour as for his technique. In 1907 he was selected by Middlesex for his first county match, against Lancashire, and whatever thoughts may have gone through his mind in the hours preceding the match, he could never have suspected that his fortunes, and those of the match, would take so bizarre a turn:

My first county match was one in which I did not get an innings. That was in 1907 against Lancashire at Lord's, the game being abandoned before lunch on the second day. There were naturally unusual circumstances. After heavy rain, a drizzle set in, but the crowd – allowed, as they were then, on the playing area – gathered in front of the pavilion and clamoured for cricket. In the middle of all the rumpus, somebody got on to the pitch itself and, accidentally or not, stuck the ferrule of an umbrella into the turf. When this was discovered by Mr Archie MacLaren, the Lancashire captain, he refused to play, even if a fresh wicket were cut out. So there was nothing for it but to pack up and go home.

P. HENDREN, 'Reflections', in *Wisden*, 1938

Wisden went into more detail. In recording the statistics of the play, Lancashire 57 for one wicket, the Almanack described the game as 'an altogether unfortunate affair', and although not saying in so many words that the visiting captain had behaved intolerably, implied as much with its mild-mannered insistence that after all the pitch appeared to have survived its ordeal virtually intact:

> ... So much rain fell during the early hours of Monday that no cricket could be attempted until after lunch. Later on there came a delay of seventy minutes owing to bad light and at five o'clock further rain put an end to play. Spooner turning out for the first time during the season and Worsley resuming his place, Lancashire had their best side for the occasion. MacLaren and Spooner put on 26 for the first wicket and afterwards the former and Tyldesley added 31 without further loss, the Lancashire captain playing particularly well. That evening the pitch was practically under water and, with a wet night, the prospects of play next day were always remote. Unhappily, there came neither sun nor wind to improve the condition of the ground. The spectators, numbering about 600, waited patiently until half-past three, but then began to clamour for the game to be resumed, demonstrating two or three times in front of the pavilion. After several visits to the wicket, the umpires made a final inspection at a quarter to five and, finding the ground still unplayable, pulled up the stumps. Thereupon, some section of the spectators walked right across the pitch and inflicted some damage, noticeably at one end. The crowd having dispersed, a prolonged discussion ensued between the captains and some of their players and the umpires, and eventually MacLaren handed the following statement to the Press: 'Owing to the pitch having been deliberately torn up by the public, I, as captain of the Lancashire eleven, cannot see my way to continue the game, the groundsman bearing me out that the wicket could not again be put right—A. C. MacLaren'. The match was accordingly abandoned. Rolled next morning for the regulation ten minutes, the pitch showed little trace of the treatment to which it had been subjected.
>
> *Wisden*, 1908

The incident was sadly typical of MacLaren, who conducted his entire career as though he were conducting a cavalry charge against the forces of darkness, when in fact he never did much more than tilt against windmills. His behaviour at Hendren's first match was so reprehensible that *Wisden* could not resist a second swipe at him. In the Almanack's summary of the 1907 Middlesex season, there is appended a more detailed description of the condition of the pitch which according to MacLaren had been 'torn up'.

> One incident during the season gave rise to a great deal of discussion and not a little ill-feeling. We refer, of course, to the abandonment on the 23rd of July of the match with Lancashire. The details of this most unfortunate affair will be fresh in the memory of everyone who follows cricket at all closely. A lot of rain fell on the first day and in

such time as was available Lancashire scored 57 for one wicket. At the ordinary time for resuming the following morning play was quite out of the question, and as events turned out it would have been much better if the umpires, who from time to time inspected the pitch, had early in the day declared cricket impracticable. As it was, the people who had paid for admission became very impatient at the long delay, and after stumps had at last been pulled up some of them went so far as to trample on the wicket. A lengthy consultation and discussion by the captains followed, and after six o'clock MacLaren handed the following official statement to the Press:

Owing to the pitch having been deliberately torn up by the public, I, as captain of the Lancashire eleven, cannot see my way to continue the game, the groundman bearing me out that the wicket could not again be put right.

A. C. MacLaren.

Opinion was very much divided as to the action MacLaren took, a letter of indignant protest being addressed to *The Field* by Mr R. D. Walker, the Middlesex president. The actual damage to the pitch did not, as it was stated, amount to more than one rather deep heel mark.

Wisden, 1908

MacLaren's petulance may have been typical of the misconduct which occasionally crept into the first-class cricket of the period, even at Lord's, but no breath of oafishness was allowed to enter the coeval world of the fictitious Lord's, which by now was beginning to feature regularly in the schoolboy fiction and some light novels of the period. Because these imaginary set pieces were invariably about public schoolboys up at Lord's for 'the Big Match', whatever it might happen to be, the ethics displayed were always of a loftiness approaching the religious, with elderly spectators conducting themselves like lovable sentimentalists who have stumbled upon the gate back into boyhood. Among those Edwardian novelists who specialised in sporting set pieces was Ernest Raymond, whose best-selling novel about the gallantry of public schoolboys at Gallipoli, *Tell England*, includes more than one sporting climax. One of his better-known works referred to Lord's, or at least to St John's Wood, in its title, *To the Wood No More*, and is revealing for the way in which it uses cricket for two extra-sporting purposes, to smooth the course of true love, and to express, however indirectly, respectable religious emotions. In the course of his match description, Raymond introduces among others, God, Jesus Christ and Lucifer.

However, as all three of those characters are dateless, Raymond has to use other names in order to locate his story in a specific season. All the actresses he names were Edwardian pin-up favourites. Their postcards were indeed a familiar sight on the walls of many an idolatrous young gentleman, and among those who, like Raymond's hero, were proud of possessing them, were Ivor Brown, one-time editor of *The Observer*, who collected Misses Dare and Studholme, Cecil Beaton, who recalled Miss Ray as 'a high-kicker with a squeaky voice', and Gertie Millar as a slender girl who became transmuted by success into a rather too spherical Countess of Dudley. The composer Vivian Ellis remembered Miss Ray as one 'who made a pretty penny from her postcards', and added, 'I have one of her masticating a piece of mistletoe.' It hardly needs to be said that none of the young ladies collected by Raymond's hero ever revealed as much of themselves as Andromeda, a fact which goes some way towards explaining the enduring popularity of Ancient Greek among public schoolboys of the period.

In terms of cricketing reference Raymond's time-scale is a shade fuzzy. In nominating Gregor MacGregor as the Middlesex captain, he is confining his period to the seasons 1899–1907. The Australian all-rounder Frank Tarrant, however, did not make his Middlesex debut till 1905, and we have already seen how Hendren made his debut for the county two seasons later. So the only possible summer in which Raymond's ingredients could have been flung into the same stew would seem to be 1907. But, from 1900 to 1912, the Gloucestershire captain was Gilbert Jessop. Sticklers for reality may care to know that in the 1907 match between Middlesex and Gloucestershire, played at Lord's on 23 and 24 May, Gloucestershire were indeed skittled by the home side, but it was Tarrant, with thirteen wickets for 87 runs, who did the damage. From these facts we can surmise that the following account is fictitious; from these facts, and also from the discovery that the poor heroine had, of all embarrassments, a windy bosom:

To the Wood No More

Now it was Wednesday, but the rain was falling, falling, upon the gardens of the wood and upon the great fields of Lord's within its high walls. It was falling, not violently, but steadfastly, so that the grass of croquet lawns looked sodden and sad, and the geraniums drooped in their window-boxes, the hollyhock stooped over the garden beds, and the limes hung their leaves heavily, drippingly, above the garden walls.

Two people watched from their windows that tireless rain of a Wednesday long ago. Susannah went often to her window and looked out at the wet grass, the stable cloud-blanket, and the grey spines of rain slanting across the darkness in the trees. She looked and looked, and found no place of comfort anywhere. 'Oh, but it mustn't rain tomorrow,' she said, with a hand at the curtains and a foot beating anxiously. 'O God, make it stop. It can't go on like this for ever. But perhaps it's a good thing that it should rain today, because it'll rain itself out and be gloriously fine tomorrow.'

Tom stood likewise at a window and stared at the rain. It was the window of his study. The little white Gothic house in Acacia Road, with its steep gable and battlements, held only Tom, his father, and their housekeeper, so Tom was able to have a sitting-room of his own on the top floor and call it his study. Here were his books and his pictures; and the pictures were more revealing than the books, which were not many. One was of Andromeda chained to her rock, and it hung there less because he was interested in the legend of Perseus and Andromeda, or because he took an aesthetic delight in the artist's draughtsmanship, than because the lovely figure of Andromeda wore nothing at all but her chains. Other pictures were of school and college groups in which Tom figured: the First Eleven at Clifton, the Freshmen's Team at Cambridge, and the Oxford and Cambridge Elevens of last year seated together before the pavilion at Lord's. On his writing desk stood a picture of his father in uniform and, opposite it, one of his dead mother in a wide picture-hat and bell-bottomed skirt. Along his mantelpiece stood a row of picture postcards, glossy portraits at twopence apiece of actresses who had delighted his eye. Here were Marie Studhome, Mabel Love, Gabrielle Ray, Phyllis Dare, and Gertie Millar – of Gertie Millar three; as well there might be, of so delicious a trifle.

Till yesterday all of these, with their smiling loveliness, had given him moments of pleasure when he wearied of reading, and glanced their way, but now Susannah had bereft them of power. They smiled at him as he stood by the window, all showing regular and radiant teeth, and some with their heads archly inclined, but he didn't turn once to look at them. The big new meerschaum pipe, which he was striving by unremitted smoking to colour a deep chestnut brown, meant more to him than they.

He, like Susannah, stared at the changeless sky. 'Oh, if only it would break up and change to bright sunlight. Then we should have a drying wicket; a beautiful treacherous wicket; a sticky-dog wicket; the perfect wicket for spin bowlers like Hearne and Tarrant and for fast bowlers like Tom Budlier.' He dreamed of a triumph on that bowler's wicket tomorrow, and of the tributes that would be paid him in the next day's papers. 'Mr T.J. Budlier and Hearne were almost unplayable, especially the former.' 'Mr Budlier took five wickets for twenty-one runs ...' 'took seven wickets for thirty-three ...' 'took all ten wickets. Tarrant also bowled well.' 'Mr T.J. Budlier is certainly a great acquisition to Middlesex.' 'On returning to the pavilion he received an ovation.' Towards evening the clouds above the rain began to whiten and brighten; they cracked and drew apart, and the travelling sun appeared in the rifts. In the morning London awoke to a sky empty of all but a jovial sun that was plainly out to make a day of it; and Tom, staring in his pyjamas at the universal brightness, exclaimed, 'My God! God is on my side. O God, send them in first. Of Thy goodness and mercy send the Gloucester lads in to bat first and let me bowl them out.'

Not that his pleasure was undiluted. Nay, diluted is the word for it. His nervousness, as the clock ticked round from nine to ten, debilitated the pleasure by diluting and melting it. His heart seemed to vary its beating with a bubbling, and his stomach to desire nothing but emptiness, so that it drove him more than once to the privy. His speech tripped over his words as he talked with his father, and his breathing stood still at certain thoughts. He didn't know, as he wandered to a window, whether he envied the people who were walking towards unpublic occupations or pitied them; he wasn't sure that he didn't want the rain to return in power and cancel the match. A crowd of twenty thousand seated round the cricket field, with Susannah among them!

He weighed the possibility of feigning sickness.

But he set his lips and closed a fist. And the fist trembled with resolve. 'I'm not going to fail. I'm going to bowl as never before. With everything I've got. O God, send them in first. This is the test of my life. I must come through it.' It seemed to him that he would be bowling not only at the Gloucester wickets but at the high barrier of disgrace between him and Susannah. Every wicket he shattered would help to smash that barrier down. And after this triumph today he would set about improving his prospects – and his character – so as to be more worthy of Susannah. He was not sure how he was going to begin this general improvement, but that misty question could wait: the immediate business, between now and sunset, was to bowl as never before in his life.

Now it was near the hour, and Albany and Susannah were in Grove End Road, approaching the gates of Lord's. They were walking fast, not because they were late, but because Albany was charged, like a super-heated locomotive, with enthusiasm and information. Susannah was dressed for the warm day in a frock of white muslin and a large flowered hat and carried her lace-fringed parasol. Her father had honoured the sun, and their purpose beneath the sun, with his lightest grey suit and a panama hat. In his enthusiasm he was saying, 'You'll see Plum Warner, and B. J. Bosanquet, who really invented the googly ball, and Warman, who's probably the fastest bowler alive – unless our Tom's as fast. You'll see some of the greatest cricketers of the day.' Of himself he was saying, with modesty, that he was never a very good batsman, only a hitter, but he gave her to understand that he'd been an uncommonly big hitter in his day. 'Had the height and reach, you see. And the strength.' He told her of some of his biggest hits. At one point there was a halt on the pavement while he showed her with his walking-stick what was meant by an off-drive, a cut, and a hit to leg. And after that demonstration, walking on, he made some doughty off-drives with the stick while he expatiated on the art, the poetry, the skills of the game. No one, he said, could really appreciate it who was not its scholar, whose eyes were not trained – just as a musical ear was trained – to detect every nuance and variation and grace-note in a supremely difficult art form. It needed trained discrimination, he said. It was beyond the understanding of Americans, he said. Susannah, though giving some response to his plan, for he was speaking with power, was thinking rather of a single performer than of these subtle nuances. Would they see Tom bowl? she asked; and her father, the expert, answered, 'I think we may probably see him both bowl and bat, since it'll be a bowler's wicket today, and one side'll be bundled out and the other side have to go in and bat before the day's over.'

Now they were at the main gate, with the crowds streaming in beside them, and here was Tom waiting for them – Tom in his white flannels and a blazer of blue and yellow stripes.

'Ah, I see you wear a Quidnunc's blazer,' said the expert. 'That's because he's a Cambridge Blue, Susannah. They don't award that to everybody.'

'No, no ... Yes ... c-come along,' Tom stuttered. 'I'm going to put you with my f-father.'

'Aren't you frightfully nervous?' asked Susannah. 'With this shocking crowd?'

'Oh, n-no. I've done this before. Before bigger crowds.' But then he recalled his vows of improvement and determined to be done with this lying. 'Yes, though – perhaps, I am – a bit. Yes, a bib-bit.'

And Susannah, seeing that his hands were trembling, said to herself, 'Oh, the poor darling!' and to God, 'O God, help him'; and then to him, for his comfort, 'I should be nearly dead. As it is, I'm nervous for you. It's rather awful when you've got someone of your own playing.'

'Of your own!' laughed her father. 'She's adopted you quickly, Tom.'

'Oh, you know what I mean,' objected Susannah, a blush flooding up under her large hat.

He took them to the seats of the privileged in the Members' enclosure beyond the pavilion, and sat them next to his father and Commander Ludlow, then with a nervous smile left them. Susannah was now between her father and the little old Colonel Budlier, who sat there with his plump hands clasped over the crook of his old ash cane, and his kind gentle smile on his round face. From the seat beyond him Commander Ludlow jerked a thumb at the smile, scanned it through his monocle, and said, 'The Colonel's trying to pretend he's not sick with pride about his boy. He's pretending it's all in the day's work to have a boy playing for his county. I'm busy assuring him there can't be anything wrong with a boy who plays cricket like Tom, because cricket develops all that's best in them. Isn't that so, Grahame?'

'I quite agree,' said Albany, who'd played cricket in his day.

The Colonel only smiled. Colonel Budlier accepted all such banter with a smile and little more, because he had no opinion of his own wit and was convinced that most men were cleverer than he. And because of this simplicity in the Colonel, Albany always felt at ease with him. Here was a man, better no doubt than he, but naïver, simpler, one whose intellectual superior he undoubtedly was.

Bait was not of the company. Albany had asked him if he was coming, but he had pish'd and pshaw'd about 'that shocking cult down the road and its enervating influence on its thousands of idle addicts'; he had expressed his astonishment that Albany could sit impounded in one of those pens throughout a whole day, and had reminded him that the ground at Lord's had once been a dairy farm with pigsties all round and that, in his view, it was not much better now; and finally he had quoted with approval a statute of Edward IV, which enacted that anyone allowing this unseemly game, this *ludus inhonestus*, to be played on his premises would be liable to three years' imprisonment, and anyone actually playing it to two years' imprisonment, a ten-pounds fine, and the destruction of his implements.

Susannah, her bosom a vessel compact of eager anticipation and windy anxiety, gazed at the huge arena before them, a brilliant green under the blazing eye of the sun. It was like a huge green salver bounded by a white rail. Behind the white rail the people were crowding on to the benches or on to the tiers of the tall white stands. Pigeons waddled and sparrows hopped about the borders of the trim turf, indifferent to the incoming multitudes and the forthcoming game, and interested only in the seeds to be found among the grass. On a soft breeze from the south-east came the scent of mown wet grass and the sounds of bats-upon-balls in the Nursery nets. From further still, from beyond the high curtain walls, came the voices of newsboys at the gates, shouting their midday sporting editions and the low murmur and purring of London's traffic on the highways and at the crossroads.

At her side, Albany, inspired by the scene, was pointing out to her what he called 'the immemorial features of an English cricket ground in summer'; the fathers with their small schoolboy sons; the unfathered urchins with pink, outstanding ears and their lunches in satchels prepared by devoted but uncricketing mothers; the parsons, old and young, sprinkled all over the stands because they alone could snatch a whole day off from their week-day labours; and the old grey men of all classes who'd done for ever with week-day labour and could sit smoking the hours away or dozing in a quiet spell or telling strangers at their sides of feats they had witnessed in the past.

Albany himself was doing exactly this. A cigar in his mouth, he was speaking with the Colonel of the immortals he'd seen in his youth; of Alfred Shaw and the Honourable Ivo Bligh and Alfred Lyttelton and A. G. Steel; of Spofforth, the demon bowler, and Blackham, the stumper who took the demon's deliveries as if they were tennis balls; of Tom Richardson, 'the greatest fast bowler England ever produced', and of a team of giants he had watched here at Lord's just twenty years ago, at the Lord's Centenary Match.

'Some of these are only men of legend now,' he said to Susannah, who was listening, for he was in lyrical mood. 'Shaw died the other day. The hungry generations tread them down. Yes, they were giants, but who knows, we may be looking at giants today who will be legendary heroes in fifty years' time.'

Oh, yes, he was in lyrical mood. He directed Susannah's eyes to the cropped and shining turf and said it was the most sacred grass in the world and had been so for a hundred years; he turned her eyes towards the crimson and ochre pavilion and assured her that, as the headquarters of cricket all over the world, it was to this most noble religion as the Vatican to the Universal Church; he spoke of the 'Noblemen and Gentlemen of the Marylebone Cricket Club', long dead now, who'd sat in that pavilion; and as a fitting coda to these dithyrambs, he concluded cheerfully, 'One day we too shall be ghosts.'

The pavilion bell. Three double chimes at noonday, as if it were a monks' bell ringing for Sext. It brought all wanderers back to their seats; it speeded the drinkers at the Tavern or pavilion bars, it hurried the feet of those who had only just threaded the turnstiles. Five minutes, and the game would begin. Susannah's heart raced.

Here came the umpires, loitering out of the players' pavilion, one of them tossing the little red ball, the sacred focus of it all, the little red apple of discord, from right hand to left and back again. And now, which captain will lead his men on to the field, MacGregor of Middlesex or Newell of Gloucester? Ah, it is MacGregor who is leading out his gentlemen amateurs, Warner, Bosanquet, Douglas and Littlejohn – and, last of them all, Tom Budlier. Tom comes shyly, for he is the youngest, the 'new boy' in this procession of celebrities. Warner and Bosanquet halt, wait, and say a few words to him, maybe for his encouragement; and Susannah can feel, across a hundred yards of grass, that Tom is flattered that the great men deign to speak with him. He is pale and palpably nervous; and she is at prayer. Now come the professionals from their humbler pavilion: Tarrant and Hearne and Trott and Hendren. A brief minute, and Gloucester's two opening batsmen appear. One goes to the popping crease at the pavilion end and takes his guard. MacGregor tosses the ball to Trott.

'We shan't see our Tom yet,' says Albany, the expert, to Susannah. 'They'll put on their spin bowlers first. You'll see. Hearne'll follow Trott, and if these two don't come off, they'll try out their new fast bowler, Mr Tom Budlier.'

Susannah is almost glad they are not going to ask Tom to bowl.

The first ball. And the first over. And the second over. Slow scoring because each batsman is poking cautiously at the spinning ball or leaving it to dance alone. Over after over with only singles hit, or stolen, here and there. Then a 'maiden over', and another to follow it.

'Why is it called a "maiden" if no one scores?' asked Susannah of her father.

'A maiden?' He is embarrassed, not liking to speak to a young daughter of a virgo intacta, a virgin unscored off. So he laughs and says, 'Perhaps it's a corruption of "made none". Eh, Ludlow?'

But look: a pause while MacGregor changes the bowling. He is tossing the ball from palm to palm. What now? Will he try out his fast bowler? Will he throw the ball to Tom? He does, and Susannah's heart is a trembling ball of solicitude, panic and hope.

'What did I tell you?' boasts Albany.

The generous crowd applauds this choice of Tom. He is young, new, full of promise, and popular with them because of some ferocious, profitable, and amusing bowling-spells last year. Tom and his captain set a new field: three slips and a gully and the stumper well back from the wicket.

'Three slips and a gully! Whoosh!' exclaims the expert. 'He's going to bowl fast.'

'And a silly mid-off and a silly mid-on,' adds Ludlow, another expert. 'He's going to bump 'em.'

Now Tom takes many, very many, strides from the bowling crease; he strides, it seems, fully quarter of the way to the boundary; and the crowd laughs because the length of Tom's run up to the wicket promises an attack packed with venom and a ball like a bullet. He scratches the grass with his boot to mark his starting place and swings his arm round and round to loosen it up. He is ready, and a silence awaits his performance – a silence in which Susannah accelerates her prayer, in some hope that God is watching the game from His pavilion in the sky. Tom begins his run, and it is indeed an extraordinary and villainous affair. He pounds towards the wicket in a menacing, head-first crouch as low as his strides are long, as if his final aim were to butt the batsman in the stomach instead of bowling a ball at him. His strides quicken as he nears the crease; a yard this side of it he leaps from off the face of the world and hurls himself and his arm forward: the ball shoots from his hand as if yonder batsman were an offence to all honest men and it would be a public service to assassinate him.

'Wide,' signals the umpire. And there is a roar of laughter. Tom's first ball is a disaster, and Susannah's heart dies.

'He's nervous,' says Albany.

Colonel Budlier's hands still rest upon his stick, but his gentle, happy smile has diminished; so Susannah prays for him too.

'Never mind,' Ludlow encourages him. 'He's not in form yet. Give the boy time. Give him time.'

Tom, a little shamed, has gone back to his starting place. He swings again his guilty arm to teach it to behave better. And now his low crouching, menacing run seems yet more vicious than before, as if he must justify himself after that first failure. Never before, surely, such a leap from the spurned earth; such a fling of his arm; would he send the arm as well as the ball at the batsman?

A full toss. The batsman slams it to the boundary. A roar of scornful laughter for the bowler; a roll of applause for the batsman. It is the first boundary of the match. And it was hit off our Tom.

'Oh, my God!' says Ludlow. And he makes a joke which pleases him all the more because it surprises him with its felicity. 'Poor Tom Bowling! Now he's gone aloft.'

'Never mind, Colonel,' says Albany. 'He hasn't really begun yet.'

'Why not let the umpire bowl instead?' calls a wag in the crowd.

But Tom is back at his base. An object of public laughter just now, he flings back his tumbled hair, palms the remainder of it away with his sweating hand, wipes his brow with his bare forearm, and rubs the ball dry on his shirt. Then he braces back his shoulders and begins a yet more malicious run.

A good ball this. The batsman lifts his bat, but decides to leave it alone.

'Ah, better!' says Ludlow. And the Colonel smiles gently again.

All the next three balls are good – untouchable – and Susannah, who has been in a deplorable state, breathes rather more easily – but not much more.

Now it is Hearne who bowls, and three runs are taken off him this over – three singles. Tom again. And Susannah at prayer again. Perhaps the prayer is answered; perhaps power from on high descends upon Tom, for the power he now puts into each ball is surely analogous with the energy which the Almighty put into the great ball of the world when He sent it spinning. Or when he sent Lucifer spinning. The ball strikes the earth and leaps off it, spurning it.

'Jesus Christ!' says Ludlow, forgetting Susannah's presence and that the Colonel's a sidesman. 'He's getting it up to an awkward height. Something'll happen soon.'

'An ugly rise that,' says the voice of an unknown behind Susannah. 'Face-high bouncers these. Something'll happen soon.'

What happened, however, was not caused by the ball's rising but its shooting. It shot and hit the batsman above the knee, so that he danced in pain. And skipped and hopped and doubtless blasphemed. He walked round and round, and round and round, lifting up his knee and sinking it, and stooping and rubbing it. And Susannah, while pitying the dancer, was guilty of a base hope that he would now be completely demoralised and very willingly yield his wicket to Tom's next ball. This wish was certainly not 'cricket', but if Tom could get a wicket it would encourage him.

The man did not, however, do this. He played Tom's last two as if they were incandescent cannon balls and, his ordeal over, began to dance again.

No wickets had fallen as yet, nor did one fall in Hearne's next over.

And Tom has the ball again. His first delivery whips past batsman and stumper both, and spins to the boundary for four byes. 'No fault of the bowler, that,' says the wiseacres. 'There was a devil in that ball. No one knew anything about it. An inch straighter and it'd have spreadeagled his wicket.'

The crowd waits in silence. Budlier is bowling well. The batsman plays the next ball respectfully. The third ball is a little short: the batsman plays forward to it, and – snick! – it's in the wicket-keeper's hands. '*How-zat?*' The shout can be heard in Baker Street, a mile away. 'How's that, umpire?'

The umpire's index finger points heavenward like the finger of the Baptist in Leonardo's picture. Small boys yell 'Got him! Got him!' The batsman walks homeward, using his bat like a walking-stick. And here comes his successor, with his bat under his arm, while he draws on his batting gloves.

He takes his guard. Tom takes the ball; he takes his long, striding, pounding run; the ball shoots on to the newcomer's pads – one hears the impact – and from the field ringside, from old men's voices and shrill boys' voices, comes the bellowed inquiry, 'HOW-ZAT?' I say it was a shout that could be heard in Gloucestershire. 'HOW WER ZAT?'

The umpire's finger points once more to the Throne of Forgiveness. The batsman returns the way he came. Small boys dance.

Two wickets in two balls. Will he get his third wicket with his next ball? Will he do the hat-trick? Twenty thousand people are loving Tom Budlier like their son. Their silent desire for his success is every whit as great as that of the Colonel, his father, behind that gentle smile. Even the ranks of Gloucestershire aren't quite sure that they don't hope he'll do it.

But he does not; the batsman plays his next ball, and a sigh of disappointment rings the field. Nor does his sixth and last ball trouble the batsman. Still, two wickets and no runs in six balls makes a fine over, and twenty thousand people, including the supporters of Gloucestershire, applaud it. So far Budlier has taken two wickets for fourteen runs.

Now Bosanquet, from the far end, is bowling his celebrated googlies, and they divert the crowd, breaking this way and that way and both ways, while the batsman stares at them, bewildered, and wondering if he is awake or sober. 'The wicket's certainly taking spin,' says the expert. 'But there's always lift and fire in a Lord's pitch.' Bosanquet, however, gets no wicket and tosses the ball back to Tom.

Some of the spectators (especially the small boys), remembering Tom's last fine over, and much liking his vehement charge and attack, give him a mutter of applause.

To their delight he looses the same cannonade, hurling his whole body after the ball so that you would think that each delivery must shoot his arm out of its socket and tear asunder the muscles of his back. But apparently it leaves him unwrecked, for he follows up each delivery in hope of a catch and, when within reach, stops the hardest ball. 'He's a wonderful fielder to his own bowling,' says the expert. Five such balls he sends down; no run is taken off them; the sixth smashes the batsman's wicket into its constituent parts. Over; and Tom, brushing his forelock off his brow with his wet forearm, resumes his cap from the umpire's hand as if he is not hearing the cheers and prolonged applause.

The wicket-keeper, before crossing to the other end, hands his cap to the umpire, as if Tom's bowling has made him sweat, and his head is seen to be bald. 'Don't wonder,' says Ludlow, 'with Tom bowling like this. He'll be white before the end of the day.'

Tom's analysis is now three wickets for 14.

And no one else has yet taken a wicket.

Good enough; but in the course of Bosanquet's next over there comes that grey disappointment which treads on the heels of success and is doubtless designed by the gods to teach a man that perfection unsullied is not to be had in this world.

Tom is fielding at extra-cover, and perhaps he is dreaming of those three sweet wickets, remembering that last ball which burst the wicket like a bomb, thinking that Susannah saw that ball and heard the cheers, but – a catch is slashed towards him off an impish Bosanquet ball; it comes into his hands before he is out of his dreams; he fumbles and drops it. The groans all round the field, twenty thousand groans, make a sound as bitter as the cheers were sweet. He hears his name from every point of the compass: 'That was Budlier ... Budlier ... Tom Budlier, and it was a dolly catch.' His sickness in this moment is not worse than Susannah's on her seat far away.

All right! Passionately he locks his lips together and vows to make amends in the next over – much as (though he has forgotten this) he resolved upon amendment after his disgrace at Cambridge.

But lest his dreams should soar too high on the wings of pride, the gods continue their chastening: they grant sight at last to the Gloucestershire batsmen so that they see his fastest balls as large as lazily drifting balloons and slam them with the best of their bats, driving, cutting, and pulling them. They score boundaries. His rich and glowing analysis begins to look like watered wine.

'They're hitting him about now,' said Ludlow. 'He's tiring.'

'Yes, he'll come off,' agrees the Colonel, since it is right to speak modestly of one's son.

'Oh no!' pleads Susannah.

And even as she begs of the distant captain to let Tom go on for a little longer, the cry goes up from Tom's very voice, a young excited voice, 'Got him!' With a run forward, a low lunge of his right arm, he has caught the driven ball five inches from the ground. Caught and bowled Budlier. And what a catch! Amends. Budlier four for 32.

And no one else has taken a wicket yet.

'He'll last till lunch-time now,' said Ludlow. 'Don't you worry, Susannah. No one's going to take him off while he's getting wickets like this.'

Bosanquet gets his first wicket before lunch, and the gods, deciding that they have chastened Tom sufficiently, suffer him to creep a little nearer the forbidden perfection. With the last ball of the last over before lunch (a pretty moment to do it in) he shatters a wicket and turns to take his cap from the umpire, as if he is now free to rest and take food.

The team comes towards the pavilion, and all the applause is for Tom. The Noblemen and Gentlemen in the pavilion stand up to clap him. At first he pretends not to realise that it's all for him, but since this deceit cannot be maintained, for they are saying 'Bravo, Budlier', and 'Good show, Tom', he touches his cap and runs up the step into the shelter of the dressing-room.

Soon, in his blue and yellow blazer, he has come to talk with his father and guests. 'I hope you're not bored,' he says to Susannah.

'Bored!' she answered. 'Bored!'

'Well done, my boy,' says the gentle old Colonel. 'You did well.'

'Did well!' scoffs the Commander. 'Why, he's done wonders.'

'Oh, but the wicket's a gift to anybody,' says Tom deprecatingly. And one of my wickets was just a fluke.'

'Still, five for 44,' says the Commander, patting him on the back.

'Oh, but I was splendidly backed up by the fielders. And I dropped one awful catch.'

The people are looking at him and Susannah. They are asking each other, Is Susannah his fiancée? And Susannah, knowing this well, is pleased to be thought so. Tom has to return to the pavilion and lunch with his fellow-players, so his guests have a meal together in the Members' Luncheon Room. After this they join the gentlemen and ladies promenading over the green grass and pausing to look at the pitch. The sun is in midday mood, so Susannah, like the other summer-dressed ladies, puts up her cream parasol, lace-edged, and feels fashionable and 'in the manner' – the grand manner of Lord's.

Ding, dong, ding dong went the monastery bell; and quickly the promenade dispersed and the green plain was empty of all except two white-coated umpires dawdling towards the wickets.

Of course, when the players came out Tom was immediately put on to bowl again. His captain lobbed the ball into his hand and Tom strolled towards his base, to the applause of the affectionate crowd. Susannah loved them all for loving Tom.

'He'll bowl unchanged throughout the innings now,' said his father. 'And he should get some of these last wickets. He's got the rabbits in front of him now.'

'Oh, I hope he gets them all,' she said, leaning forward in her seat to watch.

But Jack Hearne began the rot among the rabbits. Of the four wickets still to fall he took two, and Susannah, anxious to see Tom take them and to hear the roared appreciation of the crowd, was impatient with the man. More interested in Tom's success than in Middlesex's, she prayed in her seat, every time Hearne assumed the ball, that he would bowl very nicely and creditably, but get no wicket. He did not get a third wicket, and now Tom had his chance again. Before him was Mills of Gloucester, No. 9 in the batting order, a fine bowler but no great shakes with the bat. God give Tom his wicket.

Mills of Gloucester played the first ball of this so dangerous young bowler with an apprehensive carefulness that made the crowd laugh. He played the second ball likewise. The third, which Tom had artfully pitched a little short and much slower, he played straight into the bowler's hand. Caught! C. and b. Budlier. A wild, intemperate cheer, for seemingly the crowd, like Susannah, wants Tom to multiply his total. Budlier now six for 52. Away went Mills, taking his duck's egg back to his mates, and out came the last batsman, Dennett, like a sacrifice. A good man, Dennett, a pillar of his side, their steadiest bowler, and not the worst of batsmen. Oh, God, let Tom get him, and not that man Hearne. Dennett was drawing on his batting gloves as he came to the altar, and a loud jolly voice shouted, 'Never mind them, George. You won't need 'em.' Much laughter.

Dennett took his guard and was ready, but not, perhaps, happy, for his bat was patting and patting his block-hole. Tom had three balls left of his over: could he get him and finish off the enemy? He began his long, pounding, crouching run – for a second Susannah thought it was hardly fair to bowl as brutally at these last poor tail-enders as at the great opening batsmen, but the thought had no time to develop. Tom was at the wicket, he had leapt from off the circumference of the Earth, he had flung his arm over till head, torso and hinder leg were almost parallel with the ground. His ball, it would appear, was the fastest of the match, for no one seemed to see it, certainly the batsman didn't see it; the only thing anyone saw was the off stump leaping indignantly into the air and the middle stump throwing itself on to its back for the final count. The perfect finish to Tom's career today. Seven wickets for under 8 runs apiece. Gloucester's total only a hundred and ten, and Budlier the cause of the rout. And he the people's hero, as he walked shyly behind the older and more celebrated amateurs back to the pavilion.

It was still only three on a bright afternoon, and Albany said to Susannah, 'There's more than three hours to go. We may yet see him bat before the day's out. He goes in No. 7, and wickets are cheap today.'

'Oh, I hope we do; and I hope he does well!' exclaimed Susannah.

'He's done well enough for one day, whatever happens,' said the Commander.

They did see him bat. The Middlesex men found it as hard to make runs on this perplexing and repulsive wicket as their opponents, and as hard to protect their stumps. There was no keeping the bat above the buck-jumping ball. One by one they went sadly home to the pavilion. Save for the humour of watching these 'returned empties' going back to the cellar, the game was providing little entertainment for the crowd. Their only interest now was whether Middlesex, their home team, could reach and pass the enemy's score of a hundred and ten. It didn't look as if they could, as the afternoon wore away, and they only poked unhappily at the worrying balls for over after over, gathering no flowers by the way. If one of them did pluck a run from somewhere the crowd greeted this triumph with a prolonged sardonic cheer. But for the most part they yawned and were silent. The somnolent stillness of late afternoon came silently in and possessed the whole walled field of Lord's and all within its compass, except the white players loitering to and fro. The very flags on the two pavilion masts fell asleep. So did the trees around the ground; they slept. So did some of the old parsons in the stands, and some of the Noblemen and Gentlemen in the pavilion; they slumped in their seats and with opened mouths slept, dreaming perhaps that they were twenty again and slogging balls to a boundary. The pigeons and sparrows returned to the outfield and waddled and pecked there, confident that no more hard-driven balls would come bouncing amongst them to vex their leisure. In the stillness one heard all sounds, near or far, with an extraordinary clarity: the padding of the players' feet, the smack of bat upon ball, the gust of laughter as a batsman ducked to dodge a head-high bumper, and the clicking of turnstiles as a few late-comers hurried in to see the end of the day.

All day the sky had been clean and lustred, like the skin of a child's blue balloon, and the sun, unvisited by cloud, had laid a golden sheen on the well-trimmed grass, but now a white flocculence was piling up in the west and occasionally a grey mass passed across the sun, changing the luminous grass to a dull green and then allowing it to light up again. The clock of the Tower pointed to five, and the shadows of the pavilion began to stretch across the drowsy plain.

Five wickets down, and now a high pressure of nervousness inflated Susannah's heart, for Tom must come from the pavilion to the crease and perform in public again. He appeared, running down the steps, and the crowd, having made him their favourite for the day, applauded his long figure directly they recognised it. Susannah could hardly watch him, as he walked with a long, hurrying stride to the wicket. She suspected, from his too-quick walk, that nervousness was throbbing like an engine in his breast too. Unable to watch longer, she looked down upon her lap. And prayed.

But Tom, out there, was less nervous than she imagined. His success with the ball was a fount of happiness in his memory, and he was thinking that, even if he failed now with the bat, he'd done what he'd determined to do: he'd bowled down some of the barrier between him and Susannah. Inspired by this memory, he was telling himself that on this brute of a wicket he was going to hit out at everything and gather a boundary or two, even a six with luck, before the brute beat him. To judge from the lives of his predecessors, it was as likely to beat him if he played carefully. So away with prudence. Let's see what audacity will do.

But the wicket was even more incomprehensible than he had supposed; the ball danced about in the most illogical way, its every break, whether to off or to leg, a complete non-sequitur, and Tom's start was exceedingly shaky. It must be appearing deplorable, childish to Susannah. He could do nothing but dab the ball down cautiously or leave it to fly past him. And after two or three overs of this helpless and inglorious play the crowd began to laugh at him. This galled him, and he slammed at a ball and missed it; whereupon a group in the crowd gave him a satirical clap. He turned and looked at them, and his look said, 'So easy to play this bowling from your place in the stand, you fools.' But people, observing the look, only laughed. Off his next hit he snatched his first run, and the satirists applauded; and he loathed them for mocking him before Susannah. Still, he had now broken his duck, and his relief balanced (though only in part) the pain of ridicule. The consciousness of Susannah in her seat kept his nervousness throbbing, so that he could not stand still while his partner was batting, but must walk round and round, and up and down, by his crease. And when he took his place to bat again he must tap and tap at his block before each ball came to him. And when it came he could only make dabs at it, either putting it away or missing it altogether. The bowler, perceiving the unease, tried to finish him off with a ball so fast and merciless that Susannah flung her hand to her mouth and murmured, 'Oh, the wickedness of it!' The ball, just touched by Tom, leapt over a slip-fieldsman only an inch out of his reach.

Now the fieldsmen paid him the poor compliment – him, a hitter! – of closing in around his bat in the hope of a catch. This genial insult made the crowd laugh. Laugh in pity for him. Then something happened in Tom. Never before had the field closed in on him. Nor a crowd laughed at him for impotent play. They would treat him as a rabbit, would they? All right: he hitched up his trousers, tested his bat, and looked all round the field for a safe place to put the ball when he'd slammed it over the heads of these insolent fieldsmen. He swept his eyes over the whole of the outfield, where the pigeons were enjoying a promenade, uninterested in the game, and inexpectant of any balls in their quiet country, now that the day, with its many noises, was dwindling into the stillness of evening. A comedian, observing this sweep of Tom's eyes, shouted, 'Have a look at the wicket, too, Tom – ' and drew a laugh from every seat in the ground.

'All right, fool!' thought Tom; and he locked his lips, gripped his bat hard, and faced the bowler. The ball was a good length, but he stretched a long leg half-way down the pitch (or so it seemed) and drove it with a furious resounding smack high above these fielders who'd dared to close in on him. It flew like a howitzer shell and touched earth only a few feet from the boundary rail, scattering the pigeons like sea-spray. It banged against the white rail. A four; almost a six.

A roar of delighted laughter from the crowd, whose ridicule was now directed at the discomfited fieldsmen. And long applause, affectionate this time, not ironic.

That glorious laugh set Tom free. Set him on fire. After that, as the papers said next morning, he 'could do nothing wrong'; he played, they said, 'like one inspired'. To hell with nerves and idiotic wickets and cocksure fieldsmen! Out he went to the next ball and sent it to the leg boundary, stampeding again those loudly dissenting pigeons. Two fours in succession. Two storms of applause. Such a double is an intoxicating draught for any man, and now Tom's play flew in the face of sense and theory and succeeded everywhere. By using his long stride he converted good-length balls into bad-length balls, stepping back to make them half volleys, or running right out of his crease to hit them full-toss. One of these full tosses he slogged into the Mound Stand for six, lifting the people there to their feet in alarm and all the small boys on the ground to their feet in joy. Now it was the Gloucester bowlers and fielders who were demoralised. They bowled less well, fielded less well, and he took every advantage of this decline. Four ... two ... three ... four again. Ecstasy among the small boys.

Sir Albany did not rise with the small boys and dance on his feet, but in his enthusiasm he leaned forward with his hands on his knees and jerked up and down as if he had springs in his big buttocks. 'That's right, Tom. Smite him to the four winds of heaven.' His comments were perfervid, and sometimes they were witty, because he too was inspired. When Tom leaned back on his right foot and hit a perfect-length ball right over the head of mid-on, he exclaimed, 'But that is blasphemy, my boy; blasphemy! People don't do such things, ha, ha, ha!' When the boy scored a three immediately after a four, 'But this is gluttony,' he protested, 'gluttony.' And when Tom hit out at Dennett, Gloucester's finest bowler, and drove him along the ground for four, he shook his head in mock disapproval and declared, 'That's no way to talk to your father.' Susannah had no such wit available; overcome by this too sudden and too exciting display, she could only bewail, 'Oh, my stomach!' and, 'Oh, I can't stand this' and 'Oh, please ...'

Commander Ludlow, monocle up, hands on knees, was as exalted as Sir Albany and occasionally slapped the Colonel, his smiling and happy neighbour, on back or thigh, to congratulate him on such a son. 'Indiscreet, sir, indiscreet,' he said to the far-away Tom, as the boy ran out to a ball, 'but that's the idea. Bash the stuffing out of them!' And 'Very sweet, sir; very sweet!' as Tom cut a ball cleanly through the slips. And 'Hell, Colonel! The lad isn't stopping in his garden,' as Tom went chasséing out to a shortish ball.

'Fate generally chooses to crown one man a day,' said a voice behind Susannah. This certainly seemed true today. Fate crowned Tom its favourite, as he played on and on through an evening of sunlight and shadow. It allowed him to hit the four that lifted the Middlesex total above that of their opponents; and it allowed this hit to be a boundary. It allowed him to hit a ball so hard that it hit the pavilion railing and rolled back to the players, saving a fieldsman the trouble of running to fetch it. It allowed him, when he was in with the last man and snatching every possible run, to run runs that couldn't surely be run, but were. His young, excited voice rang over the field, 'Yes! One MORE!'

But these too-bright displays cannot last for long. The higher the flames, the sooner the ash. Of course Tom, attempting while there was yet time, a tremendous swipe for six, sent a ball like a rocket into the deep field, wild applause following it – but lo! a man running! Would he catch it! Would he? Oh, no, no, no! But he did; and a great groan assaulted the sky above Lord's. Then applause, generous applause, for a magnificent catch.

All out, and cricket over for the day, since it was now after six. Tom, returning with the Gloucester fieldsmen, was given the ovation he had dreamed of yesterday, as he watched the rain. He touched his cap to the cheering crowd and ran out of their sight into the pavilion. The people streamed away to the gates, the Commander, the Colonel, Albany and Susannah among them. As they moved slowly because of the press, Susannah heard a woman in front of her say, 'What a most attractive young man! So modest and shy!' And she knew that she was plunged into the bottom of love. 'I'm sunk,' she said to herself. 'Sunk beyond hope.' Tom's first battle was indeed won. He made a way to them, to say goodbye before they were out of the ground, and Albany said to him, 'You'll remember this day, my boy, when you're an old grey man like me, and sitting by the fire.'

He returned to the pavilion; and they passed out, and all the others with them. Lord's lay deserted. A great airy structure of excitement, like the invisible and evanescent palace it was, had collapsed into silence, and there was nothing left but the green veldt and the white railing and the empty white stands.

ERNEST RAYMOND, *To the Wood No More*, 1954

AMONG the deities invoked by Raymond are two Middlesex cricketers who rank among the most fascinating ever to appear regularly at Lord's. Bernard James Tindall Bosanquet (1877–1936) was the inventor of the Googly, a ball which is delivered with a leg-break action but spins in the opposite direction, as an off-break. Bosanquet's shattering discovery, that by adjusting the axis of the wrist at the moment of release the direction of spin can be reversed, destroyed overnight the self-confident front-foot drivers who 'read' the bowler's hand and selected their stroke accordingly. Late in life

Bosanquet took exception to his role as the scapegoat who had spoiled classic strokeplay by reducing once-triumphant batsmen to a bunch of shambling flannelled Hamlets sicklied o'er with the pale cast of thought, suggesting with comic speciousness that a googly 'is merely a ball with an ordinary break produced by an extraordinary method', much as to say that a ghost is, after all, no more than a man who happens to be transparent. Bosanquet's immortality as a bowler has tended to eclipse his considerable ability as a batsman, an irony whose force is doubled when one realises that the first-class game in which he unveiled his anarchic delivery was one in which he performed with dazzling skill as a batsman. After experiments dating from 1897, conducted on a table with a tennis ball, Bosanquet came to Lord's for a county championship match prepared to test his invention. But the *Wisden* reporter noticed nothing remarkable about Bosanquet's bowling, even though the only wicket taken by the inventor bounced, on Bosanquet's own insistence, four times.

MIDDLESEX v. LEICESTERSHIRE
At Lord's, July 19, 20, 21, 1900

This match, which they won in brilliant fashion by five wickets, marked a welcome change in the fortunes of the Middlesex eleven. The victory was badly needed, as out of nine previous matches they had only won one. All the honours were carried off by Bosanquet, who, with scores of 136 and 139, added his name to the list of those who have made two separate hundreds in a first-class match. His second innings was incomparably the better of the two, for though he hit very brilliantly for his 136, he was missed being stumped before he had made a run and had two other escapes with his score respectively at 93 and 96. His 136 lasted an hour and fifty minutes, while for his 139 he was batting two hours and fifty minutes.

Wisden, 1901

THE historic four-bouncer which had a bewildered batsman called Coe stumped when within two runs of his century, was the only successful delivery sent down by Bosanquet in the match. His final figures were one for 47 in twelve overs. But he persevered with his heretical invention and gradually gained over his errant ball a degree of control which encouraged him to try it against the visiting Australians. Again Bosanquet chose to conduct his experiment at Lord's. He later recalled 'the first time it was bowled against the Australians – at Lord's late one evening in 1902 – when I had two overs and saw two very puzzled Australians return to the pavilion. Not one of them tumbled to the fact that it was not an accident.' Later he won a Test match singlehanded at Sydney, and also enjoyed considerable success as a hammer-thrower and billiard player. Bosanquet was the perfect example of the Edwardian gentleman-athlete whose life was one long sunlit saunter from pavilion to conservatory, from flannelled grace to cuff-studded elegance. Down the years he drifted from one country house to the next, where he would play cricket, conduct himself charmingly at dinner, perform a few dexterities on the green baize and, on departing, tip the butler a couple of sovereigns for his trouble. He married very late in life and was only dimly remembered by his son Reginald. Happily, Bosanquet appears to have reserved most of his bravura performances for Lord's, and it was there in the summer of 1905 that he put on an exhibition which was forgotten by nobody fortunate enough to witness it:

MIDDLESEX v. SUSSEX
At Lord's, May 25–27, 1905

Played just before the first of the Test games, this was emphatically Bosanquet's match. Thanks chiefly to his superb batting and highly effective bowling, Middlesex, after declaring their second innings closed, won by 324 runs. For the second time in his life, Bosanquet made two separate hundreds in one match, and in all he took eleven wickets, carrying everything before him in the last innings. He hit up his 103 in an hour and three-quarters and his 100 not out in seventy-five minutes. Field played fine cricket of a far more careful kind and Warner and George Beldam were also seen at their best. Fry was kept out of the Sussex team by a damaged finger and his absence clearly dispirited the Sussex team.

Middlesex

Mr P. F. Warner, c. Goldie, B. Tate	49	b. Leach	86
Mr E. A. Beldam, b. Tate	26	lbw., b. Relf	10
Mr G. W. Beldam, c. Butt, b. Goldie	3	c. Butt, b. Cox	94
Mr E. Field, not out	107		
Mr B. J. T. Bosanquet, b. Goldie	103	not out	100
Mr G. MacGregor, b. Goldie	0		
Mr J. H. Hunt, b. Goldie	1		
Mr E. S. Littlejohn, b. Vine	3		
Mr H. D. Wyatt, C. Butt, b. Cox	13		
A. E. Trott, c. Cox, b. Goldie	20	not out	5
J. T. Hearne, c. Butt, b. Reif	17		
B 4, l-b 11, w 2	17	B 15, l-b 1, w 4, n-b 1	21
	369	(3 wkts dec.)	316

Sussex

Mr K. O. Goldie, b. G. W. Beldam	19	c. and b. Hunt	9
J. Vine, c. Bosanquet, b. Hunt	4	st. MacGregor, b. Bosanquet	31
E. H. Killick, c. Hearne, b. Hunt	32	c. and b. Bosanquet	9
A. E. Relf, c. Trott, b. Hunt	2	st. MacGregor, b. Bosanquet	5
Mr A. L. Gorringe, b. Hearne	16	b. Hunt	0
G. Cox, c. MacGregor, b. Trott	38	b. Bosanquet	8
Mr H. P. Chaplin, c. G. Beldam, b. Bosanquet	42	lbw., b. Bosanquet	0
Mr C. L. A. Smith, b. Bosanquet	41	b. Bosanquet	12
G. Leach, c. Field, b. Hearne	35	b. Bosanquet	5
H. R. Butt, not out	7	c. and b. Bosanquet	0
F. W. Tate, c. sub., b. Bosanquet	4	not out	16
B 13, l-b 6	19	B 4, l-b 2, w 1	7
	259		102

Sussex Bowling

	Overs	Mdns	Runs	Wkts	Overs	Mdns	Runs	Wkts
Relf	20	4	53	1	17	3	49	1
Cox	27	9	60	1	14	5	32	1
Goldie	33	10	80	5	10	–	50	–
Tate	25	5	81	2	11	2	46	–
Vine	15	4	54	1	10	–	42	–
Killick	6	3	24	–	11	1	43	–
Leach					8	–	33	1

Middlesex Bowling

	Overs	Mdns	Runs	Wkts	Overs	Mdns	Runs	Wkts
G.W. Beldam	8	1	29	1				
Hunt	19	3	63	3	14	5	42	2
Bosanquet ..	24.3	2	75	3	12.2	1	53	8
Hearne	18	5	38	2				
Trott	13	3	35	1				

Umpires: W. A. J. West and C. E. Richardson.

Wisden, 1906

ANOTHER Middlesex virtuoso drafted into Ernest Raymond's imaginary match was the Australian Albert Trott, even more gifted as an all-rounder than Bosanquet, and infinitely more tragic a figure. Albert Edwin Trott (1873–1914) lived a life bizarre in many ways, but none odder than his appearance as an English county cricketer. After performing brilliantly for Australia against England's 1894–95 touring side, his selection for the English tour of 1896 was regarded as a foregone conclusion. But for reasons which have never been discovered, he was overlooked, and was so outraged by his omission that he paid his own expenses to England and in time qualified for Middlesex. By 1899 he was probably the greatest all-rounder in cricket, taking 239 wickets and scoring 1,175 runs. In 1900 he took 211 and scored 1,337. In the technical sense an off-break bowler, Trott was difficult to play through his endless variations of pace and his perfecting of a fast yorker. A few cricketers have snatched at immortality through the inspired feats of a single day; Trott is one of the very few who did it twice, once with the bat, once with the ball, both at Lord's. On 31 July 1899, playing for the MCC against the Australians, Trott hit a ball from M. A. Noble over the top of the pavilion, a feat so prodigious that it appears to have tempted eye-witnesses into blatant contradiction.

Though he did not stay very long – scarcely more than 45 minutes – Trott when once he started was extremely busy. His score of 41 was in itself nothing out of the common, but he made some truly wonderful drives. He first hit Trumble over the ring at long-off, and then lifted a ball on to the top balcony of the pavilion. This caused Noble to go on, a change which as it happened brought Trott's innings to a close. Before he got the wicket, however, Noble had to suffer. Surpassing his previous efforts, Trott made a mighty hit, which cleared the pavilion roof, struck the chimney, and fell behind the building. Possibly he was a little too much elated by his success and the applause, but anyhow this great drive was the end of him. Almost directly afterwards he skied the ball to third man and was out to the easiest of catches.

The Daily Telegraph, 1 August 1899

I was sitting in the front seats of the pavilion when the hit was made, and I remember how Trott found the range with a couple of sighting shots, one pitching just short of the pavilion rails, and another on the seats. In fact, he seemed to be making a 'bracket', as the gunners say, and then came this historic hit. It was not possible to measure the distance accurately because the pavilion and the tennis-courts and Need's house intervened, and no one knew the exact spot where the ball fell.

SIR PELHAM WARNER, *Lord's*, 1946

I was on the top with H. W. Hewett, and the ball came right over our heads. Trott got only four for this hit, as the ball hit the racquet courts behind, and in those days a ball had to go out of the ground to score six.

W. N. ROE, letter to *The Daily Telegraph*, 1937

Trott's hit landed on the reverse slope of the ornamental coping along the ridge of the roof. It was not a clean hit over.

E. H. D. SEWELL, (attrib.)

Trott understandably became one of the most popular cricketers in the country, virtually a Londoner by adoption, although all over the country crowds would come to watch him in the expectation of seeing something extraordinary. Sometimes his colossal hitting caused panic in the ranks of the fielding side, as Neville Cardus has testified:

He left Australia for London and Middlesex, and became as familiar to Lord's as the Tavern and as naturally to be looked for there by the crowds, for he assimilated Cockney nature, racy and rich and uninhibited. He was as strong as a lion; huge hands and a moustache that needed copious wiping after he had swallowed a pint of ale at one pull. Trott's big hit won't be equalled until another cricketer is seized by as grandiose a conception. But Trott himself apparently spent the rest of his career trying to repeat the stroke. Ted Wainwright, of Yorkshire and England, once told me of an experience he went through while fielding in the deep at Lord's while Trott one day was seeking to conquer fresh empires in aerial space. 'Aye,' said Ted, 'Ah were standin' deep long-on, near t'Nursery, and Albert gets reight under one of Bobby Peel; and Ah saw ball goin' oop and oop, an' Ah loses 'er agenst pavilion; then Ah sees 'er reight over me, 'igh as Blackpool Tower, an' Ah gets into position an' Ah says to misel', "Tha's got 'er, Ted, aye, tha's under 'er", and Ah coops mi 'ands' – pause – 'an' then Ah thinks, "Oh, to hell with 'er," an' Ah let's 'er go.' The ball fell in front of him. 'Ah never touched it,' added Ted. 'By goom, you should 'ave 'eard 'Is Lordship; 'e coom stridin' over grass an' 'e DID carry on, 'e did an' all.'

NEVILLE CARDUS, *Cricket All the Year*, 1952

There are some cricketers whose names tend to be remembered on account of some particular feat, such as bowling Bradman for a duck, and Albert Trott is now best remembered as 'the man who hit a ball over the pavilion at Lord's'. That is unfair to a player who, in an all-too-brief career, showed supreme all-round form. Though he had already played with great success for Australia, he was not chosen to tour England in 1896, and promptly left Australia to come over and qualify for Middlesex. He immediately showed himself to be a bowler of exceptional skill, who took no less than 626 wickets in first-class matches in the course of the three seasons 1899–1900–1901, a fielder as good as anyone could be, and a batsman of enormous popular appeal.

It is his batting alone which is here to be considered. His career figures show him to have scored 9,441 runs at an average of 17.84. One's first reaction is that the figures ought to have been better, and G. L. Jessop supports this feeling. He writes: 'When he could succeed in checking his impetuosity, Albert Trott was a batsman fit for any team, for he had his moments when he was far removed from that of a hard-hitting batsman of haphazard methods. In one particular innings (112 *v.* Gloucester at Lord's in 1900) when things were going none too well for Middlesex, his cricket was entirely faultless, and it served to show to what heights as a batsman Trott could rise.' I quote this to show that Trott was never a crude agricultural tail-end swiper; if his tally of runs was less than it might have been it was on account of lack of judgement rather than technique. Gregor Macgregor, Trott's Middlesex captain, once said of his bowling, 'If you had a head instead of a turnip, Alberto, you'd be the best bowler in the world,' and the same remark might almost have referred to his batting. Like some others, Trott delighted and gave delight in the spectacular hit, especially at Lord's, where he was as popular as any player has been. Trott was a personality about whom legends grew. One is that he experimented with a super-weight bat which made the normal rhythm of good batting strokes impossible. E. H. D. Sewell whole-heartedly condemned Trott's use of this bat in the following stricture:

> Trott was an outstanding examplar of the gospel of *fortiter in re*, which resulted when he was at the crease with swooshes a many, and colossal, or distant, hits a few. After all, nobody can bat with a kind of Gog-Magog massue, weighing 3 lb, if not more. He can only swing it about, hoping that by some incidence of timing he has managed to cause its business end to cross the line of flight of the ball at the instant that matters most. Having done that much, one is not necessarily batting. Call it philandering if you like, or training to use Indian clubs, but *not* batting.

I do not know if Trott from the very start used a heavy bat, or whether after making some great hits he was led to try to improve upon them by experimenting with a heavier weapon, especially as his enormous hands were able to cope readily with any weight. As a bowler he was an arch-experimenter, and no doubt in batting also he liked to try something new. He was immensely strong, and tough as nails. Playing for MCC at Lord's, in May 1898, when it was bitterly cold, and while everyone else was draped in sweaters and ulsters, Trott appeared sweaterless and in the thinnest of shirts. Black clouds blew up round the field, and when someone suggested that it was going to snow, Trott gazed expectantly at the laden clouds: 'I hope it does,' he said, 'I've never seen snow.'

For all his strength, Trott was not very tall, not a big man in the way in which Jim Smith or Sinclair were tall. In fact, one correspondent says that when he first saw him he wondered where on earth his great strength came from: 'When he emerged from the pavilion with a slightly sardonic expression on his face there was little to suggest enormous power. But his hands were large, his shoulders were square, and he wielded a 3 lb bat.'

Another legend is that the famous 'over the pavilion' hit at Lord's in July 1899 went so much to Trott's head that for evermore he forgot to bat sensibly, and spent all his talents in attempting similar gigantic hits over every pavilion he came across. As that hit came almost at the beginning of his English career, his batting can hardly be said to have 'gone off' afterwards, and, after all, if you can hit a ball further than anyone else of your time, it seems a pity not to do so. It was fun while it lasted.

Unfortunately, Trott's career was comparatively short. He scored over 1,000 runs in 1899 and 1900, and in all his career made exactly fifty scores of 50 or over, including eight centuries – more, indeed, than other big hitters with similar averages. Six of these hundreds were made at Lord's, which was undoubtedly his happiest hunting-ground. Here is a record of his great feats there. On 4 May 1899, when playing for MCC against Sussex, he scored 64, including one drive off F. W. Tate (the father of Maurice) which struck the left-hand emblem (as you face it) of the MCC coat-of-arms which crowns the highest pinnacle on the top of the towers of the pavilion. These emblems must be a good 20 feet higher than the top of the pavilion roof, and this hit off Tate must therefore be an appreciably bigger hit than the far better-known one which he made a few weeks later. But no doubt it left Trott unsatisfied and more than ever eager to put a ball right over the pavilion. Cyril Foley, who was batting with Trott at the time of his hit off Tate, says that he can remember turning round in the middle of the pitch in time to see the ball strike the emblem fair and square. It then bounced back into the seats.

In the second innings of the match Trott scored 69 out of 82 in forty minutes, reaching 52 in twenty minutes. This match alone proved Trott to be a hitter of very exceptional powers, and from this moment he became pavilion-conscious.

A few weeks later Trott was to play the biggest and best innings of his career, against Yorkshire. On May 29th Yorkshire made 203, and Middlesex replied with 121 for four. The next morning Trott soon came in and before lunch batted for about an hour, in which he scored 17 by means of patient, copybook batting, something which an out-and-out hitter like Jim Smith, for example, could never have done. After lunch Trott cut loose and by whirlwind methods took his score to 164: the last 137 of these runs were scored out of 181 in only ninety minutes. According to the score-book, he hit 27 fours, but again, we can never know how many of his boundaries would have counted as sixes today. We do know, though, that he landed two hits on the top balcony of the pavilion and hit the Tavern many times. Three times he hit F. S. Jackson into the pavilion, and on one occasion he also drove a ball from him so hard against the pavilion railings that it bounced right back to Jackson's bowling point, so that he hardly had to move to pick it up. The fielder at square-leg on the line of the small score-box was instantly moved to protect the pavilion railings, but the very next ball went slap over where the square-leg man had been and sent the scorers diving beneath their desks as the ball crashed into the box. Trott added 33 runs to his score in six minutes, and that without sixes.

If Trott sometimes hit a ball into the air, it often went so high that no one could sight it. One of the best stories in Neville Cardus's book, *Close of Play*, is of the Yorkshire player Wainwright's refusal to cope with one such hit. The ball had risen to an enormous height. Wainwright hovered about in the deep trying in vain to sight it, but having at last seen it right above him, 'high as Blackpool Tower', he decided to have nothing more to do with it. The ball dropped at Wainwright's feet; Lord Hawke, his captain, came dashing across to see why he had refused it, but then had to laugh at Wainwright's excuse that it was simply 'too 'igh, your Lordship'.

Trott in full cry could be literally devastating, especially as he had a peculiar means of dealing with slow leg-breakers. If the ball came right for him he just turned round, faced the wicket-keeper, and helped the ball on its way to the boundary. On one occasion when trying this, he drove the ball right into the poor wicket-keeper's stomach.

Among the spectators of Trott's great 164 was the poet Francis Thompson, who for his own amusement wrote some versified notes on the game. Here is a short extract from the notes:

> For Trott, who also month-long kept
> Inert, as the batsman in him slept,
> Wakes, and with tumult of his waking,
> The many-girded ground is shaking
> With rolling claps and clamour, as soar
> Fours after fours, and ever four!
> Bowls Rhodes, bowls Jackson, Haigh bowls, Hirst, –
> To him the last is as the first:
> West-end tent or pavilion rail,
> He lashes them home with a thresher's flail.

Trott continued in great form: a week later he scored 123 against Sussex, and then, on the last day of July, came the GREAT HIT. During his first innings (of 41) for MCC against the Australians, Trott hit a ball from M. A. Noble which went over the top of the pavilion, and thus did something which has never been repeated. But though this hit is justly famous – indeed, immortal – it should be remembered that it was not so big as the one Trott had made off Tate three months earlier that season. Moreover, several other hits made by other batsmen in the direction of the pavilion would have carried even further if the building had not been in the way. In other words, it was not by any means one of the very longest hits ever made, nor even the biggest made by Trott himself. Here are some accounts of it. First, the report in the *Daily Telegraph*: 'Though he did not stay very long—scarcely more than 45 minutes—Trott when once he started was extremely busy. His score of 41 was in itself nothing out of the common, but he made some truly wonderful drives. He first hit Trumble over the ring at long-off, and then lifted a ball on to the top balcony of the pavilion. This caused Noble to go on, a change which as it happened brought Trott's innings to a close. Before he got the wicket, however, Noble had to suffer. Surpassing his previous efforts, Trott made a mighty hit, which cleared the pavilion roof, struck the chimney, and fell behind the building. Possibly he was a little too much elated by his success and the applause, but anyhow this great drive was the end of him. Almost directly afterwards he skied the ball to third man and was out to the easiest of catches.'

Sir Pelham Warner, who was playing in the match, writes: 'I was sitting in the front seats of the pavilion when the hit was made, and I remember how Trott found the range with a couple of sighting shots, one pitching just short of the pavilion rails, and another on the seats. In fact, he seemed to be making a "bracket", as the gunners say, and then came this historic hit. It was not possible to measure the distance accurately because the pavilion and the tennis-courts and Need's house intervened, and no one knew the exact spot where the ball fell.' Another witness was W. N. Roe, who in a letter to the *Daily Telegraph* in 1937 wrote: 'I was on the top with H. T. Hewett, and the ball came right over our heads. Trott got only 4 for this hit, as the ball hit the racquet courts behind, and in those days had to go out of the ground to score six.'

One can imagine Trott's immense joy at seeing the ball disappear over the top, and he showed it in the humorous gesture of shading his eyes and peering into the distance as the ball zoomed on – according to Sir Pelham Warner, who has recently given me an equally humorous demonstration of Trott's gesture. Over the top it went, with as much satisfaction to its dispatcher and his audience as a successfully launched guided missile.

I have often wondered what exactly happened to this hit, though it is not easy to find the truth of something that occurred nearly sixty years ago. There is no doubt that the ball cleared the top edge of the small roof above the back part of the balcony seats. According to E. H. D. Sewell, whose evidence is always accurate and valuable, 'Trott's hit landed on the reverse slope of the ornamental coping along the ridge of the roof. It was not a clean hit over.' After landing on the roof the ball bounced away and finished up in the garden of Philip Need, the dressing-room attendant.

As the hit was not a clean one – right over the whole building – it is impossible to know what the exact distance of the carry would have been, but one can reckon some minimum distance of a ball that would carry the whole pavilion, granting it was a howitzer-type shot that went very high and then fell almost vertically, say just outside the entrance-door to the present tennis court. It is clear that Trott's hit must have been falling if it landed on the reverse edge of the roof, so it must have been a hit which was not likely to have carried very much beyond the carriageway behind the pavilion. Now the distance from the Nursery-end wicket to the pavilion rails is 91 yards, and the distance from the railings to the wall of the tennis court (a wall which once continued both down towards the Members' Entrance and up behind the Press box and Warner Stand) I have measured at 35 yards, so the total carry from the far wicket to the entrance door of the tennis court is 126 yards. This gives some general estimate of the carry of Trott's hit. It must have been a huge ballooner, and not like a much flatter one once made by F. T. Mann when he drove a ball which struck the back row of the seats on the top balcony while still on the rise, a hit of truly vast carry if it had not been stopped before it had reached its zenith. But it is Trott's hit that is remembered; it went over the pavilion – just – and no one else has ever done it. A great feat, seeing the height it had to carry.

Trott continued his bombardment of the pavilion. In the following year when playing for MCC v. Cambridge University, he scored 22 (2 4 4 4 4 4) off an over from E. R. Wilson and, according to report, 'hit one ball among the seats on the pavilion roof, and another on to the portico balcony'. The hit 'among the seats' I reckon to be the seventh hit which I have mentioned that pitched the ball somewhere above the line of the railings to the top balcony, and I dare say there may have been others. It is an astonishing record of sustained bombardment.

There is little record of Trott's big hits to other quarters of Lord's, but Sir Pelham says that in 1902 he saw Trott in an innings of 20 v. Surrey hit a ball from Brockwell 'which sailed over extra-cover's head and landed high up in the Mound stand', a remarkable stroke for such a direction. In scoring 103 out of 136 in seventy minutes against Somerset in 1902, Trott hit 17 fours, including a hit to square-leg off Braund which went out of the ground, but not apparently counting 6.

GERALD BRODRIBB, *Hit for Six*, 1960

AFTER a few wonderful seasons with Middlesex, Trott was wiping his moustache a little too regularly, and soon his effectiveness began to decrease. By 1907 he was ready to receive that financial salute to veterans, the Benefit Match – at which point he performed one of the most inspired comic antics in the history of the game. Desperately in need of a healthy haul from the Benefit to bail him out of petty financial troubles, he went into the match against Somerset at Lord's on 20–22 May 1907, full of hopes. To some extent, alas, these hopes were dashed, by Albert himself:

MIDDLESEX v. SOMERSET
Played at Lord's, May 20, 21, 22, 1907
Albert Trott rendered his benefit match memorable by an extra-ordinary bowling performance in the second innings of Somerset, dismissing Lewis, Poyntz, Woods, and Robson with successive balls, and later on disposing of Mordaunt, Wickham, and Bailey, also with successive balls. Thus he accomplished the unprecedented feat of performing the 'hat trick' twice in an innings. Thanks to Trott's bowling, Middlesex won by 166 runs. Rain seriously interfered with cricket on the opening day, the whole time available being occupied by the home team's first innings. Middlesex blundered in the field on Tuesday, but thanks to Tarrant secured a useful lead. Litteljohn followed up his success against Hampshire with two capital displays of batting.

Middlesex

Mr P. F. Warner, b. Mordaunt	46	b. Lewis	11
F. A. Tarrant, c. Lee, b. Lewis	52	c. Palairet, b. Mordaunt	28
Mr G. W. Beldam, lbw. b. Mordaunt	12	lbw. b. Lewis	0
Mr B. J. T. Bosanquet, c. Johnson, b. Mordaunt	32	b. Bailey	29
Mr E. S. Litteljohn, c. Braund, b. Lewis	44	b. Mordaunt	52
A. E. Trott, b. Lewis	1	c. Wickham, b. Robson	35
Mr H. A. Milton, b. Lewis	3	b. Mordaunt	0
Mr G. MacGregor, c. Woods, b. Bailey	39	c. Poyntz, b. Robson	39
H. R. Murrell, b. Robson	33	c. and b. Braund	9
J. T. Hearne not out	3	not out	4
E. Mignon, b. Bailey	1	c. Wickham, b. Braund	0
B. 15, l-b. 4, n-b. 1	20	B. 3, l-b. 2, n-b. 1	6
	286		213

Somerset

Mr L. C. H. Palairet, c. MacGregor, b. Mignon	6	c. Bosanquet, b. Tarrant	35
L. C. Braund, c. MacGregor, b. Bosanquet	59	not out	28
Mr P. R. Johnson, b. Tarrant	57	c. Trott, b. Tarrant	14
A. E. Lewis, c. Tarrant, b. Mignon	31	lbw. b. Trott	1
Mr E. S. M. Poyntz, lbw. b. Tarrant	9	b. Trott	0
Mr S. M. J. Woods, c. Bosanquet, b. Tarrant	17	b. Trott	0
E. Robson not out	20	b. Trott	0
Mr F. M. Lee, b. Hearne	18	c. Trott, b. Tarrant	7
Mr O. C. Mordaunt, c. Beldam, b. Tarrant	1	c. Mignon, b. Trott	4
Rev. A. P. Wickham, c. Trott, b. Tarrant	0	b. Trott	0
A. E. Bailey, c. Litteljohn, b. Tarrant	3	c. Mignon, b. Trott	0
L-b. 14, w. 1	15	B. 4, l-b. 4	8
	236		97

Somerset Bowling

	Overs	Mdns	Runs	Wkts	Overs	Mdns	Runs	Wkts
Lewis	32	14	88	4	7	2	17	2
Bailey	16	5	33	–	16	3	58	1
Braund	13	1	33	–	13.4	1	55	2
Mordaunt	30	6	97	3	15	1	47	3
Robson	7	1	15	1	6	2	30	2

Middlesex Bowling

	Overs	Mdns	Runs	Wkts	Overs	Mdns	Runs	Wkts
Beldam	4	I	15	–	3	I	10	–
Mignon	24	6	88	2	5	I	24	–
Trott	5	I	10	–	8	2	20	7
Hearne	8	I	22	I				
Bosanquet	8	–	39	I				
Tarrant	15	4	47	6	14	4	35	3

Umpires: F. W. Marlow and S. Brown.

Wisden, 1908

Albert Trott, for whose benefit the match between Middlesex and Somerset was played, accomplished a wonderful bowling performance at Lord's yesterday morning, one indeed which has never been equalled according to the authentic records of first-class cricket. Trott twice did the hat-trick in the course of a single innings. On the first occasion he got four men out with successive balls, and he only missed the wicket by about an inch with the fifth ball. The details of his bowling are sufficiently interesting to merit exact rehearsal. Left with the task of getting 264 runs in order to win the match, Somerset began batting with Mr Palairet and Braund, and there was nothing in the early play to suggest the collapse which followed. Braund played sound cricket, and Mr Palairet made a number of excellent scoring strokes in his best style. The score was taken easily enough to 56, and then Mr Palairet was caught at cover point. Mr Beldam and Mignon had been then replaced as bowlers by Trott and Tarrant. Mr Johnson came in, made a few hits, and was then finely caught by Trott off Tarrant's bowling, the second wicket falling with the total at 74. Lewis succeeded him, and this was the beginning of the end. He was lbw to Trott after making a single. Then Mr Poyntz came in, only to be deceived by the flight and bowled first ball by Trott. Mr Woods suffered a similar fate next ball, apparently trying to make a chop stroke. With the defeat of Mr Woods Trott accomplished the hat-trick, but his success did not end there. Robson was the next man to face him, and his fate was the fate of his predecessors. He was, too, clean bowled, and he was, therefore, Trott's fourth successive victim. It was only by an accident that Mr F. M. Lee did not become his fifth. He hit at the ball bowled to him and missed it. For the moment it seemed from the pavilion that that ball had hit the wicket as well. Mr MacGregor, the wicket-keeper, evidently thought that that was so, for he did not take it, and four byes were the result. It was a wonderful over, and one is scarcely likely to see one like it bowled again in a first-class match. Mr Lee made seven runs before being caught at short slip by Trott off Tarrant's bowling. Then Mr Mordaunt, who had made four runs, faced Trott. He made a poor stroke to mid-off, and was easily caught by Mignon. Mr Wickham succeeded him, and was bowled first ball. Bailey, the last man in, had to make the one ball of the over which remained to be bowled. He hit it up into the air, and Mignon made another easy catch. Thus Trott did the hat-trick for the second time in the course of half an hour. Neither the excellence of his bowling nor the failure of the Somerset batting is to be explained away, but it is only fair to state that the light was very bad at the time. But that defective light was even the primary cause of Trott's success was not the case. Two or three of his victims he deceived in the flight of the ball, and the uncomfortable necessity of batting under unpleasantly dramatic conditions was no doubt responsible for the rather poor efforts which some others of his victims made.

Still the fact remains that his was a great achievement, and it will long be remembered by those who saw it. It is rather exceptional for a professional cricketer to do himself especial justice in his benefit match, and although Trott had made 30 odd runs in one innings, his comparative failure in this game had up till yesterday morning been generally regretted. He made the most ample amends by the way in which he brought the match to an end. In one respect his success on the field had a touch of irony in it. The game was all over by lunchtime. Had it lasted well into the afternoon, as at one time seemed probable, there would certainly have been a large attendance of the public, and Trott would have been the financial gainer thereby.

PHILIP TREVOR in *The Times*, 23 May 1907

OR, IN the unforgettable words of Cardus, 'Trott bowled himself into the bankruptcy court'. Patrick Morrah, in *The Golden Age of Cricket* (1967) echoes the identical thought by writing, 'Trott's figures for the innings were seven for 20. Fate was never very kind to Trott, and the scene ended with him kicking himself for finishing off his benefit match early on the third day.' Morrah's remark about the unkind fates has an ominous ring about it, and certainly this aspect of poor Trott's biography is the one which so many cricketing historians and anecdotists have chosen as the symbol which announced the end of Morrah's Golden Age, the season 1914 and the outbreak of the Great War.

A third player of the period who retains great interest for the student of the game is Albert E. Knight (1876–1946), a Leicestershire professional who somehow acquired certain cultural overtones of his amateur contemporaries. An opening bat good enough to play three times for England against Australia, Knight is chiefly remembered today as the author of one of the most remarkable books on cricket ever published. *Wisden*, edited by amateurs, described it somewhat condescendingly as 'containing much startling metaphor', by which it meant, presumably, that Knight, having worked as industriously on his prose style as he had on his batting technique, had finally arrived, by 1906, at the point where he could rhapsodise so extravagantly that there are moments when his text becomes distinguished, not so much for startling metaphor as for a sort of shimmering nebulosity. Knight was always immensely respectful towards his betters; after he retired he became a popular coach at Highgate School. Even before he gave up the first-class game, however, his loving appreciation of Varsity cricket shows how tenderly he embraced the game, even those areas of which he had never had direct experience:

The University game at Lord's is in so many ways the most interesting episode of each recurring year. The social aspect of the game is that most calculated to impress the ordinary observer. The miles-long line of cabs and motors which stretch adown and around the neighbourhood of St John's Wood, roughly indicates what wealth and power, what fashion and influence, still interest themselves in a game which town slum and village green alike love. Within the ground, the family companionship, the evident camaraderie, the boisterous enthusiasm, give to the battle of the Blues characteristics rarely meeting in such combination elsewhere. A plebeian spectator, wandering amid the mighty and the great like some Jude the Obscure, may be pardoned for suggesting that on the occasions privileged to his witness, the game per se was not of a very extraordinary character. Quite possibly the lack was in the critic rather than in the exposition of these youths. The whole game, however, is in many ways unique, and has an influence upon thousands who have never had the inestimable good fortune of a university education, or who, perchance, have never seen the wonderful old city on the Isis banks or the town which borders the Cam.

Of these memorable matches, indeed, one may think as less disturbed than all else by the evolution of the modern game from a pastime, to a great spectacle largely governed by the consideration of commerce and business. Matthew Arnold, musing o'er the beautiful city which did not appreciate his interpretation of the Faith of the centuries, wrote of Oxford as 'the home of lost causes and forsaken beliefs, of unpopular names and impossible loyalties'. If this were true of theologies, that Oxford bent not her knee to the passing Zeitgeist, but set aloft her lonely light amid the mists of Tubingen criticism, she may do the same for sport. The Varsity match is the last stronghold of an amateurism well-nigh extinct in first-class cricket. It manifests what, in practice at least, seems an 'impossible loyalty' to the glow and glory of pure sport, and the continuous contribution, unhappily growing less, of great university and college players, is one of the most health-giving and invaluable which the modern game receives.

A. E. KNIGHT, *The Complete Cricketer*, 1906

IF KNIGHT adored the game as a participant, Arthur Alexander Thomson (1894–1968) loved it just as passionately as a spectator. Thomson was a prolific writer, publishing more than sixty books, including several volumes of sentimental reminiscence and hero-worship concerning cricket. Being a provincial, he regarded Lord's with the same reverence as the colonials, although being also a Yorkshireman, his awe was tempered with just a dash of scepticism. Thomson died in a hospital very close to Lord's, which must have given him some solace. To the very end of his life he recalled in close detail most of the cricket he had known, and in his sixty-third year could still describe his sensations on arriving at the ground for the first time.

The first Middlesex v. Yorkshire game I ever saw was in 1910, which was odd, because I did not officially invade the metropolis until two years later. I went up to London in June 1910 in order to suffer an examination, which was to decide whether, when I was old enough, I should become a member of a university or not. This essentially unimportant question eventually settled itself, but that is another story. When the ordeal by pen and paper was over, there was still a day of happy freedom left, because matches then ended on a Saturday instead of beginning on one. When I made my way across the road to Lord's from the old St John's Wood station, I had already visited the Zoo and Madame Tussaud's and located (at any rate to my own satisfaction) the putative residence of Sherlock Holmes. Looking back, I still think this was excellent value for a Yorkshire lad's Saturday morning in the Baker Street area. As I passed through the turnstile, I had no idea that I should see the most exciting finish of the year. I was not interested in what afterwards came to be called 'thrills'. I only wanted to see my heroes.

Now any north-country boy could admire his heroes at Headingley, Park Avenue or Bramall Lane, but there, on their home grounds, he had to share them with the rest of the crowd. But on that day at Lord's, the great ones were my exclusive property, all eleven of them. The crowd were merely Londoners. Hirst and Rhodes, Denton and Haigh were not theirs; Yorkshire belonged to me. With the help of a penny scorecard and two Cockney neighbours I was able to assess the situation. In strict fact, my neighbours were not Cockney; one came from Frognall and the other from Finchley. But to me anyone born south-east of a line drawn between Arnold Bennett and Thomas Hardy was a Cockney. To do them justice, they on their side probably thought that anyone born north of Finsbury Park was a Lancashire comedian.

A. A. THOMSON, *Pavilioned in Splendour*, 1956

As a writer Thomson confined himself almost exclusively to the facts, or at least to the recording of his recollections of the facts. No doubt he and most of the other connoisseurs would have smiled behind their hands a little at the outrageous coincidences, the far-fetched eleventh-hour triumphs, the romantic final balls of so many sensational final overs, which recurred in the cricket fiction of the time. But the sceptic, before he dismisses as moonshine the innocent literary daydreams of some armchair Sobers, has to ask himself which in the end is the more absurd, the fact or the fiction of cricket. In 1910, two pulsating dreams were staged at Lord's, one attended by thousands of baying, sobbing, hysterical spectators, the other unseen by anyone apart from the dreamer.

The dream is of course absurd. But so is the fact, and more so. In the dream we are presented with a well-educated but penniless bank clerk who is a born batting virtuoso. All his elder brothers have, like the Fosters, distinguished themselves at the highest level, and now he, unexpectedly, has been given the chance to follow in their footsteps. But his opening is fraught with all the dangers facing the young amateur of the day. Our hero, if he is to snatch his chance, has to defy Mr Bickersdyke, manager of the City bank which employs him. He dashes to Lord's knowing his job is lost. What will he do to earn a living? The dispassionate observer might ask why, since the lad is clearly a cricket genius, he cannot make his living at cricket? But he has been educated at a public school. His family is genteel and well-spoken. All his brothers are amateurs. For all these social reasons and a dozen others just as pointless, the gates of professionalism are barred to him unless he is prepared to become an outcast. So he goes out to bat at Lord's with the weight of his entire future weighing him down.

Mike got to Lord's just as the umpires moved out into the field. He raced round to the pavilion. Joe met him on the stairs.

'It's all right,' he said. 'No hurry. We've won the toss. I've put you in fourth wicket.'

'Right ho,' said Mike. 'Glad we haven't to field just yet.'

'We oughtn't to have to field today if we don't chuck our wickets away.'

'Good wicket?'

'Like a billiard-table. I'm glad you were able to come. Have any difficulty in getting away?'

Joe Jackson's knowledge of the workings of a bank was of the slightest. He himself had never, since he left Oxford, been in a position where there were obstacles to getting off to play in first-class cricket. By profession he was agent to a sporting baronet whose hobby was the cricket of the county, and so, far from finding any difficulty in playing for the county, he was given to understand by his employer that that was his chief duty. It never occurred to him that Mike might find his bank less amenable in the matter of giving leave. His only fear, when he rang Mike up that morning, had been that this might be a particularly busy day at the New Asiatic Bank. If there was no special rush of work, he took it for granted that Mike would simply go to the manager, ask for leave to play in the match, and be given it with a beaming smile.

Mike did not answer the question, but asked one on his own account.

'How did you happen to be short?' he said.

'It was rotten luck. It was like this. We were altering our team after the Sussex match, to bring in Ballard, Keene, and Willis. They couldn't get down to Brighton, as the 'Varsity had a match, but there was nothing on for them in the last half of the week, so they'd promised to roll up.'

Ballard, Keene, and Willis were members of the Cambridge team, all very capable performers and much in demand by the county, when they could get away to play for it.

'Well?' said Mike.

'Well, we all came up by train from Brighton last night. But these three asses had arranged to motor down from Cambridge early today, and get here in time for the start. What happens? Why, Willis, who fancies himself as a chauffeur, undertakes to do the driving; and naturally, being an absolute rotter, goes and smashes up the whole concern just outside St Albans. The first thing I knew of it was when I got to Lord's at half past ten, and found a wire waiting for me to say that they were all three of them crocked, and couldn't possibly play. I tell you, it was a bit of a jar to get half an hour before the match started. Willis has sprained his ankle, apparently; Keene's damaged his wrist; and Ballard has smashed his collar bone. I don't suppose they'll be able to play in the 'Varsity match. Rotten luck for Cambridge. Well, fortunately we'd had two reserve pros. with us at Brighton, who had come up to London with the team in case they might be wanted, so, with them, we were only one short. Then I thought of you. That's how it was.'

'I see,' said Mike. 'Who are the pros?'

'Davis and Brockley. Both bowlers. It weakens our batting a lot. Ballard or

Willis might have got a stack of runs on this wicket. Still, we've got a certain amount of batting as it is. We oughtn't to do badly, if we're careful. You've been getting some practice, I suppose, this season?'

'In a sort of a way. Nets and so on. No matches of any importance.'

'Dash it. I wish you'd had a game or two in decent class cricket. Still, nets are better than nothing. I hope you'll be in form. We may want a pretty long knock from you, if things go wrong. These men seem to be settling down all right, thank goodness,' he added, looking out of the window at the county's first pair, Warrington and Mills, two professionals, who, as the result of ten minutes' play, had put up twenty.

'I'd better go and change,' said Mike, picking up his bag. 'You're in first wicket, I suppose?'

'Yes. And Reggie, second wicket.'

Reggie was another of Mike's brothers, not nearly so fine a player as Joe, but a sound bat, who generally made runs if allowed to stay in.

Mike changed, and went out into the little balcony at the top of the pavilion. He had it to himself. There were not many spectators in the pavilion at this early stage of the game.

There are few more restful places, if one wishes to think, than the upper balconies of Lord's pavilion. Mike, watching the game making its leisurely progess on the turf below, set himself seriously to review the situation in all its aspects. The exhilaration of bursting the bonds had begun to fade, and he found himself able to look into the matter of his desertion and weigh up the consequences. There was no doubt that he had cut the painter once and for all. Even a friendly-disposed management could hardly overlook what he had done. And the management of the New Asiatic Bank was the very reverse of friendly. Mr Bickersdyke, he knew, would jump at this chance of getting rid of him. He realised that he must look on his career in the bank as a closed book. It was definitely over, and he must now think about the future.

It was not a time for half-measures. He could not go home. He must carry the thing through, now that he had begun, and find something definite to do, to support himself.

There seemed only one opening for him. What could he do, he asked himself. Just one thing. He could play cricket. It was by his cricket that he must live. He would have to become a professional. Could he get taken on? That was the question. It was impossible that he should play for his own county on his residential qualification. He could not appear as a professional in the same team in which his brothers were playing as amateurs. He must stake all on his birth qualification for Surrey.

On the other hand, had he the credentials which Surrey would want? He had a school reputation. But was that enough? He could not help feeling that it might not be.

Thinking it over more tensely than he had ever thought over anything in his whole life, he saw clearly that everything depended on what sort of show he made in this match which was now in progress. It was his big chance. If he succeeded, all would be well. He did not care to think what his position would be if he did not succeed.

A distant appeal and a sound of clapping from the crowd broke in on his thoughts. Mills was out, caught at the wicket. The telegraph-board gave the total as forty-eight. Not sensational. The success of the team depended largely on what sort of a start the two professionals made.

The clapping broke out again as Joe made his way down the steps. Joe, as an All England player, was a favourite with the crowd.

Mike watched him play an over in his strong, graceful style: then it suddenly occurred to him that he would like to know how matters had gone at the bank in his absence.

He went down to the telephone, rang up the bank, and asked for Psmith.

Presently the familiar voice made itself heard.

'Hullo, Smith.'

'Hullo. Is that Comrade Jackson? How are things progressing?'

'Fairly well. We're in first. We've lost one wicket, and the fifty's just up. I say, what's happened at the bank?'

'I broke the news to Comrade Gregory. A charming personality. I feel that we shall be friends.'

'Was he sick?'

'In a measure, yes. Indeed, I may say he practically foamed at the mouth. I explained the situation, but he was not to be appeased. He jerked me into the presence of Comrade Bickersdyke, with whom I had a brief but entertaining chat. He had not a great deal to say, but he listened attentively to my narrative, and eventually told me off to take your place in the Fixed Deposits. That melancholy task I am now performing to the best of my ability. I find the work a little trying. There is too much ledger-lugging to be done for my simple tastes. I have been hauling ledgers from the safe all the morning. The cry is beginning to go round, "Psmith is willing, but can his physique stand the strain?" In the excitement of the moment just now I dropped a somewhat massive tome on to Comrade Gregory's foot, unfortunately, I understand, the foot in which he has of late been suffering twinges of gout. I passed the thing off with ready tact, but I cannot deny that there was a certain temporary coolness, which, indeed, is not yet past. These things, Comrade Jackson, are the whirlpools in the quiet stream of commercial life.'

'Have I got the sack?'

'No official pronouncement has been made to me as yet on the subject, but I think I should advise you, if you are offered another job in the course of the day, to accept it. I cannot say that you are precisely the pet of the management just at present. However, I have ideas for your future, which I will divulge when we meet. I propose to slide coyly from the office at about four o'clock. I am meeting my father at that hour. We shall come straight on to Lord's.'

'Right ho,' said Mike. 'I'll be looking out for you.'

'Is there any little message I can give Comrade Gregory from you?'

'You can give him my love, if you like.'

'It shall be done. Good-bye.'

'Good-bye.'

Mike replaced the receiver, and went up to his balcony again.

As soon as his eye fell on the telegraph-board he saw with a start that things had been moving rapidly in his brief absence. The numbers of the batsmen on the board were three and five.

'Great Scott!' he cried. 'Why, I'm in next. What on earth's been happening?'

He put on his pads hurriedly, expecting every moment that a wicket would fall and find him unprepared. But the batsmen were still together when he rose, ready for the fray, and went downstairs to get news.

He found his brother Reggie in the dressing-room.

'What's happened?' he said. 'How were you out?'

'Lbw,' said Reggie. 'Goodness knows how it happened. My eyesight must be going. I mistimed the thing altogether.'

'How was Warrington out?'

'Caught in the slips.'

'By Jove!' said Mike. 'This is pretty rocky. Three for sixty-one. We shall get mopped.'

'Unless you and Joe do something. There's no earthly need to get out. The wicket's as good as you want, and the bowling's nothing special. Well played, Joe!'

A beautiful glide to leg by the greatest of the Jacksons had rolled up against the pavilion rails. The fieldsmen changed across for the next over.

'If only Peters stops a bit –' began Mike, and broke off. Peters' off stump was lying at an angle of forty-five degrees.

'Well, he hasn't,' said Reggie grimly. 'Silly ass, why did he hit at that one? All he'd got to do was to stay in with Joe. Now it's up to you. Do try and do something, or we'll be out under the hundred.'

Mike waited till the outcoming batsman had turned in at the professionals' gate. Then he walked down the steps and out into the open, feeling more nervous than he had felt since that far-off day when he had first gone in to bat for Wrykyn against the MCC. He found his thoughts flying back to that occasion. Today, as then, everything seemed very distant and unreal. The spectators were miles away. He had often been to Lord's as a spectator, but the place seemed entirely unfamiliar now. He felt as if he were in a strange land.

He was conscious of Joe leaving the crease to meet him on his way. He smiled feebly. 'Buck up,' said Joe in that robust way of his which was so heartening. 'Nothing in the bowling, and the wicket like a shirt-front. Play just as if you were at the nets. And for goodness' sake don't try to score all your runs in the first over. Stick in, and we've got them.'

Mike smiled again more feebly than before, and made a weird gurgling noise in his throat.

It had been the Middlesex fast bowler who had destroyed Peters. Mike was not sorry. He did not object to fast bowling. He took guard, and looked round him, taking careful note of the positions of the slips.

As usual, once he was at the wicket the paralysed feeling left him. He became conscious again of his power. Dash it all, what was there to be afraid of? He was a jolly good bat, and he would jolly well show them that he was, too.

The fast bowler, with a preliminary bound, began his run. Mike settled himself into position, his whole soul concentrated on the ball. Everything else was wiped from his mind.

P. G. WODEHOUSE, *Mike*, 1909

A ND while Mike is battling it out, his loyal friend Psmith is also walking out of the bank for the last time. He, being the son of his father, has no real need to find any sort of job at all, but regards it as important to see what is happening at Lord's. So he seeks out his father, and the pair of them take a cab to the ground where they are delighted to find that Mike has reached 98 not out. The next chapter flashes back to the start of the innings:

For nearly two hours Mike had been experiencing the keenest pleasure that it had ever fallen to his lot to feel. From the moment he took his first ball till the luncheon interval he had suffered the acutest discomfort. His nervousness had left him to a great extent, but he had never really settled down. Sometimes by luck, and sometimes by skill, he had kept the ball out of his wicket; but he was scratching, and he knew it. Not for a single over had he been comfortable. On several occasions he had edged balls to leg and through the slips in quite an inferior manner, and it was seldom that he managed to hit with the centre of the bat.

Nobody is more alive to the fact that he is not playing up to his true form than the batsman. Even though his score mounted little by little into the twenties, Mike was miserable. If this was the best he could do on a perfect wicket, he felt there was not much hope for him as a professional.

The poorness of his play was accentuated by the brilliance of Joe's. Joe combined science and vigour to a remarkable degree. He laid on the wood with a graceful robustness which drew much cheering from the crowd. Beside him Mike was oppressed by that leaden sense of moral inferiority which weighs on a man who has turned up to dinner in ordinary clothes when everybody else has dressed. He felt awkward and conspicuously out of place.

Then came lunch – and after lunch a glorious change.

Volumes might be written on the cricket lunch and the influence it has on the run of the game; how it undoes one man, and sends another back to the fray like a giant refreshed; how it turns the brilliant fast bowler into the sluggish medium, and the nervous bat into the masterful smiter.

On Mike its effect was magical. He lunched wisely and well, chewing his food with the concentration of a thirty-three-bites a mouthful crank, and drinking dry ginger-ale. As he walked out with Joe after the interval he knew that a change had taken place in him. His nerve had come back, and with it his form.

It sometimes happens at cricket that when one feels particularly fit one gets snapped in the slips in the first over, or clean bowled by a full toss; but neither of these things happened to Mike. He stayed in, and began to score. Now there were no edgings through the slips and snicks to leg. He was meeting the ball in the centre of the bat, and meeting it vigorously. Two boundaries in successive balls off the fast bowler, hard, clean drives past extra-cover, put him at peace with all the world. He was on top. He had found himself.

Joe, at the other end, resumed his brilliant career. His century and Mike's fifty arrived in the same over. The bowling began to grow loose.

Joe, having reached his century, slowed down somewhat, and Mike took up the running. The score rose rapidly.

A leg-theory bowler kept down the pace of the run-getting for a time, but the bowlers at the other end continued to give away runs. Mike's score passed from sixty to seventy, from seventy to eighty, from eighty to ninety. When the Smiths, father and son, came on to the ground the total was ninety-eight. Joe had made a hundred and thirty-three.

Mike reached his century just as Psmith and his father took their seats. A square cut off the slow bowler was just too wide for point to get to. By the time third man had sprinted across and returned the ball the batsmen had run two.

Mr Smith was enthusiastic.

'I tell you,' he said to Psmith, who was clapping in a gently encouraging manner, 'the boy's a wonderful bat. I said so when he was down with us. I remember telling him so myself. "I've seen your brothers play," I said, "and you're better than any of them." I remember it distinctly. He'll be playing for England in another year or two. Fancy putting a cricketer like that into the City! It's a crime.'

'I gather,' said Psmith, 'that the family coffers had got a bit low. It was necessary for Comrade Jackson to do something by way of saving the Old Home.'

'He ought to be at the University. Look, he's got that man away to the boundary again. They'll never get him out.'

At six o'clock the partnership was broken, Joe running himself out in trying to snatch a single where no single was. He had made a hundred and eighty-nine.

Mike flung himself down on the turf with mixed feelings. He was sorry Joe was out, but he was very glad indeed of the chance of a rest. He was utterly fagged. A half-day match once a week is no training for first-class cricket. Joe, who had been playing all the season, was as tough as india-rubber, and trotted into the pavilion as fresh as if he had been having a brief spell at the nets. Mike, on the other hand, felt that he simply wanted to be dropped into a cold bath and left there indefinitely. There was only another half-hour's play, but he doubted if he could get through it.

He dragged himself up wearily as Joe's successor arrived at the wickets. He had crossed Joe before the latter's downfall, and it was his turn to take the bowling.

Something seemed to have gone out of him. He could not time the ball properly. The last ball of the over looked like a half-volley, and he hit out at it. But it was just short of a half-volley, and his stroke arrived too soon. The bowler, running in the direction of mid-on, brought off an easy c.-and-b.

Mike turned away towards the pavilion. He heard the gradually swelling applause in a sort of dream. It seemed to him hours before he reached the dressing-room.

He was sitting on a chair, wishing that somebody would come along and take off his pads, when Psmith's card was brought to him. A few moments later the old Etonian appeared in person. 'Hullo, Smith,' said Mike. 'By Jove! I'm done.'

'"How Little Willie Saved the Match,"' said Psmith. 'What you want is one of those gin and ginger-beers we hear so much about. Remove those pads, and let us flit downstairs in search of a couple. Well, Comrade Jackson, you have fought the good fight this day. My father sends his compliments. He is dining out, or he would have come up. He is going to look in at the flat latish.'

'How many did I get?' asked Mike. 'I was so jolly done I didn't think of looking.'

'A hundred and forty-eight of the best,' said Psmith. 'What will they say at the old homestead about this? Are you ready? Then let us test this fruity old ginger-beer of theirs.'

The two batsmen who had followed the big stand were apparently having a little stand all of their own. No more wickets fell before the drawing of stumps. Psmith waited for Mike while he changed, and carried him off in a cab to Simpson's, a restaurant which, as he justly observed, offered two great advantages, namely, that you need not dress, and, secondly, that you paid your half-crown, and were then at liberty to eat till you were helpless, if you felt so disposed, without extra charge.

Mike stopped short of this giddy height of mastication, but consumed enough to make him feel a great deal better. Psmith eyed his inroads on the menu with approval.

'There is nothing,' he said, 'like victualling up before an ordeal.'

'What's the ordeal?' said Mike.

'I propose to take you round to the club anon, where I trust we shall find Comrade Bickersdyke. We have much to say to one another.'

'Look here, I'm hanged –' began Mike.

'Yes, you must be there,' said Psmith. 'Your presence will serve to cheer Comrade B. up. Fate compels me to deal him a nasty blow, and he will want sympathy. I have got to break it to him that I am leaving the bank.'

'What, are you going to chuck it?'

Psmith inclined his head.

'The time,' he said, 'has come to part. It has served its turn. The startled whisper runs round the City, "Psmith has had sufficient."'

'What are you going to do?'

'I propose to enter the University of Cambridge, and there to study the intricacies of the Law, with a view to having a subsequent dash at becoming Lord Chancellor.'

'By Jove!' said Mike, 'you're lucky. I wish I were coming too.'

Psmith knocked the ash off his cigarette.

'Are you absolutely set on becoming a pro?' he asked.

'It depends on what you call set. It seems to me it's about all I can do.'

'I can offer you a not entirely scaly job,' said Smith, 'if you feel like taking it. In the course of conversation with my father during the match this afternoon, I gleaned the fact that he is anxious to secure your services as a species of agent. The vast Psmith estates, it seems, need a bright boy to keep an eye upon them. Are you prepared to accept the post?'

Mike stared.

'Me! Dash it all, how old do you think I am? I'm only nineteen.'

'I had suspected as much from the alabaster clearness of your unwrinkled brow. But my father does not wish you to enter upon your duties immediately. There would be a preliminary interval of three, possibly four, years at Cambridge, during which I presume, you would be learning divers facts concerning spuds, turmuts, and the like. At least,' said Psmith airily, 'I suppose so. Far be it from me to dictate the line of your researches.'

'Then I'm afraid it's off,' said Mike gloomily. 'My pater couldn't afford to send me to Cambridge.'

'That obstacle,' said Psmith, 'can be surmounted. You would, of course, accompany me to Cambridge, in the capacity, which you enjoy at the present moment, of my confidential secretary and adviser. Any expenses that might crop up would be defrayed from the Psmith family chest.'

Mike's eyes opened wide again.

'Do you mean,' he asked bluntly, 'that your pater would pay for me at the 'Varsity? No I say – dash it – I mean, I couldn't –'

'Do you suggest,' said Psmith, raising his eyebrows, 'that I should go to the University *without* a confidential secretary and adviser?'

'No, but I mean –' protested Mike.

'Then that's settled,' said Psmith. 'I knew you would not desert me in my hour of need, Comrade Jackson. "What will you do," asked my father, alarmed for my safety, "among these wild undergraduates? I fear for my Rupert." "Have no fear, father," I replied. "Comrade Jackson will be beside me." His face brightened immediately. "Comrade Jackson," he said, "is a man in whom I have the supremest confidence. If he is with you I shall sleep easy of nights." It was after that that the conversation drifted to the subject of agents.'

Psmith called for the bill and paid it in the affable manner of a monarch signing a charter. Mike sat silent, his mind in a whirl. He saw exactly what had happened. He could almost hear Psmith talking his father into agreeing with his scheme. He could think of nothing to say. As usually happened in any emotional crisis in his life, words absolutely deserted him. The thing was too big. Anything he could say would sound too feeble. When a friend has solved all your difficulties and smoothed out all the rough places which were looming in your path, you cannot thank him as if he had asked you to lunch. The occasion demanded some neat, polished speech; and neat, polished speeches were beyond Mike.

'I say, Psmith –' he began.

Psmith rose.

'Let us now,' he said, 'collect our hats and meander to the club, where, I have no doubt, we shall find Comrade Bickersdyke, all unconscious of impending misfortune, dreaming pleasantly over coffee and a cigar in the lower smoking-room.'

P. G. WODEHOUSE, *Mike*, 1909

AND so our hero is saved after all from the ignominy of embracing the serpent of professionalism. His debut at Lord's may be lit by pure moonshine, but it is hardly more far-fetched than the motivation for the espousing of the Communist cause which has characterised the attitude of his friend Psmith since the start of the saga. An outstanding leg-break bowler at Eton, Psmith had looked forward confidently to the day when he would step out on to the Lord's turf to do battle with Harrow. But his father, chagrined at his son's indifference to academic pursuits, had removed him to the minor public school where he met Mike. Psmith, outraged that he should so callously be deprived of the glory of the Lord's debut he has so richly earned, decides to embrace a revolutionary creed in protest, although it must be admitted that his grasp of Marxist principles seems to go no further than an insistence on addressing the rest of the world as Comrade. The romance between Psmith and Dialectical Materialism seems ridiculous until we encounter the following observation by the historian Barbara Tuchman on the theme of Henry Hyndman (1842–1921). The Old Etonian Hyndman was the first Englishman to form a Socialist party. Of him, Miss Tuchman writes: 'He complained of the peculiarly British technique by which the ruling class absorbed rising labour leaders who proved only too willing to sell out to the dominant minority (that is, the Liberals), "after they had obtained their education from well-to-do Socialists who have been sacrificing themselves for their sake". The tone suggests some justification for the friends who said that Hyndman, a cricketer, had adopted Socialism out of pure spite against the world because he was not included in the Cambridge eleven.' Even Miss Tuchman, one of the most eminent living historians, has missed the point. Being American, she mistakenly assumes that Hyndman had merely wished to play for Cambridge. In fact, he had, several times. The essence of his complaint was not that he had been overlooked for the side, but that he had been overlooked on the only occasion which really mattered, the game against Oxford at Lord's. As for Mike's fairy-tale century, it may be a little difficult to swallow, but, seen in the lurid light of the events at the actual Eton v. Harrow match at Lord's that very same summer, the literary contrivances of Mike's creator, the public school opening bowler P. G. Wodehouse, seem quite mild by comparison.

ETON v HARROW
Played at Lord's, July 8, 9, 1910

Eton and Harrow have been meeting on the cricket field for over a hundred years, but they have never played a match quite so remarkable as that of 1910. Indeed in the whole history of cricket there has been nothing more sensational. After following on their innings Eton were only four ahead with nine wickets down, and yet in the end they won the game by 9 runs. The nearest parallel to this finish that one can recall was one between Lancashire and Oxford University in 1888. On that occasion the county followed-on, and managed to win although when their eighth wicket fell they were still 17 runs behind. The struggle between the two public schools last season will be known for all time as Fowler's match. Never has a school cricketer risen to the occasion in more astonishing fashion. When Harrow went in with only 55 to get, Fowler took command of the game, secured eight wickets – five of them bowled down – for 23 runs and brought off what might fairly be described as a forty to one chance.

Until the second afternoon was far advanced the match proved one-sided to a degree. On the first day Harrow going in on a soft, but by no means difficult pitch, ran up a total of 232, and when bad light caused stumps to be drawn, five of Eton's best wickets had fallen for 40 runs. By far the best batting for Harrow was shown in different styles by Wilson and Hillyard. In first and out fifth wicket down at 133, Wilson took two hours and a quarter to get his 53, his play all the time being very patient and watchful. Hillyard, more vigorous in his methods, scored 62 in an hour and three-quarters, among his hits being a six to square leg and half-a-dozen 4s. On Saturday morning, Eton's first innings was soon finished off for 67, and a follow-on against a balance of 165 was involved. At first things went so badly that half the wickets were down for 65, no one being able to get the ball away on the slow pitch. The first change in the game came with the partnership between Fowler, and Wigan, 42 runs being added for the sixth wicket in fifty minutes. When Wigan left, Boswell, who had been last man in the first innings, joined Fowler and another good start was made, three-quarters of an hour's play producing 57 runs. Still despite Fowler's heroic efforts – his 64 was the highest innings in the match – the position was reached of Eton being only 4 runs ahead with a wicket to fall. Then began the cricket which will for ever make the match memorable. Kaye joined Manners, and so finely and fearlessly did Manners hit that in less than twenty-five minutes 50 runs were put on, the total being carried from 169 to 219. A remarkable catch in the slips at last brought the innings to an end, Hopley just reaching the ball and turning it to Jameson, who held it a few inches from the ground. There can be no doubt that Earle, the Harrow captain, who had made many changes in the early part of the innings, was at fault in keeping himself and Hillyard on too long. In the case of any ordinary match the ground would have been half empty before the Eton innings closed, but an Eton and Harrow crowd is a law to itself and when Harrow went in with 55 to get about 10,000 people watched the cricket. Whatever their feelings, they must have been glad they stayed as they may never see such a finish again. Probably Harrow made a mistake in having the heavy roller on. At any rate Fowler was able at once to bowl his off-break with deadly effect. He bowled Wilson in the first over; at eight he bowled Hopley; and at the same total, Turnbull, the left-handed hitter was caught in the long field. Earle seemed likely to win the match easily enough for Harrow, but after he had hit up 13 runs, a catch at slip sent him back at 21. Without the addition of a run, Monckton was bowled and Hillyard well caught low down at short mid-on. In this way, as the result of half an hour's cricket, six wickets were down for 21, Fowler having taken them all. Blount was caught and bowled at 26 by Steel, who had just gone on for Kaye, and then Jameson, who had been batting for nearly forty minutes without getting a run, was so badly hurt that for a few minutes the game had to be delayed. With victory in sight, the Eton team played the keenest possible cricket, nothing being thrown away in the field. A yorker bowled Straker at 29, and, after Graham had hit a three, Jameson was bowled by Fowler. It was not to be expected that Graham and Alexander would get the 23 runs still required, but they made a desperate effort, carrying the score to 45 or only 10 to win. Then a catch low down in the slips got rid of Alexander and a wonderful match was over. The scene of enthusiasm at the finish was quite indescribable. From the time he went on at 21, Steel with his leg breaks gave Fowler excellent support and the Eton fielding all round was magnificent.

Harrow

Mr T. O. Jameson, c. Lubbock, b. Fowler	5	b. Fowler	2
Mr T. B. Wilson, b. Kaye	53	b. Fowler	0
Mr G. W. V. Hopley, b. Fowler	35	b. Fowler	8
Mr T. L. G. Turnbull, lbw. b. Fowler	2	c. Boswell, b. Fowler	0
Mr G. F. Earle, c. Wigan, b. Steel	20	c. Wigan, b. Fowler	13
Mr W. T. Monckton, c. Lubbock, b. Stock	20	b. Fowler	0
Mr J. M. Hillyard, st. Lubbock, b. Fowler	62	c. Kaye, b. Fowler	0
Mr C. H. B. Blount, c. Holland, b. Steel	4	c. and b. Steel	5
Mr A. C. Straker, c. Holland, b. Steel	2	b. Fowler	1
Mr O. B. Graham, c. and b. Steel	6	not out	7
Hon. R. H. I. G. Alexander not out	2	c. Holland, b. Steel	8
B. 18, l-b. 2, n-b. 1	21	B.	1
	232		45

Eton

Mr R. H. Lubbock, lbw. b. Earle	9	c. Straker, b. Hillyard	9
Mr C. W. Tafnell, b. Hillyard	5	lbw. b. Alexander	7
Mr W. T. Birchenough, c. Hopley, b. Graham	5	c. Turnball, b. Jameson	22
Mr W. T. Holland, c. Hopley, b. Hillyard	2	st. Monckton, b. Alexander	5
Mr R. St. L. Fowler, c. Graham, b. Jameson	21	c. Earle, b. Hillyard	64
Mr A. I. Steel, b. Graham	0	c. Hopley, b. Hillyard	6
Mr D. G. Wigan, c. Turnbull, b. Jameson	8	b. Graham	16
Mr A. B. Stock, lbw. b. Alexander	2	lbw. b. Earle	0
Hon. J. N. Manners, c. Graham, b. Alexander	4	not out	40
Mr K. Lister Kaye, c. Straker, b. Alexander	0	c. Jameson, b. Earle	13
Mr W. G. K. Boswell not out	0	b. Earle	32
B. 10, w. 1	11	B. 2, w. 3	5
	67		219

Eton Bowling

	Overs	Mdns	Runs	Wkts	Overs	Mdns	Runs	Wkts
Fowler	37.3	9	90	4	10	2	23	8
Steel	31	11	69	4	6.4	1	12	2
Kaye	12	5	23	1	3	–	9	–
Stock	7	2	12	1				
Boswell	8	4	17	–				

Harrow Bowling

	Overs	Mdns	Runs	Wkts	Overs	Mdns	Runs	Wkts
Earle	12	9	4	1	17.3	3	57	3
Hillyard	19	9	28	2	23	7	65	2
Graham	9	7	13	2	8	2	33	1
Jameson	4	1	4	2	9	1	26	1
Alexander	4.1	1	7	3	14	4	33	2
Wilson					2	2	—	–

Umpires: J. Moss and J. P. Whiteside.

Wisden, 1911

A ND SO, within the span of a few hours of cricket, Robert St Leger Fowler (1891–1925), became a deathless hero for his class and generation. Because he made his career in the Army, Fowler subsequently dropped out of the public eye, although in 1924 he did appear twice for Hampshire in the County Championship. In the Great War he rose to the rank of Captain with the 17th Lancers and was awarded the Military Cross. He was to enjoy one more day of Wodehousean glory at Lord's, in 1920, when, batting for the Army against the MCC, he made 92 not out. To this day his phantom first-class career remains one of the great might-have-beens of amateur cricket. So overwhelming was his virtuosity in that one game that the rest of his team-mates suffered an eclipse which was perhaps not altogether deserved, especially in the case of the valiant Manners, without whose support even Fowler would have failed. Within the bosom of the Manners family during that fatal match, hope and despair swirled in violently fluctuating disorder, and it has been left to the inspired chatterbox of the Jameson Raid, Lieutenant Colonel Foley, to preserve the unforgettable scenario of Jeeves frustrated in his attempts to convey tidings of unexpected bliss to the 9th Earl. However, the veracity of Foley's account has sometimes been questioned, and it has to be said that any account of anything which confers on the supine figure of A. J. Balfour even the smallest degree of animation does sound distinctly bogus:

I was going to spend that Saturday to Monday at Coombe with General Sir Arthur Paget, and, not being in the least anxious to see an overwhelming Harrow victory, I left the ground and called in at White's Club to pick up my bag. Providentially, as it turned out, my hair wanted cutting. Half-way through the operation Lord Brackley looked in and said, 'Harrow have lost four wickets for 21 runs,' and a few minutes later, 'Harrow have lost six wickets for 21 runs.' That was enough. I sprang from the chair with my hair half cut and standing on end, and we rushed together into the street, jumped into a taxi, and said,

'Lord's! Double fare if you do it in fifteen minutes.' We got there in 14 minutes $21\frac{2}{5}$ seconds (I carry a stop-watch), paid the man, and advanced on the pavilion at a pace which is called in the French Army *le pas gymnastique*. The shallow steps leading into the pavilion at Lord's form a right-angle. Round this angle I sprang three steps at a time, carrying my umbrella at the trail. A dejected Harrovian, wearing a dark-blue rosette, and evidently unable to bear the agony of the match any longer, was leaving the pavilion with bowed head. I was swinging my umbrella to give me impetus, and its point caught the unfortunate man in the lower part of his waistcoat, and rebounded from one of its buttons out of my hand and over the side rails of the pavilion. The impact was terrific, and the unlucky individual, doubling up, sank like a wounded buffalo on to his knees, without, as far as I recollect, uttering a sound. I sprang over the body without apology, and, shouting out instructions to George Bean, the Sussex pro, who was the gate attendant, to look after my umbrella, dashed into the pavilion and up the many steps to its very summit, where I hoped to find a vacant seat.

I arrived there at the moment that Jameson was lying on the ground badly cut over, and was told that he had been batting forty minutes for no runs. As he has always been such an exceptionally quick scorer, this is worthy of record. With the total at 29, Fowler yorked Straker for 1 (29–8–1). The excitement then reached its climax. I do not think I ever saw or heard anything like it. The roars from the Harrow stand whenever a run was made were heard in the Zoological Gardens. Graham hit a 3, and then Fowler bowled Jameson. He had scored 2 and was ninth man out, and it was a thousand pities that he did not set up a record by carrying his bat through the innings for 0! (32–9–2) Alexander came in, looking horribly confident. The score crept up slowly. By now the cheering had swollen into such a volume of sound that its overtones included Paddington Station as well as the Zoological Gardens in its perimeter. Thirteen priceless runs were sneaked or stolen by the indomitable last pair. How I loathed both of them! And just as things began to look really desperate Alexander edged one to Holland in the slips off Steel, and Eton had won by 9 runs!

Needless to say the scene in front of the pavilion baffles description. I believe, though I do not vouch for it, that Lord Manners, the father of John Manners, who, gallant in his youth as in his manhood, had played such a conspicuous part in the victory, left the ground in despair at lunch-time and retired to his room with strict orders that he was not to be disturbed. It is further said that the butler knocked twice at his door with the object of telling him what his son had done, and so forth, and that he was told to 'Go away' on both occasions. If it is true that the prospect of a Harrow victory was too much for Lord Manners, his regrets that he failed to see the finish must indeed have been poignant. Sir Ian Malcolm, in his recollections of Mr A.J. Balfour, says, 'I can never forget the magnificent finish of the Eton and Harrow match in Fowler's year, when at the close of play A.J.B., Walter Forbes, Alfred Lyttelton, and two of his brothers all leapt on to the green bench upon which we had been sitting in the pavilion and waved their hats and cheered Eton in an abandonment of enthusiasm.' It has always been called 'Fowler's match'. As he made top score in both innings – namely, 21 and 64 – and took twelve wickets, such a designation is entirely justified. His analysis for the last innings was 10 overs, 2 maidens, 23 runs, 8 wickets.

C. P. FOLEY, *Autumn Foliage*, 1935

THE experience of witnessing these extraordinary events proved too much for the cool head of one of the Eton College science masters, who was visited by the divine afflatus. The evidence was later published by him in a predictably slim volume of poems:

ETON *v.* HARROW
(8, 9 July 1910)

If so be you chance to call
'Heads,' and straightway tails shall fall,
Do not make a fruitless fuss,
Do not say, ' 'Twas ever thus';
Exercise some self-control,
Cultivate a steadfast soul.

If your safest drop a catch,
Do not say, 'There goes the match.'
If so be one ball in six
Beat the bat and beat the sticks,
Still proceed your best to bowl,
Still possess your patient soul.

If, when now your turn is nigh,
Clouds and darkness fill the sky
Ere the hour of six have struck,
Say not sadly, 'Just our luck!'
Strive to keep your wicket whole,
Set your teeth, O steadfast soul.

If they make you follow-on,
Do not say, 'All hope is gone';
What though sky and fortune frown,
We may slowly wear them down.
Sure 'twill mitigate the pain
Just to put them in again.

Samuel Johnson late, like you,
Found his fame, his Boswell too,
'Manners makyth man,' God wot!
Manners maketh 'forty not.'
Put them in? Why, man alive,
Put them in for fifty-five!

Birds may 'scape the Fowler's snare;
Just as well no Bird is there.
Harrow's turn to scrape for runs,
Less like birds than furry ones.
Joy we all the same to feel
Foemen worthy of our Steel.

Swift reward for patient pluck;
Not to every man such luck.
One who cursed remains to bless—
Eton, mayst thou still possess,
When still deeper waters roll,
Thy 'unconquerable soul.'

W. D. E.

But not all the cricketing excitements at Lord's were to do with the play. There were some members who saw it as their duty to grumble about conditions at the ground and to prophecy woe and lamentation if something were not done very soon. The irony of the following letter, written by the one-time Somerset big hitter W. H. Fowler, is that it cites the Eton v. Harrow fixture as an example of a game which had recently fallen foul of the inadequate ground facilities. On the very morning that this letter appeared in *The Times*, Mr Fowler's young namesake, Robert St Leger Fowler, was just tying up his boots in preparation for one of the most sensational matches ever seen at the ground.

Sir, This ancient home of the game of cricket has of late earned an unenviable notoriety by reason of the long time the surface takes to dry after heavy rain. It will be remembered by many thousands how the Eton and Harrow match of last year had to be left as a draw, although half an hour's play on Saturday would probably have sufficed to give a definite result. Cricket was played on The Oval on that day, and there was no special circumstance why it should not have been possible at Lord's also. Then on Monday last, on a fine day, we saw the start of the Oxford and Cambridge match delayed until 4 p.m. The ground even then was in a shocking state and not really fit for such an important contest. There have been many other cases during the past few years, which go to prove that the wicket and ground hold the water on the surface far too long. The question is, can anything be done to prevent these tedious delays without tampering with the wicket?

I venture to suggest that a course of treatment similar to that which has been successfully carried out on many golf courses, where heavy clay soils have had to be dealt with, would transform Lord's from a slow to a quick drying ground. The pitch and the outfielding require different treatment. For the former the turf should be removed and the soil taken up to a depth of at least a foot. Then put in a layer of rough clinker at the bottom, and finer above, to a depth of 6 in., then fill in with the soil taken out and relay the old turf. This plan would have two advantages from a turf-growing point of view: first, the harm done by worm-casts in the spring would be largely reduced, if not absolutely stopped; and, secondly, the grass roots would become healthier and the turf would stand wet and drought far better.

For the fielding part of the ground, the plan of heavy dressings of 'coke breeze' every autumn would be found to work wonders in the way of helping the ground to absorb heavy rains. The 'breeze' should be spread on thickly at the end of September and rolled in with a light roller. The grass will soon come up through it, and it will remain just under the surface, and by the next cricket season no one would know it was there. The result to the turf, however, would be easily seen, as it would be far healthier, and in a few years it would cure the cracking which is now so often in evidence during hot weather. This treatment would not do for the pitch, as the 'breeze' would be too near the surface.

In making these suggestions, which are based on practical experience, I desire to say most emphatically that I would do nothing to 'doctor' or alter the wicket from what it has been in the past. I would use the same soil, and the only difference my suggested treatment would make would be to produce a healthier turf and ensure the quick drying of the wicket and outfield.

W. Herbert Fowler,
Letter to *The Times*, 8 July 1910

The following winter the drainage was overhauled.

IN 1912, thanks to the persistence of the South African millionaire Sir Abe Bailey, the first-ever Triangular Test tournament, between England, South Africa and Australia, was played out on English grounds. Three of the nine Tests were staged at Lord's, but the experiment proved a miserable failure, although not because the idea was an unsound one. Two factors subverted Bailey's scheme: the incessant rain which fell throughout the summer, and the refusal of more than half the Australian side to make the trip through some domestic squabble with their Board of Control. The series proved to be a walkover for the host country, but seems to have been regarded in official quarters as a useful imperial exercise.

The King, attended by Mr E. W. Wallington, Col. the Hon. Sir Harry Legge and Major Clive Wigram, visited Lord's Cricket Ground this afternoon, and witnessed the Test match being played between teams from Australia and South Africa. His Majesty was received by the Duke of Devonshire, President, and the Committee of the Marylebone Cricket Club. The members of the competing teams had the honour of being presented to the King.

Court Circular, 16 July 1912

THE citizens of the latter part of the catastrophic twentieth century tend to look back to England before the Great War as to a lost paradise, and to Lord's as the very heartland of that paradise. But England in the years leading to the outbreak of war was not quite as comfortable a place as all that. Political in-fighting over the Irish question was, by 1910, reducing Parliament to a beargarden. The Trade Unions were smouldering with discontent, and the Suffragettes were on the march. As the reign of George V began, the sound of shattering glass was heard all over London as Mrs Pankhurst's skirted army took hammers to the façades of the great West End stores. Soon the acts of violence had spread to the most exclusive of all male preserves, the sporting arena. One Sunday morning in the summer of 1912, while the court was at Balmoral, the local golf links fluttered with the purple banners of the rebellious women's movement. The insult was doubly pointed because golf was the favourite game, next to politics, of the Prime Minister himself, who one day, playing an innocent round on the links at Inverness, suddenly found himself accosted by two of the valkyries of the Pankhurst army. The point was well taken by at least one lover of cricket, who wrote to the popular weekly magazine *Cricket* to warn his fellows of the wrath to come.

Sir,
    Are the authorities at Lord's taking heed of the latest aspect of the 'monstrous regiment of women', with a view to protecting their sacred charges? After the golf greens, surely the cricket grounds in their due season? And that will be a matter of vastly larger import to the main body of the community.
              Yours,
        Verb. Sap. Suff., Letter to *Cricket*,
                26 April 1913

BUT the storm never broke. The message 'Votes For Women' may have been burned into the greens of more than one quiet country golf course, but curiously the Suffragettes left cricket alone. Was it a tactical oversight or a stroke of strategic prudence, inspired by the realisation that whereas the defacers of the links were rarely likely to be confronted by more than a handful of irate males, at a cricket match the vandals would be encircled by thousands of them? In any case, there was deep confusion as to who the vandals were. In Ford Madox Ford's *Some Do Not*, published in 1924 but dealing with the events of pre-war days, the golfers who pursue a young lady intent on spoiling their fun confirm their political maturity as well as their gentlemanly antecedents in admirable style by shouting out 'Strip the bitch naked' and 'She ought to be flayed alive'. But cricket proceeded as though nothing was happening, and nothing did.

It was during this summer that a sad accident on the field of play brought about the passing of one of the great sporting figures in English life. Alfred Lyttelton (1857–1913) was a wicketkeeper-batsman and a barrister who once defended the composer Gounod in a libel case and emerged more triumphantly than his client, who was obliged to pay out £10,000. Lyttelton went on to become Colonial Secretary, being so resourceful a man that he not only captained England at cricket and represented her at football, but also managed to overcome the distressing handicap of being Arthur Balfour's brother-in-law. In June 1913 Lyttelton scored 89 in a match against Bethnal Green Tradesmen. During this innings he was struck by the ball and suffered an internal abscess, and died after an operation, saying, 'Don't let them make too much of the cricket ball. Just a piece of bad luck.'

There was a most impressive scene at Lord's, where the University match was being played. On the stroke of twelve o'clock, the hour of the memorial service at Westminster, the umpires took off their hats. The thirteen cricketers in the field did the same and stood reverently at attention. Then everyone in the pavilion, which was filled in all three tiers, rose as did the spectators in all parts of the ground, and all remained standing for some minutes in unbroken silence. It was a most striking tribute to the general affection felt by the cricket-loving public for the man and the athlete who had gained so many of his gallant triumphs on the greatest of cricket grounds.

The Times, 9 July 1913, on the death of Alfred Lyttelton

AND so the old hero died just too soon to witness the sudden disintegration of the everlasting glory of Empire. The summer of 1914 proceeded, with interest in the County Championship unclouded by any preoccupation with Test matches. On Wednesday 22 June Lord's staged a match to celebrate the centenary of its occupancy of the premises; the Rest of England played the side which had recently won the Test series in South Africa. The Rest of England won easily, but of more interest at the time was the junket on the second evening of the match. When the grandees assembled at a spectacular hotel, as they passed the port and puffed their cigars, the thought occurred to none of them that this was to be the last cricketing social set piece of the epoch:

The most memorable event in the season of 1914 was, to my thinking, the dinner given at the Hotel Cecil by the MCC in June to celebrate the centenary of the present Lord's ground. Nothing could have illustrated more forcibly the greatness of cricket. On every hand were men whose names are familiar wherever the English language is spoken. No other game or sport could have produced such a company. Half a century of English cricket was fully represented, and in every speech there was a note of unswerving devotion to the game. It was a peculiarly happy circumstance that Lord Hawke, who has played cricket all over the world, should, as President of the MCC for the year, have had the privilege of being in the chair. One may be sure that he appreciated the honour.

S. H. PARDON, *Wisden*, 1915

A FEW weeks after this sumptuous dinner, the world it symbolised lay in ruins. The very hotel which housed the celebrations was doomed to destruction, although it did survive the war by a few years. The Cecil, built next door to the Savoy, extended, like its rival, from the Strand to the Embankment, boasting an interior almost comically voluptuous. With its Doulton tiles and its Indian-style smoking room, it had the appearance of some vast granitic mountain, indestructible, triumphant. And yet, when its time came, it vanished almost overnight. In 1930, just as the cricket season ended, the demolition crews went in and flattened it in sixteen weeks, to make way for Shell-Mex House. But in June 1914, by none of the distinguished men who sat in its lavish interior congratulating each other for being each other was any hint of nemesis perceived. Yet before that season was over, the MCC was cancelling fixtures, and Surrey, the eventual county champions, were playing home games at Lord's. The war, which all the experts had said was unthinkable, had come at last, and the reaction of the cricket world, seen in retrospect, seems quite mad. To play cricket was suddenly seen as unpatriotic, the implications being, first, that gifted athletes were by definition gifted soldiers, and second, that in a war nobody ought to be seen to be enjoying himself.

The trumpet call to duty, sounding now down the years like the gurglings of a penny bugle, consisted of a letter from W. G. Grace published in *The Sportsman*, in which physical bravery and patriotism were equated with not playing cricket. Grace, an archetypal Victorian trapped in a neo-Georgian slaughterhouse, had evidently mistaken the war for some sort of tournament. According to his good friend Sir Arthur Conan Doyle, once the realisation of what the Great War really was came home to the Doctor, the shock and the sadness killed him. But his call to duty had a stark effect on cricketers, who flocked to the colours to a man. Typical of their zeal was the behaviour of the Leicestershire batsman A. T. Sharp, engaged on the day war broke out in a match against Northamptonshire. In the first innings Sharp was out lbw for 2 runs. The scorebook for the second innings reads: 'A. T. Sharp ... absent ... 0'. On the evening of 4 August, Sharp had packed his bags in mid-match and left to join his regiment.

But he and the tens of thousands who followed him might just as well have clung to their precious peacetime lives a little longer. The government, overwhelmed by the tidal wave of volunteers, had no effective method of coping with it. Kitchener's hope had been for 100,000 volunteers in the first six months, and perhaps with luck half a million altogether. In the first month alone half a million men enlisted, and all through the winter which followed that dinner at the Cecil, the heroes lived in makeshift tents, drilling in their own clothes, and performing ancient deployments with walking-sticks –

and, no doubt cricket bats – instead of guns. Sharp might at least have completed his second innings without endangering the Empire.

But in the prevailing mood, symbolised by Grace's letter, cricket was clearly dead for the duration. And just as clearly, Lord's, as the most inviting large open space in the purlieus of north London, was marked for war service. It accommodated the Territorial Artillery, and the RAMC; and both wireless instruction and military cooking classes were held within its walls. When the RAMC moved out, the War Office moved in, using the premises to train artillery cadets. But the deepest irony was reserved for the pavilion, which was put to what was perhaps the most futile work of the entire war. For four years the fatuous generals retained their faith in cavalry as the vital military arm. For four years a vast army of horses and riders was maintained, housed, fed, groomed, all for the day when the trumpets would sound and the thunder of hooves would strike terror in the enemy. Everyone except the professional soldiers knew this to be idiotic, but as the professional soldiers were in temporary command of Lord's, it is not surprising that the ground became part of the mad conspiracy to further the cause of the cavalry arm. In all the years of *Wisden*, no more pathetic entries can be found than those pertaining to the war work carried on inside the pavilion:

During the first German War Lord's was used for military purposes. Accommodation was found for units of the Territorial Artillery, the RASC (Transport), the RAMC, wireless instruction and military cooking classes, while 2, Grove End Road was lent as HQ to the Royal Volunteer Battalion (London Regiment). When the RAMC left, the War Office used the buildings and practice ground as a training centre for Royal Artillery cadets. In the pavilion the staff and some members occupied spare time in making hay nets for horses, and some 18,000 of these were sent to Woolwich.

SIR PELHAM WARNER, Lord's, 1946

MCC in 1916: Throughout the year the War Office has continued to avail itself of the offer made by the MCC and accommodation has been found for units of Territorial Artillery, the RASC (Transport), the RAMC, wireless instruction and military cooking classes. No. 2, Grove End Road has been lent as headquarters to the Old Boys' Volunteer Battalion (London Regiment) which has trained and supplied over 400 Commissioned Officers for the Army. In the pavilion the MCC staff and one or two members and their friends have occupied their spare time in making, at the request of the War Office, hay nets for horses. About eighteen thousand nets have been completed and sent to Woolwich.

Wisden, 1917

MCC in 1917: The Long Room in the pavilion is still being used for making hay nets for horses for the Army. Owing, however, to a reduction in the staff, the number made, about 12,000, has not been so great as last year.

Wisden, 1918

ONE great cricketer fated never to witness the blasphemy of horse-nets in the Long Room was the once-rampant Albert Trott, last seen undermining the finances of his own benefit match in 1907. Since that last reckless fling, poor Trott had drunk his way to premature decline and collapse, and there is no more lugubrious event of the days leading up to the outbreak of war, and none which more terribly symbolises the death of the old order:

On the eve of the outbreak of war one of the most colourful cricketers of the age came to the saddest of ends. Albert Trott was only forty-one, but since his famous benefit match in 1907 he had gone rapidly downhill. After giving up playing in 1910 he became for a few years an umpire, but health and money troubles multiplied, and an addiction to the bottle did not help. He suffered from dropsy, his nerves went to pieces and he could not sleep. B. Bennison, in a memoir in *The Daily Telegraph*, wrote that 'a more pathetic figure of a man in later days than Trott it would be difficult to imagine'.

He was induced to enter St Mary's Hospital on July 20th, 1914, and was put under the care of Sir John Broadbent. But he could not bear the tedium of hospital life; eight days later he said he could not stand it any longer, and insisted on going home. The hospital authorities tried to dissuade him, but it was no good; he was short of money as usual, so they put him in a cab and paid his fare to his lodgings in Harlesden. His sleeplessness was worse than ever, and on July 30th he told his landlady, Mrs Crowhurst, that he could not go through another night like the last. That night he shot himself.

He had written his will on the back of a laundry bill, leaving a wardrobe, apparently his only possession, to Mrs Crowhurst. He had £4 in cash, and the MCC made themselves responsible for his funeral.

PATRICK MORRAH, *The Golden Age of Cricket*, 1967

IT was not so very long afterwards that one of his most renowned Lord's team-mates followed suit. Andrew Stoddart, captain of Middlesex and England, had by the time the war broke out declined from a prince of athletes to a wreck of a man, beset by money troubles and an unhappy marriage, and weakened by the price which so many athletes had to pay, an enlarged heart. By the start of the non-existent cricket season of 1915, he had reached the end of his rope:

On Easter Saturday, April 3rd, the Stoddart home in Maida Vale was depressed by foreboding. Andrew Stoddart had been out all day. Now, in the quiet of the evening, he took a long pistol from his pocket and placed it on the table. He told his wife he was tired of everything, and was going to finish it all. 'Life is not worth living', whispered the broken man.

She pleaded with him not to speak this way. Things could be sorted out. They would talk with friends in the morning. She picked up the pistol, but he wrested it from her after a struggle. She held the box of cartridges, knowing the pistol to be empty. He then tucked the pistol back in his pocket and left the room, saying goodnight to his wife and her companion, Isobel Dalton. Later, just before midnight, Mrs Stoddart went to his room and switched on the light. He was in bed. There was no smell of smoke and no shot had been heard, but blood was trickling down his cheek. Ethel cried out, and Mrs Dalton hurried upstairs followed soon by Constable Corrie, who found the revolver gripped in Stoddart's right hand. A second box of ammunition lay near, missing one cartridge.

'Suicide while of unsound mind': the inquest jury at Marylebone had but one verdict to return. They had been told how moody, forgetful and restless Mr Stoddart had been, how money troubles had preyed on his mind, and how a good-humoured husband had been reduced to a state of irritability where even the rustling of paper threatened to drive him mad. They had listened to clinically concise evidence from Dr Saunders (who years before had played football against him) relating to the position of the bullet-wound; to the fact that the lungs had shown impending pneumonia, which always induced despondency; to the observation that the heart was enlarged, as was common in athletes. There were many among the shocked readers of the news who could testify to the man's big-heartedness in a figurative sense besides.

DAVID FRITH, *My Dear Victorious Stod*, 1977

The tragic death of Mr Stoddart has drawn a sigh from thousands. Could nothing have been done? Thousands remembered him and his glorious batting and Rugby play; and in how many country houses is his portrait at this moment hanging with those of the other great sportsmen of our time! Had his admirers but known of his difficulties would they not gladly have ended them? Something forbade it, perhaps pride. It is all too sad for words.

Pall Mall Gazette, 1915

AND so, in the opinion of some diehards, were the events of September 1916, when, with the Empire numbed by the unspeakable slaughter on the Somme, Lord's opened its doors and staged once more a spectacle more edifying than the manufacture of nets for obsolete cavalry regiments. In retrospect it seems curious to the brink of eccentricity that charity matches in wartime were after all considered acceptable so long, apparently, as those matches were nothing to do with cricket.

> At the request of the Canadian contingent a baseball match was played at Lord's in September, 1916, between Canadians and London Americans for the benefit of a fund raised for the widows and orphans of Canadians who fall in battle. HRH Princess Louise (Duchess of Argyll) graciously gave her patronage to the undertakings and watched the game from the pavilion. The proceeds exceeded £100.
>
> *Wisden*, 1917

It has been generally forgotten since that as the war dragged on without any apparent sign of a resolution, cricket at last raised its head above the parapet and looked round at the empty grounds and the army of potential spectators. By the summer of 1917 the quaint armchair ferocity of Dr Grace had long since been rendered obsolete. The Doctor himself, heartbroken by the sheer madness and the degree of butchery of the war, had died in 1915, unable to comprehend what had happened. In the context of three years of bloodletting in the unspeakable conditions on the Western Front, a mere game of cricket no longer seemed an act of treason. In retrospect, the saddest irony of all attaches to the second of the two matches played at Lord's in the summer of 1917, for it was on this occasion that one of the greatest artists of the Golden Age, the Kentish bowler Colin Blythe, played his last match at Lord's, and indeed his last match on any county ground. He took only one wicket, that of C. G. Macartney. Three months later, he was killed in the fighting in France.

ENGLISH ARMY XI v. AUSTRALIAN ARMY XI
Played at Lord's, Saturday, July 14

It was an excellent idea to arrange two charity matches during the height of the summer, in which well-known players could be seen in the field, and from every point of view the result more than realised expectation. In the bright sunshine on the 14th of July, Lord's ground looked quite its old self. The public mustered in surprisingly large numbers, the pleasure felt in seeing even a one day match of some general interest being very keen. So good was the attendance and the sale of tickets beforehand that St Dunstan's Hotel for blinded soldiers and sailors benefited to the extent of about £620. Two capital sides were got together, the English team being composed entirely of men who before the War had taken part in first-class cricket. Several of the Australian names were unfamiliar, but the presence of Macartney, Kelleway, Matthews, and E. P. Barbour—an admirable batsman from New South Wales—lent distinction to the eleven. Some good cricket was seen but the play was too sedate in character to be exciting. The wicket, though in excellent condition, was a trifle slow and the batsmen were perhaps rendered cautious by lack of practice. Winning the toss the Australians began with a disaster, Macartney being out with the score at seven, but after the second wicket had fallen at 26 Kelleway found a most capable partner in Barbour and so long as these two stayed together there seemed every hope of a good total. Sixty-three runs were added and then Kelleway was bowled, his 53, as events turned out, being the highest score of the day. He played very well for an hour and a half. After he left the batting went to pieces. Three more wickets fell before lunch and the innings closed for 130. Lee, who was not tried till the score was up to about a hundred, bowled his slows very skilfully from the nursery end and found some easy victims. On an improving wicket the Englishmen were practically sure of victory, but even in a Test match they could not have set about their light task with greater deliberation. They left nothing to chance, Makepeace and Lee taking forty minutes to get the first eighteen runs. Two wickets were down for 24, but Ernest Tyldesley and Warner put on 65 runs in as many minutes. The match was won with five wickets in hand, but little was done after the winning hit had been made and, Franklin being absent, the Englishmen had only a margin of 32 runs in their favour at the end of the innings. Warner, apart from a chance of stumping when 26, played well for eighty minutes, but he became obviously tired and was allowed a man to run for him in the latter part of his innings. Tyldesley's batting was also very sound and steady. An auction sale during the afternoon of cricket bats, balls and pictures proved disappointing.

AUSTRALIAN ARMY XI

Lieut. C. Kelleway (N.S.W.), b Knox 53	Lieut. C. T. Docker (N.S.W.), s Franklin, b Lee....... 12
W.-O. C. G. Macartney (N.S.W.), lbw, b Douglas 0	Corpl. N. G. Dean (Melbourne), b Lee......... 8
Sergt. W. J. Munday (Adelaide), c Lee, b Blythe 8	Corpl. G. B. Inkster (Adelaide), not out..... 4
Capt. E. P. Barbour (capt.), (N.S.W.), c Hendren, b Lee 30	Pte. W. McAndrews (Queensland), b Lee 0
Pte. P. W. Docker (N.S.W.), lbw, b Lee 1	
S.-Sergt. W. S. Stirling (S.A.), run out......... 7	B 4, l-b 2 6
Corpl. T. J. Matthews (Victoria), c Franklin, b Knox 1	Total 130

ENGLAND ARMY XI

Corpl. H. Makepeace (Lancashire), c Inkster, b C. Docker 13	Corpl. D. W. Jennings (Kent), c. Barbour, b Matthews 26
Pte. H. W. Lee (Middlesex), b Macartney 7	Lieut. P. G. H. Fender (Surrey), c Barbour, b C. Docker 8
Corpl. E. Tyldesley (Lancashire), c Docker, b Andrews 38	Lieut. N. A. Knox (Surrey), c Macartney, b Barbour .. 0
Capt. P. F. Warner (capt.) (Middlesex), st Inkster, b Macartney 34	Sergt. C. Blythe (Kent), not out 2
Lieut.-Col. J. W. H. T. Douglas (Essex), b C. T. Docker 20	Capt. W. B. Franklin (Bucks), absent 0
Pte. E. Hendren (Middlesex), c Inkster, b Macartney.. 3	Byes 8, l-b 3 11
	Total 162

AUSTRALIAN ARMY XI BOWLING

	Overs	Mdns.	Runs	Wkts.
Douglas	11	1	39	1
Blythe	8	1	16	1
Fender	2	0	12	0
Knox	14	1	23	5

ENGLAND ARMY XI BOWLING

C. T. Docker	11.5	5	16	3
McAndrews	12	2	29	1
Macartney	18	5	33	3
Kelleway	9	2	17	0
Matthews	9	0	32	1
Stirling	4	1	9	0
Barbour	6	0	15	1

Umpires: E. Bale (Worcestershire) and W. Reeves (Essex)

Wisden, 1918

NAVY & ARMY v. AUSTRALIAN & SOUTH AFRICAN FORCES
Played at LORD'S, Saturday, August 18.

Arranged for the benefit of Lady Lansdowne's officers' Families' Fund, this match, owing to a showery morning, did not attract as large a company as that between the English Army and Australian Army on the same ground, five weeks earlier. Still it proved a considerable success, and in bringing into the field again so many famous cricketers, afforded keen satisfaction to some 5,000 spectators. While the English team differed only in the substitution of Hardinge and Haywood for J. W. H. T. Douglas and Makepeace, the Colonial side, although including only one South African, underwent half a dozen changes. Happily for the visitors, Macartney, Kelleway, Matthews, and Barbour were all able to turn out, and the Englishmen had to admit defeat by 136 runs. On a pitch naturally affected by the rain of the morning, the Navy and Army found runs so difficult to make against some skilful bowling that after a stay at the wickets of nearly two hours and a half, their total amounted to no more than 106. Warner batted steadily for seventy minutes, yet seven wickets fell for 64 runs, and but for a little resolute work by Fender and Franklin, the score must have been meagre indeed. Matthews and Macartney bowled to fine purpose, and R. J. A. Massie, a son of H. H. Massie of the 1882 Australian team, obtained a couple of wickets. The pitch was appreciably faster when the Australians went in to bat, but despite some capital batting by Kelleway and Taylor, there were five men out for 74. Indeed, had Blythe been in form, the finish might easily have been a close one. Unfortunately for his side the famous Kent bowler, engaging, as it happened, in his last match, was not really well enough to play. Still admitting that the English attack fell far below what might reasonably have been expected, there could be no question about the excellence of the batting shown by Barbour and Bell. The solitary representative of South Africa, Bell made some capital strokes, even if over-shadowed by his partner. So speedily did those two men master the bowling that they added 101 runs in an hour. Eighth man out at 230, Barbour obtained 101 out of 167 in 75 minutes. A few of his strokes had an element of luck, but for the most part, his hitting, especially considering the pace at which he made runs, was as good as it was powerful. He scored all round the wicket and roused the spectators to much enthusiasm with two mighty hits in front of square leg in one over. General Plumer and General Horne wired to P.F. Warner their good wishes for the success of the match, and among those present was Admiral Jellicoe. The proceeds of the match amounted to £700.

NAVY AND ARMY

C.P.O. H. W. T. Hardinge (Kent), c. Barbour b. Massie	3
Corpl. D. W. Jennings (Kent), b. Macartney	11
Corpl. E. Tyldesley (Lancashire), c. Docker, b. Macartney	4
Capt. P. F. Warner (Middlesex), c. Docker, b. Matthews	20
P.O. R. A. Haywood (Northants), c. Taylor, b. Matthews	13
Private H. W. Lee (Middlesex), st. Long, b. Macartney	0
Private E. Hendren (Middlesex), c. Docker, b. Matthews	8
Lieut. P. G. H. Fender (Surrey), b. Macartney . .	14
Capt. W. B. Franklin (Bucks), run out	21
Lieut. N. A. Knox (Surrey) not out	3
Sergt. C. Blythe (Kent), b. Massie	0
B. 6, l-b. 3	9
	106

AUSTRALIANS AND SOUTH AFRICANS

Lieut. C. Kelleway (N.S.W.), c. Fender, b. Knox	31
Lance-Corpl. W. Sewart (Victoria), b. Lee	3
W.O. C. G. Macartney (N.S.W.), c. Warner, b. Blythe	1
Gunner J. Taylor (N.S.W.), c. Hardinge, b. Fender . .	25
Capt. E. P. Barbour (N.S.W.), c. Franklin, b. Hardinge	101
Lieut. C. B. Willis (Victoria), c. Hendren, b. Knox	0
Lieut. W. Bell (South Africa), c. Fender, b. Haywood	40
Lieut. C. T. Docker (N.S.W.), c. Fender, b. Lee	8
Private T. J. Matthews (Victoria), not out	15
Major R. J. A. Massie (N.S.W.), b. Lee	6
Lieut. E. J. Long (N.S.W.), c. Hendren, b. Hardinge .	1
B. 6, l-b. 4, n-b. 1 . .	11
	242

AUSTRALIANS AND SOUTH AFRICANS BOWLING

	Overs	Mdns.	Runs	Wkts.
Macartney	22	11	37	4
Massie	14.3	2	39	2
Docker	1	0	3	0
Matthews	7	1	18	3

NAVY AND ARMY BOWLING

Blythe	11	2	51	1
Lee	18	0	73	3
Fender	9	0	36	1
Knox	11	0	33	2
Hayward	6	1	26	1
Hardinge	2.5	1	9	2

Umpires: Butt and Atfield

Wisden, 1918

THE 1918 season came and still there was no sign of peace. Lord's remained on active service, as it were, but by the time the last of the three charity matches on the programme had taken place, even the pessimists were beginning to sense that the end might be in sight. *Wisden* did not seem too clear-headed about the cricket itself. One minute everyone was out of practice, and the next the fielding was positively blinding. And the praise for Hobbs whose batting was 'by general consent the finest display of the season' sounds odd in the light of the fact that there had been no season.

ENGLAND XI v. DOMINIONS XI
Played at Lord's on Saturday, June 29th

From a cricket point of view the first of the two matches at Lord's between England and the Dominions, arranged by Captain P. F. Warner, on behalf of the Lord Roberts Memorial Workshops and King George's Fund for Sailors, proved rather disappointing, few of the well-known batsmen engaged seeming in form, but financially the result more than fulfilled expectation. The conditions were quite favourable, and a crowd of about ten thousand people watched the game. No doubt want of practice accounted to a large extent for the comparative tameness of the batting. People were obviously delighted to see so many of their old favourites in flannels again. G. T. S. Stevens, the University College School cricketer, was given a place in the England XI, and very well he acquitted himself both as bowler and batsman. Going in first the Dominions had a fairly successful but uneventful innings, chief honours resting with Kelleway, who played as carefully as if he had been engaged in a Test match. He and Macartney took the score from one to fifty-four and late in the innings, when things looked none too promising, Yeoman and Docker made a useful stand. Still the total only reached 166, and in face of such a modest score there seemed every reason to think that England would win. All hopes of this kind, however, were soon destroyed. There was a little fire in the wicket, and against Docker's very fast bowling some of the best English batsmen cut a deplorable figure. With five wickets down the score was only 28, and the match as good as lost. Warner played admirably, and received a good deal of help from McIver and Stevens, but the innings ended for 98, the Dominions winning easily by 68 runs. The victory was well deserved, the winners fairly out-playing the Englishmen at every point. Macartney bowled as well as if he had been in full practice, his length being accurate to a degree. At the end of the afternoon the Dominions went in again and scored freely until stumps were pulled up. From the English point of view by far the best feature of the match was Kirk's fine bowling.

DOMINIONS XI

Lieut. C. Kelleway, b. Horsley	30		
Capt. R. L. Park, b. Kirk	0	b. Horsley	18
W.O. C. G. Macartney, c. McIver, b. Stevens	22	b. Kirk	4
Gunner J. M. Taylor, c. McIver, b. Kirk	8	not out	22
Major A. G. Moyes, b. Kirk	22	c. Franklin, b. Kirk	1
Capt. E. P. Barbour, b. Kirk	3		
Capt. B. G. Mellé, c. McIver, b. Kirk	12		
Staff Q. M. S. Yeoman, not out	22		
Lieut. C. T. Docker, c. Horsley, b. Kirk	23		
Lieut. E. J. Long, b. Kirk	6		
Private W. H. Mars, lbw, b. Stevens	2		
B. 6, n-b. 10	16	L-b. 7, n-b. 2	9
	166		54

ENGLAND XI

Comm. C. B. Fry, b. Docker	10
E. Humphreys, A.B., b. Macartney	0
Private E. Hendren, b. Docker	0
Capt. P. F. Warner, not out	35
Rev. F. H. Gillingham, b. Docker	6
Sgt.-Major H. T. W. Hardinge, b. Docker	0
Capt. C. D. Melver, c. Docker, b. Mellé	17
Lance-Corpl. G. T. Stevens, b. Barbour	18
Sergt.-Instructor E. C. Kirk, c. Macartney, b. Barbour	0
Lance-Corpl. J. Horsley, b. Macartney	0
Capt. W. B. Franklin, c. and b. Macartney	0
B. 7, l-b. 4, n-b. 1	12
	98

ENGLAND XI BOWLING

	Overs	Mdns	Runs	Wkts	Overs	Mdns	Runs	Wkts
Kirk	21	2	55	7	5	0	21	2
Horsley	12	1	44	1	1	0	11	1
Stevens	14	0	51	2	4	0	13	0

DOMINIONS XI BOWLING

	Overs	Mdns	Runs	Wkts
Macartney	13	1	22	3
Docker	14	0	39	4
Moyes.........	3	1	8	0
Mellé	7	1	12	1
Barbour	2	0	5	2

Umpires: Atfield and Parris

Wisden, 1919

ENGLAND XI v. DOMINIONS XI
Played at Lord's, Saturday, July 13th

The second of the charity matches at Lord's was honoured by the presence of the King, but conditions were not so favourable as they had been a fortnight before, rain restricting play to rather less than four hours and a half. No definite result could be arrived at, but with a few more minutes at their disposal the Englishmen would have taken a handsome revenge for their previous defeat, the Dominions at the drawing of stumps being 123 runs behind with only two wickets to fall. P. G. H. Fender, who had been kept out of the first match by illness, was able to play for England this time, and both in bowling and fielding he was up to his Surrey form of 1914. Sent in to bat after losing the toss England made a slow but satisfactory start, scoring in an hour and fifty minutes before luncheon 87 for three wickets. This standard, however, was far from being kept up after the interval, the total, though helped by twenty-eight extras, only amounting to 157. George Gunn showed by far the best form, but he took over two hours to score his 36. The Dominions went in soon after four o'clock, but when they had had ten minutes' batting, rain fell heavily, and there was no more play for an hour and a half. The tamest of draws seemed in prospect when at last the game was continued, but those who had waited on during the rain were amply rewarded, the English team giving a dazzling display of fielding and almost snatching a victory. Seldon in the same space of time has one seen such a brilliant series of catches. Hendren surpassed himself at short-leg, and Fender, after bringing off a fine catch in the slips, caught and bowled Moyes in wonderful fashion with the right hand from a very hot return. There was not such a big attendance as at the first match, but for the falling off the weather could be held wholly responsible.

ENGLAND XI

Sgt.-Major H. T. W. Hardinge, lbw, b. Kelleway	18
L.-Cpl. G. Gunn, run out	36
Commander C. B. Fry, c. Yeoman, b. Moyes	23
Major Hon. L. H. Tennyson, c. Docker. b. Moyes	6
Pte. E. Hendren, b. Macartney	2
Capt. P. F. Warner, b. Barbour	19
Rev. F. H. Gillingham, lbw. b. Kelleway	0
Lieut. P. G. H. Fender, b. Macartney	11
Lieut. W. E. Astill, c. Park, b. Barbour	9
Sgt.-Instr. E. C. Kirk, c. D. Taylor, b. Moyes	2
Capt. W. B. Franklin, not out	3
B. 18, l-b. 3, n-b. 7.	28
	157

DOMINIONS XI

Lieut. C. Kelleway, c. Hendren, b. Fender	7
Capt. R. L. Park, c. Hendren, b. Kirk	0
W.O. C. G. Macartney, c. and b. Astill	0
Gnr. J. M. Taylor, c. Fender, b. Kirk	4
Major A. G. Moyes, c. and b. Fender	10
Major E. P. Barbour, c. Hendren, b. Kirk	0
Lieut. D. Taylor, b. Kirk	2
Capt. B. G. Mellé, c. Hardinge, b. Fender	1
Lieut. C. T. Docker, not out	0
B. 5, n-b. 5	10
	34

Staff Q. M. S. Yeoman and Lieut. E. J. Long did not bat.

DOMINIONS XI BOWLING

	Overs	Mdns.	Runs	Wkts.
Docker	6	1	8	0
Macartney	15	2	40	2
Mellé	4	1	8	0
Kelleway	18	7	35	2
Barbour	9.2	2	19	2
Moyes	10	2	19	3

ENGLAND XI BOWLING

Astill................	9	5	5	1
Kirk................	12	7	10	4
Fender	4	1	8	3
Hardinge	1	0	1	0

Umpires: Atfield and Parris

Wisden, 1919

COLONEL THE HON. F. S. JACKSON'S XI v. CAPTAIN P. F. WARNER'S XI
Played at Lord's on Saturday, August 31st

In connection with this match, played for the benefit of the Chevrons Club, there was one great disappointment, F. S. Jackson—whose return to the cricket field would have delighted everyone—being unfortunately kept away by illness. In his absence the side he had selected was captained by J. W. H. T. Douglas. The game proved a big attraction, the crowd being estimated at 8,000. Contrary to expectation the cricket proved altogether one-sided, Warner's XI winning in the easiest fashion by 161 runs and only just missing a single innings victory. Those present had the pleasure of seeing Hobbs bat in his very best form. By general consent his 86 was the finest display of the season. He and Hardinge scored 138 together for the first wicket for Warner's team, Hardinge, though a little overshadowed by his partner's brilliancy, playing extremely well. The early batting form was far from being kept up, but the total of 244 almost insured a victory. As events turned out it proved overwhelming. Jackson's XI went all to pieces in batting, the only redeeming features being Taylor's steadiness in the first innings and Hendren's free hitting in the second. Fender bowled exceptionally well, receiving capital support from Woolley and Stevens, and quite a feature of the match was Heath's fine wicket-keeping.

CAPT. P. F. WARNER'S XI

Air. Mech. J. R. Hobbs
(Surrey), c. Rotherham,
b. Barbour 86
Sergt.-Maj. H. T. W. Hardinge (Kent), c. Gibson,
b. Barbour 53
Maj. Hon. L. H. Tennyson
(Hants.), c. Gunasekara,
b. Barbour 6
Capt. P. F. Warner (Middlesex). b. Rotherham... 5
Coxswain F. E. Woolley
(Kent), lbw, b. Rotherham 9
Capt. N. Haig (Middlesex), b.
Rotherham 20
Rev. F. H. Gillingham
(Essex), b. Barbour 20

Lieut. P. G. H. Fender
  (Surrey), b. Barbour 17
Lance-Cpl. G. T. S. Stevens
  (U.C. Sch.), st. Franklin,
  b. Rotherham 0
Cadet A. P. Gregory
  (N.S.W.), not out....... 9
Capt. W. H. Heath (R.A.F.),
  b. Barbour 0
      B. 8, l-b. 3, w. 1, n-b. 7 19
                                ―――
                                244

Col. F. S. Jackson's XI

Lieut. H. W. Taylor (South Africa), ht. wkt., b. Fender	34	lbw., b. Fender	0
C. H. Gunasekara (India), b. Gregory	5	b. Fender	1
Major E. P. Barbour (N.S.W.), run out	1	b. Stevens	25
Lieut. G. A. Rotherham (Warwick), st. Heath, b. Woolley	4	c. and b. Fender	10
Private E. Hendren (Middlesex), b. Woolley	7	b. Fender	58
Lt.-Col. J. W. H. T. Douglas (Essex), c. Hardinge, b. Fender	16	b. Stevens	1
Lieut. E. L. Kidd (Middlesex), b. Woolley	5	lbw., b. Stevens	8
Capt. W. B. Franklin (Bucks.), b. Woolley	1	b. Fender	3
Sergt.-Instr. E. C. Kirk (Surrey), c. and b. Fender	1	c. Gregory, b. Woolley	18
Cadet C. H. Gibson (Eton), c. Hardinge, b. Fender	2	not out	0
Lieut. C. S. Marriott (Ireland), not out	0	not out	2
B. 4, l-b. 3	7	B. 1, l-b. 2	3
	83		129

Col. F. S. Jackson's XI Bowling

	Overs	Mdns	Runs	Wkts
Kirk	12	3	34	0
Douglas	11	0	35	0
Gunasekara	5	1	23	0
Marriott	8	1	17	0
Gibson	3	0	20	0
Barbour	13	3	53	6
Rotherham	11	1	41	4

CAPT. P. F. WARNER'S XI BOWLING

	Overs	Mdns	Runs	Wkts	Overs	Mdns	Runs	Wkts
Gregory	8	1	33	1	3	0	7	0
Woolley	11.1	3	30	4	8	2	20	1
Fender	4	0	13	4	13	3	71	5
Stevens					7	1	28	3

Umpires: F. Parris and W. Smith

Wisden, 1919

WHEN first-class cricket resumed in 1919, there was a sadly unfamiliar look about it. The authorities had decided, with dubious wisdom, to arrange a County Championship of two-day matches, a brave experiment which was tried, found wanting, and was never heard of again. The first opportunity of the Lord's public to see the new-style matches was on 16 May, when Middlesex and Notts batted far too well for any faint prospect of a result to be raised. The same tame ending occurred a few days later when the MCC played Yorkshire. As this was not a championship match, three days were allotted to it, but in spite of a first innings collapse by the visitors, a draw was the result. Sydney Pardon was in no doubt as to the reason for the failure of the two-day experiment, stating in his usual trenchant terms that the inordinately long hours of play were what upset everyone. 'The players and the umpires hated the long days and the public assuredly did not like them. Only when something quite out of the common was to be seen did any great number of people wait on the ground till half-past seven. Before that time the craving for food had as a rule become stronger than the passion for cricket. To put the matter in a prosaic way, the advocates of the two-day match overlooked the needs of the human stomach.' There was something else which deeply troubled Pardon, something he had witnessed with alarm at Lord's towards the end of the summer.

It is to be feared that a good many people who find their pleasure in watching cricket are very ignorant of the game. In no other way can one account for the unseemly 'barracking' that sometimes goes on. A particularly bad case occurred in the Middlesex and Yorkshire match at Lord's in August. J. W. Hearne, playing as well as he has ever played in his life, was doing his utmost to save Middlesex from defeat and yet a section of the crowd hooted him. A remedy for this sort of nuisance is not easy to find, as obviously the batsmen cannot leave the wickets. A stoppage of the game, however, with all the players staying on the field, might have the effect of bringing the malcontents to their senses.

Wisden, 1920

SOMETHING else happened during the 1919 season whose significance could not have been perceived at the time, but which was to have a profound effect on cricket generally. A young journalist on the *Manchester Guardian*, one Neville Cardus, had worked himself into a state of collapse fulfilling his duties as a second-string music and theatre reviewer. On his recovery he was told to go and convalesce at Old Trafford, where, it was hoped, a few hundred words on the cricket might magically materialise. The plan worked. The few hundred became a few million, many of which were devoted to descriptions of the Lord's ground, as we shall see. In time, Cardus struck up a friendship with the cricketer–playwright James Barrie, a relentless master of whimsy who once claimed to be the slowest slow bowler ever known: 'If I don't like the ball I've bowled, I run down the pitch and get it back'. One day Barrie was to attend a Lord's Test match under the tutelage of Cardus; for the moment he had to make do alone:

I went with N. to the Lord's match. 15,000 tall hats – one cad hat (mine); 15,000 stiff white collars, canes, shiny faces – one soft collar, cudgel, dreary face (mine); the ladies comparatively drab, fearing rain, but the gents superb, colossal, sleek, lovely. All with such a pleased smile. Why? Because they know they had the Eton something or the Harrow something. They bestowed the something on each other, exchanged it with each other as the likes of me exchange the time of day. I felt I was nearer to grasping what the something is than ever before. It is a sleek happiness that comes of a shininess which only Eton (or Harrow) can impart. This makes you 'play the game' as the damned can't do it; it gives you manners because you know in your heart that nothing really matters so long as you shine with that sleek happiness. The nearest thing to it must be boot polish.

J. M. Barrie, letter to Cynthia Asquith, 10 July 1920

Although his cricket-reporting apprenticeship in the sunny summer of 1919 was devoted almost exclusively to Old Trafford and the Lancashire side of Makepeace, James Heap, Parkin and the massed ranks of the Tyldesleys, Cardus's occasional excursion to Lord's was inevitable. But when he went there in the following season, it was to find that the absence of any cricket imposed upon him the onus of displaying his extra-cricketing scholarship, a challenge he met with some relish by composing dithyrambs on the works of Charles Dickens, with a defence thrown in of the crowd scenes of William Frith. It is difficult to discover exactly what match Cardus was supposed to be reporting. The almanacks of the period tell us that the rain which saturated Lord's that June fell towards the end of the month, and the only fixture which qualifies is MCC v. Oxford University, on 28 and 29 June. But this fixture was completed without undue interference from the weather. Did Cardus attend the ground on a day when no play was scheduled? Did he visit the ground at all; or compose his essay from the comfort of his hotel room? Yet in the end all speculation is pointless. Throughout his life and after it, Cardus's reputation had to endure the investigations of dullards intent on undermining his best stories. They flocked in the wake of his anecdotes like so many journalistic crows following his plough, pecking away at their tiny bones of factual contention, too dumb to perceive that Cardus was cricket literature's only writer of romantic fiction, and that players and setting were the mere pretext for his compositions. Cardus dealt in what Ford Madox Ford used to call the poetic truth, and the essay which follows is a case in point. Whatever the circumstances of its composition, where can we find a more affecting, better written, more charming impressionist portrait of the ground?

Lord's in Wet Weather – June 1920

For want of anything better to do these last two incredibly wet days at Lord's, I have been trying to understand why that place so forcibly recalls Charles Dickens's *Bleak House*. It is not merely that the rain has turned the place into another Chesney Wold; that the view from the pavilion window as I write is alternately a lead-coloured view and a view in Indian ink; that the heavy drops fall, drip, drip, drip, upon the pavilion terrace, which might be named the Ghost Walk, since the shades of so many great cricketers of other days make it murmurous. No, not simply these external and quite accidental weather effects are responsible for the mind's jumping back to Dickens's novel. Lord's is capable of reminding you of Sir Leicester Dedlock and Chesney Wold in fine weather as well as in wet, so inflexibly aristocratic is the place, so proud of the ceremonies, so insistent on blue blood.

Unless one happens to be definitely of Lord's, and a member of the mighty MCC, one is outside the pale here. You are inexorably kept at a distance. The place is a mass of signboards, teaching you your manners and position in life. Like Sir Leicester Dedlock all over, Lord's is as old as the hills, and, so it would appear, carries a general air of believing that the world might get on without hills, but would be done up without the MCC....

It is hard to imagine there is any place in the world where class distinctions are so firmly stressed as at Lord's. During a University match this is more apparent than ever. That is why, possibly, no painter in the school of Frith has given us a canvas depicting Lord's on a fine summer's day during the occasion of a Varsity match. The picture would certainly give scope for something of the multitudinous panorama in Frith's too-much abused 'Derby Day', but it would be bound to miss the broad universal appeal of the racing picture. Human nature on a large scale could hardly be got into a view of Lord's—only one aspect of it, well-bred and exclusive...

NEVILLE CARDUS, *A Cricketer's Book*, 1922

EVEN as the rain fell and the sun followed, the MCC Committee was deliberating on an issue which concerned the entire cricket community, perhaps even the nation and the Empire. What to do about the late William Gilbert Grace? Cricket was not a sport distinguished for formal memorials or monumental masonry. But surely the Doctor was a special case?

MCC Committee Report, 1920:
It is proposed to erect at the Western Entrance in St John's Wood Road, a Gateway with iron gates, and in some appropriate position on the building to place a bust of Dr Grace. The Committee proposes that the club shall guarantee the whole cost, but believing that there are many cricket clubs and many cricketers who

would desire to be associated with the memorial, they will open a subscription list for not more than a moiety of the cost. They have commissioned Mr Herbert Baker to submit a design.

MCC Committee Report, 1922:
The Committee after consideration of several designs have decided as authorised by the general meeting of May 5th, 1920, that the memorial to Dr W. G. Grace shall take the form of a gateway with handsome iron gates, at the members' entrance, to be adapted to harmonise with certain improvements at that entrance. Originally intended to be erected exclusively by the MCC, it was afterwards determined, as members may remember, to guarantee the cost of the memorial but to accept donations up to a moiety of the cost, in the belief that cricket clubs and admirers of the late Dr Grace would like to be associated with it. A tender has been accepted amounting to £2,268 and it is hoped that the work will be completed early in May.

MCC Committee Report, 1923:
Members will have had the opportunity of inspecting the Dr W. G. Grace Memorial Gateway completed in July last. Mrs Grace was asked to open it formally but did not feel able to accept the invitation.

M EANWHILE the day-to-day administration of the ground went on, never failing to prove the wisdom of Barrie's claim that everyone eventually turned up at Lord's and everything eventually happened there. The great days of the Foster brotherhood had been during the Edwardian years, but the family was yet to be involved in the founding of a publishing institution. This oversight was rectified not long after the end of the Great War:

One evening in 1920 after a day's play at Lord's I was chatting with Plum, whom I had known since my brother Tip's Oxford days in the late 1890s. I knew that it was his last season in first-class cricket and I suggested to him that in order to preserve the best interests of the game someone like he should start a paper devoted to cricket. Plum loved the idea. It was decided to form a company to run the paper. Plum thought of the name. It was accepted without question and the paper under his editorship appeared for the first time on Saturday, April 30th, 1921.

G. N. FOSTER, quoted in E. W. SWANTON, *Follow On*, 1977

I T was indeed Warner's last season in first-class cricket, and it was crowned with a story-book triumph. Despite their reputation for playing attractive cricket, and for having on call some of the outstanding amateur talent in the game, Middlesex had not won the County Championship since 1903. It was the dear wish of their captain, Warner, that he should rectify the situation in his farewell season. Which is what happened. After a moderate start to the season, Middlesex came with a late rush and snatched the title from under the nose of Lancashire.

MIDDLESEX v. SURREY
Played at Lord's, August 28, 30, 31, 1920

This was the match of the season. Middlesex and Lancashire were running neck and neck for the Championship, and as Lancashire on the same days had the simplest of tasks against Worcestershire, Middlesex knew that nothing less than an actual victory would be of real value to them. Never before has a county match proved such an attraction at Lord's. On the Saturday there must have been nearly 25,000 people on the ground, 20,700 paying for admission at the gates. A great fight was looked forward to, and as it happened all expectations were exceeded. It was a game never to be forgotten, Middlesex in the end winning by 55 runs, and so securing the Championship. Winning the toss Middlesex had the advantage of batting first on a hard wicket, but nothing could have been less promising than their start. For once Lee and Hearne failed them, and in less than an hour three wickets were down for 35 runs. After these disasters nothing was risked, and at the end of the afternoon the Middlesex score with eight men out had only reached 253. Warner was blamed in some quarters for over-caution, but he saved his side. In getting 79 he was batting for nearly four hours and a half. On the Monday there was again an enormous attendance, the number paying at the gates this time being 20,021. Owing nearly everything to Sandham, Surrey had the best of the day's cricket. Sandham had some luck—a chance of stumping at 40 and a chance at slip at 77—but for the most part he played superbly, combining an ever-watchful defence with his clean hitting. For his 167 not out he was batting four hours and twenty minutes, his figures including seventeen 4s. With the object of getting Middlesex in before the end of the afternoon Fender declared with nine wickets down, but his policy met with no reward, Skeet and Lee batting for forty minutes and taking the score to 27. For sustained excitement the third day beat everything seen in London last season. Skeet and Lee made victory for Middlesex possible, staying in until after lunch and sending up 208 for the first wicket. Lee was splendid, and Skeet, though not so certain in timing the ball, played better than he had ever played before in a first-class match. Warner declared at twenty minutes to four, leaving Surrey to get 244 in a trifle over three hours. The downfall of Hobbs—caught in the slips at 22—was discouraging, but Surrey went for the runs and, with Sandham playing even more finely than on the previous day, the 100 was up in an hour and a quarter for two wickets. However, Hendren got rid of Shepherd by means of a wonderful catch in the deep field—just in front of the screen with his hands above his head—this being really the turning-point of the game. Surrey's great hope departed when Sandham—the sixth man out—was caught and bowled from a full pitch. In the end Middlesex won with ten minutes to spare. Warner was carried off the field shoulder high, and before the crowd dispersed he and Fender had to make speeches.

Middlesex

Mr C. H. L. Skeet, c. Ducat, b. Rushby	2	c. Fender, b. Hitch	106
H. W. Lee, c. Hitch, b. Fender	12	b. Hitch	108
J. W. Hearne, c. and b. Hitch	15	lbw. b. Rushby	26
E. Hendren, b. Reay	41	c. Sandham, b. Rushby	5
Mr P. F. Warner, b. Rushby	79	not out	14
Mr F. T. Mann, c. and b. Fender	12	c. Peach, b. Fender	22
Mr N. Haig, b. Reay	18	b. Rushby	1
Mr G. T. S. Stevens, b. Fender	53	not out	21
Mr H. K. Longman, b. Fender	0		
H. R. Murrell, c. Ducat, b. Hitch	9	b. Reay	0
T. J. Durston, not out	0		
B. 12, l-b. 12, n-b. 3	27	B. 8, l-b. 4, w. 1	13
	268	**(7 wkts dec.)**	**316**

Surrey

J. B. Hobbs, c. Mann, b. Hearne	24	c. Lee, b. Haig	10
A. Sandham, not out	167	c. and b. Hearne	68
Mr M. Howell, c. Murrell, b. Durston	7	st. Murrell, b. Stevens	25
T. Shepherd, c. Murrell, b. Durston	0	c. Hendren, b. Stevens	26
H. A. Peach, hit wkt., b. Stevens	18	b. Stevens	11
A. Ducat, st. Murrell, b. Lee	49	lbw. b. Hearne	7
Mr P. G. H. Fender, c. Haig, b. Durston	30	b. Durston	1
W. Hitch, b. Durston	1	b. Stevens	6
Mr G. M. Reay, c. Haig, b. Lee	6	b. Hearne	5
H. Strudwick, b. Hearne	9	b. Stevens	10
T. Rushby, not out	6	not out	7
B. 17, l-b. 5, n-b. 2	24	B. 11, l-b. 1	12
(9 wkts dec.)	**341**		**188**

Surrey Bowling

	Overs	Mdns	Runs	Wkts	Overs	Mdns	Runs	Wkts
Hitch	32.1	10	66	2	20	5	71	2
Rushby	23	9	48	2	22	7	73	3
Fender	28	4	76	4	16.5	2	70	1
Reay	26	17	31	2	18	1	61	1
Ducat	3	1	10	–	3	–	12	–
Shepherd	6	3	10	–	4	–	16	–

Middlesex Bowling

	Overs	Mdns	Runs	Wkts	Overs	Mdns	Runs	Wkts
Durston	30	9	97	4	14	1	42	1
Haig	10	4	25	–	8	–	19	1
Stevens	16	–	72	1	13.4	–	61	5
Hearne	24	8	57	2	11	–	37	3
Lee	15	2	66	2	4	–	17	–

Umpires: J. Blake and G. P. Harrison

Wisden, 1921

The best match of the season at Lord's was the last – that between Middlesex and Surrey – and the crowd was so great that on the first day (Saturday) people were sitting two deep in front of the pavilion, the gates having to be closed early in the afternoon, and on the second day also. Middlesex had won eight matches in succession in August – and what matches they were, Kent being beaten by 5 runs at Canterbury and Yorkshire by 4 runs at Bradford! The position when the Surrey match began was this: to win the championship Middlesex had to defeat Surrey – a draw or a loss would have given Lancashire first place. The game was played on a fast wicket and in lovely weather, and was one long crescendo of excitement. The story of the match has often been told, and it will be sufficient here to state that at twenty-two minutes past six – stumps were to be drawn at seven o'clock – Stevens clean bowled Strudwick with a beautiful-length googly, which came like lightning off the pitch, and Middlesex had won by 55 runs.

It was my last match for Middlesex – my last big match at Lord's – and I should be less than human if I should ever forget it. Indeed, I can even now, after six-and-twenty years, recall every phase, every ball, every moment, of it, and the wonderful and affectionate reception the crowd gave me is the most treasured memory of my cricketing life. At one moment Surrey looked like winning, but a glorious catch in the deep field, near the screen, by Hendren changed the situation. It was a fine side of which I was in command – well-disciplined, keen, enthusiastic, and with a loyalty to its captain which has certainly never been surpassed. I had loved Lord's ever since I first saw it, and the gods were indeed good to me in decreeing that my last first-class match there should end so happily for me. I hope no one will accuse me of being boastful or arrogant – I have had too many failures in my time, including a pair of spectacles twice at Lord's, to be that – but there are some things of which one may, perhaps, be allowed to write exactly as one feels—and this is one of them. To lead the great county for which I had had the privilege of playing since 1894, under the captaincy of men like A. J. Webbe, A. E. Stoddart, and G. MacGregor, to the top of the tree in the last stage of my cricketing life was an experience which no lapse of time, no future happening, can ever eradicate from my memory.

SIR PELHAM WARNER, *Lord's*, 1946

THE reaction to this victory burst all the bounds of rational behaviour. A. J. Webbe, an ex-captain of Middlesex himself, opened his letter of congratulation to Warner as though composing a love letter to a paramour: 'As I told you last night, I could hardly bear to leave you.' The First Lord of the Admiralty sent a gushing note, and most reckless of all was the letter from C. B. Fry, who, in quoting the *Iliad*, seemed to get the Championship mixed up with the Trojan Wars and Warner with Ulysses. Most impressive of all, *The Times* devoted its leading article to the match at Lord's, seeing in Warner's leadership and Middlesex's victory a portent of the nation's future greatness:

Fortune is often fickle in cricket, but it smiled on the Middlesex captain yesterday. The close of his long and honourable period of devoted service to the best interests of the game could not have been staged in more appropriate circumstances. Yesterday's match was such as all cricketers, who are, because they play the game, all good men, desire to see and to bring about. That things do not always go so ideally in the cricket field is not a valid reason for good men to be grumbling; and true cricketers do not, in fact, dwell upon the more disappointing side of the national game. Every now and then they receive their full recompense, and the moment is well worth living for. Such a moment awaited them at Lord's last night, and 'all time's story remembers'. Mr Warner will not forget it, and no captain left the field for the last time with cheers better deserved.

The Times, 1 September 1920

FORTUNATELY for the welfare of the game, farce intruded persistently, insisting on human fallibility and raising the ribald laughter which makes a mockery of the kind of pomposity indulged in by leader-writers of the period. Whatever *The Times* may have felt about Cricket and the Empire, there were moments when the noble game came crashing down to earth. The bad old days when a batsman risked his life every time he walked out to the crease were long since past, but a few unpredictable hazards remained.

A curious incident occurred in the MCC v. Kent match at Lord's last week, Captain Jameson having to retire to the pavilion for a time owing to some sawdust getting into his eyes while batting.

The Cricketer, May 1921

BUT the England selectors that year, faced with the challenge of the first post-war Australian challenge, ended not with sawdust but with mud in their eye. In the winter of 1920–21 the game's administrators, much against their better judgement, had been persuaded by the Australians to send out a side. The outcome was predictable enough, five wins to nothing in Australia's favour, with the leadership of J. W. H. T. Douglas being dogged rather than imaginative. When the tourists stepped on the boat to sail home, it was to take their troubles with them, in the form of the Australians, now preparing to perform their execution all over again. In the event the 1921 series was little better for England than the campaign in Australia. Any faint chance of improved form was shattered by the illness of Jack Hobbs and the injury to J. W. Hearne. But some of the omissions have seemed inexplicable ever since. George Gunn, perhaps the best right-handed batsman available to the selectors after the elimination of Hobbs and Hearne, was never selected. Wilfred Rhodes played only once, but even more extraordinary is that throughout the debacles of 1920–21, England possessed indisputably the best bowler in the world, perhaps of all time, and yet made no attempt to recruit him. While the national side was being put to the Australian sword, Sydney Barnes was content to potter around in the backwaters of minor cricket, performing daily miracles for Staffordshire far into old age. It is true that Barnes, one of the most forbidding men ever to walk on to a field, was too intractable a character for any captain or committee to handle, but in view of the poverty of the England bowling at the time, it seems incredible that no overtures were attempted. Among England's three crushing defeats in the 1921 series was the second Test at Lord's, where on the first morning, 11 June, scenes of unprecedented chaos were enacted, much to the alarm and disgust of the Press:

The arrangements made at Lord's for coping with the crowd which everybody who has followed cricket at all closely during the last few years knew would assemble for the Test match, were very bad indeed. There was a most frightful crush outside the ground on the first day, ticket holders and those who had no tickets being inextricably mixed up. It is not pleasant to see women fainting in a crowd, and the authorities at Lord's cannot escape criticism for not making better arrangements. The number of turnstiles have been increased since last year, but there are even now only six or seven at most, and in order to ensure a large crowd getting into the ground, twice that number at least of turnstiles is necessary. It is also most unfortunate that all the turnstiles are in the St John's Wood Road. MCC own nearly all the property around Lord's, and one would have imagined that on this occasion entrances for ticket holders might have been made through the gardens of some of the houses at the back of the pavilion and on the north and north-east side of the ground. There were certainly not enough police to control the crowd on Saturday, and altogether the confusion was appalling, many people who were ticket holders waiting literally hours in the queue before they could obtain admission into the ground.

On Monday the arrangements were better, and the police controlled the various queues, but it is obvious that in future arrangements for dealing with a large crowd will have to be greatly improved, and, further, better seating accommodation will have to be made for the spectators. On both days the gates had to be closed, and we venture to suggest that for future Test matches MCC must keep in view a crowd of at least 40,000. The present stands at Lord's are far too low, and the grandstand in particular, a ramshackle old building, is hopelessly out of date. It takes up an enormous amount of room, and does not accommodate more than, we should imagine, 800 spectators.

The interest of cricket today is greater than it has ever been, and the MCC must, in their own interests, move with the times, and set to work strenuously to improve the accommodation of their ground. Lord's is the Mecca of cricket, and that being so, MCC should do everything in their power for the comfort of the crowd, who, after all, supply the sinews of war. The cricketing world will look with confidence to Col. the Hon. F. S. Jackson, MP, the President, to put matters right in future. He is a man of real ability, and has had great experience of organisation in other walks of life. He is in touch and sympathy with the spirit of the modern cricketing world, and with his great influence he can do much.

Nothing in the whole sorry business excited greater public indignation than the treatment meted out to disabled soldiers, whose chairs were refused admission on the ground that they took up too much space. MCC would do well to follow the example of the football authorities, both Rugby and Association, who invariably give our wounded heroes the consideration they deserve. Those in control of Lord's should remember that but for such men as these the historic enclosure might now be a German beer garden, or we might be engaged in forming fours there instead of watching and playing cricket.

The Cricketer, 18 June 1921

IN THE list of journalists reporting on the match at Lord's on that confused occasion, there was one unexpected name, that of the essayist and literary critic Robert Lynd. Not known for any specialised knowledge of sport, Lynd, when confronted by some great games-playing occasion, usually preferred to bring his Irish whimsy to bear upon it. His essay on that year's Grand National, for example, consisted mainly of a close description of the professional tipsters. His 'On Seeing the Boat Race' should really have been entitled 'On Not Seeing the Boat Race'. In the same way his reports of the 1921 Test matches are notable for their laughter and their colourful detail rather than for any profound technical insights, and are for that reason like a breath of fresh air to those students of cricket history suffering from indigestion of the spirit brought on by too many statistics. Lynd revelled in the spectacle of great masses of idiosyncratic Englishmen playing the fool, either intentionally or not, and was therefore the perfect chronicler of the events at Lord's on that long-lost June morning.

'Disgraceful scenes at Lord's'. That is the only heading that could do justice to the feelings of thousands of men and women who had bought tickets for the second Test match, and who were still attempting to blaspheme their way into the ground nearly an hour after play had begun. It was not the players, or the public, or the police who behaved disgracefully: it was the authorities at Lord's. They had sold thousands of reserved seats, but had made no arrangements for admitting ticket-holders or for informing them where they could be admitted. They seemed to have kept the secret even from the police, who were as much at sea as anyone else. I saw one old gentleman, with field-glasses slung round his shoulder, go up to a policeman in the crush and, holding out his ticket, ask, 'Where do I get in with this?' 'Nowhere', replied the policeman, with the wild smile of a man reduced to desperation. It was very nearly the truth.

I arrived an hour early and was sent to the far end of a queue that appeared to be about a quarter of a mile long. One could amuse oneself by subscribing to a flag-day, or buying from hawkers souvenirs in the shape of a small cricket ball with a photograph of an Australian player let into it, or being deafened by a lean man who came up and whistled close into one's face with one of those distressing inventions that are supposed to imitate the songs of birds, or watching the 'Chu Chin Chow' camels parading by, like turkeys that had tried to be born as horses, or listening to the endless chatter of men who explained that Douglas was a fine cricketer, but a bad captain, and who talked of English batsmen generally as though they were a lot of shivering schoolboys waiting to be caned by Mr Squeers.

After about an hour the rumour rippled along the queue that the ground was full except for ticket-holders. This meant the dropping away of some thousands of people. The queue then advanced more rapidly, till when it was just within sight of the turnstile it was attacked on the flank by a rush and crossfire of persons who had the red tickets of members of Lord's. To make things worse, a horse-policeman forced his way in and broke the queue up, and it in its turn became a mob. It gathered round the turnstile, while hundreds of people stretched their arms into the air, holding up their tickets, and yelling: 'Ticket-holders! Where do ticket-holders get in?' It was a patient crowd, but the language was on the strong side. Ladies contented themselves with 'What the devils!' and 'Gracious heavenses!' as the sun beat down on their delicate faces. Men thundered in growls, followed by vivid flashes.

Every now and then an elderly gentleman or a lady and her daughter would have to beat a way back out of the crowd in order to escape fainting. In any other country, or among the devotees of any other game, there would have been a riot. A man beside me said viciously: 'A football crowd would have had the gates down.' Meanwhile, people in front were getting in at what seemed to be the rate of about one a minute. A cynical lady said it was like a rich man trying to get through the eye of a needle. It was evident that they were examining every ticket-holder's passport and searching him for arms before admitting him. Newcomers would arrive and say to us, politely and hopefully, 'Would you mind letting us past? We've got tickets.' There would be a bitter and universal shout of 'We've all got tickets!'

After a time a merry-looking man looked out at us from a window in the back of one of the stands and, framed in ivy, shouted out: 'England 58 for no wickets!' It was not true (as we afterwards discovered) but it cheered the crowd up. Then King George arrived, and the gates opened and shut for him as if by magic. After that a horse-policeman told us to line up against the wall in a queue. We did so, and sweltered in the sun for a little longer. Then he told us to go and form a queue at another gate. 'Queueriouser and queueriouser!' a punster in the crowd relieved his feelings by muttering. And even that wasn't the end of it, for one ultimately had to leave this for yet another queue at right angles to the wall, which crept into the ground between two banks of policemen, feeling somewhat like Swinburne's 'weariest river' that 'winds somewhere safe to sea'.

But when once you were inside the ground! Is there a more beautiful view in England, I wonder, than the view you get from one of the stands in Lord's on a fine day? There is the green and white of the field – as restful as a daisy field in Chaucer. But there is also at Lord's a noble and multiple idleness that takes the imagination, not to Chaucer, but to the South Seas. It is a ground that one almost expects to be surrounded by palm trees, and, surely, if one were on the roof of the pavilion, one ought to have a view of a blue lagoon and a distant reef keeping out the noise and strife of breakers.

ROBERT LYND, *The Sporting Life*, 1922

ONCE this Test was under way, the Australians, especially Bardsley and Mailey, showed their superiority in every department of the game except possibly eccentricity, where they were hopelessly outclassed by the presence in the England side of the Hon. Lionel Tennyson, a Hampshire swashbuckler who hit 74 not out in the second innings. In the next Test, at Leeds, he hit 63, and by the fourth in the series had been installed as England's captain. The Hon. Lionel remains the only Gentleman in cricket history to have employed his valet as his wicket-keeper, although some have insisted that the reverse was the truth, that he employed his wicket-keeper as his valet. Whichever was the fact of the matter, it was W. H. Livsey who selected his employer's ties in the morning and kept wicket for Hampshire under the Hon. Lionel's instruction all summer. The Hon. Lionel saw no reason to segregate his lordly private life from his cricket career, which explains how his chauffeur came to figure in the annals of Lord's.

Lionel had a chauffeur named Bailey whose salary, to say the least, was somewhat erratically collected. The story went that master and servant had come to an understanding. In lieu of cash, if unavailable, Bailey was allowed to hire out the car; a fine vintage Austin Twenty Landaulette, for such functions as weddings, Council do's, or private assignments. There was a memorable morning at Lord's when Lionel arrived for the Hants v. Middlesex match flush with a gigantic wad of notes, the fruits of a profitable Ascot. His first gesture was to call for the faithful Bailey. Flourishing this impressive bundle and affecting an elaborately casual air Lionel said, 'Let me see, Bailey, don't I owe you some wages?' His face fell slightly when Bailey replied, 'Yes sir – three months'. But honour was satisfied by a full settlement. There was only one slight snag to domestic bliss – it rained. To while away the time Lionel joined Nigel Haig, Tommy Jameson and one or two other shrewd operators in a game of poker. Alas for human hopes and aims. Before lunch Bailey had to be summoned thrice to bail out his master's honour, and by lunchtime his original financial position had changed for the worse. If anyone had said to Bailey that he had been hard done by, he would probably have been asked to step outside.

IAN PEEBLES, *Spinner's Yarn*, 1977

THE Hon. Lionel was known in the cricket world for his courage in the face of danger, and it is certainly true that he met the arduous responsibility of being the grandson of Victoria's Poet Laureate with sublime gallantry. The world of literature remains blissfully unaware that contrary to received opinion inside that tight little world, the divine afflatus did not desert the Tennysons once Lord Alfred had passed on. The Hon. Lionel somehow found the time, between captaining England and Hampshire, and paying visits to the races, to publish a book of poems which he entitled, with impressive and thoroughly merited modesty, *From Bed to Verse*. As to his appreciation of his grandfather, it is one of the more enlightening footnotes to cricket history that one day in the Lord's pavilion the Hon. Lionel insisted that his grandfather was the author of 'Hiawatha', being so convinced of his theory as to offer inviting odds to anyone who wished to contradict him.

Douglas's deposition as England captain did not mark the end of his international career, and although he has come down as a stern, forbidding man, he too knew his moments of irreverence and levity inside the Lord's pavilion.

> CRAWLEY, Leonard George... In 1922, his last year at school, and again in 1923, he had headed the Worcestershire batting averages, actually averaging 86, but Lord Harris discovered that neither he nor the leading Worcestershire professional batsman, Fox, was properly qualified and MCC declared both ineligible for the county. This led to a famous scene in the Long Room at Lord's between Lord Deerhurst, the Worcestershire President, and Lord Harris, with J. W. H. T. Douglas, unseen it is thought by the protagonists, mimicking the actions of a boxing referee in the background.
>
> *Wisden*, 1982

A LTHOUGH by 1922 a period had elapsed since the end of the Great War which was as long as the war itself, an aftermath of the vile and shocking slaughter in the trenches was the ghostly company of dead players and followers of the game who lived on in a macabre sort of way in the club's registers. Valiantly the Lord's secretariat attempted to pick up the threads of the pre-war world, but too many had been snapped by the war for their efforts to be wholly successful:

> THE MARYLEBONE CLUB AND THE WAR
>
> At the beginning of August 1922 the MCC issued the following statement:
>
> During the war the Committee of the MCC wrote to 5,100 candidates entered in the books between 1889 and 1896 in order to ascertain if they were still desirous of becoming members of the club. Of these 1,360 decided to take up their election, 268 asked for their election to be postponed, 158 desired to take up their election but have not since applied, while from 1,650 no replies were received. In the case of 760 the letters were returned by the Post Office, 290 declined election, and the Committee are informed that 614 were killed in action or are deceased. The Committee are most desirous that no hardship should occur to those candidates who were written to during the war.
>
> In the case of those who replied, they are communicating by letter with each individual except those who have declined, but in the case of the remainder they feel that the best course they can pursue is to notify them through the Press that if they wish to be considered for election in due course and in order of entry as candidates, they should at once notify the Secretary of their desire.
>
> *Wisden*, 1923

A LTHOUGH the Georgian gentlemen's club had evolved by now into an international institution, there remained about the administration of Lord's a pleasing air of a family business whose proprietors maintained so sincere a respect for continuity that generation after generation was represented on the staff, much as the gardener's boy on some estate might in time come into the kingdom of the garden.

Richard Gaby ('Old Dick') joined the Lord's staff in 1875, retiring in 1937. He first came as a ground boy, becoming a lawn tennis professional, and subsequently was put in charge of the score-board, recalling times when numbers were hung up by hand. Gerald Maybee Gaby ('Joe') came in 1920, and from 1921–1939 was in charge of the professionals' dressing-room. After 1945 he supervised the pavilion attendants. Richard Thomas Gaby ('Young Dick') joined in 1929 as clerk to Jimmy Cannon, rejoining the staff after the war as ground superintendent where he was largely responsible for compiling the umpires' match appointments. Though a third brother, Charles Gaby, was employed at Lord's, after two seasons he fell in action during the First World War.

SIR PELHAM WARNER, *Lord's*, 1946

BY the time the Australians were due for another tour of England, in 1926, Cardus had fulfilled one of his romantic youthful dreams by becoming a friend of J. M. Barrie. Often they attended matches at Lord's together, with Barrie at first assuming the role of proud parent but soon realising that it was he who was really the cricketing child and Cardus the fatherly expert.

During 1926 I went to Lord's one morning with Barrie. We sat at right angles to the wicket, a most unprofessional place for me because I like to see the spin. But Barrie preferred the stand over the Tavern at Lord's near the dining-room; I think he imagined he was taking me to a cricket match as though I were one of his adopted grown-up children; he asked me after we had sat in the sun an hour or so whether I would like an ice-cream. Also he asked me what I thought of J. W. Hearne as a bowler: 'I mean do you call him – as an expert – fast or slow?' J. W. Hearne was a slow leg-break bowler, and I replied, 'Slow, of course; in fact, very slow.' Barrie meditated for a while, took another look at Hearne's bowling and said, 'For my part I should say he's pretty fast.' Here followed a pause for more meditation, then he added, 'You must come down to Stanway and watch me. I can bowl so slow that if I don't like a ball I can run after it and bring it back'.

NEVILLE CARDUS, *Autobiography*, 1947

CARDUS was in the unusual position of appreciating Barrie on two quite contrasting levels, for not only was he one of the game's finest descriptive writers but he had also been a drama critic, and was something of a connoisseur when it came to Barrie's oeuvre. This dual experience of his friend sometimes tempted Cardus to get them mixed up in the cause of anecdotage. In his *Autobiography*, he gives a remarkable account of a few days spent as a guest of Barrie at Robert Street, Adelphi Terrace. Throughout this visit Barrie was conspicuous by his own absence, flitting in and out like a ghost, disappearing when most expected, materialising when given up for lost. The man who ministered to Cardus's every need was the manservant Thurston, whose ability 'to correct any loose statements about Ovid that he chanced to overhear while serving dinner' suggests that perhaps he was an inspiration for Reginald Jeeves. During the long days of his visit, Cardus attended the cricket at Lord's, and returned to the apartments to find that Barrie was still absent:

After another day at Lord's I came back to the flat at dusk. Once more a cold collation and a bottle of hock waited for me. Once more the place was silent, and, as far as I could tell without poking and peering and looking under tables and behind curtains, it was unpeopled. I poured me out a glass of wine, then, as I drank, I heard the rumble of the lift and presently the door opened and a young man entered in a dinner jacket. Without a sign of curiosity at my presence or at the absence of others, he remarked to me that it had been a lovely day. He sat on a couch, smoked a cigarette, and talked for a few minutes about the cricket at Lord's; he hadn't yet been able to look in at the match himself, but he had enjoyed my account of Saturday's play in the 'M.G.'. I was liking him very much when he arose, and with an apology left the room and the flat. To this day I do not know who he was – probably young Simon out of *Mary Rose*.

NEVILLE CARDUS, *Autobiography*, 1947

FOR the sake of dramaturgic decorum, the reader hopes that the match which Cardus was attending during his eerie stay with Barrie was not the second Test of the 1926 series, when whispers of foul play were heard in the cobwebbed recesses of the Gentlemen's clubs. *Wisden* spoke of there being 'very nearly an unpleasant incident', a reference to the discovery on the second morning of the match that the middle of the pitch was mysteriously waterlogged. Sabotage was suspected, but soon it was discovered that some unidentified careless menial had left the hose-pipe connected to the water supply. Fortunately for the sanity of Empire, neither end of the pitch was affected and the game proceeded – to a draw. Cardus could no doubt have made a pretty essay out of the incident, positing the theory that the leakage had been the work of Count Fosco, or Bradley Headstone, or Professor Moriarty, or possibly all three working in concert, like a team of selectors. This literary tendency of Cardus at least once led him to a delightful experiment. Having noticed that in the two great popular sagas of middle-class life, Barchester and Forsyte, there is a neglect of cricket, in Trollope absolute, in Galsworthy very nearly so, Cardus set out to rectify the oversight by imagining what Galsworthy might have written had Jolyon been tempted to Lord's after long years of absence:

A Sentimental Journey

The taxi turned into St John's Wood Road. Jolyon recognised every part of the pavement of it; time after time he had come here on forgotten June mornings. It was quieter then, not so much traffic. He once saw Richardson and Lockwood walking along the pavement. They were very big men, and they wore blue serge, with watch-chains over their waistcoats. Both were dead now, Jolyon supposed.

He saw at once, as soon as he got into the ground, that the place had changed a bit. He was not sure about the Nursery end. Where were the arches? That stand was in the way; that was new for certain. Well it was a change for the better; it looked handsome, and there was no doubt that many more people watched cricket nowadays. He bought a match-card off a boy on his favourite Mound stand; he never did sit in the pavilion, not enough sunshine there after midday. He looked at the card: 'Gloucestershire v. Middlesex; a three-day match.' He liked the formality of Lord's. A splendid place; he really must come oftener. The pavilion possessed dignity; the whole place stood for something . . .

He was glad it was Gloucestershire who were playing; he wanted to see Hammond. He read the names on the card. Where did C. L. Townsend bat nowadays? But what was he talking about; C. L. Townsend didn't play any longer. No, it was not a piece of bad memory; he prided himself on his memory. C. L. Townsend had given up county cricket early on in life; he could not be much more than – well, fifty or so . . .

The players came into the field, and Jolyon joined in the hand-clapping. He found it hard to sort out the cricketers, though he admitted the score-board was efficiently worked. 'Bowler 10,' Goddard; a new man, evidently. And Middlesex, not Gloucestershire, were batting. He turned to a parson sitting next to him. 'Which is Hammond?' he asked. The parson pointed out Hammond fielding in the slips. 'Ah yes, of course,' said Jolyon. 'He's thickened out since last summer.' He was pleased with that reply; he was not going to give himself away.

NEVILLE CARDUS, Good Days, 1934

CARDUS published this masterly evocation of the spirit of the Forsytes at Lord's in a collection of his *Manchester Guardian* pieces called *Good Days* in 1934. Eleven years before, Galsworthy, in arriving at what ought in the artistic sense to have been the end of his Forsyte serial, *To Let*, dropped assorted members of the family into the ground, predictably for the Eton v. Harrow match. It is interesting to compare pupil and master, and to note that while Cardus, who is after all, writing a cricket essay on the sport page, filters the cricket through Jolyon's recollections, Galsworthy utilises Lord's as a mere backdrop to more portentous events:

Timothy Prophesies

On the day of the cancelled meeting at the National Gallery began the second anniversary of the resurrection of England's pride and glory – or, more shortly, the top hat. 'Lord's' – that festival which the War had driven from the field – raised its light and dark blue flags for the second time, displaying almost every feature of a glorious past. Here, in the luncheon interval, were all species of female and one species of male hat, protecting the multiple types of face associated with 'the classes'. The observing Forsyte might discern in the free or unconsidered seats a certain number of the squash-hatted, but they hardly ventured on the grass; the old school – or schools – could still rejoice that the proletariat was not yet paying the necessary half-crown. Here was still a close borough, the only one left on a large scale – for the papers were about to estimate the attendance at ten thousand. And the ten thousand, all animated by one hope, were asking each other one question: 'Where are you lunching?' Something wonderfully uplifting and reassuring in that query and the sight of so many people like themselves voicing it! What reserve power in the British realm – enough pigeons, lobsters, lamb, salmon, mayonnaise, strawberries, and bottles of champagne to feed the lot! No miracle in prospect – no case of seven loaves and a few fishes – faith rested on surer foundations. Six thousand top hats, four thousand parasols would be doffed and furled, ten thousand mouths all speaking the same English would be filled. There was life in the old dog yet! Tradition! And again Tradition! How strong and how elastic! Wars might rage, taxation prey, Trades Unions take toll, and Europe perish of starvation; but the ten thousand would be fed; and, within their ring fence, stroll upon green turf, wear their top hats, and meet – themselves. The heart was sound, the pulse still regular. E-ton! E-ton! Har-r-o-o-o-w!

Among the many Forsytes, present on a hunting-ground theirs, by personal prescriptive right, or proxy, was Soames with his wife and daughter. He had not been at either school, he took no interest in cricket, but he wanted Fleur to show her frock, and he wanted to wear his top hat – parade it again in peace and plenty among his peers. He walked sedately with Fleur between him and Annette. No women equalled them, so far as he could see. They could walk, and hold themselves up; there was substance in their good looks; the modern woman had no build, no chest, no anything! He remembered suddenly with what intoxication of pride he had walked round with Irene in the first years of his first marriage. And how they used to lunch on the drag which his mother *would* make his father have, because it was so 'chic' – all drags and carriages in those days, not these lumbering great Stands! And how consistently Montague Dartie had drunk too much. He supposed that people drank too much still, but there was not the scope for it there used to be. He remembered George Forsyte – whose brothers Roger and Eustace had been at Harrow and Eton – towering up on the top of the drag waving a light-blue flag with one hand and a dark-blue flag with the other, and shouting, 'Etroow – Harrton!' just when everybody was silent, like the buffoon he had always been; and Eustace got up to the nines below, too dandified to wear any colour or take any notice. H'm! Old days, and Irene in grey silk shot with palest green. He looked, sideways, at Fleur's face. Rather colourless – no light, no eagerness! That love affair was preying on her – a bad business! He looked beyond, at his wife's face, rather more touched up than usual, a little disdainful – not that she had any business to disdain, so far as he could see. She was taking Profond's defection with curious quietude; or was his 'small' voyage just a blind? If so, he should refuse to see it! Having promenaded round the pitch and in front of the pavilion, they sought Winifred's table in the Bedouin Club tent. This Club – a new 'cock and hen' – had been founded in the interests of travel, and of a gentleman with an old Scottish name, whose father had somewhat strangely been called Levi. Winifred had joined, not because she had travelled, but because instinct told her that a Club with such a name and such a founder was bound to go far; if one didn't join at once one might never have the chance. Its tent, with a text from the Koran on an orange ground, and a small green camel embroidered over the entrance, was the most striking on the ground. Outside it they found Jack Cardigan in a dark blue tie (he had once played for Harrow), batting with a Malacca cane to show them how that fellow ought to have hit that ball. He piloted them in. Assembled in Winifred's corner were Imogen, Benedict with his young wife, Val Dartie without Holly, Maud and her husband, and, after Soames and his two were seated, one empty place.

'I'm expecting Prosper,' said Winifred, 'but he's so busy with his yacht.'

Soames stole a glance. No movement in his wife's face! Whether that fellow were coming or not, she evidently knew all about it. It did not escape him that Fleur, too, looked at her mother. If Annette didn't respect his feelings, she might think of Fleur's! The conversation, very desultory, was syncopated by Jack Cardigan talking about 'mid-off.' He cited all the 'great mid-offs' from the beginning of time, as if they had been a definite racial entity in the composition of the British people. Soames had finished his lobster, and was beginning on pigeon-pie, when he heard the words, 'I'm a small bit late, Mrs Dartie,' and saw that there was no longer any empty place. *That fellow* was sitting between Annette and Imogen. Soames ate steadily on, with an occasional word to Maud and Winifred. Conversation buzzed around him. He heard the voice of Profond say:

'I think you're mistaken, Mrs Forsyde; I'll – I'll bet Miss Forsyde agrees with me.'

'In what?' came Fleur's clear voice across the table.

'I was sayin', young girls are much the same as they always were – there's very small difference.'

'Do you know so much about them?'

That sharp reply caught the ears of all, and Soames moved uneasily on his thin green chair.

'Well, I don't know, I think they want their own small way, and I think they always did.'

'Indeed!'

'Oh, but – Prosper,' Winifred interjected comfortably, 'the girls in the streets – the girls who've been in munitions, the little flappers in the shops; their manners now really quite hit you in the eye.'

At the word 'hit' Jack Cardigan stopped his disquisition; and in the silence Monsieur Profond said:

'It was inside before, now it's outside; that's all.'

'But their morals!' cried Imogen.

'Just as moral as they ever were, Mrs Cardigan, but they've got more opportunity.'

The saying, so cryptically cynical, received a little laugh from Imogen, a slight opening of Jack Cardigan's mouth, and a creak from Soames' chair.

Winifred said: 'That's too bad, Prosper.'

'What do you say, Mrs Forsyte; don't you think human nature's always the same?'

Soames subdued a sudden longing to get up and kick the fellow. He heard his wife reply:

'Human nature is not the same in England as anywhere else.' That was her confounded mockery!

'Well, I don't know much about this small country' – 'No, thank God!' thought Soames – 'but I should say the pot was boilin' under the lid everywhere. We all want pleasure, and we always did.'

Damn the fellow! His cynicism was – was outrageous!

When lunch was over they broke up into couples for the digestive promenade. Too proud to notice, Soames knew perfectly that Annette and that fellow had gone prowling round together. Fleur was with Val; she had chosen him, no doubt, because he knew that boy. He himself had Winifred for partner. They walked in the bright, circling stream, a little flushed and sated, for some minutes, till Winifred sighed:

'I wish we were back forty years, old boy!'

Before the eyes of her spirit an interminable procession of her own 'Lord's' frocks was passing, paid for with the money of her father, to save a recurrent crisis. 'It's been very amusing, after all. Sometimes I even wish Monty was back. What do you think of people nowadays, Soames?'

'Precious little style. The thing began to go to pieces with bicycles and motor-cars; the War has finished it.'

'I wonder what's coming?' said Winifred in a voice dreamy from pigeon-pie. 'I'm not at all sure we shan't go back to crinolines and pegtops. Look at that dress!'

Soames shook his head.

'There's money, but no faith in things. We don't lay by for the future. These youngsters – it's all a short life and a merry one with them.'

'There's a hat!' said Winifred. 'I don't know – when you come to think of the people killed and all that in the War, it's rather wonderful, I think. There's no other country – Prosper says the rest are all bankrupt, except America; and of course her men always took their style in dress from us.'

'Is that chap,' said Soames, 'really going to the South Seas?'

'Oh! one never knows where Prosper's going!'

'*He's* a sign of the times,' muttered Soames, 'if you like.'

Winifred's hand gripped his arm.

'Don't turn your head,' she said in a low voice, 'but look to your right in the front row of the Stand.'

Soames looked as best he could under that limitation. A man in a grey top hat, grey-bearded, with thin brown, folded cheeks, and a certain elegance of posture, sat there with a woman in a lawn-coloured frock, whose dark eyes were fixed upon himself. Soames looked quickly at his feet. How funnily feet moved, one after the other like that! Winifred's voice said in his ear:

'Jolyon looks very ill, but he always had style. *She* doesn't change – except her hair.'

'Why did you tell Fleur about that business?'

'I didn't; she picked it up. I always knew she would.'

'Well, it's a mess. She's set her heart upon their boy.'

'The little wretch,' murmured Winifred. 'She tried to take me in about that. What shall you do, Soames?'

'Be guided by events.'

They moved on, silent, in the almost solid crowd.

'Really,' said Winifred suddenly; 'it almost seems like Fate. Only that's so old-fashioned. Look! There are George and Eustace!'

George Forsyte's lofty bulk had halted before them.

'Hallo, Soames!' he said. 'Just met Profond and your wife. You'll catch 'em if you put on pace. Did you ever go to see old Timothy?'

Soames nodded, and the streams forced them apart.

'I always liked old George,' said Winifred. 'He's so droll.'

'I never did,' said Soames. 'Where's your seat? I shall go to mine. Fleur may be back there.'

Having seen Winifred to her seat, he regained his own, conscious of small, white, distant figures running, the click of the bat, the cheers and counter-cheers. No Fleur, and no Annette! You could expect nothing of women nowadays! They had the vote. They were 'emancipated', and much good it was doing them! So Winifred would go back, would she, and put up with Dartie all over again? To have the past once more – to be sitting here as he had sat in '83 and '84, before he was certain that his marriage with Irene had gone all wrong, before her antagonism had become so glaring that with the best will in the world he could not overlook it. The sight of her with that fellow had brought all memory back. Even now he could not understand why she had been so impracticable. She could love other men; she had it in her! To himself, the one person she ought to have loved, she had chosen to refuse her heart. It seemed to him, fantastically, as he looked back, that all this modern relaxation of marriage – though its forms and laws were the same as when he married her – that all this modern looseness had come out of her revolt; it seemed to him, fantastically, that she had started it, till all decent ownership of anything had gone, or was on the point of going. All came from her! And now – a pretty state of things! Homes! How could you have them without mutual ownership? Not that he had ever had a real home! But had that been his fault? He had done his best. And his rewards were – those two sitting in that Stand, and this affair of Fleur's!

And overcome by loneliness he thought: 'Shan't wait any longer! They must find their own way back to the hotel – if they mean to come!' Hailing a cab outside the ground, he said:

'Drive me to the Bayswater Road.' His old aunts had never failed him. To them he had meant an ever-welcome visitor. Though they were gone, there, still, was Timothy!

John Galsworthy, To Let, 1921

After two or three seasons as 'Cricketer' in the *Manchester Guardian*, Cardus's initial provincial indifference to the urbanity of Lord's gave way to a deep love of the place. Others reported the same initial failure to appreciate the blandishments of the ground, particularly the indefinable and probably unaccountable spirit of the premises, which seemed in the end to exercise an influence over regular visitors which verged on the supernatural. The hardest-headed men, politicians and empire-builders, matinee idols and industrialists, bankers and publicans alike, came to Lord's, sniffed a little, and then, either gradually as the result of regular visits or suddenly through a visitation, came to appreciate its charms. Among the many prominent men who came to their senses quite late in the day was the New Zealand millionaire philanthropist Sir Arthur Sims, who had played for W. G. Grace's side in 1912, had appeared at Lord's and gone home again without giving the matter a second thought. In 1926 he returned, and astonished himself by the depth of his feelings:

It was midsummer, and the sun was hot in a sky speckled with lazy clouds. He went into the Long Room, its pale green walls hung with portraits of men who had lived their day and made their contributions. He looked out through the broad windows, glanced from the crowded stands to the green, dappled turf, to the fieldsmen alternately rigid and relaxed, to the padded, gloved batsmen and their studious concentration ... and suddenly he knew that on no other ground had he sensed the same atmosphere of pleasure, of experience and knowledge, and competition ... of shrewd judgement and appraisal ... of appreciation and kindly criticisms ... of leisured ease and mellowness. He felt at home, that he belonged, and that, until now, he had been almost blind and insensitive. And that he was deeply contented.

ALAN MITCHELL, *84 Not out*, 1962

TAKING everything into account, 1926 was an emotional summer for English cricket. For the first time in the post-war period, the Australians were defeated and the Ashes regained. After four successive draws, England finally emerged victorious in the final Test at The Oval, in August, where Hobbs scored a masterly second innings century. The rest of the season should have been an anti-climax, but, unexpectedly, Hobbs's summer came to a climax a few days later in the match at Lord's between Middlesex and Surrey.

MIDDLESEX v SURREY
Played at Lord's, August 28, 30, 31, 1926

Hobbs seized upon this occasion to make what was at once the highest score of his wonderful career, and the highest ever made at Lord's, beating his own 266, not out, for Players against Gentlemen at Scarborough in 1925, and Holmes' 315, not out, for Yorkshire against Middlesex—also put together in the previous summer. The great batsman, who obtained his runs mainly on the on side, placed the ball with marvellous skill and did not appear to give a chance. He was at the wickets six hours and fifty-five minutes, scoring forty-one 4s, six 3s, twenty 2s, and ninety-four singles. Sandham helped to raise the total to 115—the two Surrey men's thirty-sixth three-figure first wicket stand. Ducat shared in the partnership of 101, and Jardine in one of 270. Hendren, in the first innings of Middlesex, withstood the Surrey attack for three hours and a half, and put together his seventh hundred of the season, but the home side had to follow on 304 in arrear, and Surrey, fielding brilliantly, won the match by an innings and 63 runs.

SURREY

J. B Hobbs not out.......	316	Mr A. Jeacocke run out..	26
A. Sandham c. Hendren		Mr P. G. H. Fender not out	1
b. Haig	58		
A. Ducat b. Durston.....	41	B 12, l-b 7.....	19
T. Shepherd c. and b.			
Stevens	15		—
Mr D. R. Jardine c. and		(5 wkts dec.)	579
b. Powell	103		

Mr E. R. T. Holmes, H. A. Peach, H. Strudwick and S. Fenley did not bat.

MIDDLESEX

Mr G. T. S. Stevens c.			
Strudwick b. Holmes....	2	c. Fender b. Peach	63
Mr H. L. Dales b. Jardine...	52	c. Fender b. Holmes	4
Mr G. O. Allen c. Shepherd			
b. Peach	21	c. Jardine b. Fenley.....	17
E. Hendren not out.......	101	c. Fenley b. Jardine.....	37
Mr H. J. Enthoven run out.	1	b. Fenley	5
Mr F. T. Mann c. Peach b.			
Jardine	3	not out	37
Mr N. Haig c. Strudwick			
b. Fender	12	c. Shepherd b. Fender ..	18
H. W. Lee run out	42	c. Strudwick b. Holmes .	31
H. R. Murrell c. Peach b.			
Fenley	20	c. Fenley b. Peach......	7
T. J. Durston b. Fender	0	b. Holmes	1
J. A. Powell c. and b. Fender	0	c. Strudwick b. Holmes .	4
B. 15, l-b 6......	21	B. 11, l-b 3, w 2, n-b 1.	17
	275		241

Middlesex Bowling

	Overs	Mdns	Runs	Wkts	Overs	Mdns	Runs	Wkts
Haig	37	7	118	1				
Durston	31	12	69	1				
Allen	19	3	88	0				
Stevens	22.3	1	95	1				
Lee	8	1	44	0				
Powell	27	4	109	1				
Enthoven	10	1	37	0				

Surrey Bowling

	Overs	Mdns	Runs	Wkts	Overs	Mdns	Runs	Wkts
Holmes	14	2	41	1	15.4	2	49	4
Peach	18	7	26	1	23	5	41	2
Fenley	24	4	76	1	23	4	66	2
Fender	23	5	76	3	14	2	38	1
Shepherd	9	5	22	0	8	3	12	0
Jardine	8	2	13	2	6	1	18	1

Wisden, 1927

Poets too turned their attention to Lord's, among them one of the most dedicated captains in English village cricket, Siegfried Sassoon (1886–1967), whose Kentish childhood found cricket high on the curriculum of life. Sassoon played a good standard of minor cricket, and his name may be found in the ranks of the Blue Mantles in the days before the Great War smashed his idyllic world to pieces. In 1926, Sassoon published a volume called *Satirical Poems*, which included an item entitled *The Blues at Lord's*. Musing on the oddities of modern society, Sassoon wrote the couplet often quoted since:

> One fact seems sure:
> That, while the Church approves, Lord's will endure.

evidently not perceiving that while religious observances among the mass of the English were in slow but steady decline, the popularity of Lord's was still growing.

A versifier who would have been perfectly well aware of this was Harry Graham (1874–1936), author of *Ruthless Rhymes* and that extraordinary experiment in rhymed abbreviations *Poetical Economy*. Graham was famous in his day as a writer of operatic adaptations of mittel-european imports of the most gaseous kind; to this day his words are sung in that amazing monument to human folly, *White Horse Inn*. The London production of 1931, featuring assorted horses, dogs and goats running through the snowscapes of a cardboard Tyrol, ran for over 600 performances, which must have given Graham, a former Guards officer, much leisure time to while away at Lord's. It was a spot to which he was deeply attached, especially when he felt exhausted by his poetic effusions and needed deep rest:

LORD'S

> Lord's! what tender recollections
> Does that famous name suggest!
> What a crowd of fond reflections
> Throng my antiquated breast,
> As I lounge in the Pavilion
> And, from my exalted seat,
> Watch the undistinguished million
> Surging at my feet!
>
> Hither, with a 'rover's ticket',
> In the days of youth I came;
> Glued my eye upon the wicket,
> Missed no moment of the game,
> While to feminine relations
> Whom I happened to escort
> I explained the complications
> Of this form of sport,
>
> Here, like ocean breakers roaring,
> I would stamp my feet and yell,
> When I watched my heroes scoring,
> Or opponent's wickets fell;

Here, where inningses were ended,
To the tents I turned my gaze,
Where the hock-cup subtly blended
With the mayonnaise!

Happy days! Like shadows flitting
O'er my mind, those mem'ries pass!
Now, in the Pavilion sitting,
I grow elderly, alas!
Though no tittle I am losing
Of the zeal I felt of yore,
Now and then I can't help snoozing –
Wake me if I snore!

HARRY GRAHAM, 1928

GRAHAM was, at any rate, if not a poet, at least a professional versifier. Dr Cyril Argentine Alington was neither. In 1928 Dr Alington, as headmaster of Eton College, could not claim himself to be a disinterested party at the Eton v. Harrow game. A few days before the Match of the Season, at least so far as the Doctor was concerned, he had attended the University match and been present at a tense and nerve-wracking finish, when Oxford, facing hopeless defeat, lost nine wickets with twenty minutes to go and somehow defied the Cambridge bowlers till stumps were drawn. But Alington's true ordeal did not start until his school faced Harrow. In the last moments of the match Harrow, set 308 to make in three and a half hours, made a brave attempt, but were finally undone by A. G. Hazelrigg, who took five wickets for 73. The match ended on 14 July, and two days later, readers of *The Times* were intrigued to come across a poem entitled 'Lord's, 1928', in which a poet, his identity transparently enshrouded in the initials 'C.A.A.', waxed politely hysterical about his school's victory. Today it is not Dr Alington's poetry which ensures his cricketing immortality, but the accident that a few years earlier, when headmaster of Shrewsbury School, he had offered a lifeline to the school's young cricket professional by appointing him his private secretary. This young scribe grew up to be Neville Cardus, and so the good Doctor was incorporated into the paradisical mythology of Cardus's beautiful works of fiction.

LORD'S, 1928

Lord's – Lord's on a Wednesday evening!
Cambridge fieldsmen crowding round,
Oxford's hardly a chance of saving it –
Hardly a chance, but still you found
Elderly cricketers gnawing their sticks,
Blameless Bishops, forgetful of Jix,
Publicly praying at half past six,
And prayers and curses arise from the Mound
On that head of carrots (or possibly gold)
With a watchful eye on each ball that's bowled –
And a deadly silence around the ground

Lord's – Lord's on a Friday evening!
Two men out and an hour to play –
Lose another, and that's the end of it,
Why not call it a harrowing day?
Harrow's lips are at last on the cup,
Harrow's tail unmistakably up,
And Eton? Eton can only pray
For a captain's heart in a captain's breast,
And some decent batting among the rest,
And sit and shiver and hope for the best –
If those two fellows can only stay!

Stay they did – can we ever forget it? –
Till those who had hidden us all despair
Lift their pipes with a new assurance,
Toyed instead with the word 'declare';
Harrow's glorious hours begin,
Harrow batsmen hurrying in,
One and all with the will to win,
Cheers and counter-cheers rend the air!
Harrow's down with her colours flying,
Great in doing and great in dying,
Eton's home with a head to spare!

C.A.A., *The Times*, 16 July 1928

I F Dr Alington could wax so madly about the Eton–Harrow match, what might he
not have achieved in the realms of romantic poetry had he been a West Indian
islander present at the ground a few weeks earlier when the touring side met Middlesex,
and acquitted themselves so well that the match is usually included in even the most
cursory histories of the ground? Not only was this the occasion of a famous team effort,
but it also marked one of the great individual performances:

MIDDLESEX v WEST INDIES
Played at Lord's, June 9, 11, 12, 1928

A splendid all-round performance on the part of Constantine enabled
West Indies to gain a memorable victory by three wickets. When
that player went in on Monday the tourists, as the result of more
than two hours' laborious batting, had lost half their wickets for 79,
and stood in no small danger of having to follow on. In such a
brilliant manner did he deal with the situation that, driving with
great power, and pulling in daring fashion, he made 86 out of 107
in less than an hour. Despite this fine effort, the visitors fell 122 short
of the total at which, with six men out, Middlesex had declared, but
in the county's second innings, Constantine, hitting the stumps five

times, proceeded to take seven wickets for little more than 8 runs apiece. On going on to bowl for the second time. Constantine sent down six overs and three balls for 11 runs and six wickets. Even after this deadly piece of bowling, West Indies—set 259 to win and losing five batsmen for 121—looked sure to be beaten. Coming once again to the rescue of his side, however, Constantine crowned a wonderful display by hitting up 103 out of 133 in an hour, with two 6s and twelve 4s as his chief strokes. Martin shared in his success on Monday, and in the further triumph, Fernandes was his partner. Haig, whom Hearne assisted to add 153, settled down after a moderate start to the making of a capital 100, and Hendren, who also reached three figures, was seen to advantage. In stopping a drive from Constantine, Hearne had a finger so badly damaged that he could play no more cricket last season.

Middlesex

Mr N. Haig b. Small	119	b. Constantine	5
H. W. Lee c. Martin b. Constantine	7	b. Constantine	15
J. W. Hearne c. Nunes b. Roach	75	lbw b. Small	28
E. Hendren not out	100	c. Francis b. Constantine	52
Mr E. T. Killick b. Francis	6	c. Francis b. Constantine	4
Mr G. O. Allen run out	4	c. and b. Francis	7
Mr F. T. Mann b. Francis	32	b Small	4
Mr I. A. R. Peebles not out	0	b. Constantine	0
T. J. Durston (did not bat)		not out	9
W. F. Price (did not bat)		b. Constantine	3
J. A. Powell (did not bat)		b. Constantine	1
B. 2, l-b 4, n-b 3	9	B. 3, l-b 2, n-b 3.	8
(6 wkts dec.)	352		136

West Indies

G. Challenor c. Hendren b. Durston	23	b. Haig	33
C. A. Roach c. Lee b. Durston	0	run out	10
M. P. Fernandes c. Hearne b. Allen	29	c. Allen b. Haig	54
W. H. St Hill c. Hendren b. Peebles	5	b. Durston	5
E. L. Bartlett st. Price b. Powell	13	lbw. b. Hearne	26
F. R. Martin not out	26	not out	1
L. N. Constantine b. Peebles	86	c. Haig b. Lee	103
J. A. Small c. Hendren b. Haig	7	c. and b. Peebles	5
R. K. Nunes b. Durston	17		
C. R. Browne c. Allen b. Durston	0	not out	4
G. N. Francis lbw. b. Haig	1		
B. 18, l-b 3, n-b 2	23	B. 18	18
	230		259

West Indies Bowling

	Overs	Mdns	Runs	Wkts	Overs	Mdns	Runs	Wkts
Francis	35.5	4	107	2	10	3	30	1
Constantine	20	1	77	1	14.3	1	57	7
Browne	11	2	21	–				
Small	29	5	72	1	11	3	36	2
Martin	13	–	30	–	3	–	5	–
Roach	7	–	36	1				

Middlesex Bowling

	Overs	Mdns	Runs	Wkts	Overs	Mdns	Runs	Wkts
Durston	21	10	16	4	15	3	32	1
Haig	24.4	7	32	2	22	5	80	2
Hearne	11	4	25	–	15	3	51	1
Peebles	18	2	51	2	11	2	45	1
Allen	8	2	43	1				
Powell	7	1	40	1	1	–	6	–
Lee					4.4	–	27	1

Umpires: J. W. Day and W. R. Parry.

Wisden, 1929

Against Middlesex Constantine covered himself with glory. It was his match with a vengeance, for he made scores of 86 and 103, and in the county's second innings took seven wickets in fourteen overs and three balls for 57 runs – the last six in six overs and three balls for eleven runs. Two of his strokes I shall remember to my dying day. The first was when he hit a good-length ball from Allen over extra-cover's head far up into the Grand Stand, and the second when he played back to Hearne with such tremendous force that the ball, after striking the pavilion rails, ricochetted among the seats, scattering the members of the MCC and Middlesex, and bringing destruction to woodwork and paint. On its ferocious passage from the bat Hearne very pluckily put one of his hands in the way of the ball, and was so badly hurt that he played no more cricket that season.

SIR PELHAM WARNER, *Lord's*, 1946

Constantine would be on the short list of any selector in all-time world fielders. His bowling in his early days was thrillingly fast (and, later on, just as excitingly cunning), but it is his batting which concerns us here. As with all daring and ingenious batsmen, his run-getting was disappointing, chiefly because a failure by him meant greater disappointment to the crowd than that of almost any other batsman.

His chief characteristic was an obvious wish to attack every ball if he possibly could, coupled with an apparent desire to parade the widest possible range of strokes – both orthodox and otherwise – in the shortest possible time. Like Jessop he was not primarily a long hitter, though he did hit some very big ones; it was not so much the length of his hits that was remarkable as the unusual direction of them.

Like other very great cricketers, wherever Constantine played he left some memory of his astonishing ability. In the course of a handful of appearances at Lord's he made several strokes that rank high among the famous hits on this most famous of all grounds. His performance against Middlesex there in 1928 was probably the greatest of all his achievements. He scored 86 out of 107 and 103 out of 133, and in neither of these innings did he bat for more than an hour.

When Middlesex began their second innings 122 runs ahead of the West Indies, Constantine fought back with a superb bowling spell of 6 for 11 and put Middlesex out for 136. Thus set 259 to win, the West Indies seemed well beaten when Constantine came in at 121 for 5, but his wonderful hitting enabled his side to win by three wickets. It was almost a one-man show. In this match Constantine made two strokes which Sir Pelham Warner states he will remember to his dying day. In the first innings he hit a good-length ball of G. O. Allen's slap over extra-cover's head and far up into the grandstand below the scoreboard. It wasn't a cut and it wasn't a drive; it was just Constantine. Here is his own account of the hit: 'G. O. Allen came on and I got up to drive him first ball. It was a yorker and he nearly bowled me. But afterwards he was inswinging the ball and I was glancing to leg. He placed a man fine, and I forced him past square leg. He moved outside the off stump, and I cover drove. He sent up a widish pitched-up ball, and I went at him with a horizontal bat, drive or cut as you will, but screwing the blade, and the ball fell into the seats near the scoring box. In some twenty minutes I had 50, and scored 86 in less than an hour, before Peebles bowled me with a googly.'

The other notable stroke was in the second innings, when he played back to J.W. Hearne with such tremendous force that the ball, after striking the pavilion rails, bounced about among the seats, scattering the members and bringing destruction to woodwork and paint. Hearne pluckily put up a hand in the way of the ferocious missile, and it was so badly damaged that he played no more cricket for the rest of the season. *The Times* correspondent, reporting his innings of 86, wrote: 'No one living could have shown a more pleasurable intent to score off every ball sent down to him than did Constantine yesterday. Moreover, he tried so far as he could to adopt the most unorthodox, though now frequently unexploited, method of dealing with each particular ball. Some of his scoring strokes were a revelation to those who had forgotten where runs could be made, and memorable in an innings which must rank among the very best played at Lord's this year were the way in which he hit the fast bowling over mid-wicket's head, a remarkable six over cover-point's head which landed high up in the new grandstand, and his straight driving off short balls.'

GERALD BRODRIBB, *Hit for Six*, 1960

Dr Alington was by no means the only cricket-loving writer to be moved by the Eton–Harrow match of 1928. A far less hysterical, and yet more eloquent recollection of the game was later published by someone who recalled the affair for rather different, less partisan reasons than the good Doctor, someone just beginning what was to be a career magisterial in its judgements, prolific in its wordage, and pricelessly good-humoured.

I began reporting cricket for the *Standard* in 1928, as second string to J. A. H. Cotton, and it may surprise younger readers to know that the one match I clearly recall in that year is the Eton and Harrow. Lord's in those days almost burst at the seams for this game that was so unlike any other. *Wisden* gives the paying gate for the two days in this particular year, for instance, at over 34,000. With members the company would have been around forty thousand. And for the ambulatory portion thereof, which went partly to see friends and be seen by them, and therefore paraded the perimeter, calling at the tents and arbours that covered the practice ground, or the coaches that lined the Tavern boundary, or the boxes above, the number must have seemed rather greater. Despite ropes and Keep Left signs it could take the best part of half-an-hour to circumnavigate the main ground. The throng on the field itself at the intervals, like a gently-stirring sea of confetti, was a sight to remember. Practically every man and boy was in morning-dress, every woman and girl in the height of fashion. To the stranger looking in from outside, as it were, the atmosphere was that of a mammoth family party.

E. W. SWANTON, *Sort of a Cricket Person*, 1972

NEARLY sixty years on, the cricket follower reads of such spectacular crowds at the Eton v. Harrow match and is frankly incredulous. Today the game has shrunk to a tiny incident in the Lord's summer which is hardly reported anywhere. By 1983 it had indeed dwindled to so great an extent that a decision was made to reduce it to a one-day, single innings fixture, a measure which must have been regarded as a blasphemy by those who recalled with a rosy glow the great old days of Robert St Leger Fowler and company. In fact, so great is the scepticism of the modern reader that he harbours suspicions that Mr Swanton might have imagined it all at the time or dreamed it up later. That sceptical lobby is well advised to turn to the press of the summer of 1929, when the fixture was still so elevated, socially speaking, that *The Times* treated it not only as a sporting occasion but also as part of the social diary and a dazzling exercise in *haute couture*:

ETON AND HARROW

Some of the Dresses

The Centenary Match between Eton and Harrow was begun yesterday at Lord's in perfect cricket weather, and before one of the largest crowds which have in recent years attended the match.

The favourite material for the women's gowns was flowered chiffon in all colourings on light and dark backgrounds. These were made with long uneven skirts and floating scarves and many had little coats to match. There were also many lace frocks in pale shades. There were many more large hats than small, and they were trimmed with a big posy on one side or with floating ends of velvet or ribbon. It was essentially a day for sunshades and these were seen in every variety of gay and brilliant design.

Princess Arthur of Connaught, who was accompanied by Prince Arthur, wore a gown of heavy beige crêpe de Chine, patterned with green and red flowers, and a green hat. The Duchess of Northumberland wore a gown of raspberry-pink and black printed chiffon with a large pink hat, bordered with black. She was accompanied by the Duke of Northumberland, Earl Percy, and Lord Hugh Percy, and her two young daughters, the Ladies Elizabeth and Diana Percy, who wore simple frocks of hyacinth pink and straw hats.

Mrs Stanley Baldwin, in a fawn georgette and lace dress with a feather-trimmed hat to match and carrying a pale yellow parasol, was among the early arrivals, as was also the Duchess of Roxburghe, in a black and white figured chiffon dress with a close-fitting hat. Lady Violet Astor was in a black chiffon dress patterned with small pink and blue flowers, and a small hat to match, and Marchioness Curzon of Kedleston, in white, was accompanied by her daughter, Mrs Edward Rice.

Viscountess Craigavon was accompanied by the Hon. James Craig and her daughter, the Hon. Aileen Craig, who wore a brown figured chiffon dress. Miss Ulrica Thynne wore a yellow chiffon frock with an uneven hemline and a big black hat. Others to be seen were Mr B. Thynne, Colonel Hardy, Mrs Hugh Lubbock, Mr Mark Lubbock, the Countess of Hardwicke, who wore pink and blue chiffon with a black hat, Major Guy Gold and Miss Anne Gold, and Lady Meyrick in yellow and beige chiffon. Lord North was with Lady North, who wore green flowered chiffon with a black hat, and Viscountess Folkestone, who was accompanied by Viscount Folkestone, was in chiffon patterned with large pink roses and a brown hat.

There were also to be seen Lord Harris, Mr Le Marchant, Mr Austen Leigh, Lieutenant-General Sir William and Lady Pitcairn-Campbell, who wore almond-green, Colonel W. M. Gordon, VC, Lady du Cros, and Lady Cullen of Ashbourne. Viscountess Coke, who wore a dress of flowered chiffon with a grey background, was accompanied by the Hon. Sylvia Coke, in brown crêpe de Chine, patterned with yellow and orange spots. Mrs Mills wore black and red with a large black hat. Mrs William Ogden was in a green and yellow chiffon dress, and Lady Chesham wore black. Lady Angela Scott wore white and Lady Alice Scott was in hydrangea blue and beige lace with a green hat, and Mrs Neville Chamberlain was in cool green.

Among those who entertained luncheon parties in their boxes or coaches were:–

Viscount and Viscountess Bearsted, among whose party were General and Mrs Hamilton, Miss Jean Hamilton, Mr D Parker, and their son, the Hon. Peter Samuel. Lady Bearsted wore a black and yellow figured chiffon dress with a black straw hat and a black parasol. Major Colin and Lady Margaret MacRae, the latter in pinky-beige chiffon with a brown hat, were on their coach with Miss Barbara MacRae, who wore a beige and blue flowered georgette dress with a blue picture hat to match. Lady (John) Noble was on a coach with her two daughters, Miss Noble and Miss Rosemary Noble: Lady Noble wore a beige lace dress with a large red straw hat, and she carried a blue parasol. Lord and Lady Gainford entertained the Hon. Mrs Beaumont, who wore a white georgette dress with a pale green hat.

The Earl and Countess of Bessborough, who were accompanied by Viscount Duncannon and Lady Moyra Ponsonby, entertained at luncheon the Hon. Geoffrey Brand, Lady Gweneth Cavendish, the Duchess of Roxburghe, the Marquess of Bowmont, Lady Irene Congreve, Mrs Montague Elliott, Miss Elliott, Major-General Sir John Ponsonsby, Captain and Mrs Neville Flower, Miss Anne Flower, and Mr Arthur Ponsonby.

The Duke and Duchess of Devonshire entertained a party in a box, as did Lord and Lady Leconfield, and among others who had boxes were Field-Marshal Viscount Plumer and Viscountess Plumer, who wore black and white, with a black hat trimmed with aigrettes: Brigadier-General the Earl of Lucan, Mr Anthony de Rothschild, Mrs Bulteel, who was dressed in black: the Marchioness of Crewe, the Countess of Wilton, Mrs Lionel de Rothschild, Colonel Geoffrey Glyn, Lady Penrhyn, Lord Dundas, the Marquess of Londonderry, Mrs Euan Wallace, and Mr and Mrs Gerard Leigh. Lord and Lady Hastings were in the Marquess of Abergavenny's box.

Among others who had coaches and carriages were Lord Wraxall, Brigadier-General Sir Norman Orr-Ewing, the Hon. Henry Dewar, Mr P. H. G. Gold, whose party included Sir Archibald and Lady Gold, Mr and Mrs Peter Gold, Mr Ulric Blyth and Mr Ormond Blyth, the Hon. Claud Lambton, Sir Cosmo Bonsor, Mr C. H. Goschen, Sir Edward Goschen, Sir Thomas Brocklebank, Sir Guy Campbell, Lord Cornwallis, Earl Fitzwilliam, and Mr W. W. Grantham.

Others to be seen during the day were:

The Earl of Rosebery, the Duchess of Devonshire, the Hon. Sir Harry Stoner, Lady Trenchard, Sir Godfrey Baring, Lord Wodehouse, Lord Hailsham, Archbishop Lord Davidson, Lord Armstrong, Lord and Lady Cromwell, the Earl of Chesterfield, General and Mrs Hamilton Skene, General Melliss, Mrs Humphrey Wyndham, Mr and Mrs Cator, Mrs Hamilton Cotton, Mrs Blair Oliphant, Colonel and Mrs A. F. Maclaughlin, Captain Glover and Miss Bower, Mrs Coryton, Captain S. W. Ronaldson, Mrs Cory Yeo, Mrs Bertram Hall, Mrs Frank Blundell, Mrs le Rossignol, Miss Heron Watson, Miss Hawkshaw and Miss Ruth Hawkshaw, Mr Haskett, Mrs A. Walter, Miss Broughton, Mrs H. Waller, Mrs Joseph Pike, Major Peel, the Earl of Shaftesbury, Lord Howard de Walden, the Duke of Buccleuch, Lieutenant-Colonel W. G. Lucas, and Lieutenant-Colonel G. Booker.

The Times, 13 July 1929

A FEW weeks later *The Times*, perhaps relenting, published a leader hinting at the blasphemous idea that possibly the MCC might be just a shade too stiff in its disbarring of women from the pavilion. One day, the writer seems to be suggesting, perhaps even this last male bastion will have fallen to the forces of polite society. That was more than half a century ago, and still the Long Room is sacrosanct, a masculine bolthole where the nearest approach to the rustle of skirts is the occasional arrival of a Scots member in a kilt. But the paper was wise to remind its readers that Lord's was much more than the sum of its members, that it had been subtly democratised simply by being located where it was. Lord's ground, which had once been popular among the gentry for its rusticity, its distance from Town, its countrified airs, had at last evolved, almost without anyone noticing, into one of the world's great metropolitan attractions. Those foreigners preoccupied with more childish pursuits, like baseball, or more ruffianly ones, like Rugby Union, may to this day raise an eyebrow at the claim that 'London without Lord's could hardly be considered London'. Certainly it is a ridiculous claim, justified only by the fact that it was perfectly true when the anonymous leader writer made it, and more true than ever as the century staggers to its close.

The last important game of the season has been played at Lord's, and to many it will seem that the year has ended. One sigh of satisfaction there will soon be heaved by the groundsman who has suffered agonies of anxiety in a desperate struggle against the effect of frost and drought. But his individual relief fades into nothingness before the regrets of the faithful myriads whose eyes and hearts have turned these many months, morning and evening, to the sacred city of their game.

Of that city the Pavilion is the temple. Valhalla is perhaps the better word. For there the heroes are, lining the walls in honourable portraiture, or the seats in unquestionable flesh and blood. Cheek by jowl they sit, from the elders, who could, and generally do, tell the youngsters a thing or two about hitting the ball, to the youngsters themselves, atoning for their deficiency of years by a calm confidence that no one can tell them a great deal about anything. Theirs is a sanctuary undesecrated by the foot of woman, one of the last asylums of the merely male in an epicene world. Proud sons are there, introduced by fathers, and even prouder fathers introduced by sons, but the proudest and fondest mother, wife, or daughter knocks at the door in vain. Men tolerate no such rival near this throne, where they sit, aloof like gods watching the strife of mortals, dispassionately bestowing praise and blame. Behind them, in the tranquil depths, sheltered from the tumult and the shouting lies

> 'that council hall
> Where sit the best and stateliest.'

giving law to cricket, and wielding, without other than moral sanction, a world-wide sway.

But what can they know of Lord's who only the Pavilion know? Spatially and numerically, the centre of gravity lies outside the Pavilion rails. There dwell the nameless thousands, young and old, male and, increasingly, female, for whom the humble shilling habitually opens the gateway to the Elysian field. They are no sybarites. Not for them the fat hamper on the coach-top, the collation in the private box, or even the luncheon room. Dispatch-case or brown-paper parcel

meets all the needs of the old campaigner. It is no shame to eat in the full glare
of the public eye at Lord's. The most highly respectable people in the most highly
respectable seats, even 'friends of members', unblushingly devour the homely
sandwich and banana as a preliminary to the stroll across the turf to inspect the
pitch with a knowing eye. As befits the citizens of a world centre, the Lord's
crowd is catholic in its sympathies. Its units are, first and foremost, lovers of the
game, not of a side. They will applaud a brilliant stroke, or shake their heads
over a doubtful decision, impartially for friend or foe. Rare instances of a different
deportment do but serve to throw into relief the massive good conduct of the
main attendance. The regular Lord's man unhesitatingly traces to 'visitors' any
outburst of partisanship or impatience. For these devoted thousands the glory of
life now suffers temporary eclipse. With them into the darkness go middle-aged
enthusiasts, of sedentary occupation, who make a practice of setting aside a week
or so of their holiday with the firm intention of spending every possible moment
of it at Lord's. With them go, too, the veterans, to whom membership of the MCC
is the most effective insurance against the tedium of age, and who may be heard,
pathetic inversions of schoolboys towards the end of term, mournfully counting
to one another the days of Lord's that the year still holds for them, only six days
more, three days, the very last day. For these, and for countless others, London
without Lord's could hardly be considered London. Mr Lord builded better than
he knew. It will not be thought a disproportionate reward that his name should
belong at once to the household and to the world, and should be immortal.

The Times, 7 September 1929

Bᴜᴛ if to attend Lord's was to weave oneself into the metropolitan tapestry, to play
there was to become an authentic part of cricket history. But what does it mean
to 'play' there? Does it mean to appear in a match, or to bat and bowl? Does it mean to
have played on some part of the ground which is not really The Ground? The passionate
lover of the game soon finds himself resorting desperately to the wildest semantic
deceptions in his attempt to incorporate himself into the history of Lord's. The present
writer, for example, can claim to have spent several hours batting and bowling at Lord's.
The fact that these idyllic moments were in the shape of a wartime concession by the
MCC whereby local youth clubs could take advantage of the long, double-summertime
evenings to practise in the Nursery nets is a tiny qualifying factor which is no more
than an academic quibble. In the season before Mr Swanton was serving his journalistic
apprenticeship at the Eton–Harrow match, a public schoolboy was clinging by his
fingernails to his nebulous involvement in the cricket at Lord's. He was one of the
almost-but-not-quiters of the Cheltenham eleven, but in later years satisfied himself
that he had done just enough to substantiate his harmless and touching braggadocio:

At cricket I was no star, but if, in my teens, someone had asked, 'Which would
you rather do, go in first for Yorkshire or become Prime Minister?', I might have
hesitated over the answer. In fact, I got no further than twelfth man in the
College eleven, but because I was called on to the field in the last innings of our

annual match against Haileybury, I was able to inject into subsequent articles such skilful sentences as 'the last time I played at Lord's', which suggested not only that I had played there, but that I had played there more than once.

J. P. W. MALLALIEU, *On Larkhill*, 1983

MALLALIEU was recalling his one moment of glory down the long perspective of a life now drawing to a close. He had served as a minister in Labour cabinets, and had atoned by writing some of the most readable sporting journalism of his day. But he never forgot the day he trod the Lord's turf. The experience does tend to change a man, to tempt him at last to divorce the ground from the purpose it serves, and to pay homage to it simply as an arrangement of bricks, mortar and grass. One of the stock characters in cricket reminiscences of a bygone time was the country parson come up to see his old University or school play at Lord's. He would be a quaint buffer who remembered the names of 1890 but was lost a generation later without his match-card. Most of the cricket feature writers resorted to his hypothetical presence from time to time, perhaps to make a little joke more credible, or to bring a humanising touch to columns of statistics. In fact, this imaginary rustic divine existed in his hundreds and often took to print in an attempt to convey the texture of his ecstasy. In the following extract, the writer waxes so lyrical as to commit an opening phrase which comes dangerously close to blank verse:

In bleak December, when the ground is swathed in yellow fog – when it lies buried deep in snow – or is under water, with sea-gulls standing out white like fieldsmen round the wicket – that smooth space never fails to give a thrill. Even the dull, grey wall at the Nursery end, as viewed from a bus, stirs me. For there, within those walls, memories linger – all the countless contests of a hundred years – all the shades of those who have played the great game since Thomas Lord moved his ground from South Bank, where the Regent's Canal now runs, to St John's Wood Road. History haunts Lord's. The past gives it a special atmosphere. It is the home of cricket – the place which has seen the growth and development of England's national game. No other ground can claim that heritage.

A COUNTRY VICAR, *Cricket Memories*, 1930

BUT in 1930, the sentimental Country Vicar, and tens of thousands of others, were having to come to terms with a deadly new factor in the international cricket equation. The Australians arrived full of confidence, knowing that in their ranks they had a young man who was the most comprehensive batsman, at any rate on good wickets, which the game had ever seen. Throughout the summer of 1930, Bradman drew crowds wherever he went, slaughtering the bowlers and smashing records all over the place. At the time he made it, Bradman's double century in the Lord's Test seemed a superhuman effort; only three weeks later, at Leeds, he was to surpass it with a staggering treble century. The modern student will smile a wry smile when he notices that in four days over 1,700 runs were scored and over 500 overs bowled.

ENGLAND v. AUSTRALIA.

Second Test, Lord's, June 27, 28, 30, July 1, 1930

Beating England, after a memorable struggle, by seven wickets, Australia took an ample revenge for their overthrow a fortnight previously at Trent Bridge. The batting of the Australians and particularly that of Bradman will assuredly live long in the minds of those who saw it but, while giving the visitors the fullest praise for winning so handsomely after having to face a first innings total of 425, it is only proper to observe that to a large extent England played right into the hands of their opponents. Briefly, the Englishmen lost a match, which, with a little discretion on the last day, they could probably have saved. The result of this encounter had a strong bearing on the rubber for, if England had made a draw and the Leeds and Manchester games ended as they did, the final match at The Oval would have been limited to four days. It can with truth be said, however, that the England bowling in no other game not only looked but actually was so entirely lacking in sting and effect.

Records went by the board. Australia, in putting together a total of 729 before declaring with only six wickets down, broke four—the highest score by Australia in England, 551 at The Oval in 1884; the highest score by England in this country, 576 at The Oval in 1899; the highest score by Australia, 600 at Melbourne in 1924; and the highest score in the whole series of Test Matches, 636 by England at Sydney in December 1928. Bradman himself, with a score of 254, played the second highest individual innings in the whole series of Test matches between England and Australia, while Duleepsinhji, not only made a hundred on the occasion of his first appearance in a Test match against Australia but scored the highest number of runs ever obtained by an England player in these matches at Lord's. There was one other notable point, A. P. F. Chapman, after leading England to victory six times, captaining the losing side. As some set off against that he enjoyed, for the first time in his career, the distinction of making a hundred in a Test match. In addition to Duleepsinhji, J. C. White and G. O. Allen came into the home team, Sutcliffe—owing to injury—Larwood and Richard Tyldesley standing down.

Chapman again won the toss and England, batting for five hours and fifty minutes, scored on the first day 405 runs for nine wickets. This, seeing that with the score only 13 Hobbs was out and that despite some delightful driving by Woolley and Hammond three wickets were down for 105, was a distinctly fine performance. Duleepsinhji and Hendren obtained the first real mastery over the attack, adding 104 runs in ninety minutes. The batting of these two after lunch was delightful, Duleepsinhji driving with fine power and Hendren scoring by cleverly executed strokes to the on. Chapman and Allen failing, the game took a strong turn in favour of Australia and, while the 200 had gone up with only three wickets down, six men were out for 239. Duleepsinhji, however, found a valuable partner in Tate who hit so hard as to make 54 out of 98 in seventy minutes with eight 4s—chiefly drives—as his most important strokes.

Duleepsinhji seemed certain to play out time after he had lost Robins at 363 but at quarter past six, with the score at 387, he was caught at long-off. It seems ungracious to say it, but Duleepsinhji was guilty of a bad error of judgement. He had twice driven Grimmett to the boundary in glorious fashion and in the same over lashed out wildly. Batting for four hours and three-quarters he gave a magnificent display. When the occasion demanded it he exercised restraint and at other times hit beautifully all around the wicket, having twenty-one 4s among his strokes. His innings was not faultless, for at 65 he was missed at short leg by Woodfull from a very simple chance, while at 98 he was let off by Wall at third slip. Had Duleepsinhji been patient and stayed in until the close of play there is no telling what would have been the subsequent course of events.

The next morning another 20 runs were added and then Australia, by skilful and judicious batting, remained in for the rest of the day and scoring 404 for the loss of only two batsmen left off no more than 21 runs behind—a very great performance. Tate bowled with great pluck and determination but, generally, the England attack was indifferent, Allen especially being innocuous and expensive. The Australians batted to a set plan. Woodfull and Ponsford steadily wearing down the bowling for Bradman later on to flog it. Nearly three hours were occupied over the first 162 runs, but in another two hours and three-quarters no fewer than 242 came. While in the end Bradman made most runs very great credit was due to Woodfull and Ponsford who, when England's bowling was fresh, put on 162 for the first wicket. Curiously enough the partnership terminated almost directly after a break in the play while the members of both teams were presented to the King in front of the pavilion, Ponsford, who had batted very soundly, being caught at slip. Woodfull, who was always restrained but who showed rare judgement, stayed in until twenty minutes past six, having withstood the attack for five hours and a half. His defence was remarkable and he scarcely ever lifted the ball but he enjoyed one great stroke of fortune. Just before the King arrived, Woodfull, with his score at 52, playing forward to Robins, dragged his foot over the crease. Duckworth gathered the ball and swept it back to the stumps but omitted to remove the bails. That little error cost England dear. Bradman, who went in when Ponsford was out and the bowling had been mastered, seized his opportunity in rare style and, hitting all round the wicket with power and accuracy, scored in two hours and forty minutes 155 runs and was not out at the close. The Englishmen fielded well and often brilliantly.

On the Monday, Australia kept England in the field for another four hours and a half and added 325 runs for the loss of four more batsmen before declaring their innings closed at the tea interval. The partnership between Bradman and Kippax which did not end until ten minutes to three when Bradman was caught right-hand at extra-mid-off, produced 192 runs in less than three hours. In obtaining his 254, the famous Australian gave nothing approaching a chance. He nearly played on at 111 and, at 191, in trying to turn the ball to leg he edged it deep into the slips but, apart from those trifling errors, no real fault could be found with his display. Like Woodfull, he scarcely ever lifted the ball and, while his defence generally was perfect, he hit very hard in front of the wicket. Altogether he batted five and a half hours, his chief strokes being twenty-five 4s, three 3s, and twenty-six 2s. Kippax, who was in for three hours, left three runs later at 588, but England's troubles were not over, Richardson and McCabe adding 55, and Oldfield and Fairfax 57 in the last forty-five minutes before the closure was put into force. For their huge total Australia batted ten hours and ten minutes.

England thus found themselves requiring 304 runs to escape an innings defeat. At their second attempt they lost Hobbs at 45 and Woolley at 58 but in the last forty minutes Hammond and Duleep-sinhji added 40 runs. The score was up to 129 the next morning before Hammond left but when, shortly before twelve o'clock, the fifth wicket fell at 147 England looked like losing in an innings. Indeed, but for an unaccountable misunderstanding between Richardson and Ponsford, this would probably have happened. Chapman, before he had scored, mishit a ball and the two fieldsmen mentioned stood and watched it fall to the ground between them. Eventually settling down, Chapman hit in rare style, being especially severe on Grimmett. Allen, too, batted with marked skill and aggression and 125 runs were added before he was out. It was about this time that, with a little care and thoughtfulness, England might have saved the game for at the luncheon interval, with five men out, they had cleared off all but 42 of the arrears. So far from devoting their energies to defence they continued hitting away, adding another 113 runs in an hour and a quarter afterwards but losing their last five wickets. Chapman, eighth to leave at 354, obtained his runs in just over two hours and a half. Four 6s and twelve 4s were among his strokes. He drove and pulled with tremendous power in a very wonderful display. A foolish call by Robins cost a valuable wicket when White was run out and the innings closed just before half-past three for 375.

Australia thus had to make only 72 to win but in twenty minutes there was much excitement. Ponsford was bowled at 16, Bradman caught low down at backward point at 17, and Kippax taken at the wicket at 22. Visions of a remarkable collapse arose but Woodfull, exercising sound generalship by taking most of Robins' bowling himself, tided over an anxious period and by five o'clock he and McCabe had obtained the remaining runs.

In the course of the four days, 110,000 people watched the cricket, the takings being roughly £14,500.

England

J. B. Hobbs c. Oldfield b. Fairfax	1	b. Grimmett	19
F. E. Woolley c. Wall b. Fairfax	41	hit wkt b. Grimmett	28
W. R. Hammond b. Grimmett	38	c. Fairfax b. Grimmett	32
K. S. Duleepsinhji c. Bradman b. Grimmett	173	c. Oldfield b. Hornibrook	48
E. Hendren c. McCabe b. Fairfax	48	c. Richardson b. Grimmett	9
Mr A. P. F. Chapman c. Oldfield b. Wall	11	c. Oldfield b. Fairfax	121

Mr G. O. Allen b. Fairfax...	3	lbw b. Grimmett	57
Mr W. Tate c. McCabe b. Wall	54	c. Ponsford b. Grimmett.	10
Mr R. W. V. Robins c. Oldfield b. Hornibrook	5	not out	11
Mr J. C. White not out....	23	run out	10
G. Duckworth c. Oldfield b. Wall	18	lbw b. Fairfax	0
B2, l-b 7, n-b 1	10	B 16, l-b 13, w 1 ..	30
	425		**375**

Australia

W. M. Woodfull st. Duckworth b Robins	155	not out...............	26
W. H. Ponsford c. Hammond b. White	81	b. Robins	14
D. G. Bradman c. Chapman b. White	254	c. Chapman b. Tate	1
A. F. Kippax b. White	83	c. Duckworth b. Robins.	3
S. McCabe c. Woolley b. Hammond	44	not out...............	25
V. Y. Richardson c. Hobbs b. Tate	30		
W. A. Oldfield not out.....	43		
A. Fairfax not out	20		
B 6, l-b 8, w 5.....	19	B 1, l-b 2.......	3
(6 wkts dec.)	729		72

C. V. Grimmett, P. M. Hornibrook and T. W. Wall did not bat.

Australia Bowling

	Overs	Mdns	Runs	Wkts	Overs	Mdns	Runs	Wkts
Wall	29.4	2	118	3	25	2	80	–
Fairfax	31	6	101	4	12.4	2	37	2
Grimmett	33	4	105	2	53	13	167	6
Hornibrook	26	6	62	1	22	6	49	1
McCabe	9	1	29	–	3	1	11	–
Bradman					1	–	1	–

England Bowling

	Overs	Mdns	Runs	Wkts	Overs	Mdns	Runs	Wkts
Allen	34	7	115	–				
Tate	64	16	148	1	13	6	21	1
White	51	7	158	3	2	–	8	–
Robins	42	1	172	1	9	1	34	2
Hammond	35	8	82	1	4.2	1	6	–
Woolley	6	–	35	–				

Umpires: F. Chester and T. Oates.

Wisden, 1931

ALMOST the only bowler that summer capable of embarrassing Bradman was the Middlesex spin bowler Ian Peebles, who, for two or three seasons, was one of the finest practitioners of his art in the country. But although he enjoyed an outstanding career which ended with his captaincy of Middlesex, Peebles distinguished himself at least as much when he took up journalism, in which role he never allowed his vast experience to swamp a charming mastery of whimsical humour. Before he died Peebles wrote a prize-winning autobiography, in which compassion and laughter were ever-present. Very often the laughter arose out of the mild-mannered honesty of Peebles's reporting, especially in the matter of the grandees, who, contrary to the impression they sometimes like to give, were not above the occasional loss of dignity. In this summer of 1930, when the England selectors were wriggling desperately on the end of Bradman's hook, passion sometimes got the better of their judgement:

The selectors, considering the weather to be uncertain, had sent for Tom Goddard, the Gloucestershire off-spinner. This meant that, with Walter Robins and myself, there were now three slow bowlers of whom two would play. Walter's selection had been a surprise in the first place, as he had had a sharp altercation with the Chairman of the Selectors, 'Shrimp' Leveson-Gower, during the Lord's match. At a crucial moment in the game, Walter, who was like a greyhound between the wickets, had run out Jack White. Walter was much upset by this and when he got back to the dressing-room he had high words with the Chairman, who had attacked him in somewhat intemperate terms. In the event he was the one to be omitted at Manchester, but whether this was in any way due to the scene at Lord's no one could say.

IAN PEEBLES, *Spinner's Yarn*, 1977

No ONE, that is, except Leveson-Gower, and he was saying nothing. As for Peebles, he was one of those cricketers for whom history and past techniques were as important as his own game. The pages of his autobiography soon reveal that he had one hero above all others, and that he pursued knowledge of this hero like a knight hoping to find the holy grail. The hero in question was Sydney Barnes, arguably the finest bowler of all time, an irascible, forbidding man whose indifference to glory and preoccupation with a decent wage had endowed him with independence of the cricketing Establishment. After the Great War Barnes contented himself with League and Minor County cricket, but retained into old age the ability to run through even the best sides with ease. Barnes (1873–1967), at the age of 48, took 73 wickets for Staffordshire at 7.17 each, and never lost the secrets of control which so fascinated students like Peebles. Whenever he met any contemporary of Barnes, Peebles would cross-examine them, asking about fingers and wrists and shoulders, about changes of pace, disguised spin and swerve, and all the rest of the weapons in Barnes's extraordinary armoury. Peebles finally attained Valhalla during the fifth Test at The Oval, for, during a brief respite from the Australian batsmen, he was taken across to Lord's, where he met his heart's desire.

Next day the rain poured down. By lunchtime there was no prospect of any play and my hostess, Mrs Warner, started to look up the cinemas. Suddenly she had a much better idea. 'Sydney Barnes is playing at Lord's,' she said. 'I'll take you there and introduce you to him.' Barnes was in fact playing against the MCC for Wales, where he had been living for some years. It was a splendid thought, and we set forth without delay. We found the great man sitting by himself, puffing his pipe, and possibly conjuring up visions of Victor Trumper and days gone by from the damp Lord's turf. He was delighted to see Mrs Warner, and obviously a Warner introduction was my guarantee. Having made the introduction Mrs Warner packed us off to the Long Bar where I spent one of the great hours of my life. Barnes was most expansive and, given a cricket ball, demonstrated the whole technique which was his own invention, and which has never been wholly imitated. I was much elated and, having said my thanks, parted on warm terms to return to The Oval.

There was a most unfortunate sequel. Early next morning Barnes rang Plum in considerable wrath to draw his attention to an article in the *Daily Mail*. Its headline was to the effect that Barnes told me how he would get Bradman out, and the entire article was imaginary and wholly inaccurate, giving the impression that he had been boasting freely. He was understandably infuriated, and suspected that I had given the story to the Press. Plum assured him that this was not so, and suggested that it had been the fabrication of an enterprising newspaperman on hearing that we had met. This was indeed the true explanation, and because of his faith in Plum, Barnes eventually acknowledged my innocence.

IAN PEEBLES, *Spinner's Yarn*, 1977

IT IS Peebles again to whom we are indebted for a small but fascinating contribution to the body of anecdote confirming the curious link between music and cricket. Musicians of all styles and life-styles have been familiar figures at Lord's, from eminent classical conductors to cricket-playing jazz musicians. Peebles extended this list in his autobiography by describing his attendance at a concert in Glasgow to hear one of his favourite singers, Paul Robeson. The date attaching to Robeson's recollection of Lord's is imprecise, but his mention of Percy Chapman and the fact that the London production of *Show Boat* in which he starred opened at the Drury Lane Theatre on 3 May, 1928, and ran for nearly a year would seem to place the reminiscence in the 1928 season. Chapman played in two matches on the ground that summer. In June he scored 50 against West Indies in the first Test, and at the end of August, when Kent scored 539 for nine, he was top scorer with 91. Either of these performances might easily have been regarded by Robeson as a 'flaying' exercise,

Robeson was the most charming of men, with a magnificent and gracious presence. Hearing us talk of cricket he told me that he used to sit at Lord's, but usually reading a book, until one day he saw Percy Chapman flaying the bowlers and, thereafter, took a lively interest in the game. Being somewhat of a baseball player – as well as an all-American footballer – he was induced to turn out for the Thespids, the actors' side, and was said to be a first-class cover-point.

IAN PEEBLES, *Spinner's Yarn*, 1977

IN 1930 *Wisden* published a longish, droning and quietly smug account of how the MCC administered the world of cricket. It was composed by Sir Francis Eden Lacey (1859–1946), who succeeded Henry Perkins as Secretary of the club in 1898 and who remained in strict control for the next 28 years. His prose style betrays the legal profession, to which he belonged, and so did his secretarial methods, which were efficient, impersonal and at times draconian. In his youth Lacey had been a famous batsman for Hampshire; his 323 not out against Norfolk in 1887 remained for some time the highest score in a county game. Lacey on his retirement from the secretaryship was knighted for services to cricket. Glimpses of the man behind the portfolio may be caught in E. W. Swanton's 'The Mecca' (see p. 434). Lacey's magisterial review of the game in 1930 evokes thoughts of some land-owning earl describing his estates. All is calm. No faint wrinkle of dissent ruffles the surface of English playing fields. This Panglossian portrait was soon to have risible overtones, in the uproar brought about by English tactics in the 1932–33 series against Australia. For the moment, though, to Sir Francis, looking down on cricket from the benign paternalism of honourable retirement, everything in the garden was lovely.

LORD'S AND THE MCC [1930]

THIRTY YEARS OF HISTORY

By Sir Francis Lacey

Changes are frequent in these days but it is doubtful if any place has changed more completely than Lord's cricket ground in the last thirty years or any institution grown more in administration than the MCC which owns it. Taking the physical condition first, the only part remaining of the earliest history of Lord's is the match ground. Its turf was brought from Dorset Square and North Bank over a hundred years ago and, except for a complete system of drainage supplied about twenty years ago, the usual operations of upkeep, the addition of two tanks for conserving rain water and the work of earthworms, it is the same. The tanks were made on the north and south sides to catch the rain water falling on the large stands. The value of these additions was soon shown. They provide suitable water for preparing wickets and an opportunity of reducing water rates. It is almost imperative, especially in a large town, to have an independent water supply in case of drought.

All else has undergone improvements and additions to meet the requirements of the public and the members. Outwardly the hotel (in early days 'The Tavern'), the members' luncheon room and the pavilion appear to be unchanged. Internally these buildings have been brought up to date. The hotel is the centre of the refreshment department and from it are dispensed refreshments to different parts of the ground. Its excavations extend from the hotel proper to the members' entrance. When the refreshment business was taken over in 1898, the hotel and its accommodation were found to be unsuitable and inadequate for the business it was required to carry on and bakeries, cold storage and other facilities were provided and now, although it is impossible to serve every individual in a large crowd at the same time, the conduct of the business compares favourably with any ground that has the same problem to solve. The shop adjoining the hotel was built some years later for the purpose of finding employment for some of the staff in the 'off season' and in order to reduce the loss which, owing to overhead charges, has to be faced during that period. The addition to the pavilion, on the north side, was made so as to give the Press the best position from which to watch the game in progress and in order to improve and extend the professionals' quarters below.

ADDITIONS AND FINANCES

All the present stands and seating accommodation were built within the time under review. The large mound stand followed a decision of the Committee in 1898 to give more spectators an opportunity of seeing Test matches. This involved removing the tennis and racket courts to a site behind the pavilion. Many mourned the loss of the ivy-mantled wall of this old building and the large clock it held, which offered an invitation to ambitious batsmen to reach its face with a square-leg hit. Owing to the growing popularity of Test matches these familiar and attractive features were sacrificed out of consideration for the public. The stand has answered its purpose. It is only when it is unoccupied that it offends the artistic eye. As the popularity of the big matches grew an increased demand for accommodation for entertaining arose. This was, to a great extent, satisfied by building luncheon arbours on the north, south and east sides of the practice ground. The erection of the members' extension and its south-west tower followed and all the covered seating on the ground floor was replaced subsequently by buildings of a more permanent and less dusty character. The new grandstand (replacing the one built in the middle of the last century) and the cantilever stands on the east side of the match ground, recently erected, were constructed from the plans of Sir Herbert Baker and have made a substantial addition to the seating capacity of the ground.

On the death of Dr W. G. Grace, the champion cricketer, in 1915, the Committee decided to erect a memorial in his honour. This took the form of memorial gates at the members' entrance on the south-west side of the ground.

Finance is not usually regarded as a matter of general interest; but those who are under the impression that the MCC has always been a rich club will be surprised to learn that in 1898 there was an overdraft at one bank, a loan from another bank and the balance of the purchase money of the freehold of the match ground, bought in the middle of the last century, still owing. The purchase money had been advanced by Mr W. Nicholson, a member of the Committee and in his day a famous wicket-keeper. These liabilities had to be faced in spite of the fact that £40,000 had been raised by the election of 200 life members to meet, in part, the erection of the large Mound stand and the removal and building of the tennis and racket courts. In the year above-mentioned the property of the club consisted, besides the match and practice ground, of two leasehold houses in Grove End Road, two freeholds and one leasehold in Elm Tree Road and a leasehold in Cavendish Road West. Now the MCC owns as freeholds all the houses abutting on the ground from St John's Wood Road to 22, Elm Tree Road, the Secretary's official residence. Flats for housing several of the club staff, whose services may be required at short notice, have recently been built on the north side of the practice ground.

The improvement in the financial position has enabled the club to set aside a sum of money for financing, or helping to finance, tours in different parts of the Empire, thereby enlarging its responsibilities towards Empire cricket and increasing its opportunities of strengthening family ties. Cricket finance, however, has always its problems and difficulties owing to increasing expenses and rates and taxes. Although stronger financially than it has ever been, MCC, after a few bad seasons or a decrease in the popularity of the game, might easily find, unless a large reserve is provided, that its work in promoting cricket in this country and elsewhere in the Empire would have to be curtailed. Exchanges of visits have done much to give birth to an Empire sense and it is to be hoped that a sufficiently large reserve may be secured to enable MCC's work to be continued and even increased.

THE PROFESSIONAL STAFF

MCC professionals, years ago, were recruited from the county cricket clubs which then needed help. These clubs often sent up promising but inexperienced youths. If these youngsters turned out well they were claimed for county matches, except when representative MCC matches such as those against Australia or South Africa, were played. If they did not come up to expectations they were left under the parental influence of MCC. When the counties played only eight home and away matches, this arrangement could be tolerated. As the counties increased their matches, however, MCC found itself left with elderly or second-rate players only. In these circumstances it was found necessary to train young players at Lord's conditionally on MCC having first claim on their services. The members of the professional staff used to be given a 'benefit' match in rotation, subject to an agreement to retire on receipt and to the approval of the MCC Committee with regard to the investment of the proceeds of the match. The fixture allotted was the Whitsuntide match at Lord's and the money taken fluctuated with the weather, the game more than once producing nothing. It was accordingly decided to give on retirement £500 in lieu of a match and this is always granted now on the old conditions, even when the professional has given all, or nearly all, his services to his county.

Most of the professional staff are taught the principles of coaching so that they may be available for the Easter classes. These Easter classes are held during three weeks of the Easter holidays when the MCC gives instruction in every department of the game to the sons of members and to boys introduced by them. The classes were first held 25 years ago for about ten sons of members. They are now attended by nearly two hundred boys a day and Lord's, for this purpose, cannot take more.

The Middlesex CCC has for many years used Lord's for its home matches. As, however, other county clubs thought that Middlesex was unduly favoured, a carefully considered agreement was drawn up dealing with the equities of the case and creating a situation to the mutual advantage of the MCC and the Middlesex CCC. Under this agreement Middlesex pays a fair rent and its proportion of expenses and its members are granted facilities in Middlesex and other matches.

A COURT OF APPEAL

Membership of the MCC, limited to 6,000, has naturally increased by slow degrees. It is now, roughly speaking, about 1,000 more than it was 30 years ago and, owing to wastage, it may be many years before the limit will be reached. The increased membership and the fact that the MCC is regarded as the Court of Appeal throughout the cricket world, entail a very large and wide range of correspondence. Enquiries and requests for decisions in disputes and difficulties, often couched in quaint language, are received even from remote parts of the Empire. These show a loyalty to the club such as cannot be enjoyed by many institutions. Correspondence connected with the laws of cricket and interpretations thereon became so voluminous that a pamphlet giving decisions and interpretations on all the laws and rules in cricket and its conduct, about which there can be reasonable doubt, was published by the MCC. This has a large circulation.

When the war came in 1914 the committee felt that any tendency towards scare or morbidity should be resisted and an outward show of 'carrying on' was allowed. But the ground and its buildings were, at once, placed at the disposal of the War Office and, the offer having been accepted, were used until the end of the war as accommodation and a training ground for the military. The policy of the committee was directed towards providing games for soldiers and sailors in training and on leave and for boys too young to serve. Contrary to the usual custom of changing the president each year, Lord Hawke remained President until after the war, and he and the treasurer (Lord Harris), although doing everything possible to serve their country in other ways, helped and directed in the administration of the changed conditions of the club.

TOURS AND THEIR CONTROL

While the physical outlook at Lord's was altering a less conspicuous though more valuable and potent growth was taking place in the influence and responsibility of the MCC. Tours abroad became frequent and on them, especially on those to Australia, public interest was focused. It was generally felt that tours of such importance should be controlled and conducted by some responsible body. Under pressure, the MCC, somewhat reluctantly, accepted responsibility. These tours involved money liability as well as administrative responsibility and for these reasons there was no competition for the honour. Of recent years tours to Australia have given a satisfactory return and the county clubs have shared in the profits. For some time previously MCC was out of pocket; but the deficit was honourably made good by the Australian Board of Control. There can be no doubt that Australian cricket has benefited considerably by visits from home.

Other Empire tours, financed, or partly financed, by MCC, have visited India, Egypt, Canada, the West Indies, New Zealand, Ceylon and South Africa. The South African Cricket Association has been particularly helpful as it has generally guaranteed all, or nearly all, the expenses of a tour to that country. Only those in close touch with the network of interest created by these visits can fully appreciate their value in making friendly relations and understanding.

In proportion as interest in Imperial cricket increased responsibility in selecting sides and organising Test matches, in England, also increased. In order to secure the best advice and the willing co-operation of the County Clubs, the MCC convened a meeting composed of representatives of these clubs and the constitution of a Board of Control of Test matches at home was established. This was in 1898. Besides passing rules as to the conduct of Test matches and selecting grounds on which they should be played, it was agreed that there should be an apportionment of profits, if any. One of the leading counties moved that MCC, owing to its position and the work it did for cricket, should not contribute to the pool from profits from a match at Lord's. This proposal would have been passed had not the Rt. Hon. Alfred Lyttelton MP (then President of MCC) intervened and stated that MCC wished to share equally with the county clubs. The equality arrangement was passed and has held good ever since.

Cricket legislation and control had been in the hands of the MCC for over one hundred years. The idea of a more democratic form of government had already taken root in the minds of the MCC Committee and another meeting of the county clubs was called and an Advisory County Cricket Committee brought into being. This Committee, on which all the first-class counties are represented, with three nominees appointed by the Minor Counties' Cricket Association, is consulted in cricket matters of importance and meetings can be called by the counties themselves.

Arrangements, so far, enlarged the duties and advantages of clubs at home only. The MCC owing to its close connection with clubs and cricketers throughout the Empire, realised the importance of bringing these forces within the network of cricket organisation and invited the largest clubs outside England to form governing bodies and to send delegates to an Imperial Cricket Conference. At least one meeting of this conference is held yearly. The above-mentioned consultative bodies, with the MCC, now control and manage home and Empire cricket and the organisation thus created has proved its value in many ways. The MCC still remains the parliament of cricket, holding its position by general consent, and the county clubs in framing their rules have invited it to accept the responsibility of a Court of Appeal. The MCC, apparently, assumed the position of head of cricket at the end of the eighteenth century and it is significant that through such a long time of change and criticism it has been free from any serious attack. This is, no doubt, due to the constitution of the MCC committee on which can be found famous cricketers and men of the highest repute in business and in other activities. The committee has been trusted and has never failed to aim at securing the best interests of the game as a whole and to preserve the spirit in which it should be played.

Wisden, 1931

Bᴜᴛ what exactly was the spirit in which it should be played? Not very long after Sir Francis's bromide appeared in print, Lord's was under fire from outraged colonial cricketers who were firmly convinced that the MCC was condoning, and was perhaps even implicated in, unfair and dangerous tactics. The policies of the England captain Douglas Jardine, the threat to life and limb represented by the bowling of the England fast bowlers and Harold Larwood in particular, the belated entry into the arena of politicians believed at that time to be statesmen, the abrupt ending of the international careers of Jardine and Larwood, all these sensational developments have been told and told again. But in retrospect, nothing is more astonishing about this episode than the success with which Pelham Warner, the Younger Statesman of Lord's, contrived at once to be manager of Jardine's side and yet to detach himself from any breath of guilt or complicity. In the fullness of time Warner was knighted for services to cricket, but the evidence seems to suggest that not all of those services were disclosed. Today, more than fifty years after the Bodyline controversy, questions remain unanswered, questions whose answers ought once to have been provided by Lord's.

One of the few things quite clear about Pelham Warner is that he came to detest Douglas Jardine as a result of his experiences alongside him in Australia. In his book, *A Sort of a Cricket Person*, E. W. Swanton reproduced a letter which Warner wrote in January 1934 to Sir Alexander Hore-Ruthven, subsequently the Lord Gowrie who became President of MCC in 1948. At the time he was Governor of South Australia, and as such during the Bodyline crisis he had made representations to the British Secretary of State for the Dominions, J. H. Thomas, in an effort to damp down the inflamed feelings between the two countries. When Warner wrote, the future of Jardine's leadership was in the balance. Was he to be reappointed captain for the 1934 domestic season, when the Australians would be visiting again, or not? 'At present,' wrote Warner, 'I say "No" unless he makes a most generous public gesture of friendliness, and then I am not sure I would trust him. He is a queer fellow. When he sees a cricket ground with an Australian on it he goes mad! He rose to his present position on my shoulders, and of his attitude to me I do not care to speak.'

All else about Pelham Warner's role in the Bodyline tour can be no more than inference, with many towering question marks. How, for example, does one square Billy Findlay's observation to Sir Francis Lacey that Warner had apparently not offered his views on Bodyline to Jardine, with Gubby Allen's assertion (in *The Cricketer*, May 1981) that 'Plum made numerous efforts to get Douglas Jardine to change his tactics, or at least to modify Bodyline'? How did the lachrymose Manager and Chairman of Selectors absolve himself from any of the stigmas which were attached to English cricket at this time, and especially to all who toured Australia in the winter of 1932–33? We do not know. For one of the most arresting features of the whole episode is the dearth of relevant material. As Manager of that tour, Pelham Warner submitted to the MCC Committee a report on all that had happened from the moment the party left home until the day it returned. That document, quite simply, has vanished from the archives at Lord's. So has every letter he wrote from Australia to Findlay or anyone else in the hierarchy of MCC. The protective coating, it seems, has insulated him rather well from historical research.

GEOFFREY MOORHOUSE, Lord's, 1983

BUT not all that well. Not even Warner could worm out of the contradiction between management of the tourists and his denial of any complicity in the guilt of those tourists. Moorhouse is being excessively charitable to Warner when he implies that the disappearance of the documentary evidence remains a mystery. Only Warner stood to gain from their disappearance. Harold Larwood certainly never stole them. The entire episode of Bodyline remains rather more than ancient history today because it is a model exposition of how, for all Lacey's fine words, the grandees closed ranks at the first sign of danger. The MCC was caught in a trap from which perhaps no escape existed. Having claimed to be a private club which nevertheless constituted 'the parliament of cricket', it was suddenly roused from its Victorian dream in 1933 by events which showed to what extent this honourable game, administered by civilised men of means, had outgrown the old concepts to become an international issue, a vast business enterprise, a public spectacle in which moral concepts were to be pressured from now on by financial expedience and political interests. When Warner set sail for Australia at the end of 1932 he was occupying a pleasant role which carried more prestige and diplomatic responsibility than any real duties. By the time he came back in the spring of 1933 that role had changed forever, to become a hotseat whose temperature was to increase relentlessly over the years. The spectacle of Warner suddenly realising that that seat was getting too warm, and his undignified retreat, in which he abrogated all responsibility for what had happened, may be unedifying, but it is also quite funny. Warner and Jardine may both have been Gentlemen, but they were certainly not gentlemen.

As I have said, the question was not understood in this country.

SIR PELHAM WARNER, Lord's, 1946

I do not propose to discuss it here. It would serve no good purpose.

SIR PELHAM WARNER, Long Innings, 1951

... Warner, whose behaviour at the time of the 1932–33 tour in Australia had been equivocal to put it mildly.

ROWLAND BOWEN, Cricket, 1970

The play's the thing.

DOUGLAS JARDINE, Cricket, 1936

THE claim that Lord's is the home of cricket has sometimes incensed those who, by social, geographical or colonial accident, dwell elsewhere, but there remains a substantial element of truth in the idea. Everything about Lord's, from the Edwardian serenity of the Long Room to the capaciousness of its library, from the range of its paintings to the items in the museum, from its generous nooks and crannies and arbours and backwaters to the virid glow flung off by its turf on a bright morning, all these things speak of the vast stretches of time, comparatively speaking, which are required for such effects to blend into the landscape. Everyone from idolators to lampooners, and especially lampooners, acknowledge this to be so, the idolaters because they have somehow to sustain their religious beliefs, the lampooners because the authority of Lord's provides their squibs with a focus. In 1933, in the wake of the extraordinary crises engendered by the 1932–33 Bodyline tour of Australia, a passage in the game's history which caused some to wonder if the game, by succumbing to the sins of self-importance, was not losing its head, the nation's greatest literary slapstick comedian let fly, having taken due note of the bizarre developments which caused a technical difference of opinion between the English and Australian camps to arrive at last before the walls of Westminster.

They say – ugh! those clicking tongues! – they say that disease among willow trees is already making cricketers fear a shortage of cricket bats. We must get up a campaign to make everybody save their willows, and if necessary the MCC should be empowered by a special act of Parliament to commandeer all privately owned willow trees. After all, the country's good comes first, and fine fools we should look if we had to put off a Test match for lack of bats. What would the Australians say? Perhaps they would lend us theirs – but oh, the humiliation, as the bishop said when the actress chalked a saucy limerick on his gaiter. I was talking only yesterday to a Russian cricketer –

PRODNOSE: A palpable lie!
MYSELF: Why?
PRODNOSE: They don't play cricket in Russia.
MYSELF: I know, but this man learnt it over here.
PRODNOSE: What on earth for?
MYSELF: He thinks it might be introduced into Russia, to take the place of religion, as it does here.

BEACHCOMBER, *Morton's Folly*, 1933

IN fact the English domestic campaign of 1933 was fraught with ironies, some of them painful to the rumps of English batsmen. The MCC having insisted that Bodyline bowling was a legitimate tactic to use against Australian sides, could not now complain that it was an unlawful one to unleash against English sides. The West Indian tourists, savouring the pricelessness of the situation, let fly at several grounds, including Lord's, where, however, the hostility of Martindale's bowling was eclipsed by the even more violent hostility of Constantine's batting. Those regulars at Lord's who remembered the fireworks of 1928 must have come along hoping against hope that lightning would strike twice. And that is exactly what the astonishing Constantine contrived.

Five years later – in 1933 – against the MCC Constantine played an innings of 51 out of 66 in only twenty-seven minutes. He came in late in the day and received only 22 balls from an attack which consisted of J.C. White, M.J.C. Allom, F.R. Brown and W.E. Bowes. The 22 balls were dealt with by him thus: 0 0 1 4 4 6 0 2 2 4 0 4 3 4 4 0 0 4 0 1 4 4. Every ball was hit right off the middle, and there was not a single lucky stroke. Opinion in the pavilion regarded it as the best piece of hitting seen since the 1914 war. One of his strokes off the fast bowling of M.J.C. Allom is well remembered. Let me quote Allom himself on the stroke, which he said was the most remarkable he ever saw in first-class cricket. 'I was the unfortunate bowler, and after Constantine had made a series of strokes, more impudent and fantastic than any I remember, I bowled him a "head" ball in the hope that he might mis-hit it. Instead he went through some extraordinary gyration, and struck the ball over the wicket-keeper's head; it cleared the Press box, and, in fact, was never recovered. This story I have been able to corroborate with my brother, who was watching the game at the time. I may say that many times since this incident have people come up to me, and said: "Were you at Lord's that day that Constantine, etc., etc.".'

Oddly enough for such an astonishing stroke, there has been some difficulty in reconstructing what happened, partly because it came very late in the day's play and was not fully reported. Indeed, the *Times* report refers very briefly to the innings, and mentions, rather oddly, 'a grand hit to the on for six'. Another puzzle is that Bill Bowes, both in his own *Express Deliveries* and in personal correspondence, claims that he was the bowler whom Constantine hit into the car park to fine leg. Sir Pelham Warner also refers to an amazing six made to fine leg off Bowes, but I feel that there is some misrecollection here, and that the shot in question which went over the Press box near the flagstaff was in fact off M.J.C. Allom, as that bowler and the score-book both confirm. I tell this to show how difficult it is to trace accurate evidence even of an obviously remarkable stroke that happened not so long ago at a place like Lord's, where ample evidence should be forthcoming. Whatever the exact truth of where the ball landed, the stroke was a great one, and possible only to one of amazing eye and steel wrists – in fact, a Jessop.

GERALD BRODRIBB, *Hit for Six*, 1960

When the West Indian Martindale was hurling down bumpers in 1933, Patsy Hendren persuaded his wife to fit protective side-pieces to his cap, the outcome being Sherlock Holmes looking in three directions.

KENNETH GREGORY (ed), *In Celebration of Cricket*, 1978

IN THE aftermath of the Bodyline uproar, international cricket proceeded gingerly, especially so in view of the fact that the 1933 visitors, the West Indies, possessed one or two bowlers capable of giving the opposing batsmen an uncomfortable half an hour. The whole country wanted to know more of the crisis which had suddenly flared up on the other side of the world, and of whose details they knew nothing apart from what the newspapers and a few blurred newsreels told them. The following recollection by the only England fast bowler on that ill-fated tour not to compromise himself is revealing for the shrewdness with which George V appears to have taken Jardine's measure. The background to the incident concerns Allen's recruitment as a City gent in May 1933, which curtailed his cricket so drastically that he feared he was not match-fit for the Test at Lord's. In the event he took three wickets for 46 and made 16 run out:

Gubby remembers that Test for a special reason. On the first morning the King came, and since it was raining the teams were presented to him in the pavilion. Douglas Jardine was first received for a private talk, after which the King asked to speak to Mr Allen and began questioning him about the happenings in Australia. He wasn't quite sure that the captain had told him everything. The picture remains of George V sitting in the Committee Room wearing brown leather back-ribbed gloves and smoking from a long holder. In the course of quite a lengthy talk wherein the King showed a knowledge of bowling tactics that astonished him, Gubby said, 'I didn't know you took an interest in cricket, sir'; to which came the reply in that slightly gutteral voice, 'I take great interest in my subjects.' Then he added, 'My secretaries mark items in the papers for my attention – sometimes I also look elsewhere.'

E. W. SWANTON, *Gubby Allen: Man of Cricket*, 1985

OF THE many fabulous specimens of humanity to become a familiar sight at Lord's, none was more spectacular than Charles Burgess Fry, athlete, scholar, sailor, writer, parliamentary candidate, world Long Jump champion, the only cricketer ever to be offered a European throne, a man so brilliantly many-sided that there were moments when he seemed doomed to meet himself coming the other way. In 1902 he appeared for Southampton in the FA Cup Final on the Saturday, and scored 78 for W. G. Grace's London County side against Surrey on the Monday. Part of Fry's legendary status is due to the worship he received from other writers, especially Neville Cardus and Denzil Batchelor, both of whom took care to immortalise him in print. While Cardus revelled in the Socratic side of Fry, whose disquisitions appear to have been as interminable as they were entertaining, Batchelor presented the rounded man of the world, the sort of oldtime Kiplingesque grandee for whom a woman was only a woman but a cigar was a good smoke, a conductor's baton, a knight's sword and even, in moments of demonstrative recapitulation of a dazzling cricketing career, a bat. In a famous description of Fry setting out for Lord's on Test match day, Batchelor described the Bentley, its chauffeur, the binoculars and travelling rugs, the copy of Herodotus and the box of Henry Clay cigars without which the Commander was a lost soul, the cocktails and the Traminer '26, the lobster, the strawberries, the line of celebrities, ranging from renowned composers to celebrated actresses, waiting to be invited into his box. Fry was a law unto himself, and if today that law smells of musk and mothballs, the aroma is by no means displeasing.

One May morning of 1934, at Lord's, there stood on the steps outside the pavilion a man with a monocle, writing; gaily and fluently writing. He appeared to be something between a retired admiral and an unusually athletic Oxford don. He wore marine gaiters and one of those waistcoats that are born to put the whole race of pullovers to shame. No cricket had started; so I presumed to ask him whence came the facile stream. C. B. Fry said, 'My dear fellow, I am describing my idea of how the game should go, if it were going.' The *Evening Standard* was at work. He had been given an assistant to handle his copy; and this worthy technician, meaning so very well, said to the master, 'Why, Commander, you might be a journalist yourself, instead of just an amateur.' And C. B. Fry said . . .

DENZIL BATCHELOR, *C. B. Fry*, 1943

ANOTHER visitor to the ground, just as celebrated as Fry in his own way, was Hugh de Selincourt, author of the one outstanding cricket novel, *The Cricket Match* (1924). De Selincourt was one of that group of creative artists, which included the Baxes, Edmund Blunden and Siegfried Sassoon, who found fulfilment in village cricket. But evidently when de Selincourt took the trouble to make the journey up to St John's Wood from his home in the Sussex village of Storrington, he required much sterner stuff. Noting the tendency of those who attended the Eton–Harrow match to make themselves, rather than the cricket, the main attraction, de Selincourt took exception to the stifling effect of high fashion, and actually yearned for a little more vulgarity, or, as he may well have been inclined to put it, vulgarity of an earthier kind.

Society has taken up Eton and Harrow and the Varsity match at Lord's, and the cricket is almost swamped by its attentions. Nothing fashionable can be whole-hearted. After spending an hour or two at Lord's under these conditions I have found myself thinking almost wistfully of a rude Australian crowd. I have never sat in such a crowd: I should certainly be enraged by it: but the choking respectable languor at Lord's on a fashion-day seems to affect the whole game and most of the players and spectators, myself included. Any excitement seems almost out of place.

HUGH DE SELINCOURT, *Moreover*, 1934

BUT just as, in 1930, English cricket had had other things to occupy its mind than the sentimental rhapsodising about fog and flood from country vicars, so four years later did it have its troubles excluding those of the Eton–Harrow match. The Australians, with Bradman rampant, were once again pillaging the English bowlers. The Ashes proved to be elusive once again, but an exception was the Lord's Test, where the English climate created a perfect setting for the home team to turn the tables in a most astonishing way. Once again the game was rendered legendary by a staggering feat of individual brilliance, except that this time it was not Australia that triumphed but England, and not by brilliant batting but by inspired bowling. Bradman, never a genius on a turning wicket, was for once rendered impotent.

ENGLAND v AUSTRALIA
Second Test Match
Played at Lord's, June 22, 23, 25, 1934

For their defeat at Trent Bridge, England took an ample revenge at Lord's, winning the match in three days in an innings with 38 runs to spare. This was England's first success in a Test match against Australia at Lord's since 1896 when Lohmann and Tom Richardson in a memorable struggle swept the Australians off their feet. While everyone in England naturally was jubilant over the triumph of the Englishmen it could not be denied that they were helped in a pronounced degree by the weather.

Winning the toss England stayed in until nearly three o'clock on the Saturday and put together a total of 440, but before the end of the day Australia had 192 runs on the board with only two men out. In view of this splendid start by the visitors there existed no sound reason why they should not have closely approached if not even passed the England total, but they suffered the cruellest luck, rain falling during the week-end and rendering their chances almost hopeless. Fortunately England had in the team a bowler capable of taking full advantage of the conditions that prevailed, and Verity, obtaining seven wickets in the first innings for 61 runs, followed this up with eight in the second for 43, to be the chief factor in giving England such a pronounced success. With his full record for the match, fifteen wickets for 104 runs, he excelled Rhodes's performance at Melbourne in 1904 when that even more famous left-hander took fifteen wickets for 124 runs. By a singular coincidence Rhodes was present at Lord's to see his brother Yorkshireman accomplish his wonderful performance. Verity had taken one of the Australian wickets which fell on Saturday, and on the Monday he dismissed fourteen men for 80 runs, six of them after tea at a cost of 15. This amazing achievement would probably have been only possible to a man possessed of such length and finger-spin as Verity, because although the wicket certainly helped him considerably it could scarcely be described as genuinely 'sticky' except for one period after lunch. Verity's length was impeccable and he made the ball come back and lift so abruptly that most of the Australians were helpless. The majority of them had had no experience in England of such a pitch, and they showed no ability or skill in dealing with bowling like that of Verity under these conditions. Those who tried to play forward did not get far enough, and their efforts at playing back were, to say the least, immature.

Dealing with the earlier part of the match, Walters and Sutcliffe made 70 together for the opening England wicket in just under an hour and three-quarters, but then came that series of dreadful failures which at this point of the proceedings characterised England's batting throughout the series. Hammond was out at 78, Hendren at 99, and Walters, after playing admirably for two hours and fifty minutes, at 130. In the course of his display, he showed marked skill in driving both Grimmett and O'Reilly, and altogether batted extremely well. When Walters left, Leyland went in and began what was to be a very fine exhibition. He and Wyatt put on 52 to effect a partial recovery which was consolidated by Leyland and Ames. By the time stumps were drawn these two had raised the score to 293, and next morning they carried it to 311, their partnership realising 129 runs in two and a half hours. Leyland, who batted three hours and a half, drove superbly in his great innings of 109, hitting a six and fourteen 4s. In the end he was bowled by what is known in Yorkshire as a 'long half-volley', hitting a little too late and over the ball. Ames and Geary next added 48, Ames, missed by Oldfield standing back at 96, being eighth out at 409. He hit fourteen 4s during his stay of four hours and twenty minutes, powerful driving being the outstanding feature of an inspiring display. Verity helped him to add 50 and the last wicket produced 30 runs. Neither Grimmett nor O'Reilly looked nearly as difficult as they had at Nottingham, but except when Leyland and Ames were in they bowled well.

Woodfull, who took Brown in first with him, scored 22 out of the first 68, and then Bradman, with seven 4s, hit up 36 of the next 73, but actually he never looked like staying very long, making many of his strokes without restraint. The England bowlers met with no further success that day, Brown and McCabe adding 51 and carrying the score to 192. McCabe brought off some wonderful hooks, while Brown with admirable drives and cuts completed 100 out of 184 in two hours and three-quarters. On the Monday, the light was very bad, an appeal being made against it directly the batsmen reached the wickets, but soon after the game had been resumed Brown was out at 203. He and McCabe added 62 in about an hour. Brown batted in first-rate style for three hours and twenty minutes and in his century on the occasion of his first appearance in a Test match at Lord's he hit fourteen 4s. He drove beautifully and placed the ball cleverly on the on side. His dismissal was the beginning of the end. Darling left at 204, McCabe one hour later, and Bromley at 218. Then soon afterwards came a short break while the players on both sides were presented to His Majesty the King. Chipperfield and Oldfield put on 40, but by half-past two Australia were all out for 284, the last eight wickets having gone down in two hours and twenty minutes for 92 runs. Verity took six of them for 37.

The follow-on not having been saved—Australia finishing 156 behind—the visitors had to go in again, and with only 10 on the board Brown was out to a fine catch at long leg, the ball travelling down wind at terrific speed. Verity, coming on at 17, quickly got to work again, dismissing McCabe and Bradman at 43 and 57, while after tea Woodfull, who had defended stubbornly for two hours, was fourth to leave at 94. The rest of the innings was a mere procession, for by this time the wicket had become even more difficult. There seemed a chance of Verity doing the hat-trick when he dismissed Oldfield and Grimmett with consecutive balls but he was denied this distinction. Still he took the last six wickets, and at ten minutes to six the match was all over, seven men having left in an hour for 44 runs. He was supported by brilliant fielding close to the wicket.

Ponsford being ill, Bromley came into the Australian team in his place, while England had Wyatt and Bowes for Pataudi and Mitchell. Farnes, however, was nothing like the success he had been at Nottingham, an injury to his heel preventing him from bowling in anything like his usual form. Hammond, too, was not in his best health, his back all through the match being very painful.

England

Mr C. F. Walters, c. Bromley,
    b. O'Reilly 82
H. Sutcliffe, lbw b.
    Chipperfield 20
W. R. Hammond, c. and
    b. Chipperfield 2
E. Hendren, c. McCabe, b.
    Wall 13
Mr R. E. S. Wyatt, c. Oldfield,
    b. Chipperfield 33
M. Leyland, b. Wall. 109
L. E. G. Ames, c. Oldfield,
    b. McCabe 120
G. Geary, c. Chipperfield,
    b. Wall 9
H. Verity, st Oldfield, b.
    Grimmett 29
Mr K. Farnes, b. Wall 1
W. E. Bowes not out 10
        L-b 12 12
                  440

1/70 2/78 3/99 4/130
5/182 6/311 7/359
8/409 9/410

Australia

W. M. Woodfull, b. Bowes . 22   c. Hammond, b. Verity 43
W. A. Brown, c. Ames, b.
    Bowes 105   c. Walters, b. Bowes 2
D. G. Bradman, c. and b.
    Verity 36   c. Ames, b. Verity 13
S. J. McCabe, c. Hammond,
    b. Verity 34   c. Hendren, b. Verity 19
L. S. Darling, c. Sutcliffe,
    b. Verity 0   b. Hammond 10
A. G. Chipperfield, not out . 37   c. Geary, b. Verity 14
E. H. Bromley, c. Geary,
    b. Verity 4   c. and b. Verity 1
W. A. Oldfield, c. Sutcliffe,
    b. Verity 23   lbw b. Verity 0
C. V. Grimmett, b. Bowes . . 9   c. Hammond b. Verity 0
W. J. O'Reilly, b. Verity 4   not out 8
T. W. Wall, lbw b. Verity . . 0   c. Hendren, b. Verity 1
        B 1, l-b 9 10   B 6, n-b 1 7
                  284   118

1/68 2/141 3/203 4/204   1/10 2/43 3/57 4/94
5/205 6/218 7/258 8/273   5/94 6/95 7/258 8/273
9/284   9/284

Australia Bowling

	Overs	Mdns	Runs	Wkts
Wall	49	7	108	4
McCabe	18	3	38	1
Grimmett	53.3	13	102	1
O'Reilly	38	15	70	1
Chipperfield	34	10	91	3
Darling	6	2	19	—

England Bowling

	Overs	Mdns	Runs	Wkts	Overs	Mdns	Runs	Wkts
Farnes	12	3	43	—	4	2	6	—
Bowes.........	31	5	98	3	14	4	24	1
Geary	22	4	56	—				
Verity	36	15	61	7	22.3	8	43	8
Hammond	4	1	6	—	13	—	38	1
Leyland	4	1	10	—				

Umpires: F. Chester and J. Hardstaff

Wisden, 1935

VERITY's triumph established him beyond question as the greatest left-arm slow bowler of his generation, a true artist who knew exactly how to exploit the favourable conditions he found at Lord's in the 1934 Test. But in the following summer every spin bowler in the country was eager to get to Lord's and topple the opposition. This time the explanation was to be found not in the weather but in a sudden amendment to the flora and fauna attaching to the ground. What happened at Lord's in 1935 reminded a great many club members of schoolday studies of the twelve plagues visited upon the ancient Egyptians:

Lord's and Leather-Jackets

In the second Test match South Africa won the toss and the game. In the University match Cambridge won the toss and the game. The conclusion is too obvious to be disputed. To win the toss at Lord's this summer is to win the game. The reason is not so easy to see as the fact. Creeping, materialistic minds will seek for physical causes; and some will hasten to an explanation which has been a blessed refuge to every side beaten at Lord's this summer. It is all the fault of the leather-jackets. Whereon other minds of the same order will reply that to talk of the larva of the daddy-longlegs or any other sort of long legs is a silly point: and that the dusting of Oxford's jacket had nothing to do with the leather-jackets, which had done the pitch little harm. While both sides are flatly contradicting each other, higher minds will tell them that, like the disputants in the old nursery poem about the chameleon, they both are right and both are wrong. The toss and the leather-jackets won the match for Cambridge; but not by the dull, matter-of-fact method of making the bowling difficult. No! there are such things as *imponderabilia* – causes hidden from the materialist, but perceptible by the psychologist. Oxford men – even Brasenose men and cricketers – are notoriously sensitive, imaginative, psychic. The idea means more to them than the fact, the spirit than the matter. Legions of leather-jackets, a pitch of soft mud irregularly set with pointed flints, could not have put the very feeblest of the Oxford batsmen off his game, but that the dread of something underground puzzled the will. The idea of leather-jackets, the awful spectre of leather-jackets, the mental picture of their foul and hidden orgies, the ineluctable fate of having to bat twice after Cambridge on a wicket beneath which leather-jackets might still be teeming after their creepy-crawly kind – that was the doom that turned the Oxford hearts to ice, the Oxford knees to water, the Oxford bats to walking-sticks for graceful use between pavilion and wicket and back again.

Imagination, it is rumoured, is not hotly cultivated at Cambridge; but there is no knowing what PROFESSOR SIR ARTHUR QUILLER-COUCH may not have been up to, nor what effect the science of SIR JAMES JEANS and of PROFESSOR SIR ARTHUR EDDINGTON may not insidiously have worked upon the strict Cambridge ethos. And, unless the terror that now haunts the wicket at Lord's can be exorcised before next season, the University match may be reduced to the wearing of clean flannels and blues, and tossing up, and luncheon, and nothing more. The fear of the leather-jackets may not be real; but, like the young person of Deal, sensitive players hate the fear that they fancy they feel; and, as the complaint is one of suggestion, so must the remedy be. When leather-jackets, having ruined a lot of golf greens, were under discussion in this journal in 1932, it was recorded that leather-jackets were a favourite food of starlings. Lord's has leather-jackets: Trafalgar Square has starlings. If the leather-jackets will not go to Trafalgar Square (which is unlikely), the starlings must be taken to Lord's. They might be taken by aeroplane, as the winter-bound swallows were once taken south from Austria. Small boys might be forbidden to ask for autographs until they could prove that they had brought one or more starlings to Lord's. Some grandiose political scheme might include the organisation of the unemployed into corps of beaters, to drive starlings up Regent Street and Portland Place (with the BBC making records of the starlings' chatter and of the appropriate speech of a leading politician) into Regent's Park, and so to Lord's; and flocks of starlings, collected overnight in cages, might be released each morning at the beginning of play. The thought of the presence of the avenging hosts would set to rest the imaginative terrors of sensitive cricketers; and the starling might be to Lord's what the goose was to the Capitol.

Leading Article in *The Times*, 11 July 1935

Fʀᴏᴍ time to time the Lord's crowds have taken to their hearts some cricketer who happens to appeal to their sense of what in cricket is right and proper, or, in the case of C. I. J. Smith, what is hopelessly wrong and proper. 'Jim' Smith was as homely an athlete as the name by which he was known. A fast bowler good enough to be selected for England against New Zealand and the West Indies, it was as a tail-end batsman of sensational tendencies that he was adored even by the opposition. A flailing blacksmith of a batsman, Smith had no technique, no footwork and only one stroke, yet it is no exaggeration to say that between 1934, when he joined Middlesex after being successful with his native Wiltshire, and 1939, when the outbreak of war curtailed his career, he was among the most popular batsmen in the country. Every time he came trotting down the steps to take his place at the wicket, a hum of delighted expectancy swept round the ground, and although he usually flattered only to deceive, every now and again he summoned up the whirlwind and sent his acolytes running for cover. Colourful descriptions of him are scattered through the reminiscences of the period. Cardus imagined that when he went out to bat Smith snatched up any blunt instrument which happened to be handy, a chair-leg perhaps, or a fragment of oak-beam. Ian Peebles, who partnered Smith when the big fellow made his only first-class century, called him the Supreme Haymaker and explained that when Smith mishit his only shot, a lofted drive over mid-off, the ball would fly straight back at the bowler, 'flat and low, like a shell, to the great hazard of umpire, bowler and partner'. The fullest account of Smith's exploits was published by Gerald Brodribb, who incorporated into it some of the most eloquent testimonies by other writers.

The Hon. Terence Prittie wrote a full-length study of Jim Smith in his book *Mainly Middlesex*, and here is a description of the 'windmill' in full blast:

'The Smith shot quickly became the most individual sight on the English cricket field. Smith's six feet three inches and sixteen stone give it a terrible force. It is as sudden and as violent as the first crash of the big drum in a Wagner opera, and the actual concussion of bat upon ball can be likened only to the arrival of half a hundredweight of H.E. But apart from its stark power, the stroke has an additional attraction. Even when it results in a clean miss, it causes immense amusement. The village blacksmith does this, too, but then the quality of village bowling is, comparatively speaking, so very much lower that it is, with him, by no means so frequent an occurrence. I once saw Vivian, the New Zealander, bowling his slow left-hand leg-breaks to Smith. For two whole overs the batsman failed to get a touch on the ball. Time after time the ball pitched on the middle and off stumps, to break sharply away from the batsman. Time after time Smith's bat vainly clove the air, effecting clean misses by huge margins and provoking the unrestrained delight of the spectators.'

But as Smith developed the technique of his shot, and learnt to swing his monstrous bat – a sort of Herculean club – he began to make runs; as Longfellow once said:

> You can hear him swing his heavy sledge
> With measured beat and slow.

Here is a further quotation from Terence Prittie:

'As the Smith shot was perfected, sixes became once more a common feature of the cricket at Lord's. Smith hits the ball with the same flat trajectory as the golf drive, rising steadily in its flight, only attaining its maximum some 60 to 80 yards from the wicket, and dying quickly away. The length of the carry is often out of all proportion to the height that the ball reaches – sure evidence of the tremendous power of Smith's forearms. Beside the easy elegance of a Robertson and the commanding mastery of a Compton, this shot is as incongruous as Cab Calloway swinging at an Eisteddfod or Max Miller reclining in an eighteenth-century drawing-room. For its unique qualities no better contrast of background can be imagined than Lord's.

'Against the New Zealanders I saw Smith play an innings which was a typical mixture of stupendous power and pure futility. With the slow bowlers Vivian and Dunning he could do nothing, but he knocked off Cowie, who was bowling fast and well, with a series of cruel blows over the heads of the wicket-keeper and slips. Smith's snicks have the mysterious faculty of travelling twice as fast and twice as high as those of an ordinary batsman; they are a triumph of auto-suggestion.

The prodigious nature of the Smith shot somehow communicates itself even to his mis-hits, which soar to amazing heights and fall in all sorts of unexpected parts of the field. Eventually, on this occasion, he hit Dunning clean out of the ground into St John's Wood Road, and a moment later missed a straight ball by yards. It is related that as he arrived back from this innings, after making 27 runs in ten minutes, a member leaned over from the pavilion and said, "That was a good six of yours, Smith," to which the latter replied, "Ah, but if only I had got hold of him!" This story may, or may not, be true, but the moral remains the same, for Smith did not get hold of this particular shot. He played early at the ball and his bat made the slight hollow sound which indicates that the ball has been hit high up towards the handle. Unlike his best drives, it had been lobbed into the air – although lobbing may sound a poor enough description of a carry of nearly a hundred yards.'

Unlike Trott, who seemed to reserve his best efforts for Lord's spectators, Jim Smith's great innings are spread far and wide round the country. But let us first consider his best performances at Lord's. The first hint of what he might do to county bowlers came in the Middlesex v. Gloucester match of 1934. In the first innings he scored 34 in ten minutes (chiefly by means of 4 sixes), and in the second he scored 29 in seven minutes off 9 balls bowled to him, thus: 0 4 6 6 4 4 2 3 out. This meant 63 in seventeen minutes in the match, and the *Times* correspondent prophetically wrote: 'If he plays many more innings like the two in this match he will be in danger of becoming as much a popular attraction as Bradman himself.' It may have been one of these sixes which Smith landed on the clock tower at mid-on just below the face, a hit once made off Goddard on a day when the wicket was pitched well up towards the grandstand, according to Dudley Carew. Smith's particular stroke made straight hits less likely than those to mid-on. He never hit a ball to the top tier of the pavilion, though he did once plant one in the centre balcony (in his innings of 68 against Sussex in 1938). Another memorable hit towards the pavilion was one which smashed a plate-glass panel in one of the doors. As I have said, mid-on was more his line of country, and in 1936 in scoring 69 in twenty-six minutes v. Somerset he hit 2 sixes. To quote Smith himself: 'One six had a low trajectory over mid-on and took the ridge off the new stand to the left of the pavilion, approximately 60 foot high and more than 100 yards from the wicket. A small fragment with the actual mark of the ball on it was sent to me by a spectator and is now one of my memoirs.' The drive he refers to was made off Hawkins's bowling and hit a drainpipe on the then newly built Block Q, but Smith forgets to mention that the very next ball was despatched by him in the same direction towards the now obsolete lawn tennis courts. In this innings Smith was missed four times, three off vast ballooning hits which hung an unconscionable time in the air and then plummeted down to earth past the outstretched hands of a dizzy fielder.

It was at all times impossible to place a field for him. Ian Peebles in his book *Talking of Cricket* has a glorious description of what could happen when Smith really ballooned one:

'One of the most spectacular misses it has been my lot to see was made by "Hopper" Levett of Kent, who essayed to catch Jim Smith. The stroke was a prodigious one, and so faultlessly vertical that it was really unnecessary for the wicket-keeper to claim it as his as he set about his task. This he did by revolving round and round the wicket in taut circles. With arched back and imploring hands held before his painfully unturned face, it only wanted a Voodoo drum to complete the scene. He had gone round about five times when his cap fell off, and several times more when he suddenly realised that the ball was about to arrive at the opposite side of the circle. Seeking a short cut to this point, he lurched into the castle, and went down with a crash of bails, pads and stumps, closely followed, by way of an emphatic full stop, by the thud of the arriving ball.

'It took some time to restore order. Someone then callously suggested that if "Hopper" hadn't interfered the ball would have descended on top of the middle stump and the batsman would have been out "played on".'

The Tavern was obviously in constant danger when Smith was batting. In 1938 in scoring 25 v. Lancashire he hit a ball into the open luncheon room beside the Tavern; in 1933 in his 20* for MCC v. Surrey he hit a ball from P. G. H. Fender right over into St John's Wood Road, a feat he again performed in 1937 off the bowling of J. A. Dunning, as already described by Terence Prittie. The hit off Fender was reported to have been 'one-handed' and certain of his hits to square-leg gave the impression of being swept away with one hand only. The violence of his stroke caused his right hand to lose grip on the handle of the bat.

Occasionally, by some freak of mechanics, the Smith swing sent the ball high over the boundary towards the off-side. In 1936, in the course of 30 v. Surrey, he hit a ball from E. A. Watts on to the roof of the enclosure where the Warner Stand now is, a remarkable hit; and in 1939 in 37 v. Essex, to quote *The Times*, 'he made one truly preposterous stroke with the left arm alone which propelled the ball over the boundary behind extra cover's head'.

I can recall some hits of his which started out towards mid-wicket and then changed direction towards the off-side, and which, in spite of the considerable 'slice', had enough power to carry the boundary. No wonder it was so difficult to judge his hits when waiting for catches in the deep.

Batting at the pavilion end, Smith on several occasions was able to achieve the rare carry over the Nursery-end boundary fence – a hit of at least 110 yards. In 1938 in his 25 v. Surrey he made a huge six off E. A. Watts which pitched into the terraces to the left of the screen (Blocks G/F), and he hit a ball to the same place during his innings of 69 v. Sussex in 1938. In that innings he came in on the Saturday evening with only eighteen minutes to go, but by the close of play he had scored 68, and 61 of these runs came off 21 consecutive balls bowled to him by Charles Oakes and J. H. Parks. On the Monday morning crowds flocked to Lord's with the hope of seeing Smith reach a record fast century, but he was out after making one more run.

The grandstand suffered many severe blows from Smith's hits. In his innings of 45 v. Warwick in 1939 he dislodged a tile on the roof, but his most powerful hit in the direction of the stand went right over the top, and cleared Father Time by a huge margin. This is almost certainly the biggest hit ever made over the stand. It came in his innings of 33 v. Lancashire in 1937 and was made off Pollard, the Lancashire fast-medium bowler.

Smith had been given the somewhat superfluous message to 'tread on the gas', so the first ball of the over was sent sailing into the grandstand balcony with a fearful sound of splintering wood, and then, a few balls later, came the giant hit – one which Edrich says is the biggest he ever saw at Lord's, and others affirm that it went twice as high as the height of the stand. To quote Howard Marshall in his *Daily Telegraph* account: 'It was a prodigious blow. It was as if a powder magazine had exploded, so violent was the force of it.'

Many of Smith's innings were not mere entertaining interludes, but of very definite value to his side; he could come in at a critical moment and change the course of the game in literally a few minutes. In 1938 at Lord's, for example, he came in when Middlesex, with only three wickets left, were still uncertain of victory over Gloucester. Smith scored 19*, with two colossal sixes, and the runs were knocked off. He was quite incalculable, both in how long he might stay in and in his effect on the fielding side. Also incalculable was the trajectory and direction of his hits. Smith says that none of his hits were ever measured, which seems a pity. According to Constantine, the authorities at Lord's gave specific instructions that his hits there should not be measured in case Smith might be tempted to indulge in unnecessary risky attempts to improve on his previous best. I consider this story as tall as some of Smith's own hits; for who could possibly imagine that Smith's method of batting could ever be more risky than it already was?

GERALD BRODRIBB, *Hit for Six*, 1960

Two years after Smith's arrival, there came into the Middlesex side a far greater cricketer, one of the most brilliant batsmen of all time and possibly the man who gave more sheer pleasure to Lord's regulars than any other cricketer to make his home on the ground. The debut at Lord's in the County Championship of Denis Compton was modest but quietly impressive. In the Whitsuntide match against Sussex, going in last after his side had collapsed before the onslaught of an ageing Maurice Tate, he scored 14 and, in the words of *Wisden*, 'batted ably'. It would be interesting to know what percentage of the large crowds who watched the game sensed that something altogether out of the ordinary had come to Lord's. Not till July 1937 did he make his first County Championship hundred at Lord's, against Gloucestershire. In that same summer of 1937 Compton was joined in the Middlesex side by the man destined to become known as his cricketing twin, Bill Edrich.

> In his first season since qualifying for Middlesex, Edrich not only scored his 1,000 runs in Championship engagements, but in all matches obtained more than 2,000. He and Compton, who increased his aggregate and improved his average, amply justified the high opinions that had been expressed concerning them. Neither found his form early in the summer, but each, in his different style, did splendid service later, with Edrich the more consistent and, if not perhaps so attractive to watch, the more reliable. Compton played a glorious innings of 177, the highest of his career, against Gloucestershire, and, as he scored 80 not out in 43 minutes from the Worcestershire bowling, might well have registered the fastest century of the year had not the state of the weather impelled J. H. Human, acting as captain, to declare. Against New Zealand in the Oval Test match, Compton created a very favourable impression.
>
> *Wisden*, 1938

IN THE summer of 1936, while Compton was quietly making his way up the Middlesex batting order, several small incidents of some interest occurred at Lord's. *Wisden*, unable to find the appropriate placing for them, included two items in a short but delightful passage entitled 'Miscellany':

> A sparrow was killed by a ball bowled by Jahangir Khan in the MCC and Cambridge match at Lord's. T. N. Pearce, the batsman, managed to play the ball and the bird fell against the stumps without dislodging the bails. The bird is preserved as a relic in the pavilion at Lord's. Blankets were used to dry the actual pitch at Lord's during the Test match with India.
>
> *Wisden*, 1937

NEITHER of these two items was quite as rare as might be supposed. The spectacle of a cricket pitch rendered blottesque by the weather is familiar enough to followers of the game, and, where pitches were not covered, recourse to blankets was one of the conventional weapons in the groundsman's armoury. As for the sparrow that was summarily executed by a delivery which was no more than medium-fast, it was only following where other feathered creatures had led. What was distinctive about Jahangir Khan's feat was that it took place in modern times, at Lord's, before a few thousand witnesses. Jahangir Khan went on to play for India, without ever rising to the heights of his son, Majid Khan, who was a great star for Glamorgan and Pakistan in the 1970s. But the baldness of the *Wisden* report omitted any reference to what course the umpires might have been obliged to take had the bails been displaced by the falling bird. A generation later *The Times* came to its own whimsical conclusions.

... Mr Pearce, whose experience has its memorial in the Long Room at Lord's. A ball bowled to him by Mr Jahangir Khan killed a sparrow in flight which, the batsman having played his stroke, fell dead against the wicket, but without removing the bails. Presumably, even had the wretched bird taken a bail off the verdict would have been 'Not Out'. The rule confines itself to the hitting down of the wicket with bat or any part of the person, and the sparrow was not, and had no wish to be, in any way connected with Mr Pearce.

The Times, 5 June 1953

CLEARLY there was violence in the wind throughout that summer of 1936. Not only was Jim Smith flailing away and Jahangir Khan taking deadly toll of the local wild life, but the Indian tourists were chipping pieces off the sacred pavilion. The most diverting aspect of the following recollection is that it was made by Edward Humphrey Dalrymple Sewell (1873–1947), a man who enjoyed one of the most variegated careers in the history of modern cricket. In a resumé of what it called his 'curiously varied life', *Wisden* explains that after playing for Bedfordshire, he returned to his native India, where his father had been an Army officer, and there became a civil servant. On returning to England he joined Essex as a professional, but then became a member of W. G. Grace's London County side as an amateur. Later he became coach to Surrey at The Oval, and then joined Buckinghamshire as hon. secretary and amateur player. Apart from being a hitter of great power, a famous Rugby footballer and shot putter, Sewell was in his later years a fixture in the Long Room at Lord's, and in his several books reports on what he saw there. The following recollection preserves a tiny detail about sight-screens not mentioned elsewhere. It is worth adding that Sewell remains the only author of a book on cricket to include in it a photograph of himself batting while wearing a gas-mask.

I have seen only one pavilion window broken. That was at Lord's in 1936, and it was smashed by a straight drive by Amar Nath of the Indian team. In those days they were experimenting with some kind of stiff white gauze in front of the windows directly behind the wicket, as a sort of substitute screen. I had just got up from the window behind one of these screens when the ball perforated it and smashed the window. A tale is told of one of Jim Smith's clouts at Lord's shortly before the war. This crashed through the committee-room plate-glass window. Whereupon, the story runs, a very old committeeman, awaking with a start from his post-salmon dreams, said to another: 'Yes, old man, I really think we'd better play W.G. after all.'

E. H. D. SEWELL, *Overthrows*, 1946

ALTHOUGH by this time some of the Public School matches were beginning to fade into the Lord's background, the Varsity match still attracted much attention. It also brought about considerable heartburn to those old alumni unable to reconcile themselves to the fact that the reason why their side kept failing to win had something to do with the quality of their cricket. At Lord's in July 1936 Cambridge beat Oxford by eight wickets, making it thirteen years since the Dark Blues had won. Next week, Eton and Harrow drew for the twelfth time in fifteen seasons; it was now 28 years since Harrow had last won. A pseudonymous correspondent to *The Times*, clearly an Old Harrovian who had metamorphosed into an Old Oxonian, hit on a startling extra-cricketing theory to explain away this long run of failure.

> Sir, Various explanations have been put forward to account for the lack of success which has attended Oxford (and Harrow) at Lord's in recent years. Some observers have attributed this to luck of the toss or otherwise. There is, however, an explanation which I have not yet seen advanced. I refer to the sinister fact that the inside of the scorer's box at Lord's is painted light blue. This is obviously an insuperable obstacle to the success of any dark blue side, but whether it is due to caprice or prejudice on the part of the scorers, or the MCC authorities, has not been revealed to me.
>
> I remain yours faithfully, H.H.

> Ed. Note: Light blue has since given way to cream and magnolia.

> Letter to The Times, 11 July 1936

WHETHER it was the change of paint or an improvement in the cricket which brought about a change is debatable, but the following summer Oxford won at last, and in 1939 Harrow did likewise. But the oddest fragment of Lord's history in 1936 went virtually unnoticed at the time and has since been forgotten. Did anything ever come of this revolutionary experiment? Was it hoped that success would help England's batsmen to prepare for Australian tours? How long did the empirical scientists on the ground staff persist with the experiment? We do not know, and are left only with a brief reference in *Wisden*:

> At the end of March, 1936, a strip of turf from Melbourne was laid on the practice ground at Lord's as an experiment to see how it fared in the English climate, with a possibility that such turf might be used to obviate the wearing of bowlers' footholes.

> *Wisden*, 1937

MEANWHILE the prolific and irrepressible Beachcomber, alias J. B. Morton, was persisting in his policy of flicking pellets through the Lord's Committee Room window. As cricket continued to be identified with the cause of Empire, so Beachcomber waxed more lyrical about possibilities of cricketing colonisation still undreamt of in the purlieus of St John's Wood. Once again we find the satire mocking at the MCC's pretensions to being the governing body of the game.

Carstairs has had much trouble with the natives in the matter of cricket. The chief of a peculiarly beastly tribe called the Umptitumpti discovered the other day that the witch doctor had been messing about with his bat. This old reprobate had drawn on the surface of the bat the hideous face of the tribe's favourite devil-god, Mashugu. The result was that the moment the natives saw the bat, as the chief prepared to meet the bowling, they uttered loud cries, gashed themselves with spears, beat drums, danced, prayed for rain, and hastily sacrificed a crocodile.

Carstairs wired to the MCC, who replied that though there was nothing in the rules to prevent a witch doctor from drawing pictures on a bat, yet it was undoubtedly an unsporting act, and one that could not fail to delay Africa's attainment of Test match status. Having regard, however, to the rarity of such occurrences, the MCC had decided to call a special meeting of county captains to decide on the immediate steps to be taken. It is understood that the Government is to examine at once the whole question of cricket among savage tribes.

BEACHCOMBER, *Gallimaufry*, 1936

DURING the 1937 season regulars at Lord's were moved to gestures of sentimental affection by the awareness that this was to be the last season of Elias 'Patsy' Hendren, who had played for the county since 1907, who scored 170 first-class centuries, and who was one of the few batsmen to average more than fifty runs per innings throughout the full extent of his career. Patsy was respected for his achievements and deeply loved for his personality, which was lively, puckish and devoid of malice or arrogance.

It is a big pull leaving the stage, as they call it; leaving the people I have played with and the camaraderie of the game, but we all have to come to it some time, and I thought it as well to give up while I was doing well. You know what they say about cards; bad beginning, good ending. Well, my first county match was one in which I did not get an innings. That was in 1907 against Lancashire at Lord's, the game being abandoned before lunch on the second day. There were naturally unusual circumstances. After heavy rain a drizzle set in, but the crowd – allowed, as they were then, on the playing area – gathered in front of the pavilion and clamoured for cricket. In the middle of all the rumpus, somebody got on to the pitch itself and, accidentally or not, stuck the ferrule of an umbrella into the turf. When this was discovered by Mr Archie MacLaren, the Lancashire captain, he refused to play, even if a fresh wicket were cut out. So there was nothing for it but to pack up and go home.

The fight for the Championship in my last season, 1937, provided a great struggle, but it was not the closest in which I have been concerned. I remember in 1920, when Middlesex were under the captaincy of Mr P. F. Warner (as he was then) for the last time, Lancashire, in celebration of winning the Championship, split a bottle or two of champagne before the result of the Middlesex and Surrey match at Lord's reached them. As a matter of fact, I started the turn of the game by catching Tom Shepherd in the deep – I can see myself now running from long-off to long-on to take the ball – and, with a win by 55 runs, Middlesex gained the title ... A lot has been said and written from time to time about separate exits on grounds for amateurs and professionals. So far as Lord's is concerned, the professionals have the option of going through the centre gate on to the field if they care, but they probably think it too much trouble to walk along there from the dressing-room.

PATSY HENDREN, 'Reflections', in Wisden, 1938

At Lord's on Tuesday, 31 August 1937, Elias P. Hendren went to the wicket to bat against Surrey. It was his last appearance for his native county of Middlesex in a Championship match. He was forty-eight years old. As he emerged from the professionals' gate the crowd rose to him and, when he neared the pitch, the Surrey players joined whole-heartedly in the applause. When he had made his acknowledgements, and the tumult had subsided into an equally emotional silence, he addressed himself to the business of the day. This was extremely brief, for he was immediately out. The scorebook reads, 'Hendren, lbw b. Watts... 0'.

IAN PEEBLES, 'Patsy' Hendren, 1969

IN 1938 Walter Reginald Hammond, magically transmogrified from the mere professional he had been for fifteen years into an amateur at precisely the moment when England required a captain capable of justifying his position by his play, produced one of the most famous individual performances ever seen on the ground. Although the match petered out into a draw, Hammond's display epitomised what people like to call a captain's innings. One curiosity connected with this game never noticed even by collectors of cricketing arcana is that England during this series consistently used twelve internationals instead of eleven, one of the umpires being the tiny Fanny Walden. A winger with Tottenham Hotspur, Walden won two caps for England; his cricketing feats were more modest, although he appeared for Northants over a period of nearly twenty years, scoring over 7,000 runs and taking 114 wickets.

ENGLAND v. AUSTRALIA

Second Test at Lord's, June 24, 25, 27, 28, 1938

On Saturday, the cricket was seen by the largest crowd ever to assemble at headquarters—the attendance was officially returned as

33,800. The gates were closed before the start and after hurried consultations between officials, spectators were permitted to retain positions they had taken up on the grass, the boundary ropes being moved forward a few yards, thus reducing the playing area. England definitely gained the upper hand before the close. First of all, Hammond and Ames established a new sixth-wicket record by putting on 186 and surpassing the 170 made in the Oval Test of 1930 by Sutcliffe and R. E. S. Wyatt. They had been together two hours and a half when Hammond, playing late for a good length in-swinger, was bowled leg stump. Making the highest score for England in any home Test match, and hitting 32 fours, Hammond batted over six hours. His straight, off and cover driving was magnificent; he moved to meet the ball with the ease of a master. The only semblance of a mistake occurred when a sizzling drive sped towards Chipperfield who, in trying to stop it, split a finger and did not afterwards field.

Just before his dismissal, Hammond received a nasty blow on the left elbow and the injury and also a pulled leg muscle prevented him bowling in this match and for some time afterwards. Either by instruction or on their own inclination, the other batsmen attempted to force the game but not with much success. Ames, ninth to leave, played a splendid innings at a pinch, batting three and a quarter hours without a chance to hand and hitting ten 4s. It must be added that through an innings lasting seven hours and producing England's highest total at Lord's, the Australian fielding was maintained at a high standard.

By the call of time, Australia had lost half their wickets, but a fine, fighting innings by Brown checked England's progress. Bradman played on and when McCabe's audacious hooks and hard cuts threatened another punishing effort from his bat Verity dismissed him with a brilliant catch in the gully, holding on to a hard-hit ball as he lost his balance. A longer partnership followed, Hassett batting with style and confidence but Wellard, resuming, disposed of Hassett and Badcock in one over. Barnett stayed through the last half hour with Brown, who left off with his score 140 not out, and that of Australia 299 for five.

On Monday, the Englishmen lost little time in strengthening their grip on the game. Verity, put on first thing, disposed of Barnett and Chipperfield in eight deliveries and when O'Reilly went in seventh wicket down Australia needed 37 more runs to avoid a follow-on. O'Reilly promptly hit out at the slow bowling and a serious mistake occurred in the field. It is not too much to say that had Paynter held the ball when O'Reilly skied it to long-on after scoring 11, England would have been in a position to make Australia follow their innings, and thereby secure a better chance to force a win. The fieldsman, however, misjudged the flight of the ball and came too far forward so that although he leaped up for it he could not complete a catch. Australia at this point required seventeen more runs to save the follow-on and O'Reilly, pulling two successive deliveries from Verity for 6 and taking 16 off the over, soon settled that question.

Meanwhile Brown, keeping up his strong back play and scoring with stylish drives and well timed cuts and hits to leg, had reached 150 in ten minutes under five hours and before England got down the eighth wicket, 85 runs were added in 42 minutes. Soon after

Farnes was brought back into the attack he not only bowled O'Reilly and had McCormick caught at short leg off successive balls but was deprived of a 'hat trick' owing to Compton missing a slip catch offered by Fleetwood-Smith. In his highest score against England, O'Reilly, besides his two 6s, hit five 4s.

After three hours had been lost owing to rain Brown, at 184, was also missed by Paynter, this time at mid-on, and with Fleetwood-Smith showing surprisingly good defence. Brown was able to complete a double hundred before the innings ended with a difference of 72 runs in England's favour. As already stressed, Australia's fine fight was almost entirely the work of Brown, who from start to finish of an innings lasting six and a quarter hours, played with a beautifully straight bat, kept an almost impregnable defence and, without ever appearing to make real effort to punish the bowling, hit a five and twenty-two 4s. Some of his glides and pushes towards the on side were made with remarkable accuracy.

The rain transformed an easy wicket into one soft on top and hard underneath, and England's opening pair fell for 28 so that when the last day was entered upon the match was in a fairly even position. Not even O'Reilly proved such a nuisance to batsmen as did McCormick at this juncture. After taking the wicket of Edrich in his first over, McCormick bowled Verity, who had been sent in overnight, and half the England side were out for 76 when Hammond, who owing to his injury had a runner, tried a one-hand stroke at a ball outside his leg stump and skied it. Paynter and Compton added 52 but Ames did not stay long after a blow from the ball fractured a finger. In the hour of great need, however, Compton batted superbly for England, playing fast rising balls from McCormick very coolly, driving grandly on either side of the wicket and relishing short-pitched balls from McCormick. Some hard hitting by Wellard helped to carry England clear of anxiety, the eighth partnership realising 74, including a mighty pull by Wellard which sent a ball from McCabe on to the grandstand balcony.

Hammond declared, with Compton not out after making 56 of his runs from boundaries, and left Australia an impossible task in the time available. Any thought of a failure was soon dispelled by Bradman. After the tea interval the Australian captain batted in brisk style and he and Hassett added 64, short bowling by Farnes receiving instant punishment. It had long since become evident that the Test would be another case of stalemate and Bradman kept life in the cricket by hitting his fourteenth hundred against England as the outcome of less than two hours twenty minutes' batting; his 102 included fifteen 4s. During this innings, Paynter kept wicket in place of Ames and did the job well. An interesting point of the match was that Brown was on the field from the start of play until five o'clock on the fourth day; another was that Badcock failed to score in either innings. The total number of spectators admitted to the ground on payment was 100,933—a record for Lord's—and the receipts were £28,164 11s 9d.

England

L. Hutton, c. Brown, b. McCormick	4	c. McCormick, b. O'Reilly 5
C. J. Barnett, c. Brown, b. McCormick	18	c. McCabe, b. McCormick 12
W. J. Edrich, b. McCormick	0	c. McCabe, b. McCormick 10
Mr W. R. Hammond (Capt.) b. McCormick	240	c. sub. b. McCabe.... 2
E. Paynter, lbw., b. O'Reilly.....	99	run out 43
D. Compton, lbw., b. O'Reilly....	6	not out 76
L. E. G. Ames, c. McCormick, b. Fleetwood-Smith	83	c. McCabe, b. O'Reilly 6
H. Verity, b. O'Reilly...........	5	b. McCormick 11
A. W. Wellard, c. McCormick, b. O'Reilly	4	b. McCabe 38
D. V. P. Wright, b. Fleetwood-Smith	6	not out 10
Mr K. Farnes, not out..........	5	
B 1, l-b 12, w 1, n-b 10.......	24	B 12, l-b 12, w 1, n-b 4 29
	494	(8 wkts dec.) 242

1/12 2/20 3/31 4/253
5/271 6/457 7/472 8/476
9/483

1/25 2/28 3/43
4/64 5/76 6/128
7/142 8/216

Australia

J. H. Fingleton, c. Hammond, b. Wright	31	c. Hammond, b. Wellard 4
W. A. Brown, not out..........	206	b. Verity 10
D. G. Bradman (Capt.), b. Verity.	18	not out 102
S. J. McCabe, c. Verity, b. Farnes.	38	c. Hutton, b. Verity .. 21
A. L. Hassett, lbw., b. Wellard...	56	b. Wright 42
C. L. Badcock, b. Wellard.......	0	c. Wright, b. Edrich.. 0
B. A. Barnett, c. Compton, b. Verity	8	c. Paynter, b. Edrich . 14
A. G. Chipperfield, lbw, b. Verity.	1	
W. J. O'Reilly, b. Farnes........	42	
E. L. McCormick, c. Barnett, b. Farnes	0	
L. O'B. Fleetwood-Smith, c. Barnett, b. Verity	7	
B 1, l-b 8, n-b 6	15	B 5, l-b 3, w 2, n-b 1 11
	422	204

1/69 2/101 3/152 4/276
5/276 6/307 7/308 8/393
9/393

1/8 2/71 3/111
4/175 5/180 6/204

Australia Bowling

	Overs	Mdns	Runs	Wkts	Overs	Mdns	Runs	Wkts
McCormick	27	1	101	4	24	5	72	3
McCabe	31	4	86	–	12	1	58	2
Fleetwood-Smith	33.5	2	139	2	7	1	30	–
O'Reilly	37	6	93	4	29	10	53	2
Chipperfield	9	–	51	–				

England Bowling

	Overs	Mdns	Runs	Wkts	Overs	Mdns	Runs	Wkts
Farnes	43	6	135	3	13	3	51	–
Wellard	23	2	96	2	9	1	30	1
Wright	16	2	68	1	8	–	56	1
Verity	35.4	9	103	4	13	5	29	2
Edrich.........	4	2	5	–	5.2	–	27	2

Wisden, 1939

THE shadow of the future sometimes creeps across the grass unnoticed, even by a crowd of over 33,000. While Hammond was composing his brilliant classical symphony at the expense of O'Reilly and company, technology was being born in a quiet corner of the ground. The old rustic pleasures of Beauclerk, Osbaldeston and company had long since given way to the new style, but now, in the summer of 1938, the twentieth century arrived once and for all, with a device destined to change all cricket, all sport, all national life.

The televisor brought yesterday's Test match at Lord's into the homes of thousands. The television cameras were slung smoothly about the field so that every detail of the play could be followed from the moment the ball left the bowler's hand till it reached the fielder or the boundary. The transmission was a striking example of the advance in television and the great improvement in receiving apparatus. So successful was the television of the match that a further transmission was given from 6.15 p.m. till the close of play to enable City workers to see the match in their homes. Today the match will be televised from 11.30 to 12.30, 2.30 to 3.30, at 3.50, and again, it is hoped, for a quarter of an hour before the close of play.

The Times, 25 June 1938

Test cricket was the delight of television viewers on Friday and Saturday, and long periods of play were visible, morning, noon and evening. It is a happy thing to be one with the Test crowd in your own home, and to see the batsman sending the ball to the boundary and to hear the roar of the crowd. The transmissions were indeed excellent, and at times the viewer must have felt himself almost on the pitch.

Last week was the right time to televise R.C. Sherriff's delightful comedy *Badger's Green*, for it centres in a game of village cricket which changed the course of events and saved the village from the depredations of a company promoter who wanted to ruin it. It was produced by Mr Eric Crozier, with a film of village cricket on a real village green inserted in the middle of the play to make it more actual, which was most successful.

The Times, 27 June 1938

EVEN though the camera's fishy eye was beginning to focus on cricket, a few of the old brigade lingered on, their bowed backs propped up by the tall stools in the Long Room, their sights fixed on summers long since past, cricketers long since dead and buried. They tended to be jealous of their own antiquity, the sheer length of their own recollections, and had decided views on what might put a chap beyond the pale. This poem might have been written at any time up to the outbreak of the Second World War, its point being that no matter how old a man might grow, and no matter what catastrophes the world outside might stumble into, a Ford is still a Ford and a Foster will always be a Foster. There is only one crime more heinous than confusing those dynasties, and that is to confuse them within the castle walls:

THE BLACK SHEEP

You saw that man. You wonder why
I passed him with averted eye,
Although he nodded affably?

It was a Test Match – anxious days,
Somehow he had secured a place
With us, with the habitués.

We were all there. I mean by 'we'
The Old Guard of the MCC,
And, with us, but not of us, *he*.

He talked and laughed, as if unused
To serious cricket. He confused
Fosters with Fords, and seemed amused.

You know the story of the match;
The brilliant start, the rotten patch,
And, last, the unaccepted catch:

Mid-off; a gift, no spin at all;
Pure nerves. He fumbled with the ball,
Retrieved it – and then let it fall.

Lord Nestor gave a groan; the rest
Sat silent, overwhelmed, oppress'd;
And he, that fellow, made a jest!

That man, who muddled up the Fords,
At such a moment played with words
In the Pavilion!! and at Lord's!!

G. F. BRADBY

ALTHOUGH Middlesex had been tenants at Lord's for longer than living memory, the layman still often confused Middlesex County Cricket Club with their landlords, the Marylebone Cricket Club. Towards the end of the 1930s, with Denis Compton and Edrich rampant, with Jim Smith whirling them down and Jim Sims spinning away, Middlesex had become one of the two or three strongest sides in the Championship as well as one of the most attractive to watch. Because of the location of the ground, within strolling distance of Belgravia, and a few minutes' ride of the City and Whitehall, the Middlesex sides had always tended to comprise a gallimaufry of what Cardus's battlehardened Lancashire professionals used to deride as 'coloured caps'. The dashing style of cricket which the dominant amateur presence often inspired in past Middlesex sides had been at the expense of consistency. But gradually, as the pressures on young gentlemen to get a job steadily increased, so the Middlesex side settled down into a formidable challenger for honours. Although these honours were not to come until after the war, the other counties recognised this Middlesex renaissance, much to the amusement of long-suffering Middlesex supporters, about to come into their inheritance at last.

LORD'S AND THE COUNTY GAME

He likes the country, but in truth must own
Most likes it when he studies it in town.

WILLIAM COWPER

'Wheer's Middlesex,' The Yorkshireman is said to have asked, 'is it in Lunnon?' Certainly, the county boundaries of Middlesex are elusive enough to justify the question. Middlesex has no character and no countryside, no social or territorial traditions, no sort of geographical definition. It is a county of tentacle-like town appendages, of built-up areas, ribbon-development, and the occasional blasted heath. It has little soul of its own beyond the local Woolworth and the suburban cinema. 'An acre in Middlesex,' said Lord Macaulay, 'is better than a principality in Utopia.' Today he would have plenty of reason to revise that statement.

Yet Middlesex cricket has little in common with Middlesex, the county. Since the old county grounds at Islington and Princes' closed down in the 1860's Middlesex cricket has had no home of its own. Lord's has become the headquarters of the Middlesex Club (since 1877), who now enjoy, in relation to the MCC, a sort of dual but rather subordinate position, analogous to that of Hungary in the old Austro–Hungarian Empire. Middlesex cricket has become increasingly representative of London, and essentially of the London of the West End. And although it has lost the rural spirit which was the essence of the game a hundred years ago, it has gained much in its place: the spice and sparkle that is the West End's peculiar perquisite, and a gay and impartial spirit. Middlesex cricket is not, like that of, say, Lancashire or Somerset, a raw product; it is a manufactured commodity, as skilfully blended from original and component properties as the hybrid rose or the tobacco mixture. It has the good and bad points of the hybrid and the mixture, an appeal that is aesthetic rather than spontaneous, a lack of body but a refinement of taste, an absence of root-character, but a charming, if more superficial, distinction.

Middlesex cricket may be lacking in fundamental solidity, and a Middlesex side rarely seems to have the same backbone as any of the Northern counties. Generally speaking, there has been an absence of what is vulgarly but expressively known as 'guts'. On the other hand, there has been less dull county cricket at Lord's than on almost any other ground in England. For five years only, in this century, 1930 to 1934, have Middlesex played cricket unworthy of their particular tradition of free and attractive play. For the last five years before the outbreak of war in 1939 Middlesex led, closely followed by Gloucester, Kent and Worcester, what may well be the renaissance of English cricket, a new golden age in its history. From the point of view of being leaders of the game, in the widest sense, the responsibilities of the Big Six were shouldered during these years almost exclusively by Middlesex, Kent and Yorkshire. Twenty years of the Makepeace-Hallows-Watson school of batting have necessarily retarded Lancashire's reversion to her old free-scoring methods. The willingness to return to these days only became apparent in 1937, when Paynter's personal following of Oldfield, Washbrook and Nutter began to institute the divorce from the safety-first dreariness of the previous epoch. Notts, with the bright exception of J. Hardstaff, junior, have lost much of the polished grace of a generation best represented by the brothers George and John Gunn, by Payton and the elder Hardstaff. Save for the occasional innings by Keeton, or the periodic half-hour of Harris or G. V. Gunn, Notts' batting has yielded more than that of any other county to the increased standardisation of the times. It has become unadventurous and stereotyped.

Today Middlesex's neighbours at The Oval have become almost the worst offenders of all in respect of lack of variety and imagination. The reading of the Surrey teams of 1919 and 1939 presents a sad contrast. In 1919 Surrey batted Hobbs, D. J. Knight, Ducat, Hayes, Sandham, J. N. Crawford, P. G. H. Fender, Peach, Hitch, Strudwick and Rushby. Consider the vast reservoir of character and talent here, the absolute mastery of Hobbs, the balance and polish of D. J. Knight, Sandham and Ducat, the power and daring of Crawford, Hayes and Fender, and the mighty hitting of Bill Hitch and Peach! In 1939 the Surrey team read as follows: Fishlock, Gregory, Squires, Barling, Whitfield, Parker, F. R. Brown, H. M. Garland-Wells, Mobey, Watts and Gover. F. R. Brown was a dashing all-rounder, Garland-Wells a fair comedian, but otherwise Parker alone plays cricket with any sort of claims to distinction. The side made plenty of runs, but the manner of their making lacked all kind of appeal. Fishlock had in 1939 lost most of his early promise and had fallen into line with other members of the team in developing a dull, plebeian style of play which may harmonise with the gasometers and parched, brown earth of The Oval but which has nothing in common with the grand, heroic traditions of Surrey batsmanship.

Perhaps, after all, Middlesex are lucky in Lord's, and Lord's in Middlesex. London may have robbed the county of a rustic hinterland, but it has given her generations of amateur players, who have contributed largely towards keeping Middlesex cricket fresh and attractive. There is a current witticism on this subject to the effect that, since London provides the best nursing-homes, Middlesex will always have the pre-emption on most amateurs with the means to enable them to play first-class cricket. This assertion contains a germ of truth which Middlesex supporters will hardly deny, and far less regret. Such men as Robins, Peebles, Allen, Killick, Newman and so forth have been always welcome, often invaluable, additions to the side.

It is true to say that the large amateur element has, in a sense, undermined the consistency of the side. In the early 'twenties the availability of good amateur players prevented the giving of extended trials to the brothers F. S. and J. W. Lee (later of Somerset), to North, Fowler, Beton, Powell and Paine; so that when these same amateurs were no longer able to play with any frequency, owing to business reasons or advancing years, there was no nucleus of young professionals to step into their places. Sides, too, with a high percentage of amateurs no longer win championships, for the best elevens are those that play the same eight or even nine or ten men continuously throughout the season. The most effective county side between 1919 and 1939 was probably the Yorkshire team of 1925, which consisted of A. W. Lupton, the captain, and ten professionals, Holmes, Sutcliffe, Leyland, Oldroyd, Rhodes, Robinson, R. Kilner, Macaulay, Dolphin and Waddington. Only with such a combination, hardly varying from the beginning to the end of the year, will the maximum effect of team-work in the field be achieved.

The very nature of the Middlesex side, gay, variegated and undependable, has kept it free of the partisanship which often degenerates into the worst manifestations of the competitive spirit. The real dog-fight can, it is true, be thoroughly enjoyable. I once went to Bramall Lane, ostensibly to see Yorkshire play Essex, but rather more, in fact, to see the Sheffield crowd. I witnessed some interesting play, and I learnt, I think, a little about the grand fighting spirit which has given Yorkshire cricket its unique character. O'Connor, of Essex, played a great defensive innings that day, and his mastery and courage received full appreciation. Every fine shot of his was applauded, freely and genuinely: the sportsmanship and instinctive knowledge of the crowd was never in question. But equally clear and certain were the sympathies of every Yorkshireman present. When Bowes was edged dangerously through the slips a sigh went up that was more than three parts a groan; and when Verity got his hand to the latest of late-cuts shouts of triumph arose, only to be cut short and, as it were, suspended in space, as the ball was seen to be trickling on to the boundary.

On this occasion, Smailes and Bowes attacked, not only with their obstinate Yorkshire courage and with the strength of their own right arms, but with the concentrated determination of a crowd of seven thousand behind them, urging them on and willing the Essex batsmen back into the pavilion. The very ground seemed to bristle with hostility.

Yorkshiremen are exceptional only in the concentration of their feelings. Even a Surrey or a Somerset crowd come primarily to see their own team win; only at Lord's is a balance struck by the presence of a large body of spectators who want, first and foremost, to see good cricket, and its cool and critical atmosphere serves as a reminder that partisanship has not always been attended by the happiest results. In 1924 a match at Bramall Lane provided a number of 'incidents', originating ultimately from the over-keenness of the crowd. In 1933 and '34 Larwood and Voce were allowed to bowl body-line, and their county captain entered the lists in their support and allowed himself to be entangled in a senseless controversy. Today, fortunately for the game, body-line is a thing of the past, killed and buried by the MCC's sound sense and decisive action; but it is worthy of note that more than two other Northern sides allowed the use of body-line by a single bowler, Lancashire with McDonald, and Yorkshire with Bowes. Yorkshiremen and Lancastrians are quite rightly proud of their birthright and inheritance, but when over-developed the competitive spirit is liable to run riot. 'Faction,' wrote Samuel Johnson, 'seldom leaves a man honest, however it might find him.'

The competitive spirit, too, has played its part in fostering the intricacies of recent scoring systems. This is one phase of the MCC's activities which does, I think, merit criticism. Conditions have not altered sufficiently in twenty years to justify half a dozen changes in the system of scoring points in the Championship table. In the early 'thirties the emphasis quite rightly placed on the outright win in the Championship resulted in county captains, fired by the example of B. H. Lyon, using the 'arranged declaration', as a means by which to arrive at a decision in a game limited to five or six hours. To begin with, innings were declared closed at varying, arbitrary totals, 4 or 25, or whatever number the two opposing captains had chosen. Soon it was discovered that even more time would be saved if the innings were declared closed after one over or after only one ball; and a great number of games, instead of dragging out in hours of dreary boredom, were given point, meaning and, often enough, a thoroughly exciting finish. This practice was, however, eliminated by a new declaration rule, and simultaneously an attempt was made to revise the scoring system as a compensatory measure. Other alterations followed, but even the present scoring system, as instituted in 1938, can hardly be considered satisfactory. The awarding of points on first innings to a side that ultimately loses the match is, of course, purely fantastic, and entirely contrary to the sense and spirit of the game. But more unfortunate is the present system of percentages, which may make it imperative for a side high up in the Championship to avoid winning on first innings, by forcing a 'no result'. Thus we had the miserable spectacle of a Yorkshire–Notts match in which the Yorkshire batsmen made no attempt to score runs and the Notts bowlers no effort to capture wickets. Only a return to a simpler and more logical scoring system will do away with such completely farcical situations.

Partisanship may be all very well in its way; personally, I shall always prefer watching cricket as a spectacle. 'It'll be a better world,' wrote O. Henry, 'when we quit being fools about some mildewed town, or ten acres of swamp-land, just because we happened to be born there.' There is certainly something admirable in Yorkshire's declared policy of never playing a man in the county side who was not a Yorkshireman born and bred. Yorkshiremen have every right to be proud of this policy. But they and their supporters have no particular right to criticize other counties simply because they do not follow out so laudable a precept. For Middlesex, such a system would be particularly inapplicable. It would be absurd, for instance, that a man who had lived all his life in Camden Town should be debarred from playing for Middlesex because he was born in St Thomas's Hospital on the south bank of the Thames. Yorkshire have a tradition which is built up from common geography, speech and economics, and a common method and idea of life. Middlesex have none of these things, and the importation of Minor County players (who, incidentally, would by a Yorkshire analogy be debarred through no fault of their own from playing first-class cricket at all), and even Dominion and Colonial players, has followed as a matter of course. Whether either Lancashire or Middlesex were actually the first to invite Dominion cricketers into the country need not concern us here. The only real question at issue is whether the game has suffered from their importation or not. Australians might claim that Albert Trott was lost to Test cricket by qualifying for Middlesex. But Trott came to England on his own, because he had not been invited to join the Australian touring team. Constantine and Headley, again, returned, after each summer in the Lancashire League, to the West Indies, and the former was debarred from playing only in one Test series, the latter never. McDonald probably furnishes the only real example of a Dominion losing one of its best players by reason of his emigration to England.

And how much the Lord's spectator would have missed had everyone thought and acted as Yorkshire did! A Middlesex team of 'importees' might read as follows: 1. Tarrant (Victoria), 2. Edrich (Norfolk), 3. J. H. Human (Berkshire), 4. R. H. Bettington (NSW), 5. H. G. Owen-Smith (South Africa), 6. Trott (Victoria), 7. Rawlin (Yorkshire), 8. Murrell (Kent), 9. Roche (Victoria), 10. Smith J. (Wiltshire), 11. I. A. R. Peebles (Scotland). Here is a colour, variety and 'glamour' element that has added so much to the game and to the spectator's enjoyment of it that it surely requires no apologia! These names may supply reason for envy, since 'Envy,' according to John Gay, 'is a kind of praise.' But they hardly furnish cause for contempt.

This imported element has given the Middlesex side a cosmopolitanism which is its chief characteristic. And this cosmopolitanism has, in turn, helped to give to the Lord's crowd a better-balanced appreciation and a higher degree of impartiality than to any other in England. The Lord's crowd will never suffer the self-torture and heart-searchings of Bramall Lane. The county match at Lord's has none of Bramall Lane's grim endeavour and intense, long-drawn-out agony. The Northerner, tough, hardy and self-sufficient, will revel in an atmosphere of hostility and stress – the Southerner can barely endure it for one Test match in the season.

Yet the Lord's crowd has plenty of character. I like their quick Cockney humour, and their refusal to take their pleasures seriously. I like the wild applause from the free seats when Jim Smith goes in to bat; and the deep roar from the Tavern when he hits his soaring six. I like the top hats that are brought out and dusted for Lord's Week, but I like far more that splendid piece of headgear, the Edwardian 'boater', bright with the red and yellows of MCC or Zingari colours. I do not always agree with the views of their wearers, but, if seldom very original, they are often refreshing and almost always entertaining. The straw hat seems to sit, perennially, on the top of a miniature volcano of dissatisfaction. I once saw Robins batting in his best vein against Sussex, and remarked on the fact to a friend of mine, generally known as the Orange Cockatoo and almost invariably to be found on the same perch in front of the pavilion. 'Ah yes,' he replied, 'he's not a bad player at all, but his bat's often crooked.' After 85 minutes' batting Robins ran to as brilliant a century as I ever hope to watch, but the old gentleman was still dissatisfied. 'He doesn't play a straight bat,' he grumbled; adding, as an afterthought, 'you could never imagine Archie MacLaren doing a thing like that!'

Most of all, I like the wonderful knowledge of the Lord's crowd. The true Londoner is as readily friendly as any man in the world. He will sit down beside you and talk entrancingly but simply of the game for which he has so real a love. When a schoolboy, I sat usually in the free seats by the main entrance, and often enough I would find my nearest neighbour giving a special clap for what seemed a very ordinary single to leg. But a close scrutiny of the scoreboard would show that a pair had just put on 50; or, if the scoreboard failed to reveal anything, a discreet question would discover the fact that some extraordinarily obscure or commonplace record had just been achieved, 100 runs for the match, 1,000 runs for the season, and so on. After a great game, cricket statisticians will compile critical analyses to show just how many records have been broken during its course. Many of these records will appear, to say the least, a trifle obscure. Yet it is any odds that the crowd will have spotted them as soon as they were made. Nothing escapes their notice, and batsman, bowler and fieldsman alike never fail to receive the recognition which they have merited.

There is a fundamental balance and sense of the rightness of things in the mind of every one of us, and the county game at Lord's produces an atmosphere most conducive to a state of mental equilibrium and simple enjoyment. I shall never regret a single hour of Test cricket that I have ever watched, for no single hour has failed to produce something of the vital, almost primeval excitement that one may find in even more undiluted form at Highbury or Twickenham. But all the same, the Test match is a strain, and the Timeless Test a horror. Given sensibly prepared wickets, Timeless Tests could never have come into existence. Their futility was perfectly shown up by the final Test matches, in 1930, in the West Indies, and in 1939 in South Africa. Both of these had eventually to be given up, because the England XI could continue to delay their departure no longer, if they were to arrive home in time for the forthcoming cricket season!

The fifth Test of 1938, too, was a fine example of the fatuity not only of the present policy of over-preparing wickets, but of the critical faculties of those who disapprove of scores ranging up to 1,000. When England batted for three full days and made 903 for seven wickets, more nonsense was talked and written than one would have believed possible. One was told that bowling had gone to the dogs, and harrowed with prophecies of a time to come when it would be impossible to get sides out in under a fortnight. Some blamed the weather and some the selectors of the Australian side, who had sent a team into the field with only four bowlers. In other quarters it was suggested that the Australian débâcle was the natural consequence of losing the toss!

In point of fact there was one perfectly simple, logical and all-embracing explanation. The Surrey ground staff, at the instigation of the county authorities and subject to no other sort of supervision, had been allowed to prepare a wicket that was a bowler's nightmare. Not only had no cricket been played on it for months, but far more time and attention had been given to it than to pitches which the Surrey team had used during the season. It was never intended to be part of the game of cricket that a special wicket should be created and maintained for a particular match. Obviously, the Surrey authorities wanted the best possible pitch, to give them the longest possible match and the largest possible financial return. This final consideration must be weighed against the spirit in which the game is meant to be played and, somewhere, a balance struck. Personally, I hope that the balance will be such that a score of 903 will never again be made in a Test match.

For me, at least, the county game will always have an attraction that will outweigh the 'big-match' atmosphere of the Test. 'Stillest streams,' as Cowper wrote, 'oft water fairest meadows.' The county game has given us the unmixed pleasure of watching such men as E. H. Bowley and Tommy Cook, of Sussex; Howorth, of Worcester; E. R. T. Holmes of Surrey; and Ashdown and F. G. H. Chalk, of Kent: men who never aspired to English Test teams, but who played the most attractive sort of cricket in a free and happy spirit, and whom I would far sooner see batting than some of those giants of the game, averaging 60 and 70 by masterly but laborious methods, and attaining to the game's highest honour – a place in the England side. The county game gives plenty of thrills, but its excitements are tempered by situations where one may laugh; and its realities, at least at Lord's, are never grim. A day's county cricket has the same implications as James Montgomery's lines:

> A day in such serene enjoyment spent,
> Were worth an age of splendid discontent.

After all, it is the county game which has most justified my two reasons for going to Lord's at all – to see good cricket and to get as much fun out of it as possible.

WITH the outbreak of the Second World War, a way of British life was ending for ever. When the nation picked up the pieces six years later, some things may have been better and others worse, but virtually nothing was ever the same again. Like any living social organism, the MCC showed the signs of change, among them being an alteration in the style of its membership. By the time the 1939 season ended, there were few survivors from the previous century, which meant among other things, fewer bequests. Even the most assiduous club member hardly gives a thought to the problem faced by MCC Committees year after year as the gifts come rolling in. Up to 1940 it was the policy of *Wisden* to publish each year an account of the Marylebone club's annual meeting, including details of new investments, building departures and the acknowledgement of gifts. When normal cricket resumed, and with it normal editions of *Wisden*, this practice was sadly discontinued, whether because the editors of the Almanack considered the MCC's affairs to be of scant interest to readers, or whether because the club adopted a more secretive attitude remains unknown. At any event, after 1940 it was no longer possible for members of the public to monitor proceedings at MCC meetings, which is a pity, because by taking a cross-section of the entries from the start of the century to the outbreak of the second war, it becomes possible to acquire an impressionistic effect of the multifarious activities and responsibilities of the Committee.

1900   The purchase of the freehold of No. 10, Elm Tree Road was ratified.

1901   An awning to cover 600 seats (which if desired can be extended) has been erected in the large Mound Stand, where new accommodation has been provided for the Press opposite the pavilion.

1903   Owing to the injury to the turf caused by large tents, luncheon arbours have been erected along the walls of the practice ground. These will be provided with lockers and fitted with sinks.

1904   A thorough investigation of the drainage of the match ground was made. It was found that the drainage was inadequate for carrying off the surface water in a year of abnormal rainfall. Additional pipes have now been laid.

1905   An extra refreshment bar has been erected, adjoining the hotel on the west side, in order to meet the requirements of the public in the road on crowded days.

1906   As it was found necessary to increase the number of dressing-rooms in the tennis courts, the billiard room has been converted into four dressing-rooms.

1908   It has been decided to build an additional squash racquet court. The execution of the work has, however, been delayed pending the decision of the Tennis, Racquets and Fives Association as to standardising the dimensions of squash racquets courts.

1911   Owing to complaints, the sale of daily and evening papers in the pavilion will be discontinued.

1912   The score board on the south side of the ground has been raised above the roadway between the hotel and the large Mound stand. This will increase the accomodation for spectators on the ground, and will provide about 50 additional seats on the stand.

1913 The club has purchased the freehold of Nos. 2 and 4, Grove End Road, the necessity for securing the former having long been recognised, but the owner refused to separate the two properties as affording a suitable site for flats.

1915 The wall behind the pavilion has been put back three feet and reduced in height, thus making the passage more comfortable for big occasions, and the surroundings brighter.

1916 Cricket materials have been presented to 76 Naval and Military centres in the British Isles, in France and in Holland. Some have also been sent to British prisoners in Germany.

1917 Owing to the fact that many members serving with the colours have not applied for a return of their subscriptions the finances of the club are better than could have been anticipated.

1918 The work done by the staff and others in supplying hay-nets for horses for the Army was discontinued at the request of the War Office, as other arrangements had been made – subsequently this labour was employed in netting bed stretchers. This, however, was of an intermittent character owing to a difficulty in obtaining string.

1919 The principle to be employed in paying wages to the staff at Lord's is now on a sliding scale and has relation to the purchase price of the necessaries of life. The staff were offered and have excepted [sic] a bonus of about 60% more than their pay in 1914.

1920 It has been decided to convert the top dressing-room on the north side of the pavilion into an auxiliary restaurant and bar. Attention is drawn to the fact that the confectionery shop is now doing a continuous business, and orders can be executed in the winter as well as in the season. All cakes and chocolate are made on the premises under the most careful supervision.

1921 It has been found necessary to add three new turnstiles at the entrances. Members without passes will be asked to enter by the members' entrance and write their names in the members' book. This will not entail a longer journey for those going to the pavilion.

1922 A recent decision in the High Court may result in a

levy by the Entertainment Tax Commissioners on some of the members' subscriptions. At a meeting of the Advisory County Cricket Committee it was decided to protest against such a tax where a club is carried on for cricket and not for profit.

1923 The new luncheon sheds in the garden of No. 2, Grove End Road, and the improved accomodation there, added materially to the comfort of members and their friends during the big matches in 1922. The old house in the garden which for some time had been in a very dilapidated condition has been pulled down, but it has not yet been decided to what purpose the available space shall be devoted.

1926 Last season MCC traced the case of a member of the club selling his privileges by accepting money for his Rovers tickets. The committee took a serious view of such conduct, but special circumstances were brought to their notice and they decided not to enforce the rules.

1927 The new Grand Stand and Balcony and the upper tier of seats over the north end of the Large Mound Stand were completed in time for the Test match in June. The view obtained from these stands, except in the case of a few seats in the corners of the Grand Stand, gave, it is believed, general satisfaction. The total cost of the works, exclusive of the seats, fittings and fees, should not exceed about £47,500, for which the sum of £40,000 has been received as a result of the election of 200 Life Members.

1928 Considerable expense has been incurred in connection with an up-to-date hot water system in the pavilion and tennis courts. Additional radiators have been installed which will help to keep the buildings dry during the winter months.

1929 In the hope that the inhabitants of Tristan da Cunha may be interested, sets of cricket stumps, bats, balls, etc. have been forwarded to that lonely island.

1930 In October last several of the luncheon arbours on the practice ground were wrecked by a severe gale. After taking expert advice it was considered necessary to rebuild all the arbours.

1932 The old boiler room at the south end of the pavilion below the members' bar has been converted into a ticket office, to which a special entrance has been provided for the public behind the pavilion. Members can enter this office from the inside of the pavilion.

1934   Representations having been made by the Local Authorities as to the danger to traffic occasioned by the blind corner of the junction of St John's Wood Road and Wellington Road, the Committee have agreed to a few feet of the club's leasehold property being cut off at this corner and dedicated to the public. By the generosity of Mr David Isaacs, a panel in bas-relief executed by Mr Gilbert Bayes, the sculptor, depicting 'Athletes', is being placed on the angle wall.

1937   On the advice of the club's architect, No. 20, Elm Tree Road, the official residence of the Assistant Secretary, is being rebuilt at a cost of approximately £6,000. It is hoped that when the work is completed a satisfactory modern residence will be available.

CLEARLY the brusque, businesslike style of these minutes conceals the occasional moving personal drama; the scandal of 1926, in which a member was found to be misusing his club facilities, is an example. The High Court decision of 1922, apart from disclosing the comical rapacity of the Tax Commissioners, is interesting in its revelation that at this time the MCC professed not to be carrying on cricket for profit. One wonders which traveller home from the far-flung outposts was responsible for the kindly but faintly pathetic gesture to the island of Tristan da Cunha, but it is pleasant to be enlightened as to the origins of that incongruous but not unpleasing item of bas-relief at the south-east corner of the premises.

But it is the gifts to the club which most accurately represent the old spirit of its membership. The list begins with an alarming preponderance of bits of dead animals, briskly delineated as 'heads and horns'. In this regard Mr Leatham seems to have been especially resolute. A goodish wicket-keeper who represented the Gentlemen and played occasionally for Yorkshire in the 1870s, Leatham lived considerably longer than his animal friends, and reached 81 before being mounted on the family wall in 1931. Some of the other gifts may fairly be defined as inscrutable, especially George Robey's, Lord Belper's and Earl Grey's. As for the gifts showered on the club by the likes of Lieut-Col. Heseltine, Messrs Higgins, Berners and Mugliston, thoughts are instantly evoked of Beachcomber, whose lists of useless articles included a collapsible salt-bag, a suet container, a leather grape, a dummy jellyfish, waterproof onions, a method of freezing meat-skewers, a cheese-anchor, and a hand-woven esparto grass egg-cosy which plays 'Thora' when released from the egg. Beachcomber may have been the most inspired fantasist produced by the English during this period, but even his little vanities would have paled before the cannon balls and the miniature flag.

The question which remains hovering like a mischievous ghost in the minds of club members is: what ever happened to this extraordinary gallimaufry of post-imperial junk? After all, not even the most exemplary committee has at its disposal inexhaustible supplies of grateful solicitude when confronted, year after year, with the glazed expression to which the severed heads of stuffed animals tend to be prone. Where are all those stags and deer and caribou today? And does the anonymity of 'heads and horns' conceal the exotica of tigers, elephants, camels, giraffes, wolves? Is there yet some subterranean ante-chamber of the Memorial Museum, or a floor in some suburban furniture repository, where all these glum trophies moulder down the years? Or were they surreptitiously dumped the moment their patrons were themselves eligible for stuffing? Oh my ash trays and my caribou of long ago. And was the A. Waugh who so generously donated the ball which W. G. Grace had belted all round the ground the Alec Waugh who retained his club blazer in the tropics, or his father Arthur Waugh, a publisher with cricketing affections as sturdy as those of his son?

1901 To Messrs P. Van der Byl and A. E. Leatham for heads and horns.

1902 To F. Monckton for an old cricket bat, 1793.
      To Messrs R. Wigram and Van der Byl for heads and horns.

1903 To Dr Wharton Hood for horns.

1905 To Lady Pontifex for a portrait of the late J. B. Gribble.
      To numerous gentlemen for books, portraits, heads, etc.

1906 To Sir John Rodger for a photograph of cricket in West Africa.
      To A. E. Leatham for a stuffed tufted deer from China.

1909 To George Robey for a leather statuette.
      To Sir Richard Harrison for *Recollections of a Life in the British Army*.

1912 To Mr H. W. Walker for a photograph of Samoan cricketers.

1918 To Mr E. G. Amphlett for heads and horns.

1919 To Right Hon. W. P. Schreiner for a South African flag.
      To Lieut.-Col. C. Heseltine for money notes issued by Austria for circulation in Italy.

1921 To Mr C. A. Oliver for an old map of Dorset Square.
      To Lord Gorell for heads.

1924 To Mr W. Higgins for two Sebastopol cannon balls.

1925 To Mr S. H. Berger for a china jug.

1926 To the British Ball-Games Union for a miniature Danish flag on a mounted staff.

1927 To Sir Francis E. Lacey for a small portrait of himself.

1928 To Mr T. Carlton Levick for a caribou head and a framed photograph of the MCC Argentine cricket team.
      To Lord Francis Warner for two buffalo heads.

1929   To Major-General S. H. Sheppard for a Kashmir stag's head.
       To Lieut.-Col. C. Heseltine for six ash trays.

1930   To Mr J. H. Berners for a stretcher.

1933   To Mr A. Waugh for the ball off which Dr W. G. Grace scored his hundredth century in first-class cricket.

1936   To Lord Belper for alabaster electric-light bowls.

1939   To Earl Grey for a photograph of a sculptured arm holding a ball dating from the time of the Ptolemies.
       To Mr R. K. Mugliston for a belt buckle.

THE punctuation mark of a great war marks a point in the life of many a man not normally given to dividing his past into neat sectors. For cricket watchers particularly, whose main pleasure tends to vanish once the bugles sound, war, the way it comes, the blood it sheds, the manner of its departing, is never forgotten. The following reminiscence, about one among many thousands who tended to take their pleasure at Lord's, refers to Middlesex v. Surrey, on 26, 28, 29 August, 1939, a championship match whose proceeds went to the benefit funds of two Lord's veterans, Hart and Hulme. The 'gallant Edrich innings' was one of 110 not out scored out of a total of 185 not out. It was not, however, quite the last pre-war match at Lord's. On 30 and 31 August, Middlesex trounced Warwickshire by an innings. Nor was it Edrich's last pre-war century; against Warwickshire he was caught-and-bowled Hollies for 101.

The last time I saw dapper, immaculately dressed Huntley Wright at Lord's was a few days before war was declared (28 August). He probably saw some of the war-time cricket, but I never ran into him again after that Monday morning when the balloon in the Nursery was throwing its shadow of things to come over the Mound Stand.

We watched from the Long Room the gallant Edrich innings, and equally gallant resistance from the tail-enders which helped to foil Surrey. Edrich went from 28 to his century while Gover and Co. were capturing the remaining three Middlesex wickets. As the last Middlesex wicket fell, that of Laurie Gray, Huntley Wright turned to me, and with his face expressing tragedy that gained nothing from his seventy years of service on the stage, said, 'When, Oh when, shall we see the like again.'

ROY PESKETT, *Daily Sketch*, July 1941

WHEN the First World War arrived, it was a sudden terrible irruption, out of the Georgian blue, catching the entire nation by surprise. The second war came in a very different way, by degrees, step by step, the digging of trenches, the issuing of gas masks, the registering of eligible adult males, the instructions regarding Air Raid Precautions. Crisis followed crisis. War loomed, receded, loomed again, always a little closer than last time. When at last it came, only a few fools and the occasional politician were genuinely surprised. Subconsciously cricket hoped to get through one more season, which it did, after which its finest descriptive writer, Neville Cardus, decamped for Australia, where he spent the next six years. Like so many exiles, Cardus found that distance lent not only enchantment to his memories, but clarity also, and in his *Autobiography*, one of the best-written personal memoirs of its generation, his cricketing past flowered into exotic verbal blooms. In these scattered recollections, of men and places, Cardus conveys the essence of Lord's, as a refuge, a place always to return to, somewhere to be relied upon in this most unreliable of worlds. He conveys better than anyone the sense of a glittering, glamorous centre of London, the thrill of pitching camp in one of its hotels, the keen anticipation of sunshine the following morning and a match at Lord's. He recalls one of the heroes of his youth, long in the tooth now, and reduced to playing only spectral matches from the sanctity of the Long Room. He exults in the bad weather which so often dampened the prospects of cricket but never his imagination, and he conjures up a moment, fictitious probably, to proclaim the end of an era.

I come back at midnight to London, and next morning I take a taxi in Regent Street and say 'Lord's', and the driver gives me a look that tells me he approves, and he takes his ease and rides me along the curve of Regent's Park, where we can see the boats on the lake and the children playing; and when we reach the main gates at Lord's, there is time to look round before a fresh match begins, and see Patsy Hendren arriving, also the man with the straw hat – dating from Jerome K. Jerome and *Three Men in a Boat* – who spends all his life running here and there to watch cricket.

Brearley was a gale of humanity in himself. After his career as a fast bowler for Lancashire was finished, he lived in London and, without compromising his Bolton accent and turbulence, became one of the chosen of the Long Room of the pavilion at Lord's. Often I saw him gazing for a few minutes through the great windows at some fast bowler of these latter years. He could seldom bear to look for long; his eyes popped almost out of his head; the explosive red of his face heightened. 'Ah could throw mi hat down the pitch quicker,' he would say.

I have spent whole days at Lord's and scarcely seen half a dozen consecutive overs bowled from noon to evening, yet my article of fifteen hundred words has appeared as usual next morning on the cricket page of the 'M.G.' 'So many things happen to you at Lord's,' said J. M. Barrie to me after he had spent some hours there. 'And,' he continued, 'it's astonishing the number of people you meet who know you. Yesterday a perfect stranger in the Tavern, wearing a cloth cap and a spotted handkerchief round his neck, put down his can of beer and said, "'Ello George!"'

A hundred times I have walked down the St John's Wood Road on a quiet morning – that's the proper way to enjoy Lord's: choose a match of no import-ance, for preferment one for which the fixture-card promises a 'band if possible'. I have gone a hundred times into the Long Room out of the hot sun and never have I not felt that this is a good place to be in, and if the English simply HAD to make cricket a national institution and a passion and a pride, this was the way to do it, in a handsome hall and pavilion, a resting place for the game's history, with its constitution to be found as much in *Debrett* as in *Wisden*. I have looked through the great windows on the field of play and seen the cricketers in the heat, moving like creatures in another element, the scene as though suspended in time, the crowd a painted canvas; the blue sky and the green of the trees at the Nursery end; the lordly ones slumbering on the white seats of the pavilion, or quietly talking. On the Friday morning when Hitler invaded Poland, I chanced to be in this same Long Room at Lord's watching through windows for the last time for years. Though no spectators were present, a match was being continued; there was no legal way of stopping it. Balloon barrages hung over Lord's. As I watched the ghostly movements of the players outside, a beautifully preserved member of Lord's, spats and rolled umbrella, stood near me inspecting the game. We did not speak of course; we had not been introduced. Suddenly two workmen entered the Long Room in green aprons and carrying a bag. They took down the bust of W. G. Grace, put it into the bag, and departed with it. The noble lord at my side watched their every movement; then he turned to me. 'Did you see, sir?' he asked. I told him I had seen. 'That means war,' he said.

NEVILLE CARDUS, *Autobiography*, 1947

BY FAR the most striking aspect of wartime cricket between 1939 and 1945 is that it existed at all. In 1914, the moment the Great War erupted, men as contrasted in sensibilities and usefulness as Dr W. G. Grace and Lord Roberts joined forces to insist that at this moment in the nation's destiny, to play a mere game of cricket for public entertainment was unpatriotic, the implication being that because a man was proficient in late-cutting a ball, this mysteriously endowed him with the ability to despatch Germans. This sort of fatuousness was typical of the armchair bellicosity which was rampant in the first year of the war, and was perhaps less harmful than some other manifestations of bloodthirstiness in those whose own blood was not required. But, regrettable or not, it was a misplaced sense of patriotism which removed first-class cricket from the face of English life in the Great War, although it is true that as the years went by and story-book heroics were seen to have no remote connection with the slaughterhouse of the Western Front, a certain unbending of attitudes towards cricket did take place.

In 1939 men in control were wiser. Every attempt was made to keep first-class cricket alive in some form, not only because it did no harm to the war effort but because in the opinion of heroes as huge as the Adjutant-General of the Forces and Ernest Bevin, Minister of Labour, it actually contributed towards it by showing that aspects of normal life could be sustained. The result was a curious cricketing *melange*, in many ways utterly delightful to the collector of cricketing arcana. The annals of the game were now to be enriched in a way never previously dreamed of, and it is only because of the unreal nature of the episode that I am emboldened, just for once, to scale the heights of self-idolatry by quoting myself.

It has not altogether escaped the notice of the cricket historian that what these wartime matches may have lacked in status or immediacy, they more than made up in their wonderful, extraordinary, unpredictably comic eccentricity. The annals of the game, already rich in empirical philosophers, impromptu comedians and freakish enterprises, were now enriched beyond the dreams of the wildest lunatic. The student has only to examine the events at one ground in one month to appreciate this. At Lord's, on 10 August 1940, London Counties played the British Empire Xl, the match being utterly memorable for the unexpected comeback of Frank Woolley, who not only scored 38 but also had the pleasure of dismissing Denis Compton. Five days later, a Public Schools XI found itself opposed by another veteran who had come out of retirement to chance his arm; the man following the comeback trail was Patsy Hendren. By this time patrons of the cricket were beginning to become acquainted with one of the first principles of wartime spectating, which was that you never knew who you might see in action. On the 22nd of that month it also became plain that nor could you ever predict which player would be representing which club, for on that day the West Indies side opposing Sir Pelham Warner's XI included the most improbable wicket-keeper ever to represent them. On the 31st the MCC President, Sir Stanley Christopherson, accompanied by Sir Stanley Jackson, Lord Lucan and Mr H. D. G. Leveson-Gower, who had been spending the night commanding the local Home Guard, turned up to watch a game between the Buccaneers and the British Empire XI – alas, with the Buccaneers going for victory, the match was called off owing to the Battle of Britain. On the 7th the war reduced the match between a Middlesex XI and a Lord's XI to a hopeless chaos, when an air raid warning obliged the cricketers to take cover and not resume until the All-Clear had sounded.

But there is nothing to compare with the Carrollian events surrounding the match in August 1943, at Lord's, billed as 'Middlesex and Essex v. Kent and Surrey'. With the match due to start at the usual time, torrential rain was teeming down, and, with prospects of play exceedingly thin, permission was granted for the Compton brothers to depart to play for Arsenal in the opening game of the football season against Charlton Athletic at the Valley. By half-past two, with the sun shining and the Compton brothers gone beyond recall, the covers were taken off and play found to be possible. The Middlesex–Essex side soon discovered that it was further weakened by the bizarre accident sustained by the Essex opener Avery, who, in his excitement at the prospect of playing in the match, tripped over his bag while leaving home and was unable to take any further part in the proceedings. Nor was the opposition entirely trouble-free, because Arthur Fagg, who should have been opening for them, spent the day in the less salubrious pursuit of following the mysterious spoor of his cricket bag as it wandered unattended down the labyrinth of the railways. One straw in the wind that day was a not-out half-century by a Sergeant T. G. Evans.

BENNY GREEN, *Wisden Anthology* (1940–62), 1982

APART from disclosing the identity of the surprise West Indian wicket-keeper as Leslie Compton, the 1940 edition of *Wisden*, the last for some years to bear a familiar appearance, had the sad task of winding up the old epoch and announcing the start of a new one, and making some attempt to put its readers in a more austere frame of mind. This was partly achieved by an essay called 'Cricket in Wartime' by Harry, now Major, Altham. Much of his text ranges further afield than the purlieus of St John's Wood, but intermittently the major does recall Lord's in various stages of peace and war.

The outbreak of the European War in 1914–18 will always be associated in my mind with Lord's. I was up there watching the Lord's Schools v. The Rest match and can remember buying an evening paper on the ground and reading in the stop-press column the opening sentences of the speech which Lord Grey was then making in the Commons, and subsequently travelling down from Waterloo to Esher, where I was staying with the Howell brothers, and seeing in the blood-red sunset over the Thames an omen of the years to come. The younger Howell whose batting had dominated the match and for whom no honours in the game seemed unobtainable, fell in the Salient less than a year afterwards.

For most of that August county cricket was played much as usual, though the military authorities commandeered The Oval, and Hobbs' benefit match was staged at Lord's, but then a speech by Lord Roberts and a dignified letter to *The Times* by 'W. G.' brought the first-class game to an end.

Though the 1915 *Wisden* envisaged the possibility of occasional county cricket in the coming summer, no such attempt was made or even seriously contemplated. Every county committee had encouraged the professional staff to join the forces or to engage in some form of war work, in most cases making up to them the difference between their Army pay and allowances and their cricket wage. Yorkshire took the lead in making such war service a condition of re-engagement. But cricketers everywhere needed no urging, and at the annual MCC meeting in May, Lord Hawke as President could claim that 75 per cent of first class cricketers were serving in the Army or Navy (the RFC being then of course a very small body of regular specialists).

At the same meeting he announced the MCC's intention to do all they could to help school cricket and his hope that the headmasters would co-operate to keep the game going. This hope was realised and in one respect at least the war brought real benefit to school cricket; deprived of their usual club opposition the schools naturally turned to each other and many new inter-school fixtures were arranged. Winchester, for instance, who had for sixty years met only one school—Eton—now arranged matches with Charterhouse, Wellington and Bradfield, and the policy, continued after the war, has proved an unqualified success.

The MCC played their part nobly by playing forty-four school matches, and if their sides were often rather long in the tooth this could be off-set by the youth of the school teams; for, in contrast with the far-sighted policy of to-day, no effort was made to prevent boys joining up at a bare eighteen and many were fighting or had been killed in Flanders at a time when they would normally have still been playing cricket for their schools.

The year 1917 saw a great change in sentiment about the game; the nation had by then re-adjusted its lie to the state of war and no objection was felt to an attempt to stage some exhibition matches in the cause of charity. Yorkshire had felt their way in that direction the previous year and now played four big games, whilst the MCC bestowed their official blessing by staging two matches at Lord's— The Army v. Australian Army, and Navy and Army v. Australia and S. Africa; these games, if they produced no outstanding cricket, were very popular. Charity benefited by over £1,000. Two army commanders, Generals Plumer amd Horne, wired their good wishes, and Admiral Jellicoe himself came to Lord's.

No fewer than 119 military and school matches were played that year on the Canterbury ground, and Leyton, too, saw much cricket.

The outstanding feature in the school cricket of the year was the bowling of the Wykehamist J. D'E. Firth, who took eight for 48 v. Harrow, all ten for 41 v. Eton, and with seven for 27 in the last innings at Lord's, pulled the match out of the fire for The Rest. Stevens made further progress, Gibson of Eton and Rotherham of Rugby foreshadowed their future powers, whilst at Uppingham Percy Chapman, though only 16, averaged 111 for ten innings!

The last year of the war saw a further extension of the policy of 'Exhibition' matches, both in Yorkshire and in the South.

Three such games were played at Lord's, one at The Oval, and one in September at Folkestone, and if the cricket, as was natural, hardly reached peacetime level the large crowds that attended had their moments of rich reward, in one of Hobbs' very best innings, another, almost as good, by H. W. Taylor, a piece of hurricane hitting by Fender, and the heartening spectacle of 'Plum' Warner in the familiar Harlequin cap batting almost as well as ever at the age of forty-four.

Today the horizon is again dark, and it is idle to try to look far ahead. But I believe there is a general feeling that the game can and should be kept going wherever possible. With the Military Service Act in operation, and the nation mobilised as never before for its war effort, there is no room for the charge of scrimshanking, and where cricket can be played without interfering with the national effort it can only be good for the national morale. Of course anything like county cricket is out of the question, but the MCC have arranged one or two big charity matches at Lord's with a number of minor matches, and undertaken a long programme against the schools, with the Lord's Schools and the Rest match to end the season at Lord's...

A visit to Lord's on a dark December day was a sobering experience; there were sandbags everywhere, and the Long Room was stripped and bare, with its treasures safely stored beneath ground, but the turf was a wondrous green, old Father Time on the Grand Stand was gazing serenely at the nearest balloon, and one felt that somehow it would take more than totalitarian war to put an end to cricket. *Merses profundo, pulchrior evenit.*

H. S. ALTHAM, in *Wisden*, 1940

Among those who must have mourned the loss of constant cricket between May and September was the novelist Alec Waugh, whose father omitted to put the boy's name down for MCC membership until 1914, which meant, in Waugh's words, 'that my contemporaries had a sixteen-year start of me'. However, Waugh, being a writer of fiction, concocted a plot which would expedite his entry on to the lists.

During the 1920s, however, there was devised a means by which candidates with reasonable club cricket qualifications could get their election accelerated as playing members. This involved the pulling of certain preliminary strings in order to get one's name on the list of probationary candidates. Then, to justify one's presence there, one had to play in twelve trial games for MCC in which the match manager reported on one's qualities and behaviour. It took me several years even with the backing of P. F. Warner to get on that list. Then I had to play my dozen games. It will be appreciated with what excitement, with what pride I read the announcement of my election. I could now walk into the pavilion not only for Middlesex matches – I was already a member of the county club – but for Test matches, for the Oxford and Cambridge, for the Eton and Harrow matches; I could take a guest in with me. What a pleasure to be able to take my father there. There is no comparison between the view of the play that you get when you are watching behind the bowler's arm and when you are in the members' guest enclosure, the Mound, or square in the grandstand. It was for this reason that in recent years my father and I had gone more often to The Oval, where I was a member. But we both preferred Lord's – the centre and the home of cricket. As a member of MCC I should be entitled to Rovers' tickets for Test matches, which would allow my friends a choice of seats in the various guests' enclosures. What a valued present that would make. I had known that I should be elected in the spring, but the tangible proof of my election warmed my heart.

ALEC WAUGH, *A Year to Remember*, 1975

Waugh maintained his love of the game and pride in his attachment to MCC to the end of his life. In his wandering through the tropics as an older man, he came to regard what he referred to as his Colours as though they were a talisman which could conjure a fondly recollected past; he says of his club blazer that 'it was a familiar sight in St Thomas in the 1950s when it was surmounted by a wide-brimmed cha-cha hat. I used it as a writing coat, and several press interviews recorded my wearing of it at my desk in the Algonquin. Finally it fell to pieces in the Macdowell Colony in the early 1960s. It embarrassed me on the cricket field, but it was a good friend, the companion of many contented hours'. It was inevitable that a man who wrote so well, and who loved cricket with such passion, should have studied at some depth the by now considerable body of cricket literature, and predictable that he should have published his conclusions about an era now past but still fresh in the memory of Waugh's whole generation:

Lord's and its Literature

Rather wistfully on a late summer afternoon, at the close of the last match, we walked down the pavilion steps at Lord's. For eight months Lord's would be shut; we should pass by it on the 'bus, and the white seats of the mound would be empty. A few groundsmen would be pottering about; someone would be rolling the practice pitch. We should stand up on the 'bus as we go by, for one always does stand up on a 'bus as one passes Lord's, but no longer should we crane our necks to read the figures on the telegraph, or peer eagerly to distinguish the players, to see whether it is Hearne or Hendren that was still not out. The season was not over, of course; there was still the Scarborough festival, and the champion county had to meet England at The Oval. But these games were, after all, an anti-climax; for the true cricketer the season is at an end when the last ball is bowled at Lord's.

At first we were not too sorry. Four months is a long time at even the best of games, and it was pleasant to think that in a fortnight's time we should be getting out our football jerseys and putting new bars upon our boots. It would be great fun going down to the Old Deer Park for the trial games and meeting our old friends. Soon the season would be really started, and every Tuesday morning would bring the yellow card: 'You have been selected to play for "A" XV v. Exiles or Harlequins "A" or Old Felstedians.' And then on Saturday we should let the District Railway carry us out to strange places – Northfields and Boston Manor – places whose names are familiar to us on the tubes, but are distant in the imagination, like Chimborazo or Cotopaxi, places where we never expect anyone to live. For members of an "A" XV life is always an adventure; and then, when the game is over, and we sit back in the carriage lazy and tired, it is amusing to read through the soccer results in the evening paper and learn that at Stamford Bridge 40,000 people saw 'Cock outwit the custodian and net the ball in the first three minutes.' And afterwards we go on to Simpson's and meet our friends from the other games, and eat a great deal of roast beef, and drink a great deal of beer. Oh, yes, there are many compensations for the loss of summer! The autumn passed quickly and pleasantly, but towards Christmas there came, as there always must come, an evening when we sat over the fire and remembered suddenly that it was four months since we had held a cricket bat, that May was still a long way off, and the procession of Saturdays seemed endless. On such an evening we take down *Wisden* and pore over the old scores long after our usual bedtime.

For *Wisden* is the cricketer's bible. The uninitiated make mock. 'What is it,' they say, 'but a record? We can understand your wanting to look up the scores of matches that you have seen, that will recall to you pleasant hours in pleasant company. But what possible enjoyment can you get out of reading figures and accounts of matches that you have never been to? It is no doubt an admirable work of reference for the statistician, but as literature, as a thing that is read for pleasure! Why, it reminds us of the half-pay major who spent his evenings reading the Army List of 1860!'

It is hard to explain. In the same way that the letters x and y possess a significance for the mathematician, so for the cricketer these bare figures are a symbol and a story. We can clothe the skeleton with flesh. We can picture the scene. We know exactly how it happened. We know what the score-board looked like when that seventh wicket fell, we can gauge the value of Strudwick's 5 not out, and when we read 'Ducat lbw b. Woolley 12' we know exactly the emotion of the man sitting at the end of the free seats below the telegraph. 'If only Ducat can stay in,' he had thought, 'Surrey may win yet. There are several people who might stop at the other end while he gets the runs.' But the umpire's finger rose, and we know the depression with which he wrote on the thumb-marked score-card 'lbw b. Woolley 12,' and then pulled himself together and prepared to watch in a dream 'untroubled of hope' the inevitable end delayed for a few minutes by Smith and Rushby.

And, as we study the figures of Warner's many centuries, we are sitting again on the mound, looking into that haze which covers the ground shortly after five o'clock in August, with the sun blazing on to us from the left of the pavilion, and to shield our eyes we have bent the match-card beneath our hats.

How many hours during the year, I wonder, must we spend over our *Wisden*? A great many surely, so many indeed that we cannot help thinking how small is the literature of cricket. Only two shelves in a whole library. There are one or two novels, *Willow the King*, A. A. Milne's *The Day's Play*, a few of Mr Lucas's Essays, the complete works of P. F. Warner, W. J. Ford's *Middlesex Cricket*, Lord Harris's *Lords and the MCC*, a few volumes of reminiscence, one or two textbooks, P. G. Wodehouse's delightful *Mike*, and *The Hambledon Men* – very little, really, when one thinks of the literature that hunting and fishing have produced.

Hardly any poetry has been written about the game. There is a quantity of verse, pleasant jingly stuff of the drinking-song variety, the best of it valedictory, such as Andrew Lang's *Beneath the Daisies Now They Lie*. But the few attempts that have been made at serious poetry have not been fortunate. Edward Cracroft Lefroy, for example, to whom cricket appealed chiefly as an aesthetic spectacle, included in his catalogue of the physical attributes of a bowler the

> Elbows apt to make the leather spin
> Up the slow bat and round the unwary shin.

which is not only poor verse but proves on the part of the author an inadequate knowledge of the no-ball rules.

But perhaps verse is not a happy medium through which to express an enjoyment of cricket. Phrases like 'unwary shin' will intrude themselves, and, although Pindar used to celebrate with equally appropriate ardour the feats of generals and of athletes, the very idea of commemorating in heroic couplets Woolley's two great innings at Lord's seems ridiculous. We have grown so accustomed to reading accounts of cricket matches in the prose style of the sporting press that any other treatment is impossible. Perhaps Mr Masefield will one day attempt an epic of the fifth test match at The Oval, but I doubt if it would be a success. It would be a quaint performance, as though one were to walk down the Strand in court dress of Jacobean cut. The jargon of a cricket report is unsuited to heroic verse, but it is indispensable. If, for instance, we were informed that Hendren,

> Snared into over-confidence, stept back,
> Swinging his bat as though he would eclipse
> The thundered violence of Albert Trott.
> Yet had he not correctly judged the flight
> Of the quick spinning ball.
> > Aghast he heard
> Behind his back the rattle of the stumps,

we should not be very much the wiser. We should prefer to learn of such a tragedy in straightforward narrative: 'Hendren hooked Mailey to the on-boundary twice in succession; but, in an attempt to repeat the stroke to a ball that was pitched further up to him and that went away with the arm, he was clean bowled.'

Indeed, A. E. Housman's *On an Athlete Dying Young* is the best serious poem that can be said to interpret any side of cricket, and that poem is written to a runner. But it is universal, for it contains the tragedy of all professional sport:

> Now you will never swell the rout
> Of lads that wore their honours out.
> Of runners whom renown outran,
> And the fame died before the man.

Contemporary reference to any cricketer no longer playing is made in the past tense. 'Tarrant was …'; and how many of the enthusiastic Ovalites who recall so eagerly the great days of 'Locky and Brocky' pause to consider that their hero is still alive?

The lack of prose literature dealing with cricket is, however, as surprising as it is deplorable. For a hundred years ago the game must have been able to supply an intriguing background for a novel. Lord's was like Paddington recreation ground, and, when there was no match, the public were allowed to hire a pitch there for a shilling, a sum that included the use of stumps, bat and ball: there were no mowing machines then, and the grass was kept down by a flock of sheep, which was penned up on match days. On Saturdays four or five hundred sheep were driven on to the ground on their way to the Smithfield Market. And then half a dozen small boys would run out and pick out any long grass or thick tufts that were still left. It is not surprising that there were shooters then. And never since the days of the gladiators can there have been such wholesale bribery and corruption as there was in the days of Lord Frederic Beauclerk.

Enormous bets were made. Matches were played for stakes of one thousand guineas a side – in those days no small sum, and professionals found it hard to live on their pay; indeed, they made little effort to; and in big matches where a lot of money was at stake it was not uncommon to find one side trying to get themselves out while their opponents were trying to give them easy balls to make runs off. And Lord Harris tells a story of how two professionals had a dispute at one of the annual general meetings at Lord's, and in the presence of the noble lords of the MCC such questions as 'Who sold the match at Nottingham?' and 'Who would bowl at anything but the wicket for Kent?' were bandied about to the consternation, Lord Harris says, 'of some of those present who had lost their money contrary to all calculation on the matches referred to'! There were few newspaper reporters then, and things could be done at Old Trafford news of which would come tardily to Lord's.

The only persons who appear to have remained incorruptible during these early days are, strangely enough, the umpires. Perhaps they put too high a premium on their honesty, and the bookmakers found it cheaper to have dealings with the players, or perhaps there was a general conspiracy of silence, no one being sufficiently without blame to cast a stone. At any rate, the interpreters of the law seem to have given satisfaction, and they can have had no easy time. For it was during these years that the code of rules under which we play to-day was compiled. And it was compiled in a most haphazard fashion. No committee sat over a table and weighed every possible contingency and interpretation of the laws. The authorities were worthy fellows, but lazy and unimaginative. They drew up a rough code and waited for things to happen. If any particular practice began to cause a nuisance they were prepared to put a stop to it. In the meantime let the wheel turn.

It did turn, and often with uncomfortable complications. At one time, for instance, in the days when there were only two stumps, a hole was cut between and beneath the wickets, and when a batsman completed a run he had to pop his bat into this hole. If the bowler succeeded in popping the ball there before the bat the batsman was run out. It was found, however, that bat and ball would often arrive in the hole simultaneously, with sad results to the bowler's fingers; and often enough, when a fieldsman had anticipated the bat, the defeated player would take what revenge he could by driving his bat upon the knuckles of his conqueror. After a certain number of fingers had been broken the authorities thought fit to substitute for the hole the present popping crease.

Much the same thing happened in the case of leg-before-wicket. As pads were not then invented, and as the ball was delivered with much rapidity, it had never seemed likely that any batsman would, with deliberate intention, place his unprotected legs in the path of a hard ball. But one day the cricket world was thrown into consternation by the tactics of one Ring, who placed his body in front of the wicket in such a way that it was impossible for him to be bowled out. His shins became very sore, but his score became very large. This gallant act of self-sacrifice for the good of his side did not win the admiration it deserved; it was described by a contemporary writer as 'a shabby way of taking advantage of a bowler,' so that when Tom Taylor adopted the same tactics the bowlers 'declared themselves beaten': a leg-before-wicket rule was drawn up, and another opportunity for Spartan courage was lost to an effeminate age.

The rules were altered to suit each fresh development. And when we remember the manifold and barbarous practices of that day, we cannot but shudder when we try to imagine what fearsome and horrible atrocities must have taken place before the rule about 'obstruction of the field' was invented. Cannot we picture some burly butcher skying the ball to point and then, in order to save his wicket, rushing at the fieldsman and prostrating him with his bat? Cannot we see the batsman at the other end effecting a half-nelson upon the bowler who was about to catch his partner? – The laws of Rome were not built up without bloodshed, nor were the laws of cricket. What opportunities for humorous narrative have been lost!

If only there had been some naturalistic writer who would have collected laboriously all these stories and made a novel of them! If Zola had been an Englishman we could have forgiven him his endless descriptions of gold-beaters and agricultural labourers, if one of the Macquarts had been a professional cricketer and one of those interminable novels had reconstructed the cricket world of his day. If only the caprice of things had allowed George Moore to spend his early years near a cricket field instead of a racing stable!

But even those few novelists who have included cricket in their panorama of the period appear to be woefully ignorant of the management of the game. What a sad mess Dickens made of it, and how well he might have done it! How entertaining Mr Winkle might have been behind the wicket: what sublime decisions he would have given as an umpire! But, no; Muggleton play Dingley Dell and the great Podder 'blocked the doubtful balls, missed the bad ones, took the good ones and sent them flying to all parts of the field,' which is surely the most quaint procedure that any batsman has ever followed; and as a climax Dingley Dell give in and allow the superior prowess of all Muggleton, apparently before they have had their own innings – an action without precedent in the annals of the game.

And so it has happened that our one complete picture of the Homeric days has come to us not from the novelists, the official recorders of the hour, but from John Nyren, who wrote without any thought of posterity a guide book for the young cricketer. There are some books that, like wine, acquire qualities with the passage of time, and for us to-day the *Cricketer's Tutor* possesses a value that it did not have for those for whose service it was written. To the young blood of 1840 it was merely a manual, a sort of field service regulations; to-day it is a piece of literature; it interprets its period; it reveals a personality.

As we read John Nyren's advice we can see how the game was played in 1820 on rough pitches, without pads, in top hats, and with a courage the depth of which may be gauged from the instructions that he gives to long-stop:

> When the ball does not come to his hand with a fair bound, he must go down upon his right knee with his hands before him: then in case these should miss it, his body will form a bulwark and arrest its further progress.

In those days we learn that spectators were patient folk who sat on backless seats, drank porter, smoked long pipes and made bets about the match. There was leisure then, and John Nyren believed that the batsman should wait to make his runs till bowler and fieldsmen were exhausted:

I would strongly recommend the young batsman to turn his attention to stopping: for by acting this part well, he becomes a serious antagonist to the bowler; who, when he sees a man coming in that he knows will stop all his length-balls with ease, is always in a degree disheartened. He has no affection for such a customer. Besides in this accomplishment lies the distinction between the scientific and the random batsman.

The random batsman: it is an adjective we find often in the *Cricketer's Tutor*. For Nyren had an intense hatred of unskilled success. Cricket was to him an art the technique of which could only be mastered after an elaborate apprenticeship. He distrusted the short cut, and we find him the most bitter opponent of the young idea. He is the eternal Tory of yesterday, of to-day and of to-morrow. And he is very human to us as he stands on the brink of change uttering his solemn warning. For it was towards the end of his career that round-arm bowling was introduced, and it is hard to realise the revolution this caused in the world of sport. It made as much stir and roused as many bad feelings in its own province as its contemporary the Reform Bill. This bowling was described as the 'new march of intellect – style,' and in 1827 three matches were played between Sussex and England to test the merits of the two methods. The county won the first two matches, and the nine professionals on the England side were so incensed that they signed a formal petition 'that we, the undersigned, do agree that we will not play the third match between all England and Sussex unless the Sussex bowlers bowl fair – that is abstain from throwing.' And the great Mr Ward, when asked his opinion, said, 'I can only say cricketers are a peaceable class of men. With this bowling I never see a match that might not end in a wrangle.'

John Nyren was its most fierce opponent, and it is rather pathetic to read his violent and ineffectual protest. This invention would ruin cricket. He saw a new game that would lack the grace and skill of the game as he and his friends had played it. The ball would come so fast that the batsman would not have time to prepare for it.

The indifferent batsman possesses as fair a chance of success as the most refined player. And the reason for this is obvious, because from the random manner of delivering the ball it is impossible for the fine batsman to have time for that finesse and delicate management which so peculiarly distinguished the elegant manœuvring of the chief players who occupied the field about eight, ten or more years ago.

And he goes on to state his belief that if the present system be persisted in a few years longer 'the elegant and scientific game of cricket will develop into a mere exhibition of rough, coarse horse-play.'

What would he say if he could return to the pavilion at The Oval, and see Hitch bowling at how many miles is it an hour? and Hendren hooking him to the square-leg boundary? And the last paragraph of his protest is that of every man since the beginning of time who has seen his day pass, his heroes overthrown, and a rash, irreverent generation in their place.

> I can use my eyes [he writes], I can compare notes and points in the two styles of playing, and they who have known me will bear testimony that I have never been accustomed to express myself rashly.

A forlorn figure, trusting so simply in the permanence of a static world. It is sad to think how quickly that world has passed, and how effectively the machinery of our industrial system has already taken cricket to itself. Nyren's game is no longer an entertainment for a few. It has become part of the national life, and probably, if the Bolshevists get their way here, it will be nationalised with the cinema and the theatre and association football. It is hard to find much in common between the old men who smoked long pipes and drank strong porter and watched Mr Haygarth bat three hours for sixteen runs, and the twenty thousand who flock to the Middlesex and Surrey match because the newspapers have told them to, and who barrack any batsman who plays through a maiden over. Indeed, on those big days, I do not think that you find there the survival of the old enthusiast. You will find him rather on a cold morning shivering at the back of the mound on the third day of a match that is certain to be a draw, when there are only a couple of hundred spectators. No one knows why he goes there. He will be very cold. He will not see particularly good cricket. Professional batsmen will play for a draw in the most professional manner. The fielding towards four o'clock will grow slack, and half an hour before the end the captains will decide that it is no good going on, and that they might just as well draw stumps. Your old man in the Mound knows that this must happen. But he goes there all the same, and at three o'clock he buys an evening paper to read an account of the match and he sees that the reporter says 'Hardstaff was beaten and bowled by a yorker.' And the old man will chuckle, knowing that it was a half volley and that Hardstaff hit over it. And in January, when he reads through his *Wisden*, he will put a tick against that match, with the others that he has seen, and he will add them up and find that he has spent five more days at Lord's this year than he did the year before. He will remember how his grandfather used to talk to him about Fuller Pilch; and he will smile, knowing the superiority of Hendren. And he will continue to watch cricket as his grandfather watched it on cold days as well as warm, when a draw is certain and when there is a chance of a great finish. One day he believes that the professional batsmen will fail, that there will be a collapse and a sensational victory, and only two hundred people will have seen it. He knows that many matches are played in the year and that very few of them yield great finishes, and he knows that the only way to make sure of the big occasion is to go there whenever stumps are pitched. And it is of him that we must think when we would reconstruct the cricket world of 1830.

For Nyren was the Homer of cricket and the Homeric days have passed. In

1922 the soil is no longer virgin. Cricket is a different game, and for the novelist it is less intriguing. There is no betting, there is no dishonesty, and, though we hear whispers of the questionable diplomacy of the northern leagues, it would hardly be possible to invent a cricket story with a credible villain. Nat Gould found no difficulty in writing a hundred novels of the racecourse; it is extremely difficult to write one of the cricket field. No scope is provided for dramatic narrative. Cricket in the lives of most of us is a delightful interlude – pleasant hours in pleasant company; and we do not take our success or failure very seriously. At school it is important: caps and cups are at stake, positions of authority go to the most proficient: and it so happens that the only great cricket book of recent times is a school story, P. G. Wodehouse's *Mike*. But apart from school it is hard to find in cricket a motive of sufficient strength to allow of the development and presentation of dramatic action. On the racecourse large sums of money are at stake. On the success of a horse may depend the future happiness of the hero and the heroine. But I doubt if the result of a cricket match has in recent years ever involved much more than the temporary loss or gain of personal prestige. In *Willow the King* J. C. Snaith chose a cricket match as the setting for a summer idyll, but the author of *Brooke of Covenden* would hardly rank that story highly among his other very considerable achievements. The moment for the great cricket novel has passed: irrecoverably perhaps. And in the winter months we find ourselves returning as of old to a few books of reminiscence and to our long yellow-backed, tattered row of *Wisden*, and of the two we find *Wisden* the more companionable.

ALEC WAUGH, in *London Mercury*, circa 1938

As cricket was considered to be a part of the war effort, facilities at Lord's were offered at reduced prices. In 1940 and 1941 all serving members of the forces were admitted free; the charge to the public was sixpence. In 1942 and 1943 everyone, including the forces, was charged sixpence. In 1944 and 1945 the price was raised to one shilling. At all times officers in uniform in the British and Allied forces were allowed into the pavilion, the distinction between commissioned officers and Other Ranks being maintained as sternly in war as it had been in peace. In summing up these years, Warner put on record those occasions when the premises were in genuine danger of being obliterated.

Anxiety must have been felt all over the Empire for the safety of Lord's in the Blitzes. Though Lord's received the scars of war, happily it escaped any major disaster, though it is true that all round and outside the ground itself, and, indeed, at its very gates, there was heavy damage. The first bomb was in Wellington Road on September 16, 1940. On October 16 of the same year an oil bomb fell on the ground some thirty yards to the left of the bowling screen. Out of this, when it burst, came a photograph of a young German officer with 'With Compliments' written across it.

On November 1 Lord's had a lucky escape when a high-explosive bomb wrecked the Synagogue and a corner of the flats opposite the Grace gates. On December 9 another high-explosive bomb, weighing 1,000 lb, fell just short of the stand in the north-east corner of the ground, digging an enormous crater, which the groundsmen filled up so well that no trace of it remains today. Houses belonging to the MCC adjoining the ground were severely damaged at different times, and No. 6, Grove End Road was completely destroyed. In an incendiary raid the Secretary's house, the Grand Stand, and the roof of the pavilion were set on fire, and a hole in the ceiling of the Long Room still remains as a witness to this visitation. The Lord's Fire Fighting Squad, aided by the RAF and the NFS, did splendid work on these occasions. No. 6, Elm Tree Road was wiped out by an incendiary bomb in March 1945.

When the flying-bomb attacks began many fell in and around Regent's Park. Lord's had a narrow escape when such a bomb demolished the wing of a block of flats at the corner of Grove End Road, and on the other side of the road broke the windows of the Roman Catholic Church, built in 1836, which appears in all the early prints of Lord's. Had this bomb burst a hundred yards nearer, the pavilion might have been seriously damaged. As it was, the roof of the tennis court suffered severely. On July 29, 1944, during the Army v. RAF match, a flying-bomb looked like landing on the practice ground, but fell some two hundred yards short, in Albert Road. The players and umpires lay on the ground, and spectators were to be seen in curious postures in the pavilion and round the ground. Characteristically, perhaps, the first ball bowled when the game was resumed was hooked by J. D. Robertson for six, amid tremendous cheers.

The figure of Father Time on the Grand Stand, as we have seen, was dislodged during the war, but not strictly by enemy action. A balloon in a gale got loose from its moorings, and the cables, becoming entangled with the figure, wrenched it from its setting, and it slid down into the seats in front of the Grand Stand.

SIR PELHAM WARNER, *Lord's*, 1946

As to the actual cricket, being conducted in such unusual conditions, and featuring as it did a great many cricketers who in more normal times would have been enjoying a happy retirement, it sometimes took on farcical and even tragic overtones.

On July 23, 1942, the match between Sussex Home Guard and Surrey Home Guard was abandoned because of the tragic death at the wicket of Andrew Ducat. He had made 29 when he played a ball to mid-on. The ball was returned to the bowler, who had started to deliver the next ball when Ducat collapsed at the wicket and was found to be dead when carried to the pavilion. Such an event had never happened at Lord's before, and the sudden tragic passing of this very popular Surrey cricketer and famous footballer, apparently full of health and vigour, was a severe shock to those present.

SIR PELHAM WARNER, *Lord's*, 1946

'Gentlemen queue here for Players' – Wartime notice indicating rationed cigarettes available at Services Canteen on Lord's Cricket Ground.

'In the event of an air raid good cover from shrapnel and splinters should be
obtained under the concrete stands. Public shelters will be found in St John's
Wood Church, Wellington Court, Wellington Road, South Lodge, Circus Road.
Spectators are advised not to loiter in the street.

Lord's scorecard, August 19, 1942

It was during a game between the Army and the RAF in 1944 that the descent
of a flying-bomb caused the players to fling themselves flat on the turf; and after
they had picked themselves up, the next ball was hooked famously for six by
Captain J. D. Robertson, lately of Dunkirk, always of Middlesex, and subsequently
of England.

GEOFFREY MOORHOUSE, *Lord's*, 1983

MATCHES AT LORD'S IN 1944

Until the flying-bombs arrived in London in the middle of June there
was every indication that the 1944 cricket season at Lord's would
break all war-time records in the matter of crowds and gate receipts.
As it was, the raising of the flat-rate admission charge of sixpence to
one shilling resulted in more money than ever being given to charity.
The sum, £4,217, was allocated as follows: Duke of Gloucester's Red
Cross and St John Fund £2,568, Army Cricket Association £352,
Colonial Comforts Fund £313, RAAF Welfare Fund £242, King
George's Fund for Sailors £220, and RAF War Emergency Committee
£167. Altogether the total paid to charities during the war reached
£11,557. Despite various difficulties 167,429 people paid for admission, against 232,390 in 1943. Bad weather accounted partly for
this reduction and the flying-bomb menace caused some fixtures to
be cancelled.

Wisden, 1945

THE episode of Robertson's six had a Wodehousean postcript which conveys with
admirable precision the atmosphere in the Long Room on those days when the
cricket was inclined to take second place to the exercise of eccentricity among the
gentry.

On one occasion, in 1944, I was at Lord's, sitting on the players' balcony with
Gubby Allen, who was captaining the Army against the RAF. The sinister rumble
of another of Adolf's infernal machines was suddenly audible, and soon increased
to a crescendo. Gubby pointed up at an adjacent thick cloud and, raising his

voice, said, 'I reckon it's just in there.' There was an abrupt silence followed by a sinister whistle. The players threw themselves down and everyone who could sought shelter. The public could only sit and await the arrival of this monster in their midst. In the event it fell 200 yards short, but it made a fair concussion, and we felt a strong blast at that range. There was a slight pause, the crowd laughed in relief and Jack Robertson arose and knocked Bob Wyatt into the Father Time stand for six.

Dick Twining, who had a flair for extracting bizarre comedy from the most mundane situation, was standing in the Long Room beside a very short and immensely stout man truly rather higher in his prone position than when he was standing upright. After the bomb had passed, the members had arisen, and the laughter and chat had subsided Dick became aware of a sinister and regular 'tick-tock' from behind the table. On investigation he found it was his fat friend, who had dived to the floor, and who was now see-sawing like a rocking stone on his enormous belly. The 'tick-tock' was the alternate tapping of the rim of his hat and the toes of his shoes on the parquet as he strove to arise.

IAN PEEBLES, *Spinner's Yarn*, 1977

SOME of the grander wartime matches at Lord's set standards which might surprise a more modern age reconciled to four-day draws and creeping over-rates. Although some of the names involved in the England v. Dominions scorecard in August 1943 are known all over the world, in 1943 this was not so. Trevor Bailey was a mere schoolboy, Sergeant Evans an obscure figure from the Kent Second Eleven, and Sergeant K. Miller an unknown Australian whose bowling, one day to be so fearsome, was curiously innocuous in this match, remembered with much affection, for obvious reasons, by the Compton brothers and by every one of the 40,000 people, including the compiler of this anthology, fortunate enough to be present. Even as I write these words, I can see Leslie Compton arching his tall body back across the white rails of the pavilion, keeping his foothold on the tiny upward gradient, and bagging Constantine's tremendous drive with that endearing modesty with which he was inclined to perform all his sporting feats. No more gentlemanly character ever graced the Lord's turf.

ENGLAND v. THE DOMINIONS
Played at Lord's, August 2, 3, 1943

England won by eight runs. A match remarkable for many changes of fortune and sensational incidents ended at quarter to seven in a narrow victory for England, thanks to Robertson taking the last two wickets in the only over he bowled. Robins won the toss, and England in uneven batting displays did well enough to warrant the closure of each innings. Denis Compton and Ames checked a poor start by adding 56 and, with Holmes in good form, 71 more runs came quickly, while Bailey, exercising discreet defence, helped the Kent batsmen add 112. Compton played a dashing game, but the honours belonged to Ames, who hit splendidly all round the wicket; his chief strokes during two hours forty minutes were two 6s and eleven 4s.

After scoring 93 for two wickets, The Dominions collapsed so badly before Denis Compton at the practice ground end that eight men fell for 22 runs before stumps were drawn, and when Robins in the morning decided that England, although 209 ahead, should bat again, they lost four men for 6 runs—altogether twelve consecutive wickets for 28 under conditions apparently quite favourable to batsmen. Not until Robins joined Holmes did England recover, and they played such fine cricket that 106 runs came in 55 minutes. Robins, quite in his old dashing style, made the bowling length he desired by jumping in or stepping back, and audacity brought him a 6 and ten 4s.

The Dominions did not shirk the big task of getting 360 in roughly four hours and a half. Dempster played grandly. Workman proved such a useful opening batsman that he saw the total reach 80, and Carmody, going in second wicket down, gave such assistance that 104 were added. Third out, Dempster scored his 113 out of 187 in an hour and fifty minutes, hitting ten 4s by beautiful strokes. After tea Constantine played in his own aggressive style, but from a hard drive Leslie Compton caught him with the left hand at full stretch while leaning on the pavilion rails with feet on the ground. This perfectly fair catch caused much criticism as the ball might have been over the boundary, but Constantine knew the rules and said, 'That is cricket'. With seven out for 218, The Dominions looked well beaten, but Sismey and Clarke put on 108 and the final sensation, with two very good catches, finished the match amidst much excitement. The wicket-keeping by Sismey and Evans was always high-class. On Monday the teams were presented to the Duke of Gloucester before lunch. The exact numbers paying for admission were 23,993 on Monday and 14,217 on Tuesday. The proceeds went to the Red Cross Fund.

ENGLAND

H. Gimblett (Somerset) c. Sismey b. Roper	10	b. Roper	0
Capt. J. D. Robertson (Middlesex) b. Constantine	33	c. Sismey b. Roper	1
L. Cpl L. Compton (Middlesex) b. Martindale	1	b. Martindale	1
Sgt Instr D. Compton (Middlesex) run out	58	c. Miller b. Martindale	17
Sq. Ldr L. E. G. Ames (Kent) c. and b. Clarke	133	c. Sismey b. Martindale	13
Major E. R. T. Holmes (Surrey) c. and b. Clarke	39	not out	45
Flt Lt R. W. V. Robins (Middlesex) b. Martindale	2	not out	69
2nd Lt T. E. Bailey (Royal Marines) not out	30		
L Cpl A. W. H. Mallett (Royal Marines) lbw b. Clarke	2		
Sgt T. G. Evans (Kent) b. Clarke	5	b. Roper	0
B. 5, l-b. 5, n-b. 1	11	B. 3, l-b. 1	4
(9 wkts dec.)	324	(6 wkts dec.)	150

Flt Sgt A. V. Bedser (*Surrey*) did not bat.

THE DOMINIONS

F/O D. K. Carmody (Australia) c. Evans b. Mallet.	43	c. Ames b. D. Compton .	49
Lt C. S. Dempster (New Zealand) c. Ames b. Bedser	18	b. Mallett	113
Sgt K. Miller (Australia) c. L. Compton b. D. Compton	32	c. Evans b. Bedser......	2
Sgt J. Workman (Australia) c. Mallett b. Bedser	8	b. D. Compton.........	16
L. N. Constantine (West Indies) c. Mallett b. D. Compton	2	c. L. Compton b. Bedser.	21
O/Cdt D. P. Morkel (S. Africa) lbw b. D. Compton	2	c. and b. Bedser	0
F. A. Martindale (West Indies) b. D. Compton...	4	c. D. Compton b. Bedser.	0
F/O S. Sismey (Australia) lbw b. Bedser	0	c. Bedser b. Robertson ..	70
P/O A. D. McDonald (Australia) lbw b. D. Compton	0	not out	9
C. B. Clarke (West Indies) c. and b. D. Compton ...	0	b. D Compton	52
F/O A. W. Roper (Australia) not out	0	c. Bailey b. Robertson ..	2
B. 3, l-b. 1, n-b. 2....	6	B. 11, w. 1, n-b. 5 .	17
	115		351

The Dominions Bowling

	Overs	Mdns	Runs	Wkts	Overs	Mdns	Runs	Wkts
Roper	9	–	51	1	7	1	36	3
Martindale	10	–	50	2	9	1	28	3
Clarke.........	19.7	1	89	4	3	–	29	–
Constantine....	10	–	61	1	4	–	32	–
Miller	4	1	25	–	4	1	21	–
Morkel	1	–	6	–				
McDonald	8	1	31	–				

England Bowling

	Overs	Mdns	Runs	Wkts	Overs	Mdns	Runs	Wkts
Bedser	10.6	1	33	3	25	1	108	4
Bailey	4	–	15	–	6	1	31	–
Mallett	8	1	26	1	9	4	28	1
Robins	3	–	20	–	12	–	75	–
D. Compton....	8	2	15	6	20	3	60	3
L. Compton					3	–	12	–
Holmes........					1	–	14	–
Robertson					1	–	6	2

LESLIE COMPTON'S CATCH

The two-day match between England and The Dominions at Lord's provided an example of the risk run by applying the declaration after taking first innings. R. W. V. Robins won the toss, declared with nine men out, and secured a lead of 209: yet he preferred to bat again, and his second declaration, after a collapse of batsmen who were forcing the pace, produced a grand finish: Robertson dismissed two men in the only over he bowled and England won by eight runs at a quarter to seven. The effort to get 360 in four hours and a half only just failed, and the result might and probably would have been different but for the left-handed catch by Leslie Compton leaning on the pavilion rails which dismissed Constantine. That grand catch aroused much discussion, but it was perfectly fair because Compton was standing within the boundary when he held the ball.

Wisden, 1944

A FEW weeks later occurred the game whose participants in more than one case turned out not to be participants after all. Middlesex, rendered Comptonless and also unAveried, collapsed in the face of Douglas Wright's bowling on a rain-soaked pitch. The unusual circumstances surrounding this fixture are reflected in the comparatively small attendance figures.

MIDDLESEX AND ESSEX v KENT AND SURREY
Played at Lord's, August 28, 1943

Kent and Surrey won by nine wickets. Steady rain lasting many hours suggested a wet day, but after an early lunch the downfall ceased and the precaution of covering the pitch entirely enabled a start at half-past two. Meanwhile, when everyone present regarded cricket as impossible, the Arsenal Club obtained permission for the brothers Compton to play at Charlton in the opening match of the football season. An injury to A. V. Avery of Essex, who tripped over his bag when leaving home for Lord's, further weakened what could be called the home team, and Arthur Fagg spent the day looking for his bag mislaid on the railway. This mishap merely necessitated a substitute fielding, but G. O. Allen, on winning the toss, found his side so seriously reduced in batting strength that, against an attack which always looked menacing, except in one over by A. V. Bedser, they collapsed badly. In a hundred minutes they fell for 75 runs, the best stand by Nichols and Allen realising 20. Todd started the trouble with a splendid ball, but best of the five bowlers, all in fine form, was Wright, who kept a perfect length with his leg breaks and returned a remarkable analysis. The loss of Fishlock to a juggled slip catch preceded a forcing partnership by E. A. Bedser, who shaped very well, and Ames, the runs being hit off when the innings had lasted seventy minutes: altogether they added 106 in an hour and a quarter. T. G. Evans again gave evidence of his batting ability following admirable work behind the stumps, where the beaten side were further handicapped, R. H. Twining, one of the substitutes, at the age of 53 naturally lacking the skill of Leslie Compton. After the winning hit the game was treated lightly. Considering the weather the attendance was good, 3,456 paying at the gates. The proceeds went to King George's Fund for Sailors.

MIDDLESEX AND ESSEX

Capt. J. D. Robertson, c. Mallett, b. A. V. Bedser	7
Cpl S. M. Brown, b. Todd	0
H. P. Crabtree, b. A. V. Bedser	2
Sgt Instr M. S. Nichols, c. Evans, b. Todd	11
Major G. O. Allen, b. Wright	19
Sq. Ldr R. W. V. Robins, c. Todd, b. Parker	11
G. E. V. Crutchley, b. Mallet	3
2nd Lt T. E. Bailey, c. Evans, b. Wright	7
R. H. Twining, c. Parker, b. Wright	0
Sgt J. Sims not out	11
Capt. I. A. R. Peebles, c. Parker, b. A. V. Bedser	0
L-b 4	4
	75

KENT AND SURREY

L. B. Fishlock, c. Nichols, b. Allen	3
Flt Sgt E. A. Bedser, c. Sims, b. Peebles	54
Sq. Ldr L. E. G. Ames, c. Allen, b. Robins	47
Sgt T. G. Evans not out	56
Sgt L. J. Todd not out	33
B 10, l-b 1, w 3, n-b 1	15
(3 wkts)	**208**

Major E. R. T. Holmes, Sgt J. F. Parker, L. Cpl A. W. H. Mallet, Flt Sgt A. V. Bedser, Lt D. V. P. Wright and A. E. Fagg did not bat.

Kent and Surrey Bowling

	Overs	Mdns	Runs	Wkts
Todd	7	–	17	2
A. V. Bedser	4.2	–	21	3
Parker	3	–	13	1
Wright	5	3	8	3
Mallet	4	–	12	1

Middlesex and Essex Bowling

	Overs	Mdns	Runs	Wkts
Allen	5	–	14	1
Nichols	5	1	12	–
Bailey	5	–	34	–
Sims	7	1	46	–
Peebles	6	–	54	1
Robins	3	–	33	1

Wisden, 1944

As the seasons slipped by there began to pervade the cricketing world, as all others, a sense of something ending in the not too distant future. The steady alteration in the strategic balance, from defence to attack, was reflected in a last-minute alteration to the Lord's fixture-list owing to the call of duty. What might have been the most spectacularly unfamiliar team to play on the ground this century never materialised, for reasons which *Wisden* explains. What had started out as a jocular re-run of the rivalry between the first-ever participants in an international cricket match ended in the summary despatch of a Canadian side which found itself facing, not an American eleven, but a useful local side which included several famous names.

A LORD'S XI v. CANADA

Played at Lord's, July 20, 1944

A Lord's XI won by 213 runs. Americans were to have appeared at Lord's on this date, but their team, chosen entirely from bomber crews, were too busily engaged in the initial stages of the liberation of Europe campaign. Consequently Canada found themselves against stronger opposition. They began well enough, the first ball of the day disposing of Dempster, but afterwards their bowling was mastered. Todd, the Kent left-hander, hit his 151 in two and a half hours, MacBryan and Twining helping him in stands of 111 and 145. The West Indies fast bowler, Padmore, who served in the Canadian Army, bowled almost throughout the innings. Steady slow bowling upset Canada. Northwood and Simpson put on 86 for the second partnership, but the last eight wickets went down for 22 runs. It was interesting to see the flag of Canada over the Lord's pavilion.

A Lord's XI

C. S. Dempster, c. Stacey, b. Padmore	0
J. C. W. MacBryan, c. Moffatt, b. Padmore	57
Sgt L. J. Todd, c. Court, b. Bartlett	151
R. H. Twining, b. Padmore	77
A. P. F Chapman, b. Padmore	8
E. M. Wellings not out	27
Capt. B. B. Waddy not out	0
B. 6, l-b. 2, n-b. 1	9
(5 wkts dec.)	329

Lt Col G. H. M Cartwright, Flt Lt D. Stewart, R. C. A. Fitzgerald and Sgt J. Townson did not bat.

Canada

Cpl J. Court, b. Todd	2
Capt. J. Northwood, c. Wellings, b. Cartwright	35
Capt. S. Simpson, lbw b. Stewart	60
Cpl H. Padmore, lbw b. Cartwright	3

Capt. R. Moffatt, b. Cart-
wright   0
Flt Lt E. Spriggs, b. Cart-
wright   3
CSM E. Matsuyama, c. Todd,
b. Cartwright   0
Sgt Major C. Stacey, lbw
b. Cartwright   0
Major E. S. Williams not out   6
SQMS G. McIlvenny, b.
Waddy   1
Cpl J. Bartlett, c. Townson,
b. Waddy   0
B. 4, l-b. 2   6
                          ——
                          116

Canada Bowling

	Overs	Mdns	Runs	Wkts
Padmore	21	1	112	4
Moffatt	6	—	39	—
Court	15	1	71	—
Simpson	6	—	46	—
Bartlett	8	1	52	1

A Lord's XI Bowling

	Overs	Mdns	Runs	Wkts
Todd	7	—	15	1
FitzGerald	5	—	12	—
Wellings	5	2	21	—
Waddy	4	2	14	2
Stewart	7	1	22	1
Cartwright	7	1	26	6

Wisden, 1945

THE following season, 1945, the year of victory in Europe, proved to be the last wartime season, and in the match between England and the Dominions, played almost at the end of the summer, those crowds who were so wonderfully entertained could not help looking for pointers to the form in the coming peacetime Test series. Miller, Pepper and Cristofani in particular looked as though they might plague the next generation of England Test players. In the event, Miller more than fulfilled expectations, but Pepper disappeared into the miasma of the League the moment the war was over, while Cristofani went home and never was seen at Lord's again. And despite his magnificent batting in both innings, Hammond too was to prove a spent force in international cricket. This was almost his last exhibition of virtuosity at Lord's.

ENGLAND v. DOMINIONS
Played at Lord's, August 25, 27, 28, 1945

Dominions won by 45 runs with eight minutes to spare. One of the finest games ever seen produced 1,241 runs, including sixteen 6s, a century in each England innings by Hammond, and grand hundreds for the Dominions by Donnelly, the New Zealand left-hander, and Miller, of Australia. In addition, the result was a triumph for Constantine, who, in the absence of Hassett through illness, was chosen captain by the Dominions players just before the match began. Both sides experienced various changes of fortune and the issue remained in doubt until the end. Although Craig, a left-hander from South Australia, forced the pace from the beginning, the Dominions lost half their side for 109. Then Pepper and Donnelly added 120. Always master of the bowling, Donnelly hit two 6s and eighteen 4s, being last out. With Gimblett suffering from cramp, Hammond changed his order, and before the first day ended England lost Fishlock, Robertson and Phillipson for 28.

By twenty minutes to one on Monday six England wickets were down for 96, but Hammond and Edrich lifted their side out of trouble with a stand of 177, of which Edrich's share was 65. Against keen bowling Hammond never made a mistake. Three drives off Cristofani went into the pavilion for 6, and he also hit ten 4s, getting his 121 in two hours forty minutes. Edrich, missed in the slips off Williams when 17, scored freely to the on. After Hammond left the innings was soon over, the last three wickets falling at the same total. As Gimblett and Phillipson were unfit, England fielded two substitutes when the Dominions batted again. Fell and Craig opened with a stand of 49, and the second day closed with Donnelly and Miller together and the total 145 for three wickets.

The final stage will be remembered chiefly for the glorious driving of Miller. He outshone everyone by his dazzling hitting. In ninety minutes he raised his overnight 61 to 185, and in three-quarters of an hour of superb cricket he and Constantine put on 117. Though travelling at such a pace, Miller played faultlessly. One of his seven 6s set the whole crowd talking. It was a terrific on-drive off Hollies, and the ball lodged in the small roof of the broadcasting box above the England players' dressing-room. Besides his 6s Miller hit thirteen 4s, his 185 taking him only two and three-quarter hours. This was a wonderful finish to his season at Lord's, where in four first-class matches he scored 568 runs in eight innings, twice not out, with three centuries and an average of 94.68.

England wanted 357 in four and a half hours, and thanks to Hammond, they made a worthy challenge. Always seeking runs, the England captain was twice missed in the deep before completing 50, but, though tiring, he carried on freely getting 102 out of 152 in two hours. His main strokes were one 6 and ten 4s. By hitting two separate hundreds in a match for the seventh time, Hammond set up an individual record. After he left there followed some daring batting by Davies and Griffith, who added 83 in fifty-eight minutes, but England for victory needed to get 74 in three-quarters of an hour when Phillipson joined Davies. Brilliant fielding by Constantine accounted for Phillipson, and next Pepper bowled Davies. Only fifteen minutes remained when the last man, Hollies, joined Wright. In tense excitement Ellis and Pepper each delivered a maiden with the fielders crowded round the batsmen. Constantine then brought back Cristofani, who bowled Wright, and the Dominions gained a grand victory. While some batsmen dominated the cricket, mention must be made of the splendid bowling, particularly that of Wright, who took five wickets in each Dominions innings. Hollies stood up gallantly to heavy punishment and Pepper kept going for long spells in the final innings without losing his length.

THE DOMINIONS

D. R. Fell, c. Griffith, b. Wright	12	b. Davies	28
H. S. Craig, c. Davies, b. Phillipson	56	c. Hammond, b. Davies	32
J. Pettiford, b. Davies	1	b. Wright	6
K. R. Miller, lbw b. Hollies	26	c. Langridge, b. Wright	185
M. P. Donnelly, c. and b. Hollies	133	b. Wright	29
L. N. Constantine, c. Hollies, b. Wright	5	c. Fishlock, b. Hollies	40
C. G. Pepper, c. Hammond, b. Wright	51	c. Robertson, b. Hollies	1
D. R. Cristofani, lbw b. Edrich	6	b. Wright	5
R. G. Williams, lbw b. Wright	11	c. Hammond, b. Wright	0
R. S. Ellis, b. Wright	0	st. Griffith, b. Hollies	0
C. D. Bremner not out	1	not out	0
L-b. 3, w. 2	5	B. 1, l-b. 8, n-b. 1	10
	307		336

ENGLAND

L. B. Fishlock, c. Pettiford, b. Ellis	12	run out	7
J. D. Robertson, lbw b. Constantine	4	c. Fell, b. Pettiford	5
James Langridge, lbw b. Cristofani	28	b. Pepper	15
W. E. Phillipson, b. Pepper	0	run out	14
S. C. Griffith, c. Bremner, b. Williams	15	c. Pepper, b. Pettiford	36
W. R. Hammond, st. Bremner, b. Pepper	121	st. Bremner, b. Cristofani	102
H. Gimblett, c. Pettiford, b. Cristofani	11	b. Pepper	30
W. J. Edrich, c. Pepper, b. Cristofani	78	c. Pepper, b. Ellis	31
J. G. W. Davies, lbw b. Pepper	1	b. Pepper	56
D. V. P. Wright, lbw b. Pepper	0	b. Cristofani	0
E. Hollies not out	0	not out	0
B. 7, l-b. 6, w. 2, n-b. 2	17	B. 6, l-b. 5, n-b. 4	15
	287		311

England Bowling

	Overs	Mdns	Runs	Wkts	Overs	Mdns	Runs	Wkts
Phillipson ...	16	2	40	1	2	1	1	—
Edrich	9	1	19	1	3	—	13	—
Wright	30	2	90	5	30.1	6	105	5
Davies	22	9	43	1	13	3	35	2
Hollies	20.2	3	86	2	29	8	115	3
Langridge ...	6	1	24	—	8	—	57	—

The Dominions Bowling

	Overs	Mdns	Runs	Wkts	Overs	Mdns	Runs	Wkts
Miller.......	1	—	2	—	5	—	28	—
Williams	22	4	49	1	2	—	11	—
Constantine .	15	2	53	1	6	—	27	—
Pepper	18	3	57	4	33	13	67	3
Ellis	4	3	4	1	20	4	54	1
Cristofani ...	23.3	4	82	3	21.3	1	64	2
Pettiford	5	—	23	—	14	3	45	2

Wisden, 1946

By THE time England and The Dominions had battled it out, the great *cause célèbre* of the year had already taken place. In one of those almost-but-not-quite-minor matches which were a regular Saturday affair during the war, one of the rarest forms of dismissal was seen. The Royal Australian Air Force was in the field and bowling to the captain of the South of England eleven, G. O. Allen. It is interesting to observe the similarities and differences between these two accounts of the incident, and interesting also to the editor of this anthology, who was sitting in the Mound Stand at the time, and would be willing to testify that the bowler, Roper, certainly ran after Allen imploring him to come back. However, Allen was right to dismiss the dismissal as silly, and might have been excused for calling it funny, for that was how it struck most of the spectators.

Two laws of cricket are rarely put into operation – obstructing the field and handling the ball – but the latter law was enforced in the match RAAF v. South of England on 30 June 1945. G. O. Allen played a ball from Roper, and it trickled and lay dead at the stumps, which it actually touched. Allen picked the ball up and returned it to the bowler. Roper, perhaps because he thought the bails were disturbed, or perhaps involuntarily, appealed, and Allen was given out. The umpire had no option. As he reached the pavilion Allen was asked to return, but quite rightly declined. Research into history shows that this law had not been invoked at Lord's for nearly ninety years, the last occasion being in 1857, when Grundy, playing for the MCC v. Kent, was so given out, the scorebook reading 'J. Grundy, handled the ball, b. Willsher, 15'.

'I played on to a ball from Mick Roper. Sismey, the wicket-keeper, who was standing up, and I had a good look at the bails and when we found them firmly in their grooves I threw the ball back to Roper as a friendly gesture saying "Bad luck". He then appealed to the umpire, Archie Fowler, a great friend of mine, and I was given out. Later Roper insisted he had appealed for bowled which I found totally unacceptable because of the careful check his own wicket-keeper and I had made. Frankly I think it was a silly decision as, in the light of the long delay whilst the inspection was taking place, the ball must have become 'dead'. The Australians subsequently stated that they had called me back but the only one who came near me was Keith Miller and he was not captain.'

G. O. ALLEN, quoted in E. W. SWANTON, *Gubby Allen: Man of Cricket*, 1985

THROUGHOUT the war, poets and prosodists alike continued to rhapsodise on the virid light flung up from the superlative lushness of the Lord's turf. Probably none of them ever heard of the modest man responsible for the appearance of the ground. Without his astonishing dedicated labours, that greenery would have been flecked with impurities, blotched with the sort of imperfections which have no place in a paradisical cricket ground. During the war this mute hero died unsung – except in the pages of *Wisden*, where he was rightly celebrated, and his career statistics meticulously gathered. Wicket-keepers in particular, who in their wildest dreams hardly dare aspire towards the mark of a thousand first-class victims, would have experienced the deepest depths of chagrin on reading about the number of victims concerned in this whimsical case.

MILLAR, Charles Christian Hoyer, founder and for 55 years president of Rosslyn Park Rugby Football Club, who died on November 22, 1941, aged 81, deserved mention in *Wisden* for a very special and unique reason. He undertook on his own initiative to weed Lord's turf, and Sir Francis Lacey, secretary of MCC, signed a deed of appointment making him 'Honorary Weedkiller to GHQ, Cricket'. From 1919 to 1931 he kept up his task, being particularly busy on summer evenings after stumps were drawn, and his zeal often received comment from pressmen walking to the exit when their duties were done. Mr Millar, according to his own reckoning, accounted for 624,000 victims, having spent 956 hours in his war against plantains and other unwanted vegetation.

Wisden, 1942

NOR did the war remove one iota of the prestige attaching to a Lord's connection of even the most tenuous kind. At least one of the Axis countries tended to be respectful of the overtones of a St John's Wood address, affected by the resonance of the MCC initials. If the following anecdote is based on a profound misunderstanding, that does not detract from the éclat of the Lord's ground. Like the German spies benighted enough to believe that a bowler hat and walking stick were an impenetrable disguise in wartime Britain, the Vatican authorities evidently knew too little about the finer shades of social distinction in the land of their enemy to be able to behave coherently.

In a recent conversation Mr H. Douglas Bessemer told me that when his nephew Gordon Johnston, a prisoner in Italian hands, was elected a member of the MCC in 1942, Johnston's relatives were able to send him a message through the Vatican. In case, however, the Italian authorities should attach a sinister meaning to the letters 'M.C.C.', the message just stated that he had been elected to Lord's. The Italian interpreter at his camp, apparently unaware of the existence of the well-known institution in St John's Wood Road, concluded that one of the prisoners had been raised to the peerage. From that moment Johnston was treated with great respect, and was allowed many concessions, much to his own and to his fellow-prisoners' advantage.

E. W. SWANTON

ACCORDING to the almanacks and histories of the period, little happened in 1946 of much importance. And yet everything happened. The County Championship returned. Test matches returned. A civilised man could once again open his morning weekday paper in the certitude of finding once again the much-loved rubric of the scores of yesterday's matches. For the prescient, there was one tiny straw in a very small wind which flickered across the Lord's grass in late July. It was only the most minor of fixtures except to the pupils and staffs of the two schools concerned, but anyone keeping a vigil for the future revival of English cricket might have been pardoned for assuming a great all-rounder was in the making. As events proved, a great all-rounder he was not. But he was virtually everything else.

CLIFTON v. TONBRIDGE
Played at Lord's, July 29, 30, 1946

Tonbridge won by two runs. Reputed to be the youngest player to appear in a match at Lord's, 13-year-old Michael Cowdrey, in his first match for Tonbridge, contributed largely to the success of his side. When Tonbridge were sent in to bat on a drying pitch, Cowdrey scored one more than the runs made by his colleagues and in the second innings raised his aggregate to 119. A right-arm spin bowler, mainly with leg break, he proved deadly in the Clifton second innings and with Kirch, medium, supported by smart fielding, dismissed the last five Clifton batsmen for 33 runs, so snatching a victory. Exton, with length and spin, excelled as a bowler, taking 14 wickets for 125.

TONBRIDGE

D. S. Kemp, lbw b. Exton	25	st. Lindsay, b. Exton	44
G. Bowler, b. Exton	28	b. Exton	0
M. C. Cowdrey, c. Lindsay, b. Exton	75	c. Lindsay, b. Exton	44
D. K. Horton, c. Green, b. Penny	3	st. Lindsay, b. Bird	51
J. Wrightson, c. Lindsay, b. Penny	0	c. Ritchie, b. Exton	1
G. McNichol, c. Penny, b. Exton	0	c. Lindsay, b. Ritchie	6
A. J. Turk, b. Penny	0	c. Bishop, b. Exton	8

M. J. Bickmore, c. Lindsay, b.
Penny 16   b. Exton 0
J. D. Bickmore, c. Bishop, b.
Exton 1   not out 10
J. F. MacMillan, b. Exton 1   b. Exton 2
P. N. Kirch not out 0   b. Exton 1
     B. 2, l-b. 2, w. 3 7   B. 5, l-b. 3 8
                  156   175

CLIFTON

T. S. Penny, c. Cowdrey, b.
MacMillan 25   absent 0
P. M. Crawford, c. MacMillan, b.   st. Wrightson, b.
M. J. Bickmore 57   Cowdrey 17
M. L. Green, c. Wrightson,   st. Wrightson, b.
b. Cowdrey 56   Cowdrey 6
R. N. Exton, b. M. J. Bickmore ... 9   st. Wrightson, b.
                         Cowdrey 28
M. F. Bishop not out 44   not out 45
R. K. Green, c. Turk, b. Cowdrey. 0   b. M. J. Bickmore 1
D. B. Bird, b. Cowdrey......... 5   lbw b. Cowdrey 2
D. C. Dickinson, b. Kirch 8   b. Kirch 8
R. A. M. Whyte, b. Kirch 0   b. Kirch 0
J. V. Ritchie, b. Kirch 0   c. Horton, b. Cowdrey 0
R. T. M. Lindsay, b. Kirch....... 0   b. Kirch 0
     B. 7, l-b. 1, w. 2 10   B. 6, w. 2 8
                  214   115

Wisden, 1947

W HEN the full repertoire of cricket in peacetime was resumed in 1946, from County Championship to Test matches, keen anticipation was felt and a balmy summer hoped for. In the event 1946 was a damp and discouraging season, and it was not till the following summer that English cricket could be said to have been reborn. By a pure coincidence, this rebirth was centred on Lord's, where Middlesex, for the first time since the triumphs of Warner and company immediately following the end of the Great War, carried off the Championship in dazzling style, thanks mainly to virtuoso batsmanship unmatched in living memory. The season will always be remembered as the year of Compton and Edrich, the summer of the Middlesex Twins, both of whom surpassed Tom Hayward's outstanding record of 3,518 runs in a season. Compton, in setting a new record of 3,816, also broke Jack Hobbs's record of sixteen first-class centuries; his double century for Middlesex against The Rest was his eighteenth, eleven of which came in a phenomenal six-week rush at the end of the season. Compton and Edrich, together with the county openers J. D. Robertson and S. M. Brown, scored over 12,000 runs between them. None of these records will ever be beaten, now that the structure of the county game has been amended to suit the demands of one-day cricket.

Because of this glut of runs, boundaries, centuries, huge stands, Lord's became the focus of the renaissance of English crowds. Attendances broke records; over two million spectators watched cricket in England that summer, and many tens of thousands of them watched it at its best, at Lord's. The overseas visitors that year were the South

Africans. In the second Test at Lord's they were, in that much-loved phrase of Cardus, put to the sword by the Middlesex twins. A third-wicket stand of 370 dominated the match. In the Championship, the pattern was predictable. Middlesex, bolstered by their early batsmen, scored runs in great quantity and at a fast rate; often they would declare with time for a few overs at the end of the first day, when they would snatch a cheap wicket or two and set themselves up for an overwhelming win. Ironically, it was one of their very few defeats which drew from Denis Compton perhaps the innings of the season, even, in retrospect, one of the most brilliant ever seen on the ground. The report in *Wisden* manages to contain its enthusiasm, but nobody present on the ground on the third afternoon of the match was able to do so, nor has forgotten his excitement. So astonishing was Compton's exhibition that the next day, Douglas Wright, the subtlest slow bowler in England, published a newspaper article describing the impossibility of setting any useful field against Compton in this sort of form.

It was in this context of dazzling virtuosity that day after day Lord's accommodated men come to witness more miracles, and rarely being disappointed. The lunchtime radio news programmes would recite the scores in the county matches, and if the sun shone, as it did so often in that summer, and Compton and Edrich were still there and going strong, men would leave their desks, or plead a diplomatic headache and make for the ground as quickly as possible. An anonymous cynic was once quoted as saying, 'It is a curious fact that whenever there is a Test match at Lord's, many prominent business men in the City become strangely unwell after luncheon.' In the summer of 1947 every fixture at Lord's was a Test match, and it was not only City gents who deserted their posts in the cause of great cricket, especially the cricket on view on 15 August 1947.

MIDDLESEX v. KENT
Played at Lord's, August 13, 14, 15, 1947

Kent won by 75 runs. They triumphed five minutes from the end of extra time after one of the most exciting struggles of the season. Kent scored so freely when holding a first innings lead of 72 that they were able to set Middlesex the task of getting 397 to win at more than 90 an hour. When four wickets fell for 135 an easy victory for Kent seemed in sight, particularly as Wright was bowling in superb form. Then Denis Compton found a good partner in Mann, and in ninety-seven minutes the score raced along by 161 before Wright broke the threatening stand. During the partnership most of the Kent fieldsmen were placed on the boundary. Compton hit nineteen 4s in his thirteenth century of the season. He played one of his finest innings. Upon Compton's dismissal, when he attempted another big hit, Kent again set an attacking field for Wright and Davies, who accounted for the last five wickets in thirty-seven minutes for 25 runs. In each innings Wright kept a remarkably accurate length and troubled most of the batsmen with variations of leg breaks and googlies, which brought him eleven wickets for 194 runs. Robertson hit his fifth century in successive matches for Middlesex in the first innings, when Edrich was next highest scorer with 28. All through Kent batted much more consistently. Their biggest stand was 157 by Ames and Valentine for the third wicket in the second innings.

KENT

L. J. Todd, b. Sims	62	b. Hever	7
A. E. Fagg, b. Young	66	c. L. Compton, b. Gray	6
L. E. G. Ames, c. L. Compton, b. Sims	8	c. D. Compton, b. Young	69
B. H. Valentine, b. Gray	61	c. Gray, b. D. Compton	92
J. G. W. Davies, c. L. Compton, b. Sims	4	lbw b. Young	11
G. F. Anson, lbw b. Sims	25	c. Mann, b. Young	51
T. G. E. Evans, lbw b. D. Compton	18	c. Robertson, b. D. Compton	56
R. R. Dovey run out	7	not out	10
D. V. P. Wright, b. Hever	36	c. Edrich, b. Young	11
F. Ridgway, b. D. Compton	0		
N. Harding not out	5		
B. 5, l-b. 4	9	B. 5, l-b. 6	11
	301	(8 wkts dec.)	324

MIDDLESEX

S. M. Brown, c. Valentine, b. Harding	0	b. Harding	5
J. D. Robertson, c. Evans, b. Wright	110	lbw b. Harding	12
W. J. Edrich, b. Dovey	28	c. and b. Wright	31
D. C. S. Compton, b. Wright	16	c. Davies, b. Wright	168
R. W. V. Robins, c. Harding, b. Wright	24	b. Davies	21
F. G. Mann, c. Fagg, b. Wright	1	b. Wright	57
L. H. Compton, c. Harding, b. Wright	6	st. Evans, b. Wright	7
J. Sims, b. Dovey	7	b. Davies	7
L. Gray, c. Todd, b. Wright	7	not out	4
J. A. Young, c. Fagg, b. Wright	17	c. Evans, b. Davies	0
M. G. Hever not out	8	b. Davies	2
L-b. 2, w. 2, n-b. 1	5	L-b. 4, n-b. 3	7
	229		321

Middlesex Bowling

	Overs	Mdns	Runs	Wkts	Overs	Mdns	Runs	Wkts
Gray	17	3	44	1	19	3	70	1
Hever	10.1	2	32	1	15	3	37	1
Robertson	3	1	12	–				
Young	16	8	24	1	38.2	12	65	4
D. Compton	24	2	87	2	31	10	86	2
Robins	2	–	6	–	3	–	18	–
Sims	19	–	87	1	12	1	37	–

Kent Bowling

	Overs	Mdns	Runs	Wkts	Overs	Mdns	Runs	Wkts
Harding.....	5	I	22	I	13	–	56	2
Wright	33.2	5	92	7	24	3	102	4
Dovey	28	5	59	2	20	2	69	–
Ridgway	13	I	46	–	5	–	29	–
Davies	2	–	5	–	19	3	58	4

Umpires: H. G. Baldwin and A. R. Coleman.

Wisden, 1948

AFTER the fireworks of 1947 came – the fireworks of 1948. Or so it seemed when the new season opened. When Middlesex played Somerset at Lord's in the first few weeks of the season, Compton and Edrich actually surpassed themselves. But although Compton was to bat both bravely and brilliantly against the Australians that summer, the fates had already been to visit. In his capacity as the greatest English games player since C. B. Fry, Compton had, concurrently with his cricket career, pursued his footballing destiny with Arsenal. After he and his brother Leslie had won championship medals with Middlesex in 1947, they went on to set a record with no remote chance of ever being approached, by then winning First Division Championship medals with Arsenal. But the strain began to show on Compton's legs; before the season was out the phrase 'Compton's Knee' was to cast a shadow. Certainly on those May days in the match against Somerset, everything seemed quite perfect.

MIDDLESEX v. SOMERSET
Played at Lord's, May 19, 20, 21, 1948

Middlesex won by ten wickets. The match was memorable for a stand of 424 between W. J. Edrich and Denis Compton, which beat all third wicket records in first-class cricket except the 445 by W. N. Carson and P. E. Whitelaw for Auckland v Otago at Dunedin, New Zealand, in January 1937. They stayed together four hours until Mann declared with fifty minutes of the first day still to be played. Steady bowling and keen fielding kept both batsmen comparatively quiet in the early stages of their association, but after tea 209 runs came in seventy minutes, Compton making 139. In his highest first-class innings to date Compton hit three 6s and thirty-seven 4s. Edrich hit one 6 and eighteen 4s. Somerset scored freely, but lost wickets steadily on the second day, when Middlesex claimed an extra half-hour without finishing the match, and forty-five minutes play became necessary on the final day.

MIDDLESEX

J. D. Robertson, c. Hazell, b. Buse   21   not out 22
S. M. Brown, c. Mitchell-Innes,
    b. Buse 31
W. J. Edrich not out 168
D. Compton not out 252

L. Compton (did not bat).......   not out   7
       B. 4, w. 2...........   6

     (2 wkts dec.)   478   (No wkt)   29

F. G. Mann, R. W. V. Robins, H. Sharp, J. Sims, J. A. Young and
L. Gray did not bat.

SOMERSET

H. Gimblett, b. Gray	6	b. Gray 29
M. Hill, c. L. Compton, b. Gray..	3	st. L. Compton, b.
		D. Compton 69
M. Coope, c. L. Compton, b.		
Sims	31	lbw b. Sims......... 59
M. S. Mitchell-Innes, b. D. Comp-		
ton	65	lbw b. Sims......... 8
G. E. S. Woodhouse, lbw b. D.		c. Edrich, b. D. Comp-
Compton	15	ton 8
M. T. F. Buse, c. D. Compton,		c. L. Compton, b.
b. Young	7	Young 59
M. F. Tremlett, c. Robins, b. Gray	40	c. Edrich, b. Robins .. 20
W. T. Luckes, c. Sharp, b. Young	0	c. Edrich, b. Sims.... 27
A. W. Wellard, c. and b. Edrich..	3	c. Brown, b. Robins.. 14
W. Hazell not out	4	lbw b. Robins 5
P. A. O. Graham, b. Gray	12	not out 4
B. 4, l-b. 4	8	B. 5, l-b. 3.... 8
	194	310

Somerset Bowling

	Overs	Mdns	Runs	Wkts	Overs	Mdns	Runs	Wkts
Wellard	39	4	158	–				
Tremlett	15	2	50	–	3	–	9	–
Graham.....	8	–	40	–	2.2	–	20	–
Buse........	33	9	107	2				
Hazell	19	4	56	–				
Coope	6	–	61	–				

Middlesex Bowling

	Overs	Mdns	Runs	Wkts	Overs	Mdns	Runs	Wkts
Gray	14	3	27	4	14	5	25	1
Young	13	8	14	2	19	7	41	1
Sims........	19	2	61	1	29.4	9	78	3
Edrich	9	2	29	1	3	–	20	–
D. Compton .	15	4	55	2	19	3	69	2
Robins					17	2	69	3

Umpires: H. Elliott and P. T. Mills.

Wisden, 1949

THE serious business of 1948 was not, however, breaking old records, but attempting to defeat old foes. Predictably England were outclassed in the 1948 Tests against Bradman's team, but there were consolations. The journalists who arrived in this country to report back to their readers included one writer whose last visit to Britain, in 1938, had been as the side's opening batsman. He was Jack Fingleton (1908–1981), and the fruits of his literary labours eventually appeared as the first in a delightful series of books describing the successive England v. Australia post-war matches. Unlike his English counterparts in the Press box, Fingleton had not seen Lord's for ten years, and his delight on discovering that nothing much seemed to have changed, at least externally, was made manifest in every phrase of his descriptions of his visits there.

Lord's is always a lovely sight for a Test between England and Australia. The historic ground takes on its atmosphere from dawn of the big day, but this time it began the evening before when the inevitable queue formed at ten o'clock. Heading it was sixty-year-old Bill Davies. When the Test was played there in 1938, Davies was next man to enter the ground when the order came out to close the gates. This time he took no risks.

At 11.15, as I walked from the bus to the ground, the queues outside were terrific. It was obvious there were more people who would be unable to get in than there were inside, and so it proved, the gates being closed before play started. There had been a storm to the south of London at eight o'clock and the weather, as Bradman and Yardley walked to the pitch, looked about as troubled as England's cricketing thoughts. But the setting was there. Hats and coats were off in the popular stands, flags were flying, the trees looked very green and lean, and people were squatting contently on the grass behind the white line and in front of the pavilion.

As we looked down on the ground from the Press box, the playing area seemed very small. It would be interesting to know when this habit of marking off much of the ground with a circle first was accepted. On some grounds it is necessary but not, I think, at Lord's. In the game against the MCC here, a ball had only to pass a fieldsman on the Tavern side to become four. Under such circumstances, a century score would not compare with one such when the ground was not circled off. It seems wrong to me, though I admit the anxiety to allow as many people as possible to see a Test. It does not allow a bowler to angle much for catches in the deep, and I was surprised when I put this to O'Reilly and he disagreed. He wanted to know what did it matter ... but I think he would have thought differently had he been in the middle as a bowler and saw shots earn boundaries which did not merit them.

J. H. FINGLETON, *Brightly Fades the Don*, 1949

AGAIN and again Fingleton was to join in the Lord's chorus, but before he could return to report on how Australia would fare without Bradman for the first time since 1928, other visitors were due. In 1949 the New Zealanders, in their Test at Lord's, were the victims of rules of procedure which were becoming more and more complicated as the seasons flashed by. The time was to come, with the dawn of the one-day game, when captains had to be masters of the higher mathematics in order to know what to do next, or even in some cases, to understand what they had done. A portent of this mathematical chaos presented itself at Lord's in 1949.

ENGLAND v. NEW ZEALAND
Lord's, June 25, 27, 28, 1949

Drawn. On a pitch which seemed to improve the longer the match progressed, there appeared little hope of a definite result, but the game was made memorable by an incorrect declaration on the part of F. G. Mann, the England captain, and a brilliant innings of 206 by M. P. Donnelly, the New Zealand left-hander. Shortly after six o'clock on Saturday, with England's total 313 for nine wickets, Mann closed the innings and New Zealand in fifteen minutes scored 20 without loss. At the time he did not realise his mistake, but on Sunday he issued the following statement: 'When I declared the England innings closed on Saturday evening, I thought that the experimental rule which allows a declaration to be made on the first day of a three-day match applied to the present series of Test matches. I regret very much that I was wrong in this respect, but I am very glad indeed that we did not in fact gain advantage from the declaration.' An official announcement from Lord's stated that as no protest was made at the time the match would carry on as if no breach of regulations occurred.

Wisden, 1950

NOT long before the juridical confusions of the New Zealand Test, figures of a rather different kind had arranged themselves to create a record which gave satisfaction to every spectator who had been passing through the Lord's turnstiles since the end of the war. Rising to the occasion of his own benefit match, Denis Compton thrilled the large crowd and received in return what was, by the standards of those pre-inflationary days, the huge sum of £12,000. It is, however, a reflection of the Master–Servant relationship between Gentlemen and Players which still endured as late as 1949 that the bulk of Compton's money was never given to him, but retained by his 'betters', who announced to him their decision to invest it on his behalf. This they did to such wise effect that a few years later the beneficiary of their counsel was informed that the £10,000 with which they had started was now reduced, very neatly, to nothing at all. What, one wonders, would have been the reaction of the tens of thousands of contributors to the benefit fund had they known what was going to happen to their shillings and sixpences?

MIDDLESEX v. SUSSEX
(Denis Compton's Benefit)
Played at Lord's, June 4, 6, 7, 1949

Drawn. Although early rain delayed the start until two o'clock, the match proved a great success financially. On Whit-Monday the gates were closed before lunch, and altogether during the three days

55,000 people were present, of whom 49,194 passed through the turnstiles. Denis Compton won the toss and took a wicket in his first over. Strong hitting by the left-hander, Smith, and Griffith marked the opening day. On Monday, Denis Compton celebrated the occasion by playing one of the best innings of his distinguished career. He took great pains until he became accustomed to the pace of the pitch. His hitting to the on was splendid, and when he reached 103 in two and three-quarter hours his 4s numbered seven. Afterwards Denis treated the packed crowd to a magnificent exhibition of driving and hit thirteen more 4s, his last 79 coming in forty-four minutes. When he left, his brother Leslie punished the tired bowlers mercilessly and hit ten 4s. By staying four and a half hours on the final day, John Langridge deprived Middlesex of any chance of victory, and in the closing stages Jack Oakes drove Young for four 6s and also hit six boundaries, while making 53 in twenty-five minutes. Compton's benefit realised £12,200, easily a Middlesex record.

SUSSEX

John Langridge, lbw b. Gray	1	c. L. Compton, b. Sims	131
D. V. Smith, b. Young	85	b. Edrich	8
C. Oakes, b. Young	25	c. L. Compton, b. Young	52
H. T. Bartlett, c. Young, b. Edrich	4	c. Edrich, b. Young	31
G. Cox, c. Edrich, b. D. Compton	17	lbw b. Young	20
James Langridge, b. Gray	40	lbw b. D. Compton	20
S. C. Griffith not out	68	c. L. Compton b Sims	5
J. Oakes, c. D. Compton, b. Young	1	st. L. Compton, b. Sims	53
A. E. James, c. L. Compton, b. Young	7	not out	31
J. Cornford run out	14	not out	15
J. Wood, b. Sims	0		
B. 2, l-b. 5	7	B. 5, l-b. 3	8
	269	(8 wkts)	324

MIDDLESEX

J. D. Robertson, b. Cornford	1
J. M. Brown, c. J. Oakes, b. James Langridge	66
W. J. Edrich, c. John Langridge, b. James	21
D. C. S. Compton, c. Bartlett, b. Cornford	182
F. G. Mann, b. Cornford	26
K. Sharp, c. James Langridge b. Wood	35
A. Thompson, st. Griffith, b. Wood	3

L. Compton not out.......   59
J. Sims not out..........   19
       B. 7, w. 1   8
     (7 wkts dec.)   420

B. A. Young and L. Gray did not bat.

Middlesex Bowling

	Overs	Mdns	Runs	Wkts	Overs	Mdns	Runs	Wkts
Edrich	16	2	39	1	18	3	65	1
Gray	22	7	32	2	16	7	28	–
Young	30	9	69	4	31	11	123	3
Sims........	14	–	58	1	38	3	111	3
D. Compton .	17	3	64	1	13	3	39	1

Sussex Bowling

	Overs	Mdns	Runs	Wkts
Cornford	26	9	71	3
Wood	24	7	82	2
James	32	8	85	1
C. Oakes.......	29	3	98	–
John Langridge .	1	–	4	–
James Langridge	11	–	56	1
Cox	4	–	16	–

Umpires: A. Skelding and H. Elliott.

Wisden, 1950

SOMEONE who may well have raised an eyebrow at the breaches of the law in the New Zealand Test was the all-singing, all-dancing Jimmy Cannon, who died just too soon to be amused. With Cannon's death went the last link with the old Victorian days before the present pavilion was built. Cannon was as much a part of the history and traditions of Lord's as Dark or Warner, and it says much for his tact and his devotion to the cause that after beginning as a mere servant boy at the beck and call of his betters, he should have enjoyed an old age in which he was at least a member of sorts of the club.

CANNON, Mr. James. For 65 years with MCC at Lord's, died on April 20, 1949, aged 82. He started as a ball-boy for the tennis courts when 12 and held the horses for members when they visited the ground. Gradually he climbed the ladder, becoming boot-boy in the cricket dressing-rooms, and then went into the office where for many years he was chief clerk. A small, popular figure, Jimmy Cannon was given the title 'King of Lord's' by Sir Pelham Warner. A keen gardener, he was recognised by hundreds of people by his straw-hat and buttonhole of sweet peas, rose or carnation. On his retirement in 1944 he was elected an honorary member of MCC.

Wisden, 1950

IT WAS through the dedication of men like Cannon that Lord's continued to enjoy what can only be described as an organic growth. A tiny refinement here, a new facility there, an endless succession of imperceptible advances into the new age. But the Long Room remained sacrosanct, one of the last Edwardian boltholes in London, an easy, spacious room undisturbed by the soprano of the female voice, a magnificent vantage-point from which to follow the cricket, and, on damp, windy days, something like the bridge of a great ship through whose closed windows the distant cricketers moved silently, like white ghosts across the grass. But the Long Room had become something very much more than a vantage-point. The sheer accumulation of pictures, drawings, water-colours, china, old bats of historic significance, had gradually transformed it into something between an art gallery and a museum. Later, some of the exhibits were to be removed to a newly-built museum on the premises, but at the time Warner wrote his history of the club up to 1945, everything worth studying in detail was in the Long Room. Although the MCC collection never quite aspired to masterpieces, it was always a rewarding study. While outside the twentieth century raced on its way, inside the Long Room, ancient heroes looked down from the walls, oddly juvenile old gentlemen in schoolboy caps and coloured blazers, holding bats and balls, celebrities to themselves and to each other.

The Long Room Pictures

The pavilion at Lord's, built in 1890 in order to accommodate the largely increased number of members of the club, contains a very striking feature in its Long Room. The room is over a hundred feet long, and occupies the whole of the ground floor between the two towers. During a match it is the rendezvous of members, who can obtain a fine view of the whole field from the windows, exchange their criticisms and prophecies, partake of such refreshment as may be required to invigorate their enthusiasm or dispel their depression, renew old or make new acquaintanceships, and study the tape records of the progress of matches in other places. During the intervals the collection of pictures on the walls of the Long Room, as well as those in other parts of the building, affords much interest and some amusement to the connoisseurs and amateurs of the game. When Sir Spencer Ponsonby-Fane started the collection, about 1864, he found that the pictorial property of the club was limited to two pictures only, both by Francis Hayman, RA, but both of considerable historical interest. It was a labour of love to Sir Spencer to look out for cricketing pictures, portraits, or prints as they came up for sale at the auction-rooms or in the dealer's showrooms, and as he was able to persuade the Committee to become the owners of many of them the club soon became possessed of a most interesting and valuable collection, to which the generosity of private donors has added a large number. To Sir Spencer's industry and research the club is indebted, also for the portraits of former Presidents which hang in the Committee Room at the south end of the building – but that is another story. The pictures in the Long Room may be divided into portraits and landscapes, with only one or two 'subject' pictures as well.

Prominent among the portraits is that of the foremost champion of the game, Dr. W. G. Grace. It was painted by Archibald Stuart-Wortley, the well-known painter of sporting subjects, and was subscribed for by some three to four hundred members, and presented by them to the club. It depicts W. G. at the wicket in the centre of Lord's ground, standing ready to play the ball, in the correct position, his right foot behind the popping-crease, left foot slightly advanced, with toes off the ground, his left shoulder well forward and head slightly turned to the bowler. His browned, brawny arms (sleeves turned up above the elbow), his massive frame and powerful shoulders, look like the embodiment of strength and drive. Woe betide a loose ball! If on the leg side it will infallibly fly to the boundary just below the old tennis-court and clock, which are depicted in the distance, especially as there seems to be no fielder (or even an umpire) shown in the picture who could intercept a fourer. It has been critically observed that the clock appears to point at 2.30, an hour at which there was never any play in W. G.'s time at Lord's. But this is hyper-criticism! The champion is wearing brown boots, a sign that the fashion of the pipe-clayed boot or shoe had not then come in. A fair criticism of the picture is that the boundary appears rather too distant, the stretch of green from the wicket to the tennis-court, where the Mound Stand now raises its ugly height, being excessive. For an artistic production the colouring is rather gaudy – the grass is very, very green, the red-and-yellow cap (the MCC colours) very bright, the clothes very white, and the arms very brown – but as a likeness of the 'Old Man', as he came to be familiarly called 'in his habit as he lived,' it is incontestably a most satisfying presentment.

The picture of Lord Harris is by Arthur Hacker, RA. There is no special cricket feature in this portrait. It is a pleasant, genial portrait. One would not guess that from 1868 to 1926 Lord Harris had played the game of cricket. The picture represents him leaning back in rather a *négligé* attitude, showing a considerable expanse of white waistcoat, in the armhole of which his thumb is temporarily resting, ready to talk of 'short runs' and long hits, or of the past and present doings of the club and its financial prosperity.

His immediate predecessor as Treasurer, Sir Spencer Ponsonby-Fane, is represented in a portrait painted for the club by W. W. Ouless, RA, in the Diamond Jubilee year. It is a good but not striking likeness. Sir Spencer had a very mobile mouth, often on one side, which gave him a whimsical, playful expression, but the artist has not caught this side of his physiognomy – perhaps he thought the mouth out of drawing. The light colour of the grey suit, too, is so accentuated as to distract the eye from its proper target – namely, the face of the sitter. 'Spencer', though only a name to modern cricketers, was a very familiar figure at Lord's for over seventy years. Elected in 1840, he was appointed Treasurer in 1879, and from that time until his death in 1915 devoted time, energy, forethought, and care to the interests of cricket in general, and of the MCC in particular. But cricket was not his only occupation. He was an officer of the Lord Chamberlain's Department, and was constantly in attendance upon the sovereign at official functions. He was also a keen amateur actor, and was one of the founders of the Old Stagers, who during the Canterbury Week provided theatrical entertainments in the evening for those who had been playing or watching cricket during the day.

A later addition to the portraits is one by Francis Dodd, RA, of A. J. Webbe, a figure well known at Lord's from the time when he first played as a Harrow boy until 1900, when he retired from first-class cricket. Middlesex owes a great deal to him for past services, and it was only fitting that his portrait, presented by members of the Middlesex CCC, should find a place on the walls of Lord's, with which he was for so many years closely associated. It is a good likeness and a pleasing portrait. He sits facing the spectator, in a blue suit, his flannels finally laid aside, the embodiment of friendliness and bonhomie.

Besides the portraits referred to, there is a miscellaneous collection of portraits of famous cricketers: Beldham, who played for England in 1787, and was well known as 'Silver Billy', from the very light colour of his hair; Alfred Mynn, of Kent fame, a demon bowler and a hard hitter to boot; Benjamin Aislabie, who played his last match in 1841, being then sixty-seven years of age, and served as Honorary Secretary of the club from 1822 to 1842; George Parr, of Nottinghamshire, for many years reckoned as the best batsman in England; John Wisden, of Sussex, successful with bat and ball; the Hon. Robert Grimston, a great patron of the game, and President of the club in 1883, whose heart was in Harrow cricket, and so deeply engaged therein that he often found it difficult to watch the Eton v. Harrow match when fate was adverse to his favourite school; V. E. Walker, of Harrow and Middlesex, who played for the Gentlemen when he was only nineteen – a first rate bowler and field; R. A. H. Mitchell, of Eton, commonly known as 'Mike', who was to Eton what Bob Grimston was to Harrow – a painstaking coach, and often an agonised spectator at the crucial school match; Colonel Henry C. Lowther, who played much for the MCC, early in the nineteenth century, but whose title to fame rests less on his performances in the cricket-field than in the House of Commons, where he sat for fifty years without making a speech.

But in addition to the above-mentioned portraits of well-known performers with bat and ball there are several pictures of interest and merit, of which only a few can be selected for attention. There is a delightful picture attributed to Gainsborough, and said to represent the Prince of Wales who became George IV. It was presented to the club by Mr H. Smith Turberville, and depicts a youth with long and fair hair in a picturesque blue coat, yellow waistcoat and breeches, and black shoes, leaning upon a curved bat. He is placed in a landscape which, though beautiful to look at, seems hardly suitable for cricket, as there is a substantial tree in proximity to the wicket (three stumps with a stick across), and immediately adjacent thereto a big stub or two, with a group of vegetation not usually found on a well-conducted cricket-pitch. Gainsborough, or whoever the painter, was evidently more inclined for artistic effect than accurate realism. The colouring, however, is soft and harmonious, the composition agreeable, and the effect satisfactory. This charming picture has been reproduced in colour, and copies are available to a purchaser.

'Tossing for Innings', by R. James (about 1850), is an extremely pleasing picture, perhaps the most delightful picture of the collection. It represents four ragged boys on a common. One has just tossed a bat up in the air and is watching it; so are two of the others, while the fourth is occupied in piling together the coats which the boys have taken off in order to make a rustic wicket. The composition is altogether attractive. It tells its little story of youthful and bucolic enthusiasm with simplicity and charm.

'Portrait of a Boy', attributed to Hoppner, will also arrest the attention of the picture-lover. It represents a youth in a yellow waistcoat and brown breeches, with a ruffle round his throat, holding a bat over his right shoulder. It is evidently well painted, but the general effect is somewhat marred by the addition of a big dog in the foreground, who seems as much out of place in the cricket-field as he would be on a racecourse.

'Lewis Cage' is a copy by Mrs Hughes D'Aeth of a picture by Francis Cotes, painted in 1768. Cotes was a fine portrait-painter in his day, and his pictures are still much admired, though it must be confessed that the crude colour of this one is disappointing. The subject represented is a small full-length of a youth, in green jacket and breeches, with black buckled shoes, his left stocking slipping down his leg, and exposing a bare knee. The left hand rests on his hip, and his right holds a bat, in the transitional stage of development from the curved to the straight form, with much wood in it. The artist's name and date are on the bat. Again a big dog appears, but what is more interesting is a representation of the wicket then in use. It consists of two crutched sticks about a foot high, with a long cross-stick laid over the crutches. This was one of the early forms of wicket. An earlier form was in the nature of a hoop, under which was the popping-hole, into which, while the run was being made, it was the endeavour of the fielding side to hole the ball. It is possible that this idea was derived from the game of golf, a more ancient pastime than cricket. At all events, it was from this term that 'popping-crease' is derived. It is believed that the popping-hole was discontinued in about 1775, and that the third stump then took its place.

One of the figures which should be noted is a curious and remarkable one. It represents a gentleman in a dancing-master attitude, with left leg far advanced, wearing a tightly buttoned double-breasted blue swallow-tail coat, big white choker, dark khaki breeches, and white stockings, a dress not conducive to much freedom of action. His feet are of abnormal, even ridiculous length, and he wields a bat which, looking like Hercules' club, is of gigantic proportions, and would never pass any known gauge.

The series of landscapes, each of which has a cricket match depicted in the foreground, represents the game in the stage of its development between 1745 and 1800. As a game for boys it had been known since the reign of Elizabeth, but it was not until the middle of the eighteenth century that it became fashionable. It was, in its early stages, a combination of stool-ball, cat and dog, and rounders. Horace Walpole mentions it in 1736, and Lord Chesterfield refers to it in 1740. The earliest laws of cricket were drawn up in 1774, and these pictures are extraordinarily interesting as showing the stage of development reached by the game at about that period. From that point of view the pictures give us a record of the nature of the wickets used and the dresses worn. The poet Huddesford, in apostrophising Whitsuntide, invites that season to bring with it cricket 'in slippers red and drawers white'. We should now consider that costume somewhat eccentric, but the poem was written in 1791, and it is evident from the MCC pictures that a dress something like the poet's fancy costume was worn. The players in this group of pictures are shown to be wearing loose white shirts, tight white or black breeches, and white silk stockings. Red slippers or shoes appear in one picture, and red or black caps, like jockey caps, are worn by the respective sides. In some of the pictures the players are wearing pig-tailed wigs, and the umpires always appear in their best clothes, generally also with three-cornered hats. The scorers, too, also in full dress, are often introduced 'notching' the runs on sticks, and sometimes appear to occupy prominent and somewhat 'unhealthy' places on the ground. This is probably due to artists' fancy, who would not omit the opportunity of showing the picturesque dresses and gaining credit for a complete realisation of the scene.

It is interesting to observe that in almost all these pictures the wickets are depicted as two upright forked sticks, generally erect, but sometimes sloping backwards, with a cross-stick resting on the top. In 'Cricket at Hampton Wick' (in reality Moulsey Hurst) the three-stump wicket is shown. This picture was attributed to R. Wilson, RA, who died in 1782, and must therefore have been painted before the latter date, but it is doubtful if the attribution is correct. The presence of the third stump, however, would seem to date the picture about 1775 to 1780. In all these pictures the old curved bat is in use, and some examples of this instrument are to be seen in the collection of articles preserved in the pavilion, which it would not be boastful to describe as a museum. The best of these pictures is undoubtedly that of 'A Cricket Match', by F. Hayman, RA. It is of good, uniform quality throughout, and, apart from its historical interest, is a most pleasing bit of landscape painting.

The general effect produced upon the spectator of these ancient records is that the essentials have been very slightly modified, and that in all important elements – the function of the wicket, the disposition of the field, and the position of the umpires – the game is very much the same as it was 190 years ago. If any of these old gentlemen could return to Lord's in the year of grace he would know perfectly well what was going on, and would be quite at home if called upon to take his place in a team. Some of the later landscapes show the players wearing black top hats, white yachting caps, and sometimes straw hats, and are, therefore, interesting as exhibiting the evolution of dress in the cricket-field. Pads do not seem to appear until about 1845, and it remains for us to conjecture whether they were due to faster bowling or more sensitive shins.

The last picture worthy of attention of visitors is one which, although not introducing any form of cricket, represents tennis in an early stage of development, but combines it with many other motifs. The artist is unknown, and the date, although appearing upon the picture, is not quite clear. It was probably 1534. The distance, a coast-line with steep, rocky mountains, is most delicately and minutely painted in pale blue, reminiscent of Flemish or German medieval art. The middle distance is occupied by a magnificent castle, with gardens, pools, orchards, parks, and a maze, and the foreground represents the walls and bastions of a noble fortress, in the centre of which a game of tennis is in progress. Some of the onlookers are seated along the wall inside the court, a very dangerous spot, while one is peeping through the grille and watching the progress of the game. A remarkable feature is that several of the consecutive incidents in the story of David and Bathsheba are shown as occurring simultaneously. High up on the right hand David observes Bathsheba at her ablutions. In the distance on the left the messenger is seen delivering the King's message to the lady in her bath. In the left foreground Bathsheba and her lady-in-waiting are shown approaching, and in the right-hand corner David, accompanied by two priests in scarlet and black, said to be Luther and Melanchthon, is handing to a messenger his royal orders to Joab, instructing him 'to set Uriah in the forefront of the hottest battle, and retire from him that he may be smitten and die'. The costumes are of the sixteenth century, and are German or Dutch. The delicate minuteness of the painting, its mellowed colours, and the interest of the incidents cannot fail to commend themselves to even the most careless observer. The club is indebted to Mr J. J. Freeman for this very valuable contribution to the Long Room pictures.

The portrait of Sir F. E. Lacey[1] is a good likeness, though the face is rather pale, but the general *ensemble* depicts very well an industrious Secretary working at his desk. Among more recent acquisitions is a picture of the Test match England v. Australia, at Lord's, in 1938 by Charles Cundall, RA, RWS. The picture is good in detail, bringing in successfully the various buildings and stands surrounding the ground. The pavilion itself seems somewhat dwarfed. The green of the turf is not quite satisfactory, having a rather pale tinge, while the players seem more indicated than painted. A portrait of Benjamin Aislabie mounted on a horse in hunting kit is a pleasant picture, if the horse is somewhat stiff and the pink coat rather killed by the red brick wall in the stableyard. A water-colour sketch of Lambert reading a newspaper is a clever portrait, with light but artistic touch.

From Sir Jeremiah Colman's collection was recently purchased a picture attributed to Paul Sandby, RA, painted by the gouache method, honey and gum being added to the pigments. It is an early picture, two stumps only being used in the match in progress. It has been suggested that the scene is on the Yorkshire wolds at sunset. Perhaps owing to some fading of the colouring, the first impression is of a match played upon the ice, an idea dispelled by the foliage on the trees. It is a picture entirely *sui generis*, and to be fully appreciated would be best hung apart from any other distraction.

Of all the paintings at Lord's none gives a better picture of a match than one by W. J. Bowden, dated 1852. The scene may possibly be Daniel Day's ground at Itchen, near Southampton. To the right of the picture there is a crowd of spectators in mid-Victorian costumes which is a pleasing medley of colour, and the players and umpires are well depicted. Apparently one of the sides is a naval team, for the white ensign is flying in a corner of the ground.

Outside the Long Room, on the stairs on the left side leading to the dressing-rooms, has been assembled a collection of portraits by Nicholas Wanostracht (N. Felix). The earliest, dated 1847, is of the Right Hon. Sir Spencer Ponsonby-Fane batting. There are three of Felix himself, one of Felix with Alfred Mynn, also

---

[1] I am indebted to an artistic cricketing friend for these remarks on Sir Francis Lacey's portrait and other pictures.

Alfred Mynn, William Mynn, W. Dorrington, Daniel Day, and William Clarke. Two sketches of Brighton and a print of the All England Eleven, one of Felix's best-known compositions, all show what a veritable artist Felix was, both in portraiture and landscape.

A rearrangement of all the pictures, prints, and photographs at Lord's is now *sub judice,* and a few in the Long Room may be moved to other parts of the pavilion.

In the Long Room – that historical picture-gallery of the game – you may meet men who have seen and done things – Viceroys, Governor-Generals, Prime Ministers, Cabinet Ministers, members of Bench and Bar, sailors, soldiers, and airmen, with famous Bishops and Church dignitaries (especially during the Varsity, Eton v. Harrow and Test matches), and great Civil Servants, diplomats, famous captains of industry – men of varying views and interests and ideas, but all united in a common bond and love of cricket.

The whole atmosphere is easy and pleasant, and for that the Secretaries have been largely responsible, a tradition fully maintained by those now in office – Colonel Rait Kerr and R. Aird.

And in these days, when cricket has become the interest of the whole of the British Empire and Commonwealth, and, indeed, of almost half the world, whither should cricketers turn for guidance but to the club which has grown up with the game, which has fostered it, and which has always endeavoured to preserve its finest traditions?

VISCOUNT ULLSWATER, in SIR PELHAM WARNER, *Lord's,* 1946

THOSE paintings and drawings so eloquently described by Lord Ullswater have been slumbering on the Long Room walls with the sense of permanence which comes from complete security of tenure. No Trott-impelled grenade can ever penetrate, no Jessopian catapult ever disturb the deep peace of the Long Room. But there have been rare occasions when the serenity of the building has been rudely broken by some unexpected event. In 1949 the Derbyshire bowler Gladwin was dismissed in a way which ruffled his sense of what was right and proper. *Wisden,* the soul of tact, gave him the benefit of the doubt so blatantly that posterity may be forgiven for discerning the grin behind the hand:

MIDDLESEX v. DERBYSHIRE
Lord's, August 24, 25, 26, 1949

The equanimity of the Lord's pavilion was disturbed when Gladwin, after being run out by his partner, accidentally put his bat through the dressing-room window.

Wisden, 1950

BY 1949 the status of the great Lord's hero, Denis Compton, had become virtually legendary, and, at the age of thirty, he had become the subject of a biography, in which glimpses of the workings of the Lord's ground, with particular stress on its accommodation of apprentice-cricketers, remain of some interest.

The practice ground is called the Nursery because it was once a market garden, but the name is doubly appropriate since the Nursery is the home of the junior players on the Lord's staff. If you hear a twittering from the ivy-clad Clock Tower at the Nursery End it may not all be coming from the sparrows, for on its flat roof in their time off perch the fifteen-year-olds who pull the roller, sell scorecards, clean up the ground when play is over, and generally answer the call of the groundsman. The Lord's staff is divided into four classes, and only those who have graduated into the First have their headquarters in the pavilion. Young Compton, of course, toed the line in the Fourth Class. He saw all he could of the cricket in the intervals of doing his job, played on two afternoons a week in the nets under the wise instruction of George Fenner and, later, of Archie Fowler, the senior professionals, and looked forward to his matches on Sundays with his father's team, or with Stamford Hill.

E. W. SWANTON, *Denis Compton, a Sketch,* 1949

THIS was the year in which a major shift in the balance of power was discerned in Test cricket. The West Indians under Frank Worrell came to England and blazed a trail, through the brilliance of their batsmen, especially Weekes, Walcott and the captain himself, and through the great strength of their spin attack represented by A. L. Valentine and S. Ramadhin. It was at Lord's, in the second Test, that the tourists not only scored their first ever Test victory in England, but achieved it in a style so mature, and before crowds so huge, that from now on the primacy of Australia as visitors to English cricket grounds was no longer to be taken for granted. The gaiety of the occasion was underlined by the great increase in the number of West Indian immigrants, who were able to attend the match and to lend a serious occasion a tinge of carnival. Calypso and multi-coloured shirts had arrived at the bastion of the old grandees.

ENGLAND v. WEST INDIES
Second Test Match
Played at Lord's, June 24, 26, 27, 28, 29, 1950

West Indies won by 326 runs. They fully merited their first Test victory in England, which, to their undisguised delight, was gained at the headquarters of cricket. In batting, bowling and fielding they were clearly the superior side, with Ramadhin this time the more successful of the two 20-year-old spin bowlers who during the 1950 summer wrought such destruction among English batsmen. In the match Ramadhin took eleven and Valentine seven wickets.

England, already without Compton, suffered further setbacks before the game began by the withdrawal through injury of Simpson and Bailey. In view of heavy rain on Friday, the selectors gambled on the pitch being helpful to spin by choosing Wardle, left-arm slow, to replace Bailey, but instead the turf played easily from the start, and Yardley found himself with three slow bowlers who turned the ball from leg; he would have wished to bowl all of them from the same end. The teams were presented to the King just before the start when 30,500 were inside the ground, the gates having been closed.

Although Wardle took a wicket with his first ball in Test cricket in England by getting rid of Stollmeyer at 37, West Indies were so much on top that shortly after four o'clock the total stood at 233 for two. Brilliant stroke-play came from Worrell, who drove delightfully and made some astonishing late cuts, and Weekes, whose 63 in ninety minutes contained ten 4s, but Rae, in much less spectacular manner, performed even more important work for West Indies.

A fine ball by Bedser which swung away and broke back after pitching shattered the wicket of Weekes at 233, and from that point England fought back splendidly. Clever slow bowling by Jenkins, in particular, raised England hopes after tea. In a twenty-minute spell of seven overs he sent back Walcott, Rae and Gomez. Rae, who was badly missed in the gully off Bedser when 79, made no other mistake during a patient innings lasting four hours forty minutes, in which he scored 106 out of 273. At times he appeared content to continue a passive defensive policy, but occasionally he would abandon these tactics, as when in one over he hit Jenkins for three of his fifteen 4s. Largely through the inspiration of Yardley, England atoned for earlier catching errors by first-class ground fielding, and in view of the nature of the pitch they could feel satisfied with their performance of taking seven wickets for 320 runs on the opening day. Bedser was the most consistent and reliable bowler, but luck went against him, especially when he saw two catches missed off him during a fine spell of 22 overs for 17 runs with the new ball.

No more than ten minutes were required to finish the innings on Monday, but England's reply was disappointing in the extreme. Neither Hutton nor Washbrook was in his best form, but both played well enough to take the score to 62 before Hutton dashed down the pitch and was stumped yards out. This began a rout which was checked only by spirited hitting by Wardle, who punched six 4s and took part with Berry in the second highest stand of the innings, 29 for the last wicket.

No blame could be attached to the pitch. It gave slow bowlers a little help, but only to those who used real finger spin as did Ramadhin and Valentine. Ramadhin bowled with the guile of a veteran. He pitched a tantalising length, bowled straight at the wicket and spun enough to beat the bat. No English batsman showed evidence of having mastered the problems of deciding which way Ramadhin would spin and he was too quick through the air for any but the most nimble-footed to go down to meet him on the half-volley with any consistency. Valentine lent able support, but the English batsmen might, with profit, have tackled him more boldly. England's score was their lowest for a completed innings in a home Test against West Indies.

Thanks to a remarkably sustained spell of bowling by Jenkins, England prevented West Indies in their second innings from placing themselves in an impregnable position until the association of Walcott and Gomez. Previously Weekes, Worrell and Stollmeyer gave another exhibition of masterly stroke-play, but with only a twenty-minute rest Jenkins kept one end going from the start until tea, and deserved the reward of the four wickets which fell to him.

Unfortunately for England a second series of fielding blunders played into the hands of West Indies at a time when a slight prospect of victory seemed to exist. The most expensive of these occurred when Walcott had scored nine. He was missed at slip off Edrich, who bowled with plenty of life in using the new ball. Before England met with another success Walcott and Gomez put on 211, beating the record for the sixth wicket in England v. West Indies Tests established a few weeks earlier at Manchester by Evans and T. E. Bailey. Walcott and Gomez also set up a record Test stand for any West Indies wicket in England. When Goddard declared, setting England 601 to get to win with nearly two days to play, Walcott, the six-foot-two wicket-keeper-batsman, was only one short of the highest score by a West Indies player in Test cricket in England, 169 not out by G. Headley in 1933. As usual, Walcott scored the majority of his runs by drives, even against the good-length or shorter ball, and leg sweeps. He hit twenty-four 4s. Gomez did not put such force into his strokes, but he provided an admirable and valuable foil.

Two batsmen distinguished themselves in England's second innings. For five hours and a half Washbrook withstood the attack, and his only mistake occurred when, at 93, he gave a hard chance to mid-on. Otherwise he batted excellently; although for the most part refusing to take a risk he hit one 6 and fourteen 4s.

The only other success was Parkhouse, who signalised his first Test with a very good innings, in which he showed encouraging confidence and a variety of strokes until he hit a full toss straight to silly mid-off in the last over of the fourth day when wanting only two runs for 50. This mistake came at a time when thoughts were raised that Washbrook might be capable of saving the match if someone could stay with him. Hutton again was dismissed curiously. He made no stroke at a ball which came with Valentine's arm and hit the middle stump.

England started the last day with six wickets left and 383 runs required to win, but when Ramadhin yorked Washbrook, who did not add to his score, the end was in sight and nothing happened to check the inevitable defeat. Ramadhin and Valentine were again the chief executioners. During the five days the full attendance was 112,000.   R.J.H.

West Indies

A. F. Rae, c. and b. Jenkins	106	b. Jenkins 24
J. B. Stollmeyer, lbw b. Wardle	20	b. Jenkins 30
F. M. Worrell, b. Bedser	52	c. Doggart, b. Jenkins 45
E. Weekes, b. Bedser	63	run out 63
C. L. Walcott, st. Evans, b. Jenkins	14	not out 168
G. E. Gomez, st. Evans, b. Jenkins	1	c. Edrich, b. Bedser . 70
R. J. Christiani, b. Bedser	33	not out 5
J. D. Goddard, b. Wardle	14	c. Evans, b. Jenkins . 11
P. E. Jones, c. Evans, b. Jenkins	0	
S. Ramadhin, not out	1	
A. L. Valentine, c. Hutton, b. Jenkins	5	
B 10, l-b 5, w 1, n-b 1	17	L-b 8, n-b 1.. 9
	326	(6 wkts dec.)425

1/37 2/128 3/233 4/262 5/273
6/274 7/320 8/320 9/320

1/48 2/75 3/108
4/146 5/199 6/410

England

L. Hutton, st. Walcott, b. Valentine	35	b. Valentine 10
C. Washbrook, st. Walcott, b. Ramadhin	36	b. Ramadhin....... 114
W. J. Edrich, c. Walcott, b. Ramadhin	8	c. Jones, b. Ramadhin 8
G. H. G. Doggart, lbw, b. Ramadhin	0	b. Ramadhin....... 25
W. G. A. Parkhouse, b. Valentine. .	0	c. Goddard, b. Valentine 48
N. W. D. Yardley, b. Valentine	16	c. Weekes, b. Valentine 19
T. G. Evans, b. Ramadhin........	8	c. Rae, b. Ramadhin 2
R. O. Jenkins, c. Walcott, b. Valentine	4	b. Ramadhin....... 4
J. H. Wardle, not out............	33	lbw. b. Worrell..... 21
A. V. Bedser, b. Ramadhin.......	5	b. Ramadhin....... 0
R. Berry, c. Goddard, b. Jones....	2	not out 0
B 2, l-b 1, w 1...........	4	B 16, l-b 7... 23
	151	**274**

1/62 2/74 3/74 4/75 5/86
6/102 7/110 8/113 9/122

1/28 2/57 3/140
4/218 5/228 6/238
7/245 8/258 9/258

England Bowling

	Overs	Mdns	Runs	Wkts	Overs	Mdns	Runs	Wkts
Bedser....	40	14	60	3	44	16	80	1
Edrich....	16	4	30	—	13	2	37	—
Jenkins ...	35.2	6	116	5	59	13	174	4
Wardle ...	17	6	46	2	30	10	58	—
Berry	19	7	45	—	32	15	67	—
Yardley...	4	1	12	—				

West Indies Bowling

	Overs	Mdns	Runs	Wkts	Overs	Mdns	Runs	Wkts
Jones.....	8.4	2	13	1	7	1	22	—
Worrell...	10	4	20	—	22.3	9	39	1
Valentine .	45	28	48	4	71	47	79	3
Ramadhin	43	27	66	5	72	43	86	6
Gomez ...					13	1	25	—
Goddard ..					6	6	—	—

Umpires: D. Davies and F. S. Lee.

Wisden, 1951

Troubles of a different kind were looming over the heads of the governors of English cricket. Defeat at the hands of the West Indians was one thing, but the coming tour of Australia was quite another. Death duties, high taxes, and the Welfare State were conspiring to cut off the supply of moneyed amateurs with enough leisure and talent to lead the national side. The stopgap ex-professional Walter Hammond had retired; G. O. Allen, who had so gallantly led the team to the West Indies in 1947–48 at the advanced age of 46, was no longer available. The selectors then offered the captaincy in Australia to the Middlesex captain F. G. Mann, who was obliged to reject the offer because of business commitments. The selectors then turned to Norman Yardley of Yorkshire, but he too declined for similar reasons. At this point the Gentlemen v. Players match was played at Lord's. The captaincy of the Gentlemen, a post generally recognised as being of deep significance with reference to the England leadership, was offered, and was accepted, by F. R. Brown, captain of Northants. The announcement caused great surprise. Brown, whose career had been interrupted by the same business demands which restricted the movements of Mann and Yardley, had not been connected with international cricket since as a youngster he had toured Australia as a leg-break bowler with Douglas Jardine's Bodyline army in 1932–33. His spirited, swashbuckling style of leadership had revived the flagging fortunes of Northants, for whom during the season he had scored over 800 runs and taken 70 wickets. Even so, the contortions apparently being performed by the selectors in their efforts to find a captain struck most people outside Lord's as ungainly.

The last week has not gone by without some more than usually virulent criticism directed against the MCC for its handling of current affairs. It may be that through history Lord's has thrived on criticism. Certainly, in cricket's evolution, daily writings, as well as the more permanent literature, have had a deep and it could be said usually constructive influence. But the insulting insinuations as to a prejudice against the professionals that have been made in connection with the finding of a captain for Australia do not come into this category. I cannot discover either from correspondence or in conversation that among the keener or more enlightened enthusiasts much of the mud has stuck, but the more casual follower, in whose imagination the hierarchy at Lord's probably bears some faint resemblance to the cartoonist's dream, featuring tall hats and an abundance of watch-chain and whisker, may well be wondering what is behind all the fuss.

E. W. Swanton, in *The Daily Telegraph*, 1950

What was behind the fuss was the realisation among the administrators of English cricket that at last the once endless supply of suitable gentlemen-cricketers was drying up. In retrospect this simple fact, with no social or political riders attached, seems so obvious as to be a truism. But at the time, with everyone falling over himself not to offend anyone, it must have been difficult to the brink of impossibility for the facts of the case to be acknowledged. When Brown was announced as the captain of the Gentlemen, desperate measures certainly seemed in the wind. If Brown had never remotely pushed himself into Test contention in his prime, how could his possible selection be justified at the age of forty? At which point fate came to the rescue of the selectors. Brown performed brilliantly for the Gentlemen at Lord's, playing what Jack Fingleton later described as 'one of the greatest innings in the whole history of these matches, making 122 in an hour and fifty minutes, and this 122 out of the last 131 scored by the Gents'. A more interesting reaction to Brown's famous innings is Swanton's: 'Brown's runs were the product of a style of play which is essentially that of a cricketer not under the restraint and taboos of one who plays the game for a living.' And this indeed was the theory behind the belief that only an amateur could encourage brighter, braver cricket, although the annual evidence of the Oxford–Cambridge match, in which all twenty-two players were inclined to bat like insurance policy holders, was laughing in the face of what once might have been a valid theory. It was not professionalism which was robbing cricket of its light, but the times themselves. Cardus's belief that societies get the cricket they deserve was, and will remain, perfectly true, and in post-war, rationed, austerity Britain the days of the swashbuckler were strictly numbered. For the moment, however, Brown staved off the *zeitgeist* and went to Australia as captain, where he conducted himself so effectively that although England lost again, they did so with much honour. The game at Lord's which was to settle the fate of England's captaincy proceeded from sport to politics in a matter of moments, as the accounts of the game disclose. No sooner had Brown's great innings ended than he was called in before the committee, like a candidate for a coveted job being interviewed by the board of directors – which is exactly what he and they were.

GENTLEMEN v. PLAYERS
Lord's, July 26, 27, 28, 1950

Drawn. A match worthy of the traditions of its title became specially memorable because of two features. One was the gloriously thrilling finish. The Players accepted the challenge of a declaration by Brown which set them 253 to win in two and a half hours so spiritedly that with twenty minutes left and seven wickets in hand they required 36. From this point such a transformation occurred that in seventeen minutes six more batsmen were out, three the victims of a hat-trick by Knott. When Hollies, the last man, joined Wright five balls remained and eleven runs were needed for victory. Amidst tense excitement Hollies managed to keep the last deliveries out of his wicket and away from the clutching hands of the ten fieldsmen crouched in a circle only a few yards from the bat.

A superb display by Brown, reminiscent of H. T. Bartlett's magnificent innings in the 1938 game, also placed the contest above the ordinary. On the opening day, after his side had been put in, Brown launched a remarkable attack on the bowling. His fierce driving recalled memories of bygone days. So completely was he the master that he scored all but nine of the 131 runs made in the 110 minutes he batted. He hit sixteen 4s and celebrated his century with a six into the pavilion. Other good innings for the Gentlemen were those of Dewes and Doggart. Dewes, in an unusually free mood, put much power into his hits, which included one 6 and ten 4s, and Doggart charmed by his varied stroke-play.

Just as Brown pulled round the Gentlemen, so Dollery, the Players' captain, rescued his side after four wickets, three in succession to Brown, went down for 71. Dollery never looked in difficulty and he cut, drove or hooked with strength and expert placing. He received good assistance from Bedser in a seventh-wicket stand of 116. As soon as the Gentlemen team left the field upon Dollery's declaration on the second day Brown was invited to captain the side to Australia during the winter, and by the time his team began batting he was sitting in Committee discussing the first cricketers to be picked for the tour. Simpson and Dewes opened the Gentlemen's second innings with a stand of 103, and Doggart and Insole also batted well, as did Parkhouse a second time for the Players. Of the bowlers, Wright showed good form, Tattersall kept a tantalisingly accurate length with off-breaks rolled rather than spun, and Knott grasped his opportunities cleverly when the Players were racing for runs in the final dramatic overs.

Gentlemen

R. T. Simpson, c. and b. Bedser...	10	lbw b. Hollies......	69
J. G. Dewes, c. Washbrook, b. Tattersall....................	94	b. Tattersall.......	48
G. H. G. Doggart, b. Wright......	75	lbw b. Wright......	36
D. B. Carr, b. Tattersall.........	0	c. Bedser, b. Wright.	17
D. J. Insole, c. Evans, b. Wright...	4	not out..........	38
N. W. D. Yardley, run out........	5		
T. E. Bailey, c. Parkhouse, b. Bedser	5		
F. R. Brown, b. Tattersall........	122	not out..........	22
J. J. Warr, b. Wright...........	2		
D. V. Brennan, b. Hollies........	0		
C. J. Knott, not out............	1		
B 5, l-b 2..............	7	B 1, l-b 3, n-b 1..	5
	325	(4 wkts dec.)	235

Players

H. Gimblett, lbw b. Brown.......	23	c. Knott, b. Bailey..	14
C. Washbrook, c. Insole, b. Bailey.	0	c. and b. Brown....	43
W. G. A. Parkhouse, b. Brown....	29	c Brown, b. Knott..	81
D. J. Kenyon, lbw b. Brown......	5	c. Brennan, b. Bailey	54
H. E. Dollery, c. Brennan, b. Doggart	123	c. Yardley, b. Knott.	20
T. G. Evans, b. Bailey...........	19	st. Brennan, b. Knott	9
D. Shackleton, c. Simpson, b. Knott	25	c. Insole, b. Knott..	2
A. V. Bedser, c. Dewes, b. Knott..	59	b. Bailey..........	10
R. Tattersall, lbw b. Doggart.....	12	st. Brennan, b. Knott	0
D. V. P. Wright, not out.........	6	not out...........	2
W. E. Hollies, not out...........	1	not out...........	0
B 2, l-b 4..............	6	B 2, l-b 5...	7
(9 wkts dec.)	308	(9 wkts)	242

Players Bowling

	Overs	Mdns	Runs	Wkts	Overs	Mdns	Runs	Wkts
Bedser....	23	2	77	2	12	—	41	—
Shackleton	18	3	51	—	13	—	60	—
Tattersall .	16.4	6	38	3	10	—	35	1
Hollies ...	23	8	49	1	12	1	43	1
Wright ...	25	4	103	3	9	—	51	2

Gentlemen Bowling

	Overs	Mdns	Runs	Wkts	Overs	Mdns	Runs	Wkts
Bailey	25	6	65	2	14	2	59	3
Warr.....	21	5	66	—	8	1	38	—
Yardley...	10	1	23	—	4	—	13	—
Brown ...	28	3	63	3	10	—	59	1
Knott	21	2	63	2	11	—	66	5
Carr	2	—	11	—				
Doggart ..	4	1	11	2				

Umpires: K. McCanlis and A. Skelding.

Wisden, 1951

No sooner had the excitement over Brown's captaincy died down than a fresh storm broke at Lord's. In the side to tour Australia there was no Edrich. This was a piece of selectorial insanity which has never been explained, although Fingleton in his book of the tour sensed that no matter who might refuse a trip to Australia that winter, and no matter what replacement batsmen might be required, Edrich would never be asked. The nature of the misdemeanour he may have committed has never been breathed, but it could hardly have been to do with his cricket. On form, Edrich would have been one of the automatic choices for the tour.

His omission caused general surprise, although neither his form nor his health had been good. There was a period in that summer when Edrich was in plaster because of spine injury. There was an occasion, too, when Edrich joined in the general laughter at Lord's against himself. He was playing against the West Indians and had been making exceedingly heavy weather of things against Ramadhin and Valentine. He was in all sorts of bother and, from the Tavern, the barrackers were chiding him. In mock disgust, at the end of the over, Edrich lifted his bat to his shoulder and, using it machine-gun style, ran it along the rows of barrackers. Next minute he was out.

A voice from the Tavern: 'Now go away and shoot yourself!'

J. H. FINGLETON, *Brown and Company,* 1951

IN that same summer, amid great issues like the England captaincy and the banishing of Edrich, the cricket-lovers of England found other worries to exercise their minds. Not even a ground as meticulously regulated as Lord's can always insure against calamity. And when it does allow its etiquette to slip for a moment, we can be sure that no matter how tiny the congregation present, the eagle eye of fussiness will spot the error and come swooping down on the heads of the Committee. The following letter to the editor of *The Times* suggests that there are those whose interest in the cricket is sometimes secondary to the search for solecism. No matter that the game was minor, that the crowd was small, that nobody else took offence. The crime was a heinous one and the culprits must be castigated.

Sir, The guardsman who dropped his musket on
parade is forgotten – outclassed. Today at Lord's,
during the Royal Navy v. Royal Air Force match,
the White Ensign flew above the pavilion upside
down! From before the match until the luncheon
interval 'Old Glory' hung on her mast,
immediately above the Navy's dressing-room, limp
and listless in the still breeze, shy or sad because of
the indignity imposed upon her; but occasional puffs
of wind displayed her sorry state – while two
commanders and one lieutenant, RN, smote the ball
with vigour and squadron leaders and flight
lieutenants scurried to and fro, oblivious of the
heinous crime perpetrated before their eyes at the
headquarters of cricket's majesty. It was not until
a mere civilian pointed out the error that it was
rectified. Thereafter the Ensign was lowered, and
rehoisted, the right way up, at 13.38 hours, amid
the faint cheers of the few spectators viewing the
spectacle. In case this memorable occurrence has
skipped your notice I venture to record it. No doubt
Wisden will mark it with reverence in due course.

M. NEVILLE KEARNEY,
Letter to *The Times*, 10 August 1950

SLOWLY the veterans who could remember the Victorian Lord's were passing away.
In 1951 there died William Williams, born 1860 and an MCC member since 1900.
In his youth a considerable all-rounder, he kept wicket for Middlesex in 1885–86,
dropped out of the first-class game for fourteen years and suddenly returned, showing
he had not frittered away the intervening time, for he was now the possessor of a more
than useful leg-break which he tweaked on behalf of the county intermittently till
1905. His last season was in 1934 when, his seventy-four years notwithstanding, he
turned out for MCC against the House of Lords, taking three for 16, the three in
question being Lord Dalkeith, Lord Tennyson and Major K. George, a feat of such
political catholicity that he was presented with the ball by a grateful Marylebone Club.
But for all his long cricketing life Williams won his real fame in a different game, and
may be said to be one of the few men whose monument has given intense pleasure
literally to millions.

Billy Williams was a robust and upright old fellow who sported an MCC cap as
well as a sash and also a clipped white moustache. He had bowled for Middlesex
in his youth before reverting to leg-breaks, but his chief achievement was, as a
moving spirit on the Rugby Union, to urge the purchase of Twickenham. The
ground was considered too remote from London to be suitable as the game's

headquarters and was scathingly referred to in its early days, before the first war, as 'Billy Williams's cabbage patch'. Very late in life Billy, who was something of an old buck, was cited as co-respondent in a divorce suit, and was said to be highly indignant when the case was dismissed.

E. W. SWANTON, *Follow On*, 1977

IN October 1952 the *News Chronicle* columnist Ian Mackay died. His comradeship with John Arlott, especially in the world of wine, led Arlott to write a glowing and very moving portrait of his friend, whose incidental pleasures included the casual contemplation, not merely of cricket, but of cricket at Lord's. Arlott's appreciation of his old friend makes a point about the lure of cricket, which it expresses in an oxymoron of memorable originality. The reference is fleeting, but the picture it conjures is vivid, of a man for whom duty calls walking unwillingly away from the ground with his head turned towards 'the quiet noise of cricket over the wall'.

He liked nothing better, of a summer afternoon, than watching cricket at Lord's. At one time he had a flat overlooking Lord's and, when he heard the quiet noise of cricket over the wall, it was hard for him to pass on to Fleet Street.

JOHN ARLOTT, *The Great Bohunkus*, 1953

IN 1953 English cricket took a deep breath and prepared to make yet another bid to regain the Ashes, encouraged by the discovery of a genuine fast bowler in Trueman of Yorkshire, who, on his Test debut against India in 1952, had carried all before him. The expedient of appointing Brown captain had staved off the inevitable, but now, for the first time in history, the selectors had emerged from their meetings at Lord's to announce the appointment of a professional captain in Leonard Hutton of Yorkshire, in which departure they were more enlightened than the committee of Hutton's own county, which never did entrust him with the leadership of their side. For the first time since 1926, an Australian side was visiting England without Bradman, in itself a great bonus for the home side. The captain of the tourists was Lindsay Hassett, who, in the second Test at Lord's, was the hero of a tiny incident in which new ground was broken in the placing of the field.

'Lindsay Hassett has not changed his field, except to hurry along two fellows crossing the sightscreen while carrying trays of beer.'

BRIAN JOHNSTON at Lord's, 1953

THE season opened with great interest in and concern for the Lord's scoreboards. Because the ground was a national institution as well as a sporting arena and a place of public entertainment, there were those who objected to all change on principle, among them the anonymous writer of the following *Times* leader. The unease was perfectly understandable. When men spoke of returning to Lord's after long years of absence, perhaps from the other side of the earth, they invariably expressed the sentiment that although the world outside was beginning to contort itself into all sorts of unfamiliar shapes, at least Lord's remained faithful to its own past. Just as in palmier days veterans from the outposts of Empire returning home on leave made a beeline for the Criterion Long Bar or the Trocadero on the assumption that there they would be sure to pick up the pieces of the old life, so the veterans of spectating at Lord's tended to resent the slightest tinkering with the accoutrements of paradise. The scoreboards were an integral part of this comforting familiarity, like the face of an ancient family clock which has wheezed on in the hall down the generations. It is typical of a game which so baffles those who have not been let into the secret that in a year when tense battles were looming, an essay in a leading newspaper should busy itself over a question of sentiment and never so much as refer to the actual cricket. But then, where would cricket be without sentiment?

With everybody tumbling over themselves to be thought up-to-date and progressive, last ditches today are unoccupied areas, but surely a few stalwarts will man them and make their protest against the alterations which have now been made to the scoreboards at Lord's. The numbers one to eleven have been added, with the letter S for substitute, and when the ball is caught or fielded the scorer will press a button and a light above the player's score-card number will shine out on the board. Lord's, indeed, will be more like Piccadilly Circus than a respectable cricket ground, and gone will be the favourite occupation of the expert on-looker, that of gently but firmly correcting the erroneous notions of his neighbour. When the man in the row in front has loudly applauded a piece of fielding and confided to his impressed companion that Dash is the best cover-point in the country, no longer will he be able to remark, with an air of mild yet unmistakable superiority, 'That, sir, was not Dash, the ex-Cantab, but Blank, the old Oxonian.'

Besides, to carry through such a reckless revolution at this particular moment is to surrender a point in the psychological warfare which is now the recognised prelude and accompaniment to all respectable games. Even when the Australians were rolling us in the dust, there was always comfort in the thought that at least we did things in our own, and therefore, the superior way. If Sydney and Melbourne chose so to conduct their business that the crowd could turn its back on the game and watch its progress on boards huge in size and correspondingly lavish with information, that was their own affair, and we had no intention of following suit. In the good old days of not so very long ago it was part of the fun to bamboozle the paying spectator and keep him in a state of comic ignorance as to what was going on. If it rained and then stopped, he was seldom told when play was likely to begin again, and, on some grounds, scorecards before luncheon were a treat. He, stout fellow, stood it all with the utmost good humour, but now all is changed. The man is positively pampered, a decent anonymity is no more, and cricketers, to all intents and purposes, are as the poor footballers who carry numbers as though they were horses or articles at an auction sale. Still, last ditches are uncomfortable places to linger in, The Oval and Trent Bridge have already gone part of the way with Sydney and Melbourne and the hope is that this summer the lights of Lord's may shine out as brightly as the sun itself.

The Times, 12 March 1953

Bᴜᴛ Lord's had *two* scoreboards, and even as the MCC was replacing the one on the north side of the ground, it found itself being attacked by another lobby for not replacing the board on the south side. Here was one instance of a letter to *The Times* bearing fruit. Once the letter was published, the Committee must have taken note of its contents and decided to act upon them. After some hasty deliberations, extending over a mere sixteen years, down came the offending southern scoreboard and up went the new one so passionately demanded by Mr Walton, who by then may or may not have been in the best position to enjoy it.

> Sir, May I suggest to the powers that be in the MCC that they celebrate the year of the Coronation by erecting a new scoreboard on the south side of what I presume to be the premier cricket ground in the world? The present board is a confused jumble of figures, a jumble now made the worse by the addition of the numbers 1–11 and S, squeezed in at the top to denote the fielders. The spacing and arrangement of words and figures would bring a blush to the cheeks of even a third-rate printer.
>
> W. H. Mᴜʀʀᴀʏ Wᴀʟᴛᴏɴ,
> Letter to *The Times*, 26 May 1953

NB: In 1969 the scoreboard was replaced at the age of nearly 80. The MCC annual report thoughtfully acknowledged that it 'had reached the end of a most useful life'.

As preparations began for what was to be one of the tensest and most closely followed of all battles for the Ashes, the overseas journalists arrived to cover events. Especially eager to savour the cricket played out against the unique background of the coronation of a new queen was Jack Fingleton, who arrived hotfoot at Lord's only to be rebuffed almost before he had set foot inside the ground. The oafishness of the MCC in the affair seems, in retrospect, so maladroit as to be comical. But Fingleton, looking back on the year in the book he published in 1954, failed to see the joke.

It is lovely sunshine at Lord's. Painters, sitting on the ground and discussing the day's winners, dab at the rails. The nearby power-house, showering soot, is a constant menace to Lord's. It is five years since I last saw old Father Time with his scythe, revolving above the scoring board, lifting the bails for 'stumps drawn'. He is a weather-vane and moves gently to and fro with the breeze, but the old boy has been dotted in the eye himself by his own commodity. Lord's has capitulated to the times and just underneath him now on the scoring board are the figures:– 1 2 3 4 5 6 7 8 9 10 11 and then the letter S. Electric bulbs are above them and so now this season we are to be able to identify the fieldsmen (if first, of course, we buy a scorecard). This, indeed, is a concession from Lord's but, having at last abandoned a system that concealed the names of the most famous players behind a colourless number, Lord's has now gone in off the deep end. Eleven fieldsmen and a substitute. It is pleasant to sit dozing in the warm sun, the numbers on the board all at zero, wondering what the season has ahead. Soon the numbers will be whirring and the ball thudding up against the new paint-work.

Lord's has something no other cricket ground quite possesses. There is an enveloping atmosphere of tradition and peace about the place. Red balls, newly painted and shining in the warm April sun, are perched in two sets of two, above the letters MCC, at either end of the Long Pavilion. Tall, white flag-poles rise up beside them from the pavilion roof, one flag above each dressing-room.

I would have enjoyed my pilgrimage to Mecca more had the Secretary Aird possessed more of a cricketing soul. What could be more natural than that one should like to wield a bat again at the Nursery nets? I hinted, gently, as he gave us Honorary Membership cards for the season, that a few among us who had worn the Australian colours more than a few times at Lord's would appreciate, sometime, a net at Lord's. Just for old times' sake. The answer was interesting: 'It might make it difficult. It might create a precedent.' Membership, then, with provisos? A sentimental journey, snapped short at the booking-office and stripping some of the tinsel from the pious remarks of the week about the traditions and the memories of 'this glorious old game'. Next time, if ever, we come this way, we will be past caring whether we have a joust at the Lord's nets. A few former Test cricketers, still with some active blood in their veins, and besieged with requests to play in games in various villages and towns, would hardly desecrate the venerable turf. We would not only get the nets out in Australia, for former English internationals, but also, so to speak, the flags.

J. H. FINGLETON, *The Ashes Crown the Year*, 1954

B UT by the time the second Test of the series was due to start at Lord's, Fingleton, his grumpiness discarded except for a wistful sigh over the smallness of the accommodation, dashed to the ground as eagerly as any schoolboy, his adjectives primed for one of the great occasions in the sporting calendar. It is surprising that Fingleton should have found it surprising that the match was sold out before it started. The first two or three days usually are. And unlike some reporters, Fingleton was acute enough to perceive that the prelude to any game of such grandeur is not in the moment when you pass through the turnstiles within the enchanted castle, nor even as you stop at the turnstiles, but outside, in the streets, where the entire district is fizzing with a kind of vicarious expectation. Housewives who actually loathe the very thought of cricket, and who profess not to know the difference between fine leg and a broken leg, lean with muscular forearms on window sills, watching the hurrying streams of men with benign condescension. Boys playing in the surrounding streets work up a little extra hysteria in deference to what they sense is a great occasion, and the sellers of newspapers, chestnuts, pirate programmes, favours, lend a hint of carnival to the morning, as do the policemen keeping a schoolmasterly watch.

25 June, 1953: To Lord's by underground and a strange sight all along the tube stations of blackboards with chalked notices:– 'Cricket: Test match at Lord's. Ground Full'. What a disappointment this is for tens of thousands. Along the road to Lord's from St John's Wood station I met people with packed hampers and faces of disappointment. At a guess I would say there were some 10,000 mingling outside Lord's before play began. Goodness knows how many had not even attempted the impossible, not even coming to the ground.

One could visualise a crowd of 100,000 at Lord's if there were sufficient accommodation. There is room, too, for expansion, but the cost of extensive alterations to accommodate many more people would not be justified by such a crowd once every four years when the Australians visit.

26 June, 1953: The same blackboard tale on the underground route to Lord's: – 'Ground full. Gates closed'. The streets outside the ground this morning are an awful litter of old newspapers, the remnants of the all-night camp by many people. Scalpers are on the job, and they are interesting studies with their alert sideways looks and poker faces. They live by their wits, and they look like it. It is doubtful whether any have seen the inside of a sporting ground, but they are always outside all grounds here when big sporting fixtures are on. They ask today £5 for a £1 reserved seat.

J. H. FINGLETON, *The Ashes Crown the Year*, 1954

IN the event, the melodrama was to take place not at Lord's, but across the town at The Oval, where in the fifth and final Test England broke a run of four successive drawn matches and reclaimed the Ashes at last. Fingleton was delighted to find himself contemplating the pleasure not of one queen but of two. One wonders if either Fingleton or Queen Salote was aware of the long traditions of cricketing fanaticism attaching to the Tongas, a fanaticism dutifully recorded by *Wisden* in its obituary to one of Queen Salote's royal predecessors, George Tubow, who died in 1918 having made himself famous in the annals of his island by saving the nation from catastrophe: 'His subjects became so devoted to the game that it was necessary to prohibit it on six days of the week in order to avert famine, the plantations being entirely neglected for the cricket field.' In 1953 the plantations of London, from the City to the East End, were likewise neglected several times during the summer, as the battle proceeded. It has been calculated that the last rites were intoned over more grandmothers in 1953 than in any other year, and that once the final Test had been concluded, the plague disappeared as mysteriously as it had arrived.

18 May, 1953: Queen Salote, of the Tongas, is a visitor to Lord's today. She is just emerging from her car, a dominating figure and personality; as I walk around the back of the pavilion I whistle quietly: 'E otun mafi ro noman eiki koe', the beautiful hymn of the Islands, and am rewarded with a glittering and royal smile.

J. H. FINGLETON, The Ashes Crown the Year, 1954

WHEN the captains and the kings depart, it appears, much to the amazement of the general public, that other captains and other kings make their entry into the ground. To the man who lives for the summer, and for cricket, Lord's in mid-winter, glimpsed perhaps from the top of a London omnibus as it sways past the Nursery en route to some mysterious assignation in Swiss Cottage, or seen as a sludgy blur as the cab races through the murk of St John's Wood Road, makes a lugubrious if greatly impressive sight, like a castle abandoned by the garrison. In fact a great many activities take place at Lord's throughout the long London winters. I have attended dinners there in December when the place is humming with those peripheral activities which do so much to transform Lord's from a mere cricket ground to a self-contained world. Even as we dug the spoons into the vegetable dish, men were racing around the tennis court, while upstairs some late student pored through the leaves of forgotten books in the library. Shadowy ground staff might be glimpsed through the gloom transporting a rake or a hoe from point A to point B, while the man on the gate stamped his toes against the weather. What almost always goes unreported is the occasional indulgence in other games. Within a few weeks of England's triumphant recapture of the Ashes, other battles were being fought out on the same turf which had once swished under the skirts of Etonian and Harrovian mothers, sisters and girlfriends.

There is a place for Lord's Cricket Ground in the hearts of all lacrosse players, for besides its congenial surroundings and excellent turf, it has a long historical connexion with the sport. Indeed, a history of lacrosse at Lord's covering the last seventy years would make fascinating reading.

Although the appearance of the players today and the form of their equipment have changed since the Canadian pioneers of 1833 played at Lord's, the skill, teamwork and character have been maintained. This Saturday Kenton and Old Thorntonians, meeting there in a championship match, begin a new chapter in this history. Other games will follow every Saturday until November 14.

The Times, 7 October 1953

IN 1955 the poet-editor-cricketer Alan Ross found himself at Lord's reporting the England–South Africa match for the *Observer*. Coming out of the Long Room, he happened to notice two old gnarled men walking arm-in-arm, one blind, the other leading him. Although these things are always arguable, what the poet was contemplating was the sight of the greatest bowler of all time taking a stroll with the greatest left-arm bowler of his generation. At the time of this encounter Sydney Francis Barnes was 82, Wilfred Rhodes 77. To young Ross they must have looked like men very nearly at the end of their day. Amazingly Barnes lived on till his 94th year, Rhodes till his 96th. The poignancy of the moment drew from Ross one of the loveliest elegies in the repertoire of cricket literature.

TEST MATCH AT LORD'S

Bailey bowling, McLean cuts him late for one.
I walk from the Long Room into slanting sun.
Two ancients halt as Statham starts his run.
Then, elbows linked, but straight as sailors
On a tilting deck, they move. One, square-shouldered as a tailor's
Model, leans over, whispering in the other's ear:
'Go easy. Steps here. This end bowling.'
Turning, I watch Barnes guide Rhodes into fresher air,
As if to continue an innings, though Rhodes may only play by ear.

ALAN ROSS

IN 1956 the Yorkshireman A. A. Thomson waxed rhapsodic about the ceremonial visit to Lord's at the start of the season. For even Yorkshiremen acknowledge that there is nothing quite like the resumption of youth symbolised by a return to Lord's at the end of April, especially as, by a sort of unofficial tradition, the first first-class game to take place there is MCC v. Yorkshire. And Thomson is quite right to accent the rigours of the long winter preceding the opening day of the season. The bitterness of the gales, the depressed readings on the barometer, the depth of the snow, only render the new affirmations of the cricket season more delicious than ever.

For me the supreme moment in all the glad New Year is the moment when I pass through the turnstiles at Lord's at the opening of the season. I generally, like other wise men, approach from the east, but it does not matter. Having paid your two shillings (and better value for even a north-countryman's money it would be hard to find) you pass through the broad canyon between the high south wall and the Mound stand; quickening your pace, you swing round to the right by the bookstall and the full glory of the picture bursts upon you.

With a lover and his lass, the reality, when he sees her once more, is even more beautiful than the image he has been carrying in his heart. So it is with Lord's. All through the winter, while the north-east wind howls round the eaves and the snow lies thick on the garden borders, you have comforted yourself with the imagined picture of this last Saturday in April. Now it breaks upon you if more grandly than you imagined. To your left is the great terra-cotta bulk of the most renowned pavilion in the world; and it is a solemn thought that the original building had a thatched roof; to the right, beyond the Mound, the widely curved high bank of the open stands, with the sight-screen before and the Nursery behind. (It once really was a market garden nursery.) The sight-screen for most of its life has been painted in a very slight variant of the ancient dead-white; now it is a delicate shade of blue, reminiscent of a sea-gull's egg. Right in front of you across the green width of the playing area is the Father Time stand, with the main scoreboard, virginally blank, in the middle, and the old gentleman himself on top.

You set out in your first walk round the estate (which is a kind of sacred pilgrimage); past the Tavern, under whose veranda you see a gentleman, probably a well-known actor, appreciatively holding up a glass of golden ale to the light; past the clock tower; the Q (members and friends) stand; the closed court behind the pavilion where the schoolboys linger with their autograph albums, hopeful and eager as the first snowdrops, waiting for a glimpse of one of the earth's great ones.

By the time you have made the circuit of the other half of the great round-edged rectangle past the Father Time tea-bar and round by the opening where lie the covers which you hope will never be required, you hear the sound of music which affects you as the skirl of the pibroch affects a Scot or the fire-iron infelicities of a contemporary symphony affect those who take their pleasures in that sad way. It is the sound of the pavilion bell, playing a carillon unique in music: delightful though dignified, solemn but genial. You hurry round to stake your claim to a place on the wooden seats in front of the Tavern. The seats are hard, and you can soften them for sixpence, but if you are a hardy northerner, you scorn soft seats. You look round. The crowd is not very large – it will be considerably bigger after lunch – but it is composed of lovers of the game, people who, like yourself, want at the moment nothing so much in life as to see another season launched upon its happy voyage. It would be well worth cracking a bottle of champagne over. Before you stretches the magic expanse of emerald green that has seen struggle and drama, character and comedy, on good wickets and bad, for nearly a hundred and seventy years. In the nearest corner the Lord's sparrows flit and twitter, as they or their ancestors have undoubtedly flitted and twittered for the same hundred and seventy years.

The bell tolls again. Then with that measured tread which is the acme of official dignity the umpires come down the steps and out through the wicket gate. Their long white coats have something of the reverend quality of ecclesiastical vestments. You inevitably contrast them with the truncated garments of the Australian umpires, who, in the newsreels at least, are hardly distinguishable from grocers or even dentists. Compare the English and Australian umpire, each in his characteristic costume; one is a bishop, the other might well be a barber. It is perhaps fortunate that it is not really a small world. Our two bishops reach their appointed stations. Figures in white flannels are moving in the pavilion's main doorway. Then you settle down to perfect happiness because the first match of the season has for a long time been MCC v Yorkshire. If Yorkshire field first, well, there you are; you will see them troop out all at once, familiar figures under the white rose cap, with perhaps one or two unfamiliar ones, too. And if Yorkshire are having first turn of the wicket, you may see the finest batsman in the world. The bell, the umpires, the fielding side and at last the two batsmen. Blossom by blossom the spring begins.

A. A. THOMSON, *Pavilioned in Splendour*, 1956

ANOTHER essay on the same theme, less dithyrambic but perhaps truer to the whimsicality of life as it is glimpsed at Lord's, was rendered by Raymond Charles Robertson-Glasgow (1902–1965) of Oxford, Somerset and the Gentlemen, who graduated to the eminence of one of the game's outstanding essayists. While Thomson strains for allegories of Spring, Robertson-Glasgow concentrates on the vagaries of humanity and the telegraph board. Those readers who sometimes feel that the recollections of famous writers on the game are rendering them outsiders will warm to the reference in this essay to the man whom, Robertson-Glasgow claims, 'I always see on my first day at Lord's. He was waiting for his brother; who is always late.' I have seen that man myself, although never his brother.

To Lord's Again

By foot, once again, is the way to approach Lord's, drinking the slow, deep draught of anticipation. The cigarette shop on the way had not changed. The proprietor and his wife emerged from behind their photographic gallery of film stars, as ever readier for a conversation than a sale. Business could wait. Life is too short for hurry. When the proprietor heard that I'd been to Australia, he looked at me as if to make sure of my identity. He knew someone, he said, who'd been over there, and he never came back.

Round the corner the street was as quiet as ever. The only change was that one more house had been taken over by the Government, for the Sanitary Inspector. But the other signs were reassuring. An errand-boy rode past on a bicycle far too large for him, whistling. A young navigator tested his new boat on a string in the Regent's Canal, to the obvious annoyance of the angler who never had any luck.

Inside the W. G. Grace gates I saw the same spectator whom I always see on my first day at Lord's. He was waiting for his brother; who is always late. And there was the field itself. How green, after the huge, glaring, yellowy arenas of Australia.

But I missed the member with his telescope which he balances on the front rail of the pavilion, bending low to fix his eye on the footwork of the batsmen and the very texture of the pitch. He will surely arrive, when the sun is stronger, and he has finished cataloguing the ships at sea, or the stars in the May sky. He will, of course, bring his field-glasses as well, for double verification.

In the afternoon sun the Tavern grew more argumentative. On the grassy plot behind the Rover stand, one man sat with his back to the match, achieving that elusive triumph of thinking of absolutely nothing at all. Another spectator lay fast asleep, content with the mere fact of cricket and his own absence from the roar of traffic, from invoices, or the blare of his neighbour's radio. He would wake in an hour or so, and tell them, all wrong, all about the cricket, when he reached home. Near these two, a lady sat and took everything out of her handbag and put everything back in a slightly different order, as is the way of the ladies.

On the top of the grandstand Father Time, the weathercock, fiddled eternally with the bails, and pointed his wind-arrow, hopefully, to the west. And, behind the scoreboard, the men in charge of the telegraph-numbers went agreeably mad, and said that Number Seven, long out, had made 173, then 29, then 46, then a pair of noughts.

Meanwhile, two attendants persuaded some fifty spectators who had emerged on to vacant benches in the sun to return to the cold shade of the covered seats. They would not have retired so obediently at Sydney.

R. C. ROBERTSON-GLASGOW, *Crusoe on Cricket*, 1966

Iɴ writing about cricket, all commentators have felt free to ignore chronological sequence from time to time, especially in pursuit of comparative judgements. Some feats remain contemporary no matter how long ago they were performed. Freeman's three hundred wickets in an English season, Compton's eighteen centuries, W. G. Grace's thousand runs in May at the age of 46, Jim Laker's nineteen wickets in one Test against Australia. All these impossible feats have dates attached to them, but they exist also in a sort of cricketing limbo, time-free and always to be deployed as measuring rods against the scores in the morning newspaper. Among these feats is Albert Trott's drive over the Lord's pavilion. Never since equalled, the stroke grows in prodigiousness as the seasons slip past without anyone quite matching it. Anecdotes about the stroke, and about Trott, continued to appear more than half a century after the great moment. One of the most evocative writers of the past when discussing the present was E. W. Swanton in the days when his column in *The Daily Telegraph*, year after year, maintained the perfect blend of erudition and entertainment. Swanton used sentiment sparingly but with unerring aim, as in these two fragments to do with the multitudinous history of his favourite ground.

The Old Lord's Press Box

I was, it so happened, the last cricket writer to leave the Press box after the Middlesex–Worcester match; the last, therefore, I reflected, ever to put pen to paper in the place where the game has been written about for half a century. For the new stand, which will be completed before next season, includes Press accommodation, built into the back of the upper storey. The appointments will be far superior, in keeping with modern requirements, though the angle will be less satisfactory. So passes the old box where the Pardons reigned supreme, where one remembers as a young man being appropriately awed by Charles Stewart Caine, where Neville Cardus at first was too shy to enter.

E. W. SWANTON in *The Daily Telegraph*, 1958

Over the Pavilion

June 1958. Apropos Albert Trott's hit (the only one to have cleared Lord's pavilion) the late Cyril Foley, who was batting with him at the time, used to tell how he went up to Trott and said he thought it was going to snow. Trott, an Australian, said he hoped it would because he had never seen snow. He was wearing a silk shirt but seemily grew chilly, and warmed himself with his celebrated stroke. It was always said that he got out many times afterwards trying to repeat it.

Sticking for the present to Lord's, I myself only recall once seeing the ball hit over the Nursery Stand (not the sight-screen) into the practice ground. That was by A. M. Crawley in the University match. It has, however, been done several times, including, according to legend, an occasion when the ball hit by F. T. Mann is said to have gone running on right across the Nursery until it hit the far Wellington Road wall. Frank Mann probably made more big hits at Lord's than any other of more or less modern times. He is credited with hitting two 6s off Rhodes into the middle balcony, one after the other. The first woke up an old member as it hit the stonework close to his head. He had hardly got off to sleep again when an almost identical stroke crashed against the stonework the other side of his head. This, it is said, convinced him that the assault was personal. He therefore picked up his hat and umbrella and hurriedly made off – out of cricket history for ever.

E. W. SWANTON in *The Daily Telegraph*, September 1957

IN June 1959 the Indians came to Lord's and were defeated by eight wickets in a pleasant but unmemorable game. No centuries were scored; no bowler took more than seven wickets. The weather was fine and the crowds fairly large. But the match incorporated one moment when the struggle was lifted out of the ordinary into the realms of the whimsical. From time to time, lounging away an uncommitted afternoon up in the Mound Stand, I have been diverted by the antics of some dog which has trotted on to the field of play and stopped among the close fielders, staring incuriously at these crazed bipeds behaving so strangely. The choreography on these occasions never differs. One of the fielders makes a sudden grab for the interloper, who, entering happily into the spirit of the game, gallops away. Sometimes, when the game was allowed to develop unhindered by the cricket, you might see as many as five or six cricketers diving at the dog, throwing their caps at it, grabbing at its tail, falling over themselves, all to the accompaniment of cheers from the crowd.

I have sometimes wondered where these dogs came from. How did they gain entry into the ground? Or were they residents, the privileged pets of some groundsman or caretaker? I never discovered, but did notice that these dogs, so varied in breed and disposition, had one thing in common, their ability to evade capture and choose their own moment for departure. But cats are different. They are, in fact, not dogs, and on the very rare occasions when they deign to field for a while, nobody attempts to chastise them. In the England–India match the reporter from *The Times* was much moved by a certain cat, one with proprietory rights to his position.

Walking by Himself

A fair-minded man might well assert that the most composed of all those who have taken the field at Lord's during the past two days was the resident cat – the cat which, in the middle stages of India's first innings and in fine full view of the spectators and the television camera, fielded for a short period at square leg, changed comfortably to mid-off at the end of an over and then stalked majestically off the field. Though he was unable to improve on his pause before the last ten yards by taking off a cap or waving a bat, many a player must have envied him the easy grace and the absence of self-consciousness with which he made the long walk between the wicket and the pavilion. That walk, whether it is at the school fathers' or at one of the more skilful if less exciting contests that take place at Lord's or The Oval, tries even the strongest nerves. The difficult thing, on a lone public occasion, is to have nothing to do except just walk. The occasional century-maker has, it is true, various gestures of acknowledgement as well as his inner joy to sustain him. Even the duck-maker can indulge in some comic by-play – provided his ducks are rare enough. The poor wretch who has made about five, and usually does, has no saving grace.

But the real test is the walk to the beginning of a performance, whether at a wicket or, say, a rostrum. Slow speed, like that of the Lord's cat, is certainly the essence of the technique – confident slowness, conveying the impression of knowledge that the crowd is expectant and that the walker has something so good to bestow that he can well keep them waiting. Mr Pickwick would never have kept such a grip on the Club if he had not 'slowly mounted into the Windsor chair'. Of no body less than a Beatrix Esmond can it be said that their 'motion, whether rapid or slow', is 'always perfect grace'. It is useful to keep to a practised standard gait and mien; though this is little help to the hardest tested of all solitary walkers – the young athlete who is called up successively at the school sports prize-giving to receive the trophies of, say, the 100 yards, 220, 440, long jump, high jump, hurdles and Victor Ludorum. In all these things cats have it over human beings. They are used to walking slowly and by themselves, and they are creatures of habit. A long, solitary walk suits them, and they share with all animals the lack of self-consciousness which creates public dignity. They gain by the facility for doing a bit of what comes naturally. At which point truth compels us to admit that the Lord's cat directed his stately walk from the wicket not to the pavilion but to the bar.

The Times, 20 June 1959

ALTHOUGH the correspondent seems to have been conversant with the basic list of characters in *The Pickwick Papers* and *The History of Henry Esmond*, he evidently did now know either the name, age or gender of the cat in question. These facts were disclosed in *Wisden* a few years later when the animal, having lived out his ninth and final life, went where all pavilion cats have earned the right to go, into the obituary columns of the Almanack.

CAT, Peter, whose ninth life ended on 5 November 1964, was a well-known cricket watcher at Lord's, where he spent twelve of his fourteen years. He preferred a close-up view of the proceedings and his sleek, black form could often be seen prowling on the field of play when the crowds were biggest. He frequently appeared on the television screen. Mr S. C. Griffith, Secretary of the MCC, said of him: 'He was a cat of great character and loved publicity.'

Wisden, 1965

EVER since cricket began, there has been the vexed question of How to Dress for a Cricket Match. The answer has shifted as the unwritten rules of society have themselves shifted. Photographs of the set pieces at Victorian and Edwardian Lord's suggest that a man without a top hat and morning coat would have been refused admission, likewise any lady not attired in a hat carrying an assortment of dead birds and a dress whose hem picked up the whitewash from the crease-marks. But as England since then has been steadily unbuttoning itself, so have cricket watchers. The problem has always been a delicate one for the MCC, which likes to keep up declining standards as far as is practical. To this day, the gentlemen who guard the portals of the pavilion will politely refuse entry to any man not wearing a tie. The rebuff is administered with consummate tact, as though the culprit thought he was wearing a tie and required the services of the doorman to jog his memory. But it is still a rebuff. Out in the stands the club's holy writ does not apply, and spectators in the great public stands can dress as they please, within reasonable limits. But what are reasonable limits? These too have been shifting down the century. By the end of the 1950s a small *cause célèbre* took place when MCC officials took action against indecorous dress. The official reason given for the need to act sounds extraordinary. Little did the world of cricket know how much further down the primrose path the game was destined to go.

About thirty men sitting shirtless in the sun watching the Middlesex v. Yorkshire match at Lord's on Saturday were asked by an MCC attendant to replace their shirts. The attendant said this move was a result of complaints from women spectators during the recent hot spell. 'After all, Lord's is Lord's,' he added.

Later, a Lord's official said there was no ground rule enforcing the wearing of shirts. 'But we do have regular complaints from ladies who object to seeing men with bare chests. We do our best to comply with their views and to persuade men to wear shirts.'

The Times, 17 August 1959

THE 1960s dawned with a crisis of a very different kind, one of those technical debates which never fail to convulse the cricket world while reducing the uninitiated to stony bafflement. The central figure in the controversy was the fast bowler G. Griffin, spearhead of the visiting South African side, a young prospect whose bowling action was deeply suspect. To the spectator there was no doubt that Griffin was not so much a bowler as a thrower, the bend of his elbow at the moment of delivery confirming that each time he released the ball he broke the rule governing the bowling action. But what is obvious to the naked eye is not always apparent in the juridical sense, and before Griffin could be chastised officially, measures had to be taken. It must be said in defence of the authorities that their position in these matters is invidious. If they take no action they are seen to be in default of their own responsibilities as custodians of the game. If, however, they are resolute, they are taking drastic action in the knowledge that they are curtailing and perhaps even concluding the career of a dedicated cricketer. Griffin, however, seems to have been too blatant an offender for even the most dropsical of judges to ignore. The official account of Griffin's amazing mixed fortunes in the second Test at Lord's in 1960 appeared in the following spring's edition of *Wisden*.

ENGLAND v. SOUTH AFRICA
Lord's, June 23, 24, 25, 27, 1960.

England won by an innings and 73 runs with over a day to spare and placed themselves two up in the series. The game was made memorable by the several incidents which occurred while Griffin was bowling. He became the first South African to achieve a hat-trick in a Test match and the first man for any country to accomplish this feat in a Test at Lord's. He also gained a less enviable record, for he became the first player to be no-balled for throwing in a Test match in England. There had been two previous instances abroad, E. Jones of Australia against England at Melbourne in 1897–98 and G. A. R. Lock of England against West Indies at Kingston, Jamaica, in 1953–54.

Griffin was called eleven times during the course of the England innings, all by F. Lee at square leg. Then, when the match ended at 2.25 p.m. on the fourth day, an exhibition game took place and Griffin's only over consisted of eleven balls. S. Buller no-balled him for throwing four times out of five. On the advice of his captain, McGlew, who had spoken to Buller, Griffin changed to under-arm bowling, but was promptly no-balled again by Lee for forgetting to notify the batsman of his change of action. Griffin's last three balls were bowled under-arm.

Wisden, 1961

B̲ᴜᴛ behind the scenes the Griffin case had been brewing since the start of the season. It so happened that the administrator responsible for such matters as illegality of bowling action was G. O. Allen, the ex-England and Middlesex captain who had always stood by the Rule of Law in cricket. Weeks before the Lord's Test he went to study Griffin's by now notorious action and became convinced that something should be done about it. But how? The only sensible course was to photograph the bowler in action. But the MCC, no doubt uneasy at the degree of subterfuge required to take moving pictures of the culprit, declined. Allen then took matters into his own hands, with the result that Griffin's action was judged to be illegal, the judgement being announced in the most public of all pulpits, a Test match. Allen's morality was then, as always, unimpeachable. Ever since, as a young player, he had dissociated himself from Douglas Jardine's hysterical strategies in Australia in 1932–33, his stature had grown as the conscience of English cricket personified. He was to go on to fill every prestigious office in the game, and was finally knighted for services to cricket in the Birthday Honours list of 1986 – about thirty years later than most Englishmen committed to the game might have expected it.

In his capacity as Chairman of the MCC Cricket Sub-Committee Gubby was very much on the war-path against illegal actions, and if ever there was a blatant case it was that of Griffin, who had twice been no-balled in South Africa. In the MCC–South Africans match at Lord's in May Gubby and Wilf Wooller went around Lord's looking at him from every angle. As a result of this Gubby arranged with Leslie Deakins, the secretary of Warwickshire, that Griffin, and also the other fast bowlers engaged in the first Test, should be secretly filmed – and he himself paid the cameraman's fee of £22 since MCC had declined to authorise the matter. By the time of the Lord's Test Gubby had his evidence which amply supported the six umpires who, between them, had already no-balled Griffin seventeen times in three matches. At Lord's he was no-balled eleven times, whereupon it was announced he would not bowl again on the tour – a thoroughly unhappy business for all concerned. Gubby, though it was distasteful to do so, invited Geoff Chubb, president of the South African Cricket Association, and the manager, Dudley Nourse, to see the film, but they declined. Gubby presented his film to Lord's, where it now reposes with a number of subsequent shots of suspect actions in what he calls 'The Rogues' Gallery'.

E. W. SWANTON, *Gubby Allen: Man of Cricket*, 1985

IN THE following summer Lord's was the scene of delightful pleasantries which sadly faded away almost as soon as they arrived. The idea of providing music at cricket matches was a venerable one dating back to the Victorians and perhaps beyond. John Small, the celebrated Hambledon cricketer, was such an accomplished violinist that once, when confronted by a belligerent bull while crossing a field, he soothed the breast of the savage creature by giving it a chorus of violin music to think about; it is hard to believe that such a resourceful and devoted musician would not have whiled away idle hours in the pavilion by playing to himself and his team-mates. The presence of music at the match can, of course, prove a dangerous distraction to those gifted with perceptive musical ears, men like that irrepressible comic among virtuoso batsmen, George Gunn (1879–1958). In 1907–8, convalescing from illness in Australia during an England touring side led by Gunn's Nottinghamshire captain, Arthur Owen Jones (1872–1914), Gunn was called up in the emergency caused by Jones's illness. Gunn duly turned out for his country at Sydney, where he scored 119 and 74. Gunn always insisted that he might have made much more than 119 in his maiden test innings had it not been for the lunch-interval music provided by a band whose cornettist was never quite in tune. The possibility of a recurrence of this nightmare was chanced by the MCC in June 1961, on the first day of a Middlesex home fixture. On that first morning Warwickshire, perhaps fevered by the prospect of orphean enticements, slumped to 36 for six, and were well beaten.

For the first time in memory there will be music played at Lord's during a county cricket match. The Middlesex Regiment's Band, in this country during a summer for the first time since the last war, offered its services and the Middlesex club accepted. So musical selections will be played during the lunch and tea intervals at the Middlesex and Warwickshire match today. Bands do play at Lord's during the season, but only when Services teams are taking part.

The Times, 3 June 1961

MEANWHILE, the University match was still causing irate letters to be written to the Press, and to be published. Any doubt that the modern age had finally arrived is dispelled by the first reference in the annals of Lord's to the spectre of inflation. The writer of the letter seems to have been labouring under the misapprehension that the only entertainment on offer at a cricket match is the cricket. The truth of the matter is that there have been many days at Lord's when the tea interval was found to be a lively diversion from the play.

> Sir, This afternoon, on the last day of the Varsity match, I arrived at Lord's at 4.20 and on tendering the prescribed entrance fee of 3s. was informed that if I waited until 4.30 I should save 1s.6d. Remembering Mr Getty's prudent philosophy, I decided to wait. On peering through the gate I saw that the playing area was deserted, as the tea interval was in progress. Surely, Sir, the MCC does not include the tea interval in the hours of play, and, if it does, is it not adding to the inflationary spiral?
>
> LEONARD HUMPHREY RAZZALL,
> Letter to *The Times*, 22 July 1961

ONE previously uncolonised part of the world which remained uncolonised during 1961 was the territory administered by a Certain Foreign Power. The last known overtures on behalf of cricket towards the Soviet Union had been at an unspecified date in the life of one Edward Rae, otherwise unknown, whose one-line obituary in *Wisden* after his death in the summer of 1923 at the age of 76 recorded the fact that 'he introduced the game into Russian Lapland', but taking into account Rae's dates it seems likely that his brave gesture was performed in pre-revolutionary days. Ever since Rae's death, any possibility of cultural exchange between St John's Wood and the Kremlin had remained untested, and by 1961 seemed so remote that a cricket satirist was prompted to imagine the might-have-been.

Tovarich at the Test

As the 1961 May Day Parade in Moscow was covered by the BBC, reciprocal arrangements might have been made for the Lord's Test.

The time is three in the afternoon. Mackay has yet to add to his one o'clock score and the England captain signals for drinks. E. W. Swanton, J. H. Fingleton, B. Johnston and P. West are interpreting the excitement to television viewers at home while the Russian commentator Y. K. Slobin initiates his countrymen into the mysteries of the game.

FINGLETON: I liked the way Mackay let that long-hop pass safely outside his off-stump. Wouldn't you agree, Brian, that Australia are definitely getting on top?

JOHNSTON: Well, it's a bit early to say. Anything can happen in cricket as you well know.

FINGLETON: True. I remember in 'thirty-eight...

SLOBIN: English viewers are at present hearing the views of the Australian Fingleton. He is a member of his country's ruling class, his last book was introduced by Prime Minister R. Menzies, the reactionary oppressor of the Canberra Communist Party.

JOHNSTON: By Jove! that was a near thing. Mackay nearly hit that one. Let's ask Jim Swanton what he thought about it.

SWANTON: Pretty good ball. Moved a bit off the seam.

JOHNSTON: I should have thought more than a bit.

SWANTON: A good 'un. Incidentally I must tell Jack Fingleton that I've just seen in the pavilion an old friend of his, Sir Holtby Humby. Looks very fit.

FINGLETON: All Australians will be pleased to hear that. We remember Sir Holtby when he was Governor of Northern Territory.

SWANTON: Played for Harrow in 'ninety-eight.

SLOBIN: At one end of the ground there is a fortress called the pavilion. Only aristocrats are permitted to sit in it. The names of all English babies of the ruling class are written down as they are born in the pavilion book. Many of the people who sit there are princes; their leader is the Grand Duke Altham.

JOHNSTON: And Mackay has taken a quick single. Risky in the circumstances. Still, four and a half days left.

WEST: My word! Indeed! Yes!

FINGLETON: I think I can see a beard growing out of the Press-box. It must be.

SLOBIN: No member of the English Communist Party is allowed in the pavilion.

SWANTON: It's Alan Ross of the *Observer*.

FINGLETON: If Mackay doesn't soon get out we shan't be able to distinguish Alan from Father Time.

SLOBIN: Nowhere in England is the mastery of the English aristocracy so perpetuated as here at Lord's field. On top of a stadium there is the figure symbolic of the depressed classes. The Lords who owned this field once seized a serf called F. Time and compelled him to cut the grass with a scythe.

JOHNSTON: The Tavern seems to be doing a good trade.

FINGLETON: Probably the Press-box emptying.

SLOBIN: In England the majority press is in favour of the cult of personality. Only this morning the *Express* openly encouraged cricket player Trueman with the words 'Freddie! Slam! Wham! Whoosh!' The newspapers like *The Times, Guardian, Observer* and *Sunday Times* which are the organs of the ruling class all employ journalists carefully conditioned by the university at Oxford.

SWANTON: Our spinners are not flighting the ball as Laker did five years ago. I think Jack Fingleton would agree?

FINGLETON: Well, Jim, as one who was not unacquainted with the pre-war generation of England spinners...

SLOBIN: To enter this field one has to pass through the Grace Gates. It is noteworthy that when tribute had to be paid to the medical profession the English chose a man who did not work under their National Health Service. For daring to criticise this and other decisions of the ruling class, cricket player J. Laker was recently purged.

SWANTON: Looking through my glasses I can see some very comely young ladies at the top of the open stands. We'll ask Peter West what he thinks. Peter?

WEST: My word! Indeed! Yes!

SLOBIN: The English bourgeoisie are not allowed to sit in the pavilion but use a covered stand. Their spokesmen, the plutocrats Clore and Cotton, slobber as they think of taking-over the pavilion but the Whites will defend their privileges by calling in the Brigade of Guards.

FINGLETON: I prefer the ladies' stand at Sydney.

SLOBIN: Pictured now is the English proletariat herded together in a stand where there is no protection from the snow. They are dressed much as their forefathers were when the novelist C. Dickens visited Muggleton.

FINGLETON: There's one question I should like to ask Jim Swanton – has he ever seen Colin Cowdrey wearing a Harlequin cap?

SLOBIN: Patrolling the nursery and preventing the proletariat from realising their political aspirations are members of the Secret Police. Their uniform explains why they are called White Shirts. They are Fascist beasts, the dreaded Lord's PROs.

SWANTON: I've never seen Cowdrey wearing a Harlequin cap.

SLOBIN: English cricket players are either aristocrats or members of the proletariat. The aristocrats used to wear the so-called Harlequin caps but these enraged the masses and their aristocrats now wear them only in the House of Lords.

JOHNSTON: Trueman is taking the new ball. I'll ask Jack...

SLOBIN: The expression on the face of English bowler Trueman contrasts strongly with the happiness displayed by our glorious Soviet athletes. Trueman is a member of the proletariat, he is clearly outraged that he should be compelled to carry the cricketing bags of E. Dexter to and from Dexter's hotel. Dexter is a member of the ruling royal family.

FINGLETON: Interesting to see two short-legs. Let's ask Jim...

SLOBIN: To play cricket at Lord's field a country must be a member of the Imperialistic Cricket Conference.

SWANTON: We haven't seen two short-legs since half-past twelve.

SLOBIN: The men and women now debauching themselves is a sure indication that capitalism is working itself out in the Tavern.

JOHNSTON: Well, look who's here! John Arlott having a rest from the old steam radio. Enjoying Mackay, John?

ARLOTT: An amiable man, Mackay, square-shouldered...

SLOBIN: English viewers are now hearing the voice of J. Arlott, who speaks to those Wessex serfs too poor and exploited to own a television. Arlott was once a member of the State Police until he started writing bourgeois poetry.

SWANTON: That was mighty close to a catch at the wicket.

WEST: My word! Indeed! Yes!

SLOBIN: The first full description of a cricket match was written in 1706. That was exactly five years after Peter the Great introduced the game to England...

KENNETH GREGORY, *In Celebration of Cricket*, 1978

ONCE upon a time attendance at an Oxford–Cambridge match would have been a guarantee of cricket of the very highest class, with a sprinkling of embryonic Test players and national leaders on view. But gradually the democratisation of Britain was making inroads on university cricket. Fewer undergraduates were able to devote as much time to the game as their fathers and grandfathers. Very few of them were able to contemplate a career in county cricket as amateurs subsidised by the family business. For the moment the Oxford and Cambridge sides retained their first-class status, justifiably so. In the last great flowering of the amateur game, the England side was buttressed by the skills of Sheppard, May, Cowdrey, Barber, Subba Row, Bailey and others. But a generation after the appearance of this letter in *The Times*, there were those who glanced at the crushing defeats being sustained by Oxford and Cambridge at the hands of even the weaker counties and wondered whether the time had not come to expunge such games from the first-class averages. So drastically had the Varsity fixture receded into the realm of minor cricket, of little interest to the public, that casual readers who happen to come across the following poem in some anthology, must have wondered to themselves at the cruel way that the whirligig of Time really does bring in its revenges.

THE BLUES AT LORD'S

Near-neighboured by a blandly boisterous Dean
Who 'hasn't missed the match since '92',
Proposing to perpetuate the scene
I concentrate my eyesight on the cricket.
The game proceeds, as it is bound to do
'Till teatime or the fall of the next wicket.

Agreeable sunshine fosters greensward greener
Than College lawns in June. Tradition-true,
The stalwart teams, capped with contrasted blue,
Exert their skill; adorning the arena
With modest, manly, muscular demeanour –
Reviving memories in ex-athletes who

Are superannuated from agility –
And (while the five-ounce fetish they pursue)
Admired by gloved and virginal gentility.

My intellectual feet approach this function
With tolerance and Public-School compunction;
Aware that, whichsoever side bats best,
Their partisans are equally well-dressed.
For, though the Government has gone vermilion
And, as a whole, is weak in Greek and Latin,
The fogies harboured by the august Pavilion
Sit strangely similar to those who sat in
The edifice when first the Dean went pious –
For possible preferment sacrificed
His hedonistic and patrician bias,
And offered his complacency to Christ.

Meanwhile some Cantab slogs a fast half-volley
Against the ropes. 'Good shot, sir! O good shot!'
Ejaculates the Dean in accents jolly...
Will Oxford win? Perhaps. Perhaps they'll not.
Can Cambridge lose? Who knows? One fact seems sure;
That, while the Church approves, Lord's will endure.

SIEGFRIED SASSOON

SOMETHING else which was being democratised was the MCC itself. Passing rapidly were the days when devotees like Alec Waugh could bemoan the fact that their fathers had omitted to enter them for membership at birth, thus causing their entry into the Long Room to be delayed until middle age. Acceptance for membership by the club was still a matter to be pursued with patience, but as that membership expanded, so did the social range represented on the books. For a great many, the process had a halfway stage, a sort of way-station on the road to Valhalla. This was membership, if not of MCC then at least of Middlesex. The benefits were almost as gratifying, for after all, the great blessing of belonging to the club is the privilege of watching the cricket through the glass of the Long Room windows, of wandering through the corridors of the pavilion, of studying the hypnotic array of team photographs from the past hanging on the tea-room walls, of examining the tickertape which tells the latest scores around the country, of trudging up to the high balconies and contemplating that long-lost drive of Alfred Trott's. The man who has never succeeded in penetrating the defences of the MCC may, by being deliberately ambiguous in his remarks, give the impression that he is one of the select by letting it be known that he is as familiar as the next man with the inside of the Long Room, the next man no doubt being a Middlesex member like himself:

How to be One Up at Lord's
Without Actually Being a Member of the MCC

This is a complex subject. It would be an over-simplification to say that Lord'smanship is the art of watching big cricket without actually being a member of the MCC – the phrase is too limiting. But it does help to remind us that Lord'smanship itself belongs to the vast subject of Badge Play, sub-section How to be in the Right Place with the Wrong Tie.

First, a personal note, which I only bring in here because, although I loathe mentioning myself, I do happen to be typical. The fact that I am not actually a member of the MCC is in itself a small news item of which I am surprised that the Press has not made more use. Everybody knows that from 1917 to 1923 I was a rowing man. Marylebone Cricket Club would not invite me for my play. Indeed, it may be of interest to fact specialists if I reveal that I only played cricket once, in June 1926, when I batted tenth for Toppesfield village and was out second ball, which gives me a career average of 0.00. Honorary membership must have been mooted at HQ, but I always feel that perhaps there was a letter going astray there, a clerical slip here; anyhow, it was not for me to enquire.

By the time my lifetime of cricket watching set in I might surely have got J.C.O. and Frank C. to put me up. They know me quite well. But I have been in a constant state of thinking, for the last forty years, that I hadn't the slightest chance of still being alive by the time my name came through. Now I have regrets. At Henley my tie may be pink enough. Even at golf I may have squeezed my nose round the door of the club which my wife called, as soon as they let me in, the Royal and Senile. But at cricket I have never been a Pav. man. This fact is somehow feebly irritating. Year after year my MCC friends offer me Rover tickets for the Lord's Test match. This year, so far as Days Four and Five are concerned, dozens of people have flooded me with Rover seats, and in an easily recognisable tone of voice, during the match, 'Where are you sitting?' they say, having spent most of the morning demonstrating to me beyond possible doubt where it was that they themselves were to be found.

There are thousands of people in my position, and again and again I have seen in their expressions the unspoken cry: Is there a Membership Counterploy?

The answer, of course, is 'Yes'. More precisely, there are two basic gambits, each with a ploy of its own.

The A approach is this. Be a specialist. Know about cricket and know about Lord's. Be detailed about Lord's. Be detailed, indeed, about the pavilion. It is not the slightest use simply making vague references to the Long Room. Talk of the extraordinary drawing of J. H. G. Mudderghi just outside the Committee Room door which shows the extraordinary position of his middle finger at the moment of release of his faster ball. Disapprove of the new position of something. Say something else isn't what it was. Know Lord's history. Know *Wisden*. I have recommended, in a pamphlet, the copy of *Wisden* specially bound so that it looks as if it was a copy of an ABC. While appearing to look up a train, you can in reality be finding out the figures for eighth-wicket stands, Middlesex v. Northants.

The question of knowing celebrated cricketers personally is a difficult one. On the basis of a twelve-minute conversation with Mr Bailey, in 1960 at Romford, am I justified in referring to him as Trevor? This is a question which every individual must decide for himself. Let him look in his heart, and ask. If I do this, I invariably find the answer is 'Yes'. Last year I tried a difficult ploy, which was, I think, successful. I do not know Mr Denis Compton personally, though I know him by sight. He does not know me by sight. He was standing in front of the Tavern, chatting to a friend on his left while he watched the cricket. I placed myself on his right, but a little behind. I turned towards him, smiled, and moved my mouth, *as if talking to him*. He of course took no notice; but three men standing on the steps of the Tavern did have the impression that I was talking to Compton.

The second great counter-membership gambit, which has its weaknesses and strengths, is to pretend that you don't really care about not belonging, even that you're rather glad. Here the basic ploy is to be a Tavern man. To like the Tavern and the Mound Stand is by no means a difficult frame of mind to assume. There is a certain nearness of drink. The wish to take off a coat in hot weather and reveal a rather crumpled blue shirt, sleeveless, is not only allowed but may be considered correct dress play. Many support, in this area, the shouting of restrained comments on play, though never of course in 100 per cent Oval Gasworks style. It is the perfect position in which to observe a pull to leg, the most satisfying shot in cricket. One finds oneself, in general, a good deal nearer to everything, including especially the players. On an empty day, deep square leg may occasionally seem to give one a smile. It is possible to discover, by use of the large specialist padded field-glasses recommended by us, whether or not the wicket-keeper is wearing a vest under his shirt – a practice which, we wish to record without comment, is on the increase. The Tavern-and-Mound position may be inferior to the Pavilion, but it is certainly better than the rest of the ground, the seats of which often represent unexplored desert on the map (though today I saw a little cluster to the north-west, obviously a school treat; and one box, to the left of the scoreboard, full of men huddled together in overcoats and revealed, by the binoculars, to be gloomily drinking Scotch).

Some people, counter-membering, say what a pity the pavilion was built before the sunburn age, and that it is impossible, after noon or in one corner after six, to enjoy there 'the blessing of sun on one's face' (see Open Airmanship, Section Three). But in general it is the jolly democracy of South Lord's which appeals to you, be you who you may.

As everybody knows, there is a short cut into pavilion land, and I'm bound to say I have taken it. The process of becoming a member of the *Middlesex County cricket Club* is quicker. It is even, I say in gratitude, rather easy. Everybody realises that 'I am a member of the MCCC' is a phrase in which 'MCCC', the initials, are indistinguishable, after two gin and tonics, from 'MCC'. And one can really go in on certain occasions (see printed instructions) to the pavilion itself. In a sort of way, one has made it. It's good. It's worth it. And members are NOT like Osbert Lancaster caricatures, NOT like the American view of cricket. They are nice. They are human. They may even, at heart, be sensitive artists, intro-spects, fond of Bach. Many have beards. I have spoken to some of them. 'Well,' I say, 'it's certainly warmer in here.' They do not actually answer me, but I fancy I notice a softer look in the eye. Once again, the world problem of loneliness.

Or the problem of unfulfilled ambition. Because the member is conscious of inferiority.

He is embroiled in the unending frustration of Badge Play. He is a member. But he is not a member of the Committee.

Every now and then, indeed extraordinarily often, I trot back to the Tavern, and having made crystal clear the position of the Place in which I have just been sitting, I demonstrate that I am still one of them at heart; that they can treat me just as if I was one of themselves – that I am now, in completeness, a Lord'sman.

STEPHEN POTTER in LESLIE FREWIN (ed.), *The Boundary Book*, 1962

B Y NOW the crude empirical experiments staged at Lord's in 1938 had blossomed into an industry so all-pervading that the day had arrived when the great cricket audiences were to be found, not in the stands, but at home, or in offices, glued to the television screen. Even though the sophistications of colour, of computerised career figures, of multi-camera coverage of every shot, were still in the future, the nation was beginning to savour the delightful proposition that no matter where you might happen to be when a Test match was in progress, you could watch every ball, and see much more of the game than from the view in the Long Room. Televised cricket was to prove, indirectly, to be the most devastating new factor in the equation of the game's development. It was to pull in a vast new audience, to tempt sponsors and advertisers, to revolutionise the social status of star players. A great many unpredictable developments, to do with history rather than with cricket, had for three generations been wresting control of the game from the MCC. Of these, none was more pervasive than television. While it is impossible to nominate one moment, or one session of play, or even one game, which marks the transition of cricket from an open air sport to a part of the entertainment industry, there was once a Test at Lord's which stopped the nation in its tracks, which brought company directors and their messenger boys alike thronging to the screen, profit and loss forgotten as two international sides battled out the final hours of a thrilling struggle.

ENGLAND v. WEST INDIES
Second Test Match
Played at Lord's, June 20, 21, 22, 24, 25, 1963

Drawn. One of the most dramatic Test matches ever to be played in England attracted large crowds and aroused tremendous interest throughout the country. All through the cricket had been keen and thrilling, but the climax was remarkable, Cowdrey having to go in with a broken bone in his arm. About 300 people rushed the ground at the end of the match seeking souvenirs and patting the players on the back. The West Indies supporters called for Worrell and Hall, who appeared on the balcony, sending them home happy.

When the final over arrived any one of four results could have occurred—a win for England, victory for West Indies, a tie or a draw. The match was drawn with England six runs short of success and West Indies needing one more wicket. Most people felt happy about the result, for it would have been a pity if either side had lost after playing so well.

The England selectors sprang a surprise by recalling Shackleton, aged thirty-eight, after a gap of more than eleven years. His form at the time plus the fact that he had a fine record at Lord's, influenced them. He replaced Statham, and to strengthen the batting Parks came in for Andrew as wicket-keeper. West Indies preferred McMorris as opening batsman to Carew.

Worrell won the toss for West Indies, and after rain had delayed the start for twenty-three minutes the game began on a high note with Hunte taking 4s off the first three balls of the match, bowled by Trueman. Shackleton frequently worried Hunte, who offered two sharp chances off him. The scoring dropped right back, and at lunch the total was only 47. The first wicket fell at 51 and the next at 64. Then Sobers and Kanhai, in an entertaining stand lasting sixty-five minutes, added 63. A fifth wicket partnership of 74 between Kanhai and Solomon put West Indies in a useful position, but with Worrell failing to score England were well in the picture. At the close West Indies were 245 for six, and they carried the total to 301.

Shackleton failed to take a wicket on the first day, but he terminated the innings with three in four balls, dismissing Solomon, Griffith and Gibbs. Trueman bowled well for long spells and claimed six for 100.

Edrich fell to the first ball he received, and with Stewart also going early England were 20 for two at lunch. Afterwards Dexter gave a thrilling display of powerful driving, hooking and cutting. He took only forty-eight minutes to reach 52, and when leg-before he had made 70 in eighty-one minutes off 73 balls received. His hits included ten 4s, and the way he stood up and punished the fiery fast bowling of Hall and Griffith was exciting to see. Barrington played a minor role in helping Dexter add 82 in sixty-two minutes but later took over command.

Cowdrey again disappointed, but Parks shared a sixth wicket partnership of 55 in an hour. Barrington, still searching for his first Test century in England, drove a catch to cover after batting three hours, ten minutes for 80. England finished with 244 for seven. On the Saturday, when the gates were closed ten minutes before the start, Titmus played a sound innings and England finished within four of the West Indies total. Griffith took five for 91, always being awkward to play.

When West Indies lost their opening pair for 15 the issue was wide open. Cowdrey, at slip, held his third successive catch to dismiss Kanhai, and with Sobers and Solomon going cheaply, West Indies were 104 for five with England apparently on top. Then came a complete swing. Butcher, showing excellent form and hitting the bad ball hard, checked the slide and with Worrell carried the score to 214 for five by the close. West Indies then led by 218 and were well placed only to lose ground again in a remarkable twenty-five minutes on Monday morning when the last five wickets went for 15 in six overs.

Butcher, ninth out for 133 (two 6s and seventeen 4s) batted splendidly for nearly four and a half hours. He and Worrell put on 110. Trueman, with five for 52, claimed eleven for 152 in the match, one of his best performances for England. Shackleton supported him well with seven for 165 in the two innings.

So England went in to get 234 to win. Their hopes sank when

Edrich, Stewart and Dexter were out for 31, but Barrington again rose to the occasion. He and Cowdrey had to withstand some fierce bowling from Hall, who often pitched short and struck the batsmen on the body and fingers. Eventually Cowdrey received such a blow that a bone just above the left wrist was broken and he had to retire, having shown his best form of the series and helping to carry the score to 72. Close took his place and the England fight back continued, Barrington hitting Gibbs over mid-wicket for two 6s in an over. Bad light handicapped the batsmen, and there were two stoppages before the game was given up for the day at 4.45 p.m. with England 116 for three, needing another 118.

To add to the tenseness of the situation, rain and poor light delayed the resumption next day until 2.20 p.m. Hall and Griffith, bowling at their best on a pitch which had remained lively throughout the match, made the batsmen fight desperately for every run. Barrington added only five in fifty-five minutes, and the first hour brought no more than 18 runs.

Close and Parks took the score to 158, and Titmus also fought well. At tea, it was still anyone's game with England 171 for five, Cowdrey injured and 63 needed in eighty-five minutes. With West Indies averaging only 14 overs an hour, this was a harder task than it looked on paper. The game moved back in West Indies' favour when Titmus and Trueman fell to successive balls. Close, who had defended with rare courage despite being hit often on the body and finishing with a mass of bruises, decided the time had come to change his methods. He began moving down the pitch to Hall and Griffith to upset their length. He succeeded for a time, but eventually he just touched the ball when trying a big swing and was caught at the wicket. Worrell said afterwards that while not wishing to detract from a very fine innings, he thought Close's changed tactics were wrong. Others paid high tribute to what they termed a magnificent and courageous innings which lasted three hours, fifty minutes. He made 70, easily his highest score for England.

Shackleton joined Allen with nineteen minutes left and 15 runs required. They fell further behind the clock and when Hall began his last dramatic over eight were needed. Singles came off the second and third balls, but Shackleton was run out off the fourth when Worrell raced from short-leg with the ball and beat the batsman to the bowler's end. That meant Cowdrey had to come in with two balls left and six wanted. He did not have to face a ball, Allen playing out the last two. If he had to shape up, Cowdrey intended to turn round and bat left-handed to protect his left arm.

Hall, in particular, and Griffith, showed remarkable stamina. Hall bowled throughout the three hours, twenty minutes play was in progress on the last day, never losing his speed and always being menacing. He took four for 93 off forty overs in the innings. Griffith bowled all but five overs on the last day.

The game which attracted 110,287 paying spectators and approximately £25,000 all told, gave cricket a fine boost which was reflected immediately in improved bookings for the third Test at Edgbaston. The receipts were £56,300, not far short of the record for any match. Those who saw it, and the millions who followed the game's progress over television and radio, were kept in a constant state of excitement. It was a game to remember.

West Indies

C. C. Hunte, c. Close, b. Trueman .	44	c. Cowdrey, b. Shackleton	7
E. D. McMorris, lbw b. Trueman . .	16	c. Cowdrey, b. Trueman	8
G. S. Sobers, c. Cowdrey, b. Allen .	42	c. Parks, b. Trueman	8
R. B. Kanhai, c. Edrich, b. Trueman	73	c. Cowdrey, b. Shackleton	21
B. F. Butcher, c. Barrington, b. Trueman	14	lbw b. Shackleton	133
J. S. Solomon, lbw, b. Shackleton .	56	c. Stewart, b. Allen .	5
*F. M. Worrell, b. Trueman	0	c. Stewart, b. Trueman	33
†D. L. Murray, c. Cowdrey, b. Trueman	20	c. Parks, b. Trueman	2
W. W. Hall, not out	25	c. Parks, b. Trueman	2
C. C. Griffith, c. Cowdrey, b. Shackleton	0	b. Shackleton	1
L. R. Gibbs, c. Stewart, b. Shackleton	0	not out	1
B 10, l-b 1	11	B 5, l-b 2, n-b 1.	8
	301		**229**

1/51 2/64 3/127 4/145 5/219
6/219 7/263 8/297 9/297

1/15 2/15 3/64
4/84 5/104 6/214
7/224 8/226 9/228

Bowling: *First Innings*—Trueman 44–16–100–6; Shackleton 50.2–22–93–3; Dexter 20–6–41–0; Close 9–3–21–0; Allen 10–3–35–1. *Second Innings*—Trueman 26–9–52–5; Shackleton 34–14–72–4; Titmus 17–3–47–0; Allen 21–7–50–1.

England

M. J. Stewart, c. Kanhai, b. Griffith	2	c. Solomon, b. Hall .	17
J. H. Edrich, c. Murray, b. Griffith .	0	c. Murray, b. Hall . .	8
*E. R. Dexter, lbw b. Sobers	70	b. Gibbs	2
K. F. Barrington, c. Sobers, b. Worrell	80	c. Murray, b. Griffith	60
M. C. Cowdrey, b. Gibbs	4	not out	19
D. B. Close, c. Murray, b. Griffith. .	9	c. Murray, b. Griffith	70
†J. M. Parks, b. Worrell	35	lbw b. Griffith	17
F. J. Titmus, not out	52	c. McMorris, b. Hall.	11
F. S. Trueman, b. Hall	10	c. Murray, b. Hall . .	0
D. A. Allen, lbw b. Griffith	2	not out	4
D. Shackleton, b. Griffith	8	run out	4
B 8, l-b 8, n-b 9	25	B 5, l-b 8, n-b 3.	16
	297	(9 wkts)	**228**

1/2 2/20 3/102 4/115 5/151
6/206 7/235 8/271 9/274

1/15 2/27 3/31
4/130 5/158 6/203
7/203 8/219 9/228

Bowling: *First Innings*—Hall 18–2–65–1; Griffith 26–6–91–5;
Sobers 18–4–45–1; Gibbs 27–9–59–1; Worrell 13–6–12–2. *Second
Innings*—Hall 40–9–93–4; Griffith 30–7–59–3; Gibbs 17–7–56–1;
Sobers 4–1–4–0.

Umpires: J. S. Buller and W. E. Phillipson.

Wisden, 1964

THAT match, always to be remembered as the one in which Brian Close all but bared
his chest in defiance of the West Indies pace attack, and one which was played out
as the shadows lengthened and the light faded to the point where the pictures on the
TV screen gave an impression of someone's destiny being settled in the murk, was one
of the great set pieces in the history of Lord's. But history cannot consist in its entirety
of set pieces. There are also the less emotional but, in their whimsical way, just as
essential issues, forever being scrutinised by an uncomputed army of watchers over the
destiny of Lord's, an army whose every member is prepared, on the slightest pretext,
to snatch up a pen and indulge in the age-old prerogative of an English gentleman, to
compose a letter to the Editor of *The Times*.

Sir, Your Cricket Correspondent today laments the
present drainage problem at Lord's. It was ludicrous
to all of us watching despondently yesterday to see
the falling rain run off the playing area, by
hosepipe, to the very parts of the ground which
need redraining. It is an elementary thought that
the water could have been drained into mobile tanks
or containers. In future may this be considered for
the benefit of thousands of cricketers for whom the
Lord's Test is the one event each year which takes
precedence over all else?

KEITH FALKNER,
Letter to *The Times*, 23 June 1964

NB. A new drainage system was installed in 1964.

THE resolution of the drainage crisis coincided with the centenary of the Middlesex
County Cricket Club, which had spent all but a few early years of that century as
tenants at Lord's. Newcomers to the game, and especially apprentice schoolboys, still
have trouble distinguishing the MCC from the MCCC, and are visibly shocked when
comparing for the first time the vast patrician confidence of the Pavilion with the modest
bungalow alongside which comprises the Middlesex office. But most of the first-class
cricket on view at Lord's is Middlesex cricket, and when one thinks of artists from
Stoddart, McGregor and Tarrant, through Hendren and the Hearnes, Compton and
Edrich, down to Brearley and company, the debt owed to the county by the cricket
world needs no advocacy. On the occasion of the centenary, the best writer among
Middlesex captains contributed an essay.

A MIDDLESEX CENTURY [1964]

On December 15, 1863, a number of gentlemen met in the London Tavern, Bishopsgate, to consider a momentous project. This was the formation of a Middlesex County Cricket Club, and the proceedings were conducted with admirable energy and decision.

Indeed, so assured is the report of the meeting, immediately released to the London newspapers, that it has some resemblance to the announcements following more recent and very much less pleasant events. It opens with a sweeping and surely debatable assumption. 'Sir,' it says, 'Middlesex being the only cricketing county in England that has no County Club'. It proceeds to say that a provisional committee had been formed, and that a general meeting would be held in the London Tavern in February of the following year.

As a result of this benevolent coup d'état events rushed forward. At the promised meeting the secretary, Mr C. Hillyard, recorded the names of a fair nucleus of members, a regular committee of 16 was appointed, a ground hired in Islington, and four bowlers engaged. The staff was completed by the arrival of a groundsman, happily named George Hearne, and an umpire. A president, in the person of Viscount Enfield, followed soon afterwards.

The Middlesex team burst into action in 1865, with matches against Sussex, Bucks, Hants and MCC, with several lesser fixtures. Challenges from the established and powerful counties of Surrey and Lancashire were shrewdly side-stepped for the time being.

Such a dynamic start was not to be maintained. By 1869 Middlesex lost the use of Islington ground, and could not then afford to accept the MCC terms to play at Lord's. A melancholy two years on the rough Amateur Athletic Association Ground at Lillie Bridge was followed by another abortive tenancy of Prince's ground, near Hyde Park Barracks, which never gave much promise of permanency. At a meeting in 1877 it was decided to take the major step of playing at Lord's, starting the following year with four matches. From this time onwards the fortunes of Middlesex were inevitably bound up with those of MCC, yet the tenants have always maintained a sturdy independence in the conduct of their affairs, a state of affairs which exists to this day. From the formation of this partnership starts the real progress of Middlesex as a County Cricket Club.

Many enthusiastic members, players, and administrators had seen the club through these early vicissitudes. It is not possible to mention many of these deserving names but that of Walker has ever been immortal in Middlesex. 'The Walkers of Southgate' was a brotherly triumvirate whose initials R. D., V. E. and I. D. are still fresh and familiar in the annals of the club. All were competent administrators as well as being fine cricketers and so contributed to every aspect of the club's establishment and progress.

The County Championship Birth and Residential qualifications had been introduced in 1873 and Middlesex had competed from that year with varying, but seldom more than modest success except in 1878 when they led the counties. The start of the new tenancy marked no spectacular advances in these fortunes but very soon some very famous names came to support and perpetuate the foundations laid by the Walkers. In 1876 C. I. Thornton made his first appearance and was soon recognised as a hitter of unprecedented power. A.J. Webbe's active association with the club began in 1875 and was to last until 1937, as player, captain and President. Webbe played for England but once and his interests were almost entirely focused on Middlesex. In light of this undivided devotion he may justly be described as the greatest figure in the county's hundred years of history. Aided by two Lytteltons and three Studds and, a little later, by Sir Timothy O'Brien, and the great A.E. Stoddart, Middlesex scored more attractively than ever in the eighties but, despite G. Burton's consistent slows, were a somewhat ineffective bowling side.

The names of Stoddart and O'Brien were linked as those in later years of Hearne and Hendren, and Compton and Edrich. Stoddart is still regarded by many competent judges as the greatest amateur batsman ever to represent Middlesex. In the course of an outstanding county career he went four times to Australia, twice as captain. His average of 35.57 for 30 innings against Australia was remarkable for the figures of his time. His record on the Rugby football field was no less illustrious.

It was in 1888 that J.T. Hearne made his first appearance, to reach his full powers in 1892, when he took 163 wickets. On the fast side of medium pace he had a beautiful wheeling action, spun the ball sharply from the off, and soon made his mark as the finest bowler of his type in the country. Through the next decade he was the mainstay of the attack with the support of J.T. Rawlin, a serviceable fast bowler. It was not until 1897 that Albert Trott had qualified to spin his leg-breaks from a prodigious hand. (In passing it may be said that this was regarded as the largest hand in cricket until lost in the enveloping grip of A.D. Nourse.)

In the first half of the nineties Middlesex, with a wealth of amateur batting, and the unflagging talents of J.T. Hearne, kept well to the fore, being third in the table in 1893 and 1894. The names of the amateur batsmen were nigh legion but collectively they had a certain mercurial quality to thwart that consistency which makes for champion counties. Thus, although thrice third and twice runners-up in the nineties Middlesex were bested in the first half by neighbouring Surrey and, latterly, by Yorkshire and Lancashire. Surrey were at one time almost invincible with the irresistible force of Richardson and W.H. Lockwood to exploit the performances of a dependable batting order.

Middlesex entered the twentieth century well established as one of the major powers in the County Championship. In the North, Yorkshire always had a slight ascendancy in the struggle for power with their Lancashire neighbours. Nottinghamshire ruled the Midlands. In the South, Middlesex and Surrey dominated the scene. Through the nineties Surrey had a great deal the better of the argument but, by the turn of the century, the relative strengths of the rivals had altered so that Yorkshire succeeded as champions in 1900 and 1902 and Middlesex were top in 1903.

Although Middlesex did not again head the table before the outbreak of war, the county prospered greatly under the enlightened captaincy of P.F. Warner who, after a spell during which G. MacGregor led, had succeeded Webbe. In fact, as deputy captain Warner had handled the side frequently during MacGregor's tenure. Warner was very much greater in the international scene than Webbe, but

Middlesex was still his first and greatest love. During his term of office he became one of the greatest all-round amateur batsmen in the country if not quite in the same category as C. B. Fry, K. S. Ranjitsinhji and F. S. Jackson. An indomitable defence was allied to sound orthodox scoring strokes, especially to the on, and the whole technique was applied with great intelligence and concentration. Warner brought the same qualities to his captaincy and had, at all times, an observant eye for every detail of the play. He used the extraordinary and occasionally erratic talents of A. E. Trott to best advantage. These consisted of a commendably aggressive attitude to batting, and a great power of leg-spin allied to a remarkably fast and accurate yorker. Many thought the first attribute unduly exaggerated by Trott's determination, on every occasion, to repeat his monumental straight drive which cleared the Lord's pavilion. All players found it instructive and enormously pleasant to be a member of Warner's side.

The start of the century was quite promising but 1902, a wet season, brought almost unprecedented disaster. Only two matches were won by a Middlesex side which, for one reason or another was seldom fully represented. It was a surprise to all, including the winners, when Middlesex went to the top of the table in the following year. Warner was now at the height of his powers as a batsman and was well supported by the normal Middlesex reservoir of amateur talent. Trott and Hearne were a formidable pair in this wettest of seasons and had the support of B. J. T. Bosanquet whose 'googlies' had a considerable impact on the game as a whole. Bosanquet, like some other pioneers, never mastered his invention to the extent achieved by many successors, but the novelty was too much for many batsmen, as the Australians found at Sydney and Trent Bridge. He was in addition a fine batsman with a short pick-up but plenty of power.

In 1908 Warner became the official captain of Middlesex. By this time he had wide and varied experience of his craft and got the best out of his side for the next nine playing seasons, culminating in the glorious win of 1920.

Trott's career came to an end in 1909 but F. A. Tarrant had now developed into a splendid all-rounder. A sound and dependable batsman, his left-hand spinners were regarded as being equal to those of Wilfred Rhodes and Colin Blythe in all but accuracy. Further to enhance the county's prospects, J. W. Hearne and E. (Patsy) Hendren had just embarked. Hendren was to take some time to come to full bloom but Hearne's progress was so rapid that within a couple of years he was thought of in the same context as Rhodes and G. H. Hirst. He was a neat, precise batsman who preferred the back foot as a general base of operation. His leg-breaks he spun more than any Englishman within memory, and was only outspun on the arrival of A. A. Mailey. His googly was at least serviceable in an era as yet not wholly familiar with this form of deception. H. R. Murrell, a man of great personality, who was to play a lasting part in Middlesex affairs, kept wicket and batted with great spirit when the occasion demanded.

In an era when county cricket flourished and opposition from the North, Midlands and South bank of the Thames was formidable, Middlesex were always in the first six of the Championship. In 1910 and 1911 they were third and in 1914 ran into second place. With

Warner, Tarrant and Hearne at the height of their powers, and Hendren verging on his potential greatness, Middlesex might well have gone further but for the untimely interruption. There were many young men whose names were to become prominent in the twenties, F. T. Mann, N. E. Haig, C. N. Bruce, R. H. Twining, S. H. Saville and G. E. V. Crutchley, to name a few, who brought a fine youthful zeal to support the professional skill.

The year of 1919 was an uneasy one for English cricket which, like many other institutions, was striving to re-organise a wholly disrupted institution. The experiment of three two-day matches a week was found to be a strenuous and unsatisfactory arrangement. The most pleasing development at Lord's was the batting of Hendren whose form far outstripped any hope based on pre-war performances.

In the following year P. F. Warner ended his long and brilliant career by leading his side to the top of the Championship table. His unsurpassed qualities as a captain and tactician made full use of a very talented side. Hendren and Hearne were the foundation of a very good batting side. G. T. S. Stevens, largely a protégé of the perspicacious Warner, was a great amateur addition to the professional core of batsmen, and bowled a dangerous mixture of leg-breaks and googlies. It was not, however, until late in the season that the Middlesex challenge became apparent, and not until the closing moments of the last match of the season that the prize was finally grasped. Middlesex won a very important toss but were headed by 73 runs on the first innings. Centuries by H. W. Lee and C. H. L. Skeet got Middlesex well on the way to a good second innings but time ordained that Warner should set Surrey, a strong, aggressive batting side, 244 to make in three hours. At one point Surrey seemed to be well on the way to victory but, appropriately, a typically shrewd move from Warner turned the day. Seeing Fender on the balcony give the signal to the batsmen for 'general chase' he removed Hendren from short leg to deep long-on. Very soon Shepherd was caught in that position, and the spin of Hearne and Stevens saw Surrey defeated by 55 runs with only ten minutes to spare.

Warner, departing gloriously, handed over to F. T. Mann, who for eight years led the county with a firm but happy touch which gained him the lasting affection and admiration of all who played for or against Middlesex. His reign opened auspiciously when, in 1921, Middlesex again won the Championship. With T. J. Durston and Haig to open, the bowling was now a very fair complement to the plentiful batting. Without ever repeating this success Middlesex were well amongst the leaders for the remainder of the twenties. The flow of amateur batting was undiminished with Twining, Bruce, Crutchley, H. J. Enthoven and H. L. Dales all available for reasonable periods. Haig, Stevens and G. O. Allen were a tower of all-round strength, and Mann was ever liable to dominate the game with his explosive hitting powers.

During the season 1929 Mann, although still officially captain, was prevented by matters of business from playing more than occasional matches. In his absence Haig took over, and proved himself another most able captain. The season, with Hearne and Hendren still fine cricketers, despite the latter's lean patch early on, was brightened by the splendid all-round cricket and dazzling fielding of R. W. V. Robins. His leg-breaks, bowled at medium pace, were occasionally erratic, but had a most devastating power of spin and were coupled to a well concealed googly. Middlesex seemed on the threshold of another splendid decade but, in the early thirties, fortunes declined to a low ebb. As occasionally happens, to any side, the powers of several important members suffered a sudden decrease, and others were removed by business calls. It was not until Robins took over in 1935 that once again things got under way.

The side was now largely reconstituted. C. I. J. ('Big Jim') Smith, imported from Wiltshire, had found his best form with the new ball and, employing one basic stroke, hit the ball higher and further than anyone before or since. Soon the great batting partnership of D. C. S. Compton and W. J. Edrich was to take shape while J. D. Robertson had developed into a most polished Number One. H. G. O. Owen-Smith and J. H. Human played the same dynamic cricket as their captain and Joe Hulme continued to fly round the deep. J. M. Sims developed into a medium-pace leg-spinner. Only a superb Yorkshire side stood between Middlesex and the Championship. This they succeeded in doing until the war, with Derbyshire at the top in 1936. The season of 1939 saw the retirement of Robins but the momentum he had generated carried the team to second place in the table on the eve of the war, a position they had occupied in the previous three seasons. This was a fine period in Middlesex play, for Robins made the most positive use of the young and energetic talent at his command.

In 1946 Robins returned to the helm and immediately set about reorganising affairs. After a season's effort and experiment Middlesex were poised for the triumph of 1947. The summer was a fine one and the Middlesex batting calculated to make the most of good wickets and bowling which had not yet regained pre-war standards. Robertson and S. M. Brown regularly opened and both scored over 2,000 runs. They were followed by the truly devastating power of Compton and Edrich, both of whom topped the three thousand. This mass of runs was acquired with a speed which gave a good attack, led by L. H. Gray and sustained by J. A. Young, ample time to despatch the opposition. Having won the Championship, Robins retired and F. G. Mann took over. In 1948 the presence of the Australians robbed him of his best players for long periods but, in 1949, he was better served, and Middlesex shared first place with Yorkshire. At this Mann, the only son to succeed a Championship winning father, retired and Middlesex fortunes flagged.

Robins returned for the third time as captain for 1950, before a joint captaincy, shared by Compton and Edrich, fared no better for two years than such compromises incline to do. Edrich took over for five years, but the form of the great fluctuated and little glory came to Lord's.

Compton and Edrich retired in 1957 but J. J. Warr brought a strong reviving influence to bear in 1958, and Middlesex again pushed forward. F. J. Titmus was now a splendid all-rounder and A. E. Moss, who had done so well for almost a decade, still had a fair head of steam to call on. A promising crop of young batsmen including R. A. Gale, W. E. Russell and P. H. Parfitt helped Middlesex to reach third place in 1960 and when P. I. Bedford succeeded Warr in 1961 he achieved the same success. He, in 1963, gave way to C. D. Drybrough and, whilst the record has been moderate, the prospects are indeed bright at the moment of writing.

Titmus will captain a side which, with himself, includes five of the party that toured South Africa. In addition, Russell has advanced to be a most promising batsman.

After one hundred years of continued existence most institutions, and certainly county cricket clubs, take on a distinct character. That of Middlesex is pre-eminently of cheerfulness and enjoyment. These qualities permeate from the players to all associated with the club. Perhaps the best testimony to this spirit was the fact that, after ninety years of harmonious life, it was accidentally discovered that, as the original rules had been lost, the club had operated without any written code for almost its entire existence to that date.

Ian Peebles in *Wisden*, 1965

In its long and at times turbulent history, the MCC could be said to have involved itself in some controversial decisions, delivered the occasional questionable judgement, taken the periodic rash action. But always there were Fors as vociferous as the Againsts, always a feasible argument to support as well as to oppose. It took the great social revolution of an escalation in property values and the effect of television on the ground as a centre for providing lavish hospitality, to tempt the club into an act, or series of acts, which were felt by the vast majority of those who used the ground to be indefensible. One of the most delightful of all the various nooks and crannies of Lord's was the Tavern, an ancient building whose age and architectural vagaries had lent it an aspect of the asymmetrical. To walk out of bright sunshine into its cool, shadowed interior, and there to hear the clank of glasses and the buzz of small talk was to enjoy one of the sweetest delights any cricket ground, or indeed any public institution of any kind in England, could offer. On the walls were photographic talismans of the past, and upstairs was a bright, airy dining room from which it was possible, if you acquired the right table, to take your food while watching the cricket. Places like the Tavern are never designed or built, they evolve, slowly, by accident, and when they do they are always to be cherished as a happy fluke. Sadly the MCC did not cherish the Tavern enough to preserve it.

Beer-drinking spectators outside the Tavern at Lord's this summer will need to order an extra pint to drown their nostalgia. For at their backs, as they drink, time's winged chariot will be drawing near in the form of a redevelopment plan which will obliterate their century-old haven behind cover-point, or mid-wicket, depending on which end is bowling. MCC yesterday published the details of the comprehensive £1m redevelopment plan for the south-west corner of cricket's headquarters. In the plan the Tavern will be demolished and rebuilt with an added restaurant next to the Grace Gates and out of sight of the wicket.

A new stand, seating about two thousand spectators, will be built on the site of the existing Tavern, members' dining-room, and clock tower. In the background a twelve-storey block of flats will be erected, partially overlooking the ground, and presumably in great demand as a vantage-point during Test matches. But thirsty spectators can sip their pints in security all this summer and next, while they watch the run-stealers flicker to and fro; demolition of the existing Tavern will not start until September 1966, when the new Tavern will be ready for them.

MCC have also realised that there is a need for some therapeutic haven with a view of the cricket in which their customers can find liquid inoculation against bitter weather and tedious stonewallers. So on the site of the present Tavern they will build a smaller Tavern bar. And from here in the future, as in the past, hearty cries of comment and advice will be hurled at any batsman who tries to put up the shutters in the last few overs before luncheon.

The Times, 6 May 1965

With impressive speed – only five months after the announcements in the daily Press – the conservative element in the club made some attempt to muster its forces to resist the new plans, deploying with some bitterness the word 'grandiose' to describe the plot about to be implemented. But the resistance soon crumbled, or was brushed aside. Before long the Tavern, possibly the most endearing subsection to be found within the club estates, was demolished in the cause of banqueting suites and what are often laughingly defined as executive suites.

Full members should attend special general meeting 5.30 p.m., Wednesday, 20 October 1965, to oppose proposals to provide funds for grandiose building programme. Proposals include increasing members' subscriptions by 50 per cent, pledging property, selling investments and building site lease. Members have received no explanations. Financial justification very large expenditure seems very slender. Inserted by a member of the Club.

The Times, Personal Column, 18 October 1965

In place of the Tavern was erected a microscopic bar dispensing assorted beverages in cardboard cups, thus underlining the most puzzling of all the anomalies about Lord's, which is that within this beautiful, prestigious, meticulously maintained ground, the standard of food and drink available to the general public and, for the most part, to members, is hardly worthy of some ancient decrepit seaside boarding house. The gaping hole left by the removal of the Tavern removed any possibility of sitting down while refuelling, or of arranging a trysting spot, or of viewing the estate at leisure. An institution much loved had been exchanged for an eyesore universally derided, and from now on customers could enjoy the comfort and camaraderie of the old Tavern only by exercising the powers of recollection, for which reason the following general description of the ground, accurate in detail, endearing in spirit, has a special sentimental value, being almost the last comprehensive attempt to describe the totality of Lord's before those grandiose changes.

My first visit to Lord's as a contestant is one of my personal landmarks. For months before the match I'd been wondering about the long, lonely walk to the wicket through the little wooden gate, even though – as number ten batsman – little was to be expected of me. My secret, terrible fear was that the gate would not open... On the previous night I did not sleep. But the reality was an anticlimax, for by some quirk of fate twenty-two schoolboys contrived to bat thoroughly well and only seventeen wickets fell in two days. I never even put on my pads!

The game was made for ever memorable by the visit of the then King and Queen, with the newly-engaged Princess Elizabeth and Prince Philip. The crowd was very large on the Friday and hundreds surged round the Royal Box. I found myself drawn again and again to the dressing-room balcony to gaze over this amazing scene. I have been sentimental about the ground ever since.

Lord's has an apostrophe 's'. Cricket had only one Lord: Thomas – who filled, in his generation, the role of a Jack Solomons-cum-Prince Littler more nearly than that of Mr Ronald Aird, MC, TD, the Secretary of MCC, or his successor, Mr S. C. ('Billy') Griffith, DFC. Three times Lord moved his cricket field, the area of his business, and he finally settled at the present site in 1814. Ultimately he sold his interest in the ground for £5,000 – a good benefit – and he died in 1832, aged seventy-six.

If you take a man out from the Tavern, drunk or sober, stand him on the grass facing Father Time, blindfold him and tell him to walk across and touch the railings in front of the grandstand, the most extraordinary gyrations result. Old inhabitants of Lord's say that no one has ever succeeded. They will volunteer that Patsy Hendren tried and failed and that it is therefore impossible. Apparently everyone has one leg shorter than the other and cricketers are especially crooked-limbed. Hence the blindfolded figure staggers out across the green, veering here and there, and his course will either take him left, towards the pavilion, or away down the hill to the tiered stand at the Nursery end – according to which leg is the shorter. If the victim is part-filled with what the Yorkshiremen call 'bar-ile', he is, so they say, likely to turn right round and return to the counter, where the next round is very definitely his.

The concrete in front of the Tavern is the best place from which to look Lord's over. The dominating figure is Father Time; though, in fact, quite young he is very authentic and utterly ageless. He was an architect's surprise, for Sir Herbert Baker, who planned the grandstand, consulted nobody about the weathervane. In the last war a barrage balloon cable dragged it off its perch, but it has otherwise remained well-loved and unmolested. I don't believe he has ever been offered a catch by any batsman, although on the last Saturday of April 1955 Vic Wilson hit a ball only just below him. The bowler's name...?

The grandstand was ready for the Australians in 1926. It cost a lot of money, holds very few people and was therefore a poor investment. Some of the spectators sitting there cannot even see the entire field. Nevertheless, it is an impressive building.

The great scoreboard is its centre-piece. From a 'Bridge' above it the 'notchers' peer down; and theirs is probably the best view of all. The scoreboard seldom lets the public down, and when its does its efforts to right itself are greeted with jeers. If the cat-callers could only see the chaotic mass of bands and wheels behind its impeccable face they would be silent, for the strangeness of the machine is made even more grotesque by its size.

At either end of it are the boxes. These are always well decorated and well filled at the Eton and Harrow match, and used to be so for the 'Varsity match. Apart from these occasions and Test matches, they stand empty, being ideal places for those who enjoy watching great events at their leisure to the accompaniment of gentle carousal.

Below them is the Grandstand Balcony, which merges with the concrete stands at the Nursery end. These perches afford a fine broadside view and are among the most expensive seats at Lord's. Under them are the dark, cavernous regions on the ground level and the long thoroughfare in the Tunnel, which always seems to be full of people who are shaping to pass you on the same side that you were shaping to pass *them*. I have never made so many 'Excuse me' or 'I am *so* sorry' detours as in that Tunnel, and if you stand and watch at one end on a busy day the whole world seems bent on bumping into its neighbour. Perhaps it is the fault of the bars beneath; but even these have not the draw of the cricket, for a burst of applause drags everyone in the passage to the side and heads peer over to see if they can discover what it is they've missed.

The stands at the Nursery end provide as good a view of the cricket as there is at Lord's and these are the so-called 'free seats', where very many of the expert watchers are to be found. The Nursery – which used to grow the best pineapples in London – was acquired in 1887. In the course of the next year the Great Central Railway tried to buy it – with the rest of Lord's! – by compulsory purchase, but happily they lost their case. Now, however, the ex-LNER line from Marylebone passes under the Practice Ground and British Railways still, I believe, own a strip of land near the boundary wall.

The Nursery End is usually a very busy place, for it is here that the Cricketers' Factory is situated. Coaches from several organisations try to make cricketers of members' sons, young professionals, Middlesex players and members themselves, who are of various ages, complexions and measurements. The net wickets there are invariably good from the first day of the season to the last – and they get a most horrid pasting. They are well looked after and the contact of the ground with the pavilion is nowhere better illustrated than by the Nets Notice-Board, which hangs in the members' dressing-room and which affords some protection against the 'Must have a net in any weather' man.

There is a great gap in the Cantilever – or 'M' – stand, which serves the groundsman's purposes. Through it are trundled all the modern paraphernalia of covers, rollers and drying machines. Some time ago an imitation hostelry appeared there and elsewhere to draw some of the congestion away from the Tavern proper.

The Mound stand, built on the site of the old rackets court, adjoins. This is the respectable stand; one sees no unconventional figures there and nothing uproarious happens to disturb its quiet. Yet, if Lord's has any equivalent to the famous Hill at Sydney, this is it. The Mound was not always quiet; in 1899 the spectators whistled and stamped out the 'Dead March' from *Saul* when Darling took three hours to make 38. A disappointing building, perhaps – but it effectively fills this corner of the ground and is tall enough to block out some of the chimneys across the St John's Wood Road.

We are now back at the Tavern, jumping off the top of the bookstall and passing under the main scoreboard's younger brother. The Tavern is the traditional home of noise. Here the expert cricket barrackers collect and from here most of the insults are hurled at the players. Bickering individuals also produce laughter and amusement; the boozier the contestants, the more fun there is in it. But recently apathy has come to the Tavern. Its noise has been replaced by a more widespread phenomenon, the slow hand-clap – which is about the most unhelpful noise that anyone can make. It is infectious and depressing and more often than not has utterly the wrong effect on the object of disapproval. A good old-fashioned taunt is far more likely to do the trick, and the Cockney and other cads are very much missed in front of the Tavern for this reason and there are, of course, the Lord's Taverners themselves.

In the good old days the Tavern was never quiet; now, it is often at the Eton and Harrow match that the uproar breaks out, though one can recall some pretty funny shouts during a prolonged Oxford stand in the 1952 'Varsity match; John Bush, the Oxford opening batsman, was the target, and we – the opposition in the field – were told several ways of digging him out.

The members' dining rooms adjoin the Tavern and above are the main boxes, including the Royal Box. However, it is the pavilion and its two satellite members' friends stands which dominate this side of the ground. Pavilions at Lord's have not always been lucky and all the old records of the game were destroyed in a pavilion fire at the beginning of the nineteenth century. The present building has stood some seventy or more years and it is the real hub of the ground.

Behind it, across the carriage-way where the autograph hunters collect in their clamouring hordes, are the gardens and the tennis and squash courts. Occasionally these provide a refuge for cricketers, but more often are the home of a very different clientele. The rackets court has been turned into the Memorial Museum, and it is in this newly created building that one can see just what the ground and its owners, the MCC, stand for.

The fact that the MCC was founded in 1787 and has flourished ever since is important enough. However, Lord's has a deeper significance born in its tradition and the MCC has wider powers than a mere club could ever have envisaged. Lord's has always been the centre of things and it is on this ground more than any other that the great cricketers have played their greatest matches. Tradition seems to evoke a response which is hardly definable. Each person makes an analysis of his own personal reaction; the fact is that Lord's expects more from its visitors than do other grounds and casts a formidable spell upon them. Not even the most hardened Middlesex man, for whom it should be very much the ordinary ground, is left untouched by the extraordinary influence of Lord's.

Nor is it probable that a player appreciates the ground only because he eats well at Lord's. Furthermore, it is a case of 'all this and Hatfields too'; for a Hatfield out of a silver mug, Lord's own exclusive concoction in the sling line, has spurred more than one player on to bolder and more successful post-prandial efforts. Nor is it the fact that there are no better baths to be had in all England than those at Lord's – better than any others for several reasons, not the least being the luxurious sponges sending water, sweeter than any shower, down a tired back. Creature comforts there are in plenty, and though by themselves they may mean little they are signs of civilisation which, *in toto,* proclaim Lord's the leading cricket field.

These things do not happen of themselves; they are brought about by men. Ultimately, the club and its secretariat are responsible for the upkeep and preservation of the ground. In the particular period on which I am qualified to pass judgement they were very much aware of their responsibilities.

Much of the atmosphere of Pall Mall was banished from the pavilion and its magnificent Long Room by a liberal dose of paint, which brightened the rooms and staircases, showing up to good advantage those treasures of the past which the MCC possess – apart from its living, though sometimes semi-conscious, members. For Lord's is a permanent art gallery. The pictures can be *seen*; they are moved round and effectively hung, year by year. Many of them have been reproduced in a glorious book, the combined achievement of Miss Rait-Kerr, the custodian, and the late Sir Norman Birkett, who wrote a charming introduction to the work. Lord's is a handsome place; no member of the MCC has any excuse for ignoring its beauties.

The MCC leads the cricket world and succeeds in doing so without appearing deliberately to enhance its prestige or widen its powers. The position it holds is secure, because it is unchallenged. After the financial failure of the Shaw-Shrewsbury tour to Australia in 1887–88, it was Shaw's opinion that the MCC should run all cricket tours. MacLaren took the last private tour to Australia at the beginning of this century and since then the MCC has certainly been the perpetual Foreign Minister of the game.

It would be difficult to say who is Prime Minister. In theory it is a body meeting occasionally as representatives of all the first-class counties, which has power to change the laws. The leading first-class counties also have a majority vote on the Board of Control. This Board (which has a strong MCC contingent) administrates Test matches in this country. These bodies seem very loosely co-ordinated and, indeed, the only central organisation is the MCC, in theory and in practice still a private club with its subscription-paying members, whose welfare the club must always consider. There is, therefore, no democracy behind cricket's main authority.

Such a state of affairs has attracted severe criticism in some quarters for very many years. It has all centred upon the MCC. The club's defenders are unable to appeal to the widest public, whereas the severest critics feel that they represent the main body of the cricketing public, who, it is asserted, resent the MCC's overpowering influence.

The MCC, they say, moves too slowly and is a cumbersome, inefficient body unable to serve the best interests of the game.

These grounds for attack have always existed. Indeed, Sir Pelham Warner, who wrote the history of Lord's – as he was supremely qualified to do – constantly refers to the slow progress in development of the game and to the abuses which continued for so long without any action being taken by the MCC to remove them.

Such a one was the system of private tours; another he mentions is an old chestnut – bad umpiring, together with unfair play of one sort and another; there were the terms of professionals' employment, as well.

The MCC have taken notice of all these things and have, after deliberation, influenced the game by passing laws or by appointing a body to do so. The problems which exist now are very much the same as they were in the younger days of Sir Pelham, when W.G., the irreplaceable high priest of cricket, was still enthroned. If the MCC moves slowly, it also acts wisely; its impressive display of collective wisdom through the long years has made it the one authoritative body in the game. Basically, their problem has been to decide whether cricket should endeavour to keep up with the life of the world outside the Grace Gates and, if so, what changes are necessary to preserve cricket as an entertaining and profitable game.

Each individual must have his own answer to this problem, but the MCC represents the sum total of the best-informed views of cricketers, past and present. Its voice is not often heard; when it is heard, it merits respect.

One more thing: Lord's is not administered solely in the interests of its members, but of all the people who go to watch cricket there. The object of increasing the facilities all over the ground is to satisfy all comers and to widen its appeal. The only people at Lord's whose interests have not always been considered are the gentlemen of the Press. Cricket correspondents for many years were never adequately housed, enduring conditions like the days when Mr Knight 'stood all day in the bushes inside the rails, this being the only place from which to view the cricket on a crowded day, with no scoreboard or cards to tell him the state of the game, and having to record the score of the whole of the match in his own score-book'. The Press box today, however, compares favourably with those in Australia and elsewhere.

As for the mass of people who go to Lord's, they go to see cricket and therefore the better it is the more they are likely to be pleased. The MCC can be blamed if the paint comes off the seats, but they cannot be held responsible for uninspired batting or poor play generally. Some visitors are there for other purposes. Occasionally one hears a lady talking of Lord's as a place to sit and – 'you know, dear, it is really quite nice there ... Not that I know anything about the game, but one can get lunch there ...'

Some days there is good cricket, some days bad, and the vast majority of people will appreciate the one and recognise the possibility of the other. There are those who moan continually – one finds some of them on the Pavilion balconies. Their complaints are re-echoed on the upper storey at the other end of the ground; only the real pundit prefers the view behind the bowler's arm. At Eton and Harrow matches Brian Johnston generally manages to take a day off from official commentating and becomes a vociferous and highly amusing Old Etonian, holding court above the sight-screens. As a rule those couples who do not sit in the Mound get together under the grandstand balcony, unless they are prepared to shed various garments and expose themselves to the sun.

There is one figure who used to come to Lord's to take up two seats under the Balcony in the front row. Yorkshire Annie was a whole host in herself – a great ambassadress. Her comments, 'Come on, Yorkshire, give 'em another' or 'Go on, Frankie, bash 'im again', were straight from the ring-side – wrestling, not boxing. A conversation with her at the Pavilion back door revealed a most engaging character and a heart of gold. She adored cricket and was the self-appointed 'mother' of most of the players; nor was she as violently partisan as her comments would have had you believe. There have been many characters, Lord's 'regulars', who have had their own circle of followers and their own special seats.

Test matches and Whitsun weekends are still the main occasions which bring the public to Lord's and deepen their affection for it. Eton and Harrow is still one of these occasions and was the first Lord's tradition that I experienced. No one could grow up at any of the schools which play their vital match at Lord's without realising what the ground means and how inseparably linked it is with all the cricket that we played as boys. At Harrow this feeling was particularly strong because the school was generally 'coming from behind' and needed spirit to make up for lack of technique.

'Willow the King is a Monarch Grand,' we used to sing; and later another song was written, dedicated to F. S. Jackson. It contains this verse, of which the last three lines ought to be inscribed on the mind of every cricketer:

> Light Blues are nimbly fielding
> And scarce a hit can pass,
> But those the willows wielding
> Have played on Harrow grass.
> And there's the ball a-rolling
> And all the people see
> A gentleman's a-bowling
> And we're a-hitting he

There have been songs about other, more recent and more important, matches. The West Indian victory at Lord's in 1950 was a fantastic 'crowd match'. A small Caribbean contingent brought so much life and happiness to the ground on the last day that hardly an Englishman can have been sore about his country's defeat. The result was that splendid calypso about

> Those two pals of mine,
> Ramadhin and Valentine.

Lord's, though, is still primarily the Londoners' ground, and the Middlesex supporter, perhaps a little more sophisticated than the Oval habitué, is fortunate in his home territory. Sometimes even the gatemen are dumbfounded by the dialect. "Ere, Jack,' one was asked, 'can I go out to my jam-jar? I've left my ticket in the Lucy of my Nannie.' Which, being interpreted, meant that his coat (Nannie-goat) was in his car (jam-jar) and his ticket in its pocket (Lucy Locket)!

Jack Young was for years the Professor of Cockney rhyming slang and knew as much about Lord's as most people. Jack – like the present Middlesex players – was among those who spent their working days at Lord's. The visiting public sometimes see the 'native' workers but seldom get to know them. The man who pulls the numbers round on the scoreboard, for instance; in the summer he is a midget to everyone on the ground – only binoculars reveal him, dark and 'miniature'. I remember seeing one such in his overalls working on the ground alongside a famous umpire. He was one of the nameless ones; other Lord's men are better known. Jack O'Shea, whose expression of deep cunning was that seen on the faces of leg-break bowlers and who always reminded me of Eric Hollies for that reason, had a lot to put up with from selfish cricketers and uncontrolled temperament. But the Lord's staff seem rarely to change, they never seem to be older when one returns next year.

'Watty' – W. R. Watkins, the head MCC coach – who could tell a county cricketer a thing or two but who never gives advice unless it is asked for, is typical of the many men who always seem to find some good reason for being at Lord's, whatever the season. Bill Harrington, once one of his deputies, was a cricketing Jack-of-all-trades – bowler, batter, fielder, umpire and coach – for years one of the invaluable cogs in the MCC wheel. As was Maisie, who used to preside over the players' dining-room. She noticed all the cricketers, their habits and their wants, but was herself generally overlooked in the rush of eating. Today, some remain, some are gone, there are new faces.

But all have the tie of everyday things; and everyone connected with the game is somehow tied to the ground which is called 'the Mecca of cricket'. At times nothing about it seems right and everything is dreary. Incredible deeds break the monotony. Keith Miller, while an Australian airman, played at Lord's at the end of the war and hit the ball on to the top deck of the pavilion. Not long ago he drove three balls in one day clean over the Tavern. Will some other at last emulate Albert Trott and clear the whole pavilion with a mighty drive? Perhaps.

'Perhaps' is the fascination of the game, and if the story of Fowler's Match, the Eton victory of 1910, means more to me than any other cricketing miracle it is because of an educational accident. Other cricketers, other heroes—Lord's has seen them all. The gates which lead out to the busy world are named after the greatest cricketer, of whom Father Time, the *Zeitgeist* of Lord's, might well say:

> He was a man. Take him for all in all,
> I shall not look upon his like again.

ROBIN MARLAR in LESLIE FREWIN (ed.), *The Boundary Book*, 1962

WHEN the smoke and dust had cleared, and the appalled eyes of Lord's devotees fell on the spectacle of the new Barbarism, there was an attempt by some correspondents to pretend that nothing much had changed. Nothing much had, except that a diminutive slum had been installed as the headstone of a charming hostelry. It may be that putting a brave face on it was the best policy, because nothing now could ever redress the damage. But the expression of deep disgust at what had been done was a necessary thing, if only to let the decision-makers know where they had erred, and that they ought never to err in the same direction again.

Magic of Lord's – Even Without the Tavern

It is no use arranging to meet a friend on the Tavern forecourt, as it used to be called, or under the Clock Tower boxes during next week's Test match against India at Lord's. If you do, you will find yourself hidden by boarding from a view of the play and in the way of men working on the new stand, which it is hoped will be finished by the start of the 1968 cricket season.

The Tavern today means the new pub which has just been opened to the west of the Grace Gates, complete with banqueting facilities. For old times' sake, the MCC were keen to erect a temporary bar in front of where the original Tavern stood; but the contractors resisted lest it should delay their progress. As things are going, it will be possible to watch next year's Test match against Australia from where the workmen's sparks now fly.

That, of course, is a great occasion. England against Australia at Lord's, like the Royal meeting at Ascot, has nothing quite to match it. Yet for any touring side this particular Test match is the showpiece of their tour. It will be the same for the Nawab of Pataudi's side next Thursday, in spite of the steel girders and the building operations, and happily the Indians have found the form which should enable them to enjoy themselves.

May is now a bad and costly memory – for the majority of counties as much as the Indians themselves. I shall always remember, though never willingly, the lugubrious expressions of Mr T. Tarapore, who is their manager, and his treasurer, Mr Chinnaswamy, who was always huddled at his side, in those melancholy weeks. Only at Headingley at the beginning of this week did they allow themselves a smile as India, against all the odds, made their highest total against England.

Each touring side brings to Lord's its own distinctive cricketing character. And in some felicitous way they generally manage, when they come there, to be at their best, at least for a time. The Australians are still the toughest of them all and their feathers the most prized. Only a pair of Australians would spend the day on their feet, barracking from the stand reserved for members' friends. And only Keith Miller, two of whose many friends they were, would have put them there in the first place.

Only an Australian, too, would pay off a taxi at the Grace Gates a quarter of an hour before the start of play on a Monday morning when he was the 'not out' batsman. Richie Benaud, having been caught in the traffic on the way, did so in 1956, and in the next two hours he increased his score from three to 97. Yet the Australians are the first to say that no other ground in the world has the same quelling atmosphere as Lord's, that great 'cathedral of cricket' as Sir Robert Menzies has called it.

The New Zealanders offer more homespun methods, and a modesty that is inhibiting except when they have a Donnelly or a Sutcliffe in their side. Of all the fine innings played at Lord's since the war, Martin Donnelly's double century in the second Test of 1949 is among the very best. Donnelly had the irresistible qualities, when they are allied to one another, of greatness and humility. You will find him now, unchanged except that his hair is grey, fishing the mountain streams of Australia or boating with a large family in Sydney harbour.

South Africans have a special affection for Lord's as being the scene of their first Test victory in England. In 1935, when leather jackets lived in the wicket, Xenophon Balaskas, a Greek chemist from Johannesburg, destroyed England with his leg-breaks. Sir Pelham Warner described Lord's that season as looking like 'the sand on the sea shore'.

It was at Lord's, too, that the West Indies beat England for the first time over here. That was in 1950, when the calypso writers set Ramadhin and Valentine to music, and gaiety and passion broke loose. It was the start of the West Indies' rise to power. On their next tour, in 1957, Everton Weekes played so magnificently on a flying wicket that Mr Ronnie Aird, secretary of the MCC, wrote on the club's behalf to congratulate him.

In 1963 came the epic match which ended in a draw, with England three runs short and West Indies needing only the wicket of Cowdrey, whose arm was encased in plaster. Several West Indians who got drunk that night were excused the next day by a magistrate. 'I don't blame you,' he said. 'It was worth it.'

Now it is India and Pakistan whom people will go to Lord's to watch; and many of the pleasures will be the same as if the Australians were there. Planters from Assam will arrange to meet sheep farmers from Victoria in the Long Room Bar, as they did when last they were at home. Whoever the visitors, it is always a full and beautiful time of year, with the hay being mown, strawberries in the Memorial Garden, and the buttonholes matching the members' complexions.

Next week the Indians may feel with a sense of relief that they have already proved themselves after their great recovery at Leeds. Their bowling is critically weak, and at any time, as Trueman had a way of proving, a genuine spell of fast bowling tends to find them out. Probably they have too many weaknesses to win.

But if all goes well they will show with the bat those gifts peculiar to them-selves – of quickness of foot and eye, and flexibility of wrist – that can make them so attractive at the crease. If Pataudi, Chandra Borde, Hanumant Singh and Farrokh Engineer feel the sun on their backs and a firm and true wicket at their feet, the grazier and his friend will soon leave the bar.

JOHN WOODCOCK in *The Times*, 17 June 1967

WHILE memories of the lost Tavern were still clear in his mind, John Arlott looked back further still, to the days of the predecessors to the recently demolished inn. His essay puts a brave face on it, but his last thoughts have proved to be not quite accurate. Drinkers still congregate on the spot, still brandish pint glasses, still chant their disenchantment at moments of crisis. But there is no longer a real focus to their location. No more can they disappear into replenishing shadow to refill their glasses. The seductive rival attraction to the play, which the old Tavern used to constitute, has disappeared, and the premises are much the poorer for it.

One Tavern After Another

The new 'public bar and concourse', MCC officially assured us in their plan of development, 'will retain the traditional atmosphere of the present Tavern Bar'. More, if semi-authoritative stories are to be believed, the new concourse will be sloped or stepped so that Taverners will not, as hitherto, have to be graded – 'shortest to the front, tallest to the rear' – in order to watch the play over the rims of their tankards.

The positive and practical advantage, however, may not allay alcoholically nostalgic regrets for the Tavern which is gone. These are sentiments which should not be discouraged; certainly not ignored, for they spring from the tenderest of emotions.

Fortunately, however, history may allay these feelings. It would be a short-sighted Lord's Taverner, devoid of feeling for tradition, who was not prepared to consider the feelings of his spiritual predecessors when, exactly one hundred years ago, the original Tavern – for ours was the second – was demolished to make way for the place where he has so often satisfied simultaneously his appetites for beer and batting, tipple and Titmus, or crisps and Compton.

Thomas Lord started to build the first Tavern in what was then open country in 1813, but St John's Wood Church and several houses were going up by the time it was ready for the opening of the present ground – Lord's third – on 9 May 1914. During the week before the opening, according to the *St James's Chronicle*:

'A shocking accident occurred at the New Lord's Cricket-ground public-house, Marylebone Fields. The landlady of the house had occasion to use a small amount of gunpowder, and whilst in the act of taking same from a paper containing a pound weight, a spark from the fire caught it, and it went off with a great explosion. The landlady, her sister, and two little girls who were in the room were seriously burnt. The two former are in a dangerous way. The explosion broke every pane of glass in the room and set it on fire.'

Did no one think it odd that the landlady 'had occasion to use a small amount of gunpowder' sufficient to cause a great explosion? Or take it from a paper containing a pound weight?

The original Tavern was 'a low rustic building' with bow windows, fronted by a row of leafy trees, and the green at the front had tables and chairs for the patrons. By 1838 an assembly room had been built over the parlour, the long room at the end had been turned into a billiard room, and a railed-in bowling green was laid at its western end.

Owen Swift was a boxer, a large, heavy and lazy man who, in his brief career as a cricketer, was extremely reluctant to field. So he used to arrange for an easy chair to be placed outside the Tavern for him and while his side was in the field he would sit back in it, smoking a churchwarden pipe and with a quart pot of porter at his side – a good Taverner. His rest was disturbed on one occasion, if not for good, when one of his opponents lofted a big hit straight into his stomach.

To Swift, and many another, it must have seemed something near desecration when, in 1867, their familiar Tavern was demolished and what was to them the new, and to us the old, Tavern was built on the site.

Taverns – or rather The Tavern – may change: but I doubt there is much change in the character, the pleasure or the habits of those who frequent it: only Swift had a *quart* pot!

JOHN ARLOTT in Lord's Taverners Ball Programme, 4 November 1968

SOMEBODY who died just too soon to witness the changes, and who might, one fondly hopes, have said a word in favour of the old Tavern, was Sir Pelham Warner (1873–1963), a man who had held virtually every executive post which existed in cricket, who was knighted for services to the game, who always attempted to be the very soul of probity, and yet whose reputation has left floating on the air the faint aroma of bad fish. No amount of whitewash can ever quite erase the stain of the 1932–33 Bodyline tour, when he served as manager of an England side which behaved in direct contravention of the spirit of cricket he was always so keen to define and defend. Warner was, in fact, a slippery customer, and it somehow comforts posterity to know that he did not always escape from the implications of his own conduct scot free. Long after he died, the writer Alan Gibson recounted in *The Times* the emnity festering between Warner and the Gloucestershire left-arm bowler Charlie Parker. Parker had a brilliant career, taking over 3,000 wickets for less than twenty runs each, yet played for his country only once, a neglect due, apparently, to Warner's detestation of him. In Gibson's story, one night after a cricket dinner at Bristol, the two men found themselves enclosed in the same hotel lift, at which Parker, shrewd tactician as ever, perceiving that he was alone with his deadly enemy for the first and probably the last time, with no witnesses present, took advantage of the moment and landed one on Warner's nose. Perhaps it is kinder to leave him basking in the glow of a more congenial relationship, with one of the game's longest standing enthusiasts.

I met 'Plum' Warner only once and that was only for a few minutes in the Long Room in Lord's pavilion when he was far gone in years and I was gone a pretty long way myself. In the Lord's library on the same day I had been one of a small audience listening to C. B. Fry recounting his 'Varsity days when he used to take a standing jump from floor to mantelpiece, and he offered to repeat the performance for our benefit.

BEN TRAVERS, 94 *Declared*, 1981

EVEN as the old order passed, antiquarians were still raking the embers of long-forgotten controversy in their attempts to clarify even the tiniest issues of cricket history generally and of Lord's in particular. The rule which bars the female sex from the Long Room has continued to stand with astonishing longevity, although it surely seems only a matter of time before some resolute amazonian all-rounder takes the owners of the ground to court and invokes the Sex Discrimination Act. In 1966 a vigilant lady from the wild west of Britain addressed to the editor of *The Cricketer* the following communication, one which seems to suggest that for some obscure reason connected either with chivalry or patriotism or both, the rule debarring ladies from the Lord's pavilion was relaxed momentarily in deference to the blood that was still being shed in the name of freedom.

Dear Sir,

On looking at the picture of King George V watching England v. The Dominions at Lord's in 1918, I was amazed to see ladies sitting in the pavilion enclosure. Was this as unusual an occurence in those days as it would be today?

JULIA F. WHITE,
Letter to *The Cricketer*, 1966

WHILE ladies like Miss White take the legitimate path to equality in the cricket world, others pursue more devious and much, much, more reprehensible methods to make the feminine presence felt. The possibility that sorcery may after all have its place in the history of the game had not, until 1968, been one worthy of much serious consideration, but the claims of a married lady from London W14 certainly gave some pause for thought. That the all-powerful hypnotist had been responsible all these years for the prolific rainfall in and around Brisbane was a theory which brought a momentary glow to the mundane arts of the meteorologist, and although nothing more was ever heard of the lady's intervention in first-class cricket after the following report, there must remain a slight unease in the minds of all those victims of freak dismissals, unpredicted weather, broken limbs and unreasonable umpires, all of which phenomena may simply have been the unbending Mrs Munday at work.

Cricket and the occult make strange companions. But last Thursday a woman telephoned Lord's when the ground was covered in hailstones and said, 'I'm responsible for this storm. And there will be more such storms until the Australians pay their debts.' Mr Donald Carr, Assistant Secretary of Lord's, told a colleague of the incident at the dinner which the MCC gave on Saturday night to commemorate the 200th Test match between England and Australia. The Lord's switchgirl, he said, asked the caller for a little more information about herself: 'I have occult powers so far as the weather is concerned,' said the voice. 'Several years ago I used these powers to break the drought in Australia. The Australians have not yet paid me for my services. My spell over their matches will continue.' The Australian fast bowler Graham McKenzie received a similar call during the rainy second match at Leicester, evidently from the same person. Again the drought debt was her main theme. 'The woman said she wasn't fooling,' continued Mr Carr, 'and she proceeded to put a spell upon our Jean over the telephone. At the end of a few seconds, Jean felt so dizzy that she cut the caller off.'

In fact, using my own highly developed occult powers, I can tell Mr Carr precisely who the sinister caller was: Mrs Doris Munday, of Applegarth Road, W14.

'I've been doing this for a long time,' she confessed, clearly not in the least rattled at being discovered. 'It was three years ago when the Australians asked me to break up their seven-year drought, and when I did it, they gave all the credit to the aborigines. They also promised to take up a collection for me, and didn't; not that I wanted the money, but I was annoyed. So I started off by smashing the Brisbane Test in 1966. I've been bashing them ever since.'

Mrs Munday, who is 49, broke into the psychic business a long time ago as a hypnotist; then about four years ago she was told by a hypnotist friend that she was a 'weather manipulator'. 'I was so shocked I told him to leave at once. But then I took a few tests in psychic phenomena, and sure enough I found I could do it,' she recalls. Since then she claims to have broken droughts in India, China and the United States, brought freak storms throughout Britain and given countless friends sunny holidays.

The Times, 24 June 1968

JUDGING from the tone of her proclamations, which sound much more like the outrages of Beachcomber's Mrs McGurgle than they do of a lady of cultural discernment, Mrs Munday would not have thought much of a milestone in the history of cricket literature which had appeared two seasons before the disclosure of her hectoring sorcery. This was the most comprehensive encyclopaedia of the game ever published, a work of scholarship whose literary quality may be gauged from the superlative review of the history of Lord's contributed by one of its most passionate Australian boosters, notwithstanding the rebuff at the hands of maladroit officials half a lifetime before.

Lord's and the MCC

I think it was the No. 13 bus that I used to catch from the bottom of the Strand to go to Lord's. We would do some jogging past Nelson in Trafalgar Square, as he kept his good eye on things up Whitehall, and then, making speed, move out of Cockspur Street into Regent Street. It sometimes happened that long before we got to Piccadilly Circus the bus 'Clippie', with a discernment common to those of his and her ilk on the London buses, would gather from my accent the nature of my journey. Up Regent Street, then, there would be some tart and direful asides upon how the Australians would fare this day at Lord's, and by the time the bus had reached Oxford Street we would be on the best of swapping terms. From Oxford Street we turned into Baker Street, thence across Marylebone Road, and so on to the disembarkation point, the 'Clippie' having the parting thrust. The bus largely emptied itself at the Lord's stop. Most of the ties of my travelling neighbours I could recognise – MCC, the Forty Club, an occasional Middlesex one, the Purchasers and, sometimes, the distinctive one of the Hong Kong Cricket Club or a club in South Africa. One felt an affinity with them all. We were all off with hope to Lord's for the Test, and it was fitting, one always thought, that this particular route should have led along some of the best-known streets in the world because Lord's, of a surety, is as much part of the London scene as

Buckingham Palace, the House of Commons, the National Gallery, the red double-deck buses and so on.

Some (and particularly from Australia because it is not a national characteristic of ours to take care to conceal our first impressions) have expressed disappointment on seeing Lord's for the first time. It has not the ample open-space proportions of the Sydney Cricket Ground. It has not the immense tier upon tier of concrete construction that has hidden the gaunt Melbourne ground from the adjacent parklands and given it the character of a Coliseum. Lord's lacks, for instance, the idyllic charm and splendour of the hills that frame the fields of Adelaide and Cape Town. But no other ground, as I have seen them, can compare with Lord's in its calm and peaceful majesty. The Holy of Holies it has been exaggeratedly called by some of its disciples. I prefer to think of it as the Mecca of Cricket because I think it true to say that there has never been an outstanding player from any country who hasn't played at Lord's. I saw it first in 1938, enveloped by the slight mist of a departing spring. It was awakening to a new season, full of pride in its long and historic past yet looking forward with youthful zest to more great deeds in the sun. Old Father Time, I told myself as I caught a glimpse of him over the sight-board as he was removing the bails at the day's end, knew what it was all about!

There is that thought, suggested above, of every great and good international cricketer of every age having been seen at Lord's. That is one aspect of it – the travellers to cricket's Mecca – yet there is another important one that flits through the mind as it takes in Lord's for the first time. From here the game has spread to those countries, incredibly many, in which cricket is played. From here has come the spirit of the game, the changes in Laws, the mellowed and qualified lead that spreads through the game wherever it is played. A1 at Lloyd's is a well-known distinction. To be A1 at Lord's at the end of an international career and to be accepted into life membership by this immortal club is an accolade that warms the cricketing hearts that receive it.

On hearing of Lord's for the first time one is understandably apt to associate it with the aristocracy; to imagine it as the possible cavorting (if such a term can be used in this context) place of those members of the House of Lords set free, for the nonce, from their duties of the nation. But the naming of the places is as far apart in actuality as they are in being, although membership of both has been common to many. The House of Lords is on the River Thames at Westminster; the club is in Marylebone, from which parish its name originates, some miles away. There was a prisoner of war once who found the erroneous association to his well-being. The story is told of one Gordon Johnston who was elected a member of MCC when he was a prisoner of the Italians in 1942. His relatives decided to send him the glad tidings through the diplomatic channels of the Vatican yet, knowing that cricket would mean little to the Italians, they hesitated to use the initials 'MCC' in case some sinister meaning should be attached to them. The message, then, merely stated that he had been elected a member of Lord's. The Italian interpreter concluded that one under his charge had been elevated to the peerage. From that moment on, Johnston (and his fellows profited with him), was given prisoner-of-war treatment which the Italians thought commensurate with his lordly standing!

The name comes from Thomas Lord, 'the pivot around whom the formation of the Marylebone club turned'. Lord was a Yorkshireman, and his father, a substantial yeoman of Roman Catholic stock, had his lands sequestrated when he espoused the Stuart cause in the rising of 1745, so that he had to work as a labourer on the very farm which he once owned. We can imagine the feelings of the Lord family when it moved south to Norfolk, where Thomas Lord spent his young days. Thence he migrated to London and found employment at the White Conduit Club as a bowler and factotum around the club.

THE BLOSSOMING ACORN

This club was the acorn which blossomed into the gigantic oak to be known as the Marylebone club. Formed in 1782, it was an offshoot of a convivial West End club called the *'Je-ne-sais-quoi'*, some of whose members frequented the White Conduit House and played cricket matches on the adjoining fields near Islington. In spite of their club name, the cricketers did know what they wanted in the shape of a permanent cricketing home. Prompted by the Earl of Winchilsea, who could be considered the founder of MCC, and Charles Lennox, later to be the Duke of Richmond, a guarantee against loss was made to Lord if he would start a new private cricket ground. Lord was most willing and in May 1787 he opened his first ground on what is now Dorset Square. Middlesex beat Essex by 93 runs in the first game played there. The first recorded MCC match was in June 1788, when the club beat the White Conduit Club by 83 runs. Lord put a fence around the ground but the site was now an invaluable building one and became too costly for Lord's purse. The last match was played there in 1810. Foreseeing the future with some acumen, Lord in 1808 rented two fields on the St John's Wood Estate for a term of eighty years, free of land-tax and tithe, at £54 a year. The new ground was ready in 1809, so that for two years Lord had two grounds on his hands, the St John's Wood CC using the new enclosure. This club was afterwards incorporated in the MCC. The new Lord's was officially taken over on May 8th, 1811, the turf having been removed from the original ground in Dorset Square so that 'the noblemen and Gentlemen of the MCC should be able to play on the same footing as before'. The move was not popular with many members of the MCC and the club did not play a single match there in 1811 or 1812 – and only three the following year.

But London was spreading, and yet another move was enforced upon Lord as Parliament decreed that the Regent's Canal should be cut through the centre of the ground. The Eyre family, on whose ground the second estate was situated, were willing to grant Lord another plot. So Lord lifted his roots and his turf again and made yet another headquarters, this time on the site where Lord's is today. The rent was to be £100 yearly and the ground was to open in 1814. Lord was now a man of some substance in the parish of Marylebone. He was made a member of the Marylebone Vestry in 1807 and he also conducted a wine-and-spirit business. The ground had an inauspicious beginning. Four days before it opened the landlady of the public house at the fields was handling some gunpowder (and odd substance, surely, for such a one to be handling). A spark from the fire caught it and it went off with a great bang, seriously injuring the landlady, her sister and four little girls. It cast a shadow over the first game played there which MCC won against Hertfordshire by an innings and 27 runs.

THE WARD TAKE-OVER

The ground was immediately popular with the players and the public, but Lord, who could have had well-developed business instincts by this time, was anxious to turn more shillings. He obtained permission from the Eyre Estate to develop the ground as a building site to enhance the value of the sixty-eight years remaining of the lease, and plans for building houses were actually drawn up which limited the playing area to 150 square yards. Had Lord been able to sell out, there would have been no Lord's of today. William Ward, a director of the Bank of England and later to be MP for the City of London, saved the situation by buying Lord's interest in the ground for £5,000. Thus Lord's contact with the famous ground ceased in 1825. He continued to live in the adjoining St John's Wood Road until 1830 and died in Hampshire in 1832, aged 76. In 1835 Ward and his four daughters, who joined in the lease to bind any interest they had in the property, transferred it to one J. H. Dark, who gave £2,000 for it and undertook to pay the Ward family an annuity of £425 during the unexpired term of the lease, which was to be fifty-nine years from 1834, at a yearly rental of £150. When Dark first leased Lord's there were two ponds, one in front of the present Mound stand and the other at the west end of the ground. One of the groundsmen learned to swim there. Dark, himself, lived in a house near the present members' luncheon-room.

E. H. Budd, in 1816, hit the first century at Lord's, 105. He played with a bat weighing three pounds, which is in the pavilion today. William Ward, the saviour of the ground when Lord wished to sell it, hit 278 for the club against Norfolk in 1820 and that record as the highest score on the ground stood until Percy Holmes, of Yorkshire, hit 315 not out in 1925. Jack Hobbs beat that next year with 316 not out, which still remains the highest score made at Lord's. Middlesex were on the receiving end in both instances. Ward was a pretty powerful fellow. In that record innings he used a bat weighing four pounds – and, moreover, used the same bat for fifty years.

A wooden pavilion was built in 1814, and was later enlarged and improved by Ward. In 1825, a few hours after the Winchester–Harrow match, it was destroyed by fire and all the club's original possessions, records, score-books and trophies were lost. A new pavilion was built in 1826, it was enlarged in 1865, and in 1889 the first stone of the present pavilion was laid. A tennis court was put down in 1838 and pulled down in 1898 to make way for the Mound stand. The present tennis court behind the pavilion, to which a racquets court and squash courts were later added, was then built. In 1838 the pavilion was lighted by gas and the tavern, which had been erected by Lord when he opened the ground in 1814, had an assembly-room built over it. As far back as 1825, Eton, Harrow and Winchester used to meet at Lord's and did so until 1854 when the headmaster of Winchester, thinking London held too many temptations for his boys, forbade the fixture.

Pony races were held at Lord's in the 'forties and 'fifties after the cricket season had finished. A balloon, too, once made its ascent from Lord's which, however, had nothing to rival The Oval, where executions were sometimes held. Over these years the pitch and outfield at Lord's were notoriously rough. Sheep used to be brought in before a game began to nibble the outfield and only a small roller was used to condition the pitch. It is interesting that when a machine-mower made its first appearance strong objection was made to it by some members. In 1864, the first groundsman was engaged, at 25s. a week. A crisis arose in 1860, when the Eyre Estate sold the freehold of Lord's at a public auction. Dark and others wanted the club to bid but, strangely, they didn't and the ground was bought by Isaac Moses for £7,000. When, eventually, the ground became the property of the club on August 22nd 1866, £18,333 6s. 8d. had to be paid to Moses for the freehold. An old Harrovian, William Nicholson, advanced the sum and, justly, became President of MCC in 1879. In 1887, £18,500 was paid for 3¾ acres of what was known as Henderson's Nursery. It reputedly grew the best pineapples in England and was famed also for its tulips. Hence the origin of the Nursery end, where the practice pitches and car parks are. Four years later, MCC acquired the Clergy Female Orphan School from the then Manchester and Sheffield Railway in exchange for leave to tunnel under the practice ground. To-day the British Railways own a strip of ground forty yards wide where the arbours are situated and for which the club pay an annual rent of £200. The 99-year lease dates from May, 1897.

In 1888 the Great Central Railway promoted a bill in Parliament to acquire Lord's in order to run their line through it. This would have meant the end of Lord's, but the club made such a fuss that this part of the bill was withdrawn. Thus entrenched, the foundation stone of the present pavilion was laid in 1889. The cost, including extras and furniture, was £21,000. There have been some internal alterations since, but mostly the pavilion today is as it was first built. The Press stand was added in 1906, and was in use until the building of the splendid stand named after Sir Pelham Warner in 1958. The Press now sits at the top of this stand in a special enclosure that lacks nothing. It accommodates, too, broadcasting and television.

AN ARCHITECT'S INSPIRATION

After the First World War, MCC built a new grandstand and the cantilever stands on the east side of the ground. In 1934 an additional stand for members and their friends was built between the south clock tower and the pavilion. It cost £46,000. Sir Pelham Warner was one who thought it should have been better. In Churchillian terms he once said that never in the history of cricket had so large a stand been built at such a cost to hold so few people. Sir Herbert Baker was the architect of this, as he had also been of the grand stand about which a similar criticism might have been made. However, to his eternal credit Baker threw in a superb surprise in the Father Time weather-vane. Nobody on the committee knew that Father Time was to be placed on top of the grandstand. It is now one of the characteristics of Lord's, bails being taken off at the end of play by the Old Man with his scythe over his shoulder. In an air raid in 1940, during the Second World War, Father Time was caught up in the cable of a balloon barrage and slid gently down on to the balcony seats. He spent the rest of the war in the committee-room. Even today, however, Lord's does not hold very big crowds. Its capacity would be about 34,000 and that with a lot of people sitting on the grass. Many a time in Tests against Australia have the gates been closed before play began. It was no uncommon occurrence to see people leave the ground after a day's play and then join the over-night queue for play next day. That, to my mind, has always been one of the saddest sights in English cricket – to see thousands queued up outside grounds with no possible hope of gaining admittance.

It wasn't until 1877, when Middlesex began to use Lord's as their home ground, that the area realised its full potential. It is interesting to know that the ground was of heavy clay and badly drained and the outfield always rough and treacherous. There were no boundaries – except the pavilion – no stands or fixed seats of any kind, nothing but the small old pavilion and a line of loose benches running part of the way around the ground. The MCC Committee at this time was said to be stuffy and unimaginative. One who thought the club in dire danger of losing its character was the enthusiastic secretary, R. A. FitzGerald. He was intent on making Lord's the great centre of cricket but his Committee was lethargic and indifferent. FitzGerald hoped to induce Middlesex to use Lord's as its home ground but there was delay and Middlesex found another ground in Prince's. But later FitzGerald induced MCC to invite Middlesex again, and this time they accepted.

Down the years, Lord's has had the reputation of being conservative. Evidently it was true in the last century. FitzGerald induced E. Rutter and C. E. Green to nominate for the Committee, in order to liven it up, and Rutter relates how they sat in conclave with their elderly and reactionary fellow-members. 'At first we were distinctly ignored and Charlie Green was so utterly disgusted with the supercilious manner in which he was received that he declared he would never sit on the Committee again. Nor did he, but stuck to his resolve. Oddly enough, the next official appearance he made in the club was many years later (1905), when he was elected President.' Sir Pelham Warner notes that Green himself was not altogether free of reactionary tendencies. 'When I suggested early in the present century,' writes Warner, 'that there should be a wider screen at Lord's, Green remarked, "I never knew you were such a radical, Warner".' Warner, of course, was referring to the Nursery end. One wonders what the reactions of both him and Green would have been in 1964 when MCC agreed to a sight-screen being put up in front of the sacred pavilion for the first time. The rough nature of the ground must have been a trial. It cost the life of a Nottinghamshire player, George Summers, in 1870 when a ball reared from the pitch and hit his head. He died a few days later. During 1873, the ground was re-levelled and Lord's lost its proverbial reputation of being the most dangerous ground in the country.

SHADOW OF THE DOCTOR

Dr W. G. Grace was now casting his huge shadow on the game and its fields. With both bat and ball he did big things at Lord's for the Gentlemen against the Players and obviously he must have had a tremendous capacity for the game to make hundreds on such dubious pitches. In 1875, Grace made 7 and 152, run out, and took twelve for 125 against the Players. Next year in the same game he made 169 and took nine for 122. Fitzgerald resigned from the secretaryship that year, after thirteen years, and it is worth noting that during his time the membership grew from 650 to 2,080. Now the famous names stream across Lord's: A. J. Webbe, A. P. Lucas, Edward and Alfred Lyttelton, A. G. Steel, I. D. Walker – and the Australians of 1878. They shocked English cricket almost immediately by beating a powerful MCC side at Lord's by nine wickets in a single day. *Wisden* describes the scene on the ground: 'A stream of at least a thousand men rushed frantically up to the pavilion, in front of which they clustered and lustily shouted, "Well done, Australia!" "Bravo Spofforth!" "Boyle, Boyle!", the members of the MCC keenly joining in the applause of that maddened crowd, who shouted themselves hoarse before they left to scatter far and wide that evening the news how in one day the Australians had so easily defeated one of the strongest MCC elevens that had ever played for the famous old club.'

The Australians played two other games at Lord's that year. One was against Middlesex, whom they beat by 98 runs, a game memorable for a magnificent innings of 113 by the Hon. E. Lyttelton, the bearer of a renowned name in English public life and cricket, who thus became the first Englishman ever to score a century against Australia at Lord's. In honour of it Spofforth presented him with his walking-stick. At Lord's too the Australians played Cambridge who, under Lyttelton's captaincy, won a famous victory by an innings and 72 runs. As an Australian perhaps one could be forgiven for noting that this first team from our country took England unawares. Nobody thought there was strength in any cricket outside of England, and so a very haphazard fixture-list was drawn up for this tour. It might be true to say that England has never since taken an Australian team in England too easily – though some, before the 1964 tour, were disposed to regard Simpson's men as easy for the plucking! The Australians, under W. L. Murdoch, came again in 1880 but didn't play a single game at Lord's. Trouble had arisen two years earlier over the status of Australians as amateurs, but the most trouble arose over a decision in Sydney during the tour of Lord Harris's English team when Murdoch was given run out. Oddly, Dave Gregory, the NSW captain, went on the field and asked that the English umpire, Coulthard, should be retired. There were violent crowd scenes and Lord Harris, who was assaulted in the mêlée, said he had no wish to play against an Australian team again. The atmosphere towards my countrymen in England was icy, but Lord Harris nobly relented and helped to arrange the first Test against England in England, at The Oval, and England won a good game by five wickets. Dr Grace made 152, and Murdoch 153 not out for Australia. Australia played its first Test at Lord's in 1884, England winning by an innings and five runs. A. G. Steel was England's hero with 148.

Lord's now became in all ways the central point of cricket. Changes in the laws emanated from there, and in 1899 a Board of Control was set up, being chaired by the President of MCC, to decide upon finance, payment of professionals, hours of play, umpires and so on. As five Tests were played against Australia for the first time in this year, the Board also nominated English Test selectors. The South Africans sent their first side to England; the West Indians followed soon afterwards and a team from Philadelphia (USA) also played at Lord's. And so, down the years, every visiting team has played there and, like the Australians, I'll wager every team considers that its Test at Lord's is the big match of the tour. No player has walked on to Lord's for the first time without his heart beating infinitely faster. There is something about Lord's, something in its somnolent yet majestic atmosphere, that no other ground in the world possesses. The Saturday of the Lord's Test is without parallel – a crowded ground bathed in sunshine (if the sun is shining!), the arch-critics looking down from the boxes, Father Time keeping a gentle eye upon things, the learned 'Professors' in the Long Room (and the Press box, might I add) passing sonorous judgement. What honour indeed – to play at Lord's on such an occasion – and happy is the cricketer who, on tour, has notched his century there.

SENTIMENT IN THE BATH

It is an odd thing, but I sensed the traditions of Lord's most in the biggest and deepest bath I have ever seen – with the smallest plug-hole, incidentally. Lucky was the man who got first bath there, because it took an eternity to drain and refill and the gentlemen in the Long Room, not aware of our social engagements, must often have wondered as we moved with speed through the Long Room and scampered up the stairs for first bath after play. It was an intriguing thought to laze in that bath, ignoring the knocking at the door, and reflect that no doubt in its water had floated the whiskers of the great Doctor. Lord's is chock full of tranquil history and close association with the past. It is interesting to reflect upon all the great players who have gone down the steps from the pavilion, all fated to do so some day for the last time. I can see the ground again in 1948 when the clamouring thousands swarmed over it the day Don Bradman had played there for the last time. They stood in front of the pavilion and called for their hero to appear on the balcony. He didn't come. Possibly he was deep in his own thoughts. I can remember seeing Miller and Lindwall walk from the field for the last time. There is something tragic in this, and yet few, I think, recognise their final curtain call when it comes. If so, they would surely pause on the threshold of the Long Room and look back with a last, longing and lingering look.

Yet, when the playing days are gone, Lord's always beckons back. Many a lovely hour have I spent in the Long Room (and, indeed, in the committee-room) just walking around, yarning and looking at the relics of other days, in which Lord's abounds. In that Long Room you will meet all manner of Englishmen. Not everybody, in the English tradition, is prepared to pass the time of day with his neighbour. Be that as it may, I think all who enter Lord's are entitled to be alone with their own thoughts, if they feel that way. Of all the manifold stories of Lord's I like best the one of two strangers in the Long Room watching a match there one day and each ignoring the other – until a workman sauntered in, covered the bust of Dr Grace and carried it off. 'My God,' said one member to the other, 'that can mean only one thing. That means war.' And it did – the Second World War. One of the most dramatic photographs ever taken at Lord's shows cricketers lying prone to the ground during a match as a Doodle-Bomb speeds overhead.

There is much at Lord's upon which I haven't touched, but then Lord's has filled many a volume and my effort is but to give an Australian impression of cricket's holy of holies. It is well to reflect that from Lord's comes the sage guidance and wisdom in the game. And unlike our own Australian Board of Control, which not even yet seems to have forgotten the great cleavage between the players and officials in 1912, Lord's gathers to its bosom those who have served the game best on the field. Sir Donald Bradman is the only one I can recall in recent years who has been made welcome by our Board. We suffer, as I see it, from the desire of many unknowns to impress themselves in a sphere which they never graced in a playing manner. That is the beauty of Lord's, or, at least, one beauty that impresses itself upon me. One walks with cricket's past, present and future at Lord's. Long may Father Time reign there!

J. H. FINGLETON in E. W. SWANTON (ed.) *The World of Cricket,* 1966

IN 1972 the vagaries of pitch, slope, climate, humidity and the swing of the bowler transformed a moderate performer into a hero for a day. Apart from this one Test, the international career of R. A. L. Massie was undistinguished, yet he remains one of the few players to be rendered unforgettable through the accolade of having a game in which he played named after him.

ENGLAND v. AUSTRALIA
Second Test Match
Played at Lord's, June 22, 23, 24, 26, 1972
Australia won by eight wickets on the fourth day with nine and a half hours to spare. So Australia soon avenged their defeat at Manchester in a contest which will be remembered as Massie's match. The 25-year-old fast bowler from Western Australia surpassed all Australian Test bowling records by taking sixteen wickets for 137 runs; in all Tests only J. C. Laker, nineteen for 90 for England against Australia in 1956, and S. F. Barnes, seventeen for 179 for England against South Africa in 1913–14, stand above him. Moreover, Massie performed this wonderful feat on his Test début, the previous best by a bowler on his first appearance for his country being as far back as 1890 when at The Oval, Frederick Martin, a left-arm slow to medium pacer from Kent, took twelve for 102 for England against Australia on a pitch that had been saturated by rain.

Not for the first time, particularly in recent years, England were badly let down by their specialist batsmen, who failed lamentably in all respects. From the start they allowed the Australian bowlers to take the initiative and their excessive caution met with fatal results.

Illingworth won the toss for the seventh consecutive time and one must admit that the hard fast pitch—it remained true to the end—was ideal for men of pace. During the first three days, too, the atmosphere was heavy and ideally suited to swing. Massie maintained excellent length and direction and his late swing either way always troubled the England batsmen. The conditions would also have suited Arnold, but England's best bowler at Manchester was suffering from hamstring trouble and on the morning of the match was replaced by Price, who proved rather disappointing. That was England's only change, whereas Australia brought in Edwards and Massie, who had recovered from a strain. Both were making their Test début and for the first time Western Australia had four representatives in the Test XI.

One must also stress the important part Lillee played in Australia's victory. Perhaps he was inspired by his six for 66 in England's second innings at Manchester. Anyhow, although this time his reward was confined to two wickets in each innings he looked a far better bowler. He had tidied his long fast approach of 22 strides, he was truly fast and he sent down far fewer loose deliveries. Massie capitalised on the hostility of his partner.

A light drizzle delayed the toss and the start for twenty-five minutes. Australia lost little time in taking the initiative, Boycott, Luckhurst and Edrich being removed for 28 runs before any substantial resistance was offered. At times Massie bowled round the wicket, but Smith and D'Oliveira raised the score to 54 for three at lunch. Afterwards, D'Oliveira struck three fine boundaries only to be leg-before to Massie's slower ball, whereupon Greig proceeded to hit his third successive fifty for his country.

Greig and Knott enabled England to make a satisfactory recovery in their stand of 96, but immediately after tea at 147 Knott spooned Gleeson gently to mid-wicket where to everyone's amazement Francis dropped the catch. In the end both batsmen fell to casual strokes, but Illingworth and Snow played well so that at the close of a momentous and exciting first day England were 249 for seven.

Next morning the new ball was due after two overs and Massie snatched the remaining three wickets and led his team back to the pavilion. Of the 36 bowlers *Wisden* lists who have taken eight wickets in a Test innings, only A. E. Trott, for Australia against England at Adelaide in 1895 and A. L. Valentine, for West Indies against England at Manchester in 1950 had previously accomplished the performance on their Test début.

A superb century by G. S. Chappell made the second day memorable after Australia had received early shocks in the loss of Francis and Stackpole for seven runs. Ian Chappell set a noble example as captain, leading the recovery with an aggressive display. He used his favourite hook to some purpose while his brother remained strictly defensive. Ian struck one 6 near Smith before he fell to a fine running-in catch that Smith held rolling over near his ankles.

Snow, if not so fast as Lillee, bowled splendidly and soon induced a catch from Walters, but Greg Chappell, in for three hours before he hit his first boundary, now took charge, excelling with the off drive. Edwards gave valuable support, but with the light murky Illingworth brought on Gifford and then himself, tempting Edwards into indiscretion for Smith to bring off another fine running catch on the leg side. Chappell duly completed his hundred on the stroke of time and Australia wound up 71 behind with half their wickets intact.

On Saturday the gates were closed at 11.10 a.m. with 31,000 inside. Greg Chappell lasted another hour and a half, batting altogether for six and a quarter hours and in his splendid upright style hit fourteen 4s. Australia, who did not wish to face a huge target in the fourth innings, went ahead through another gallant display of powerful hitting by Marsh. He struck two 6s and six 4s in his 50, which came in seventy-five minutes and Australia gained a useful lead of 36. Snow, five for 57, alone of the England bowlers excelled.

Only the most optimistic Australian could have anticipated the success which so soon attended the efforts of Lillee and Massie. The England collapse—half the side were out for 31—began when a fast shortish ball from Lillee lifted and Boycott, instead of dodging, preferred to let it strike his body while his bat was lifted high. It bounced off his padded front left ribs over his shoulder and dropped behind him on to the off bail. It was most unlucky for Boycott as well as England. Obviously, the Australians, having captured so valuable a wicket so cheaply, now bowled and fielded like men inspired. Luckhurst had no positive answer to Lillee's pace and soon went, to be followed by Edrich who was compelled to flick at a late outswinger (to him) that would have taken his off stump.

Again, Smith, getting right behind the ball, kept up his end, but the remainder were bemused by Massie's accuracy and late swing which meant that at the end of a miserable Saturday for England they stood only 50 runs ahead with nine wickets down.

It remained only for the weather to stay fine on Monday for Australia to gain their just reward. Gifford and Price put on 35 in the best stand of the innings but Australia needed only 81 to win and Stackpole saw them comfortably home.

With 7,000 present on the last day, the match was watched by just over 100,000 (excluding television viewers) and the receipts of £82,914 were considered to be a world record for a cricket match with the possible exception of India.   N.P.

England

G. Boycott, b. Massie	11	b. Lillee	6
J. H. Edrich, lbw. b. Lillee	10	c. Marsh, b. Massie	6
B. W. Luckhurst, b. Lillee	1	c. Marsh, b. Lillee	4
M. J. K. Smith, b. Massie	34	c. Edwards, b. Massie	30
B. L. D'Oliveira, lbw. b. Massie	32	c. G. S. Chappell, b. Massie.	3
A. W. Greig, c. Marsh, b. Massie	54	c. I. M. Chappell, b. Massie.	3
†A. P. E. Knott, c. Colley, b. Massie	43	c. C. S. Chappell, b. Massie.	12
*R. Illingworth, lbw. b. Massie	30	c. Stackpole, b. Massie.	12
J. A. Snow, b. Massie	37	c. Marsh, b. Massie	0
N. Gifford, c. Marsh, b. Massie	3	not out	16
J. S. E. Price not out	4	c. G. S. Chappell, b. Massie.	19
L-b. 6, w. 1, n-b. 6.	13	W. 1, n-b. 4	5
	272		116

1/22 2/23 3/28 4/84 5/97   1/12 2/16 3/18 4/25 5/31
6/193 7/200 8/260 9/265   6/52 7/74 8/74 9/81

Bowling: *First Innings*—Lillee 28–3–90–2; Massie 32.5–7–84–8; Colley 16–2–42–0; G. S. Chappell 6–1–18–0; Gleeson 9–1–25–0. *Second Innings*—Lillee 21–6–50–2; Massie 27.2–9–53–8; Colley 7–1–8–0.

Australia

K. R. Stackpole, c. Gifford b. Price	5	not out	57
B. C. Francis, b. Snow	0	c. Knott, b. Price	9
*I. M. Chappell, c. Smith, b. Snow	56	c. Luckhurst, b. D'Oliveira	6
G. S. Chappell, b. D'Oliveira	131	not out	7
K. D. Walters, c. Illingworth, b. Snow	1		
R. Edwards, c. Smith, b. Illingworth	28		
J. W. Gleeson, c. Knott, b. Greig	1		
†R. W. Marsh, c. Greig, b. Snow	50		
D. J. Colley, c. Greig, b. Price	25		
R. A. L. Massie, c. Knott, b. Snow	0		
D. K. Lillee, not out	2		
L-b. 7, n-b. 2	9	L-b. 2	2
	308	(2 wkts)	81

1/1 2/7 3/82 4/84 5/190   1/20 2/51
6/212 7/250 8/290 9/290

Bowling: *First Innings*—Snow 32–13–57–5; Price 26.1–5–87–2; Greig 29–6–74–1; D'Oliveira 11–5–48–1; Gifford 11–4–20–0; Illingworth 7–2–20–0. *Second Innings*—Snow 8–2–15–0; Price 7–0–28–1; Greig 3–0–17–0; D'Oliveira 8–3–14–1; Luckhurst 0.5–0–5–0.

Umpires: D. J. Constant and A. E. Fagg.

Wisden, 1973

T IMES and life-styles were changing so rapidly in the land outside the walls of the castle in St John's Wood that it was inevitable for infiltrators to pierce the defences. The increasing say of politicians in the affairs of cricket led to the pathetic insistence that politics had no place in sport. But then, nor ought sport to have any place in politics, and like it or not, nations and governments were tending more and more to see games of cricket and football as issues of national pride and prestige. In recent years three great schisms have left scars on the face of cricket. As the 1960s ended, so did the connections between South Africa and Commonwealth cricket. The issue centred round the right of the English selectors to send whichever players they pleased on a tour to South Africa. Among their selections was Basil D'Oliveira. The fatuousness of the South African government knew no bounds, and culminated in the insistence that they and not the England selectors should pick the team. When your opponent insists on selecting your team as well as his, then that mutual assumption of civilised codes of conduct which is essential to all sophisticated team games finally flies out of the window; the MCC, after a certain amount of dithering, took the necessary action.

The second great watershed was the passing of power from the MCC to the Test and County Cricket Board, to some extent the same animal with a longer name, but certainly with a few drastic modifications. The third was the attempt by an Australian entrepreneur called Kerry Packer to break the monopoly of employment possessed by established cricket boards. Packer's sole aim, to do with the inner politics of Australian television, was fulfilled, but its side-effects included a telling blow to the autocracy of the MCC, who banned players who had succumbed to his financial blandishments, only to be taken to court by the banned players who claimed wrongful deprivation of income. The MCC lost, and players in England have, ever since, seen their hypothetical earnings rise to previously undreamed-of heights. In the 1970s these and many other troubles transformed the cricket world, bringing into its green fields both the violence of political disaffection and the sheer daftness of a morality which was becoming so relaxed as to be in danger of falling in a heap.

ENGLAND v. WEST INDIES
Lord's, August 23, 24, 25, 27, 1973

West Indies won by an innings and 226 runs. This match will assuredly be known in cricket history as 'The Bomb Scare Test'. There was drama on the Saturday afternoon when 28,000 people were ordered to leave the ground following a telephone warning that a bomb had been planted. The call proved to be a hoax, but no chances could be taken with the safety of players and spectators because an IRA bomb campaign was in full swing in London at the time. The incident caused the loss of 85 minutes' playing time and it was agreed that half an hour would be added to the day's play and further extra time provided for on Monday and Tuesday. But the triumphant West Indies had no need of it and they won with a day and a half to spare.

Wisden, 1974

Arlott: And a freaker, we've got a freaker down the wicket now. Not very shapely, and it's masculine. And I would think it's seen the last of the cricket for the day. The police are mustered, so are the cameramen, and Greg Chappell. And now he's had his load, he's being embraced by a blond policeman, and this may be his last public appearance, but what a splendid one. And so warm...

Voice off: He flashed through the covers.

Arlott: Many, of course, have done this on cold rugby grounds, but this chap has done it before twenty-five thousand people, on a day when he doesn't even feel cold. And he's now being marched down in the final exhibition, past at least eight thousand people in the Mound Stand, some of whom, perhaps, have never seen anything quite like this before. And he's getting a very good reception, which he's acknowledged in an extremely gracious fashion, and at least he's being escorted off by an Inspector, and no play will be re-started until he's gone. Fine performance, but what will they do about finding him swimming trunks?

BBC Radio Commentary, England v. Australia, Lord's, 4 August 1975

Michael Angelow, who ran naked across Lord's cricket ground on Monday, was fined £20 when he appeared at Marylebone Magistrates' Court yesterday. Mr Angelow, aged 24, a merchant seaman, of St Albans, Hertfordshire, admitted insulting behaviour. When told that the escapade was for a £20 bet, Lieutenant-Colonel William Haswell, chairman of the bench, said, 'The court will have that £20. Please moderate your behaviour in future.'

The Times, 6 August 1975

THE death of Sir Neville Cardus (1889–1975) removed from the scene a man who had done as much as anyone to convey the idea of Lord's to those who had never experienced it at first hand. Although he ended his life living in a block of flats in Marylebone Road, no more than a few minutes' octogenarian saunter from Lord's, Cardus remained to the end what he had always been, a child of Old Trafford, whose turn-of-century giants had introduced him to the game he loved so deeply and about which he wrote with such genius. But Lord's became his local ground, and right to the end he was to be seen, often alone, gazing through the glass of the MCC room to the left of the Long Room, his eyes masked with the recollection of other days and other ways. He was in love with the tradition of Lord's, its pageantry and its antiquarian aspect, and was sometimes inclined to gild the patrician lily just a shade. But he always did it with such faultless literary aplomb that only a jackass could take exception. Before he died I had several conversations with him, but always at his home, and twice on the telephone. I never spoke to him at Lord's, feeling, whenever I saw him there, that this was a private affair between himself and the ground. I think in a way he belonged to it and it to him just as completely as Old Trafford. The best description I know of Cardus at Lord's, apart from those written by himself, of course, was contributed in the post-war years by his publisher.

Almost any fine summer's day will find him at Lord's, high in the Press box, wandering from the Tavern to the Long Room and back, or sitting alone in one of the stands. Even those minor games for which the match-card used to promise 'Band if possible' draw him in. He smokes a pipe and carries a book under his arm. Often he seems not to be watching the players at all, but experience has shown that little escapes him. If one eye is on the Eternal Verities, the other is firmly fixed on Denis Compton.

RUPERT HART-DAVIS (ed.), *The Essential Neville Cardus*, 1949

BUT still Lord's struggled on, doing what it could to maintain its grace and dignity in an age seemingly indifferent to both those qualities. Towering buildings began to pierce the skyline behind the Mound Stand, although the observation of a few years before, that the expensive apartments towering over the ground would be much coveted because of the free view they afforded of the play, proved to be a pipe-dream; one of the most striking features of the New Brutalism glowering down on the mild Edwardian mannerism of the pavilion was that, all along these new terraces, the balconies were empty. But Lord's remained Lord's, ineffable, inimitable, indefinable. In a murder novel about cricket published in the summer after the affair of The Streaker, co-written by an ex-England captain, there appeared the following incidental observation.

Lord's is still reckoned to be the greatest cricket ground in the world. The old Tavern has gone and its replacement is appalling enough; miniature skyscrapers disfigure the horizon as Central London steadily devours the village of St John's Wood, but the ground has retained its sense of proportion and the superb Victorian pavilion (Architect, Mr T. Verity) still subdues all innovations.

TED DEXTER AND CLIFFORD MAKINS, *Testkill*, 1976

BUT if Lord's was to a great extent the same, the game over which it presided had changed so much that a virtuoso of the old school, W. G. Grace for one, would not have been able to make any sense of what was going on. Most of the rule-changes – finicky, fussy amendments – were in the cause of that ancient chimera, Brighter Cricket. But somehow the tinkering with over-rates and run-bonuses only confused the spectators while it did less than nothing to render the cricket brighter. At last, the poor captains and umpires, obliged to keep several different sets of rules at their fingertips, for the County Championship, for the various one-day leagues and competitions, for Test matches, understandably made errors from time to time. Years before, when F. G. Mann erred on the side of mathematical confusion while captaining England against New Zealand, the writing had been on the wall. But nobody seemed to take any notice, with the result that by the end of the decade, the *Wisden* reports were obliged to delve into the Higher Mathematics in order to explain what the umpires did wrong.

MIDDLESEX v. GLOUCESTERSHIRE
Lord's, July 20, 21, 22, 1977

Drawn. An extraordinary match with two distinct halves reached a controversial, tense climax after seeming all over on the second afternoon. Brearley batted all the first day for his 145 and both he and Gatting were missed twice. After tumbling from 48 for no wicket to 80 all out Gloucestershire came back strongly with an unbroken opening stand of 145 on the second day. The second innings could hardly have provided a greater contrast, for every batsman fought tenaciously after the first three had fallen in the opening hour of the third day. While Edmonds and Emburey toiled through a vast number of overs—Edmonds' 77 has rarely been surpassed in the Championship—their colleagues gradually showed the strain and substitutes were needed, including their coach, Don Bennett, for Brearley, Smith, Featherstone and Selvey. The last wicket fell at 5.12, but umpire Alley allowed Middlesex only 12 overs to make 75 (as five had already been bowled since 5.00), seeming to ignore the regulation that when a new innings starts inside the last hour it should contain one over for every three minutes. 38 minutes should have meant 13 overs, but a note from Brearley to the umpires as Middlesex vainly tackled their task proved fruitless. Against Procter at his fastest Middlesex sacrificed wickets recklessly, but finished 12 short.

Middlesex

M. J. Smith, c. Stovold, b. Brain	1	c. Vernon, b. Brain	22
*J. M. Brearley, b. Procter	145	run out	0
G. D. Barlow, b. Childs	55	c. Shepherd, b. Brain	0
C. T. Radley, c. Stovold, b. Childs	28	b. Brain	10
M. W. Gatting, c. Stovold, b. Brain	79	not out	21
N. G. Featherstone, c. Vernon, b. Procter	7		
P. H. Edmonds, not out	0	c. and b. Procter	1
†I. J. Gould (did not bat)		run out	1
J. E. Emburey (did not bat)		not out	0
M. W. W. Selvey (did not bat).		b. Brain	0
B. 11, l-b. 8, w. 2, n-b. 7	28	B. 3, l-b. 4, n-b. 1	8
(6 wkts dec.)	343	(7 wkts)	63

1/4 2/146 3/211 4/310 5/332 6/343

1/18 2/22 3/53 4/57 5/59 6/59 7/63

W. W. Daniel did not bat.

Bowling: *First Innings*—Procter 32–4–85–2; Brain 22.5–4–85–2; Vernon 17–2–58–0; Childs 28–3–87–2. *Second Innings*—Procter 6–0–28–1; Brain 5.5–0–27–4.

Gloucestershire

Sadiq Mohammad, c. Radley, b. Emburey	32	c. Emburey, b. Edmonds	82
†A. W. Stovold, c. and b. Edmonds	19	c. Emburey, b. Edmonds	81
Zaheer Abbas, b. Edmonds	0	b. Emburey	6
A. J. Hignell, c. Gatting, b. Emburey	1	b. Edmonds	26
*M. J. Procter, lbw. b. Edmonds	0	c. Radley, b. Edmonds	38
D. R. Shepherd, lbw. b. Edmonds	5	c. Gatting, b. Edmonds	22

J. C. Foat, lbw. b. Emburey . . .	0	c. Smith, b. Edmonds . . .	17
J. H. Shackleton, st. Gould, b. Edmonds	5	c. Gatting, b. Emburey . .	28
M. J. Vernon, c. Radley, b. Emburey	2	lbw. b. Edmonds	3
B. M. Brain, not out	2	c. Gatting, b. Edmonds . .	0
J. H. Childs, b. Edmonds	0	not out	0
B. 6, l-b. 6, n-b. 2	14	B. 19, l-b. 5, n-b. 10 .	34
	80		337

1/48 2/48 3/49 4/52
5/58 6/59 7/76 8/76 9/79

1/155 2/168 3/186
4/241 5/270 6/277
7/316 8/326 9/335

Bowling: *First Innings*—Daniel 4–0–12–0; Selvey 5–0–24–0; Edmonds 16–6–18–6; Emburey 13–6–12–4. *Second Innings*—Daniel 13–4–27–0; Selvey 4–2–5–0; Edmonds 77–13–132–8; Emburey 66.4–26–91–2; Gatting 5–2–17–0; Featherstone 12–3–29–0; Smith 2–0–2–0.

Umpires: W. E. Alley and J. van Geloven.

Wisden, 1978

ONE predictable effect of the widespread changes, inside Lord's and outside even more so, was a growing appetite for what was now regarded as the good old days, when privilege walked across the grass and a gentleman was a Gentleman. One of the most famous fictitious characters ever to acknowledge applause at Lord's had been the amateur cracksman, A. J. Raffles, whose fingers were equally eloquent whether flipping out leg-breaks or closing round some valuable object. His creator, E. W. Hornung, brother-in-law of Sir Arthur Conan Doyle, had stopped publishing the Raffles stories in 1909, although he lived on until 1921. In 1932 a writer called Barry Perowne was invited to revive Raffles, which he did with several amusing short stories, the vital difference being that while Hornung had been romancing with the raw materials of his own age, Perowne was unashamedly trafficking in the sentiment attaching to a world on the far side of Flanders Fields. In a tale called 'Raffles of the MCC', the cracksman and his friend Bunny, whose relationship with Raffles is suspiciously reminiscent of the attachment between Holmes and Watson, decide to steal an ancient and very valuable tennis racket from Lord's, an episode which gives Mr Perowne the opportunity to pause for a moment to describe the view of Lord's from an uncommon vantage-point, in the dank fog of a winter's night.

The stands and terraces, so vividly stippled in summertime with the confetti hues of ladies' parasols and men's boaters and blazers, loomed now deserted, spectral in the dank, persistent fog. Only from the tennis-court building, in its secluded corner of the famous demesne, did gleams of gaslight faintly mitigate the muffling vapour. Capped, scarved and ulstered, we entered the building. Just inside the entrance stood a glass case. In this was housed the token trophy of the tournament – token only, as it was one of the priceless treasures at Lord's and never left the grounds.

BARRY PEROWNE, *Raffles of the MCC*, 1979

By now, the tradition of Test matches between England and Australia was venerable enough for prestigious anniversaries to loom, and to be celebrated with some style. In 1977 the centenary of England v. Australia in Australia had been marked by a commemorative match played with great spirit and watched by a small army of retired Test cricketers. It was the most obvious thing in the world for the same kind of friendly contest to be played three years later to mark a hundred years of England v. Australia in England, and even more obvious that this match should be staged at Lord's, again with as large an army as could be mustered of ex-Test players. In the event, everything that could go wrong did go wrong, from the inconclusive result to the weather. Neither of these two disappointments might have been too hard to bear had it not been for a third mishap, about which *Wisden*, the MCC, the Press, in fact everyone involved, was tight-lipped.

ENGLAND v AUSTRALIA
Cornhill Centenary Test
Played at Lord's, August 28, 29, 30, September 1, 2, 1980

Drawn. It had been hoped that England's Centenary Test, to mark the centenary of the first Test played in England—at The Oval in 1880—might be played in late summer sunshine with many a nostalgic reunion, some splendid fighting cricket and a finish to savour.

Over 200 former England and Australian players assembled from all over the world; it was impossible to move anywhere at Lord's without meeting the heroes of yesteryear. The welcoming parties, the dinners and the take-over by Cornhill Insurance of a London theatre for a night were all hugely successful. Sadly, however, the party in the middle was markedly less so.

Almost ten hours had been lost to rain in the first three days, the match ended in a tepid draw, with many people disappointed that England did not make a bolder bid to meet Australia's final challenge to score 370 in 350 minutes. With Boycott 128 not out and Gatting 51 not out they had reached only 244 for three at the finish.

As much as for the cricket, though, the game will be remembered for a regrettable incident, seen by millions on television on the Saturday afternoon, in which angry MCC members were involved in a momentary scuffle with umpire Constant as the umpires and captains moved into the Long Room after their fifth pitch inspection of the day. Ian Botham, the England captain, and Greg Chappell, his Australian counterpart, saw to it that matters got no worse. When play finally started at 3.45 p.m., police escorted the umpires through the Long Room and on to the field.

Two MCC members, identified by Chappell, were questioned by the Secretary, Mr J. A. Bailey, after the incident on Saturday afternoon. This was followed, on the Monday, by the following statement:

'Enquiries instituted today into the behaviour of certain MCC members towards the umpires and captains on Saturday leave no doubt that their conduct was inexcusable in any circumstances. Investigations are continuing and will be rigorously pursued with a view to identifying and disciplining the culprits. Meanwhile the club is sending to the umpires and to the captains of both sides their profound apologies that such an unhappy incident should have occurred at the headquarters of the game and on an occasion of such importance.'

Fifty minutes had been lost to rain on the first day and all but an hour and a quarter on the second. On the third, the Saturday, ninety minutes' rain in the early morning left a soft area around two old uncovered pitches on the Tavern side of the ground. The ground staff, however, thought play could have started by lunch, as did a crowd of some 20,000 who were growing increasingly impatient in sunshine and breeze. Umpires Bird and Constant were the sole judges of when play should start, with one captain noticeably keener to play than the other; Australia being in the stronger position, Chappell was the more eager of the two. They conducted inspection after inspection, seemingly insensitive to the crowd's rising anger and the need for flexibility on such a special occasion. By the time the President of the MCC, Mr S. C. Griffith, exerted pressure on the umpires to get the game started, the pavilion fracas had occurred. Although the authorities decided, when play did resume, that it could continue until eight o'clock that Saturday evening, it was fairly certain the light, by then, would not have been fit for play. In the event it soon rained again. An extra hour was also added to each of the last two days of the match.

On the field Australia were much the more convincing side, making a nonsense of the pre-match odds of seven to one against an Australian victory. After Chappell had won the toss Australia batted well through repeated interruptions before declaring on the Saturday evening for 385 for five. Wood contributed a battling 112, before being brilliantly stumped by Bairstow off Emburey, and Hughes graced the occasion with a highly talented and spirited 117 in which he hit three 6s and fourteen 4s, every stroke being played according to the fighting intentions of his side. Against such aggression England's bowling, with the exception of Old, looked very ordinary.

Lillee and Pascoe, with faster and more skilful bowling than their opponents', routed England for 205 on the Monday with enough time left that evening for Australia to score 106 for two, taking their lead to 286. In England's first innings Boycott, Gower and Old were the only batsmen to pass 20. Lillee, superbly controlled, removed the first four batsmen, and Pascoe finished the innings with a spell of five for 15 in 32 balls. Both bowlers took all their wickets at the Nursery end, once so infamous for its ridge. Chappell insisted that the ridge was still plainly visible and very much in play although the pitch had been shifted some four or five feet away from the pavilion end in an effort to escape its influence.

England's first innings collapse, in which they lost their last seven wickets for 68 runs, had left Australia in a potentially winning position when the last day began. They hammered a further 83 runs in under an hour before Chappell's second declaration left England to score for almost six hours at over a run a minute. In Australia's second innings Chappell made a sound 59 and Hughes a brilliant 84. Moving into his shots with zest and certainty Hughes played the most spectacular stroke of the match when he danced down the pitch to hit the lively Old on to the top deck of the pavilion.

England did not attempt to meet Chappell's challenge. When Lillee trapped Gooch lbw for 16 and Pascoe removed Athey, to a bat-pad catch, for 1, survival became the priority. The in-form Boycott dropped anchor and Gower curbed his attacking instincts as they consolidated. When the score had reached 112 for two by three o'clock, with play possible until seven o'clock, many felt it would have been fitting if Botham had come in himself and had a fling. But the highest total England have ever made in a fourth innings to beat Australia in England is 269 for nine, at The Oval in 1902, and now they looked upon their first innings collapse as good enough reason for not risking another. Amid more boos than cheers they moved unhurriedly towards a draw. During the match the insatiable Boycott passed the Test aggregates of both Sir Leonard Hutton (6,971) and Sir Donald Bradman (6,996) and took his own Test aggregate to 7,115 runs. Boycott's second innings hundred was his sixth against Australia and his nineteenth in Tests.

The Cornhill Trophy and cheque for £500 as Man of the Match went to Hughes, and the prize-money of £4,500 was split between the sides. The official attendance was 84,938; takings were £360,850.50.

Australia

G. M. Wood, st. Bairstow, b. Emburey	112	(2) lbw b. Old	8
B. M. Laird, c. Bairstow, b. Old	24	(1) c. Bairstow, b. Old ..	6
*G. S. Chappell, c. Gatting, b. Old	47	b. Old	59
K. J. Hughes, c. Athey, b. Old	117	lbw b. Botham	84
G. N. Yallop, lbw b. Hendrick	2		
A. R. Border, not out	56	(5) not out	21
†R. W. Marsh, not out	16		
B. 1, l-b. 8, n-b. 2	11	B. 1, l-b. 8, n-b. 2..	11
(5 wkts dec.)	385	(4 wkts dec.)	189

1/64 2/150 3/260 4/267 5/320

1/15 2/28 3/139 4/189

D. K. Lillee, A. A. Mallett, R. J. Bright and L. S. Pascoe did not bat.

Bowling: *First Innings*—Old 35–9–91–3; Hendrick 30–6–67–1; Botham 22–2–89–0; Emburey 38–9–104–1; Gooch 8–3–16–0; Willey 1–0–7–0. *Second Innings*—Old 20–6–47–3; Hendrick 15–4–53–0; Emburey 9–2–35–0; Botham 9.2–1–43–1.

England

G. A. Gooch, c. Bright, b. Lillee	8	lbw b. Lillee	16
G. Boycott, c. Marsh, b. Lillee	62	not out	128
C. W. J. Athey, b. Lillee	9	c. Laird, b. Pascoe	1
D. I. Gower, b. Lillee	45	b. Mallett	35
M. W. Gatting, lbw b. Pascoe	12	not out	51
*I. T. Botham, c. Wood, b. Pascoe	0		
P. Willey, lbw b. Pascoe	5		

†D. L. Bairstow, lbw b.
Pascoe 6
J. E. Emburey, lbw b.
Pascoe 3
C. M. Old, not out 24
M. Hendrick, c. Border, b.
Mallett 5
    B. 6, l-b. 8, n-b. 12... 26   B. 3, l-b. 2, n-b. 8.. 13

                         205   (3 wkts) 244

1/10 2/41 3/137 4/151   1/19 2/43 3/124
5/158 6/163 7/164
8/173 9/200

    Bowling: *First Innings*—Lillee 15–4–43–4; Pascoe 18–5–59–5; Chappell 2–0–2–0; Bright 21–6–50–0; Mallett 7.2–3–25–1. *Second Innings*—Lillee 19–5–53–1; Pascoe 17–1–73–1; Bright 25–9–44–0; Mallett 21–2–61–1.

                    H. D. Bird and D. J. Constant.

                            Wisden, 1981

To mark the occasion, *Wisden* invited G. O. Allen to write an essay comparing the Lord's Test in which he made his international debut, in 1930 against the Australians, and the 1980 centenary match whose every ball he had watched with rapt attention. By now Allen was English cricket's Grand Old Man. Ever since the death of Warner he had been growing into this position, and by 1980 it was a puzzle to many people that he had not been knighted for services to cricket. (The honour finally came to him in the Birthday List six years later.) Allen, whose home may be found in the row of quietly detached Victorian houses backing on to the ground, with access to it, was the senior administrator in the game, who had captained his country and represented her 25 times. He had participated in all the Lord's set pieces, Eton–Harrow, Oxford–Cambridge, Gentlemen–Players, England–Australia, and no one was better placed to make a comparative assessment.

FIFTY YEARS ON

By G. O. Allen

The Test match against Australia at Lord's in 1930 was my first. Now, 50 years later, presumably because I am, sadly, the only surviving member of that England team, I have been asked to record my impressions of, and draw some comparisons between, that match and the Centenary Test match against Australia at Lord's last summer.

    That the former was one of the great games in cricket history and the latter was not was due partly to chance. For one thing, the weather in 1930 was perfect. So, though on the slow side, was the pitch, which had been specially prepared, this being the first ever four-day Test match at Lord's. In 1980 it rained often enough and hard enough on the first three days to have confounded even the 1930 sides from providing as much entertainment and fine cricket as I believe they did half a century ago. To that extent, Chappell and Botham and their two sides were up against it from the start. On the other hand, I am sure that in 1930, in conditions similar to those on the Saturday of the Centenary Test match, play would have started much earlier than it did. In fact, looking back to the thirties, when pitches were uncovered and there was much less covering generally, I think that play was often started too soon; but surely the pendulum has now swung too far in the opposite direction.

It must seem incredible to many who play and watch the game today that England could have made 425 in the first innings of a four-day match, as they did at Lord's in 1930, and yet have lost. In reply, Australia scored 729 for six declared. In the last two hours forty minutes on the second day, Australia went from 162 for one to 404 for two—255 runs, that is, in 160 minutes, of which Bradman made 155. At the start of the last day England, in their second innings, were 98 for two, still 206 behind with Hobbs and Woolley out, and it needed a great innings of 121 in two and a half hours by Chapman to save his side from an innings defeat. In the end Australia, losing three wickets (including that of Bradman) for 22 runs, had a minor crisis to surmount before winning with an hour to spare.

But this was the age of the batsman, the age before the lbw law was changed, and this was a batsman's match throughout. The pitch, for reason I have mentioned, was easy-paced, and the bowlers, the leg-spinners and White excepted, were perhaps slightly below standard, Tate by then being a little over the top.

For England the outstanding innings were those of Chapman and Duleepsinhji, though Woolley's 41 in very quick time on the first morning was a gem. Duleepsinhji's 173 in his first Test match against Australia was one of the most graceful exhibitions of batting I have ever seen: he was a superb player of spinners as he proved on this occasion. Chapman's was a fine effort, particularly the second half of it, though he played and missed many times in his first fifty. I can vouch for this as I was in with him, and he should have been out before scoring. I can see it now; he failed to spot Grimmett's googly and hit a skier on the off side. Woodfull, Richardson and Ponsford all could have caught it easily, but at the last moment, no one having called, each left it to the other. Amidst much laughter and some apologies all Grimmett said was 'Never mind, I'll get him out next over'. When watching the Centenary match with Ponsford, I mentioned the incident to him. He remembered it well, but to our mutual enjoyment he was disinclined to admit to more than a minor share of the guilt.

For Australia, the first four, Woodfull, Ponsford, Bradman and Kippax, all played fine innings, each in his own rather different style; Woodfull with his short backlift, very sure but always looking for runs; Ponsford mainly on the back foot or up the wicket to the spinners and a superb timer of the ball; Kippax a very elegant stroke-player on both sides of the wicket—and then, of course, Bradman. The best comment on Bradman's innings is probably his own. When asked which was the best innings he ever played, he is on record as saying: 'My 254 at Lord's in 1930 because I never hit a ball anywhere than I intended and I never lifted one off the ground until the stroke from which I was out.' Some believe he was unorthodox. Well, perhaps he was when he was really on the rampage, but in defence and when necessary, none was more correct. It was his early judgement of length, his quickness of foot and his ruthless concentration which made him the undoubted genius he was.

The Centenary Test match is a different story. As I have already said, conditions were unfavourable from the start. Even had MCC acquired an additional cover, and before the match the captains and umpires had been requested by the authorities to be rather less stern in their judgement as to fitness for play, I doubt if it would have helped greatly as it is always difficult to make a game flow once it has been subject to frequent interruptions.

I hate saying it, but I do not think either looked a very good side. There were, of course, several high-class batsmen amongst them, and in Lillee certainly the best fast bowler in either match. Although perhaps not quite as fast as he was, his rhythm, his ability to move the ball and vary his pace, and his unbounded determination were a feature of the match.

For Australia, Wood played a sound first innings and Chappell two good, though for him rather subdued, innings. In form, with all his strokes going. Chappell must rank high amongst batsmen of our time. But in this match it was Hughes who caught the eye, at least mine. Of course he took some chances and had his moments of luck, particularly in the second innings, but he was reluctant to be dictated to, moved his feet well, and with a wholesome backlift was able and prepared to play all the strokes. After 50 years one's memory is hazy, but of one thing I am sure—his straight six off Old was unquestionably the best hit in either match, indeed possibly the most remarkable straight hit I have seen. To take two paces up the wicket to a fast-medium bowler of Old's class and hit a flat 'skimmer' on to the top of the pavilion at Lord's takes some beating. Goodness only knows where it might have gone had he, to use a golfing term, taken a slightly more lofted club.

For England, the batting, with two exceptions, was below Test match standard, even after making allowances for the excellent fast attack of Lillee and Pascoe and the fact that the match took place late in the season after a difficult series against some relentless West Indian fast bowling. Boycott showed his undoubted class in two typically determined innings. Technically he is head and shoulders ahead of any other batsman in England, indeed his technique is so good it is surprising he does not tear the attack apart more often. Gower twice played some fine strokes and was beginning to look the batsman all Englishmen hope and believe he will be, only to get out to two bad shots. Unfortunately Gooch, who is now an extremely good opener and a powerful striker of the ball, failed in both innings.

So much for my impressions of the two matches; now for some comparisons. My first and foremost must be regarding the pace at which they were played, and the Centenary match is a fair example of how the game has slowed down over the span of years. I may have some regrets about the present-day game, but this is my one real criticism of it. Statistics are often boring and can be unjust, but in this instance I think they are interesting and revealing in that they provide some indication as to how much and why this state of affairs has come about.

In the 1930 match 1,601 runs were scored in 23 hours 10 minutes, that is at an average of 69 runs per hour, whereas in the Centenary match 1,023 were scored in 21 hours 7 minutes, an average of 48.4 per hour. A difference of 20 runs an hour is disturbing, to say the least; yet if one looks at the runs per 100 balls one finds very little between them, there being 53 runs in 1930 and 51.2 in 1980. If one then takes into account the importance nowadays attached by captains to containment and the present high standard of fielding, it is clear the batsmen must be exonerated.

And so, inevitably, to the over rate. In 1930, 260 overs of pace and 245 of spin were bowled at an average of 21.50 an hour: in 1980, 210 overs of pace and 122 of spin were bowled at an average of 15.82 an hour. These figures for pace and spin suggest to me that it is not solely the predominance of fast bowling that is responsible for the loss of 5.68 overs an hour. The endless discussions between bowlers and captains, the frequent changes in field-placing—and the waiting for new batsmen to reach the crease before making some of them—waste part of the time. But it is the absurdly long run-ups of many of the fast bowlers, and even of some of the medium-paced bowlers, often coupled with a funeral walk back to their marks, that are the real cause of the trouble. For those who saw little or no cricket before World War Two, I can assure them one could count on the fingers of one hand the number of fast bowlers who ran more than 25 yards: nowadays one can count on the fingers of one hand those who do not—and some run 40 or 50 yards. Of course a few of these long-runners are a fine sight coming in, but please let us be spared their country strolls.

One last statistic, a sombre thought. In a 30-hour Test match, the loss of 5.68 overs and 20 runs an hour could mean the loss of as many as 170 overs and 600 runs. Put another way, the debit, in terms of the modern rate as compared with the old, is roughly two whole days' play.

The comparison between the number of paying customers and the takings for the two matches is illuminating; in 1930, 110,000 people paid £14,500 to watch the four-day match; in 1980, 84,938 over the five-day match paid £360,850 and had the weather been kinder that figure must have been in excess of £400,000. At the moment the situation is clearly very satisfactory, but might not the crunch come if the tempo is not increased, especially when the opposition is less glamorous?

As regards the fielding there can be no argument. In the 1930 match it was moderate. For England Hammond and Duleepsinhji were two fine 'slippers': I still maintain that the former was the best I have ever seen. Chapman, who made magnificent catches to dismiss Bradman in both innings, was excellent anywhere, as was Robins. Hobbs, Hendren and Woolley, who had all been of the highest class, were by then getting on in years. For Australia only Bradman and Richardson really stood out. In the Centenary match the general standard was far superior, the ground fielding and throwing being superb. The catching was not put to the test, but knowing something of both sides I am certain it, too, would have been of the highest order. The 'sliding tackle' is a spectacular innovation. In the thirties, even if I had thought of it, I could barely have afforded the additional cleaning bills.

In addition to the tempo there was another fundamental difference between the two matches, namely the approach and tactics of the sides in the field. In 1930, with both teams relying heavily on a leg-spinner and slow left-armer, the theme was always likely to be attack. In the modern game, though rather less in evidence in the Centenary match, defensive field placing, containment, call it what you will, plays an important rôle. Hence the attraction for the crowds lies more in the brilliance of the fielding and perhaps a fiercer sense of conflict engendered by the menace of the fast bowling. It is not surprising that defensive tactics have crept into cricket—they are common to most sports today. No doubt more or earlier use of them might have been advantageous in the thirties, but strange, even crazy, as it may seem now, I simply do not think that was the way either captains or players wanted to play their cricket.

I said earlier that I might have some regrets about the present-day game. Well, I do have one or two. I particularly regret the lack of variety, once one of the charms of cricket, and for much of this I blame, each in its own way, the change in the lbw law introduced way back in 1935 and the lack of pace in many of the pitches. The change in the lbw law was designed to prevent 'padding-up'; it was also argued that it would help all types of bowlers equally and increase off-side play. In the event, apart from reducing the use of the pads to some extent, it has, in my opinion, done more harm than good. As it has helped disproportionally bowlers who bring the ball into the batsman, it has swung the game more towards the leg-side and has contributed in no small degree to the demise of both the leg-spinner and the slow left-armer. Then, with pitches getting slower and slower, containment was bound to become the order of the day. I, for one, do not blame the players, I simply pray for more variety. But how to restore it is the baffling question.

I regret, too, the predominance of the 'forward prod' to balls short of a length; that can certainly be blamed on the lbw law. It is safer forward. But excessive forward play must restrict the batsman's range, there being so many attractive and lucrative strokes to be found off the back foot.

And my last lament: I find the incessant noise on many big-match days thoroughly irksome. I welcome the enthusiasm, the cheering and the clapping, but the banging of cans and the endless alcoholic shouting is not for me.

But I have no wish to end these thoughts on a critical note. The game has undoubtedly changed in some respects, mainly in the last 25 years, but in saying this I am not suggesting that it is not in a healthy state: it is. Sadly, circumstances conspired against the Centenary match; yet it was a happy, nostalgic occasion, wherein old rivalries were recalled and old friendships renewed. There is, after all, nothing in cricket to compare with England v. Australia, the oldest of all Test match fixtures.

G. O. ALLEN in *Wisden*, 1981

IN the aftermath of the scuffle at the Centenary match, there was an official investigation by senior members of the MCC, whose President, Peter May, later assured members that action had been taken against the culprits without offering even the faintest hint what that action was. This comical reticence left the bulk of the membership baffled. If the members of a gentlemen's club cannot behave like gentlemen, why are they members? The question remains unanswered to this day, one of hundreds which have accumulated in the two hundred years since Thomas Lord began dabbling in land.

THE CENTENARY FRACAS

This great jamboree, arranged to celebrate 100 years of Test cricket between England and Australia in England, had been eagerly awaited. Its counterpart, at Melbourne in 1977, had been a wonderful success. As will be clear from the account of it elsewhere in this Almanack, last summer's match was ill-fated from the start. Some would say that the hours from eleven o'clock until six o'clock on the Saturday were like a nightmare. So incensed were certain members of MCC by the middle of the afternoon that play was not in progress, owing, as they thought, to the obstinacy of the umpires, that a scuffle took place on the steps of the pavilion, in which the umpires, one or two members, and the captains were involved. As a result of it, the umpires were shaken, the reputation of MCC was damaged and the occasion impaired.

Two and a half months later, following what MCC described as a 'thorough inquiry'—which included taking the evidence of the umpires, the captains and a number of members, and studying a BBC film recording of the incident—Peter May, President of MCC, wrote in a letter to all members of the club that 'appropriate disciplinary action' had been taken. He made the point, too, that it was no more fitting for members of a club publicly to question the decision of the umpires, let alone abuse them, than for players to do so on the field. If good is to come from a sorry affair, it will be to see that efforts are redoubled to provide the best possible covering on all first-class grounds, especially those where Test matches are staged. As many have said, it seems laughable to be able to land a man on the moon yet to have discovered no adequate way of protecting the square at Lord's.

Wisden, 1981

THE nearest thing to an eye-witness account of the fracas appeared in *The Times*, whose correspondent had taken the trouble to interview both the MCC Secretary and the England captain, Ian Botham. The latter, who was to know a time when the full weight of the MCC disciplinary committee would come down on his head, was here placed on the side of the angels, and spoke his mind. In retrospect, the irony is that on the occasion of the Disgraceful Scene in Lord's Pavilion, the honour of cricket should have been defended by an Australian captain whose great tactical contribution to the game was to instruct his bowlers to roll the ball along the ground, and an England captain one day to be suspended for bringing the game into disrepute.

Language of the Terraces Comes to Lord's

Has civilisation as we know it ended with the disgraceful scenes in the Members Enclosure at Lord's before the start of the third day of play in the Cornhill Centenary Test?

Even the august and dignified members of the world famous MCC would appear to have among their numbers an element who are not averse to using a rather coarser sort of language than one expects on the cricket field.

The abusive language and jostling that took place as the two captains and umpires returned to the Long Room is the kind of behaviour we have come to expect on the football terraces but not from the gentlemen of the pavilion at Lord's.

It just is not cricket and today the MCC will start an inquiry into this most unsporting behaviour.

Many might prefer a dignified veil of silence to be drawn across the unseeming incidents on Saturday in which Ian Botham, the England captain, was hit on the head and David Constant, an umpire, grabbed by the tie and jostled. But they have received so much publicity that an investigation will begin with Botham and Greg Chappell, the Australian captain, being seen by Mr Jack Bailey, secretary of the MCC.

He had heard a complaint from Chappell that intimidatory and abusive language was being used and that one of the umpires had been jostled as they returned from making a fourth inspection of the pitch, where 22,000 spectators were waiting for play to start. Mr Bailey investigated this and spoke to two members pointed out by Chappell but said he thought, from what they had told him, that they had not been behaving unreasonably.

Mr Bailey said: 'I spoke to the men and felt they were innocent, but of course it could have been a case of mistaken identity. There is no question about it, the members were not pleased at having to wait and made their feelings known, but I thought they were doing it in the reasonable English way and that it would not go beyond this.'

From the hotel where he is staying in London, Botham described the incidents as 'the behaviour one expects from football hooligans'. He added, 'I was walking out to make the final inspection with Chappell and the two umpires when I was hit on the back of the head by a hand.

'I did nothing about it but as we were all walking in a man in his twenties grabbed the umpire David Constant by the tie and shoved and jostled him. Greg Chappell and I moved in to break it up.'

He said the man thought he was being clever and added that the abusive language being shouted in the pavilion had disgusted him. 'It was a disgrace, especially as it involved the captain of an opposing team. I feel very sorry and embarrassed about people who to my mind are a disgrace to the game.'

So the language and behaviour of the football hooligan has at last invaded the home of English cricket. W. G. Grace would turn in his grave at the thought.

RICHARD FORD in *The Times*, 1 September 1980

SOMETHING else happened at Lord's in the summer of 1980, something more important than the tantrums of a few oafs, and very much sadder. John Arlott, known across the world to tens of millions as The Voice of Cricket, delivered his last Test match commentary. At the age of 66 he had grown weary of the constant travelling up and down the land, improvising conversational descriptions of wonderful freshness and poetic originality. Arlott, an ex-policeman turned radio producer-cum-poet, had taken up the microphone for the first post-war Test match, against the Indians in 1946, and had been there ever since. Long before his retirement his had become one of the most-impersonated vocal styles in the world, a rustic tenor softened by a burr which lent his speech the resonance of country wisdom. He was also one of the most prolific, most graceful, of all cricket writers, a considerable historian of the game, and a bibliophile of such perception that by his retirement his collection of rare books, first editions and manuscripts was priceless. Of few men could it be said that their retirement left a hole in the national life never to be filled, but it was certainly true of Arlott, who told me that last day at Lord's that he was indescribably tired. In the season before his departure to the peace of the Channel Islands, he had published a book called *An Eye for Cricket*, in which the following passage occurs: 'Few cricketers ever receive the accolade of a standing ovation at Lord's, when as a batsman approaches the pavilion, by a strange unanimity of recognition, and with no suggestion of pre-arrangement, the whole company of the members rise to their feet with a rustling noise like the passing of a great flock of birds, and the clapping gradually mounts to a crescendo.' A year later he himself was to receive that very accolade, in a match noted at the time for a fracas but remembered for all time as a farewell:

Farewell to the Box

Everybody knew that 1980 was to be John's last season as a commentator. He had announced his intention to retire well in advance, and yet when the moment arrived with the Centenary Test against Australia, still one was shocked by the immediacy of the end. Assuredly, there was the one-day fling in the Gillette to come, but the celebration of a hundred years' cricket between the two old adversaries was undeniably the fitting occasion in which to hold his closing words. This was to be his final commentary.

Long before, during and after the match, John had been nearly overwhelmed by a frenzied host of farewell dinners, receptions and parties, liberally interspersed with written and spoken pieces for practically every platoon in the army of communication – an exhaustive and exhausting requirement that was not sought, but to which he subjected himself with not only will and gratitude, but also a promise to sleep for six months.

His last twenty-minute period was uneventful and somehow timeless. That, perhaps, is how it should be:

Arlott: The sun bright, the wind still, and just fluttering the flag, the MCC flag on the Works Office. And Lillee turns, six feet tall and wide shoulders he comes up, a little stammer in the middle of his run, but then he gets it straight again, bowls short and [applause] Boycott hooks that. That looks like being four, it is four [applause] and I imagine we're going to hear somebody on the Public Address at any moment asking the spectators over there to get back inside the boards, because several of them are lying on the grass inside the playing area – any moment now I think the voice of Alan Curtis will be heard in the land – and Lillee turns then, 60 for 2 now, 8 to Gower, 26 Boycott.

Two more to Boycott then – 28, 69 for 2, and the batsmen out in the England innings – remembering they were set 370 to win in a minimum of 350 minutes – now it's Bright to

Boycott – pushes this away on the on side – little trouble in reading the flight there – Gooch bowled Lillee 16, Athey caught Laird bowled Pascoe 1, that was 19 for – 43 for 2, and Bright again going round the wicket to the right-handed Boycott, and Boycott pushes this away between silly point and slip, picked up by Mallett at short third man, that's the end of the over, it's 69 for 2, nine runs from the over, 28 Boycott, 15 Gower, 69 for 2, and after Trevor Bailey it'll be Christopher Martin-Jenkins. [Suddenly the unexpected sound of spirited clapping from within the commentary box]

Bailey: [Over applause] Well, the applause is ... [clapping] ... I'm very lucky to have been on while John completed his last commentary, and on behalf of the Test Match Special team and listeners ... we thank him very much indeed, and would he open that bottle of champagne a bit quickish....

Martin-Jenkins: ... and let's hope it's launching a happy retirement rather than finishing a great career. Here comes Lillee bowling on the off stump to Gower, who plays that up to mid-off, and there is no run. Gower now 15 – 28 to Boycott, 69 for 2 – the cricket full of tension ... but the box, in a way, tense too, because that was the final twenty-minute session of John Arlott's career as a Test broadcaster, although he'll be back on Saturday here for the Gillette Cup Final, and I sincerely hope will be broadcasting and writing, at least occasionally, during his – what we hope will be a long and happy retirement ... [Public Address announcement].

Bailey: And the applause was for John Arlott, his last commentary.

Martin-Jenkins: And Trevor, the entire Australian field is clapping. Geoff Boycott having a clap there, and I'm sure the entire ground is clapping at that announcement by Alan Curtis that John has just done his final Test match session ... a moment indeed of nostalgia in a very nostalgic match. [Prolonged applause]

(BBC Radio Commentary, England v. Australia, Centenary Test, Lord's 1980)

At the end of the Test, John presented the Man of the Match award. As he came on to the Lord's balcony, the vast congregation below burst into a spontaneous and rapturous ovation that lasted several minutes.

If they had not been on their feet already, they would have stood. It was a most moving and heart-warming gesture of admiration and affection that nobody wanted to end; indeed, the applause seemed to continue for so long that it appeared the crowd did not want to allow John to speak. If that were really so, it would be the first and only time that anybody did not wish to hear what he had to say.

DAVID RAYVERN ALLEN (ed.), *A Word from Arlott*, 1983

A PROFESSION weakened immeasurably by Arlott's decision to declare rose to the occasion in the person of the most graceful and idiosyncratic of the remaining writers on cricket, Alan Gibson, who, in the pages of *The Times*, marked the moment. In the years since, Arlott's retirement has fortunately turned out to be slightly operatic; the occasional book review or obituary, or essay on wine, still appears, proving that his hand has lost none of its skill even though exiled to so resolutely non-cricketing an island as Alderney.

The Voice of Cricket Declares

When the Centenary Test match came to its end yesterday, there also came to an end, at least as far as Test matches were concerned, the most famous of cricketing voices.

Broadcast cricket commentary began soon after broadcasting itself, but for a long time it was rather amateurishly done. The usual practice was to find some distinguished old cricketer, such as Pelham Warner, prop a microphone in front of him, and leave him to get on with it.

In the 1930s, Howard Marshall appeared, and after him E. W. Swanton (and we must not forget Arthur Wrigley, who founded the technique of modern scoring).

But it was only after the war that we heard the voice of them all, John Arlott.

He came from Basingstoke, and his Hampshire accent was in those days sharp. The Hampshire accent is not naturally a mellow one, such as that of Dorset, which helped to make Ralph Wightman such a broadcasting success.

It took a year or two for the public, brought up on Marshall and Swanton, to grow accustomed to Arlott. He did not sound like a member of MCC. But by 1948 he was established, and ever since has remained, for every Test in England, a necessary part of the scene.

He did that because he was a cricketer and a poet. He was never, I think, expected to be an outstanding cricketer, though he had a passion for the game, and when he abandoned his first-class ambitions he was determined to stay in touch with it somehow.

He became very knowledgeable, partly because he pestered cricketers for information: not the dressing-room gossip, but technical stuff. 'What does he *do*? What's his dangerous ball?' he would demand if a new bowler appeared.

'We all loved and admired John in the Hampshire dressing-room,' said his old friend, Desmond Eager, then the Hampshire captain, 'but we did sometimes wish he would stop asking questions.'

The greatest honour that he feels he has been paid is to have been invited to be chairman of the Cricketers' Association, a post he will retain in retirement. Not that he really retired; he is going to live in his beloved Alderney, but he will speak and write as long as he lives. He has immense industry, a constant urge to work, more than any man I have known.

But he would not have become so famous had he not been a poet. He was considered one of the most promising post-war poets. He gave that up too ('The words don't come any more'), but his adventures in poetry gave him a command of words, a gift of phrase such as no other cricket commentator has possessed.

He also had an unforced sense of humour. When he used phrases such as 'the fieldsmen are scattered in the wilderness like missionaries', people used to think he had thought them up beforehand. Sometimes, I suppose, he may have done, but he never needed to.

I remember one Test morning at Trent Bridge when I was in the commentary box with him and Trevor Bailey. Trevor began, as usual, with his introduction about the state of the game, finishing with 'and now come the umpires in their new-style short coats, looking like dentists. Over to John Arlott.'

John immediately said: 'It occurs to me, Trevor, that it is rather suitable for the umpires to look like dentists, since one of their duties is to draw stumps.'

ALAN GIBSON in *The Times*, 3 September 1980

As partial consolation for the rowdiness in the pavilion there was the decorum in the Post Offices of two nations. The incident reflects the sad loss of prestige of the erstwhile Mother of Empire, but at least the old colonies still understood what was what, and where. Perhaps the item should inspire no surprise, for after all, Canada was playing Test matches when the English were still pottering about inside their tight little island.

From the Curator of Lord's Cricket Ground, 27th March, 1980, to *The Times*:

Sir, I realise that Britain's role in the world has changed somewhat since the days of, say, Dr W. G. Grace, but it was still a shock to receive a letter addressed to 'Lord's Cricket Ground, London, Ontario'. I must, however, congratulate the Canadian and British Post Offices on delivering it safely.

Yours faithfully,

Stephen Green.

Each year the followers and fanciers of metropolitan cricket await the opening day of the season at Lord's, when the MCC fields a side against Middlesex. (It used to be Yorkshire, but there has recently been a minute tinkering with the administrative machinery.) No matter how arctic the weather, that first day is the signal for summer to begin. All winter it has been awaited eagerly, and when it comes it can never be a disappointment unless torrential rain actually closes the ground. To step inside the premises is itself an act of faith independent of the play, and these days one of the more exciting duties of the returning wanderer is to check all his favourite amenities and make sure none of them have been removed, or modernised, or otherwise tampered with. (The disappearance of the old bookstall to make way for the new Tavern was a particularly horrible accident.) Although the visitor takes this experience for granted, an instinct informs him somewhere at the bottom of his boots that in order for him to be able to stroll in so nonchalently and find the whole complex circus whirling away requires much thought, common sense and hard labour. These days the MCC is among the most complicated social organisms open to the public, which is why editors never tire of essays describing some of the inner machinery.

Pavilioned in Splendour

Today's cricket match at Lord's between MCC and Middlesex, the county champions, is not only the traditional opening fixture of the season, when Test match hopefuls aim to impress the selectors. It is also the cricket follower's annual opportunity to cast off the leaden cares of winter and imbibe the sight, sounds and smells that are an irreplaceable part of an English summer. More than that, it enables him to escape into a time-warp.

The ground, which opened in 1814 as the home of MCC, is universally regarded as the Mecca of cricket. Despite many structural changes to the international game it remains the administrative headquarters; the President and Secretary of MCC still automatically occupy the same positions within the International Cricket Conference, cricket's supreme body, and MCC still makes the laws of the game.

Hardly surprising, perhaps, that Lord's today should remain cocooned in traditions that comfort those who belong there and warn strangers to mind their manners.

Unless you have a match ticket, a membership card or a specific appointment you will have trouble passing through the huge wrought-iron Grace Gate. Middlesex players arriving for practice in a car they have used all the previous season have been known to find difficulty getting in.

Bill Leonard, at 81 the most venerable of those who mind the gate, arrived at Lord's in 1922. He became a gateman in 1965; six years ago, when his wife died, he was told he could stay in the job as long as he liked. The club's generosity is the reward for his instinctive loyalty, and epitomises the benevolent feudalism fundamental to Lord's and the Marylebone Cricket Club – a well-defined hierarchy which perpetuates, in subtle ways, the old cricketing distinction between 'gentlemen' (amateurs) and 'players' (professionals).

The home of the gentlemen of Lord's is, of course, the member's pavilion, a magnificent late Victorian three-tier stone building, a bastion of male privilege, where women and children are admitted only at specially ordained times.

Downstairs, the members take their ease, strolling among the cricketing memorabilia in the famous Long Room, or in the reading room and bars, while on the first floor Jack Bailey, the Secretary, and his three assistant secretaries run the show.

Mr Bailey cut short a holiday in Majorca last week to return for another in a seemingly endless round of committee meetings. At the back of his mind is the special meeting later this summer when the members will decide whether or not to send an MCC team to South Africa, an issue that threatens to throw the cricketing world into a turmoil with repercussions as far-reaching as those of the D'Oliveira Affair. This morning, however, his main concern will be the weather.

That, too, will be the chief preoccupation of Lieutenant-Colonel John Stephenson, assistant secretary in charge of cricket, who will have bicycled in from Swiss Cottage shortly before 9 a.m., and will soon be on the telephone to RAF Northolt for the latest forecast.

Known to everyone as 'Colonel' ('It's not quite pally-pally, but it's not too formal,' he says), his is the unmistakably military figure that strides out to the wicket during weather-induced stoppages in matches to talk to the umpires and discuss the prospects for resumption of play with Jim Fairbrother, the groundsman. His arrival – as impressive in its way as the famous walk to the wicket of 'Lord Ted' Dexter, or that of the arm-swinging superman Ian Botham – invariably prompts a cheer.

In his office, with its fine view of the pitch, the Colonel was explaining last week how the MCC organizes its 260 annual away fixtures and its foreign tours.

The average MCC club side is rather stronger these days than it used to be. Probationary playing members, of whom there are between two and three hundred, are given five matches in which to prove their worth under the eye of the match manager, before their applications are considered in August. Half are rejected.

Match managers' reports and records of every player's performances are kept in the Cricket Office, at the corner of the pavilion, where they are constantly updated by the manager, Steven Lynch, assisted by a clerk and a typist. In the files lie such fascinating details as the performances of I. T. Botham in his first MCC match in 1972 against the Universities Athletic Union. He made nought and took no wicket for 23 runs.

Botham was once an MCC Young Cricketer, a group of 20 school leavers taken on by Lord's for up to three seasons. It is their chance to learn the game (28 of them have gone on to be current county players), with the benefit of daily coaching, but they have to earn their keep by doing odd jobs, bowling at members, and occasionally being drafted into MCC sides at short notice.

They arrived fresh faced on Monday to be given a pep talk by the Colonel. Today they will sell scorecards, man the scoreboards and be ready to help Jim Fairbrother with the covers.

The chief coach is Don Wilson, a genial 45-year-old Yorkshireman who played for England just before the sudden explosion in cricketers' pay in the 1970s, and who keeps a fatherly eye on the Young Cricketers, the schoolboys who come to Easter coaching classes, and even some seasoned professionals.

Few games encourage such eccentricity and give so much time for contemplation as cricket; it is no coincidence, for example, that many cricketers love music.

One day recently the indoor school was brought to a halt by a sudden burst of beautiful choral singing. Those familiar with Don Wilson's eccentricities may have carried on playing, but others dropped their bats and listened. He had been coaching the boys of the Westminster Abbey choir school, and at the end of their net, he asked them to sing. He always does.

Another music-lover is Christopher 'Gus' Farley, a small, rotund, Pickwickian figure who is the ground superintendent, responsible for policing, general upkeep, and hiring winos. Winos? Surely they'd never get through the gate?

'Without them this place wouldn't be open,' he replies. 'They know there's casual work here, so they come from the arches at Charing Cross to paint the seats and clean. We give them a meal and pay them in cash.

'Mind you,' he adds, 'you have to look closely at their eyes before you take them on. And if there's one propped up between two others, you have to make sure he can stand up.'

Two of the regular winos are, curiously enough, trained opera singers. Sometimes, after dark, when the cleaning is done, their fine voices echo across the deserted square.

In lyrical mood Mr Farley describes the peculiar atmosphere of Lord's; how it livens up on the Monday when the Young Cricketers arrive, how on the morning of a match the ground 'opens out like a flower', and how the life drains out of it at the end of the day as the last spectators leave.

Elsewhere in the pavilion Roy Harrington, the 62-year-old dressing-room attendant, prepares to bring the players their 10 a.m. tea, attend to any repairs to equipment, then bring lunch, towels, tea, and clean up the showers and baths afterwards.

This summer there will be no Geoffrey Boycott, always grabbing one of the two dressing-tables with a looking-glass. And Roy regrets the departure of characters like Denis Compton, who would often arrive late and rush out to smite centuries with a borrowed bat.

Behind the scenes, undoubtedly the most important figure is Jim Fairbrother, the groundsman. Foreign visitors, anxious to learn from the man who, as curator of the Lord's pitch, is the most distinguished practitioner of his art in the world, assume that he earns at least £20,000 a year, and drives a Mercedes. He does not.

To the cricket watcher, the square over which he presides is just a flattish patch of grass, albeit carefully trimmed. To Jim Fairbrother, it is 18 numbered pitches. The Test match pitch is No. 10, bang in the middle; no one else will play on it all year. He and the Colonel will have decided yesterday whether pitch No. 12, on the Tavern side of the centre, has dried out sufficiently to be used for today's game, or whether to switch to pitch No. 3, higher up on the square. (There is a notorious 'hill' at Lord's which runs down towards the Tavern.)

By the end of the season, the earth on the whole square has tightened as hard as a pavement. It has to be softened up by sprinkling over two days; then it must be raked with a scarifier, brushed with a besom, hollow-tined by machine, treated with a sorrel at the batting ends, grass seed inserted to a special formula, holes filled in with a top-dressing of soil with a high clay content, then covered with more soil and levelled with a lute. Jim illustrates this highly sophisticated procedure with an artist's hand gestures.

He had been thinking of taking a holiday last week, but the weather put paid to that. With rain about, it is all a matter of hairline decisions: which roller to use, how low to cut the grass, when to allow the Middlesex players to have nets or use the practice ground.

Under the Grand Stand work the Lord's printers, a team of three long-serving men, updating scorecards during matches, printing annual reports, invitations and notices for the club's 18,000 members.

'It's not like working in a factory,' says 62-year-old Charles Reason. 'They are not unreasonable people here. Also you've got the atmosphere of the match, with people coming in and out wanting scorecards. You get caught up in it. I used to belong to a union, but you don't need it here.'

A similar attitude prevails elsewhere round the ground. The Clerk of Works, Ted Collins, has an office next to the Grand Stand. His deputy, Dave Norman, is also the Lord's electrician – happy to work round the clock if necessary to get the place ready for a big game. Like many others, he often works seven days during peak cricketing periods.

The staff canteen, a homely place with cricket pictures on the walls, is run by Sharon Clarke, the 22-year-old manageress, and her mother, Anne. They provide special lunches at Christmas and at the end of the season when the nursery ground comes into its own for the use of the Cross Arrows, the club for permanent members of MCC staff. Finally there is the annual staff fixture between two fairly ramshackle teams, one captained by Colonel Stephenson, the other by Wing Commander Lawrence, the chief accountant. The result doesn't matter, of course. The game's the thing.

RUPERT MORRIS in *The Times*, 27 April 1983

ARRANGEMENTS of a special nature are necessary for the relay by radio and television of matches from Lord's. The Test Match Special team, manfully plugging the huge gap left by John Arlott, have now become themselves an English institution. Deriders have said that some of the chatter is so peripheral that the actual cricket is hardly required for its flow. But this is a high compliment, not a criticism. One of the greatest of all pleasures to be derived from cricket is the allusive conversation it inspires. The television commentators provide what utilitarian talk people desire, but for the good-natured smalltalk cloaking encyclopaedic knowledge, there is nothing to surpass the Test Match Special team. Ladies with no interest in the game, but who have encountered the talking team by accident or through the browbeating of an insistent husband, have ended by baking their most sumptuous savoury recipes and sending them to the heroes of the radio team. There was a time when I doubted the existence of some of the myriad cakes which seemed to be drawn on angels' wings to the commentary box. If it were all true, how was there room for the team itself to get into the tiny room? But one day I was myself invited to be the luncheon interval interviewee. As this was the fulfilment of a schoolboy ambition, I was pleased just to be there, and paid less attention to the routine than I might otherwise have done. But I did notice that during my forty minute occupancy of the box, during which time I drank two glasses of champagne and was offered several more, four and possibly more tins containing cakes were delivered. This glut of pastry inspired more talk, off-microphone, concerning which hospitals or schools might be appreciative, the waistbands of the team having already reached that degree of rotundity considered acceptable in a member of Test Match Special.

A day or two beforehand the tempo of preparation increases with the arrival of outsiders who have backstage parts to play in the dramas to come. Squads of people are drafted in by the BBC to erect bits and pieces of equipment around the playing area. Microphones for sound effects are carefully taped to the balcony railings of the pavilion. The mobile gantry bearing one of the television cameras is manoeuvred behind the sight-screen at the Nursery end, where its yellow arm will be periodically flexed during five days, tracking some of the action and exposing a cameraman to vertigo. The broadcasters themselves begin to wander in, checking this and that, sniffing atmosphere, chatting everybody up. Brian Johnston, who will soon be giving the nation copious earfuls of rather Old Etonian (circa 1925) humour, makes a first leisurely circuit of the ground in his own Test Match specials, his co-respondent shoes. The cricket writers, having detached themselves from the humdrum of the county game, drop by the pavilion, where a notice has been pinned up to establish where they shall sit in the Press box above the Warner Stand. There are 105 places for reporters up there and each is earmarked for a particular journalist.

GEOFFREY MOORHOUSE, *Lord's*, 1983

IN 1983 Moorhouse had undertaken the very necessary task of bringing the literature of Lord's up to date. The author of several distinguished books on the Empire and travel, Moorhouse was, so far as the MCC was concerned, an Outsider. In his introduction he actually states his belief that a writer should never join anything because once he does he forfeits that impartiality without which no book is worth the paper it is printed on. While this is taking to extremes the old dictum that a writer should maintain his independence, and while one wonders whether Mr Moorhouse has ever enrolled as a customer of a bank or a library, one takes his point. His book on Lord's is indispensable to the reader interested in being told how the place works without being assaulted either by a torrent of invective or half-drowned in the porridge of conformity. Many of the aspects covered in Mr Moorhouse's book will be familiar enough to many readers, but some of the newer aspects and one or two of the old strike us as not only judiciously expressed but positively educational.

In the great buff shed of the Indoor School beyond H Stand at the Nursery end, batsmen and bowlers are liable to be working out at any time from shortly after breakfast until ten o'clock at night. The building looks rather like a small aircraft hangar from the outside, or some place where the Ministry of Defence might be conducting secret experiments that nobody in his right mind would want to know about. Inside, in a chamber 120 feet by 88 feet, the cavernous echo of ball on bat is not much reduced by the nets which hang in rows from ceiling to floor to separate one 'pitch' from the next. At one end is a viewing gallery, with cricketing pictures on the wall between it and a bar; and spectators are almost always there, while their offspring, or their spouses, or their colleagues are jumping to it on the Uniturf below.

The idea of an indoor school at Lord's was first raised by Middlesex in 1955. But it would have needed a grant, as well as permission from MCC, which was then going through one of its financial crises, and the matter was dropped. The county eventually acquired a school in Finchley, and Lord's did not see its like until the end of 1977, when MCC opened this one of its very own. It cost £200,000 to put up, which would certainly have been more if both the architect and the builder hadn't been members of MCC; and the hole this knocked in club finances would have been bigger than it was if £75,000 hadn't been donated by 'Union Jack' Hayward, the millionaire engineer who delights in spending his fortune patriotically, in ways other than those schemed by the British income tax system, from his base in the Bahamas. As a result of this generosity, the school's interior is known as the Hayward Hall, and it has been a total asset from the day Gubby Allen performed the opening ceremony, regretting only that he was unable to bowl the first ball ('I'm afraid,' he said at seventy-five, 'it's just beyond me now').

There are seven strips laid in plastic Uniturf on the board floor and they have been carefully designed for the two chief types of bowling. Four of the nets are regarded as fast; the other three, made from softer PVC containing more air cells, take more spin and produce less bounce. Orthodox cricket balls are mostly used, though sometimes they come in two colours for instructional purposes, so that novices can see the spin more clearly, or whether the seam is really being kept up as the young fast bowler intends. Hordes of novices now go through the school every year, ranging in age from seven to rising sixty, some with a natural talent that can be developed into something impressive, others with no hope from the outset of anything more than great pleasure at having been coached at Lord's. Apart from the novices, scores of good club cricketers, as well as first-class players in need of a net on a rainy midsummer's day at Lord's, have found the indoor school a boon. The Parliamentary cricketers who represent the teams fielded by the Lords and Commons practise there; so do those optimistic chaps from the *Guardian* newspaper, with their ambitions set on yet another tour of California or somewhere on the Indian sub-continent. The demand is such that people are clamouring to reserve evening nets in March for the following winter, at £9.60 an hour for a group of six, an arrangement which means that each one of them gets about ten minutes of batting. Continous, though; no waiting for every bowler to take a constitutional between delivering each ball.

On top of the practice sessions, there are also the six-a-side competitive games, with the nets down and the entire chamber open to play, with batsmen hitting balls that rebound from the walls (often straight to a fielder, which accounts for the fact that sixty per cent of the dismissals are run-outs). The Laws of Cricket, obviously, are somewhat rearranged for this sort of thing. An innings lasts for twelve overs, bowling and batting are confined to one end apiece. It's said to be great fun by those who've become addicted to it, as many have, about 200 games a year taking place now, with competition sometimes disconcertingly fierce. It obliges a batsman to control his shots very finely, a bowler to be very accurate because the umpires are extremely strict about wides. It peps up a fielder's reflexes and it requires batsmen to run and call more nimbly than they sometimes do in the open air. But no one, certainly not at Lord's, pretends that indoor cricket has any major contribution to make to real cricket, apart from keeping cricketers in trim during the off-season. As it patently does.

GEOFFREY MOORHOUSE, *Lord's*, 1983

MOORHOUSE covers one venerable aspect of Lord's which has not been written about at any length, concerning the problem of how the addicted patron of Lord's copes with the withdrawal symptoms of early September. Few experiences are more tinged with sadness than the last day of the season, any season, anywhere. At Lord's in recent years this occasion has been cloaked in the ribaldry of the One-Day Cup Final, at which chants are screamed, flags waved, beer-cans banged and groups of young men in an advanced stage of undress express their allegiances by kind permission of the brewers of Old England. Perhaps this is no worse than the old style, when the last championship fixture might drift on to a pointless conclusion, or an MCC side jousted with a team of veterans from the universities. But there is an interim stage whereby the devotee can, without actually attending a Lord's match, watch cricket at Lord's. I was introduced to the touching ritual of the Cross Arrows fixtures by a friend who tended to hibernate once the season was over, and not put his head over the parapet again till the following April. He explained to me that the Cross Arrows club played its home matches on the Nursery pitch, often quite late in September, at which I instantly made for the ground one September Saturday afternoon when the official cricket was finished, and was delighted to watch an interesting afternoon's cricket in which the Cross Arrows fielding was rendered lively by the promptings of its long-on, whom I recognised as a mature R. W. V. Robins. But I was never quite clear, until I studied Moorhouse's book, exactly what the Cross Arrows club comprised, and how one qualified for membership.

The Cross Arrows Cricket Club is nothing less than the works team at Lord's. Everyone employed there is entitled to be a member and its players are a jumble of fellows who may labour during the year in any one of the departments at headquarters, augmented by the occasional MCC member and cricketer from the Middlesex staff (the 1982 fixtures saw Emburey, Cowans and Williams turning out for the side). The club was founded just over a hundred years ago with the express purpose of allowing MCC employees to have a spell of fun and games themselves after providing so much for others in the course of the season proper. At first it called itself the St John's Wood Ramblers Cricket Club, but then discovered that the name had already been pre-empted by another team in the same part of London. Therefore, in 1880, it designated itself the Cross Arrows; supposedly because an early fixture was away against the Northwood club and, on enquiring which direction that was, one of the team was told that 'It's 'cross 'arrow way' – beyond Harrow.

Nowadays all the Cross Arrows games are played at Lord's, on the practice ground, where they put up a dapper little scoreboard of the kind familiar to all properly equipped village clubs, and rope the boundaries off, and set up a beer tent, and bring out the deck chairs for spectators who prefer not to sprawl on the grass. At 11 a.m. sharp each game begins, a different one every day with the exception of Sundays, right through to the end of September. A motley collection of visitors provide the opposition – Stage, Leprechauns, Tunbridge Wells, Mashonaland Country Districts, Ex-MCC Young Professionals, Frogs, Metropolitan Police D Division, Barclays Bank and the like – and all the results go into fine print on the sports pages of *The Times*, because the Cross Arrows have a special place in cricket's affections. Gary Sobers once turned out for this lot, and so would Frank Worrell if he hadn't had to cry off at the last minute; and a sixteen-year-old called Titmus in 1949 scored 660 runs for the club in eleven innings, at an average of 94.28. Cross Arrows matches are usually pretty high-scoring affairs, what with the short boundaries on the practice ground, and the fact that although the bowlers are trying hard enough, not one of them is taking himself quite as seriously as he might if he were performing in the big time on the other side of the Nursery End stands. Five hundred runs in the day are not uncommon, and in 1982 the home side hit 310 in 172 minutes against the Young Professionals. This is not a bad way to finish a season at Lord's. It's the way a lot of people there think cricket ought to be played more often than it is.

There is a Cross Arrows dinner every November, just like any other cricket function of its kind, with much tobacco smoke in the air, much booze going where it loosens tongues, much sentimentality, much mingling of the gentlemen and the players, much gossip making some sit up and others droop with boredom. There is a guest speaker, chosen for his knack of rolling people in the aisles above all, though occasionally his reputation has been misconstrued and he just about paralyses them instead. If he's really been hand-picked, though, ballpoints and the backs of menus are surreptitiously brought into action all over the Lord's banqueting suite, as the uninventive take careful note of the better jests, which are destined to resurface later in winter before impressed audiences all over the home counties of southern England. The President of Cross Arrows, who is always the Secretary of MCC, steers the evening adroitly from the top table. The captain of Cross Arrows, who is currently the Assistant Secretary (Cricket) of MCC, reports on the fortunes of September and distributes floral arrangements to one or two ladies without whom the evening, and some of the club's cricket, wouldn't at all be what it is.

GEOFFREY MOORHOUSE, *Lord's*, 1983

ONE amenity at the ground which has been improved most spectacularly is that part of the building, connected to the main pavilion but separated from it by the public right of way past the entrance to the Long Room, where is housed the library, recently refurbished lavishly through the support of the Agatha Christie Foundation, and, beneath, the Memorial Gallery and Museum, wherein are housed assorted relics ranging from the Ashes to the unfortunate sparrow killed in flight half a century ago by Jahangir Khan. The following note, however, serves very ill the shade of John Wisden, Sussex fast bowler and founder of the almanack which perpetuates his memory. It was not the almanack, but John Wisden himself, who coined the Wildean epigram concerning the magnitude of the Atlantic breakers.

The Cricket Memorial Gallery at Lord's holds consolation and frustration for hard-pressed England supporters. The Ashes are there, come what may, but the men who won matches are there only in effigy.

There is much W. G. Graceiana – two portraits, one severe, one rather bucolic, and the gold plate which celebrates his hundredth hundred in 1895. The coffin-shaped snuffbox of his brother, the coroner-cricketer, is the most charming of many cricket trinkets. Old bats bear traces of strokes well struck and there's a right-handed smiting stick used by Dick-a-Dick, a star of the Aborigine tourists of 1868.

The old photographs of teams of moustachioed and bearded Victorians may suggest placidity, non-commercialism and good sportsmanship. If so, they mislead. The first England team to tour America in 1859 survived hitting an iceberg en route … 'All the sea needed was ten minutes of the heavy roller,' says *Wisden*.

The first England tour of Australia (1861) was sponsored by a commercial firm who sent them when Charles Dickens refused to tour. The Government wanted to stop the 1872 tour of America for political reasons, and the first Australian team to play a Test here (1880) came in a maelstrom of hostility generated by the unruly behaviour of Australian tours the winter before.

DAVID ROBSON in *Sunday Times Magazine*, 1984

CRICKET lovers know that their game is changing too fast when they read an item which would have been literally incomprehensible to W. G. Grace, or even Sir Jack Hobbs in his prime. Were the players of the old days to visit Lord's for a modern match, the biggest single difference between their cricket and what was on offer would be perhaps, not the disgraceful decline in over rates, nor the finicky rules pertaining to different competitions, but the physical appearance of the batsmen.

The match between Middlesex and Leicestershire at Lord's this week was marked by tiny crowds and devastatingly hostile bowling. The most spectacular effort was from the Middlesex quick bowler Neil Williams, who struck Nigel Briers such a fearsome blow on the helmet that the bolt securing the visor was dislodged. It was eventually found at mid-on. There were suggestions that the bolt should be given a place of honour at Lord's.

The Times, summer 1985

AS THE occasion of the bi-centenary approached, club members conducted nervous reconnaissance trips to see what was being done to the old Mound Stand in the name of progress. A seven-figure gift from the Getty family had made the new development possible, which meant in turn that by the time the two hundredth birthday arrived, all existing descriptions of Lord's would be out of date. But that is as it should be. Only by subtle modulations has the club contrived to survive for so long. It has changed its style, changed its appearance, while remaining what it has always been, the central point of world cricket. Fresh generations of the faithful rise up to replace the departed. The writer of the following appreciation rightly admits that, for him, 'Lord's is the best of all cricket grounds because it was the first'. The most interesting point of all raised by the writer is the pleasure derived from strolling round the ground. It was Cardus who first drew attention to the truth that watching a cricket match is not all cricket. There are the peripheral pleasures, the peeping at the pin-ups on the wall of the printers' shop, the examination of ancient rollers left to doze in the sun by the Nursery end sight-screen, the atmosphere in the betting tent where once the pineapples bloomed, those mysterious private houses winking over the wall beyond the north grandstand. Lord's is not a cricket arena, it is an estate, and needs to be surveyed at regular intervals.

Cricket grounds are like seaside resorts. They come alive in summer with the sunshine and the deck chairs and the bunting and the bands, but like seaside resorts I find them oddly appealing out of season when they are empty and windswept. I see that this is perverse, but there is something romantic about the melancholy of deserted stands, the odd piece of flapping canvas, sea-gulls standing on the square, dejected but undisturbed.

One chill day in winter I came in to Lord's for a game of Real Tennis. They were rebuilding the squash courts and changing-rooms, so for once the tennis players, usually consigned to a rather poor relation status behind the pavilion, were allowed to change in the Middlesex and England dressing-room. The dressing-room felt as if it had been untouched since about 1947 and the days of the Compton–Edrich ascendancy and, perversely, that too gave it a strange romance. When it is titivated, as it presumably will be, it will become much harder to think of those Brylcreem heroes actually padding up in that very room. It had snowed during the night and I was playing early. The whole of the ground was covered in white and there wasn't a footmark on it. I have never seen Lord's looking better.

Even in season there is something about being at Lord's on a very quiet day. One day early in summer I was walking towards the Nursery end when MCC were playing the MCC professionals. I had vaguely assumed that MCC would be represented exclusively by retired majors in Eton Rambler sweaters. I paused. The scoreboard said that MCC's opening bat was 58 not out. He looked oddly familiar and not a bit like an Old Etonian major. It was Geoffrey Boycott. I bought a scorecard and settled down. Seconds later there was a bowling change. The captain was bringing himself on. 'Mr D's bowling,' said a knowledgeable voice, and sure enough it was the tall thin figure of the Lord's coach. He beat him once too, going for the sweep, hit him on the front pad. Not out, of course, but a moment to savour. G. Boycott, Yorkshire and England, versus D. Wilson, Yorkshire and England. I suppose there might have been thirty of us in the ground. Better that, oddly enough, than thirty thousand.

The inescapable Cardus seems to have had a similar notion, though not quite so extreme. 'A hundred times,' he wrote in his autobiography, 'I have walked down the St John's Wood Road on a quiet morning – that's the proper way to enjoy Lord's: choose a match of no importance, for preference one for which the fixture card promises "a band if possible". I have gone a hundred times into the Long Room out of the hot sun and never have I not felt that this is a good place to be in; and if the English simply had to make cricket a national institution and a passion and a pride, this was the way to do it.' I particularly like 'a band if possible'! Lord's, of all grounds, should always have a band.

Playing Real Tennis at Lord's – a new recreation in danger of becoming obsessive – I've seen the place often out of season and also learned something about that curious extramural activity which takes place behind the pavilion (no, not THAT sort of activity). Real Tennis seems to come naturally to cricketers, at least to batsmen. Douglas Jardine was the Oxford number one; F. R. Brown was good; Colin Cowdrey and Ted Dexter especially so. 'The stroke is like a cover drive,' says Henry Johns, leaning elegantly into a textbook batless demonstration in the pro shop. 'Batsmen find it easier than bowlers because they can read the spin and follow the flight.' Norman Cowans, who spent a winter as a young pro, impressed everyone with his cheerfulness and his dedication but it was obvious that he was never going to be one of the world's great tennis players.

Mr Johns is the doyen of tennis and a keen observer of the cricketing scene as well. Years ago he had a flat overlooking the ground. From it he could see the queues forming the night before the Australian Test match and he would watch early on the morning of the first day as MCC's secretary Colonel Rait Kerr (who played Real Tennis for the club) came out and made a ritual presentation of two free tickets to the people at the very head of the queue. There were buskers to entertain the queue and vendors hawking food and drink. On the morning of the Eton and Harrow match Henry could see the flower sellers turning up at six and dyeing their carnations in the traditional light blue of Eton. (It was, as Etonians are always pointing out, Eton blue long before being appropriated by Cambridge.) Harrow wore dark blue carnations, and the nobbier supporters of both schools brought horse-drawn carriages which they parked at the Nursery end, where they picnicked on the grass.

The final of the Gold Racquet was moved from Oxford and Cambridge to Eton and Harrow at Douglas Jardine's insistence (he was involved in both the Varsity match and the tennis final) and drew capacity crowds. Harold Macmillan always came; ladies were not allowed on the closely packed benches in the dedans but watched from the galleries high above the court. One year, just as Henry Johns was about to start the game, a lady dropped her handbag which burst open on the penthouse scattering its contents, including powder, all over the court. Henry had to postpone the tennis and get a step ladder to retrieve the bag. Even when the Gold Racquet was not being played it was customary for the Etonians and Harrovians to pause from their gentle amble round the ground and meet for a brief chat in the court. All changed now, however. In the shires, especially the north, men will mutter caustically about the feudal aristocratic traditions of

Lord's and say that the Eton and Harrow match is the high point of the year for the MCC committee, but it's not true. The game nowadays *is* an anachronism and if the truth be told should really go the way of all those other anachronisms which were banished from cricket HQ years ago – Beaumont and Oratory, Clifton and Tonbridge. Yet they like to put on *one* public school match, and nowadays there are Lord's games for representative sides of state schoolboys too.

Many of the Real Tennis professionals around the country are men who came to the Lord's court from 'the cricket side' and were taught the game by Henry Johns: David Johnson at Queen's (he won the bat for most promising young batsman three years running); Brian Church at Cambridge; Peter Dawes at Hayling Island. The present chief pro, David Cull, came over twenty-five years ago as a young medium-pacer and was quickly transformed by the coach Bill Watkin into an off-spinner.

'I gave it a season,' he says, 'then I came over one day for a game of squash with the lads.' He had scarcely heard of squash, let alone played it, but he thought it was fun and stayed through the winter as the most junior of four pros on the tennis side. He was supposed to go back to cricket next summer but stayed on behind the pavilion. He never told Gus Farley, the ground superintendent in charge of the boys, and got a rollicking from him.

He was so small then that he could barely see over the net. Indeed the Assistant Secretary of MCC, S. C. 'Billy' Griffith, had been seriously concerned about whether he could stand up to the workload. 'These boys now have it so easy' is David Cull's verdict on the modern generation. 'We had to get here at eight in the morning and sweep the whole ground. Then help the fellows with the roller. On match days you sold scorecards – you got a farthing for each one. Another thing I did was work in the scorebox. That was my bunce.

'Crumbs, I loved it though. I remember when I first came here and I was the only boy without a bat and pads. They said get changed and I got changed and they said, "Where's your bat and pads?" and I said, "I'm a bowler." I mean I thought at Lord's they'd provide all the gear. But my mother, she was so proud of me she found the money and got me the bat and pads.'

For me Lord's is the best of all cricket grounds because it was the first. I have been going there for over thirty years and I have been a member of MCC for more than a decade. I think the pavilion is one of the world's most evocative buildings. It suggests elegance and escape and on big match days it and the whole ground still have a buzz for me. I love watching a great cricketer, past or present, making a stately progress during the lunch or tea interval. During the last of the England–Australia one-day matches I saw Colin Cowdrey, nut-brown and beaming, walking very slowly along the tarmac behind the pavilion and acknowledging greeting and reverence. And you could sense the crowd all thinking, 'Ah, Cowdrey ... if only he were playing.'

As it was, Gooch and Gower made hundreds, and although they were only playing for the plate, England thumped Australia. I was in the Long Room when Gower came in, bat raised high and punching the air with his fist. It was the end of an appalling run of low scores, and the members seemed as relieved by the century as the England captain himself. Often I have seen players come through the Long Room staring moodily at the floor or the ceiling, apparently determined to ignore the members. Too often there seems an unbridgeable gulf between the young professionals earning their living and the clubbable members taking time off to be spectators.

That day the place was so packed that the only place I could find was on the bridge between the pavilion and Q Stand. A lot of members aren't really aware of this, because you have to go down a private-looking passage past the England dressing-room to get to it. The view is excellent, and that day it was full of serious and gossipy cricketers who were happy to fill me in on the proceedings so far, and particularly gleeful in describing how cross Phil Edmonds had been at being left out and how he had come straight out of the dressing-room looking like thunder and made a series of phone calls. I would have played him myself because, like Randall, he is always doing something, even if it's only chatting up the umpires.

'I know you from somewhere,' said the member on my left suddenly. 'Where do you play your cricket?'

I said I hadn't played cricket since my golden duck, opening the innings against Great Tew in 1965. He didn't believe me.

'I know,' he said. 'You play for the Nomads. That's it. You're a Nomad.'

And try as I might, I could do nothing to shake this belief.

1985 was a surprisingly good Lord's summer because, despite the pervading damp, the sun shone on St John's Wood when it mattered. The Test was won by Australia by four wickets, a victory memorable chiefly for an innings of 196 from Border and for the fact that it was started on time. (Everybody was full of stories about how they had walked on to the outfield and found water coming over their insteps. Somehow the ground staff, working all through the night, managed to dry it out.) There was sun for the one-day Texaco which England won by eight wickets; sun for the B&H final; and sun for the NatWest.

I quite enjoyed the Benson and Hedges, though it has never been my favourite final. There always seem to be more rowdies than usual, perhaps because the game is played so emphatically outside the soccer season. I always feel the crowd is nearer to a soccer one than on any other cricket occasion. More booze, more mindless shouting. Not that it was too bad this time, though for the first time in my life I was heckled under the Grandstand for wearing an MCC tie.

In this one Leicester beat Essex by five wickets with three overs to spare. It sounds easy, but it wasn't until a fine sixth-wicket stand between Willey and the sprightly Garnham, a young wicket-keeper who soon afterwards announced a premature retirement, that the thing was settled. They made an unbeaten eighty together and got them in twelve overs.

The NatWest final was more exciting, carrying on into the murk of a September evening with Nottingham almost snatching an unlikely win over Essex. They were chasing 280, and got hopelessly behind the clock. Randall, at his most chirpy, almost pulled them back, but they still needed 18 off the last over. Despite the most defensive field imaginable he somehow took sixteen runs off Pringle's first five balls, only to hole out off the sixth. There is nothing like being part of a Lord's crowd on occasions like that.

Of course it is not everyone's cup of tea. 'It's not Wembley,' remarked Jack Bailey, MCC's Secretary, gazing across at the builders working on the new Mound Stand (courtesy of J. Paul Getty). But a lot of people think it *is* cricket's Wembley and find it hard to reconcile the notion with the fact that MCC is a private club with a twenty-year waiting list. It seems rather strange to me too, but I find that I can accept the idea. But then, enjoying the privileges of membership, I would, wouldn't I? On the other hand all county cricket clubs are private members' clubs, it's just that they don't have the good fortune, like MCC, of being over-subscribed. You can hardly blame MCC for being desirable. And isn't it better to have a club owned by several thousand members, none of them necessarily very rich, than a club owned by one millionaire and dictated to by a board of directors? Give me MCC and Lord's rather than any soccer club in the League. Yet how often do you hear about Old Trafford or White Hart Lane being 'undemocratic'?

In fact non-members have freer access at Lord's than many county grounds. At Headingley and Northampton, to pick two at random, you are not allowed to walk right round the ground. But at Lord's you can watch the teams limbering up in the nets at the Nursery end – there were huge crowds contemplating the Australians in their incongruous yellow-and-green tracksuits. And you can walk under the Grandstand and behind the pavilion, gawping as you go. The new Mound Stand, financed by Getty, has been designed with a special arched walk-way to maintain this principle. It's just the pavilion which is a clubhouse. Only members are allowed in the pavilion, to snooze in the reading room, sit in one of the high chairs in the Long Room, or sample the sea food in the restaurant at the top.

You could write a book about Lord's. Geoffrey Moorhouse did. Moorhouse is a Lancashire lad and not a natural MCC ally, but the book is scrupulously fair and meticulous, and by and large the club and ground emerge with credit. 'If that's the worst anyone can write about us then we're not doing badly' was one mainstream MCC verdict I heard. For the 1987 bicentenary MCC has commissioned Tony Lewis, a former captain of Cambridge, England and Glamorgan as well as the *Sunday Telegraph* cricket man. (Moorhouse used to write for the *Manchester Guardian*.) Lewis is a more obvious choice but, as it turned out, the Moorhouse book was a wonderful piece of public relations. You expect an encomium from a fancy hat like Lewis. Not from a cloth cap like Moorhouse.

Lord's does change, but it changes with measured tread. There will, for instance, be bucket seats in the new Mound Stand but not elsewhere. At least not yet. When I asked Jack Bailey about them he said that there was something to be said for bench seating. On a quiet day you could put your feet up, spread out, have room for the sandwiches and the scorebooks. And you can always hire a cushion if you have a sensitive backside. There will be 'improvements' at Lord's but not much in the way of dramatic change. 'It's like buying a new pair of shoes,' says Bailey. 'The minute you've got them that serviceable old suit suddenly starts to look a bit shabby and you feel you have to get a new one.' So the minute the new Mound Stand is finished people will turn their attentions to the newly evident tattiness of the Grandstand and the Nursery stands.

If you want chapter and verse about Lord's you must refer to Moorhouse.

Moorhouse has a map. And several pages devoted exclusively to Gubby Allen. And the precise number of pints consumed on Cup Final days.

For me, Lord's has a special and inimitable atmosphere; a compound of personal memory and corporate nostalgia; of anachronistic hierarchies and deferences and rules; of the best cricket I ever watch; of a sense of occasion no matter if the ground is packed full of noisy partisans or if only a single slow handclap echoes round the stands. There is something about the place which is as timeless as a cathedral or a village green, and there is far more to it than cricket...

The timeless continuity of Lord's withstands all its changes. I've been going there so long that I feel it is always the same even when – in detail – it manifestly isn't. I recognise the gatemen these days, and I look out for Henry Johns and David Cull standing in those ducky new white track-suits the tennis players now affect, guarding their territory behind the pavilion. I know where to look for Jonners and Blowers and the rest of the BBC commentary team as they scale the steps to their turret high above the play. I hope to see journalists like Mark Boxer, the editor of the *Tatler*, or Godfrey Smith of the *Sunday Times* or Michael Davie of the *Observer*; or the novelist Simon Raven; or the poet P. J. Kavanagh; or David Webb Carter, the Brigadier from Belize. I remember days with family and friends; hundreds from Gooch and from Gower; pyrotechnics from Dexter and Richards and Botham; Brearley's captaincy; Titmus's spin; and Edmonds and Emburey; and Peter Parfitt and Don Bennett. I like to walk slowly round the ground, moving from rowdiness in the claustrophobic dark under the Grandstand to a murmur in the pavilion balcony and euphoric excess at trestle tables in the old arbours at the Nursery end. I always pause before that wonderful portrait of the founders of I Zingari and walk slowly through the Long Room, enjoying the ancient bats and balls in glass cases and the ancient members perched on chairs and tables.

It's elusive, the true character of cricket, and you can find aspects of it everywhere the game is played and watched, but nowhere more than here at Lord's, headquarters of the game, where they have been playing for almost two hundred years and are still going strong.

TIM HEALD, *The Character of Cricket*, 1986

ALTHOUGH it is already some years out of date, the best all-round portrait of Lord's which conveys both its physical appearance and what might be called its incorporeal spirit, is the one written in a volume of memoirs in 1977 by Mr E. W. Swanton, who, like God, moves in mysterious ways in the cause of Lord's, having been instrumental in getting the Indoor School built and in bringing true the dream of a new library, of whose committee he remains chairman. Those who have never been to Lord's may feel, having read Swanton's essay, that there is no longer any need for them to do so. But then, those who have never been to Lord's suffer, by definition, from impaired judgement.

The Mecca

There is only one starting-point for anyone, and especially for an Australian, anxious to explore the mysteries of cricket, and that is its headquarters at St John's Wood called Lord's. For anyone with a fondness for cricket who has any spark of imagination the story of MCC, and of Lord's which has been its home since the time of Waterloo, must have a strong romantic appeal. Much of my own enjoyment of cricket has centred on Lord's, too, so I feel something of a personal involvement in its history.

The game was played, of course, and flourished in and around the Weald – had even reached as far north as Nottingham and Sheffield – long before Thomas Lord and the new Marylebone Cricket Club first became associated, to their mutual advantage. But from that time – and remember we are now only ten years short of the Bicentenary of the foundation of MCC – cricket had a metropolitan focal-point, and henceforward to a large extent the growth and development of the game and of MCC went hand in hand.

The interplay of chance and coincidence that are the stuff of history are fascinatingly evident if we trace the evolution of the club and of its premises. Thomas Lord's father is a prosperous yeoman farmer in the North Riding of Yorkshire and a Catholic who, with his own troop of 500 horse, goes to the aid of Prince Charlie in the '45 Rebellion, suffers in consequence the confiscation of his lands, and so migrates from Thirsk (where in the pavilion of the cricket club there is today a Lord commemorative plaque) to the quiet Norfolk market-town of Diss.

In due course the handsome Thomas moves on to seek his fortune in London, enters the wine trade, and also becomes ground bowler and general factotum to the aristocratic White Conduit Club which plays on the public fields of that name at Islington. The White Conduit decide they want the privacy of an enclosed field, and they back young Lord to procure one. First they inhabit a ground in the rural area which became Dorset-square, at which point (1787) the White Conduit became Marylebone whose noble members, according to popular request, promptly undertake a revision of the first Laws of 1744.

The great days of Hambledon are over by this time, as its patrons shift their interest from Hampshire to London, and there is no disputing the authority of what from its earliest days was recognised as the leading club. The expansion of London in the first years of the new century forces Lord farther north, first (taking his precious turfs with him) to a plot that became absorbed into the Regent Canal and thirdly and lastly, turfs and all, to its present situation to the west of the newly-built St John's Wood Church, of which parish, by the way, he, now presumably Anglicanised, becomes a vestryman.

To every cricket historian this is all familiar ground: lo! is it not written in the book of the prophet and evangelist, Altham? But it may be new to my young Australian friend, and if I am to conduct him round a sentimental English cricket pilgrimage there is only one possible place to start.

When I first knew Lord's, from the late '20s on, my generation used often to refer to it, in inverted commas, you understand, as 'The Mecca'. It has had several subsidiary titles. The Press have often used the tag 'Headquarters', which is explicit enough, while Plum Warner used to quote, with an ecclesiastical intonation and a twinkle in his eye, Sir Robert Menzies's description, 'The Cathedral of Cricket'. After the clamour of Melbourne and Sydney the holy calm of Lord's used to strike visiting Australians with particular emphasis, and Bob Menzies's appellation perhaps might still be applied over most of the season though he would have something more pungent to say about the can-banging and the slogan-chanting by the minority that now take away so much of the pleasure from Test matches and Cup Finals.

Again, some of the old pre-war landmarks have gone, notably the Tavern and members' dining-room, the low stands, A and B and P and Q, flanking the pavilion on either side, cosier and more personal places, all of them, than their more commodious, efficient successors. Yet withal Lord's is still 'The Mecca', the shrine to which pilgrims come from wherever in the world cricket is played, and which has still an atmosphere quite distinct, exclusive to it.

Suppose my friend and I come in from St John's Wood Road and make a tour of the ground before entering the cathedral sanctuary. We pass through the Grace Gates which were put up in 1923 – suitably imposing and substantial – simply inscribed to 'William Gilbert Grace, The Great Cricketer'. Plum records that there was much discussion in committee about the wording of the commemorative stone, and many suggestions were received, in English, Latin and even Greek – which would no doubt have caused the Old Man to pluck at his beard a bit – before Stanley Jackson came up with the phrase that says all that needs be said.

I will postpone making an assessment of W. G.'s unique place in the game as we pass on, leaving the new Tavern, practical if unlovely, to our left. Next comes a pleasant memorial to another of the great men of cricket (like W. G. what would now be called a *controversial* figure), the Harris Garden. It is in the shape of a lawn-tennis court, which is exactly what it used to be...

Directly following the garden is the block comprising the Real Tennis and squash courts and also the War Memorial Gallery which replaced the old Racket Court. I played tennis – the real or royal game – just enough to be able to imagine the extraordinary fascination it has for all who take it up. I only did not continue because of so many absences abroad in winter, which was the only time I would otherwise have been able to play. The court at Lord's is rarely empty, and neither for that matter are the squash courts.

The Imperial Cricket Memorial Gallery as it is today conjures in me mixed emotions – on one hand admiration and approval for its dignified and handsome appearance, and for the good taste surrounding the wide range of cricketana, pictures, bats and relics of every sort that make up the exhibits; on the other sadness that the chance was missed of erecting a more practical tribute to the fallen such as a cricket school which at long last has come, after subsequent plans had foundered, a quarter of a century later.

The original memorial plan incorporated a library as well as a gallery, and it was certainly at least as necessary to display to the best advantage MCC's unique book collection as its other valuable treasures. But soaring costs limited the scheme and so Diana Rait Kerr, daughter of the then secretary and for upwards of a quarter of a century MCC's brilliant curator, had to make do as library with a converted office in the pavilion, which was adequate possibly but far from ideal. Now the library is less accessible, having been moved across and up too many stairs for old legs to the court block.

It was the Hon. George Lyttelton, the Eton master, not the least distinguished member of the famous family, who this time produced the approved line: Secure from change in their high-hearted ways', below the inscription:

> To the memory of cricketers of all lands who gave their lives in the cause of freedom, 1914–1918; 1939–1945.

The author is the nineteenth-century poet James Russell Lowell, he who wrote:

> Once to every man and nation comes the moment to decide,
> In the strife of Truth with Falsehood, for the good or evil side.

Once? Or twice? Or three times?

Many of MCC's best landscape pictures are hung in the Memorial Gallery, for they came largely from the bequest of Sir Jeremiah Colman, who asked that in so far as was possible they should be hung together. Dominating the far Gallery wall is one such, the celebrated composite by H. Barrable and R. Ponsonby Staples, showing the ground as it was in the late '80s with a great match in progress. W. G. has hit to the extra-cover boundary in the foreground, and T. W. Garrett is fielding the ball immediately in front of the old 'A' Stand which was then the focus of beauty and fashion. Those present seem to be giving only perfunctory attention either to the cricket or to the Prince and Princess of Wales who have arrived almost unnoticed. They are equally oblivious to the discomfort of the lady whose slim waist seems to be wedged between the back-rest of one seat and the lower bar of the one in rear, with nothing to sit on!

The eye as one enters the gallery takes in two objects: one is the picture just referred to, the other the marble bust of W. G., placed centrally on the first elevation as though on the quarter-deck of his ship – as maybe in a sense he is. This is the bust, then in the Long Room, about which Cardus told his ever-popular story. The last game of the summer of 1939 – Middlesex v. Warwickshire – was pursuing its placid way when Cardus saw two overalled figures approach the statue and, between them, with no word spoken, bear it carefully away. Two old members also witnessed the scene, whereupon one, according to Cardus, gravely remarked to the other: 'Mark my words: this means war.'

We move on round the periphery with an admiring look at the Coronation Garden with its weeping ash and seats among other shady trees and air of peaceful refuge behind the Warner Stand. This stand is part of the newer Lord's, two-storeyed, confined to members and friends, with a big bar and buffet, giving on to the field, and surmounted by the Press box, ample and well-equipped, appropriate maybe in that Plum was among many other things in the game a cricket-writer, but ill-placed in that the view is over extra-cover and long-leg. The senior writers have a medallion which admits to all pavilions, Lord's included, yet the fact is they are at a disadvantage compared with their brethren of TV and radio.

They are better placed than I was at the Lord's Test of 1930, in a Press annexe, under the canopy of the new Grand Stand, more or less behind cover-point – but, naturally, I was pleased enough to be there, watching, as it turned out, one of the most memorable and spectacular of all games, wherein among other things Don Bradman sealed his fame with his chanceless 254, in his own view *the* innings of his life.

What can one say about the Grand Stand? It is greatly in its favour that it has dignity, and blends well with the pavilion. On the other hand, considering its size it gives a satisfactory field of view to the minimum number. Some seats are unsaleable since from them can be seen only one set of stumps! At its rear is a honeycomb of stairs and passages, and some of the dining-rooms are situated in bizarre relation to the boxes they were designed to serve.

It cost £46,000 – no flea-bite in 1926 – and on its completion MCC were reputedly none too happy with their bargain. The architect, Sir Herbert Baker, disarmed criticism, however, by affixing at its apex, and immediately above the main scoreboard, as a surprise present, the Father Time weather-vane showing the old man with the scythe affixing the second bail – at least it is to be assumed he is putting them on rather than taking them off – which is now a symbol of Lord's all over the world. And there is at least a splendid view from the Grand Stand balcony.

We come next to the North Clock Tower where are inhabited the ground staff. Here many who became famous had their initiation to the game, from young Jack Hearne, Pat Hendren and Denis Compton to John Murray and Fred Titmus downward. On either side of the sight-screen is the two-storey stand known as the 'Free Seats', seeing that admission to the ground (with certain reservations now, I think) gives access to them. From them one gets as good a view as anywhere, plus as much sun as there is – in contrast to the pavilion seats which are in shadow from noon on. Curious how allergic the Victorians were to the sun!

Come to that, they were allergic to a good deal, including almost any sort of change – such, for instance, as the new-fangled mower, which only won grudging and belated acceptance. This north-east corner was the site of the sheep-pens, the inhabitants of which kept the turf cropped, their efforts augmented on Saturdays by four or five hundred sheep who were driven through Lord's, almost perhaps for their last square meal, on their way to Smithfield market. The coarser grass, unpalatable to the sheep, was pulled out by hand by groups of boys – much, I suppose, as rows of black women moving forward almost imperceptibly on their haunches picked out the weeds one by one on the old Wanderers' ground at Johannesburg when I first saw it nearly forty years ago.

The Nursery or practice ground, which extends behind the Free Seats right back to Wellington Road, has had any number of uses and now, most importantly, inhabits the MCC Indoor School. The nets are here, and here throughout September the Cross Arrows, drawn from past and present playing staff and also MCC members, fulfil a match programme. Although the straight boundaries are on the short side the Nursery square is ample to take a lot of cricket and there are those who would like to see MCC and other matches played there during the summer when the main ground is not being used.

Part of the Nursery is a car park, and the arbours round the perimeter, hired to members for the big matches, remain as a reminder of the days when for the Lord's Week, comprising the University match and the Eton and Harrow, the Nursery was the social centre of London, sprinkled with club tents from which flags flew, and wherein champagne, salmon mayonnaise and strawberries and cream were the order of the day. It got its name, by the way, because it had been a market garden known as 'Henderson's Nursery', famous, according to Plum, for its tulips and pineapples.

Proceeding clockwise, we flank the Mound stand, the oldest public accommodation remaining, before coming on the big modern development which comprises the long row of boxes with bars and seats below and another members' friends enclosure above them. Thus we have made the circle, leaving for my Australian's scrutiny the pavilion which we enter from the main door in the rear.

Lord's pavilion, since the pulling-down of the Hotel and members' dining-room to make way for the new Tavern stand, is now the oldest building on the ground. Look at it front on from the field of play and anything of the kind better symbolising the later-Victorian age would be hard to envisage. There it stands, solid, ample, serene, the epitome of an Empire on which the sun would never set, headquarters of the game above all others that helped to bind it. The foundation stone was laid in September 1889, and eight months later to the day it was ready for the Annual General Meeting.

The only external change since has been the addition of the narrow parapet which protects from the weather the last few rows of seats at the back of the top storey. This did not exist when in 1899 Albert Trott, the Australian who played for Middlesex, hit his fellow-countryman, M. A. Noble, over the pavilion. The ball glanced off a chimney en route, which makes one wonder whether Trott would have cleared the top as it now is...

The Long Room will impress my Australian with its wide panoramic view of the field and, around the walls, its selected treasures. Sometimes the human scene is more interesting than the cricket, as the late 'Buns' Cartwright was acknowledging when a friend asked him why he was sitting behind the sight-screen. 'Because,' he said with a steely eye, 'it's the only place from which I can't see that beggar Bolus'; in fairness to whom let me add that there has been many another staunch England batsman who has not exactly rated top marks for ease and elegance. Brian Bolus – this also gives me a chance to say – has done good service to cricket as captain of Derbyshire – which has never been a sinecure yet, nor ever will be.

Brian is one of not a few modern cricketers who refute the lament of those who say that there is no humour left in the game. He and I have often laughed since over the time when we two and Brian Close were supposed to be the star speakers at the annual dinner of that excellent and, I hope, still prosperous institution, the York and District Cricket League. Unfortunately for us Mr Close was first in the order, and we two waited our turn, first in patience, then in irritation, finally in amused incredulity as the oracle meandered interminably on, in a flow of uncoordinated reminiscence, until if he had been a more sensitive man he might have noticed that (in the late Lord Birkett's phrase) the audience, receptive enough for the first half-hour or so, had ceased just looking at their watches but, metaphorically at least, were shaking them to see whether they were still going. For myself, I tried to detach myself from the actual situation and to recall Close's hour of honour and glory against the West Indies' fast bowling at Lord's in '63 when his innings of 70 so nearly won the day for England. For that at least he should never be forgotten.

Perhaps the performance at York lasted no more than fifty minutes or so, though it seemed longer; but what after-dinner speaker, anxious to deliver himself of his modest offering, has not known his spirits sink as his glass and all others around him grow empty and another's spate continues to flow unquenched? I hold firm views on the length and style of after-dinner speeches – but ... as may have been noted already, the subject is not strictly connected with Lord's pavilion. Occasionally, it is true, one hears longish speeches there, in the Committee Room, but at least they are in the afternoon.

Let us then return to the Long Room, preferably when it is empty so that the eye can fully enjoy it. The pictures are occasionally transposed between the Long Room and other parts of the pavilion and also, of course, the Memorial Gallery, for MCC's art collection is now so large that certain pictures, though not the most distinguished and important, are always being 'rested' in the basement.

To the right of the handsome showcase of bats and other cricketana (including the Ashes urn) which forms the focal point of the long West wall hangs one of the best-known of all cricket pictures, 'Tossing for Innings'. The artist is Robert James, the date around 1850, and the bat is shown in mid-air thrown up by one of four young urchins while another is about to make the momentous call, 'round' or 'flat'.

High over the showcase, indeed above the deep decorated frieze that extends the length of the main wall, is the polished oak panel on which are written in chronological order the names and respective years of office of the Presidents of MCC since the first-known incumbent in 1825. There were, no doubt, duly elected Presidents from the club's inception in 1787, but their identity vanished along with the rest of the club records in the fire that destroyed Lord's first pavilion. This panel is the room's most recent addition of note, and one feels that one day a resting-place for it may be found nearer eye level.

On the far wall the four men gazing out in neat array are, from right to left, and in order of age, Plum Warner, Douglas Jardine, Don Bradman and Gubby Allen. Of these four three have been everything in cricket, players and captains of their countries, selectors, administrators and legislators, holders of the highest offices. During my time their influence off the field has been unrivalled. To this extent Jardine is in inappropriate company, with the added irony that he hangs between his manager in Australia, Plum, who so hated Jardine's brain-child, Bodyline, and the Don, for whose subjugation it was devised. None of these four pictures has, I think, any great intrinsic merit. Plum is shown half-length, in white shirt and Harlequin cap, much as he must have looked when he led Middlesex as county champions off his beloved Lord's pitch for the last time. With him, as with Jardine, wearing the MCC touring blazer, it seems as though the picture was painted on photographic evidence.

The Don is shown not as the pre-eminent cricketer but shrewd, confident, and with the hint of a smile, through horn-rimmed spectacles, looking just what he now is, a director of companies and a bank, as well as the voice of post-war Australian cricket authority.

Next door, appropriately enough, is the Don's parallel English figure in the councils of the game, as well as his rival on the field, Gubby Allen: the only captain, by the way, who ever won two successive Test Matches against him. Gubby is pictured wearing an England tie, looking out on to the field from the side Committee Room window as he has done for so long, notably in his seven-year stint as chairman of selectors. It is no doubt a fair likeness of the subject in introspective mood, but the artist, John Ward, has not quite captured that blend of charm and determination, that persistence in argument which all at Lord's know so well.

So from the south door we pass, noting John Ward's agreeable line and wash impressions of the three most recent secretaries, R. S. Rait Kerr, Ronald Aird and S. C. Griffith, in the intervening passage, into the Committee Room. Here round these tables, which nowadays take the form of a large fat 'U', most of the substantial cricket issues for all but ninety years have been decided: not only the Laws and all other things touching Marylebone as a club, but the affairs of English cricket in all its aspects, and also those of international import as covered at the annual meetings of the ICC. Though MCC have handed over their over-all responsibilities – implicit though never clearly defined – to the Cricket Council and its adjunct, the Test and County Cricket Board, these new bodies still meet in the old time-honoured sanctum.

As might be expected, much of the modern history of Lord's is expressed by the portraits of the Presidents, Treasurers and Secretaries that look down on the committees and sub-committees and boards and conferences. The treasurership perhaps needs an explanatory word. It is the senior and semi-permanent (unpaid) office, round which, in complement with the secretariat, the management revolves. As an ex-officio member of every sub-committee (of which there are ten!) the Treasurer is the link man who with the Secretary and his assistants dovetails all this effort. Apart from the present Lord Cobham, who held the treasurership for one year before relinquishing it for wider duties outside cricket, there had been five treasurers only in this century when J. G. W. Davies took over from Gubby Allen in the autumn of 1976. Of Mr Allen's four predecessors on display in the Committee Room the portrait of Harry Altham is almost the least flattering likeness in the MCC collection, though happily it is now augmented by Edmund Nelson's posthumous portrait of Harry in flannels and Harlequin cap, presented by his son, Dick, with the special request that it be hung in the Indoor School.

Harry held the Treasurer's reins from 1950 to 1963, taking over from the ninth Lord Cobham whose work spanned the war years and to either side,

1938–49. Generally speaking, the figureheads at Lord's, in my recollection, have personified a conspicuous charm of manner, and none more so than this tall military figure, who always found time for a word or a smile.

Before this Lord Cobham's treasurership was Lord Hawke's short span of six years which began in 1932 with the death of Lord Harris. Martin Bladen Hawke was truly the founder of Yorkshire cricket, for when he took over the captaincy in 1883 the side was something near a drunken rabble. In his long reign of 27 years Hawke not only brought discipline and self-respect into the Yorkshire XI but in so doing greatly improved the status of county cricketers everywhere. So it is appropriate enough that his is the only Committee-Room portrait in cricket dress. He is wearing the Yorkshire blazer with the white rose on the pocket, and when I see it I often think of the story of the youthful Gubby Allen, fresh to the Committee, making, under Hawke's chairmanship, a spirited address in favour of some cause on which he held strong views.

Gubby, as he talked, was a little disconcerted to notice that Hawke was inclined to shake his head and occasionally mutter, 'No, no – oh, no, no!' As Gubby eventually sat down, Hawke was heard to ask his neighbour, Sir Stanley Jackson: 'Tell me, Jacker, what was he saying?' The word 'martinet' was not coined in respect of Martin Hawke, but he would have seemed a formidable figure on such an occasion. In any case, the young were not expected to make noises in those days! Gubby recalls that when he was elected to the Committee – in 1937 – he was, at 33, six years younger than Guy Jackson, who in turn had almost as many years in hand of the next junior man. Let it be added that Gubby must now have spent more hours in the Committee Room than anyone either before or since, and I would have thought it unlikely that he has ever afterwards been put off his stroke in debate – or, for that matter, elsewhere.

There are two Committee-Room portraits which I suspect most who use the room might be unable to name. One is of Herbert Jenner-Fust, and the other Sir Spencer Ponsonby-Fane. The latter, a figure of rare benignity, would seem to have earned his place in perpetuity since until only a year or two ago he was not only a member of MCC for what was then the record span of 75 years but was Treasurer for almost half that time, from 1879 to his death in 1915 aged 91. A player on the field by day and on the boards by night with the Old Stagers at the first Canterbury Week, one of the three founders and the first Governor of I Zingari, Ponsonby-Fane clearly typified the sort of man around whom the club's high repute in Victorian England was built. For many years he was the oldest link with the past. He knew Lord's from the days when the membership mustered around 300: at his death there were 16,000 names on the waiting-list (a number sadly reduced by war casualties) and the estimated time-lag before election was forty years. That was excessive enough, of course, but they were the days when males were apt to be automatically entered at birth!

In his *Wisden* obituary F. S. Ashley-Cooper records that Ponsonby-Fane, a diplomat by training, 'brought from Paris the treaty ending the Crimean War', was private secretary to the great Palmerston, and Comptroller of the Lord Chamberlain's office; but Ashley-Cooper does not answer the intriguing question why he 'several times' declined the supreme honour of the Presidency. This grizzled patriarch who, among so many other things, was the founder of the MCC Art Collection, may still be vaguely remembered by a few of the dozen or so members still living who were elected before the date of his last visit to Lord's in 1913.

Jenner-Fust's career goes back even farther for he captained Cambridge (without the Fust) in the first University match of 1827, and was President of MCC six years later at the age of 27. Perhaps he owes his place to having been the youngest of all Presidents: otherwise he seems lucky to hold it if only because for some reason unexplained by the historians he resigned from MCC many years before his death at the age of 98. Talking of links and longevity I recall having a talk at Canterbury in 1946 with a spry, amusing F. A. Mackinnon, 35th chief of the clan, who on the eve of my going to Australia spoke of his tour there with Lord Harris's team of 1878–79. (In the only Test, at Melbourne, he was the middle man in the first-ever Test hat-trick by 'the Demon' Spofforth.) The Mackinnon, likewise then 98, was reckoned an odds-on bet to become the first first-class cricketer to reach 100, and Hubert Preston, editor of *Wisden*, records the old man's reply to a telephone enquiry as to his health: 'I am going to hospital tomorrow – but only for the annual meeting at which I shall preside. I am very well: weeds don't like me at all.' However, the hard, hard winter of 1946–47, in Morayshire as elsewhere, was too much for him, and though he beat Jenner-Fust by a few months he just failed to reach 99.

The member who has been so much longer than anyone else in the recorded annals of MCC is at the time of writing still with us and has furthermore reached his hundred: E. C. Wigan. Mr Wigan has been a member for 77 years, and has just nosed ahead of the Hon. R. E. S. Barrington, the previous title-holder, who died two years ago. Aspirants after the honour won't need reminding that the subscription is waived for all of 60 years' standing and beyond.

The best picture in the Committee Room, and almost in the MCC collection, is of Lord Harris, painted as he was in his late sixties by Arthur Hacker. Below his wing collar is a Band of Brothers bowtie. His right hand lightly holds the lapel of a double-breasted waistcoat, grey like his moustache. He gazes straight down the room in a steady, appraising way, gently dominating the scene. There, too, hang Stanley Christopherson, most long-serving of all presidents since he held the fort all through the Second World War, and William Findlay, Secretary 1926–36 and President 1951–2, whose urbanity masked, I always felt, a strong reactionary vein. This pleasant likeness was definitely painted from a photograph.

Over the mantelpiece, sitting at a desk covered with papers, is a figure with a pale, ascetic face – Francis Edwin Lacey, the Secretary who brought the administration of cricket quietly, firmly out of its easy Victorian tempo through the first quarter of the twentieth century. When, a practising barrister aged 38, Lacey took office in the new pavilion in 1898 no other part of the present ground was standing, though only a year afterwards the Mound stand replaced the old tennis and racket courts. There was no special machinery for administering Test matches either at home or abroad, though the formation of the Board of Control also immediately followed. It was another six years before MCC acceded to the request to set up an Advisory County Cricket Committee. In 1906, after spirited protest at the conditions under which they worked, the Press were provided with a box over the Professionals' quarters. (They had previously obtained no amelioration except under duress: for the first half-century of Lord's the only recognised representative, Mr Knight of *Bell's Life*, which became the *Sporting Life*, stood all day in the shrubbery beside the pavilion recording the play in his own score-book.) In 1909 the three then Test-playing countries formed the Imperial Cricket Conference, with its headquarters, inevitably, at Lord's.

'Ben' Lacey, so Plum tells us, on his appointment was advised by his predecessor, Henry Perkins, 'Don't take any notice of the – – Committee.' But MCC now had at the helm a different personality from the easy-going 'Perkino', who was said to have got so drunk at a Club dinner that after a temporary failure of the lights he was observed on the floor going through the motions of swimming, apparently under the impression that he was crossing the Styx. Lacey found the finances in poor shape, took them in hand, and generally put things in order. He personally reorganised the Refreshment Department which – not for the last time – was causing dissatisfaction, and did so to such effect that his stipend was raised from £500 to £700. The MCC minute approving the extra £200 added, 'so long as he shall continue to act in that capacity'. How often in the voluminous records of today's affairs does one notice a similar note of business prudence! He also began the Easter Coaching Classes, and, himself a highly reputable player, proclaimed firm views on the theory of the game.

Lacey well merits his continued presence over the committee fireplace. He initiated and organised so much over his 28 years – most of it personally and by hand. For a great deal of his time he had no recourse to a typewriter, and he inherited one telephone – in the basement. On his retirement in 1926 he was accorded the first knighthood ever bestowed for services to cricket, and lived to enjoy the distinction a further twenty years, during which time Plum Warner was similarly honoured, as also was the secretary of Yorkshire and manager of three MCC touring teams at Australia, F. C. Toone.

It is time to leave the Committee Room, our final gaze beside the doorway drawn perhaps to Lord Harris, the dictator of Lord's during his treasurership, which began with Ponsonby-Fane's death in 1915 and ended with his own seventeen years later. He was the keenest of competitors certainly who, like W. G., wanted his pound of flesh. A captain of Eton at Lord's, he, when bowling, retained the ball and ran out a certain unlucky Harrovian called Walroth, an action that might have determined the outcome of a close-fought match which Eton just won. In his old age, playing at Lord's against the Philadelphians, he is supposed to have had recourse to under-arm 'sneaks' in order to save the game.

The professionals took good care to keep the right side of him – did not one of them, after having run himself out at Canterbury, as his lordship bore down on the dressing-room, clamber out of the back window to keep out of his way? But we have Frank Woolley's word that he was the players' best friend. They can indeed all revere his memory today for the fact of benefits being tax-free goes back to the test case of Rex v. James Seymour, the latter being backed by Harris all the way to the House of Lords, which in 1927 decided in Seymour's favour.

Autocrat he certainly was, with everyone at his beck and call in a way barely credible today. Kent Committees (now never completed in under a couple of hours and often nearer three) used to be called for 4.30 at Cannon-street Hotel adjoining the station. If everything hadn't been tersely concluded by five o'clock the last of the proceedings were tidied up as with his retinue he progressed up the platform to his carriage to catch the 5.16 to Faversham. As with W. G. at Paddington I expect the station-master awaited his convenience before blowing the whistle.

Even Plum Warner, most charitable of critics, allows that he could be 'a little testy'. He also wrote that in committee he was 'deferential to the opinions of others, did not force his own views, and was fair and balanced'. When general agreement seemed unlikely he was inclined to adjourn for lunch or tea, saying, 'it helps us to adjust our ideas'. What could never be in dispute was his deep, abiding love of cricket. Though his career was a varied and busy one he wrote in his memoirs, *A Few Short Runs*, 'My whole life has pivoted on Lord's.' When he was abroad as Governor of Bombay he did more probably than anyone to export into India the English enthusiasm for cricket.

Continuing to try and convey an impression of the spirit of Lord's and the men who have made it – for the benefit, if you approve the fiction, of my young Australian companion – we must have another look at the likenesses of the three most recent secretaries hanging immediately outside the Committee Room.

Senior in age of service was Colonel R. S. Rait Kerr, known universally as 'R-K', whose span was cut in two by the war. R-K was not everyone's cup of tea, for he could have a curt way with members, and far from not suffering fools gladly at times it was with difficulty he suffered them at all. Still, with Ronny Aird at his elbow this did not so greatly matter, and his merits easily outshone a brusqueness of manner which may have derived from shyness and in latter years from ill-health. R-K was essentially a superb staff-officer who brought to Lord's a military efficiency that became all too necessary to match the difficult times into which cricket was moving when he arrived in 1936. By all account he was a faultless author of agenda and minutes, while on the practical side of the Lord's 'plant' his sapper training was of equal value.

R-K made another inestimable contribution to MCC in the shape of his daughter, Diana, who was recruited directly after the war to the new post of curator, and in the course of her appointment not only looked after and supervised the distribution of MCC's art collection and library but established a unique reputation as an authority on every variety of object that comes under the broad heading of cricketana.

I tried to portray in *Sort of a Cricket Person* Ronny Aird's special contribution as the purveyor, through his own personality, of an extraordinary harmony as between all at Lord's: members and secretariat: secretariat and staff: staff and members. Under him MCC was a happy family of a sort impossible now to foster to the same degree if only because the membership has jumped so steeply. Here are some figures: when Ronny went to Lord's in 1926 there were around 6,000 members. By 1949 it had risen only to 7,500, with a wait estimated at thirty years. A great many members knew a great many other members. In 1962, when he retired, it was still under 12,000, including the fairly recent class of

Associates, and there was still a very long waiting list. In the last fifteen years the figure has jumped by sharp stages to 18,000, with associate status abolished and the queue largely absorbed.

It so happens, too, that the wonderful staff which served at the time, say, of my election in 1936 have now departed either to still greener fields or to live in retirement. The last of the old links went with the sudden death last year of 'Joe', brother of 'Dick', sons of 'Old Dick' Gaby who worked at Lord's for a lifetime. There had been either one Gaby or more at Lord's for 116 years. Such gaps are irreplaceable. R. T. retired from the office of Club Superintendent in 1973 and now frequents the pavilion, as an honorary member, a repository of old stories and the idiosyncrasies of bygone members. Joe commanded the main pavilion door, knew more members by name and sight than anyone, and had a genial word with all of them.

There were many oddities in the Aird era – and still are some, but they are not so easy to identify since the pavilion is apt to be either terribly full or disappointingly empty. Many old-'uns, and indeed the now middle-aged whom he favoured, may recall the little man who took up his station near the Long Room door on to the field at the boys' matches and consolingly offered a bag of sweets to dismissed batsmen on their return. In cold print it might be wondered whether this Mr Haddock's motives were all that was to be desired, but one look at his simple, smiling face must have disarmed suspicion. What response he may sometimes have had from young hopefuls out for small scores at the sight of this unexpected and probably unwanted offering is more questionable.

Billy Griffith, after eleven years under Ronny Aird as joint Assistant Secretary with Jim Dunbar, took over the secretaryship in 1963 and held the reins for the twelve momentous years that followed. During this time the 'administrative tail' at Lord's grew vastly in size and scope with developments of the utmost significance both on the field and off. On the cricket side the three one-day competitions, making their successive bows, altered the general shape of the first-class game involving long debate – and, for a secretary therefore, an interminable succession of minutes and agenda. There was also a new state of things in that the amateur ceased to be: all were now dependent cricketers.

More crucial than all this from the secretary's point of view was that MCC voluntarily abjured their ancient status, universally accepted though never put into words, as the instigators, administrators and arbiters, of everything in the world of English cricket as well as the permanent hosts and organisers of the International Cricket Conference. Now there was to be a British constitution for cricket with a democratic flavour; the Cricket Council at the top, comprising in its turn the three essential bodies, the Test and County Cricket Board, to control what its title implies, the National Cricket Association, to coordinate and encourage every form and facet of cricket short of the top class, and MCC themselves, officially now only the law-makers. They had 'started it all' – 'the Advisory', as it was called, for county cricket, the Board of Control for Test matches, the MCC Youth Cricket Association and the MCC National Cricket Association – these latter, subdivided into county organisations, now brought together under the NCA.

But for all that this meant in secretarial terms the most testing aspect of Billy Griffith's time was the almighty rumpus that became known as the D'Oliveira Affair: first the cancellation of MCC's tour to South Africa because their Government had said that Basil D'Oliveira, the Cape Coloured who had emigrated here, would be unacceptable as a member of our team; then the last-minute abandonment of the South African tour to England on the plea of the British Government. Friends took up irreconcilable positions on this most controversial event in cricket since the Bodyline tour, and there was that dreadful meeting at Church House, Westminster, wherein the MCC Committee had to fight off votes of no-confidence in their handling of the business. Church House, indeed! The general spirit was not overflowing with Christian charity, nor would the general standard of debate (though with an exception or two) have commended itself to the illustrious forerunners of those chiefly concerned whose respective impacts on Lord's I have been talking about in this chapter.

Billy Griffith, though he had a fine war record and won his DFC on D-Day as a lieutenant-colonel in the Glider Pilot Regiment, was and is essentially, like Plum Warner, a man of peace: what more ironic than that each should have been closely involved in the biggest two rows ever to darken the face of cricket?

I have many happy pictures of Billy in my mind's eye: as a Cambridge undergraduate of the famous sporting generation of the '30s in the congenial atmosphere of Mr Goggs's wine bar behind Leicester Square where in the fashion of the day we used to drink quantities of hock-and-seltzer – a mild enough quencher in all conscience: of his return to the dressing-room at Queen's Park, Port-of-Spain – utterly exhausted, having been pressed into service because of injuries as opening batsman, and answering the call with a hundred in his first Test – the heat was so humid and intense that the sweat was coming through the front of his pads, something I've never seen before or since: of his brilliant wicket-keeping as George Mann's vice-captain in South Africa where for two Test matches he was preferred to Godfrey Evans: of his brief years as *Sunday Times* cricket-writer and a summer Sunday at Bolton Abbey in Wharfedale where he was so over-burdened with work for other papers that for the one and only time in my life I ghosted a Test report, I think for the long-deceased *Daily Graphic*.

John Ward's water-colour, done shortly before his retirement, shows him looking up from his desk with the tired expression that he often indeed could not disguise. It was the only defect of his qualities that he loved Lord's and cricket too well. However, though he spent many hard months of his retirement slogging away at a recodifying of the Laws, there he is now at Arundel, taking the utmost pleasure from the game, running the cricket at that most beautiful of grounds on behalf of Lavinia Duchess of Norfolk, looking distinctly younger than when he left St John's Wood the best part of three years ago.

There are many others known to fame who have either decorated Lord's in the past or who do so today, to whom or about whom my young friend might have liked to talk. We might have seen Doug Insole hurrying about on the business of the TCCB whose chairman he now is; or George Mann, chairman of Middlesex, or John Warr, who represents the Australian Cricket Board in England; or a hundred and one other cricket notables to whom Lord's and the Long Room is a focus in summer. But there is a limit to what can be digested at one visit, so let us leave the pavilion as we came in, pausing only to admire the likeness of the man who 'bestrode the game like a colossus', who won men's hearts for cricket in a way unknown before, but for whose career even this pavilion might not be standing, rich alike in treasures and history.

Archibald Stuart-Wortley's picture, a signed print of which commands the wall beside my desk as I write, shows W. G. in the moment before he begins to shape the stroke. The left shoulder is forward, the eyes bright and steady above the dark, square beard, and beneath the MCC cap of red and yellow. The bat is slightly raised, equally ready to play back or forward, though the left leg is a foot in front of the crease with the toe of his brown boot slightly raised. So a forward stroke, whether punitive or otherwise, is the likeliest outcome. W. G. was 42 when the painting was done, and the lissom lines of youth have given way to an ample frame. He isn't fat but looks as though, in the modern phrase, he'll soon have to 'watch it'. No doubt he must have done, for those thousand runs in the May of 1895 that finally sealed his fame, the last of them made at Lord's, were still five years into the future.

The peculiar cocking of the toe was a 'W. G.-ism' that caught on among a certain sort of gentry, to the peculiar fury of Charles Kortright of Essex, reputedly the fastest bowler of his day. W. G. could do as he liked, but if anyone cocked a toe in the direction of 'Korty' he pursued only one ambition, to land a full-pitch on it in the quickest time possible. Kortright might have cried, as W. G. is reputed to have done in some moment of argument – 'I *can't* have it, and I *won't* have it.'

This is no place, nor am I the authority, for a dissertation on the moral principles of W. G. Stories spread of his being a bit sharp: of pointing up into the sun and observing to the young man he was bowling to, 'Look at they ducks' – whereupon the victim is duly dazzled and bowled out. There are many such – to which there seemed more point, no doubt, if they were attributed to the Old Man. There's no doubt he was an enthusiastic practical joker. I would only add that I never met anyone who knew him and did not greatly like him. As I wrote on the occasion of one of his anniversaries in the *Daily Telegraph*:

> I prefer to think of him as a devoted country doctor, who during a match in which he made two hundreds stayed up all night because he had promised to see a woman through her confinement: who at Christmas bade the parish poor bring two basins which were filled by him and his wife, one with roast beef and vegetables, the other with plum pudding.

He was a legend beyond compare in his lifetime, yet never lost his humility, his love of a joke, the common touch. Is not this a sure explanation for the affection in which he was held by so many generations of Englishmen?

E. W. SWANTON, *Follow On*, 1977

BUT even as those essays and books were published, by Swanton, by Moorhouse, by Heald, the nature of cricket at large and Lord's in particular was subtly shifting. Like the philosopher's river, you cannot step into it unchanged twice, or even once, because somewhere, whether on the field of play, or out in some obscure corner where they oil the rollers, or store the paint for the sight-screens, or where the birds peck away disrespectfully in the Lord Harris garden, something is being altered, or introduced, or amended, or reshaped, so that everything may be made to appear as if nothing has changed. Since Swanton took us on his guided tour, the Library has been most beautifully extended and refurbished; in 1985 the Mound Stand was demolished and its rebuilding completed in time for the bi-centenary celebrations. There have also been changes of a rather different nature. In the two hundredth year of its history, a photograph of a sweater-laden blonde appeared in *The Times*. She was leaning over a set of stumps, and holding up an admonitory finger. The caption read:

Dawn Trousdale, aged eighteen, who today becomes the first woman to umpire a men's cricket match at Lord's. She is to take charge at the finals of the national indoor cricket championships.

The Times, summer 1986

THE same newspaper published another item about Lord's which illustrates the ways in which cricket may be drawn into the day-to-day life of the outside world. Today along the St John's Wood Road the land is filled for the most part by huge hotels. The largest exception in architectural terms is the house of worship exactly across the road from the Grace Gates.

Lord's cricket ground could soon play host to worshippers at the neighbouring liberal Jewish synagogue. Its rabbis want to pull down the building because of its 'serious and deteriorating structural defects' and hope to hold services in a marquee on the sacred turf until a new one is built. The proposals are contained in a report passed anonymously to me yesterday. The rabbis say the potential £3m repair bill is too much for the synagogue's 'aging and declining' membership of 2,500 and have come up with an ingenious idea to get a new synagogue for nothing: a partnership with a commercial developer who would use the rest of the site for offices and twenty-four flats.

Relations with Lord's have been strong since the friendship of their first rabbi, Israel Mattuck, and Plum Warner, star of the 1920s MCC. Certainly, if a marquee is erected it would not be the first unlikely mix of overs and Passover; after the synagogue was bombed in the war, services were held in Lord's pavilion.

The Times, summer 1986

Oᴺᴇ last event remains to be recorded in the annals of the first two hundred years of the Marylebone Cricket Club. Early in the summer of 1986, during a Test match with India, a young lady dashed on to the field while play was in progress. Such an incident may be regrettable, but it is certainly not unprecedented. Often in modern times when a player reaches his hundred, especially in an international contest, idolaters tend to invade the pitch and slap their champion's back to the point where his concentration is broken irrevocably. But this young lady was different from all others before her. She had no clothes on. One wonders what the reaction would have been from the ancient grandees of two hundred years ago to such an outrage. A picture forms of the outraged virtue of Beauclerk, Aislabie, Osbaldeston, Ward and the rest of them.

Then again, on the other hand...

The severance of Lord's from its almost immemorial rights and uses, would cause many a pang and deep regret.

WILLIAM DENISON, *Sketches of the Players*, 1846

I can never walk about Lord's without some such reflections as may be supposed in Rip Van Winkle after his sleep of twenty years; the present and the past come in such vivid contrast before my mind.

JAMES PYCROFT, *Oxford Memories*, 1886

At The Oval, men seem to have rushed away with some zest from their City offices. At Lord's there is a dilettante look, as of men whose work, if ever, has yet to come.

JAMES PYCROFT, *Oxford Memories*, 1886

It is a curious fact that, whenever there is a Test match at Lord's, many prominent business men in the City become strangely unwell after luncheon.

ANON., 'Sheep at Lord's in Early Days', late 19th Century

The Mecca of cricket must be
In the beautiful classic arena,
The home of the old MCC

Mr Punch's Book of Sports, 1906

Iredale says that he can never see a ball at Lord's when he is facing the pavilion, and English cricketers have told me the same thing.

WALTER A. BETTESWORTH, *Chats on the Cricket Field*, 1910

From its inception, the Marylebone Club has been known for its sportsmanlike spirit, and to this day there is no ground whereon the game is more strictly played, none where the sporting element is more predominant, none whose habitués are more truly lovers of the game, or more free from partisan spirit.

A. E. KNIGHT, *The Complete Cricketer*, 1906

There never was a better way of watching cricket than at Lord's.

ERIC PARKER, *Playing Fields*, 1922

The Oval, Canterbury, Brighton and Fenner's always produced good wickets; but Lord's was terribly bad, and it was said that the only respect in which its pitch resembled a billiard table was the pockets.

H. S. ALTHAM, *A History of Cricket*, 1926

In the evening light Lord's is a place of infinite peace and quiet and friendly charm.

HON. T. C. F. PRITTIE, *Mainly Middlesex*, 1947

It is the best of all games, and I thank my stars that my early footsteps took me to Lord's, for, with all respect to the other great grounds, to me it is the best place in the world to play.

DENIS COMPTON, quoted in E. W. SWANTON, *Compton, a Cricket Sketch*, 1948

It is a wonderful thing to walk from the pavilion out to the middle at Lord's for the first time. In recent years I have been on some of the biggest barrack squares in the country, but they have nothing on Lord's for vastness and when it comes to feeling lost.

DENIS COMPTON, *Playing for England*, 1948

The name is magic. It is also magnificently Debrett. It has an aura loftily unique — a cachet unmatched. It conjures in the mind not merely the aristocratic among the world's cricket fields but a social rallying point. Indeed there are many human beings, a trifle vague as to its origin and functions, who believe that it is firmly associated with our peerage rather than plain Mr Lord.

JOHN MARSHALL, *Lord's*, 1969

For cricket-lovers there is no place quite like Lord's during a Test match. Lord's must be a bit like Heaven. There are many mansions in it. It caters for all tastes, classes, colours, ages, points of view, degrees of skill, levels of knowledge.

T. C. DODDS, *Hit Hard and Enjoy It*, 1976

Lord's – it's a magical world to me, the 'open sesame' to a lifetime of happiness.

MARGARET HUGHES, *All on a Summer's Day*, 1953

I always feel as though I am stepping into history.

J. M. KILBURN, *Overthrows*, 1975

I know of nowhere else on earth where so much of cricket's flavour is so readily concentrated.

Ibid.

Lord's is the Mecca of all cricketers and a pilgrimage thereto when they are in London provides a hallowed memory that must sustain the faithful in many a barren outpost.

E. W. SWANTON, *Compton, a Cricket Sketch*, 1948

Lord's is a world apart. It is a community, an establishment, a living monument, an atmosphere.

T. C. DODDS, *Hit Hard and Enjoy It*, 1976

Yes, that ring at Lord's shows me every gradation in the scale of life – the once active now stiff and heavy, the youthful grey, the leaders of great elevens passing unrecognised and alone.

JAMES PYCROFT, *Oxford Memories*, 1886

My own personal feeling is that the laws and regulations of cricket generally could not have been entrusted to better hands than those of the MCC. The club has always set a high standard to the cricket world, and has never refused to consider reasonable suggestions from responsible cricketers. It has acted with the impartiality of the High Court of Appeal, and has always safeguarded the best interests of the game, without unduly interfering with the rights and liberties of cricketers, individually or collectively.

W. G. GRACE, *Cricketing Reminiscences and Personal Recollections*, 1889

For your good cricketer the ends of the earth have come to a resting-point at Lord's, and wherever he may be at the fall of a summer's day his face should turn religiously towards Lord's.

SIR NEVILLE CARDUS, *Days in the Sun*, 1924

INDEX

Numbers in bold type refer to contributors

Abel, R., 141
Abercorn, Duke of, 100
Absolom, Bos, 53, 54
Advisory County Cricket Committee,
   250, 285, 442, 445
Aird, Ronald, 332, 345, 376, 384,
   440, 444–5
air raid shelters, 304, 305
Aislabie, Benjamin, 21–2, **35**, 38, 328,
   331
Albert, Prince-Consort, 7, 40
Alexander, R. H. I. G., 183, 184, 185,
   186
Alington, Dr C. A. ('C. A. A.'), **229–30**,
   233
Allan, F. E., 83
Allen, D. A., 366, 367
Allen, David Rayvern, **415–16**
Allen, G. O. (Gubby), 227, 231, 232,
   233, 240, 241, 242, 243, 251,
   255, 278, 304–5, 308, 309, **314–
   15**, 337, 355–6, 372, **408–12**,
   424, 433, 439, 440, 441
Allen, William, 366, 367
Alley, W. E., umpire, 404
Allom, M. J. C., 254
Altham, H. S., 18, **19–20**, 32, **45**, 47,
   83–4, 292–3, 434, 440, **450**
Amar Nath, 267
American Base Ball Players (1874),
   65–9
Ames, L. E. G., 257–8, 259, 271, 272,
   273, 305, 306, 307, 308, 309,
   318, 319
Anson, G. F., 319
Appleby, A., 68, 69, 100
Arlott, John, 37, 39, **342**, 360, 384,
   385–6, 400–1, 414–18, 422
Armstrong, Warwick, 116
Army v. RAF match (1944), 303, 304
Arnold, G. G., 397
Arnold, Matthew, 172
art collection, MCC, 326–32, 379,
   436, 439–42
Artillery Field, Finsbury, 6
Arundel Castle, 446
Ashdown, W. H., 282

Ashley-Cooper, F. S., **8–9**, 13, **14–15**,
   16, **18–19**, **21–2**, 24, 25, **26–8**, 30,
   32–3, **38–9**, 40, 42, 44, **46–7**, 48,
   59–60, 71, 83n, **89–90**, **131–2**,
   441
Astill, W. E., 203, 204
Athey, C. W. J., 406, 407, 416
Attewell, W., 108, 114
Australia, 81, 86, 442; 'Bodyline' tour
   (1932–3), 251–2, 253, 254–5,
   386; Centenary Test (Melbourne,
   1977), 405, 413; Kerry Packer,
   400; MCC tours, 213, 240, 249–50,
   337, 338, 339, 340, 356, 379, 427
Australian tourists in England, 90, 93,
   94, 105, 114, 119, 120, 160, 162,
   337, 393; Army v. English Army
   (1917), 196–8, 293; v. Cambridge,
   85, 394; Cornhill Centenary Test
   (1980), 405–17; first visit (1878),
   81–4, 85; Middlesex v., 85, 93, 115,
   394; One-Day matches, 430, 431;
   RAAF v. South of England, 314–15;
   and South African Forces v. Navy
   and Army (1917), 198–200, 293;
   Test matches, 107–8, 113, 140,
   162, 165, 166–8, 213–17, 219,
   220, 226, 239–43, 244–5, 256–
   60, 270–4, 281–2, 322, 331, 342,
   344–7, 383, 387, 394, 395, 396–
   9, 400–1, 414, 415–16, 417, 427,
   431; Triangular Test (1912), 190
Avery, A. V., 291, 308

Badcock, C. L., 271, 272, 273
Bailey, Sir Abe, 190
Bailey, A. E., 168, 169, 170
Bailey, G. H., 83
Bailey, J. A., Secretary of MCC, 405,
   414, 419–20, 432
Bailey, T. E. (Trevor), 305, 306, 307,
   309, 333, 334, 335, 339, 340,
   348, 460, 362–3, 416, 418
Bairstow, D. L., 406, 407
Baker, Sir Herbert, 209, 247, 376,
   392, 437
Balaskas, Xenophon, 384

Baldwin, H. G., umpire, 320
Bale, E., 198
Balfour, A. J., 185, 186, 191
Bannerman, Charles, 82, 83, 85
Barbour, E. P., 196, 197, 198, 199,
   201, 202, 203, 204, 205
Bardsley, W., 217
Bardswell, G. R., 110, 111, 112
Barling, T. H., 277
Barlow, G. D. (Graham), 403
Barlow, R. G., 95, 97
Barnes, Sydney, 213–14, 244–5, 348,
   396
Barnes, W., 94, 95, 96, 98, 99
Barnett, B. A., 271, 272, 273
Barrable, H., 436
Barrie, J. M., **207**, 209, 219–20, 289
Barrington, K. F., 365, 366, 367
Barrington, R. E. S., 442
Bartlett, E. L., 231
Bartlett, H. T., 324, 338
Bartlett, J., 310, 311
baseball matches, 65–9, 195
Batchelor, Denzil, **255–6**
Bates, W., 95, 98, 99
Bax, Clifford, 116, 256
Bayes, Gilbert, 1, 286
Beachcomber (J. B. Morton), **253**, **269**,
   286, 388
Beagley, Tom, 33–4
Bean, George, 186
Beaton, Cecil, 145
Beauclerk, Lord Frederick, **15–19**, 20,
   21, 25, 28, 33, 34, 35, 37, 38, 274,
   297
Beaufort, Duke of, 88
Beckett, Ernest W., 106
Bedford, P. I., 373
Bedser, A. V., 306, 307, 308, 309,
   334, 335, 336, 339
Bedser, E. A., 308, 309
Beerbohm, Sir Max, 38
Beldam, E. A., 161
Beldam, G. W., 161, 162, 169, 170
Beldham, William ('Silver Billy'), 9, 17,
   19–20, 328
Bell, W., 198, 199

452

Bell's Life, 34–5, 51, 62, 64, 78, 80, 87, 443
Belper, Lord, 286, 288
Benaud, Richie, 383
Bengough, C. W., 91–2
Bennett, Don, 403, 433
Bennison, B., 194
Benson and Hedges final (1985), 431
Bentinck, Lord George, 14
Bentley, John, 25
Berry, R., 334, 336
Bessborough, Earl of, 100, 101
Bessborough, Earl and Countess of, 236
Bessborough, Frederick, Lord, 37, 38
Bessborough, George P. W., Lord, 24–5
Bessemer, H. Douglas, 316
Bettesworth, Walter, 32, 83n, **449**
Bettington, R. H., 280
Bevin, Ernest, 290
Bicentenary celebrations (1987), 432, 434, 448
Bickmore, J. D., 317
Bickmore, M. J., 317
Bircham, S., 132
Birchenough, W. T., 184
Bird, D. B., 316, 317
Bird, G. E., 68, 69
Bird, H. D., 406, 408
Birkett, Sir Norman, 379
Bishop, M. F., 316, 317
Blackham, J. McC., 150
Blake, J., umpire, 211
Bland, Jim and Joe, bookmakers, 12
blankets used to dry Lord's pitch, 266
Bligh, Ivo, 150
Blitz/bombing (2nd World War), 302–5
Blofeld, Henry, 433
Blount, C. H. B., 184
Blunden, Edmund, 116, 256
Blythe, Colin, 196, 197, 198, 199, 200, 371
Board of Control, 379, 395, 442, 445
'Bodyline' tour of Australia (1932–3), 251–5, 279, 337, 386, 439
Boer War, 116, 117, 132
Bolus, Brian, 438–9
Bonnor, G. J., 94
Booth, C., 82
Borde, Chandra, 384
Border, A. R., 407, 408, 431
Bosanquet, B. J. T., 148, 150, 153, 154, 159–62, 169, 170, 371
Bosanquet, Reginald, 160
Boswell, W. G. K., 183, 184, 185
Botham, I. T., 405, 407, 408, 413–14, 420, 433
Bowden, W. J., 331
Bowen, E. E., 102, **103–4**
Bowen, Roland, 11–12, **16–17**, 19, 252
Bowes, W. E., 254, 258, 259, 260, 278, 279
Bowler, G., 316
Bowley, E. H., 282
Boxer, Mark, 433
Boycott, Geoffrey, 397, 398, 405, 406, 407, 410, 415–16, 421, 428
Boyle, H. F., 82, 83, 84
Bradby, G. F., **275–6**
Bradley, Don, 113
Bradman, D. G. (Sir Donald), 240, 241–2, 243, 256, 258, 259, 263, 271, 272, 273, 322, 342, 395, 396, 407, 409, 411, 437, 439, 440
Brain, B. M., 404
Brain, W. H., 104, 164

Bramall Lane, 172, 278, 279, 280
Braund, L. C., 168, 169, 170
Bray, E. H., 109, 110, 111, 112
Brearley, J. M., 368, 402, 403, 433
Brearley, W., 289
Bremner, C. D., 313
Brennan, D. V., 339
Briers, Nigel, 427
Briggs, Johnny, 94, 95, 97, 98, 99
Bright, R. J., 407, 408, 415–16
British Empire XI (1940), 291
Broadbent, Sir John, 194
broadcast cricket commentary, 400–1, 414–18, 422–3, 433
Brockwell, W., 168
Brodribb, Gerald, **22–4**, **92**, 93, **163–8**, **232–3**, **254**, **262–5**
Bromley, E. H., 258, 259
Bromley, James, 50
Bromley-Davenport, H. R., 104
Brookes, Christopher, 9
Broughton, R. J. P., 24, 43, 44
Brown, F. R., 254, 277, 337–40, 342, 429
Brown, Ivor, 145
Brown, Lionel H., **140**
Brown, J. M., 324
Brown, S., umpire, 170
Brown, S. M., 309, 317, 319, 320, 373
Brown, W. A., 258, 259, 271, 272, 273
Browne, C. R., 231, 232
Bruce, C. N., 372
Buckingham, W. S., 24
Buckland, F. M., 61, 80
Budd, E. H., 16, 17, **20–1**, 29, 31, 33, 391
Burgoyne, R., 68, 80
Buller, C. F., 72–3, 74, 75
Buller, J. S., umpire, 368
Buller, S., 355
Burnup, C. J., 109, 110, 111
Burrell, Sir Peter, 6
Burton, G., 370
Buse, M. T. F., 320, 321
Bush, John, 378
Butcher, B. F., 365, 367
Butt, H. R., 117, 161
Buttress, Billy, 47–87
Byron, George Gordon, Lord, 22–4

Caine, Charles Stewart, 351
Caldecourt, William ('Honest Will'), 27, 28, 32
Cambridge, 85, 168, 394; *see also* Oxford v. Cambridge matches
Canada, Lord XI v. (1944), 310–11
Cannon, James, 219, 325, 326
Canterbury Cricket Week, 66, 327, 441
Cardus, Sir Neville, **163**, 166, 171, 206–7, **208**, **219–21**, 225, 229, 255, 262, 276, **289–90**, 338, 351, 401–2, 428, 429, 436, **451**
Carew, Dudley, 263
Carmody, D. K., 306, 307
Carr, D. B., 339, 340
Carr, Donald, 387
Carr, J. L., 26
Carson, W. N., 320
Carter, David Webb, 433
Cartwright, 'Buns', 438
Cartwright, G. H. M., 310, 311
Case, Professor, 6
Cathcart, G. Devonshire, 25
Causton, R. K., 106
Centenary Match (MCC v. England) and Dinner (Lord's, 1887), 94–102, 150

Centenary Match (MCC v. Rest of England), and Dinner (Lord's 1914), 191–2
Centenary Test: Australia v. England (Melbourne, 1977), 405, 413
Centenary Test: England v. Australia (Lord's, 1980), 405–17
Chalk, F. G. H., 282
Challenor, G., 231
Chaplin, H. P., 161
Chapman, A. P. F. (Percy), 4, 240, 242, 243, 245, 293, 310, 409, 411
Chappell, G. S. (Greg), 397–8, 399, 400, 405, 406, 407, 408, 410, 414
Chappell, I. M. (Ian), 397, 398, 399
Chelsea, Viscount, 106
Chester, F., umpire, 243
Chesterfield, Lord, 329
Childs, J. H., 404
Chinnaswamy, Mr, 383
Chipperfield, A. G., 258, 259, 260, 271, 273, 274
Chitty, Mr Justice, 100
Christian, E. B. V., **9–10**, **114**
Christiani, R. J., 335
Christopherson, Sir Stanley, 291, 442
Chubb, Geoff, 356
Church, Brian, 430
Churchill, Lord Randolph, 99
Clarke, Anne and Sharon, 422
Clarke, C. B., 306, 307
Clarke, C. C., 129
Clarke, William, 332
Clarke's All-England Eleven, 39
Clayton, R., 72, 74, 75, 76
Clifton v. Tonbridge (1946), 316–17
Close, D. B., 366, 367, 368, 438–9
Cobbett, J., 49
Cobbold, P. W., 110, 111, 112
Cobden, F. C., 52–4
Cobham, Lord, 109, 112, 440; 9th, 440–1
Coleman, A. R., umpire, 320
Colley, D. J., 398, 399
Collins, Ted, Clerk of Works, 422
Colman, Sir Jeremiah, 331, 436
Colmer, Francis, 116
Committee Room, MCC, 440–3
Compton, D. C. S. (Denis), 265–6, 272, 273, 276, 291, 305, 306, 307, 308, 317, 318, 319, 320, 321, 323–5, 334, 363, 368, 370, 373, 402, 421, 437, **450**
Compton, L. H. (Leslie), 291, 292, 306, 307, 308, 319, 320, 321, 324, 325
Constant, D. J., umpire, 399, 405, 406, 408, 414
Constantine, L. N. (Learie), 133, 230–1, 232–3, 253–4, 265, 280, 306, 307, 308, 312, 313, 314
Constantine, L. S., 133
Conway, John, 81
Cook, Tommy, 282
Coope, M., 321
Cornford, J., 324, 325
Coronation Garden, 436
Cotes, Francis, 329
Cotton, J. A. H., 234
County Championships, 77, 185, 209, 210–13, 265–6, 276–82, 316, 317–21, 402; Middlesex Centenary (1964), 368–74; scoring systems, 279; two-day matches (1919), 206; *see also* Middlesex; Surrey, etc.
Court, J., 310, 311
Courtenay, C., 66, 68
Cowans, Norman, 425, 429
Coward, Noël, 132

Cowdrey, M.C., 316, 317, 359, 360, 364, 365, 366, 367, 429, 430
Cowie, J., 263
Cowper, William, 276, 282
Cox, G., 161, 324, 325
Crabtree, H.P., 309
Craig, H.S., 312, 313
Crawford, J.N., 277
Crawford, P.M., 317
Crawley, A.M., 352
Crawley, Leonard George, 218
Creevey, Thomas, 14
Cricket, 140, 190
Cricket Council, 440, 445
The Cricketer, 57–8, 130, 213, 214–15, 251, 386–7
Cricketer's Association, 417
Cristofani, D.R., 311, 312, 313, 314
Crosfield, S.M., 142
Cross Arrows (formerly St John's Wood Ramblers), 89, 422, 425–6, 437
Crowhurst, Mrs, 194
Crozier, Eric, 275
Crutchley, G.E.V., 309, 372
Cull, David, 430, 433
Cundall, Charles, 331
Cunliffe, F.H.E., 109, 110, 111, 112
Curtis, Alan, 415, 416
Curzon, Viscount, 106

D'Aeth, Mrs Hughes, 329
Daft, Richard, 48, 49, 73, 75
Daily Mail, 132, 245
Daily Telegraph, 162, 163, 166–7, 194, 265, 337, 351–2, 447
Dales, H.L., 227, 372
Dare, Phyllis, 145, 147
Dark, Ben, 50
Dark, James Henry, 7, 22, 34–46 passim, 49–51, 52, 57, 102, 391, 392
Dark, John, 50
Dark, Sidney, 49–51
Darling, J., 108, 115
Darling, L.S., 258, 259, 260
Dartmouth, Earl of, 105
Darwin, Bernard, 46
Davidson, G., 108
Davie, Michael, 433
Davies, Bill, 322
Davies, D., umpire, 336
Davies, J.G.W., 312, 313, 314, 318, 319, 320, 440
Dawe, Henry, 21–2
Dawes, Peter, 430
Day, Daniel, 331, 332
Day, J.W., umpire, 232
Deakins, Leslie, 356
Dean, James, 42, 90
Dean, N.G., 197
Deerhurst, Lord, 218
Dempster, C.S., 306, 307, 310
Denison, William, 35, 42, 122–5, 127, 128, 449
Dennett, E.G., 155–6, 158
Denton, D., 173
Derbyshire, 119, 332, 373
Devonshire, Duke(s) of, 107, 190, 236
Dewes, J.G., 338, 339
Dexter, E.R. (Ted), 359, 365, 366, 367, 402, 420, 429, 433
Dickens, Charles, 207, 208, 299, 427
Dickinson, D.C., 317
disabled soldiers, 214–15
Docker, C.T., 197, 198, 199, 200, 201, 202, 203
Docker, P.W., 197
Dodd, Francis, 327–8

Dodds, T.C., 450, 451
Doggart, G.H.G., 335, 336, 338, 339, 340
D'Oliveira, Basil L., 397, 398, 399, 400, 420, 446
Dollery, H.E., 338–9
Dolphin, A., 278
Donnelly, M.P., 312, 313, 323, 383
Dorrington, W., 332
Dorset Square, Lord's ground at, 6, 7, 9, 17, 34, 96, 246, 390, 434
Douglas, J.W.H.T., 150, 197, 198, 204, 205, 213, 217–18
Dovey, R.R., 319, 320
Doyle, Sir Arthur Conan, 113, 142–3, 192, 404
Druce, N.F., 109, 110, 111, 112
Drybrough, C.D., 373
Ducat, A., 211, 226, 227, 277, 296, 303
Duckworth, G., 241, 243
Duleepsinhji, K.S., 240–1, 242, 409, 411
Dunbar, Jim, 445
Duncan, A.S., 72, 73, 75
Dundas, Lady Jane, 25
Dunning, J.A., 263, 264
Durston, T.J., 211, 227, 231, 232, 372

Eady, C.J., 108
Eager, Desmond, 417
Earle, G.F., 183, 184, 185
Easter Coaching Classes, 248, 443
Ebury, Lord, 59
Eddington, Professor Sir Arthur, 261
Edgbaston, 140, 366
Edmonds, P.H. (Phil), 403, 404, 431, 433
Edrich, J.H., 365, 366, 367, 397, 398
Edrich, W.J. (Bill), 265, 266, 273, 274, 276, 280, 288, 312, 313, 314, 317, 318, 319, 320, 321, 324, 325, 335, 336, 340, 368, 370, 373
Edward, Prince of Wales (Edward VII), 89
Edwards, R., 397–8, 399
Elizabeth, Princess (Elizabeth II), 376
Elizabeth, Queen-Mother, 376
Elliott, H., umpire, 321, 325
Ellis, R.S., 313, 314
Ellis, Vivian, 145
Emburey, J.E., 403, 404, 406, 407, 408, 425, 433
Emmett, Tom, 46
Engineer, Farrokh, 384
England v. Dominions: 1918: 200–4, 387; 1943: 306–8; 1945: 311–14; see also Australia; New Zealand, etc.
English Army XI v. Australian Army XI (1917), 196–8, 293
Enthoven, H.J., 227, 372
Essex, 12, 119, 264, 278–9, 308–9, 390, 431
Eton v. Harrow matches, 29, 30, 31, 38, 43, 47, 52, 55–9, 60–4, 69, 76, 80, 93, 102–4, 138–9, 221, 229–30, 233–6, 256, 268, 377, 378, 380, 381, 382, 391, 429, 430, 438; Byron's match (1805), 22–4; Centenary match (1929), 234–6; Fowler's match (1910), 182–8; reduced to one-day fixture (1983), 234
Eton v. Winchester matches, 43, 391
Evans, T.G., 291, 306, 307, 308, 309, 319, 335, 336, 339, 446
Exton, R.N., 316, 317

Eyre family/Estate, 27, 34, 43, 390, 391, 392

Fagg, A.E., 291, 308, 309, 319, 399
Fairbrother, Jim, groundsman, 420, 421–2
Fairfax, A., 242, 243
Falkner, Keith, 368
Farley, Christopher 'Gus', 421, 430
Farnes, K., 258, 259, 260, 272, 273, 274
Father Time weather-vane, 265, 293, 303, 305, 345, 349, 351, 358, 376, 382, 389, 392–3, 395, 437
Featherstone, N.G., 403, 404
Felix, N. (Nicholas Wanostrocht), 39–40; paintings of, 331–2
Fell, D.R., 312, 313
Fellows, Harvey, 45, 128–9
Fender, P.G.H., 197, 198, 199, 200, 202, 203, 204, 205, 206, 210, 211, 227, 264, 277, 293, 372
Fenley, S.E., 227
Fenner, George, 333
Fernandes, M.P., 231
Field, E., 161
The Field, 76, 94, 145
Findlay, William, 251, 442
Fingleton, J.H. (Jack), 273, 322, 338, 340, 344–7, 358–9, 388–96
Firth, J.D'E., 293
Fishlock, L.B., 277, 308, 309, 312, 313
Fitzgerald, R.A., Secretary of MCC, 43, 44, 58, 60, 62, 63, 64, 65, 66, 68, 69–71, 77, 78, 101, 393, 394
Fitzgerald, R.C.A., 310, 311
Fitzhardinge, Lord, 88
Fitzroy, Hon. A., 6
Fleetwood-Smith, L. O'B., 272, 273, 274
Flowers, W., 82, 95, 96, 98, 99
flying bombs, 304–5, 396
Foat, J.C., 403
Foley, Cyril Pelham, 116–17, 165, 185–7, 351–2
Forbes, Walter, 186
Ford, Ford Madox, 191, 207
Ford, Bill, 93
Ford, Richard, 413–14
Ford, W.J., 6, 296
Forjonnel, Catherine, 33
Forster, H.W., 105, 106
Foster, G.N., 209
Foster, H.K., 110, 111, 112
Foster, R.E., 133
Fowler, Archie, umpire, 315, 333
Fowler, Robert St Leger, 182, 183–4, 185, 186–8, 234, 382
Fowler, William Herbert, 92–3, 188–9
Francis, B.C., 397, 399
Francis, G.N., 231, 232
Franklin, W.B., 196, 197, 198, 199, 201, 203, 205
Freeman, A.P., 46
Freeman, J.J., 331
Fremantle, T.F. (Lord Cottesloe), 41
Frewin, Leslie, 362–4, 375–82
Frith, David, 194–5
Frith, William, 207, 208
Fry, C.B., 6, 8, 128, 141, 142, 161, 201, 203, 212, 255–6, 371, 386
Furniss, Harry, 133–5, 136, 137

Gaby, Charles, 219
Gaby, Gerald Maybee ('Joe'), 219, 445
Gaby, Richard ('Old Dick'), 219, 445

Gaby, Richard Thomas ('Young Dick'), 219, 445
Gainsborough, Thomas, 328
Gale, Frederick, 37, 42, **45**, 90
Gale, Norman, **114–15**
Gale, R. A., 373
Galsworthy, John, 220, **221–5**
Garland-Wells, H. M., 277
Garnerin, M., balloonist, 25
Garnham, M. A., 431
Garrett, T. W., 83, 436
Gatting, M. W. (Mike), 403, 404, 405, 407
Geary, G., 258, 259, 260
Geloven, J. Van, 404
Gentlemen v. Players, 7, 33, 45, 47, 48, 49, 52, 54, 76, 77, 78, 87, 137, 226, 337–40, 394
George IV (Prince Regent), 328
George V, King, 117, 190, 202, 241, 255, 387
George VI, King, 334, 376
Getty, J. Paul, 432
Gibbs, L. R., 365, 366, 367, 368
Gibson, Alan, 386, **417–18**
Gibson, C. H., 204, 205, 293
Giffen, George, 107, 108, 114
Gifford, N., 397, 398, 399
gifts to MCC, 286–8
Gillingham, Rev. F. H., 201, 203, 204
Gimblett, H., 306, 312, 313, 321, 339
Gladstone, H. J., 106
Gladstone, W. E., 105, 107
Gladwin, Cliff, 332
Glamorgan, 266
Gleeson, J. W., 397, 399
Gloucester, Duke of, 306
Gloucestershire, 80, 91, 97, 146, 164, 263, 265, 266, 277, 402–4
Goddard, J. D., 335, 336
Goddard, T. W., 221, 263
Goldie, K. O., 161
Gomez, G. E., 334, 335, 336
Gooch, G. A., 406, 407, 410, 416, 430, 433
Goodford, Dr., Provost of Eton, 55
googly balls, 148, 153, 159–60, 371, 372
Gorringe, A. L., 161
Goschen, George, 99–101, 107
Gould, I. J., 403
Gover, A. R., 277, 288
Government v. Opposition (1893), 105–6
Gower, D. I, (David), 406, 407, 410, 415, 430, 433
Grace, E. M., 86, 92
Grace, G. F., 54
Grace, W. G., 34, 46, 47, 52, 53, 58, 69, 72, 73, 74, 75, 77, 82, 83, 84, 85, 86, 87–9, 90, 92, 94, 95, 96, 97, 98, 99, 100, 101, 107, 108, 112, 113, 120, 142, 192, 193, 196, 226, 287, 290, 351, 380, 394, 427, 435, 436, 443, 447, 451; bust of, 290, 396, 436; London County Eleven of, 142, 143, 255, 267; Memorial Gateway to, 208–9, 247, 435; portraits of, 326–7, 447; Testimonial to (1879), 88–9
Grace, W. G., Jr, 110, 112
Grace Gates, 2, 4, 208–9, 247, 303, 350, 359, 374, 383, 419, 435
Graham, H., 108
Graham, Harry, **228–9**
Graham, P. A. O., 321
Graham, O. B., 183, 184, 185, 186
Grandserre, John Joseph, 36

Grandstand and Balcony, 51, 55, 56, 63, 84, 137, 214, 247, 265, 285, 303, 376, 377, 349, 422, 432, 437
Gray, L. (Laurie), 288, 319, 321, 325, 373
Great War (1914–18), 171, 185, 190, 192–206, 218, 244, 284, 288, 292–3
Green, C. E., 393
Green, M. L., 317
Green, R. K., 317
Green, Stephen, 418
Gregory, A. P., 205, 206
Gregory, David, 81, 83, 394
Gregory, J. M., 81
Gregory, Kenneth, **254**, **358–60**
Gregory, R. J., 277
Gregory, S. E., 81
Gregory, S. F., 108
Greig, A. W., 397, 398, 399
Greville, Colonel, 17
Griffin, G., 354–6
Griffith, C. C., 365, 366, 367, 368
Griffith, S. C., Secretary of MCC, 312, 313, 324, 354, 376, 406, 430, 440, 445, 446
Grimmett, C. V., 241, 242, 243, 257, 258, 259, 260, 409
Grimston, Hon. Robert (Earl of Verulam), 24, 32, 36–7, 328
Grundy, J., 314
Gunasekara, C. H., 204, 205
Gunn, George, 202, 203, 213, 277, 356
Gunn, G. V., 277
Gunn, John, 277
Gunn, W., 95, 98, 99, 107
Guy, Earl, 286, 288

Hacker, Arthur, 327, 442
Hadow, W. S., 61, 72, 73, 74, 75, 76, 100
Haig, N. E., 204, 211, 217, 227, 231, 232, 372
Haigh, S., 141, 173
Hall, Sir John, 8
Hall, Louis, 94, 95, 98
Hall, W. W., 364, 365, 366, 367, 368
Hambledon Club, 7, 434
Hamid, Ronnie, 3, 4–5
Hamilton, Lord George, 100, 101
Hamilton, Marquis of, 68
Hammond, W. R., 92, 240, 242, 243, 257, 258, 259, 260, 270, 271, 272, 273, 274, 311, 312, 313, 337, 411
Hampshire, 33, 185, 217
Hanumant Singh, 384
Harding, N., 319, 320
Hardinge, H. W. T., 198, 199, 200, 201, 203, 204
Hardstaff, J., 301
Hardstaff, J., Jr, 277
Hardy, Thomas, 131
Harrington, Bill, 382
Harrington, Roy, 421
Harris, Lord, 8–9, 13, 14–15, 16, 18–19, 21–2, 24, 25, 26–8, 30, 32–3, 38–9, 40, 42, 44, 46–7, 48, 56, 59–60, 71, 73, 75, 89–90, 100, 101, 113, 131–2, 218, 249, 296, 298, 394, 441, 442, 443–4; portrait of, 327, 442, 443
Harris Garden, 435, 448
Harrison, George Pickering, 129–30, 211
Hart, G. E., 288
Hart-Davis, Rupert, **401–2**
Hartley, J. C., 109, 110, 111, 112

Hassett, A. L., 271, 272, 273, 312, 342
Hawke, Hon. M. B. (Lord Hawke), 94, 95, 98, 120, 124, 125, 141, 166, 249, 292, 441
Hay, George, 93
Hayes, E. G., 277
Haygarth, Arthur, **40**, 42, 301
Hayman, Francis, 326, 330
Hayward, T. W., 142, 317
Hayward, 'Union Jack', 424
Haywood, R. A., 198, 199, 200
Hazell, W., 321
Hazelrigg, A. G., 229
Headingley, 172, 383, 432
Headley, G. A., 280, 335
Heald, Tim, **428–33**, 448
Heap, James, 207
Hearn, W., umpire, 111, 140
Hearne, Alec, 89, 113
Hearne, Frank, 89
Hearne, G. F., 89
Hearne, G. G., 82, 89, 95, 96, 98, 369
Hearne, J. T., 107, 108, 115, 130, 147, 150, 152, 155, 161, 162, 169, 170, 368, 370, 371, 372, 437
Hearne, J. W., 206, 211, 213, 219, 231, 232, 233, 368, 371
Hearne, Thomas, 89–90, 141, 142
Hearne, Thomas, Jr, 89
Heath, W. H., 205
Hemingway, W. M. G., 110
Henderson's Nursery, 392, 438
Hendren, Elias 'Patsy', **143**, 144, 146, 150, 197, 199, 201, 202, 203, 205, 210, 211, 212, 226, 227, 231, 240, 242, 254, 257, 259, **269–70**, 289, 291, 297, 300–1, 368, 370, 371, 372, 376, 411, 437
Hendrick, M., 407, 408
Henry, O., 279–80
Henty, umpire, 117
Herbert, A. W., 73, 75
Hever, M. G., 319
Hewett, H. T., 167
Hewett, H. W., 163
Hignell, A. J., 403
Hill, M., 321
Hillyard, C., 369
Hillyard, J. M., 183, 184, 185
Hirst, G. H., 140, 141, 173, 371
Hitch, W., 211, 277, 300
hitting for six, 27, 92–3, 162–8, 231, 233, 254, 262–5, 267, 303, 304, 305, 351–2, 382, 410, 438
Hobbs, J. B. (Sir Jack), 200, 204, 210, 211, 213, 226, 227, 240, 242, 277, 292, 293, 317, 391, 409, 411
Hobhouse, C. E. H., 106
Holland, W. T., 184, 186
Hollies, W. E., 312, 313, 314, 338, 339, 382
Hollins, F. H., 140
Holmes, E. R. T., 227, 282, 305, 306, 307, 309
Holmes, P., 29
Holmes, Percy, 226, 278, 391
Hopley, G. W. V., 183, 184
Hoppner, John, 329
Horan, T., 83
Hore-Ruthven, Sir Alexander, 251
Hornby, A. N., 82, 84, 95, 97, 98, 100
Hornby, Rev. Dr J., 100, 101
Horne, General, 198, 293
Hornibrook, P. M., 242, 243
Hornung, E. W., 404
Horsley, J., 201, 202
Horton, D. K., 316
Housman, A. E., 297

Howard, T. C., 15
Howe, Lord, 129
Howell, M., 211
Howorth, R., 282
Huddesford, poet, 329
Hughes, K. J. (Kim), 406, 407, 410
Hughes, Margaret, **451**
Hulme, J. H. A., 287, 373
Human, J. H., 266, 280, 373
Humphreys, E., 201
Humphreys, George, 60
Hunt, J. H., 161, 162
Hunte, C. C., 365, 367
Hutton, A. E., 106
Hutton, L. (Sir Leonard), 272, 273,
    334, 335, 336, 342, 407
Hyde, Captain, 93
Hyndman, Henry, 182

Illingworth, Ray, 397, 398, 399
Imperial Cricket Conference, 443
India, 249, 266, 267, 342, 352–3,
    383, 384, 414, 444
Indoor School, MCC, 5, 420, 423–5,
    433, 435, 437, 440
Inkster, G. B., 197
Insole, D. J., 339, 446
International Cricket Conference (ICC),
    419, 440, 445
Iredale, F. A., 108, 449
Isaacs, David, 286

Jackson, F. S., 102–4, 107, 108, 109,
    165, 204, 214, 371, 381
Jackson, Sir Stanley, 291, 435, 441
Jackson, Rt Hon. W. L. (Baron
    Allerton), 102
Jackson's XI v. Warner's XI (1918),
    204–6
Jahangir Khan, 266, 267, 426
James, A. E., 324, 325
James, R., 'Tossing for Innings', 328–
    9, 439
James of Hereford, Lord, 132
Jameson, Dr Leander Starr, 117
Jameson, T. O., 183, 184, 185, 186,
    217
Jameson, Captain, 213
Jardine, D. R. (Douglas), 226, 227,
    251, 252, 255, 337, 355, 429,
    439, 440
Jeacocke, A., 227
Jeans, Sir James, 261
Jellicoe, Admiral, 198, 293
Jellicoe, F. G., 80
Jenkins, R. O., 334–5, 336
Jenner, Herbert, 21, 22
Jenner-Fust, Herbert, 441, 442
Jennings, D. W., 197, 199
Jessop, Gilbert, 84, 108, 110, 111,
    140, 142, 146, 164, 232
Johns, Henry, 429, 430, 433
Johnson, David, 430
Johnson, P. R., 140, 169, 170
Johnson, Samuel, 279
Johnston, Brian, **342**, 358, 359, 360,
    380, 423, 433
Johnston, Gordon, 316, 389–90
Jones, Arthur Owen, 356
Jones, E., 93, 140, 355
Jones, P. E., 335, 336
Jordan, groundsman, 48

Kanhai, R. B., 365, 367
Kavanagh, P. J., 433
Kaye, K. Lister, 183, 184, 185
Kearney, M. Neville, **341**
Kelleway, C., 196, 197, 198, 199,
    200, 201, 203

Kelly, J. J., 107, 108
Kemp, D. S., 316
Kent, 31–2, 60, 89, 97, 98, 113, 212,
    213, 245, 277, 308–9, 318–20
Kenyon, D. J., 339
Kidd, E. L., 205
Kilburn, J. M., **451**
Killick, E. H., 161
Killick, E. T., 231, 278
Kilner, R., 278
Kippax, A. F., 241, 242, 243, 409
Kirch, P. N., 316, 317
Kirk, E. C., 201, 202, 203, 204, 205
Kitcat, (Marlborough Captain), 91
Knight, Albert E., **171–2, 450**
Knight, D. J., 277
Knight (*Bell's Life* reporter), 51–2, 380,
    443
Knott, A. P. E., 397, 398, 399
Knott, C. J., 338, 339, 340
Knox, N. A., 197, 199, 200
Kortright, Charles, 447
Kynaston, Roger, 44, 130

Lacey, F. E. (Sir Francis), 94, 122, 143,
    246–50, 251, 252, 287, 315, 331,
    442–3
lacrosse, 347
Laird, B. M., 407, 416
Laker, J. C. (Jim), 351, 359, 396
Lambert, William, 15, 17
Lancashire, 97, 143–5, 182, 207,
    210, 212, 264, 265, 269–70, 277,
    279, 280, 370
Landseer, Edwin, 41, 49, 50
Lang, Andrew, 296
Langridge, James, 313, 314, 324, 325
Langridge, John, 324, 325
Larwood, Harold, 240, 251, 252, 279
Latham, Lord, 100, 101
Lawrence, Wing-Commander, 422
Laws of cricket, 298–9, 329, 389, 402,
    424, 434; 'bodyline' controversy,
    251–2, 253, 254–5, 279, 337;
    follow-on law, 104–5, 109–13;
    handling the ball, 314–15; lbw law,
    118–29, 298, 412; obstruction of
    the field, 299, 314; 'the over' (law
    XIV), 90–1; throwing the ball, 354–
    6
Leach, G., 161
Leatham, A. E., 286, 287
leather-jackets at Lord's, 260–1, 384
Lee, F. M., 169, 170
Lee, F. S., 278, 336, 355
Lee, H. W., 196, 197, 199, 200, 210,
    211, 227, 231, 232, 372
Lee, J. W., 278
Leese, J. F., 106
Lefroy, Edward Cracroft, 296
leg-before-wicket (lbw) law, 118–29,
    298, 412
Legge, Sir Harry, 190
Leicestershire, 160, 171, 192, 427,
    431
Leigh, Sir Edward Chandos, 100, **101–2**
Lennon, Hon. Colonel, 6
Lennox, Hon. Charles (4th Duke of
    Richmond), 13, 96, 390
Leonard, Bill, gateman, 419
Leveson-Gower, H. D. G., 101, 110,
    111, 112–13, 244, 291
Levett, W. H. V. ('Hopper'), 264
Lewis, A. E., 168, 169, 170
Lewis, R. P., 110, 111
Lewis, Tony, 432
Lewisham, Viscount, 101
Leyland, M., 257–8, 259, 260, 278
Library, 426, 433, 435, 436, 448

Lillee, D. K. (Dennis), 397, 398, 399,
    406, 407, 408, 410, 415, 416
Lillywhite, Frederick, 24, 49, 97
Lillywhite's Almanack/Annual, 79, 83n,
    87
Lillywhite's Eleven, James, Australian
    tour of (1876–7), 81
Lindsay, R. J. M., 316, 317
Lindwall, R. R., 395
Littlejohn, E. S., 150, 161, 168, 169
Livsey, W. H., 217
Lloyd, Charles (J. A.), 23, 24
Lock, G. A. R., 355
Locker, E. H., 25
Locksley, Mrs Emma, 26, 27
Lockwood, W. H., 370
Lohmann, George, 94, 95, 98, 99, 257
London Counties v. British Empire XI
    (1940), 291
London County Eleven, 142–3, 255,
    267
Long, E. J., 199, 201, 203, 252
Long, Walter, 106, 107
Longman, H. K., 211
Long Room, 3, 92, 193, 194, 226,
    237, 267, 275, 288, 289–90, 293,
    303, 304–5, 361, 379, 384, 386,
    395–6, 405, 419, 429, 430, 431,
    432, 433, 436, 438, 439–40, 443,
    446–7; pictures, 326–32, 379,
    439–40; removal of W. G.'s bust
    from (1939), 290, 396, 436;
    women barred from, 236–7, 386–7
Lord, Thomas, 4, 6, 8–11, 13, 14, 17,
    18, 21, 24, 25, 26–7, 28, 29, 30,
    31, 41, 56, 96, 131, 239, 376, 385,
    390–1, 434
Lord, Thomas, Jr, 10, 34
Lord, Mrs Thomas, 8
Lord's School v. The Rest (1914), 292
Louise, Princess, 195
Love, Mabel, 147
Lowell, James Russell, 436
Lowther, Colonel Henry C., 328
Lubbock, Alfred, 56, 66, 68, 69
Lubbock, R. H., 184
Lucan, Lord, 291
Lucas, A. C., 68
Lucas, A. P., 394
Luckes, W. T., 321
Luckhurst, B. W., 397, 398, 399
Lupton, A. W., 278
Lynch, Steven, 420
Lynd, Robert, **215–16**
Lyons, B. H., 279
Lyons, J. J., 114
Lyttleton, Hon. Alfred, 80, 100, 105,
    112, 118–21, 122, 123, 125, 127,
    128, 137, 150, 186, 191, 250, 370,
    394
Lyttleton, Hon. Edward, 85, 109, 112,
    370, 394
Lyttleton, Hon. George, 436

McAndrews, W., 197, 198
MacBryan, J. C. W., 310
McCabe, S. J., 242, 243, 258, 259,
    260, 271, 272, 273, 274
McCanlis, K., umpire, 340
Macartney, C. G., 196, 197, 198, 199,
    200, 201, 202, 203
Macaulay, G. G., 278
McCormick, E. L., 272, 273, 274
McDonald, A. D., 307
McDonald, E. A., 279
McGlew, D. J., 355
MacGregor, Gregor, 108, 115, 146,
    150, 151, 161, 164, 169, 170,
    212, 368, 370

McIlvenny, G., 311
McIntyre, Martin, 72, 73, 75
McIver, Capt. C.D., 200, 201
Mackay, Ian, 342
Mackenzie, Gordon, **13–14**
McKenzie, Graham, 387
McKibbin, T.R., 107, 108
Mackinnon, F.A., 442
MacLaren, A.C. (Archie), 123, 128,
  143, 144, 145, 269–70, 281, 379
Macmillan, Harold, 429
MacMillan, J.F., 317
McMorris, E.D., 365, 367
McNichol, G., 316
Mailey, A.A., 217, 297, 371
Majid Khan, 266
Makepeace, H., 196, 197, 198, 207,
  277
Makins, Clifford, **402**
Malcolm, Sir Ian, 186
Mallalieu, J.P.W., **238–9**
Mallett, A.A., 407, 408, 416
Mallett, A.W.H., 306, 307, 309
Manchester Guardian, 206, 221, 225,
  432
Mann, F.G., 318, 319, 321, 323, 324,
  337
Mann, George, 446
Mann, F.T., 211, 227, 231, 352, 372,
  373, 402
Mann, Sir Horace, 31, 32
Mann, Noah, 32
Manners, Hon. J.N., 183, 184, 185,
  186
Manners, Lord, 186
Marchant, F., 108
Marlar, Robin, **375–82**
Marlow, F.W., umpire, 170
Marriott, C.S., 205
Marriott, H.H., 110
Mars, W.H., 201
Marsh, R.W., 398, 399, 407
Marshall, Howard, 265, 417
Marshall, John, **450**
Marsham, Charles, 53
Marsham, C.H.B., 140
Martin, F.R., 231, 232
Martin, Frederick, 396
Martindale, E.A., 253, 254
Martindale, F.A., 306, 307
Martin-Jenkins, Christopher, 416
Massie, H.H., 198
Massie, R.A.L., 396, 397, 398, 399
Massie, R.J.A., 198, 199
Matsuyama, E., 311
Matthews, T.J., 196, 197, 198, 199
Mattuck, Israel, 448
Maurois, André, 22
May, Peter, 360, 412, 413
Meek, H.E., 47
Melbourne, 240, 389, 435, 442;
  Centenary Test (1977), 405, 413
Mellé, B.G., 201, 202, 203
Melver, C.D., 201
Memorial Gallery and Museum, 378,
  426–7, 435–6, 439
Menzies, Sir Robert, 383, 435
Middlesex County Cricket Club, 12, 79,
  80, 89, 98, 100, 117, 130, 146,
  162, 164, 168, 209, 248–9, 261,
  276–82, 301, 317–21, 328, 343,
  361, 363, 391, 393, 418–19, 424;
  v. Australia, 85, 93, 115, 394;
  Centenary (1964), 368–74; v.
  Derbyshire, 332; v. Essex, 264, 390;
  v. Gloucestershire, 146, 164, 263,
  265, 266, 402–4; v. Kent, 212,
  213, 245, 318–20; v. Lancashire,
  143–5, 269–70, 264, 265; v.

Leicestershire, 160, 427; v.
  Nottinghamshire, 130, 141, 206; v.
  Somerset, 168–71, 194, 263–4,
  320–1; v. Surrey, 168, 210–13,
  270, 226–7, 264, 265, 270, 288;
  v. Sussex, 161–2, 265–6, 323–5; v.
  Warwickshire, 265, 436; v. West
  Indies, 230–2; v. Yorkshire, 165,
  172–3, 206, 212, 354
Middlesex and Essex v. Kent and
  Surrey (1943), 308–9
Midwinter, W., 82
Mignon, E., 169, 170
Millar, Charles Christian Hoyer, 315
Millar, Gertie, 145, 147
Miller, K.R. (Keith), 307, 311, 312,
  313, 314, 382, 383, 395
Mills, P.T., umpire, 321
Milne, A.A., 296
Milton, H.A., 169
Minor Counties' Cricket Association,
  250
Mitchell, Alan, **226**
Mitchell, Frank, 109, 110, 111, 112
Mitchell, R.A.H., **77–8**, 100, 126–8,
  258, 328
Mitchell-Innes, M.S., 320, 321
Mitford, John, 21
Mobey, G.S., 277
Moffatt, R., 310, 311
Mold, A.W., 141
Monckton, W.T., 183, 184
Montgomery, James, 282
Moorhouse, Geoffrey, **251–2**, **304**,
  423–6, 432–3, 448
Mordaunt, G.J., 110, 111, 112
Mordaunt, O.C., 168, 169, 170
Morkel, D.P., 307
Morland, George, 8
Morley, F., 73, 75, 82, 83
Morning Post, 30
Morrah, Patrick, 171, **194**
Morris, Dave, 3, 4
Morris, Rupert, **419–22**
Morton, P.H., 85
Moses, Isaac, 7, 43, 44, 392
Moss, A.E., 373
Moss, J., umpire, 185
Moulsey Hurst match (1735), 96–7
Mound Stand, 2, 3, 4, 5, 36, 94, 115,
  135, 136, 137, 168, 247, 283,
  285, 314, 363, 377–8, 391, 427–
  8, 438, 442; new, 5, 427–8, 432,
  448
Moyes, A.G., 201, 202, 203
Munday, Mrs Dorris, 'weather
  manipulator', 387–8
Munday, W.J., 197
Murdoch, J.A., 90
Murdoch, W.L., 82, 83, 117, 394
Murray, D.L., 367
Murray, John, 437
Murrell, H.R., 169, 211, 227, 280,
  371
music at Lord's, 356–7
Mycroft, T., 91, 93, 96, 106
Mynn, Alfred, 28, 32, 40, 97, 328,
  331–2
Mynn, William, 332

Napier, Hon. Mark F., 106
Nash, John, 10
National Cricket Association (NCA),
  445
NatWest final (1985: Notts. v. Essex),
  431
Navy and Army v. Australian and
  South Forces (1917), 198–200,
  293

Need, Philip, 167
Nelson, Edmund, 440
Newman, G.C., 278
Newnes, George, 106
New Zealand, 142, 249, 263, 266,
  322–3, 373, 383
Nichols, M.S., 308, 309
Nicholson, William, 7, 43, 44, 46,
  100, 130, 131, 247, 392
Noble, M.A., 162, 166, 167, 438
Norfolk, Lavinia Duchess of, 446
Norfolk, MCC v. (1820), 29, 391
Norman, Dave, 422
Norman, Philip, 22
Northamptonshire, 132, 337, 432
North Bank, Lord's at, 6, 7, 26–8, 96,
  246
North Clock Tower, 437
North v. South (1878), 84–5
Northwood, J., 310
Norton, George Rose, 135–6
Nottingham Twenty-Two, 18
Nottinghamshire, 48–9, 72–6, 81,
  97–8, 130, 141, 277, 370, 431
Nourse, A.D., 356, 370
Nunes, R.K., 231
Nursery or practice ground, 5, 36, 51,
  96, 238, 333, 345, 377, 392, 437–
  8; Cross Arrows matches on, 422,
  425–6, 437
Nutter, A.E., 277
Nyren, John, **18**, 299–301

Oakes, Charles, 265, 324, 325
Oakes, Jack, 324
Oates, T., umpire, 243
O'Brien, Sir Timothy, 92, 370
O'Connor, J., 278
Old, C.M., 406, 407, 408, 410
'Old Cricketer' 's letter to *The Times*,
  136–7
Oldfield, N., 277
Oldfield, W.A., 242, 243, 258, 259
Oldroyd, E., 278
Old Trafford, 65, 80, 140, 206–7, 298,
  401
O'Reilly, W.J., 257, 258, 259, 260,
  271, 272, 273, 274, 322
Osbaldeston, 'Squire' George, 13–16,
  17, 274
Oscroft, William, 73, 75
O'Shea, Jack, 382
Ouless, W.W., 327
The Oval, Kennington, 25, 32, 45, 65,
  78, 188, 277–8, 292, 293, 294,
  295, 300–1, 344, 392; England v.
  Australia, 94, 140, 226, 240, 244–
  5, 271, 281–2, 346, 394, 405, 407,
  427; England v. New Zealand, 266;
  see also Surrey
Over Thirty v. Under Thirty (1879), 88
Owen-Smith, H.G., 280, 373
Oxford v. Cambridge ('Varsity
  matches'), 62, 76–7, 80, 104–5,
  133, 138, 139–40, 171–2, 182,
  188, 256, 260, 268, 357, 360–1,
  377, 378, 429, 438; Cobden's
  match (1870), 52–4; follow-on
  incident (1896), 108–11

Packer, Kerry, 400
Padmore, H., 310, 311
Paget, General Sir Arthur, 185
Pakistan, 266, 384
Palairet, L.C.H., 142, 169, 170
Palmer, G.E., 94, 121
Pankhurst, Mrs, 190
Pardon, Sydney H., **138**, **192**, 206
Parfitt, P.H., 373, 433

Park, R. L., 201, 203
Parker, Charlie, 386
Parker, Eric, **450**
Parker, J. F., 277
Parkhouse, W. G. A., 335, 336, 339
Parkin, C. H., 207
Parks, J. H., 265
Parks, J. M., 365, 366, 367
Parr, George, 328
Parry, Gambier, 41
Parry, W. R., umpire, 232
Pascoe, L. S., 406, 407, 408, 410, 416
Pataudi, Iftikhar Ali, Nawab of, 258
Pataudi, Mansur Ali, Nawab of, 383, 384
Paulton, J. M., 106
Pavilion, 8, 32, 35, 38, 41, 46, 55, 56, 175, 193, 246, 326, 358, 362, 363, 378, 379, 391, 392, 419, 430, 438, 439–41; Centenary Test fracas in (1980), 405, 412–13; Committee Room, 440–3; destroyed by fire (1825), 29–31, 391; hitting over and into the, 92–3, 162–8, 233, 263, 351–2, 382, 410, 438; pictures in, 326–32, 379, 439–41; women barred from, 236–7, 386–7; *see also* Long Room
Paynter, E., 271, 272, 273, 277
Payton, W. R. D., 277
Peach, H. A., 211, 227, 277
Peacock, Wadham, 99n
Pearce, Peter, 76, 85–6, 87
Pearce, T. N., 266, 267
Pease, J. A., 106
Peebles, I. A. R. (Ian), **217**, 231, 232, **244–6**, 262, 264, **270**, 278, 280, 309, **368–74**
Pelham, A. G., 116
Penny, T. S., 316, 317
Pepper, C. G., 311, 312, 313, 314
Perkins, H., Secretary of MCC, 70, 78, 80, 90, 91, 100, 130, 443
Perowne, Barry, **404**
Peskett, Roy, **288**
Peter the cat (at Lord's), 353–4
Pettiford, J., 313, 314
Philadelphians, 124, 125, 395, 443
Philip, Prince, 376
Philips, James, 141
Phillips, J., umpire, 108, 140
Phillipson, W. E., 312, 313, 314, 368
Pickering, F. P. U., 69
Pilch, Fuller, 16, 40, 301
Pilkington, C. C., 110, 111, 112
Pilling, R., 95, 97
Plumer, General, 198, 293
Pollard, R., 265
Ponsford, W. H., 241, 242, 243, 258, 409
Ponsonby-Fane, Sir Spencer, 8, 19, **37–9**, 100, 118, 128, 129, 326, 441–2, 443; portraits of, 327, 331, 441
Ponsonby Staples, R., 436
Potter, Stephen, **362–4**
Pougher, Dick, 107, 108
Powell, J. A., 227, 231, 232
Poyntz, E. S. M., 168, 169, 170
Press, Press Box, 5, 51–2, 100, 101, 135, 137–8, 322, 351, 358–9, 380, 395, 401–2, 423, 436–7, 443
The Press, **17**
Preston, Hubert, 442
Price, J. S. E., 397, 398, 399
Price, R. G. G., 133
Price, W., 54, 106
Price, W. F., 231

Prince's Ground (Belgravia), 65, 78, 79, 276, 369, 393
Pringle, D. R., 431
printers, Lord's, 422
Prittie, Terence, 262–3, 264, **450**
Procter, M. J., 403
Punch, 81, 133, 141–2
Pycroft, Rev. James, **17**, 19, 28, 31, 32, **33–4**, **449**, **451**

Q Stand, 349, 431
Quaiffe, William, 141
Quiller-Couch, Sir Arthur, 261

RAAF v. South of England (1945), 314–15
Radley, C. T. (Clive), 403
Rae, A. F., 334, 335
Rae, Edward, 357
Rait-Kerr, Diana, curator, 379, 436, 444
Rait-Kerr, Colonel R. S., Secretary of MCC, 332, 429, 440, 444
Ramadhin, S., 333, 334, 335, 336, 340, 381, 384
Randall, Derek, 431
Ranjitsinhji, Prince K. S., **6–8**, 107, 128, 141, 371
Raven, Simon, 433
Rawlin, J. T., 95, 96, 98, 115, 280, 370
Ray, Gabrielle, 145, 147
Raymond, Ernest, **145–59**, 162
Razzall, Leonard Humphrey, **357**
Read, Maurice, 95, 98
Read, W. W., 95, 98, 99
Real Tennis, 428, 429–30, 435; Gold Racquet final, 429
Reason, Charles, 422
Reay, G. M., 211
Redgate, S., 32–3, 49
Reese, Daniel, **142–3**
Reeves, W., 198
Reid, R. T., 105, 106
Relf, A. E., 161
Renny-Tailyour, H. W., 73, 75, 76
Rhodes, Wilfred, 128, 140, 173, 213, 257, 278, 348, 352, 371
Richards, I. V. A., 433
Richardson, C. E., umpire, 162
Richardson, Tom, 150, 257, 370
Richardson, V. Y., 242, 243, 409, 411
Ridgway, F., 319, 320
Ridley, A. W., 72, 73, 74, 75, 76, 82, 83, 100
Risqué, W. (pseudonym), 139
Ritchie, J. V., 316, 317
Roach, C. A., 231, 232
Robertson, J. D., 303, 304, 305, 306, 307, 309, 312, 313, 317, 318, 319, 320, 324, 373
Robertson, W. P., 140
Robertson-Glasgow, R. C., **350–1**
Robeson, Paul, 245–6
Robins, R. W. V. (Walter), 241, 242, 243, 244, 278, 281, 305, 306, 307, 308, 309, 319, 321, 372–3, 411
Robinson, Emmott, 278
Robson, David, **427**
Robson, E., 168, 169, 170
Roche, W., 115
Roe, W. N., 163, 167
Roper, A. W., 306, 307, 314–15
Rose, W. M., 68, 69
Rosebery, Earl of, 105, 107
Ross, Alan, **347–8**, 358
Rotherham, G. A., 204, 205, 293
Round, J., 66, 68

round-arm bowling, introduction of, 31–2, 34, 300
Royal Box, 376, 378
Rugby v. Marlborough (1886), 90–1
Rushby, T., 211, 277
Russell, Lord Charles, 88–9, 99
Russell, W. E., 373, 374
Rutter, E., 393
Rylott, A., umpire, 83

Sadiq Mohammad, 403
St Hill, W. H., 231
St James's Chronicle, 26, 385
St John's Wood Ramblers *see* Cross Arrows
Salisbury, Lord, 99, 107
Salote, Queen of the Tongas, 346, 347
Salt, Henry S., **55**
Samuel, Sir Saul, 100, 101
Sandby, Paul, 331
Sandham, A., 210, 211, 226, 227, 277
Sassoon, Siegfried, 116, 228, 256, **360–1**
The Saturday Review, 62
Saville, S. H., 372
Scarborough Festival, 130, 295
Scarborough: Players v Gentlemen (1925), 226
scoreboards, 51, 90, 96, 219, 283, 343–4, 345, 349, 351, 376–7, 378, 382, 420
score-cards, 420, 422; first issued (1848), 41, 51
Scott, H. J. H., 93
Scott, S. W., 92
Seacox Heath (Kent) cricket week, 99–100
Second World War (1939–45), 282, 288–93, 302–16, 396
Selby, J., 73, 75
Selincourt, Hugh de, 116, **256**
Selvey, M. W. W., 403, 404
Sewart, W., 199
Sewell, E. H. D., **163**, 164, 167, **267**
Seymour, James, 443
Shackleton, D., 339, 365, 366, 367
Shackleton, J. H., 403
Sharp, A. T., 192
Sharp, H., 321, 324
Shaw, Alfred, 49, 71, 72, 73–4, 75, 76, 82, 83, 150, 379
Shaw, J. C., 73, 75
'She Didn't Know Enough About the Game' (song), 139
Shepherd, D. R., 403
Shepherd, Tom, 210, 211, 227, 270, 372
Sherriff, R. C., 275
Sherwin, M., 83, 95, 98
Shine, E. B., 109, 111, 112
Shrewsbury, Arthur, 73, 75, 94, 95, 98–9, 129, 379
Shuter, John, 121–2
Simpson, R. B., 394
Simpson, R. T., 333, 339
Simpson, S., 310, 311
Sims, Sir Arthur, 226
Sims, J., 276, 309, 319, 321, 324, 325, 373
Sismey, S., 306, 307, 314–15
six-a-side competition games, 424–5
Skeet, C. H. L., 210, 211, 372
Skelding, A., umpire, 325, 340
Slatter, 'Steevie', 27, 37, 39, 131
Slatter, W. H., 27, 30, 131
Smailes, T. F., 278
Small, J. A., 231, 232
Small, John, 7, 356

Smith, Hon. Mr Justice A.L., 101
Smith, C.A., 94
Smith, C.I.J, ('Big Jim'), 4, 92, 165, 261–5, 267, 276, 281, 373
Smith, C.L.A., 161
Smith, D.V., 324
Smith, G.O., 108, 110, 111, 112
Smith, Godfrey, 433
Smith, J., 280
Smith, M.J., 403, 404
Smith, M.J.K., 397, 398, 399
Snaith, J.C., 302
Snow, J.A., 397, 398, 399
Sobers, G.S. (Sir Garfield), 27, 365, 267, 268, 426
Solomon, J.S., 365, 367
Somerset, 92, 93, 168–71, 263–4, 279, 320–1
South Africa, 190, 198–200, 248, 260, 293, 317–18, 347, 354–5, 384; cancellation of MCC's tour to (D'Oliviera affair), 399–400, 420, 446; MCC tours in, 250, 281, 374; Test matches in England, 190, 260, 317–18, 354–6, 384, 395
Southerton, James, 54–5, 81
Southerton, S.J., 54
Spender, J.A., 118
Spofforth, F.R., 82, 83, 84, 85, 150, 394, 442
Spooner, R.H., 144
The Sporting Magazine, 14, 25
Spriggs, E., 311
Squire, Jack, 116
Squires, Stan, 277
Stacey, C., 311
Stackpole, K.R., 397, 398, 399
staff canteen, 422
Staffordshire, 213, 244
The Standard, 76
Stanhope, Hon. E., 100, 101
Statham, J.B. (Brian), 348, 365
Steel, A.G., 94, 121, 122, 125–6, 127, 150, 394
Steel, A.I., 183–4, 185, 186
Stephenson, Lieut-Col John, 420, 422
Stevens, G.T.S., 200, 201, 202, 205, 206, 211, 212, 227, 372
Stewart, D., 310, 311
Stewart, M.J., 365, 366, 367
Stirling, W.S., 197, 198
Stock, A.B., 184, 185
Stoddart, A.E., 94, 95, 98–9, 107, 108, 114–15, 194–5, 212, 368, 370
Stoddart, Mrs Ethel, 194–5
Stollmeyer, J.B., 334, 335
Stovold, A.W., 403
Straker, A.C., 183, 184, 186
Strathavon, Lord, 6
streakers, 400–1, 402, 449
Strudwick, H., 211, 212, 227, 277, 296
Stuart, Leslie, 139
Stuart-Wortley, Archibald, 326–7, 447
Studd, Charlie, 121
Summers, George, 48—9, 51, 62, 393
Studholme, Marie, 145, 147
Subba Row, R., 360
Suffragettes, 190–1
Surrey, 20, 98, 119, 192, 264, 267, 277–8, 279, 308–9, 370; Middlesex v., 168, 210–13, 226–7, 264, 265, 270, 288, 372; see also The Oval
Sussex, 60, 97, 117, 119, 161–2, 165, 166, 263, 265–6, 300, 323–5

Sutcliffe, H., 240, 257, 259, 271, 278, 383
Swanton, E.W., 209, **234**, 238, 251, 255, 315, **316**, **333**, 337, 338, **341–2**, **351–2**, **356**, 358–60, **388–96**, 417, 433, **434–47**, 448, 450, **451**
Swift, Owen, 385, 386
Sydney Cricket Ground, 240, 389, 435

Tafnell, C.W., 184
Tarapore, T., 383
Tarrant, F.A. (Frank), 146, 147, 150, 168, 169, 170, 280, 297, 368, 371, 372
Tate, F.W., 161, 165
Tate, Maurice, 165, 265
Tate, W., 240, 241, 243
Tattersall, R., 339
Tavern, Lord's, 2, 5, 7, 13, 26, 35, 37, 38, 46, 92, 246, 264, 349, 350, 358, 359, 363, 374–5, 376, 378, 382, 383, 384, 385–6, 402, 419, 435
Taylor, Alfred D., 49
Taylor, D., 203
Taylor, H.W., 205, 293
Taylor, J.M., 198, 199, 201, 203
Taylor, Tom, 298
televised cricket, 274–5, 364, 400, 422
tennis and racquet courts, 35, 36, 37, 41, 45, 59, 94, 100, 378, 391, 428, 435
Tennyson, Alfred Lord, 217
Tennyson, Hon. Lionel H., 203, 204, 217
Test and County Cricket Board (TCCB), 400, 440, 445, 446
Thanet, Earl of, 35
Thomas, J.H., 251
Thompson, A., 325
Thompson, Francis, 80, 166
Thomson, Arthur Alexander, **172–3**, **348–50**
Thornton, Buns, 117
Thornton, C.I., 47, 93, 369–70
Timeless Tests, 281
The Times, 12, 16, 29, 36, 42, 60–2, 70, 94, 96–9, 109, 113, 120, 122, 137, 138, 191, 212–13, 233, 234–6, 237–8, 254, 260–1, 264, 267, 274–5, 343–4, 347, 352–3, 354, 357, 374–5, 387–8, 401, 427, **448**; Alan Gibson, 417–18; 'C.A.A.', 229–30; John Woodcock, 383–4; letters to, 43, 92–3, 133–7, 188–9, 268, 340–1, 344, 357, 368, 418; Personal Column, 375; Philip Trevor, 170–1; Richard Ford, 413–14; Rupert Morris
Titmus, F.J., 365, 366, 367, 373, 374, 426, 433, 437
Todd, L.J., 308, 309, 310, 311, 319
Toll of Esher, 12
Townsend, C.L., 221
Townshend, Rev. Charles, **34**
Townson, J., 310, 311
Travers, Ben, **386**
Tremlett, M.F., 321
Trent Bridge, 240, 257, 344
Trevor, Philip, **170–1**
Triangular Test tournament (1912), 190
Trott, A.E. (Albert), 128, 150, 161, 162–71, 194, 263, 280, 351–2, 361, 370, 371, 382, 397, 438
Trott, G.H.S., 108
Trousdale, Dawn, umpire, 448

Trueman, Freddie, 92, 342, 359, 365–6, 367, 384
Trumble, H., 107, 108, 167
Trumper, Victor, 245
Tubow, George, 346
Tuchman, Barbara, 182
Turberville, H. Smith, 328
Turk, A.J., 316
Turnbull, T.L.G., 184
turnstiles, 59, 214, 284
Twining, R.H., 305, 308, 309, 310, 372
Tyldesley, Ernest, 196, 197, 199, 207
Tyldesley, J.T., 144, 207
Tyldesley, R.K., 207, 240

Ullswater, Viscount, **326–32**
Ulyett, G., 94, 95, 98, 99

Valentine, A.L., 333, 334, 335, 336, 340, 381, 384, 397
Valentine, B.H., 318, 319
Varsity matches see Oxford v. Cambridge
Verity, H., 257, 258, 259, 260, 271, 272, 273, 274
Verity, T., 402
Vernon, G.F., 82
Vernon, M.J., 404
Victoria, Queen, 94
Vine, J., 161
Vivian, H.G., 262, 263
Voce, W., 279

Waddington, A., 278
Waddington, M., French Ambassador, 99, 100, 101
Waddy, B.B., 310, 311
Waddy, P.S., 110, 111
Waintwright, E., 163, 166
Walcott, C.L., 334, 335
Walker, I.D., 72, 74, 75, 100, 369, 394
Walker, J.G., 93, 95, 98
Walker, R.D., 145, 369
Walker, Tom, 18
Walker, V.E., **32**, 68, 69, 100, 328, 369
Wall, T.W., 241, 242, 243, 259
Wallington, E.W., 190
Wallroth, C.A., 56, 443
Walpole, Horace, 329
Walters, C.F., 257, 259
Walters, K.D., 397, 399
Walton, W.H. Murray, **344**
Wanostrocht, Nicholas see Felix, N.
Ward, Rev. A.R., 53
Ward, John, 440, 446
Ward, William, 7, 16, 28–9, 30, 34, 44, 51, 130, 300, 391
Wardle, J.H., 333–4, 336
Warner, P.F. (Sir Pelham: 'Plum'), **15–16**, 17, 47, **48–9**, **51–2**, 56, 79, **83**, 85, 90, **91**, **94–5**, **99–100**, **101–2**, **104–5**, 110, 111, **112–13**, 115, 120, 122, 128, **133**, **140**, 148, 150, 161, **162–3**, 167, 168, 169, **193**, 196, 197, 198, 199, 200, 201, 203, 204–6, 209–10, 211, 212–13, **219**, **232**, 233, 245, 254, 270, 291, 293, 294, 296, **302–3**, 325, **326–32**, 370–1, 372, 379–80, 384, 392, 393, 417, 435, 436, 438, 443, 444, 448; portrait of, 439–40; role in 'Bodyline' controversy, 251–2, 386
Warner Stand, 137, 168, 264, 392, 423, 436
Warr, J.J., 339, 340, 373, 446

Warwickshire, 119, 265, 356–7, 436
Washbrook, C., 277, 334, 335, 336, 339
Watkin, Bill, 430
Watkins, W. R., 382
Watts, E. A., 264, 265, 277
Watts, G. F., 39
Waugh, Alec, 187, 294–302, 361
Waugh, Arthur, 187, 188
Webbe, A. J., 72, 82, 94, 95, 96, 98, 100, 130, 212, 327–8, 370, 394
Weekes, E., 334, 335, 384
Weigall, G. J. V., 142
Wellard, A. W., 271, 272, 273, 274, 321
Wellings, E. M., 310, 311
Wells, C. M., 104–5, 112, 115
West, John, umpire, 96
West, Peter, 358, 359, 360
West, W. A. J., 108, 111, 162
West Indies, 132–3, 291; MCC tours in, 249, 281, 337; Middlesex v. (1928), 230–2; Test matches in England, 245, 253–5, 333–6, 340, 364–8, 381, 384, 395, 400, 439
Wheeler, umpire, 91
Wheeler, C. A., 20–1, 28–9
White, J. C., 240, 242, 243, 244, 254, 409
White, Julia F., 386–7
White Conduit Club, 6, 9, 11, 28, 96, 390, 434
Whitfield, E. W., 277
Whitelaw, P. E., 320

Whitlom, Dick, 12
Whiteside, J. P., umpire, 185
Whyte, R. A. M., 317
Wickham, Rev. A. P., 168, 169, 170
Wigan, D. G., 183, 184
Wigan, E. C., 442
Wigram, Major Clive, 190
Willes, John, 31–2
Willey, Peter, 407, 431
Williams, E. S., 311
Williams, Neil, 425, 427
Williams, R. G., 312, 313, 314
Williams, William, 341–2
Willis, C. B., 199
Wilson, C. E. M., 109, 110, 111
Wilson, Don, 420–1, 428
Wilson, E. R., 140, 168
Wilson, R., 'Cricket at Hampton Wick', 330
Wilson, T. B., 183, 184, 185
Wilson, T. S. B., 104
Wilson, Vic, 376
Winchester v. Harrow, 7, 43, 391
Winchilsea, Earl of, 6, 13, 96, 390
Wisden, John, 328, 426–7
Wodehouse, P. G., 174–82, 196, 302
Wood, G. M., 406, 407, 410
Wood, J., 324, 325
Woodcock, John, 383–4
Woodfull, W. M., 241, 242, 243, 258, 259, 409
Woodhouse, G. E. S., 321
Woods, S. M. J., 142, 168, 169, 170
Wooller, Wilf, 356

Woolley, F. E., 204, 205, 206, 240, 242, 243, 291, 409, 411, 443
Worcestershire, 117, 210, 218, 266, 277
Workman, J., 306, 307
Worrell, F. M., 333, 334, 335, 336, 364, 365, 366, 367, 368, 426
Worsley, W. A., 144
Wright, D. V. P., 273, 274, 308, 309, 313, 314, 318, 319, 320, 338, 339
Wright, H., 66, 68
Wright, Huntley, 288
Wrightson, J., 316
Wrigley, Arthur, 417
Wyatt, H. D., 161
Wyatt, R. E. S., 257, 258, 259, 260, 271, 305
Wyld, F., 72, 82, 83

Yallop, G. N., 407
Yardley, N. W. D., 322, 334, 336, 337, 339, 340
York, Duke of, 13
Yorkshire, 98, 165, 172–3, 206, 212, 226, 277, 278–9, 280, 348, 349–50, 370, 373, 441
Yorkshire Annie, 380–1
Young, J. A., 319, 321, 324, 325, 373
Young, Jack, 381
Young Cricketers, MCC, 420, 421
Youth Cricket Association, MCC, 445

Zaheer Abbas, 403

ACKNOWLEDGEMENTS

The author and the publishers wish to thank the copyright holders for permission to reprint extracts from the following copyright material:

John Arlott, *Cricket, The Great Bohunkus*, two BBC radio commentaries, © John Arlott; John Arlott and David Rayvern Allen, *A Word from Arlott*, © Michael Joseph Ltd; Roland Bowen, *Cricket: a History of its Growth and Development*, © Eyre & Spottiswoode; Gerald Brodribb, *All Around the Wicket, Hit for Six*, © Gerald Brodribb; Christopher Brookes, *English Cricket*, © George Weidenfeld & Nicholson Ltd; Lionel H. Brown, *Victor Trumper and the 1902 Australians*, © Secker & Warburg Ltd; Sir Neville Cardus, *Autobiography*, © Collins Publishers; Sir Arthur Conan Doyle, *Memories and Adventures*, © John Murray Ltd; A Country Vicar, *Cricket Memories*, © Methuen & Co. Ltd; Bernard Darwin, *W. G. Grace*, © Gerald Duckworth & Co. Ltd; Ted Dexter and Clifford Makins, *Testkill*, © Allen & Unwin; Jack Fingleton, *Ashes Crown the Year, Brightly Fades the Don, Brown and Company, Lord's and the MCC*, © Messrs Glasson, Gemmell & McGill; C. P. Foley, *Autumn Foliage*, © Methuen & Co. Ltd; Leslie Frewin (editor), *The Boundary Book* ('The Game', 'How to be One Up at Lord's'), © Leslie Frewin; David Frith, *My Dear Victorious Stod*, © James Clarke & Co. Ltd, The Lutterworth Press; Kenneth Gregory, *In Celebration of Cricket*, © A. P. Watt Ltd; Tim Heald, *The Character of Cricket*, © Pavilion Books Ltd; Gordon Mackenzie, *Marylebone*, © Macmillan & Co. Ltd; J. P. W. Mallalieu, *On Larkhill*, © Allison and Busby Ltd; Alan Mitchell, *84 Not Out*, © Harrap Ltd; Geoffrey Moorhouse, *Lord's*, © Hodder and Stoughton; Patrick Morrah, *The Golden Age of Cricket*, © A. M. Heath & Co. Ltd; Ian Peebles, *Patsy Hendren, Spinner's Yarn*, © A. R. T. Peebles; Barry Perowne, *Raffles of the MCC*, © Macmillan & Co Ltd; Ernest Raymond, *To the Wood no More*, © Macmillan Publishing Inc.; Daniel Reese, *Was it all Cricket?*, © Allen & Unwin; Alan Ross, 'Test Match at Lord's', © Alan Ross; Siegfried Sassoon, 'The Blues at Lord's', © George Sassoon; Hugh de Selincourt, *Moreover*, © Oxford University Press, *Over*, © The Bodley Head; E. H. D. Sewell, *Overthrows*, © Century Hutchinson; E. W. Swanton, *As I Said at the Time, Denis Compton, a Sketch, Follow On, Sort of a Cricket Person*, © Collins Publishers; *Gubby Allen: Man of Cricket*, © Century Hutchinson; all extracts from *The Daily Telegraph* ©The Daily Telegraph Ltd; all extracts from *The Times*, © Times Newspapers Ltd; A. A. Thomson, *Pavilioned in Splendour*, © John Farquharson Ltd; Sir Pelham Warner, *Lord's 1787–1945*, © Emilia Warner; Alec Waugh, *A Year to Remember, Lord's and Its Literature*, © A. D. Peters & Co Ltd; P. G. Wodehouse, *Mike*, © A. P. Watt & Son Ltd.

Every effort has been made to trace the holders of copyright material used in this anthology. We apologise for any omissions in this respect, and on notification we undertake to make the appropriate acknowledgement in subsequent editions.